A Publication Sponsored by
the Society for Industrial and Organizational Psychology, Inc.,
A Division of the American Psychological Association

Other books sponsored by the Society include:

The Changing Nature of Performance
Daniel R. Ilgen, Elaine D. Pulakos, Editors

Career Development in Organizations
Douglas T. Hall and Associates

Productivity in Organizations
John P. Campbell, Richard J. Campbell, and Associates

Training and Development in Organizations
Irwin L. Goldstein and Associates

Organizational Climate and Culture
Benjamin Schneider, Editor

Work, Families, and Organizations
Sheldon Zedeck, Editor

Personnel Selection in Organizations
Neal Schmitt, Walter C. Borman, and Associates

Team Effectiveness and Decision Making in Organizations
Richard A. Guzzo, Eduardo Salas, and Associates

The Changing Nature of Work
Ann Howard, Editor

Individual Differences and Behavior in Organizations
Kevin R. Murphy, Editor

New Perspectives on International Industrial/Organizational Psychology
P. Christopher Earley and Miriam Erez, Editors

Multilevel Theory, Research, and Methods in Organizations

Multilevel Theory, Research, and Methods in Organizations

Foundations, Extensions, and New Directions

Katherine J. Klein

Steve W. J. Kozlowski

Editors

Foreword by Sheldon Zedeck

JOSSEY-BASS
A Wiley Company
San Francisco

Jossey-Bass books and products are available through most bookstores. To contact Jossey-Bass directly, call (888) 378-2537, fax to (800) 605-2665, or visit our website at www.josseybass.com.

Substantial discounts on bulk quantities of Jossey-Bass books are available to corporations, professional associations, and other organizations. For details and discount information, contact the special sales department at Jossey-Bass.

Library of Congress Cataloging-in-Publication Data

Multilevel theory, research, and methods in organizations : foundations, extensions, and new directions / Katherine J. Klein, Steve W.J. Kozlowski, editors ; foreword by Sheldon Zedeck.
    p. cm. — (Frontiers of industrial and organizational psychology)
    Includes bibliographical references (p.) and indexes.
    ISBN 0-7879-5228-1
    1. Psychology, Industrial. 2. Complex organizations. I. Klein, Katherine J. II. Kozlowski, Steve W.J. III. Series.

HF5548.8 .M815 2000
158.7—dc21

00-025343

FIRST EDITION
HB Printing   10 9 8 7 6 5 4 3 2 1

A joint publication in
The Jossey-Bass
Business & Management Series
and
The Jossey-Bass
Social & Behavioral Sciences Series

Frontiers of Industrial and Organizational Psychology

Contents

Part Two: Analyzing Multilevel Data

Part Three: Commentary

Foreword

The Society for Industrial and Organizational Psychology (SIOP) established the Frontiers of Industrial and Organizational Psychology series in 1982, in part to advance the scientific status of the field. The series was designed to include edited volumes that would each deal with a single topic considered to be of major contemporary significance in the field. Each volume editor, a leading contributor to the topic, would take responsibility for developing the volume, with the goal of presenting cutting-edge theory, research, and practice in chapters contributed by individuals doing pioneering work on the topic. Each volume was to be aimed at SIOP members: researchers, practitioners, and students. The volumes were to be published on a timely basis rather than on a fixed schedule.

The first editor of the series was Raymond Katzell, who was followed in that role by Irwin Goldstein. My term as series editor began in May 1993 and ended in May 1998, when Neal Schmitt succeeded me. (Because the present volume was initiated during my term as editor, I continued to see it through to publication.) The practice that I followed for choosing volume topics and editors is the one that was successfully established by my predecessors. Specifically, the topics and volume editors are chosen by the *Frontiers* series editorial board. There is considerable exchange between the board and the volume editor in the planning stages of each volume. Once the volume is under contract, the series editor collaborates with the volume editor to coordinate editorial activity with the activities of the board and then works with the publisher to bring the manuscript into existence as a book in the series.

Under the excellent leadership and guidance of the premiere editor, Raymond Katzell, three major volumes were developed and published: *Career Development in Organizations,* edited by Douglas Hall (1986); *Productivity in Organizations,* edited by John Campbell and Richard Campbell (1988); and *Training and Development in Organizations,* edited by Irwin Goldstein (1989). Under the equally excellent stewardship of Irwin Goldstein, four additional volumes were produced: *Organizational Climate and Culture,* edited by Benjamin Schneider (1990); *Work, Families, and Organizations,* edited by Sheldon Zedeck (1992); *Personnel Selection in Organizations,* edited by Neal Schmitt and Walter Borman (1993); and *Team Effectiveness and Decision Making in Organizations,* edited by Richard Guzzo and Eduardo Salas (1995).

Since my term began, we have published four volumes: *The Changing Nature of Work,* edited by Ann Howard (1995); *Individual Differences and Behavior in Organizations,* edited by Kevin Murphy (1996); *New Perspectives on International Industrial/Organizational Psychology,* edited by P. Christopher Earley and Miriam Erez (1997); and *The Changing Nature of Performance,* edited by Daniel R. Ilgen and Elaine D. Pulakos (1999). The success of the series is evidenced by the high number of sales (more than thirty-five thousand copies have been sold), by the excellent reviews that the volumes have garnered, and by the frequency with which scholars cite the volumes and their individual chapters.

The present work, edited by Katherine Klein and Steve Kozlowski, continues the tradition of publishing volumes that are designed to move the field forward and present new thinking and approaches. The general purpose of this volume is to illuminate and explicate the complexity and interdependence of today's organizations. Traditionally, we have studied organizations from different perspectives; we have divided the study of organizations into such units of analysis as the organization, the group, and the individual. Accordingly, we have created separate disciplines, theories, and approaches, and this practice has resulted in an organizational science that is not integrated. This volume bridges the gap between micro and macro approaches to the study of organizations and presents organizational science from a multilevel framework. This approach should produce an integrated conceptual and methodological paradigm for the future study of organizational issues. The chapters of this volume identify the central issues for the development of multilevel theory and research. They provide examples of the development of integrative, multilevel theoretical models for topics that are of concern to industrial/organizational psychologists, and they present the areas of agreement and disagreement that exist among the different systems that have been designed to study multilevel issues. The goals of the volume are to stimulate and guide research for the future and particularly to convince researchers that multilevel analysis should be considered in the study of virtually all phenomena that occur in organizations.

The editors of the present work have done an excellent job of identifying the topics, selecting a diverse group of authors, and working with them to provide a focused volume that is sure to direct research for many years to come. SIOP owes the editors and the chapter authors a considerable debt of gratitude for undertaking such an ambitious volume. We expect it to serve as an important stimulus for researchers seeking to move forward in understanding behavior in today's organizational environments.

The production of a volume such as this one requires the cooperation and effort of many individuals. The volume editors, the chapter authors, and the series editorial board all played, obviously, a major role. They deserve our sincere appreciation and thanks for devoting their time and effort to a task that was undertaken for the sole purpose of making a contribution to the field, with no remuneration whatsoever. Also to be thanked are Cedric Crocker and his colleagues at Jossey-Bass, especially Julianna Gustafson. They worked with us during the planning, development, and publication of this volume, and we owe them a significant debt of gratitude as well.

January 2000   SHELDON ZEDECK
                                          University of California at Berkeley
                                          Series Editor, 1993–1998

Preface

Levels of analysis issues have frustrated and fascinated us throughout our academic careers. We each tackled multilevel research in our doctoral dissertations, bravely—if naively—grappling with multilevel theory development, data collection, and analysis. Working on our doctoral dissertations in the early 1980s, we were surprised by the paucity of explicit multilevel theory in industrial and organizational psychology (I/O) and by the absence of clear, accepted answers to the conundrums of multilevel data analysis. We found important guidance and encouragement from the few organizational scholars who advocated multilevel theory development and research. Their seminal work answered some of our questions and, perhaps just as important, assured us that we were asking the right questions—questions about the reciprocal relations among individuals, groups, and organizations.

During the past fifteen years, multilevel theory and research have increasingly become more common in I/O psychology and organizational behavior (OB). During this time, our fascination with multilevel theory and research has increased and our frustration has diminished, although certainly not disappeared. Multilevel theories integrate micro- and macro-organizational perspectives. They are rich, complex, and meaty. Multilevel research tests such theories, rigorously assessing the relationships among constructs at multiple levels of analysis. For these reasons, multilevel theory and research are fascinating. But because multilevel theory and research are complex and challenging, and because they remain rare and the object of continuing debate, they are frustrating.

Purpose of This Book

We conceived of and edited this book in the hopes that we might build on recent advances in multilevel theory building and research, increasing readers' fascination and diminishing readers' frustration with multilevel theory and research.

More specifically, we hoped that the chapters of this book might demonstrate the power and relevance of multilevel theory to a broad range of I/O topics. Some topics—organizational climate, team effectiveness, leadership—are relatively widely recognized as multilevel. But the issues of concern to multilevel theorists transcend these few topics. Multilevel theories rest, most fundamentally, on the premise that individual, group, and organizational characteristics interact and combine to shape individual, group, and organizational outcomes. A multilevel perspective may thus add depth and richness to theoretical models and studies of topics traditionally examined at just one level of analysis.

Further, we hoped that the book might clarify the choices available to researchers in collecting and analyzing multilevel data. In many cases, we feared, debates regarding the relative merits of different techniques to analyze multilevel data had confused and put off potential researchers. We hoped that the chapters of this book might illuminate the history, assumptions, and logic underlying differing data analytic systems, thus helping readers to identify the most appropriate technique(s) to answer their multilevel questions.

The subtitle of the book—*Foundations, Extensions, and New Directions*—succinctly captures our goals. We designed the book to articulate the solid theoretical, methodological, and analytical foundations that undergird multilevel organizational research. Beyond the apparent confusion in the literature, there is a solid base on which to build understanding. The book is also intended to push the state-of-the-art, extending current theoretical perspectives and positing new directions for multilevel theory building and research.

Contents

Reflecting these goals, the book is divided into three parts: Part One ("Extending Multilevel Organizational Theory"), Part Two ("Analyzing Multilevel Data"), and Part Three ("Commentary"). The first chapter in Part One is our own. In this chapter, we have attempted to offer a broad and thorough foundation in multilevel theory building. We explore the epistemological roots of multilevel organizational theory; articulate principles for theory development, data collection, and analysis; and lay the groundwork for new conceptual and empirical analyses of emergent processes in organizations.

The next four chapters in Part One offer new and rigorous multilevel theoretical models of traditional I/O topics. The chapters pose—and begin to answer—new questions about the multilevel processes and effects of selection, performance appraisal, training, and human resource management. Together, the four chapters are innovative—even radical—in their redefinition of traditional I/O topic areas. In Chapter Two, Schneider, Smith, and Sipe propose a new conceptual model of the multilevel consequences of employee selection. DeNisi next examines the multiple levels of performance appraisal and performance management in Chapter Three. Kozlowski, Brown, Weissbein, Cannon-Bowers, and Salas examine training effectiveness from a multilevel perspective in Chapter Four, highlighting vertical transfer processes that link individual training outcomes to group and organizational performance. And in Chapter Five, Ostroff and Bowen describe the multilevel consequences of human resource practices on individual skills, attitudes, and behaviors and on organizational performance.

The last two chapters of Part One examine topics newer to I/O psychology. In Chapter Six, Klein, Palmer, and Conn offer a multilevel conceptualization of interorganizational relationships (IOR), challenging the common assumption within the IOR literature that an organization's boundary spanners are homogeneous in their attitudes about and behaviors toward their organization's IOR(s). And in Chapter Seven, Chao provides a multilevel analysis of cross-cultural interaction, examining the ways in which individual personality, group membership, organizational culture, and national culture may interact to influence the dynamics and outcomes of cross-cultural interaction.

The chapters in Part Two clarify the assumptions, logic, and procedures of differing multilevel data analytic approaches, as well as the commonalities and differences among these approaches. In Chapter Eight, Bliese explains how information regarding within-group agreement, non-independence, and group mean reliability may influence a researcher's decision to aggregate individual-level data to the group- or organization-level to represent constructs at these higher levels. In Chapter Nine, James and Williams consider the effects of situations on persons, explaining the assumptions, logic, and mechanics of the cross-level operator in regression, analysis of covariance, and contextual analysis. Dansereau and Yammarino then describe in Chapter Ten the questions that guided the development of WABA (within and between analysis) and the assumptions and statistical procedures used by WABA researchers to address these questions. In Chapter Eleven, Hofmann, Griffin, and Gavin discuss the roots, uses, assumptions, and steps of hierarchical linear modeling (HLM), one of a class of random coefficient modeling techniques. The authors of Chapter Twelve identify commonalities and differences among the data analytic procedures described in Part Two of the book, illustrating these commonalities and differences in a series of analyses of a simulated data set designed for this purpose.

Finally, Part Three of the book provides commentary from two scholars prominent in the application and development of multilevel theory in I/O and OB. In Chapter Thirteen, Brass comments on the importance of the levels perspective to the historical development of our science and on the increasing influence of multilevel work on mainstream organizational theory and research. Rousseau closes by reflecting in Chapter Fourteen on the promise and continuing challenges of multilevel theory and research, highlighting the still largely untapped potential of multilevel theory to unify our science and to provide a foundation for influencing organizational policy and practices. We have come quite far, but still have a long way to go.

Acknowledgments

Our fascination with multilevel theory and research is greater than ever. Our frustration with multilevel theory and research is lower than ever. For that, we have the chapter authors to thank. They delivered us informative, creative, and insightful drafts of their chapters and then kindly and graciously responded to our suggestions for changes.

We thank Shelly Zedeck, too, who offered us encouragement, kept us from falling too, too far behind, and gave constructive feedback on each chapter. We thank our colleagues and students at our respective universities for serving as our sounding boards, listening to us and educating us with their questions, insights, and suggestions. We also thank Julianna Gustafson at Jossey-Bass for seeing us through the publication process with efficiency, patience, and good humor. And, finally, we thank the members of the SIOP Frontiers Series Board for their enthusiastic belief in the merits of a book on multilevel theory and research.

This project was a truly collaborative effort of the two editors. We did it together, watching it evolve from an idea to a rich and thought-provoking volume. In this process, we've learned a tremendous amount, had a lot of fun, and strengthened a strong friendship. What will we argue about now that the book is done?

January 2000

KATHERINE J. KLEIN
College Park, Maryland

STEVE W. J. KOZLOWSKI
East Lansing, Michigan

The Authors

KATHERINE J. KLEIN, associate professor of industrial and organizational psychology at the University of Maryland, received her Ph.D. degree in community psychology from the University of Texas. Her research focuses primarily on levels-of-analysis issues and on workplace innovation. More specifically, she is interested in the development and testing of multilevel theory; the measurement, antecedents, and consequences of within-unit variability in employee attitudes and perceptions; the influence of leadership and climate on the implementation of workplace innovations; and parttime work, work-family conflict, and other time-related aspects of work. She is a fellow of the Society for Industrial and Organizational Psychology and the American Psychological Association. Her articles have appeared in the *Journal of Applied Psychology*, the *Academy of Management Review, Leadership Quarterly*, and the *Journal of Vocational Behavior*. She currently serves on the editorial boards of the *Academy of Management Review*, the *Journal of Applied Psychology*, and the SIOP Frontiers Series.

STEVE W. J. KOZLOWSKI, professor of organizational psychology and program head at Michigan State University, received his Ph.D. degree in industrial and organizational psychology from Pennsylvania State University. His major interests are in the application of multilevel theory to understanding innovation, change, and adaptability at the individual, team, and organizational levels. His theory and research address organizational downsizing, innovation, continuous learning, adaptive performance and expertise, leadership, team development, climate, and socialization. His current work, which focuses on team leadership, training and development, and adaptive performance, has been supported by the Naval Air Warfare Center Training Systems Division and the Air Force Office of Scientific Research. His work has been published in many journals, including the *Academy of Management Journal, Human Performance, Human Resource Planning, International Review of Industrial and Organizational Psychology, International Review of Selection and Assessment,* and *Journal of Applied Psychology.* Kozlowski has also authored or coauthored numerous book chapters. He serves or has served on the editorial boards of the *Journal of Applied Psychology, Organizational Behavior and Human Decision Processes,* and the *Academy of Management Journal.* He is a fellow of the American Psychological Association and the Society for Industrial and Organizational Psychology.

PAUL BLIESE received his Ph.D. degree in organizational psychology from Texas Tech University in 1991. After graduation, he worked in the Office of Research and Evaluation at the Bureau of Labor Statistics, studying cognitive and social factors that might influence economic statistics. In 1992 he joined the Walter Reed Army Institute of Research (WRAIR), where he is a member of an interdisciplinary team studying stress and adaptation among U.S. Army soldiers. At WRAIR, he has studied the Gulf War syndrome, the effects of downsizing, the adaptation of soldiers deployed on various peacekeeping operations, and the effects of implementing new technology. His research interests center on conceptual and statistical issues involved in modeling the effects of contextual factors on soldiers' well-being and performance. He has published articles in *Armed Forces and Society,* the *Journal of Applied Psychology,* the *Journal of Applied Social Psychology,* the *Journal of Management, Organizational Research Methods, Parameters,* and *Work and Stress.*

MICHELLE C. BLIGH is a doctoral candidate in the School of Management at the State University of New York at Buffalo. She specializes in organizational behavior and is affiliated with the Center for International Leadership. Her research interests include organizational culture and culture change, identification, leadership, and levels-of-analysis issues.

DAVID E. BOWEN, professor of management in the Department of World Business, Thunderbird/American Graduate School of International Management, received his Ph.D. degree in business administration from Michigan State University. His research, teaching, and consulting focus on the organizational dynamics of delivering service quality and on the effectiveness of human resources management departments. His articles have appeared in the *Academy of Management Review,* the *Academy of Management Journal,* the *Academy of Management Executive,* the *Journal of Applied Psychology,* and *Human Resource Management.* He coedited the *Academy of Management Review's* 1994 special issue on total-quality management and has published six books on service management, including *Winning the Service Game* (1995, with Benjamin Schneider). He serves on the editorial boards of the *Journal of Management Inquiry, Human Resource Management,* the *Journal of Quality Management,* and the *International Journal of Service Industry Management.*

DANIEL J. BRASS, professor of organizational behavior at Pennsylvania State University, received his Ph.D. degree in business administration from the University of Illinois–Urbana. His research focuses on the antecedents and consequences of social networks in organizations. He has published articles in *Administrative Science Quarterly,* the *Academy of Management Journal,* the *Academy of Management Review,* the *Journal of Applied Psychology, Organizational Behavior and Human Decision Processes, Human Relations, Business Horizons, Organizational Behavior Teaching Review, Research in Personnel and Human Resources Management, Research in Politics and Society,* and *Research in Negotiation in Organizations.* He has also published numerous book chapters and currently serves as associate editor of *Administrative Science Quarterly.*

KENNETH G. BROWN, assistant professor of management and organizations at the University of Iowa, received his Ph.D. degree in industrial and organizational psychology from Michigan State University. His research interests center on the role of learner choice and activity in determining training effectiveness, particularly in learner-controlled and technology-mediated training environments, such as Web-based training. He has conducted training evaluation projects for Ford Motor Company and the National Center for Manufacturing Sciences and is currently working on evaluation projects with Boeing Flight Safety and the Stead New Media Center at the University of Iowa. He has published several book chapters in addition to articles in the *Journal of Applied Psychology* and *Human Resource Planning.*

JANIS A. CANNON-BOWERS, senior research psychologist in the Science and Technology Division of the Naval Air Warfare Center Training

Systems Division (NAWCTSD), received her Ph.D. degree in industrial/organizational psychology from the University of South Florida. Her research interests include investigation of training needs and design for multioperator training systems, training effectiveness and transfer-of-training issues, tactical decision making under stress, the impact of multimedia training formats on learning and performance, and training for knowledge-rich environments. As team leader for advanced surface-training research at NAWCTSD, she has been involved in a number of projects directed toward improving training for complex environments. To date, she has authored or coauthored more than one hundred publications in the areas of her research interests.

GEORGIA T. CHAO, associate professor of management at Michigan State University, received her Ph.D. degree in industrial and organizational psychology from Pennsylvania State University. Her primary research interests are in the areas of organizational socialization and work adjustment, career development, and international human resources management. Her current international work examines the role of cultural values in multinational organizations, particularly their impact in China. She serves on the editorial boards of the *Journal of Applied Psychology,* the *International Journal of Selection and Assessment,* and *Human Resource Management Review.* She is a member of the Academy of Management and the Society for Industrial and Organizational Psychology and has served on executive committees in both organizations. In 1995 she received the Academy of Management's award for Outstanding Publication in Organizational Behavior.

AMY BUHL CONN, currently employed at Personnel Decisions International in Boston, is a doctoral candidate in industrial and organizational psychology at the University of Maryland. Her major research interests include training, selection, networking, and the dynamics and consequences of interorganizational relationships. Her dissertation focuses on the effectiveness of self-directed learning programs as a training platform.

FRED DANSEREAU, associate professor of organization and human resources in the School of Management at the State University of New York at Buffalo, received his Ph.D. degree in organizational behavior from the University of Illinois. He has extensive research experience in the areas of leadership and managing at the individual, dyadic, group, and collective levels of analysis. Along with others, he has developed a theoretical and empirical approach to theorizing about and testing theories at multiple levels of analysis. He has served on the review boards of the *Academy of Management Review, Group and Organization Management,* and *Leadership Quarterly.* He is associate editor of *Group and Organization Management,* the author of four books and more than sixty articles, and a consultant to a number of organizations, among them the Bank of Chicago, Occidental, St. Joe Corp., Sears, TRW, the U.S. Army and U.S. Navy, Worthington Industries, and various educational institutions.

ANGELO S. DENISI, B. Marie Oth Professor of Management and director of the Center for Human Resource Management at Texas A&M University, received his Ph.D. degree in industrial/organizational psychology from Purdue University. He has published mostly in the areas of performance appraisal and job analysis. His publications include *A Cognitive Approach to Performance Appraisal* (1996). He has served as editor of the *Academy of Management Journal* and is coauthor of a forthcoming textbook on human resources management. He is a fellow and 1999–2000 president of the Society for Industrial and Organizational Psychology as well as a fellow of the American Psychological Association and the Academy of Management.

MARK B. GAVIN, assistant professor of management at Oklahoma State University, received his Ph.D. degree in organizational behavior/ human resources management from Purdue University. His research interests include employee attitudes, group/team dynamics, trust, and extra-role behaviors. His methodological interests include issues surrounding the application of hierarchical linear modeling and structural equation modeling to organizational research.

MARK A. GRIFFIN, principal research fellow in the School of Management, Queensland University of Technology, received his Ph.D. in industrial/organizational psychology from Pennsylvania State University. His primary research interests concern the link between workplace characteristics and measures of individual well-being and performance. He is interested in the methodological and practical implications of such research issues as the impact of organizational climate on individual affect and the impact of individual performance on workplace safety outcomes.

DAVID A. HOFMANN, associate professor of management at Michigan State University, received his Ph.D. degree in industrial/organizational psychology from Pennsylvania State University. His primary research interests include how individual, group/team, leadership, and organizational factors relate to safety problems, to the interpretation of accident causes, and to the occurrence of accidents, and to perceptions of commitment and accountability for both safety and quality performance. His other interests include multilevel modeling, organizational surveys and assessment methodologies, and organizational change. In 1992 he was awarded the Society of Human Resource Management's Yoder-Henemen Personnel Research Award.

LAWRENCE R. JAMES holds the Pilot Oil Chair of Excellence in Management and Industrial-Organizational Psychology at the University of Tennessee. He is the author of numerous articles, chapters, and papers and is coauthor of a book on causal analysis. He is a current or former member of the editorial boards of the *Journal of Applied Psychology, Organizational Behavior and Human Decision Processes, Human Performance, Human Resources Management,* and *Organizational Research Methods.* He has chaired Division 19 of the Academy of Management and has also held a number of positions in Divisions 5 and 14 of the American Psychological Association.

CHERI OSTROFF, associate professor of management at Arizona State University, received her Ph.D. degree in industrial/organizational psychology from Michigan State University. Her research interests include levels-of-analysis issues, person-environment fit, human resources management systems, training, and socialization. Her articles have appeared in the *Academy of Management Journal,* the *Journal of Applied Psychology, Personnel Psychology, Organizational Behavior and Human Decision Processes, Group and Organizational Management,* and the *Journal of Vocational Behavior.* She has also served as associate editor of the *International Journal of Selection and Assessment* and serves on the editorial boards of the *Journal of Applied Psychology* and *Personnel Psychology.* In 1994 she received the Society of Industrial and Organizational Psychology's Ernest J. McCormick Award for Early Career Contributions and the American Psychological Association's Distinguished Scientific Award for Early Career Contribution in Applied Research.

SHANNON L. PALMER, currently employed at the Center for Creative Leadership in Greensboro, North Carolina, is a doctoral candidate in industrial and organizational psychology at the University of Maryland. Her major research interests include team process and decision-making effectiveness, organizational change and innovation, the dynamics and consequences of interorganizational relationships, and levels-of-analysis issues. Her dissertation focuses on the influences of diversity, norm development, and role-development processes on decision-making effectiveness among top management teams.

DENISE M. ROUSSEAU, H. J. Heinz II Professor of Organizational Behavior and Public Policy at the Heinz School of Public Policy and Graduate School of Industrial Administration, Carnegie Mellon University, earned her Ph.D. in industrial/organizational psychology from the University of California. Her research focuses on the changing employment relationship and on psychological contracts in employment. She is coauthor of *Relational Wealth* (with Carrie Leana), *The Boundaryless Career: A New Employment Principle for a New Organizational Era* (with M. Arthur), and *Psychological Contracts in Employment: Cross-National Perspectives* (with Rene Schalk). Her book *Psychological Contracts in Organizations: Understanding Written and Unwritten Agreements* (1995) won the Academy of Management's Terry Award.

EDUARDO SALAS, professor of psychology at the University of Central Florida, where he also holds an appointment as principal scientist at the Institute for Simulation and Training, received his Ph.D. degree in industrial and organizational psychology from Old Dominion University. His research interests include team training and performance, training effectiveness, tactical decision making under stress, team decision making, performance measurement, and learning strategies for teams. He has coauthored more than 150 journal articles and book chapters and has coedited eight books. He is on the editorial boards of *Human Factors, Personnel Psychology, Military Psychology,* the *Interamerican Journal of Psychology, Transportation Human Factors Journal,* and *Training Research Journal* and currently edits an annual series for JAI Press, *Human/Technology Interactions in Complex Systems.* He is a fellow of the American Psychological Association and the Human Factors and Ergonomics Society. He has also received the Department of the Navy's Meritorious Civil Service Award.

BENJAMIN SCHNEIDER, professor of psychology and chair of the program in industrial and organizational psychology at the University of Maryland, received his Ph.D. degree in psychology from the University of Maryland. His interests include service quality, organizational climate and culture, staffing issues, and person-organization fit, especially the role of the manager's personality in organizational effectiveness. He has published more than eighty-five journal articles and book chapters and six books, the most recent of which is *Winning the Service Game* (1995, with David E. Bowen). He also serves on the editorial review boards of the *Journal of Applied Psychology* and other journals. He is a fellow of the American Psychological Association, the American Psychological Society, and the Academy of Management and has served as president of the Organizational Behavior Division of the Academy of Management and of the Society for Industrial and Organizational Psychology.

WILLIAM P. SIPE, currently working with William M. Mercer's productivity group, is a doctoral candidate in psychology at the University of Maryland. His primary research interests are influences on perceptions of leadership, levels of analysis, alignment of human resources practices, and group decision making. His work with William M. Mercer's productivity group involves examining the alignment of human resources practices with an organization's strategy and empirically linking human resources practices to organizational productivity.

D. BRENT SMITH, assistant professor of organizational behavior in the School of Industrial and Labor Relations at Cornell University, received his Ph.D. degree in psychology from the University of Maryland. His research interests concern level-of-analysis issues, personality processes, person-organization fit, and quantitative methodology. His research has been published in the *Journal of Applied Psychology, Personnel Psychology,* and *Human Performance.* In 1998 he was co-recipient of the Scholarly Achievement Award, presented by the Human Resources Division of the Academy of Management.

DANIEL A. WEISSBEIN, currently consulting for numerous organizations in the public and private sectors, is a doctoral candidate in industrial/organizational psychology at Michigan State University. His areas of particular interest include training and organizational development.

LARRY J. WILLIAMS, professor of management at Virginia Commonwealth University, received his Ph.D. degree in organizational behavior from the Indiana University School of Business. He was founding editor of *Organizational Research Methods* and continues to serve as the journal's editor. He also serves as director of Virginia Commonwealth University's Center for the Advancement of Research Methods and Analysis, an interdisciplinary center devoted to helping faculty and students advance their knowledge of social science research methods and data-analysis techniques.

FRANCIS J. YAMMARINO, professor of management at the State University of New York at Binghamton, where he is also fellow and associate director of the Center for Leadership Studies, received his Ph.D. degree in organizational behavior from the State University of New York at Buffalo. His research interests include superior-subordinate relationships, leadership, self-other agreement processes, and multiple levels-of-analysis issues, and he is among the developers of the Varient/WABA approach to multiple-level theory building and testing. He has authored or edited four books and numerous book chapters and has published extensively in the *Academy of Management Journal,* the *Academy of Management Review,* the *Journal of Applied Psychology, Leadership Quarterly, Personnel Psychology,* and *Research in Personnel & Human Resources Management.* He has also authored about sixty technical reports or working papers and has delivered approximately seventy conference presentations. He is a past senior editor of the *Leadership Quarterly* and serves on the editorial review boards of the *Academy of Management Journal, Group & Organization Management, Journal of Applied Psychology, Journal of Organizational Behavior, Leadership Quarterly,* and *Organizational Research Methods.* He is a fellow of the Society for Industrial and Organizational Psychology (Division 14 of the American Psychological Association) and the American Psychological Society. He has received more than $1.2 million in research grants from various public and private organizations and has served as a consultant to numerous organizations, such as IBM, Textron, TRW, Medtronic, Loral, Lockheed Martin, United Way, and the U.S. Army, Navy, Air Force, and Department of Education.

Multilevel Theory, Research, and Methods in Organizations

PART 1

Extending Multilevel Organizational Theory

CHAPTER 1

A Multilevel Approach to Theory and Research in Organizations

Contextual, Temporal, and Emergent Processes

Steve W. J. Kozlowski
Katherine J. Klein

Organizations are multilevel systems. This axiom—the foundation of organizational systems theory—is reflected in the earliest examples of organizational theory, including the Hawthorne Studies (Roethlisberger & Dickson, 1939), Homans's theory of groups (1950), Lewin's field theory (1951), sociotechnical systems theory (Emery & Trist, 1960), Likert's theory of organizational effectiveness (1961), Thompson's (1967) theory of organizational rationality, and Katz and Kahn's (1966) social organizational theory, to name but a few. Further, this axiom continues to provide a foundation for virtually all contemporary theories of organizational behavior. Yet, despite the historical tradition and contemporary relevance of organizational systems theory, its influence is merely metaphorical. The system is sliced into organization, group, and individual levels, each level the province of different disciplines, theories, and approaches. The organization may be an integrated system, but organizational science is not.

There are signs that this is beginning to change, that we are moving toward the development of an integrated conceptual and methodological paradigm for organizational science. We have witnessed the evolution, over the last two decades, of multilevel frameworks that have well-developed conceptual foundations and associated analytic methodologies. Organizational science is moving toward the development of a paradigm that can bridge the micro-macro gap in theory and research. We are witnessing the maturation of the multilevel paradigm in organizational science.[1]

As with all maturation, however, the process has not proceeded without pain. The roots of the multilevel perspective are spread across different disciplines and literatures, obscured by the barriers of jargon, and confused by competing theoretical frameworks and analytic systems. Although there are some explicit efforts to specify general multilevel frameworks for organizational science (e.g., Dansereau, Alutto, & Yammarino, 1984; House, Rousseau, & Thomas-Hunt, 1995; Klein, Dansereau, & Hall, 1994; Roberts, Hulin, & Rousseau, 1978; Rousseau, 1985), real and apparent differences among the frameworks have created the impression of little common ground (e.g., George & James, 1994; Klein, Dansereau, & Hall, 1995). Further, the best way to evaluate multilevel theories (e.g., George & James, 1993; Yammarino & Markham, 1992) and establish emergent constructs (e.g., James, Demaree, & Wolf, 1993; Kozlowski & Hattrup, 1992; Schmidt & Hunter, 1989) is much contested. No single source exists to cut across these differences and to guide the interested researcher in the application of multilevel concepts. This contributes to confusion and limits the development of multilevel theories. Accordingly, a review of the current literature is likely to leave those who are tempted to test multilevel theories intrigued yet confused—inspired yet wary.

Our goal in this chapter is to help resolve this confusion by synthesizing and extending prior work on the development of multilevel theory and research for organizations. The chapter is organized into three sections. In the first section, we review the theoretical roots of the multilevel perspective as it relates to theory building and research in organizations. The epistemological foundation and several basic assumptions for the levels perspective are rooted in general systems theory (von Bertalanffy, 1968) and related variants. Early and enduring applications of the levels perspective to research on organizational characteristics and organizational climate had a formative impact on the development of the levels perspective and continues to exert considerable influence.

In the second section, we clarify, synthesize, and extend basic principles to guide multilevel theory development and to facilitate empirical research. We first provide principles to guide the development of multilevel theory. We discuss theoretical issues pertaining to the origin and direction of phenomena across levels, unit and entity specification, time, and factors affecting the degree of coupling or linkage of phenomena across levels. With this theoretical foundation in place, we next explain and illustrate how to specify and operationalize multilevel models. Critical issues focus on establishing an alignment among levels of theory, constructs, and measures. We also specify different types of levels models, examine implications for research sampling, and provide an overview of data-analysis issues.

In the third section, we extend multilevel organizational theory by drawing particular attention to relatively neglected *bottom-up* processes. Many organizational theories are implicitly or explicitly *top-down,* addressing the influence of macro levels (for example, organization or group characteristics) on micro levels (for example, individuals). Such models focus on contextual factors at higher levels that constrain and influence lower-level phenomena. Bottom-up models describe phenomena that have their theoretical origin at a lower level but have emergent properties at higher levels (for example, psychological and organizational climate, individual and team effectiveness, individual and organizational learning). Models of emergence have been largely restricted to isomorphic composition processes, which has limited the development of bottom-up multilevel theory and research. We elaborate discontinuous, configural compilation processes and describe how they allow the conceptualization of alternative manifestations of emergence. We use this perspective to extend extant models of emergence. We develop a *typology of emergence* to illustrate and explain several alternative models that range from isomorphic composition to discontinuous compilation. We are hopeful that these alternative models of emergence will stimulate and guide research on these central but neglected multilevel phenomena.

Foundations for Multilevel Theory in Organizations

Conceptual Underpinnings

General Systems Theory

General systems theory (GST) has been among the more dominant intellectual perspectives of the twentieth century and has been shaped by many contributors (e.g., Ashby, 1952; Boulding, 1956; Miller, 1978; von Bertalanffy, 1972). Systems concepts originate in the "holistic" Aristotelian worldview that the whole is greater than the sum of its parts, in contrast with "normal" science, which tends to be insular and reductionistic. The central goal of GST is to establish principles that generalize across phenomena and disciplines—an ambitious effort that is aimed at nothing less than promoting the unity of science.

Systems principles are manifest as analogies or *logical homologies*. Logical homologies represent identical concepts (that is, *isomorphism*), and parallel processes linking different concepts (that is, *homology*), that generalize to very different systems phenomena (von Bertalanffy, 1972). For example, it is noted that open systems counteract the second law of thermodynamics—entropy—by importing energy and information from the external environment, and transforming it, to maintain homeostasis. Feedback and servomechanisms are the basis for the purposive responses of cybernetic systems. Organizational systems are proposed to have analogous structures and processes (e.g., Katz & Kahn, 1966; Miller, 1978).

Whether one takes a more macro (Parsons, 1956, 1960) or micro (Allport, 1954) perspective, the influence of GST on organizational science has been pervasive. Unfortunately, however, that influence has been primarily metaphorical. The bureaucratic-closed systems–machine metaphor is contrasted with a contingent-open systems–living organism metaphor. Although metaphor has important value—virtually all formal theory is rooted in underlying metaphor (Morgan, 1983)—lack of specificity, formal identity, and precise definition can yield truisms that mislead and fail the test of science (Pinder & Bourgeois, 1982; Bourgeois & Pinder, 1983). GST has exhibited heuristic value but has contributed relatively little to the development of *testable principles* in the organizational sciences (Roberts et al., 1978). It is to this latter concern that the multilevel perspective is directed.

As social systems, organizations are qualitatively distinct from living cells and other concrete physical systems. The goal of the multilevel perspective is not to identify principles that generalize to other types of systems. Although laudable, such an effort must often of necessity gloss over differences between qualitatively different systems in order to maintain homology across systems (compare Miller, 1978). *The primary goal of the multilevel perspective in organizational science is to identify principles that enable a more integrated understanding of phenomena that unfold across levels in organizations.*

Macro and Micro Perspectives

Fundamental to the levels perspective is the recognition that micro phenomena are embedded in macro contexts and that macro phenomena often emerge through the interaction and dynamics of lower-level elements. Organizational scholars, however, have tended to emphasize either a micro or a macro perspective. The macro perspective is rooted in its sociological origins. It assumes that there are substantial regularities in social behavior that transcend the apparent differences among social actors. Given a particular set of situational constraints and demographics, people will behave similarly. Therefore, it is possible to focus on aggregate or collective responses and to ignore individual variation. In contrast, the micro perspective is rooted in psychological origins. It assumes that there are variations in individual behavior, and that a focus on aggregates will mask important individual differences that are meaningful in their own right. Its focus is on variations among individual characteristics that affect individual reactions.

Neither single-level perspective can adequately account for organizational behavior. The macro perspective neglects the means by which individual behavior, perceptions, affect, and interactions give rise to higher-level phenomena. There is a danger of superficiality and triviality inherent in anthropomorphization. Organizations do not behave; people do. In contrast, the micro perspective has been guilty of neglecting contextual factors that can significantly constrain the effects of individual differences that lead to collective responses, which ultimately constitute macro phenomena (House et al., 1995; Klein et al., 1994; Roberts et al., 1978; Rousseau, 1985).

Macro researchers tend to deal with global measures or data aggregates that are actual or theoretical representations of lower-level phenomena, but they cannot generalize to those lower levels without committing errors of misspecification. This renders problematic the drawing of meaningful policy or application implications from the findings. For example, assume that we can demonstrate a significant relationship between organizational investments in training and organizational performance. The intuitive generalization—that one could use the magnitude of the aggregate relationship to predict how individual performance would increase as a function of increased organizational investments in training—is not supportable, because of the well-known problem of ecological inference. Relationships among aggregate data tend to be higher than corresponding relationships among individual data elements (Robinson, 1950; Thorndike, 1939). This fact continues to be a significant difficulty for macro-oriented policy disciplines—sociology, political science, economics, education policy, epidemiology—that attempt to draw individual-level inferences from aggregate data.

Micro researchers suffer from an obverse problem, which also makes the desire to influence human resource management policy difficult. We may, for example, be able to show that individual cognitive ability increases individual performance. However, we cannot then assert that selection systems that produce higher aggregate cognitive ability will necessarily yield improved organizational performance. Perhaps they will, but that inference is not directly supported by individual-level analyses. Misspecifications of this sort, however, are not unusual (Schmidt, Hunter, McKenzie, & Muldrow, 1979). Such "atomistic fallacies," in which organizational psychologists suggest team- or organization-level interventions based on individual-level data, are common in our literature.

A levels approach, combining micro and macro perspectives, engenders a more integrated science of organizations. House and colleagues (1995) suggest the term *meso* because it captures this sense that organizational science is both macro and micro. Whatever it is called, we need a more integrated approach. The limitations that the organizational disciplines suffer with respect to influencing policy and applications can be resolved through the development of more complete models of organizational phenomena—models that are system-oriented but do not try to capture the complexity of the entire system. Instead, by focusing on significant and salient phenomena, conceptualizing and assessing at multiple levels, and exhibiting concern about both top-down and bottom-up processes, it is possible to build a science of organizations that is theoretically rich and application-relevant.

Formative Theory Development: The Emergence of a Levels Perspective

Early efforts to conceptualize and study organizations as multilevel systems were based in the interactionist perspective (Lewin, 1951) and focused on the construct of organizational climate.[2] Those early efforts played a significant role in developing a "levels" perspective. Interactionists see behavior as a function of both person and situation, with the nature of the combined effect broadly conceived (as, for example, additive, multiplicative, and reciprocal; see Schneider, 1981; Terborg, 1981). Thus behavior is viewed as a combined result of contextual and individual-difference effects. The interactionist perspective has had a pervasive influence on organizational research. It has played a dominant role in shaping research on climate, first posited by Lewin, Lippitt, and White (1939). It continues to exert influence through research on person-organization fit.

As organizational psychology developed as a distinct subdiscipline in the 1950s, organizational climate emerged as a central construct for understanding organizational effectiveness. Researchers of this era described climate as a representation of "organizational stimuli" or "environmental characteristics" presumed to affect individual behavior and attitudes. Forehand and Gilmer (1964) reviewed the climate literature, highlighting problems of conceptualization and measurement. They criticized researchers' failure to consistently and clearly distinguish whether climate was viewed as an objective property of the organization or as an individual perception, and they bemoaned the resulting confusion regarding whether climate should be assessed at the organizational level, via objective characteristics, or at the individual level, via perceptions.

James and Jones's (1974) subsequent review helped to dispel much of this confusion. They distinguished objective characteristics of the organizational context, which are the antecedents of climate, from individuals' interpretive perceptions, which ascribe meaning to the context. This conceptualization views climate perceptions as a result of both contextual and individual influences. In addition, James and Jones distinguished psychological (that is, individual-level) climate from organizational climate, arguing that homogeneous perceptions could be aggregated to represent climate as a property of the organization. James and Jones's conclusions influenced the nature of climate research for the next two decades.

There were two critical contributions of this formative research on the development of a levels perspective in organizational science. First, this research made top-down cross-level contextual effects salient, establishing the need to conceptualize and assess organization, subunit, and group factors that had the potential to affect individual perceptions, attitudes, and behavior. This energized a stream of research that linked organizational structure and technology to individual attitudes (e.g., Herman & Hulin, 1972; James & Jones, 1976; Rousseau, 1978b). As this research progressed, models were elaborated to include mediating perceptions. Many studies were conducted that demonstrated that individual-level climate and/or job-characteristics perceptions mediated the linkage between contextual factors at higher levels (group, subunit, or organization) and individual-level outcomes (e.g., Brass, 1981, 1985; Oldham & Hackman, 1981; Kozlowski & Farr, 1988; Rousseau, 1978a). This work emphasized the importance of top-down cross-level contextual effects on lower-level phenomena. *Thus group and organization factors are contexts for individual perceptions, attitudes, and behaviors and need to be explicitly incorporated into meaningful models of organizational behavior.*

The second contribution of this research was to make salient emergent phenomena that manifest at higher levels. Although organizational policies, practices, and procedures are the antecedents of individual-level climate perceptions, individuals in organizations do not exist in a vacuum. People in groups and subunits are exposed to common features, events, and processes. They interact, sharing interpretations, which over time may converge on consensual views of the group or organizational climate (James, 1982; Kozlowski & Hattrup, 1992). Processes such as attraction, selection, and attrition; socialization (Schneider & Reichers, 1983); and leadership (Kozlowski & Doherty, 1989) also operate to reduce the variability of individual differences and perceptions, facilitating common interpretations of the climate. In such conditions, individual-level perceptions can be averaged to represent higher-level group, subunit, or organizational climates (Jones & James, 1979; Kozlowski & Hults, 1987; Schneider & Bowen, 1985). This work emphasized the importance of bottom-up emergent processes that yield higher-level phenomena. *Thus individual social-psychological processes can be manifest as group, subunit, and organizational phenomena and need to be explicitly incorporated into meaningful models of organizational behavior.*

Multilevel Organizational Theory and Research

Overview

Although interest in the development and testing of multilevel theoretical models has increased dramatically in the past decade, there have been relatively few efforts to provide multilevel theoretical frameworks for organizational researchers (e.g., House et al., 1995; Klein et al., 1994; Rousseau, 1985). Multilevel theory building presents a substantial challenge to organizational scholars trained, for the most part, to "think micro" or to "think macro" but not to "think micro *and* macro"—not, that is, to "think multilevel." Our goal is to explain fundamental issues, synthesize and extend existing frameworks, and identify theoretical principles to guide the development and evaluation of multilevel models.

In the first part of this section, we describe multilevel theoretical processes, providing insights into and principles for "thinking multilevel." The issues we examine are central to the development of multilevel theories and provide conceptual guidance for theorists seeking to develop specific multilevel models. In the second part of this section, we focus on model operationalization. Most of the difficulties of conducting multilevel research have concerned the consequences of incongruent levels among constructs, measures, or analyses (for example, misspecification errors, aggregation biases, ecological correlation; see Burstein, 1980; Firebaugh, 1979; Freeman, 1980; Hannan, 1991; Robinson, 1950; Thorndike, 1939). We provide principles to guide the interested researcher through the problem of model specification.

The principles we derive are intended to be general guidelines applicable to most circumstances; they are not immutable laws. We acknowledge at the onset that the complexity of the issues involved in multilevel theory makes exceptions to the general principles inevitable. In such cases, theory takes precedence—that is the one overarching principle.

Principles for Multilevel Organizational Theory Building

This section describes fundamental theoretical processes that provide the underpinnings for developing multilevel theories. We hope to assist readers in emulating and extending the best of current multilevel thinking. Toward this end, we highlight established principles and consider provocative new possibilities for multilevel theory building and research. For ease of presentation, we present central principles of multilevel theory building and research organized around the *what, how, where, when,* and *why* (and *why not*) of multilevel theoretical models.

What

On what should multilevel theory building and research focus? The possibilities are virtually endless, reflecting the full breadth of organizational processes, behavior, and theory. Nevertheless, a few guidelines regarding the process of choosing a focus for study are possible. First, we urge scholars to begin to fashion their theoretical models by focusing on the endogenous construct(s) of interest: What phenomenon is the theory and research attempting to understand? The endogenous construct, or dependent variable, drives the levels, constructs, and linking processes to be addressed by the theory. Too frequently, researchers begin theory development with the antecedents of interest: "These are interesting constructs; I wonder how well they predict generic outcomes." Such an approach invites the development of a trivial or misspecified theory. Without careful explication of the phenomenon of interest, it is exceedingly difficult to specify a meaningful network of potential antecedents.

PRINCIPLE: *Theory building should begin with the designation and definition of the theoretical phenomenon and the endogeneous construct(s) of interest.*

Second, multilevel theory is neither always needed nor always better than single-level theory. Micro theorists may articulate theoretical models capturing individual-level processes that are invariant across contexts, or they may examine constructs and processes that have no meaningful parallels at higher levels. Similarly, macro theorists may develop theoretical models that describe the characteristics of organizations, distinct from the actions and characteristics of organizational subunits (groups, individuals). Although we think that such phenomena are likely to be rare, in such cases multilevel theory building is not necessary.

Finally, theorists may also find it impractical to develop multilevel models for processes, relationships, and outcomes new to organizational science; that is, when tackling phenomena previously unexplored in the organizational literature, a theorist may find it helpful to initially act as if the phenomena occur at only one level of theory and analysis. In this way, a theorist temporarily restricts his or her focus, putting off consideration of multilevel processes for a period. Huselid's work (1995) on strategic human resource management provides an example. Huselid has documented organization-level relationships among human resource practices, aggregate employee outcomes, and firm financial performance, but what are the cross-level and emergent processes—the linkages of individual responses to human resource practices—that mediate the relationship between organizational human resource practices and organizational performance? The time is now ripe for such multilevel theory building (Ostroff & Bowen, Chapter Five, this volume).

Having acknowledged that there may be instances in which multilevel models may be unnecessary, we also offer the following caveat: given the nature of organizations as hierarchically nested systems, it will be difficult in practice to find single-level relations that are unaffected by other levels. The set of individual-level phenomena that are invariant across contexts is likely to be very small. Similarly, the set of group- or organization-level phenomena that are completely uninfluenced by lower levels is also likely to be small. Failure to account for such effects when they exist will yield incomplete or misspecified models.

PRINCIPLE: *Multilevel theoretical models are relevant to the vast majority of organizational phenomena. Multilevel models may, however, be unnecessary if the central phenomena of interest (a) are uninfluenced by higher-level organizational units, (b) do not reflect the actions or cognitions of lower-level organizational units, and/or (c) have been little explored in the organizational literature. Caveat: Proceed with caution!*

How

By definition, multilevel models are designed to bridge micro and macro perspectives, specifying relationships between phenomena at higher and at lower levels of analysis (for example, individuals and groups, groups and organizations, and so on). Accordingly, a multilevel theoretical model must specify how phenomena at different levels are linked. Links between phenomena at different levels may be top-down or bottom-up. Many theories will include both top-down and bottom-up processes.

Top-down processes: contextual influences. Each level of an organizational system is embedded or included in a higher-level context. Thus individuals are embedded within groups, groups within organizations, organizations within industries, industrial sectors within environmental niches, and so on. Top-down processes describe the influence of higher-level contextual factors on lower levels of the system. Fundamentally, higher-level units may influence lower-level units in two ways: (1) higher-level units may have a direct effect on lower-level units, and/or (2) higher-level units may shape or moderate relationships and processes in lower-level units.

An organization has a direct effect on the behavior of its individual employees when, for example, its culture determines the accepted patterns of employee interaction and work behavior (for example, how formally employees address each other, or the extent to which employees question their supervisors' directives). An organization has a moderating effect on lower-level relationships when the relationship between two lower-level constructs changes as a function of organizational context. Thus, for example, the relationship between employees' conscientiousness and performance may vary across organizational contexts. In contexts that provide autonomy and resources, conscientiousness may be associated with performance. However, contexts low on autonomy and resources are likely to constrain the effects of conscientiousness on performance, hence the relationship will be weak.

PRINCIPLE: *Virtually all organizational phenomena are embedded in a higher-level context, which often has either direct or moderating effects on lower-level processes and outcomes. Relevant contextual features and effects from the higher level should be incorporated into theoretical models.*

Bottom-up processes: emergence. Many phenomena in organizations have their theoretical foundation in the cognition, affect, behavior, and characteristics of individuals, which—through social interaction, exchange, and amplification—have emergent properties that manifest at higher levels. In other words, many collective constructs represent the aggregate influence of individuals. For example, the construct of organizational culture—a particularly broad and inclusive construct—summarizes the collective characteristics, behaviors, and values of an organization's members. Organizational cultures differ insofar as the characteristics, behaviors, and values of organizational members differ.[3]

Bottom-up processes describe the manner in which lower-level properties emerge to form collective phenomena. The emergence of phenomena across increasingly higher levels of systems has been a central theme of GST. Formative efforts to apply GST focus on the structure of emergence—that is, on the higher level, collective structure that results from the dynamic interactions among lower-level elements. The broad system typologies of Boulding (1956) and Miller (1978) attempt to capture the increasingly complex collectivities that are based on lower-level building blocks of the system. Thus, for example, interactions among atoms create molecular structure, or interactions among team members yield team effectiveness. This perspective views an emergent phenomenon as unique and holistic; it cannot be reduced to its lower-level elements (e.g., Dansereau et al., 1984).

A more contemporary perspective, one that has its roots in GST, derives from theories of chaos, self-organization, and complexity, and it views emergence as both process and structure. This perspective attempts to understand how the dynamics and interactions of lower-level elements unfold over time to yield structure or collective phenomena at higher levels (Arthur, 1994; Gell-Mann, 1994; Kauffman, 1994; Nicolis & Prigogine, 1989; Prigogine & Stengers, 1984). This perspective is not a reversion to reductionism; rather, it is an effort to comprehend the full complexity of a system—its elements, their dynamics over time, and the means by which elements in dynamic interaction create collective phenomena (e.g., Cowan, Pines, & Meltzer, 1994). The two perspectives are compatible but different. We draw on this latter perspective and attempt to understand both process and structure in our conceptualization of emergence.

Emergence can be characterized by two qualitatively distinct types—composition and compilation—that may be juxtaposed as anchors for a range of emergence alternatives. To simplify the discussion that follows and make distinctions more apparent, we treat composition and compilation as ideal or pure types. Later in the chapter, we further elaborate their underlying theoretical differences, discuss interaction processes and dynamics that shape emergence, and explore forms of emergence that are more akin to composition or more akin to compilation. *Composition,* based on assumptions of isomorphism, describes phenomena that are essentially the same as they emerge upward across levels. Composition processes describe the coalescence of identical lower-level properties—that is, the convergence of similar lower-level characteristics to yield a higher-level property that is essentially the same as its constituent elements. *Compilation,* based on assumptions of discontinuity, describes phenomena that comprise a common domain but are distinctively different as they emerge across levels. The concepts are functionally equivalent—that is, they occupy essentially the same role in models at different levels, but they are not identical, as in composition. Compilation processes describe the combination of related but different lower-level properties—that is, the configuration of different lower-level characteristics to yield a higher-level property that is functionally equivalent to its constituent elements.

The distinction between composition and compilation forms of emergence is best illustrated with examples. Consider the composition model for psychological and organizational climate

(James, 1982; Kozlowski & Hattrup, 1992). It indicates that both constructs reference the same content, have the same meaning, and share the same nomological network (Jones & James, 1979; Kozlowski & Hults, 1987). For example, an organization's climate for service is a reflection of organizational members' shared perceptions of the extent to which organizational policies, procedures, and practices reward and encourage customer service (Schneider & Bowen, 1985). An organization's climate for service—whether positive or negative—emerges from the shared, homogeneous perceptions of organizational members. Thus individual and organizational climates are essentially the same construct, although there are some qualitative differences at higher levels. Organizational climate is more inclusive and may have some unique antecedents relative to its lower-level origin in psychological climate (Rousseau, 1988). Composition models based on isomorphic assumptions have been the primary means of conceptualizing emergent phenomena (Brown & Kozlowski, 1997; House et al., 1995). We describe collective phenomena that emerge through composition processes as shared properties, and we discuss them in more detail in a subsequent section.

Sometimes lower-level characteristics, behaviors, and perceptions may not coalesce. Instead, lower-level characteristics, behaviors, and/or perceptions may vary within a group or organization, and yet the configuration or pattern of lower-level characteristics, behaviors, and/or perceptions may nevertheless emerge, bottom-up, to characterize the unit as a whole. Consider, for example, individual and team performance. The compilation model for individual and team performance references performance as a functionally equivalent domain but specifies different antecedents and processes at different levels (Kozlowski, Gully, Nason, & Smith, 1999). Individual performance entails task-specific knowledge, skills, and abilities. Dyadic performance entails coordinated role exchanges. Team performance is a complex function of specific individual and dyadic—networked—contributions. Thus, in compilation models, the higher-level phenomenon is a complex combination of diverse lower-level contributions (Kozlowski, 1998, 1999). The form of emergence described by compilation is not widely recognized and yet is inherent in many common phenomena, including the domains of learning, performance, norms, power, conflict, and effectiveness, among many others. Compilation-based emergent processes are relatively little explored from a multilevel perspective in the organizational literature. We describe collective phenomena that emerge through compilation processes as *configural properties* and discuss them in more detail in a subsequent section.

The type of emergent process is fundamentally affected by the nature of social-psychological interactions and can vary for a given phenomenon; that is, a particular emergent phenomenon may be compositional in some circumstances and compilational in others. Consider team performance once again. Team performance emerges from the behaviors of individual team members. But does team performance emerge as a result of the coalescence of the essentially identical behaviors of individual team members so that team performance simply reflects the sum or average performance of individual team members? Or is team performance the result of the array or pattern of individual team members' performance— the complex culmination of one team member's excellence on one task, another team member's excellence on a second task, and a third team member's fortunately inconsequential performance on yet a third task? The first conceptualization is an example of composition; the second is an example of compilation. Neither conceptualization is "right" in all circumstances. Rather, the determining factors are the dimension of interest for team performance, the nature of the team's work-flow interdependence, and the organizational context in which the team exists, among others. This example hints at the challenges inherent in explicating the precise bottom-up processes that yield many higher-level constructs. Despite the challenges, however, precise explication of these emergent processes lays the groundwork for operationalizing the construct— a point on which we elaborate later in this chapter.

PRINCIPLE: *Many higher-level phenomena emerge from characteristics, cognition, behavior, affect, and interactions among individuals. Conceptualization of emergent phenomena at higher levels should specify, theoretically, the nature and form of these bottom-up emergent processes.*

Where

Virtually inseparable from the question of *how* is the question of *where*—that is, precisely where do top-down and bottom-up processes originate and culminate? The answers to these questions specify the focal entities—the specific organizational levels, units, or elements—relevant to theory construction. Suppose, for example, that a theorist is interested in the influence of unit climate on individual actions. What is the level of interest? For example, is it group climate? division climate? organizational climate? the climate of the informal friendship network? In the passages that follow, we will first explore the nature of organizational units as evoked by multilevel theory and then describe processes that determine the strength of the ties that link organizational levels or units.

Nature of organizational units. All but the smallest organizations are characterized by differentiation (horizontal divisions) and integration (vertical levels). These factors yield myriad entities, units, or levels. In organizational research, levels of *theoretical interest* focus on humans and social collectivities. Thus individuals, dyads, groups, subunits, and organizations are relevant levels (units, or entities) of conceptual interest. The structure is hierarchically nested so that higher-level units encompass those at lower levels. Many writers (Brown & Kozlowski, 1997; Freeman, 1980; Glick, 1985; Hannan, 1991; Simon, 1973) assert the importance of using formally designated units and levels for specification; for example, leadership research typically defines the "leader" as the formal unit manager. Generally speaking, formal units can be defined with little difficulty, although there can be exceptions, where unit boundaries or memberships are fuzzy.

Yet organizations are social systems in which people define their own informal social entities (Katz & Kahn, 1966). A variety of phenomena may define units or entities that do not correspond with formal unit boundaries. For example, vertical dyad linkage (VDL) theory (Graen, 1976) posits the formation of in-and out-groups as distinctive entities within a formal unit. Rentch (1990) demonstrates that patterns of social interaction across formal units influenced consensus on organizational climate, indicating that informal entities affect sensemaking processes. Often unit specification is based on expedience rather than on careful consideration. This can be problematic when the phenomena of interest are examined within formal units but are driven by informal processes that yield nonuniform patterns of dispersion (Brown & Kozlowski, 1997). Therefore, levels and units should be consistent with the nature of the phenomenon of interest (Campbell, 1958; Freeman, 1980).

PRINCIPLE: *Unit specification (formal versus informal) should be driven by the theory of the phenomena in question. Specification of informal entities that cut across formal boundaries, or that occur within formal units and lead to differentiation, requires careful consideration.*

Determinants of the strength of ties linking organizational levels or units. One overgeneralization of the systems metaphor is that everything is related to everything. In reality, some levels and units are much more likely than others to be strongly linked, through what Simon (1973) refers to as *bond strength.* The theorist needs to chose appropriate units and levels or risk a misspecified or ineffective theory. Bond strength and related concepts help to explain what is likely to be connected across levels, and why.

Simon (1969, 1973) views social organizations as nearly decomposable systems. In other words, limited aspects of the larger system can be meaningfully addressed without compromising the system's integrity. A social organization can be conceptualized as a set of subsystems composed of more elemental components that are arrayed in a hierarchical structure. The linkage among levels— individual, group, and organizational—and subsystems is determined by their bond strength, which refers to the extent to which characteristics, behaviors, dynamics, and processes of one level or unit influence the characteristics, behaviors, dynamics, and processes of another level or unit (Simon, 1973). The greater the implications of one unit's actions for another unit, the greater the strength of the bond linking the two units. Therefore, meaningful linkages increase in strength with proximity and inclusion, and they decrease in strength with distance and independence.

Other researchers have used similar concepts to express the same basic principle. Weick (1976) uses the concept of *coupling* to reference decomposable subsystems. House and colleagues (1995) describe *inclusion* as the proportion of a lower-level unit's activities that are devoted to a higher level; units that are highly included will be more closely linked to the higher level. Kozlowski and Salas (1997) use the term *embeddedness* to describe how lower-level phenomena are aligned with contextual factors and processes that originate at higher levels in the organizational system; alignment reflects strong bonds or inclusion across levels. Technostructural factors such as organizational goals, technology, and structure, as well as enabling processes such as leadership, socialization, and culture, influence embeddedness. From an interactionist perspective, Indik (1968) and James and Jones (1976) assert that strong interactions between levels require propinquity of structure and process and alignment of content. Constructs and processes implicated in bond strength, coupling, inclusion, and embeddedness will be more strongly linked across levels for relevant units.

This has obvious implications for models that incorporate multiple levels or units. Proximal, included, embedded, and directly coupled levels and units exhibit more meaningful relations than distal levels or loosely coupled units. Moreover, the content underlying constructs at different levels has to have some meaningful connection. For example, work-unit technology and structure exhibit cross-level effects on individuals because they constrain the characteristics of jobs (Kozlowski & Farr, 1988; Rousseau, 1978a, 1978b). The levels are coupled and the content is meaningfully related in a common network of relations. In contrast, the potential effects of organization-level strategy on individual jobs is likely to be quite small. This does not mean that strategy has no effect; rather, its effects are mediated through so many intervening levels, units, and content domains that direct effects are likely to be very difficult to detect at the individual level because bond strength is weak and the focal content is not meaningfully related. The effects of strategy are likely to be indirect.

PRINCIPLE: *Linkages across levels are more likely to be exhibited for proximal, included, embedded, and/or directly coupled levels and entities.*

PRINCIPLE: *Linkages are more likely to be exhibited for constructs that tap content domains underlying meaningful interactions across levels.*

When

Time is rarely a consideration in either single-level or multilevel organizational models (House et al., 1995), yet it is clearly the case that many if not most organizational phenomena are influenced and shaped by time. Here we explore three ways in which time may be incorporated into a multilevel model, increasing the rigor, creativity, and effectiveness of multilevel theory building.

Time as a boundary condition or moderator. Many organizational phenomena have a unidirectional effect on higher- or lower-level organizational phenomena, but multilevel relationships are not always so simple; instead, over time the relationship between phenomena at different levels may prove bidirectional or reciprocal. A given phenomenon may appear to originate at a higher or lower level according to the theorist's assumption about the current time point in a stream or cycle of events. The failure, quite common, to make such assumptions explicit can lead to apparently contradictory models of the same phenomenon and to debates about its "true" level.

For example, organizational culture is more likely to be based on emergent processes, either when the organization is at an early point in its life cycle or when the organization is undergoing dramatic change. In effect, individual sensemaking and social construction are more active and have a greater impact when the organizational context is ambiguous or in a state of flux. Therefore development or change in organizational culture will appear to be a bottom-up process. Over time, however, culture becomes stable and institutionalized. Formative events that were salient during emergence become the stuff of myth, legend, and tradition. Founding members move on. New members are socialized and assimilated into enduring contexts that resist change. Therefore, organizational culture appears to have a top-down influence on lower-level units.

The distinction between the two perspectives just sketched does not have to do with which one represents the "true" model of organizational culture; both are veridical. A variety of factors and processes can influence the apparent direction, top-down or bottom-up, of a cross-level process. This illustrates the necessity for the theorist to explicitly specify the temporal assumptions for the phenomenon in question. Thus time may serve as a boundary condition for the model; for example, the theorist states that the model applies only to mature organizations, or only to new ones. Alternatively, in a theoretical model, time may serve as a moderator of the phenomenon; for example, the theorist posits that the direction (top-down or bottom-up) and effects of the phenomenon vary as a function of the organization's maturity.

PRINCIPLE: *The temporal scope, as well as the point in the life cycle of a social entity, affect the apparent origin and direction of many phenomena in such a way that they may appear variously top-down, bottom-up, or both. Theory must explicitly specify its temporal reference points.*

Time-scale variations across levels. Differences in time scales affect the nature of links among levels (Simon, 1973). Lower-level phenomena tend to have more rapid dynamics than higher-level and emergent phenomena, which makes it is easier to detect change in lower-level entities. This is one reason why top-down models predominate in the literature. For example, efforts to improve organizational outcomes (for example, quality) through training (for example, total-quality management, or TQM) assume emergent effects that originate at the individual level. Models of training effectiveness focus on the transfer of trained skills to the performance setting. Higher-level contextual support (for example, a transfer climate; see Rouiller & Goldstein, 1993) enhances transfer in such a way that the effects of TQM training on quality are relatively immediate. However, the effect of individual-level TQM training on organizational outcomes is emergent and requires a much longer time scale. Individual cognition, attitudes, and behaviors must combine through social and work interactions. Depending on the nature of the vertical transfer process, individual outcomes will compose or compile to the group level and, over longer time frames, will yield organizational outcomes (Kozlowski & Salas, 1997; Kozlowski, Brown, Weissbein, & Cannon-Bowers, Chapter Four, this volume). Thus contextual or top-down linkages can be manifest within short time frames, whereas emergent, bottom-up linkages necessitate longer time frames.

PRINCIPLE: *Time-scale differences allow top-down effects on lower levels to manifest quickly. Bottom-up emergent effects manifest over longer periods. Research designs must be sensitive to the temporal requirements of theory.*

One implication of this effect of time scale is that phenomena at different levels may manifest at different points in time. For example, Kozlowski and his colleagues have proposed that team performance compiles and emerges across levels, from individuals to dyads to teams, at different points in the team-development process (Kozlowski et al., 1994, 1999). Others, in related fashion, have noted that level of a relationship in a multilevel model—homogeneous groups, heterogeneous groups, or independent individuals—can be influenced by factors that, over time, change the level of the relationship (Dansereau, Yammarino, & Kohles, 1999).

Entrainment: changing linkages over time. The term *entrainment* refers to the rhythm, pacing, and synchronicity of processes that link different levels (Ancona & Chong, 1997; House et al., 1995). Coupling across levels or units is tightened during periods of greater entrainment. Entrainment is affected by task cycles and work flows, budget cycles, and other temporally structured events that pace organizational life (Ancona & Chong, 1997). For example, the concept of entrainment has been used in the group and team performance literature to capture the idea that work-flow interdependence is not necessarily uniform over time; rather, the degree of interdependence or coupling can vary significantly depending on the timing of events or acts that require a synchronous and coordinated response (e.g., Fleishman & Zaccaro, 1992; Kozlowski, Gully, McHugh, Salas, & Cannon-Bowers, 1996; Kozlowski et al., 1999; McGrath, 1990). Thus levels or units that ordinarily are loosely coupled will be tightly coupled during periods of synchronicity.

Accordingly, entrainment processes must be considered during theory construction. Further, entrainment has rather obvious implications for research designs that intend to capture entrained processes. At some points in the cycle, two entities or levels may be tightly coupled or entrained, whereas at other points they will be decoupled and will appear independent. This variability creates demands for precise theory and measurement in order to capture the coupling; data collection must be sensitive to entrainment cycles and periods.

PRINCIPLE: *Entrainment can tightly couple phenomena that ordinarily are only loosely coupled across levels. Theories that address entrained phenomena must specify appropriate time cycles and must employ those cycles to structure research designs.*

Why and Why Not?

Argument by assertion is invariably a poor strategy for theory building. Argument by logical analysis and persuasion—argument that explains why—is always preferable. In multilevel theory building, explaining why is not merely preferable but essential. A great deal of organizational multilevel theory building spans organizational subdisciplines (industrial/organizational psychology and organizational theory, for example). Therefore, the unstated assumptions in a multilevel theory may be obvious to the members of one subdiscipline but not to the members of another, who are also interested in the new multilevel theory. Furthermore, multilevel theories often incorporate novel constructs (for example, team mental models, or organizational learning). The meaning of such constructs may well be obscured in the absence of thorough explanations concerning why. Finally, multilevel data analysis has been the subject of considerable and continuous debate. Conflicts regarding the best way to analyze multilevel models abate considerably, however, in the presence of carefully and fully explicated theoretical models (Klein et al., 1994) that make the choice of analytical strategy clear (Klein, Bliese et al., Chapter Twelve, this volume). Thus multilevel theorists must not only specify what, how, where, and when but also why: Why are relationships in the model conceptualized as top-down rather than bottom-up? Why are constructs conceptualized as compositional rather than compilational? Why are predictors assumed to have immediate rather than long-term consequences for the outcomes of interest?

Nearly as important as the question of why, and perhaps even more interesting, is the question of why not. Why might bottom-up processes *not* yield a group-level property? That is, why might members' perceptions *not* converge to form a shared unit norm or climate? Why might top-down processes *not* constrain relationships in an organizational subunit? Why might predictors, hypothesized to be influential over time, prove instead to have immediate consequences? In exploring why not, theorists may refine their models, incorporating important insights and nuances. This adds diversity and depth to theory; it is how a science is built.

PRINCIPLE: *Multilevel theoretical models must provide a detailed explanation of the assumptions undergirding the model. Such explanations should answer not only the question of why but also the question of why not.*

In sum, rigorous multilevel theories must carefully consider what, how, where, when, why, and why not. In what follows, we explicate how these basic questions inform the definition and measurement of constructs in multilevel models. We then describe distinctive forms or frameworks that multilevel models may take, the kinds of research designs and samples necessary to test multilevel models, and possible data analytic strategies.

Principles for Model Specification: Aligning Constructs, Measures, Models, Design, and Analyses

Many of the controversies and problems associated with multilevel research are based on misspecifications or misalignments among the theoretical level of constructs, their measurement, and their representation for analysis. Misalignment is a problem for any research design that incorporates mixed levels, but it is also a problem for single-level research that incorporates emergent constructs. The nature of these misalignments is well documented elsewhere (Burstein, 1980; Firebaugh, 1979; Freeman, 1980; Hannan, 1991; Robinson, 1950; Rousseau, 1985; Thorndike, 1939). The following are some common problems: blind aggregation of individual-level measures to represent unit-level constructs, use of unit-level measures to infer lower-level relations (the well-known problems of aggregation bias and ecological fallacies), and use of informants who lack unique knowledge or experience to assess unit-level constructs.

Misalignments degrade construct validity and create concerns about generalizability. To build theoretical models that are clear and persuasive, scholars must explicate the nature of their constructs with real care. Precise explication lays the foundation for sound measurement. Constructs that are conceptualized and measured at different levels may be combined in a variety of distinctive multilevel models. Research design and analytical strategies need to be aligned with the levels inherent in these models. Principles relevant to these concerns are considered in the remainder of this section.

Constructs in Multilevel Theory

Construct level and origin. Constructs are the building blocks of organizational theory. A construct is an abstraction used to explain an apparent phenomenon. The level of a construct is the level at which it is hypothesized to be manifest in a given theoretical model—the known or predicted level of the phenomenon in question. Although organizational theorists have often discussed "the level of theory," we prefer to use the phrase *level of the construct* because mixed-level models, by definition, include constructs that span multiple levels; that is, generalizations are constrained by the level of the endogenous construct ("the level of the theory"), but other constructs in a model may be at higher or lower levels. Thus, in mixed-level research, the theoretical explanation will span several levels in the effort to understand an endogenous construct at a given focal level.

The first and foremost task in crafting a multilevel theory or study is to define, justify, and explain the level of each focal construct that constitutes the theoretical system. Remarkably, the level of many organizational constructs is unclear. This problem, we have noted, once plagued the climate literature. Researchers and critics asked whether climate was to be conceptualized and measured as an organizational (unit) construct or as a psychological (individual) one. Climate researchers resolved this question, differentiating explicitly between a consensual unit climate and its origins in psychological climate. However, the question of level is often unasked in other research. Consider the familiar construct of worker participation. What is its level? Is worker participation an individual-level phenomenon, describing the influence an individual exerts in unit decisions? Or is worker participation at the unit level, describing a set of formal structures and work practices (for example, quality circles) characteristic of units, not individuals? For the most part, the participation literature reveals neither clear consensus regarding the level of the construct nor explicit discussion of its level (Klein et al., 1994).

PRINCIPLE: *The theorist should explicitly specify the level of each construct in a theoretical system.*

In specifying the level of a construct, the theorist must build a targeted theory, or "minitheory," of the phenomenon, explicating where, when, and how the construct forms and is manifest. Many phenomena we study in organizations have their theoretical origins in the cognition, affect, and behavior of individuals but emerge, through compositional or compilational processes, to manifest as higher-level phenomena. A given construct may be an individual-level construct in some circumstances and a unit-level construct in others. When a theorist specifies that a construct originates at the individual level and manifests at a higher level, the theorist must explicate when, how, and why this process occurs. The theoretical foundation for emergent effects must be at the level of origin. When psychological and social-psychological phenomena are emergent at higher levels, the researcher needs to distinguish the level of theoretical origin and the level at which the focal construct is manifest—the level of the construct. The researcher must also explain the theoretical process that yields higher-level emergence—the conditions in which the higher-level construct exists or does not exist. This is essential to determining an appropriate means of assessing and representing the emergent higher-level construct.

PRINCIPLE: *When higher-level constructs are based on emergent processes, the level of origin, the level of the construct, and the nature of the emergent process must be explicitly specified by the theory.*

We elaborate further in what follows, explaining links between the previously described principles of multilevel theory (what, where, when, how, why, and why not) and the definition, explication, and measurement of theoretical constructs. Our quarrel with much of the existing theoretical literature on organizations is not that authors are too complex in characterizing the multiple, even shifting, levels of their constructs but just the opposite: that, too often, authors' conceptualizations of the theoretical processes and levels of their constructs lack important detail, depth, and complexity. We now consider different types of higher-level constructs and address the implications for measurement.

Types of unit-level constructs. Unit-level constructs describe entities composed of two or more individuals: dyads, groups, functions, divisions, organizations, and so on. In the organizational literature, many problems and controversies revolve around the definition, conceptualization, justification, and measurement of unit-level constructs. The "level" of many higher-level constructs (culture, leadership, or participation, for example) is often debated. The debate is due in part to the potential for these constructs to emerge from lower-level phenomena.

To help resolve the controversies and confusion that often surround the definition, meaning, and operationalization of unit-level constructs, we distinguish three basic types:

1. Global unit properties
2. Shared unit properties
3. Configural unit properties

Global unit properties differ from shared and configural unit properties in their level of origin. Global unit properties originate and are manifest at the unit level. Global unit properties are single-level phenomena. In contrast, shared and configural unit properties originate at lower levels but are manifest as higher-level phenomena. Shared and configural unit properties emerge from the characteristics, behaviors, or cognitions of unit members—and their interactions—to characterize the unit as a whole. Shared and configural unit properties represent phenomena that span two or more levels. Shared unit properties are essentially similar across levels (that is, isomorphic), representing composition forms of emergence. In contrast, configural unit properties are functionally equivalent but different (that is, discontinuous), representing compilation forms of emergence. Configural unit properties capture the variability or pattern of individual characteristics, constructs, or responses across the members of a unit. We elaborate in what follows, and then we discuss how the nature of a unit construct influences its measurement.[4]

Global unit properties. Global constructs pertain to the relatively objective, descriptive, easily observable characteristics of a unit that originate at the unit level. Global unit properties do not originate in individuals' perceptions, experiences, attitudes, demographics, behaviors, or interactions but are a property of the unit as a whole. They are often dictated by the unit's structure or function. Group size and unit function (marketing, purchasing, human resources) are examples of global properties. There is no possibility of within-unit variation because lower-level properties are irrelevant; indeed, any within-unit variation is most likely the result of a procedure that uses lower-level units to measure the global property. If, for example, group members disagree about the size of their group, someone has simply miscounted. Unit size has an objective standing apart from members' characteristics or social-psychological processes. In contrast, "perceived group membership" is an entirely different type of construct.

Shared unit properties. Constructs of this type describe the characteristics that are common to—that is, shared by—the members of a unit. Organizational climate, collective efficacy, and group norms are examples of shared unit-level properties. Shared unit properties are presumed or hypothesized to originate in individual unit members' experiences, attitudes, perceptions, values, cognitions, or behaviors and to converge among group members as a function of attraction, selection, attrition, socialization, social interaction, leadership, and other psychological processes. In this way, shared unit properties emerge as a consensual, collective aspect of the unit as a whole. Shared unit properties are based on *composition* models of emergence, in which the central assumption is one of isomorphism between manifestations of constructs at different levels; the constructs share the same content, meaning, and construct validity across levels. When researchers describe and study shared unit properties, they need to explain in considerable detail the theoretical processes predicted to yield restricted within-unit variance with respect to the constructs of interest: How does within-unit consensus (agreement) or consistency (reliability) emerge from the individual-level characteristics (experiences, perceptions, attitudes, and so on) and interaction processes among unit members?

Configural unit properties. Constructs of this type capture the array, pattern, or configuration of individuals' characteristics within a unit. Configural unit properties, like the shared properties of a unit, originate at the individual level. Unlike shared unit properties, however, configural unit properties are not assumed to coalesce and converge among the members of a unit. The individual contributions to configural unit properties are distinctly different. Therefore, configural unit properties have to capture the array of these differential contributions to the whole. Configural unit properties characterize patterns, distribution, and/or variability among members' contributions to the unit-level phenomenon. Configural unit properties do not rest on assumptions of isomorphism and coalescing processes of composition but rather on assumptions of discontinuity and complex nonlinear processes of *compilation*. The resulting constructs are qualitatively different yet functionally equivalent across levels.

Configural unit properties are relatively rare in the organizational literature, but they are not rare in organizations. We can distinguish two types of configural unit properties: *descriptive characteristics,* which reference manifest and observable features, and *latent constructs,* which reference hypothetical and unobserved properties of the unit in question. Descriptive characteristics are straightforward. For example, diversity—the extent to which unit members' demographic characteristics are dissimilar—is a configural descriptive unit property. However, whereas diversity is a manifest unit characteristic, it most likely has effects through latent constructs that tap underlying psychological differences (e.g., Millikin & Martins, 1996). For example, diversity in unit-level sex or age are descriptive characteristics that may be linked to unit-level variability for the constructs of attitudes and values.

Unit-level conceptualizations of constructs are often configural.[5] For example, the combination of team members' abilities or personality characteristics constitutes the configural properties of the unit (Moreland & Levine, 1992). Configural constructs may also capture the pattern of individual perceptions or behavior within a unit. For example, team performance is often regarded as a global property of the team, yet when individual team members perform different but interdependent tasks, team performance may be conceptualized as a configural construct; team members do not engage in identical behaviors (Kozlowski et al., 1999). Finally, network characteristics (for example, network density) are configural insofar as they depict the pattern of the relationships within a unit (or network) as a whole (Brass, 1995). Configural unit properties are based on compilation models of emergence (e.g., Kozlowski et al., 1999). When studying configural unit properties, researchers need to explain in detail the theoretical processes by which different individual contributions combine to yield the emergent unit property—that is, how are the individual origins represented in the summary, pattern, configuration, or array of the unit-level property?

PRINCIPLE: *Theorists whose models contain unit-level constructs should indicate explicitly whether their constructs are global unit properties, shared unit properties, or configural unit properties. The type of unit-level construct should drive its form of measurement and representation for analyses.*

Levels of Measurement

Basic issues. The level of measurement is the level at which data are collected to assess a given construct. Individual-level constructs should, of course, be assessed with individual-level data. Unit-level constructs, in contrast, may be assessed with either unit-level or individual-level data. When unit-level constructs are assessed with unit-level measures, an expert source (a subject matter expert, for example, or an objective archive) provides a single rating of each unit. When unit-level constructs are assessed with individual-level measures, unit members provide individual-level data (for example, individual ratings of climate, or individuals' reports of their own demographic characteristics), which are subsequently combined in some way to depict the unit as a whole. Rousseau (1985, p. 31) advises researchers to measure unit-level constructs with global (that is, unit-level) data whenever possible: "Use of global data is to be preferred because they are more clearly linked to the level of measurement, avoiding the ambiguity inherent in aggregated data." Klein and colleagues (1994, p. 210) note that when a researcher uses "a global measure to characterize a group, he or she lacks the data needed to test whether members are, indeed, homogeneous within groups on the variables of interest." Accordingly, Klein and colleagues (1994, p. 210) recommend that researchers use global measures to capture unit-level constructs only when the level of the construct is "certain" or "beyond question." Here, we elaborate on Rousseau's (1985) and Klein and colleagues' (1995) admonitions, advising that the level of measurement should be determined by the type of the unit-level construct.

Individual-level constructs. Individual-level constructs should, as already noted, be assessed at the individual level. For example, individuals may complete measures of their own job satisfaction, turnover intentions, self-efficacy, psychological climate, and so forth. In some cases, one or more experts may provide assessments of the characteristics of other individuals. This procedure can be used when the characteristic is observable, or when the informant has unique access to relevant information (Campbell, 1955; Seidler, 1974). A supervisor may describe his or her individual subordinates' performance behavior, an observer may record individual demographic characteristics, or a researcher may use archival records to assess individuals' ages, tenure, or experience. In each case, data are assigned to individuals and are considered individual-level data. Issues of measurement quality are, of course, still relevant.

Global properties. The measurement of unit-level variables is often more complex and more controversial. Least complex and least controversial is the measurement of the global properties of a unit. By definition, global properties are observable, descriptive characteristics of a unit. Global properties do not emerge from individual-level experiences, attitudes, values, or characteristics. Accordingly, there is no need to ask all the individuals within a unit to describe its global properties. A single expert individual may serve as an informant when the characteristic is observable, or when the informant has unique access to relevant information. Thus a vice president for sales may report his or her company's sales volume, a CEO may report a firm's strategy, or a manager may report a unit's function. Although these examples each use an individual respondent, the data are considered global unit-level properties.

Shared properties. In contrast, shared properties of a unit emerge from individual members' shared perceptions, affect, and responses. The theoretical origin of shared properties is the psychological level, and so data to assess these constructs should match the level of origin. This provides an opportunity to evaluate the composition model of emergence underlying the shared property;

that is, the predicted shared property may not in fact be shared, in which case the data cannot be averaged to provide a meaningful representation of the higher-level construct. Therefore, the data to measure shared unit properties should be assessed at the individual level, and sharedness within the unit should be evaluated. Given evidence of restricted within-unit variance, the aggregate (mean) value of the measure should be assigned to the unit. Several empirical examples of this approach to the conceptualization, assessment, and composition of unit-level constructs can be found in the literature (e.g., Campion, Medsker, & Higgs, 1993; Hofmann & Stetzer, 1996; Kozlowski & Hults, 1987). This approach ensures both that the data are congruent with the construct's origin and that they conform to the construct's predicted form of emergence, thereby avoiding misalignment.

Configural properties.   When a construct refers to a configural property of a unit, the data to assess the construct derive from the characteristics, cognitions, or behaviors of individual members. Individual-level data are summarized to describe the pattern or configuration of these individual contributions. As before, theory—the conceptual definition of the emergent construct—drives the operationalization of the measure. Configural properties emerge from individuals but do not coalesce as shared properties do. Thus a researcher, in operationalizing the configural properties of a unit, need not evaluate consensus, similarity, or agreement among individual members except to rule out coalescence. The summary value or values used to represent the configural property are based on the theoretical definition of the construct and on the nature of its emergence as a unit-level property. A variety of data-combination techniques may be used to represent, capture, or summarize configural properties, including the minimum or maximum, indices of variation, profile similarity, multidimensional scaling, neural nets, network analyses, systems dynamics and other nonlinear models, among others. The mean of individual members' characteristics is generally not an appropriate summary statistic to depict a configural unit property, although it may be combined with an indicator of variance or dispersion (Brown et al., 1996). In the absence of within-unit consensus, means are equifinal, ambiguous, and questionable representations of higher-level constructs.

PRINCIPLE: *There is no single best way to measure unit-level constructs. The type of a unit-level construct, in addition to its underlying theoretical model, determine how the construct should be assessed and operationalized. As a general rule, global properties should be assessed and represented at the unit level. Shared and configural properties should be assessed at the level of origin, with the form of emergence reflected in the model of data aggregation, combination, and representation.*

Establishing the construct validity of shared properties. The assumption of isomorphism that is central to the conceptualization of shared constructs requires explicit consideration. There are two primary issues relevant to testing models with one or more shared unit properties:

1. Establishing the measurement model
2. Evaluating the substantive theoretical model

The issue of the measurement model addresses the construct validity of aggregated lower-level measures as representations of higher-level constructs. It is generally addressed through examining patterns of within-group variance. Consensus- or agreement-based approaches—for example, $r_{wg(j)}$—evaluate within-group variance against a hypothetical expected-variance (EV) term. Agreement is examined for each shared property measure for each unit: a construct-by-group approach. Consistency- or reliability-based approaches—for example, ICC(1), ICC(2), and within-and-between analysis (WABA)—evaluate between-group variance relative to total (between and within) variance, essentially examining interrater reliability for each shared property across the sample: a construct-by-sample approach (Kozlowski & Hattrup, 1992; Bliese, Chapter Eight, this volume).

These different treatments have been the source of some debate (e.g., George & James, 1993; Yammarino & Markham, 1992). Consensus approaches treat issues 1 and 2 as distinct (e.g., James, Demaree, & Wolf, 1984; James et al., 1993; Kozlowski & Hults, 1987; Kozlowski & Hattrup, 1992). The strength is that construct misspecification, for any construct in any group, is avoided. The disadvantage is that there may be insufficient between-group variance for model evaluation, and this problem will not be revealed until data analysis. Consistency-based approaches treat the issues as more unitary (e.g., Yammarino & Markham, 1992). The strength is that both within and between variance are considered in the computation of reliability, and so aggregated measures also have adequate between variance for the evaluation of substantive relations. The disadvantage is that some constructs may not actually have restricted variance in some groups, and so there is some potential for construct misspecification, which may be masked in the construct-by-sample approach.

We assert that consideration of both within-group and between-group variance is critical. However, the particular approach chosen is a matter of consistency with one's theory and data. Both approaches have different strengths and drawbacks. In the appropriate circumstances, either of the approaches is acceptable; there is no universally preferable approach.

PRINCIPLE: *The assumption of isomorphism of shared unit properties should be explicitly evaluated to establish the construct validity of the aggregated measure. The selection of a consensus- or consistency-based approach should be dictated by theory and data; no approach is universally preferable.*

Data source, construct, and measurement levels. Individuals as sources of data play different roles in measuring the three different types of unit constructs. This observation highlights the distinction between the data source, on the one hand, and the level of the construct and its measurement, on the other. For example, a knowledgeable individual may act as the data source for a global unit property such as size, function, or strategy, but in such a case the level of measurement is not considered the individual but rather the unit as a global entity.

A single informant may provide the data to measure the configural or distributional properties of a unit when the properties are directly and reliably observable, or when the informant has unique access to relevant information. For example, a supervisor may report the distribution of males and females in a unit. A manager may report unit members' tenure, thus providing the data necessary for the calculation of a unit's variability with respect to tenure. Individual-level performance data may be reported by a team leader to assess the configuration of team performance. In these examples, the configural construct is a unit-level construct even though the source is a single expert.

In contrast, a single individual may rarely if ever serve as the data source regarding a shared property of the construct. For example, it is generally not appropriate to use single informants (for example, a supervisor or a CEO) to assess unit or organizational climate; climate originates as individual interpretations and emerges via social interaction, and single informants are not uniquely situated to know the inner interpretations of multiple perceivers. Thus assessment should model the theory regarding the origin and nature of the construct.

PRINCIPLE: *Individuals may serve as expert informants for higher-level constructs when they can directly observe or have unique knowledge of the properties in question. As a general rule, expert informants are most appropriate for the measurement of global unit-level properties and observable (manifest) configural properties. They are least appropriate for the measurement of shared properties and unobservable (latent) configural properties.*

Item construction. Several authors have provided guidelines for item construction, primarily for the measurement of shared properties. In general, the advice is to focus respondents on description as opposed to evaluation of their feelings (James & Jones, 1974) and to construct items that reference the higher level, not the level of measurement (James, 1982; Klein et al., 1994; Rousseau, 1985). In practice, research has tended to use items framed at both the individual level (data source) and at higher levels. Recently, Chan (1998) distinguished these practices as representing different composition models of the constructs in question. For example, Chan views climate items referencing self-perceptions (for example, "I think my organization . . .") as constructs distinct from items that tap the same content but reference collective perceptions (for example, "We think the organization . . .")—what he refers to as "reference shift consensus."

Research that has tested the merits of this advice is, however, very limited. Klein, Conn, Smith, and Sorra (1998) have found that survey items referencing the unit as a whole (for example, "Employees' work here is rewarding") do engender less within-group variability and more between-group variability than comparable survey items that reference individual experiences and perceptions (for example, "My work here is rewarding"). However, many climate researchers assessing shared unit properties have used self-referenced items and have demonstrated meaningful within-unit consensus (e.g., Kozlowski & Hults, 1987; Ostroff, 1993; Schneider & Bowen, 1985). It may well be the case that item content is critically important to the unit of reference. Perhaps climate-related content (for example, "I think the reward system . . .") that taps the broader work environment may be more robust to differences between self-reference versus collective reference. The perspective, whether the self or the larger unit, may be largely the same, whereas content that taps more variable properties (for example, "My job is . . .") may be more sensitive to the point of view incorporated in the item.

Clearly, more empirical work is needed to establish which item characteristics are critical to construct fidelity and which ones are not essential. In the meantime, we suggest that researchers employ measures consistent with the conceptualization of their constructs, using unit-level referents, if possible, to assess shared unit-level constructs. However, without more definitive empirical evidence, we do not encourage this as a litmus test and do not offer a principle. We do encourage more empirical research on guidelines for the construction of items to assess emergent constructs.

Types of Multilevel Models

Theoretical models describe relationships among constructs. A multilevel perspective invites—indeed, necessitates—special attention to the level of the constructs united within a theoretical model. In this section, we build on the preceding section by describing broad types of models distinguished by the levels of the constructs they encompass, as well as by the links they propose among constructs. Model specifications are illustrated in Figure 1.1. Following our description of basic models, we note further complexities in the creation of multilevel models.

Single-level models. Single-level models, as their name suggests, specify the relationship between constructs at a single level of theory

Figure 1.1. Model Specification.

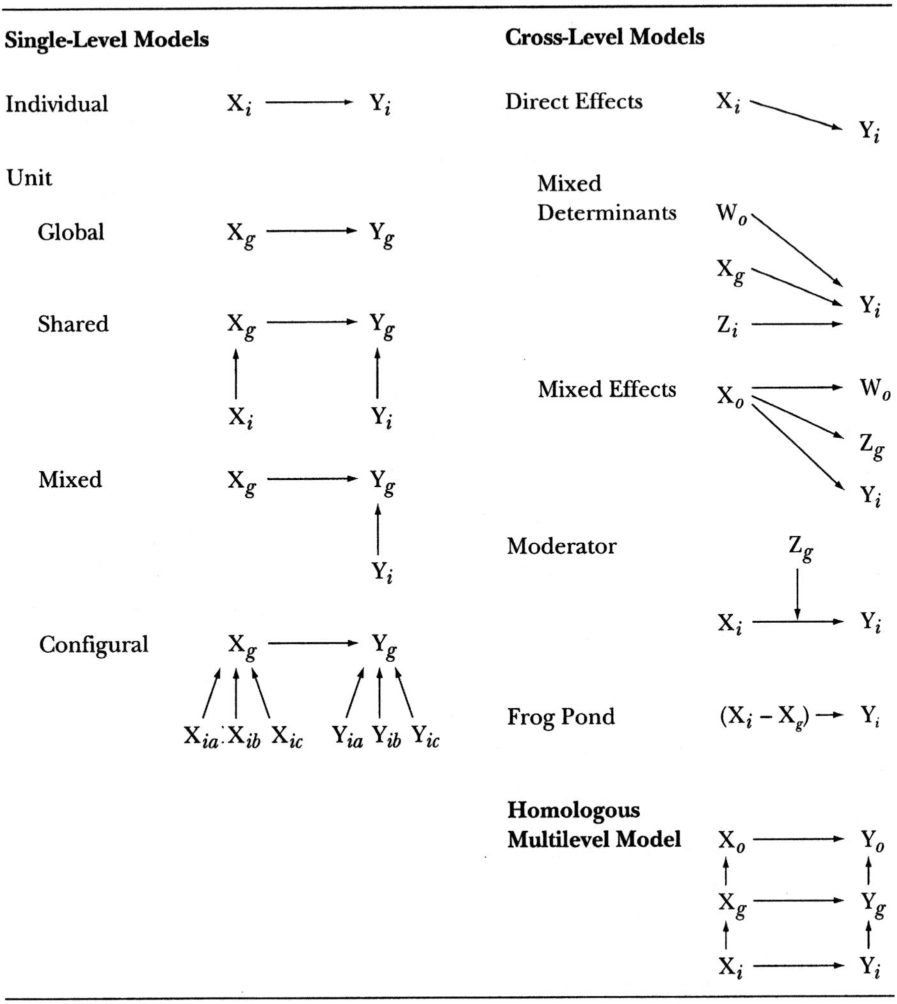

Single-Level Models

Cross-Level Models

Individual $\quad$ $X_i \longrightarrow Y_i$

Unit

Global $\quad$ $X_g \longrightarrow Y_g$

Shared $\quad$ $X_g \longrightarrow Y_g$
$\qquad\quad$ $\uparrow \qquad\quad \uparrow$
$\qquad\quad$ $X_i \qquad\quad Y_i$

Mixed $\quad$ $X_g \longrightarrow Y_g$
$\qquad\qquad\qquad\qquad \uparrow$
$\qquad\qquad\qquad\quad Y_i$

Configural $\quad$ $X_g \longrightarrow Y_g$
$\qquad\qquad$ $X_{ia} \; X_{ib} \; X_{ic} \quad Y_{ia} \; Y_{ib} \; Y_{ic}$

Direct Effects $\quad$ $X_i \searrow$
$\qquad\qquad\qquad\qquad\qquad Y_i$

Mixed
Determinants $\quad$ W_o
$\qquad\qquad\qquad\quad X_g$
$\qquad\qquad\qquad\qquad\qquad\qquad Y_i$
$\qquad\qquad\qquad\quad Z_i \longrightarrow$

Mixed Effects $\quad X_o \longrightarrow W_o$
$\qquad\qquad\qquad\qquad\qquad Z_g$
$\qquad\qquad\qquad\qquad\qquad Y_i$

Moderator $\qquad\qquad Z_g$
$\qquad\qquad\qquad\qquad \downarrow$
$\qquad\qquad X_i \longrightarrow Y_i$

Frog Pond $\quad (X_i - X_g) \longrightarrow Y_i$

Homologous
Multilevel Model $\quad X_o \longrightarrow Y_o$
$\qquad\qquad\qquad\qquad \uparrow \qquad\quad \uparrow$
$\qquad\qquad\qquad\qquad X_g \longrightarrow Y_g$
$\qquad\qquad\qquad\qquad \uparrow \qquad\quad \uparrow$
$\qquad\qquad\qquad\qquad X_i \longrightarrow Y_i$

and analysis. Such models are common in our literature and generally represent particular disciplinary perspectives. Psychologists are likely to find *individual-level* models the most familiar and straightforward type of single-level model. Individual-level models may be conceptually complex, specifying intricate interactional relationships among numerous constructs. However, individual-level models, by definition, ignore the organizational context of individual perceptions, attitudes, and behaviors. Thus the simplicity of individual-level models is in many cases a major limitation. Indeed, ignoring the context when it is relevant will lead to biases in the examination of construct relations (that is, the standard-error estimates of parameters will be biased).

Potentially far more complex are *unit-level* models, for these models may combine the three types of unit constructs in a variety of ways, in some cases necessitating mixed-level conceptualization, data collection, and analysis. Group-level models that depict the relationship of two global constructs are, from a levels perspective, the least complicated. To test these models, a researcher gathers unit-level data, consulting objective sources or experts to operationalize constructs. Tests of the effects of organizations' global human resource practices (for example, the presence or absence of merit pay and quality circles) on objective measures of organizational performance provide an example. But such models are very simple—perhaps too simple, like their individual-level counterparts. We suggest possible elaborations in what follows.

More complex, from a levels perspective, are unit-level models that include shared constructs. Consider a model linking two shared constructs: perhaps, for example, unit climate is hypothesized to predict unit morale. In proposing such a model, a scholar must explicate not only the processes linking the independent and dependent variables but also the processes engendering the emergence of climate perceptions and feelings of morale to the unit level: How do climate perceptions and feelings of morale, respectively, come to be shared by unit members? Further, to test such a model, a researcher must gather data from the level of origin— that is, from unit members—ascertaining the presence of restricted within-unit dispersion prior to aggregating data measuring the independent variable (climate) and the dependent variable (morale) and conducting unit-level analyses. Thus a seemingly simple unit-level model may, if it includes shared constructs, effectively include a multilevel (compositional) model in the very definition and operationalization of each shared construct.

Unit-level models may also link global and shared constructs in direct and mediated relationships. A researcher may predict, for example, that global organizational human resources practices enhance global organizational performance by increasing the level of (shared) organizational citizenship behavior. In proposing such a model, a theorist moves beyond the simple unit-level model of global constructs (already outlined), offering a richer and more sophisticated analysis of the possible determinants of organizational performance. Ideally, such a theory explicates the influence of human resources practices on organizational citizenship behavior, the emergence of shared organizational citizenship behavior to the organizational level, and the influence of shared organizational citizenship behavior on global measures of organizational performance. Further, to test such a model, a researcher must, as before, collect individual-level data to tap the shared construct of interest.

Unit-level models incorporating configural constructs are also plausible. For example, the variation in cognitive ability within a unit may be predicted to influence global measures of unit performance. Or consider a more complex model: perhaps the personality configuration of a unit is predicted to influence unit creativity; that is, units with more diverse personality types may develop more creative ideas than units with less dissimilarity. Such a model requires not only the careful definition and operationalization of personality configuration but also the careful definition and operationalization of unit creativity. How does unit creativity emerge from the ideas and behaviors of unit members? Is it a shared construct—a unit average—or a configural construct, reflecting a more complex weighing, or configuration, of individual contributions? These questions hint at the rigor that a multilevel perspective may bring to the processes of theory building and theory testing. At first glance, the construct of unit creativity appears straightforward, unremarkable. But a further, multilevel examination indicates much work to be done in defining, explicating, and operationalizing the nature and emergence of unit-level creativity.

Cross-level models. Cross-level theoretical models describe the relationship between different independent and dependent constructs at different levels of analysis (Rousseau, 1985). Typically, organizational cross-level models describe the top-down impact of higher-level constructs on lower-level constructs (outcomes and processes). Although theory often conceptualizes the potential impacts of lower-level constructs on higher levels (the impact of newcomers on group cohesion, for example), bottom-up cross-level modeling is a distinct rarity in the empirical literature because of its analytic limitations. We should note, however, that recent work is beginning to address this problem (Griffin, 1997). Here, we outline three primary types of top-down cross-level models:

1. *Cross-level direct-effect models* predict the direct effect of a higher-level (for example, unit-level) construct on a lower-level (for example, individual-level) construct. Typically, such models predict that the higher-level construct in some way constrains the characteristics (for example, perceptions, values, or behaviors) of lower-level entities. Thus, for example, a cross-level direct-effect model may highlight the influence of unit technology on the nature of the individual job characteristics in each unit. Routine unit technologies are likely to yield jobs that are low in discretion, variety, and challenge. Conversely, uncertain technologies are likely to yield jobs high in discretion, variety, and challenge (e.g., Kozlowski & Farr, 1988; Rousseau, 1978a). Cross-level direct-effect models may, of course, highlight the effects of global, shared, or configural unit properties on lower-level constructs. For example, unit norms (a shared construct) may constrain individual behavior, or the density of a unit's social network (a configural construct) may influence individual satisfaction and turnover within the unit. Finally, cross-level direct-effect models may describe the influence not only of units on individuals but of other, higher-level entities (for example, industries) on lower-level entities (for example, organizations). Variants of cross-level direct-effect models include *mixed-determinant* and *mixed-effect* models (Klein et al., 1994). A mixed-determinant model specifies multilevel determinants (for example, both unit and individual) of a single-level (for example, individual-level) outcome or outcomes. A mixed-effect model specifies multiple-level outcomes of a single-level predictor. Thus, for example, an organiza-

tion's adoption and implementation of a new computerized technology may engender changes in the image of the organization to outsiders, in the extent to which distinct groups within the organization coordinate their work tasks, and in individual employees' feelings of job security as a function of their technical expertise and trust in the organization. Mixed-determinant and mixed-effect models may be combined to create complex cross-level models of antecedent and outcome networks.

2. *Cross-level moderator models* suggest that the relationship between two lower-level constructs is changed or moderated by a characteristic of the higher-level entity in which they are both embedded. One may also formulate the model so that a cross-level relationship between a higher-level construct and a lower-level construct is moderated by another lower-level construct. These two forms are actually identical because each model specifies direct and interactional effects of the higher- and lower-level constructs on a lower-level outcome measure. As an example, consider the effects of unit technology on the relation between individual cognitive ability and individual job performance. Generally, higher ability is associated with higher performance. However, routine unit technology limits individual discretion, thereby limiting the relevance of cognitive ability to performance. Conversely, uncertain unit technology fosters high individual job discretion, allowing cognitive ability to enhance job performance. Unit technology thus moderates the relationship of individual ability and performance.

3. *Cross-level frog-pond models* highlight the effects of a lower-level entity's relative standing within a higher-level entity. The term *frog pond* captures the comparative or relative effect that is central to theories of this type: depending on the size of the pond, the very same frog may be small (if the pond is large) or large (if the pond is small). Also called *heterogeneous, parts,* or *individual-within-the-group* models (Dansereau et al., 1984; Glick & Roberts, 1984; Klein et al., 1994), theoretical models of this type are cross-level models in that the consequences of some lower-level (typically individual-level) construct depend on the higher-level (typically group-level) average for this construct: where one stands relative to the group average. Consider, for example, the relationship between an individual's amount of education and his or her influence in problem-solving discussions within a group. A college-educated individual

may have a great deal of influence if his or her group members' average amount of education is relatively low (few graduated from high school), or very little influence if his or her group members' average amount of education is relatively high (most have postgraduate degrees). Thus the relationship between an individual's education and his or her influence in a group depends on the individual's relative standing within his or her group's degree of education. Frog-pond models of this type, we should note, may be categorized in different ways in levels typologies. We have classified frog-pond models as cross-level models, but we recognize that frog-pond models do not evoke unit-level constructs in the same way as the other cross-level models already described. The "group average" specified in a frog-pond model is not conceptualized as a shared property of the unit. Indeed, were the construct predicted to be shared within each group, then it would make no conceptual or empirical sense to assess individual standing on the construct relative to the mean—the hallmark of frog-pond models (X_i – the group mean of X). Nor is the "group average" considered a global property of the unit; perhaps the group average, in combination with deviations, may be considered a configural property of the unit. This insight is subtle and complex, but it may help clarify why the frog-pond effect has been classified by some scholars as a distinct phenomenon or even as a distinct level of analysis. Just as we have created a distinct category for configural unit-level properties—unit properties that are characteristics of the unit but are neither global nor shared (isomorphic)—so others (e.g., Klein et al., 1994; Dansereau & Yammarino, Chapter Ten, this volume), in their conceptualizations, have designated frog-pond (heterogeneous or parts) models as a distinctive level.

Homologous multilevel models. These models specify that constructs and the relationships linking them are generalizable across organizational entities. For example, a relationship between two or more variables is hypothesized to hold at the individual, group, and organizational levels. Such models are relative rarities. The most commonly cited example of such a model is Staw, Sandelands, and Dutton's (1981) model of threat rigidity. Staw and his colleagues posit that the way in which individuals, groups, and organizations respond to threat is by rigidly persisting in the current response. By arguing for parallel constructs and homologous linking processes, they have developed a homologous multilevel model of threat-rigidity effects. However, the model has not been tested empirically, its propositions are open to debate (e.g., House et al., 1995), and its attention to construct composition is limited. Lindsley, Brass, and Thomas's model (1995) of efficacy-performance spirals is an excellent example of a homologous multilevel model that carefully attends to the composition of its constructs. However, we know of no empirical test, in the published organizational literature, of a fully homologous multilevel model.

Given their generalizability across levels, homologous multilevel models are, at their best, uniquely powerful and parsimonious. At their worst, however, multilevel homologies may be trite. A search for parallel and generalizable constructs and processes may so reduce and abstract the phenomenon of interest that the resulting model may have little value at any level. The basic notion that goals influence performance at the individual, group, and organizational levels may be valid but not, at least in its bare-bones formulation, very interesting or useful. A hypothesis that is readily applicable to many levels may be a very basic hypothesis, indeed. In the literature there are examples of efforts to develop and apply homologous multilevel models to organizational behavior (e.g., Kuhn & Beam, 1982; Tracy, 1989), although these models have had little influence on theory or research. Thus the theorist must be aware of the tension inherent in the construction of multilevel models: good ones have the potential to advance and unify our field, but weak ones offer little to our understanding of organizational phenomena.

Sampling in Multilevel Research

Sampling within and across units. When testing individual-level theoretical models, researchers endeavor to ensure that their samples contain sufficient between-individual variability to avoid problems of range restriction. Sampling issues in multilevel research are more complex but comparable. In testing unit-level theoretical models (for example, the relationship between organizational climate and organizational performance) and mixed-level models containing unit- and individual-level variables (for example, the relationship of organizational human resources practices and individual organizational commitment), researchers must endeavor to ensure that their samples show adequate variability on the constructs of interest, *at all relevant levels in the model.* Thus, for example, it may be inappropriate to test a cross-level model linking a group construct to an individual outcome in a single-organization sample. If a higher-level organizational characteristic constrains between-group variability, it will yield range restriction on the measure of the group construct and preclude a fair test of the model. Unfortunately, this problem is all too common in levels research.

In testing models containing shared unit-level constructs, researchers must endeavor to obtain samples showing within-unit homogeneity *and* between-unit variability on the shared constructs. Thus, for example, if a theoretical model asserts that units develop shared norms over time and that these norms influence unit-level or individual-level outcomes, then a test of the model requires units in which individuals have worked together for a considerable period; newly formed task groups, for example, would provide an inappropriate sample for the study. The researcher's sampling goal, then, is to obtain experienced units showing shared norms that differ between the units. Alternatively, a researcher may explicitly model and gather data to test the hypothesis that the length of time unit members have worked together predicts the emergence of shared norms, which in turn influence unit-level or individual-level outcomes. In this scenario, the researcher's sample should contain units showing substantial variability in the length of time that unit members have worked together. This strategy allows a researcher to test the variable (time that unit members have worked together) hypothesized to engender the emergence of shared norms. The outcome measure for this hypothesis, then, is not the level or nature of a shared norm but the extent to which the norm is shared (or, conversely, its dispersion across group members).

The collection of data to test a multilevel model, or even a single unit-level model, is thus likely to be labor-intensive and time-consuming. It is not enough to sample many people in one organization. The multilevel researcher, whose variables include measures of shared and configural constructs, must sample many people in many units that are nested in many higher-level units. In other words, multilevel research generally necessitates sampling several organizations, units within these organizations, and individuals within these units. To be forewarned is to be forearmed: it is not reasonable to whine about range restriction in mixed-level data after the fact!

PRINCIPLE: *In the evaluation of unit-level or mixed unit-level and individual-level theoretical models, the sampling strategy must allow for between-unit variability at all relevant levels in the model. Appropriate sampling design is essential to an adequate test of such models.*

Sampling across time. In the section on theoretical principles (see "Principles for Multilevel Organizational Theory Building," pp. 21–25), we highlighted the importance of time, as well as its general neglect in theory construction for processes that link different levels. However, temporal considerations are important not only for theory; they are also essential to research design. Two issues are central: differential time scales across levels, and entrainment.

The first issue, differential time scales across levels, concerns the fact that higher-level and lower-level phenomena operate on different time scales. In general, lower-level phenomena change more quickly, whereas higher-level phenomena tend to change more slowly, and so it is easier to detect change in lower-level entities. This means that top-down cross-level relations, if present, can be readily detected with cross-sectional and short-term longitudinal designs. In related fashion, emergent phenomena generally need longer time frames to unfold and manifest at higher levels, and so bottom-up emergent effects require longitudinal designs.

PRINCIPLE: *Time-scale differences allow top-down cross-level effects to be meaningfully examined with cross-sectional and short-term longitudinal designs. Bottom-up emergent effects necessitate long-term longitudinal or time-series designs.*

The second issue, entrainment, concerns the fact that the links between some phenomena are cyclical; that is, the strength of a link may vary over time and will be detectable only during periods of entrainment. Therefore, a theory that includes entrained phenomena necessitates a very carefully timed research design that can sample relevant data during periods of entrainment. To the extent that such a theory represents an effort to evaluate entrainment as a process, the design must also be capable of sampling relevant data during periods when the phenomena are not entrained.

PRINCIPLE: *Entrainment tightly links phenomena that are ordinarily only loosely connected across levels. Sampling designs for the evaluation of theories that propose entrained phenomena must be guided by theoretically specified time cycles, to capture entrainment and its absence.*

Analytic Strategies

Several techniques are available for the analysis of multilevel data: analysis of covariance (ANCOVA) and contextual analysis using ordinary least squares (OLS) regression (e.g., Mossholder & Bedeian, 1983); cross-level and multilevel OLS regression; WABA (Dansereau et al., 1984); multilevel random-coefficient models (MRCM), such as hierarchical linear modeling (HLM; Bryk & Raudenbush, 1992); and multilevel covariance structure analysis (MCSA; Muthen, 1994). The techniques differ in their underlying theoretical assumptions and are designed to answer somewhat different research questions. Therefore, no single technique is invariably superior in all circumstances; rather, the choice of an analysis strategy is dependent on the nature of the researcher's questions and hypotheses. Here we see again the primacy of theory in dictating the resolution of levels issues. The best way to collect and the best way to test multilevel data will depend on the guiding theory. The more explicit and thorough the guiding theory, the more effective data collection and analysis are likely to be. We provide a brief overview of these analytic approaches here but direct the reader to later chapters in this volume for in-depth consideration of contextual and regression analysis (James & Williams, Chapter Nine), WABA (Dansereau & Yammarino, Chapter Ten), and multilevel random-coefficient models (Hofmann, Griffin, & Gavin, Chapter Eleven).

ANCOVA and contextual analysis. Among the earliest approaches to the analysis of cross-level data were adaptations of ANCOVA and the use of OLS regression to conduct contextual analysis (Firebaugh, 1979; Mossholder & Bedeian, 1983). The ANCOVA approach is used to determine whether there is any effect on an individual-level dependent variable that is attributable to the unit, beyond the effect accounted for by individual differences. Essentially, this approach treats the individual-level variables as covariates and then uses unit membership as an independent variable to determine how much variance is attributable to the unit. Unit membership as a variable accounts for all possible remaining differences across units. Therefore, this approach cannot identify the specific constructs relevant to unit membership that are actually responsible for observed differences among groups; such effects are unexplained. Nevertheless, to the extent that there are any differences attributable to the grouping characteristic, this approach will capture it (Firebaugh, 1979).

The regression approach to contextual analysis typically uses aggregation and/or disaggregation to specify contextual constructs of interest. Although it is typically used to determine the effects of one or more higher-level contextual constructs on an individual-level dependent variable, it is actually flexible with respect to level. "Classic" contextual analysis includes individual-level predictors and unit means on the same predictors, to assess the relative amounts of variance attributable to the unit (Firebaugh, 1979). To the extent that unit means on the variables of interest account for variance beyond that explained by their individual-level counterparts, a contextual effect is demonstrated. This approach generally explains less variance than ANCOVA because the substantive unit variables are usually a subset of the total group composite effect, but it does identify the unit characteristic responsible for differences. Note that the aggregation process in classic contextual analysis is typically atheoretical (that is, no theoretical model of emergence is modeled), and isomorphism is not evaluated.

Cross-level and multilevel regression. In the organizational literature, OLS regression has been adapted to examine cross-level and multilevel effects and is quite flexible with respect to the type of model it can evaluate. Contemporary uses of this approach treat aggregation as an issue of construct validity (James, 1982; Kozlowski & Hattrup, 1992) so that a model of emergence is first evaluated before individual-level data are aggregated to the group level (e.g., Kozlowski & Hults, 1987; Ostroff, 1993). Therefore, with respect to the specification and measurement of construct types, this approach is relevant to the issues we have discussed in this chapter. Once the measurement model of the higher-level (aggregated) constructs is established, the analysis proceeds to test substantive hypotheses. For example, if the theory assumes shared perceptions of unit climate as predictors of individual satisfaction, then one establishes restricted within-unit variance on climate, aggregates the data to the unit level (that is, computes means), and then disaggregates to the individual level of analysis (that is, assigns the means to individuals in the unit). The analysis then estimates the amount of variance in individual satisfaction that is attributable to unit climate. Individual-level analogues of the contextual construct are not necessarily controlled (as in contextual analysis) unless the question is of substantive interest (James & Williams, Chapter Nine, this volume).

Within-and-between analysis. The basic WABA equation (Dansereau et al., 1984) is modeled on the classic decomposition of within-and-between variance terms formulated by Robinson (1950) to model individual-level and aggregate group-level correlations. The "classic" WABA analysis examines bivariate relationships, assumes measures at the lowest level of analysis for all constructs, and proceeds in two phases. The first phase, WABA I, establishes the level of the variables. The second phase, WABA II, evaluates the level of relations between all the variables in the analysis (Dansereau et al., 1984). WABA I is designed to assess whether measures, treated one at a time, show variability in the following ways: both within and across units (as typically with an individual-level construct), primarily between units (as typically with a unit-level construct), and primarily within units (as with a frog-pond, parts, or heterogeneous construct). WABA II is designed to assess whether two measures covary in the following ways: both within and across units (as typically with individual-level relationships), primarily between units (as typically with unit-level relationships), and primarily within units (as typically with a frog-pond, parts, or heterogeneous relationship; see Klein et al., 1994). Although WABA was originally developed to examine bivariate relations at multiple levels, it has been extended to address multivariate relations (Schriesheim, 1995; Dansereau & Yammarino, Chapter Ten, this volume).

Multilevel random-coefficient modeling. The MRCM analysis strategy is represented by several packages of statistical software (for example, PROC MIXED in SAS; MLn; lme in S-PLUS), of which

HLM is probably the most familiar. HLM analysis assumes hierarchically organized, or nested, data structures of the sort that are typically encountered in organizations: individuals nested in units, units nested in organizations, and organizations nested in environments. Models of theoretical interest typically represent multiple levels of data. For instance, many cross-level models involve an outcome variable at the lowest level of analysis, with multiple predictors at the same and higher levels. HLM is well suited to the handling of such data structures.

The logic of HLM involves a simultaneous two-stage procedure. Level 1 analyses estimate within-unit intercepts (means) and slopes (relations). To the extent that unit intercepts and/or slopes vary significantly across units, Level 2 analyses treat them as outcomes. Thus Level 2 analyses model the effects of unit-level predictors on unit intercepts and slopes so that effects on intercepts are indicative of direct cross-level relations, and effects on slopes are indicative of cross-level moderation. HLM relies on a generalized least squares (GLS) regression procedure to estimate fixed parameters, and on the EM algorithm to generate maximum-likelihood estimates of variance components. This provides many statistical advantages over analogous OLS regression–based approaches (Hofmann et al., Chapter Eleven, this volume).

An in-depth description of these techniques is beyond the scope of this chapter; assumptions, applications, and differences among the techniques are addressed elsewhere in this volume. However, we will note here that all these techniques have the potential to be misused in an atheoretical attempt to establish "the" level at which effects occur. We reiterate that the conceptual meaning of higher-level aggregations (however they are statistically determined) must have an a priori theoretical foundation.

PRINCIPLE: *There is no one, all-encompassing multilevel data-analytic strategy that is appropriate to all research questions. Particular techniques are based on different statistical and data-structure assumptions, are better suited to particular types of research questions, and have different strengths and weaknesses. Selection of an analytic strategy should be based on (a) consistency between the type of constructs, the sampling and data, and the research question; and (b) the assumptions, strengths, and limitations of the analytic technique.*

Extending Models of Emergent Phenomena

Some of the most engaging and perplexing natural phenomena are those in which highly structured collective behavior emerges over time from the interaction of simple subsystems [Crutchfield, 1994, p. 516].

A central theme woven throughout this chapter is the need for a more extended understanding of emergence as a critical multilevel process in organizational behavior. There is evident dissatisfaction with the overreliance on isomorphism-based composition as the primary model for conceptualizing collective constructs (House et al., 1995; Rousseau, 1985). Indeed, there is increasing recognition that emergence based on isomorphism may well be the exception rather than the rule. Although isomorphic emergence is a very powerful conceptual model, it is but one possible model. Emergent phenomena are not necessarily shared, uniform, and convergent. In their discussion of dispersion theory, a precursor to our typology, Brown and Kozlowski (1997, p. 7) note that nonuniform "phenomena marked by differentiation, conflict, competition, coalition formation, and disagreement are common" in organizations.

There are many theories, in our literature and others, that implicitly or explicitly address alternative forms of emergence. Power, conflict, and competition all involve compilational, discontinuous forms of emergence. The *varient paradigm* (Dansereau & Yammarino, Chapter Ten, this volume), with its interest in "parts" relationships, shows a recognition of the plausibility of compilation. This is a good beginning, but the "parts" perspective captures but one form of compilation among many. We argue that there is a need to extend the conceptualization of emergence, to make it more inclusive, so that our theories and research can encompass more varied and diverse emergent phenomena. We need to elaborate compilation forms of emergence.

Conceptual Goals

Purpose

Our purpose is to take a step toward this elaboration, describing forms of emergence that until now have received little attention in the organizational literature on levels of analysis. In preceding sections of this chapter, we contrasted composition (shared unit properties) and compilation (configural unit properties) as distinctive, ideal types of emergence. This contrast was useful in making salient the important differences that affect conceptualization, measurement, and sampling. However, composition and compilation are not necessarily clear-cut dichotomous categories; rather, they are end points for a diverse set of emergence alternatives, with some forms of emergence being more akin to composition and some forms being more akin to compilation.

We now explore varying forms of emergence, hoping to foster increased attention to the structures and processes underlying emergent organizational phenomena. We undertake this exploration here by elaborating the theoretical underpinnings of emergence. First we consider, in greater depth, the theoretical foundation for emergence. A primary focus of our attention is the central role that interaction processes and dynamics among individuals play in shaping the form of the emergent phenomenon. Next, with this foundation in place, we identify more specific theoretical assumptions that distinguish the ideal or pure types of composition and compilation forms of emergence. We describe and illustrate how the assumptions change when one is considering discontinuous compilation relative to isomorphic composition. Finally, we develop a typology, posing a set of emergence exemplars that range between the ideal types of composition and compilation. We discuss each exemplar, providing examples from the literature that consider unit performance, unit learning–cognition–knowledge, and other unit phenomena, to illustrate how the theoretical assumptions help to explicate the nature of emergence for that exemplar. Our use of the typology is intended to help elaborate the theoretical underpinnings that shape the conceptualization of alternative forms of emergence.

Contributions

There are three primary conceptual contributions of this effort. First, our intent is to be inclusive, encompassing multiple perspectives. Several recent theoretical efforts have started to explore emergence and the ways in which it may be manifest (Brown & Kozlowski, 1997, 1999; Brown et al., 1996; Chan, 1998; Kozlowski, 1998, 1999; Morgeson & Hofmann, 1999a, 1999b). Although these efforts are for the most part compatible, they have also chosen different points of theoretical departure, different language, and different organizing structures. It is not our goal to explicitly integrate these efforts, but we believe our framework makes their compatibilities more explicit. We build on the strong theoretical and research foundation provided by isomorphism-based composition and elaborate it to embrace different, alternative, and neglected forms of emergent organizational phenomena that follow from a consideration of discontinuity-based compilation. Because compilation entails less restrictive assumptions, it allows for many more possible emergent forms relative to composition. We argue that a broader range of alternatives, from composition to compilation, is necessary to more fully capture complex emergence.

Second, an important contribution of our perspective is the recognition that higher-level phenomena do not necessarily exhibit universal forms of emergence; that is, a given phenomenon may emerge in different ways depending on the context and the nature of lower-level interaction processes. We need to attend to the ways in which interaction processes and dynamics shape the form of emergence. Therefore, the search for universal models of emergence, to be applied in each and every instance, may be misguided. Our perspective emphasizes that a collective phenomenon—unit performance—may emerge in a variety of different ways in different units. We need flexible conceptual tools that allow us to seek out, explore, and characterize variation in forms of emergence.

Third, our intent is to stimulate a more extended conceptualization of the theoretical mechanisms that characterize different forms of emergence. We develop a typology of emergence that explicitly links exemplars of different emergent forms to key theoretical underpinnings. Our focus is on theory development, not on mere classification. We are not advocating simple reductionist explanations for higher-level phenomena. We recognize that many organizational phenomena are top-down rather than bottom-up. Further, as we have already explained, many phenomena reflect *both* top-down and bottom-up processes unfolding over time. Moreover, we are not rejecting macro single-level approaches that do not explicitly address the emergent origins of the higher-level phenomena. Rather, we seek to promote more inclusive, extensive, and coherent explanations of collective phenomena. We are interested in both structure *and* process. We wish both to understand the whole *and* keep an eye on the parts.

The issues we address go to the conceptual meaning of higher-level phenomena that are rooted in individual characteristics and actions. Consider, for example, the global outcome of a baseball game score. One can examine a global predictor of this outcome (for example, average ability of team members), but this predictor can only provide a limited understanding of the team's performance. Baseball team scores are equifinal. True fans know this. They follow box scores so that they can understand how individual team members, in *dynamic interaction,* compiled the team score. We believe that a similar degree of conceptual understanding can pay big dividends in our effort to comprehend meso organizational behavior.

Theoretical Underpinnings of Emergence

What Is Emergence?

Emergence is bottom-up and interactive. The concepts undergirding emergence have broad expression in the biological, social, and physical sciences and are represented in theories of chaos, self-organization, and complexity (Arthur, 1994; Gell-Mann, 1994; Kauffman, 1994; Nicolis & Prigogine, 1989; Prigogine & Stengers, 1984) which address the dynamics of emergence. Our focus is on emergent phenomena that occur within the boundaries and constraints of organizational systems. Emergence is particularly relevant in the continuing effort of our science to understand how individuals contribute to organizational effectiveness. This is a central theme in several of the chapters of this book, including those focused on selection (Schneider, Smith, & Sipe, Chapter Two), performance appraisal (DeNisi, Chapter Three), training effectiveness (Kozlowski et al., Chapter Four), and human resources management (Ostroff & Bowen, Chapter Five). Emergence plays an important role in the linkages involved in interorganizational relationships (Klein, Palmer, & Conn, Chapter Six) and cross-cultural relations (Chao, Chapter Seven).

A phenomenon is emergent when it originates in the cognition, affect, behaviors, or other characteristics of individuals, is amplified by their interactions, and manifests as a higher-level, collective phenomenon (Allport, 1954; Katz & Kahn, 1966). Individual cognition, affect, behavior, and other characteristics denote *elemental content.* Elemental content is the raw material of emergence. Team mental models (cognition), group mood (affect), team performance (behavior), and group diversity (other characteristics) all represent emergent group properties that have their origins in the elemental content provided by individuals. *Interaction* denotes process. Individuals communicate and exchange information, affect, and valued resources. They share ideas. They communicate mood and feelings. They perform acts and exchange work products. Communication and exchanges may be direct, as in face-to-face interaction, or indirect, as when information or other resource exchange is mediated via some form of technology. The form of the interaction process, in combination with the elemental content, comprises the emergent phenomenon.

Emergence is shaped and constrained. Although emergent phenomena have their origins in lower levels, the process of emergence is shaped, constrained, and influenced by higher-level contextual factors. Interaction in organizations is constrained by a hierarchical structure that defines unit boundaries. The individuals in a unit tend to interact more dynamically and intensely with each other than with individuals outside their unit (Simon, 1973). Moreover, work-flow transactions—the ways in which people are linked to accomplish the work of the unit (Thompson, 1967)—pattern interactions and exchanges. Individuals directly linked by the work flow tend to interact more with each other than with individuals who are only linked indirectly (Brass, 1995). Thus, for example, professors tend to interact more intensely with the students who are involved in their research than with the other students in their programs, and they interact more with students in their programs than with students in other programs. This patterning of interaction by formal structure and work flow shapes emergence.

In addition, informal patterns of interaction—social interaction that transcends formal boundaries and work flows—also shape emergence. People who cross unit boundaries to bond socially are more likely to communicate common perspectives. For example, Rentch (1990) shows that individuals from different organizational units who met informally developed a shared conception of the organization's culture. In organizations, emergent phenomena are shaped by a combination of formal structure and work flows, and by informal social-interaction processes, with the relative importance of one, the other, or both dependent on the phenomenon of interest.

There are also a variety of other forces—such as attraction, selection, and attrition (ASA); common stimuli; socialization; and sensemaking—that affect interaction processes and dynamics. These forces, in combination with formal structures, work flows, and social structures, as already described, shape the nature of emergent phenomena. Generally, these forces have been conceptualized as constraining either the range of elemental content or the interaction process. Given these assumptions, the forces have been used to explain composition-based emergence, but they can also explain compilation. For example, the result of the ASA process is a workforce that is relatively more homogeneous in terms of ability, personality, attitudes, and values (Schneider & Reichers, 1983) and therefore more likely to have viewpoints in common. Organizational environments tend to expose employees to common stimuli—policies, practices, and procedures—that shape common perceptions (Kozlowski & Hults, 1987). Socialization can operate as a powerful force that shapes shared sensemaking (Louis, 1980). In these ways, the forces act as constraints shaping composition forms of emergence that are characterized by stability, uniformity, and convergence.

Sometimes the forces operate to expand rather than limit the range of elemental content or the nature of the interaction process. Compilation is based on the assumption that ASA, socialization, and related processes are not so powerful as to eliminate all meaningful differences in individual organizational members' elemental characteristics. Indeed, these processes may preserve or even engender variability within organizations, at least with respect to many important elemental qualities. For example, selection, attrition, and reward processes are unlikely to eliminate all variability in individual performance. Moreover, some organizations may well select individuals for their varying and idiosyncratic strengths, much as a sports team needs some players who are good on offense and other (typically different) players who are good on defense. Further, interactions among organizational members may engender similarity or dissimilarity; social interactions may unite or polarize employees. Finally, a variety of contextual factors limit an organization's ability (and often its desire) to build an organization of perfectly homogeneous individuals. Some measure of demographic variability is inevitable in most organizations, for example.

Further, diversity in an organization—with respect to organizational members' demographic characteristics, work experiences, education, and so on—may foster organizational creativity and innovation. In these ways, the forces create differences and discontinuities, shaping compilation forms of emergence that are characterized by irregularity, nonuniformity, and configuration.

Emergence varies in process and form. As already noted, interaction dynamics can lead to variation in the ways in which a higher-level phenomenon emerges; that is, a given phenomenon, such as team performance, can arise in a variety of different ways, even in the same organization. Individual characteristics, cognition, affect, and behavior are constrained by their context. Over time, interaction dynamics acquire certain stable properties; stable structure emerges from a dynamic process. Katz and Kahn (1966) describe this as recurrent patterns of interaction. Thus the emergence of a collective phenomenon is the result of a dynamic unfolding of *role exchanges* (Katz & Kahn, 1966), *ongoings* (Allport, 1954), or *compilation processes* (Kozlowski et al., 1999) among individuals. It is from these dynamics that a stable collective pattern emerges.

Morgeson and Hofmann (1999a) describe Allport's notion of *ongoing* as a recurrent pattern representing the intersection of individual action in its context. Individual ongoings encounter one another, creating interaction *events*. Subsequent interactions solidify a recurrent *event cycle*, which represents the emergence of a stable collective phenomenon. Similarly, Kozlowski and colleagues (1999) describe how team performance *compiles* upward from individual behaviors and work-flow transactions: individuals work out transaction patterns that regulate dyadic work flows, and as these dyadic exchanges stabilize, team members develop extended work-flow networks that stabilize around routine task demands. Gersick and Hackman (1990) characterize these stable patterns in teamwork as *habitual routines.*

However, because emergent phenomena are based on patterns of interaction, even small changes in individual behavior or dyadic interaction can yield big changes in the nature of emergence. For example, Kozlowski and colleagues (1999) also propose that task environments can change dramatically and unpredictably. Unexpected shifts, and the novel tasks they present, necessitate adaptation of team networks, an adaptation that is based on individuals and dyads developing alternative work flows. In this model, team performance and adaptability emerge across levels from individual action and dyadic transactions, creating enormous flexibility in the formation of adaptive work-flow networks that may resolve the novel situation. *The implication is that collective phenomena may emerge in different ways under different contextual constraints and patterns of interaction. Emergence is often equifinal rather than universal in form.*

This important implication of our conceptualization of emergence sets our framework apart from most others: a given phenomenon or construct domain does not necessarily have to exhibit a universal form of emergence;[6] that is, a given emergent phenomenon may be the result of composition processes in one situation and of compilation processes in another. A consideration of the examples shown in Figure 1.2 illustrates this point. Consider, for example, how personality makeup can differ across teams (Jackson, May, & Whitney, 1995; Moreland & Levine, 1992). Teams may be characterized by the high homogeneity indicative of personality composition, or by the heterogeneity indicative of personality compilation. There is no a priori theoretical reason to suppose that one or the other is a universal form for the way in which team personality emerges.

Consider collective cognition, for example. The construct of shared mental models (Klimoski & Mohammed, 1995) assumes that team members hold identical mental representations of their collective task. In contrast, alternative conceptualizations assume that team members' mental models have compatible configurations but are not necessarily identical. Group members have somewhat different mental representations of their collective task, based on their specific roles within the team. Members' different mental representations fit together in a complementary way, like the pieces of a puzzle, to create a whole that is greater than the sum of its parts (Kozlowski, Gully, Salas, & Cannon-Bowers, 1996). Similarly, collective knowledge may be conceptualized as the sum of individual knowledge; more nonredundant information is better, and collective knowledge is the sum of the parts. Alternatively, collective knowledge may be conceptualized as configural spirals: some individual knowledge is more useful than other knowledge; useful knowledge is selected and crystallized, and it then attracts

Figure 1.2. Theoretical Underpinnings of Emergence.

Emergent Process	Composition ◄·····················► Compilation	
Variation in Emergence	⬇	⬇
	• Personality similarity	• Personality diversity
	• Shared mental models	• Compatible mental models
	• Classical decision making (single optimal solution)	• Naturalistic decision making (multiple solutions)
	• Pooled team performance	• Adaptive team networks
	• Organizational learning (sum of individual knowledge)	• Organizational learning (knowledge spirals)
Theoretical Assumptions		
Model	Isomorphism	Discontinuity
Elemental contribution		
Type	Similar	Dissimilar
Amount	Similar	Dissimilar
Interaction process and dynamics	Stable	Irregular
	Low dispersion	High dispersion
	Uniform	Nonuniform
Combination	Linear	Nonlinear
Emergent representation	Convergent point	Pattern

and amplifies related knowledge, in a spiral of collective knowledge acquisition (Nonaka, 1994).

The point of these examples is that given phenomena may emerge in different ways. A variety of contextual and temporal constraints operate to influence interaction dynamics among individuals, which in turn shape the emergent form, yet the dominance of composition models based on isomorphism has tended to limit consideration to shared models of emergence, and to the dichotomous presence or absence of emergence (Brown & Kozlowski, 1997). Theory needs to be able to capture the rich complexity of emergence rather than limiting emergence to universal conceptualizations that often do not exist.

Theoretical Assumptions

Our framework is formulated around theoretical distinctions between ideal forms of composition and compilation, considered in earlier sections of this chapter. Here we turn our attention to three sets of overlapping assumptions, shown in Figure 1.2, that are useful for more finely distinguishing these alternative forms of emergence. The assumptions include the following elements:

1. The theoretical model of emergence, and the type and amount of elemental contribution implicated by the model
2. The interaction process and dynamics that shape the form of emergence
3. The resulting combination rules for representing the emergent form.

At the risk of some redundancy, we will outline these assumptions and apply them to the contrasting of composition and compilation forms of emergence. We will then present a typology, using the assumptions to distinguish alternative forms of emergence ranging between composition and compilation ideals.

Model and elemental contribution. Composition and compilation are distinguished by their underlying theoretical models. Composition is based on a model of isomorphism, whereas compilation is based on a model of discontinuity.[7] Isomorphism and discontinuity represent differing conceptualizations with respect to the nature and combination of the constituent elements that constitute the higher-level phenomenon.

Isomorphism essentially means that the type and amount of elemental content—the raw material of emergence—are similar for all individuals in the collective. In other words, the notion of isomorphism is based on an assumption that all individuals perceive climate, for example, along the same set of dimensions, or that all team members possess mental models organized around the same content. In addition, isomorphism means that the amount of elemental content is essentially the same for all individuals in the collective. In other words, the climate or mental model is shared. Hence, within-unit convergence (that is, consensus, consistency, homogeneity) is central to composition. Morgeson and Hofmann (1999a, 1999b) describe this similarity in the type and amount of elemental content as *structural equivalence.* Thus isomorphism allows the theorist to treat a phenomenon as essentially the same construct at different levels (Rousseau, 1985). Note that isomorphic constructs are also *functionally equivalent.* That is, they occupy the same roles in multilevel models of the phenomenon; they perform the same theoretical function (Rousseau, 1985).

Discontinuity means that either the amount or type of elemental content is different, or both the amount and type are different. The notion of discontinuity is based on an assumption that the kinds of contributions that individuals make to the collective are variable, not shared and consistent. Essentially, there is an absence of structural equivalence in the nature of the elemental content and in the ways in which it combines (Kozlowski, 1998, 1999; Morgeson & Hofmann, 1999a, 1999b). Nevertheless, there is functional equivalence because the constructs perform the same role and function in models at different levels (Rousseau, 1985), as we shall explain.

The elemental content comes from a common domain—performance, personality, cognition—but the nature of individual contributions can be quite different. For example, baseball players contribute qualitatively different types and amounts of individual performance to accomplish team performance. The pitcher pitches, fielders field, and batters hit. In any given game, some will excel and others will make errors. Different dominant personality traits characterize each team member. Team members possess different but compatible mental models of the game. Therefore, variability and pattern are central to compilation. Because the diverse elemental content is drawn from a common domain and contributes to a similar collective property, there is functional equivalence across levels. This functional equivalence allows the theorist to treat compilational properties as qualitatively different but related manifestations of the phenomenon across levels (Kozlowski, 1998, 1999; Morgeson & Hofmann, 1999a, 1999b).

Interaction process and dynamics. The hallmark of composition forms of emergence is convergence and sharing. In climate theory, for example, a variety of constraining forces have been proposed that are thought to shape the emergence of a shared collective climate. Individuals are exposed to homogeneous contextual constraints—common organizational features, events, and processes (James & Jones, 1974). They develop individual interpretations of these characteristics, yielding psychological climate. ASA processes operate to narrow variation in psychological climate (Schneider & Reichers, 1983). Interpretations are filtered and shaped by leaders (Kozlowski & Doherty, 1989). Individuals interact, communicate perspectives, and iteratively construct a common interpretation. Variations in individual interpretations dissipate as a collective interpretation converges. This is an incremental process that, over time, promotes stability, characterized by reduced dispersion as outliers are trimmed and by increased uniformity as perceptions are pushed to a convergent point. An equilibrium is achieved.

The hallmark of compilation forms of emergence is variability and configuration. Team performance requires that individuals coordinate and dynamically combine distinct individual knowledge and actions. The emergence of team performance is largely shaped by work-flow interdependencies—that is, the linkages that connect individual performance in the team work system (Brass, 1981). Consider once again the performance of a baseball team. There are any number of ways in which team members, working together, can achieve a particular score. They may excel because power hitters recurrently hit home runs. They may have a stable of good but not exceptional hitters; by consistently getting players on base the team is able to accumulate good scores. They may excel by limiting the success of the opposing team; exceptional pitching, for example, will keep opposing scores low, and good defensive fielding, along with solid teamwork, will be needed to support the pitcher. Each player on the team will make distinctive individual contributions that combine in myriad ways to yield the team's performance. The *score* may be no more than the sum of its parts (that is, runs), but *team performance* is more than a simple sum of parts. Decomposing team performance necessitates an understanding of who did what, when, and of how it all fits together. This is an irregular process rather than incremental, stable interaction. There will be considerable dispersion and nonuniformity in the ways in which individual contributions are coordinated and combined to yield the compiled team performance (Kozlowski et al., 1999).

Combination rules and representation. The representation of an emergent construct is an effort to capture or freeze the result of a dynamic process. The assumptions identified earlier provide the basis for different combination rules—guidelines for summarizing or capturing a collective representation from the elemental content. For composition, similar types and amounts of elemental content that evidences relative stability, uniformity, and low dispersion will generally be summarized with linear additive or averaging rules. This procedure will yield a single indicator—a convergent point capturing the shared unit property. Collective climate, based on composition assumptions, is generally represented by unit means (Kozlowski & Hattrup, 1992). Homogeneous perceptions of worker participation are likewise represented as unit means (Klein et al., 1994).

For compilation, a variety of different nonlinear combination rules may be used to combine the different types and amounts of elemental content. Compilation interaction processes are irregular, high in dispersion, and nonuniform. Elemental content may vary in amount, kind, or both. Therefore, the combination rules for compilation are more varied and complex than those used to characterize composition. A sampling of potential combination rules includes disjunctive, conjunctive, and multiplicative combination models, and indices of variance, proportion, configural fit, and network characteristics, among others (Levine & Fitzgerald, 1992; Meyer, Tsui, & Hinings, 1993). The key issue is that the combination rules should be consistent with the conceptualization of emergence. For example, if the compilation theory emphasizes team networks (Kozlowski et al., 1999), then the representation should capture such meaningful variation in network characteristics as centrality, transaction alternatives, and substitutability (Brass, 1981). If the theory emphasizes the formation of dyadic relationships, as in leader-member exchange (Graen, 1976), then the representation should capture relative standing on the basis of differences between leader-member pairs (Dansereau & Dumas, 1977). If the theory focuses on the formation of in-groups and out-groups (Kozlowski & Doherty, 1989), then the representation should capture in-and out-group standing and differences (Brown & Kozlowski, 1997, 1999).

Summary of distinctions between composition and compilation. The key assumptions that distinguish composition and compilation, respectively, involve the question of whether the following elements are present:

1. Elemental (that is, individual) contributions to the higher-level phenomenon are similar (isomorphism) or dissimilar (discontinuity) in type, amount, or both
2. Interaction processes and dynamics are incremental and stable, exhibit low dispersion, and are uniform in pattern, or interaction processes and dynamics are irregular, high in dispersion, and exhibit nonuniform patterns
3. The emergent phenomenon is consequently represented by a linear convergent point (composition), or the emergent phenomenon is represented as a nonlinear pattern or configuration (compilation)

A Typology of Emergence

The purpose of our typology is to promote a more expansive conceptualization of the theoretical mechanisms that characterize different forms of emergence. Our typology of emergence, shown in Figure 1.3, juxtaposes composition and compilation. The theoretical underpinnings derived previously are used to distinguish a variety of exemplars—specific emergence models. We discuss each exemplar, illustrating the exemplars with examples regarding

Figure 1.3. Typology of Emergence.

Emergence Theory and Features	Isomorphic Composition		
	↓	*Pooled*	*Pooled*
Exemplars	*Convergent*	*Constrained*	*Unconstrained*
• Performance ⟶	Rowing crew Synchronized swimming	Tug of war Group sales	Social loafing Free riding
• Learning/ Knowledge ⟶	Shared mental models/ knowledge	Group information exchange	Organizational learning/ knowledge
• Others ⟶	Collective Climate Efficacy		Unit rates Absence Turnover Accidents

Elemental Contribution			
Type	Similar	Similar	Similar
Amount	Similar	Moderately similar	Similar to dissimilar

Interaction Process, Combination Rules, and Representation			
	Low dispersion Uniform Sum or mean **(linear)**	Moderate dispersion Uniform Sum or mean **(linear)**	Moderate to high dispersion Uniform Sum or mean **(linear)**

···➤ **Discontinuous Compilation**
⬇

Minimum/ Maximum	*Variance*	*Patterned*
Climbing team Jury decision making	Jazz improvisation Dance	Adaptive team performance Performance spirals
Crew ability/ knowledge	Creativity Knowledge/ diversity	Knowledge spirals Compatible mental models/knowledge Transactive memory
	Norm cystallization Culture strength Personality diversity	LMZ Intragroup conflict
Similar Dissimilar	Variable Variable	Dissimilar Dissimilar
Dispersion NA Uniform NA Minimum/Maximum **(nonlinear)**	Variable dispersion Uniform Variance **(nonlinear)**	High dispersion Nonuniform Patterns Profiles Networks Proportion **(nonlinear)**

collective performance, learning–cognition–knowledge, and other phenomena. We include exemplars for the following types of emergence: convergent, pooled constrained, pooled unconstrained, minimum/maximum, variant, and patterned. Each exemplar describes a different emergence process, based on contextual constraints and interaction processes, for how a lower-level phenomenon is manifested at a higher level. The nature of elemental contributions, in type and amount, and the combination rules applicable to each exemplar are indicated. Although we have used the individual and group levels to make the examples easier to explain, the models are applicable to higher levels as well. The typology is intended to help elaborate the theoretical underpinnings that shape the conceptualization of alternative forms of emergence.

Convergent Emergence

The exemplar for this type of emergence represents the ideal form of composition that we have discussed throughout this chapter. The model is based on the assumption that contextual factors and interaction processes constrain emergence in such a way that individuals contribute the same type and amount of elemental content. Therefore, the phenomenon converges around a common point that can be represented as a mean or a sum. For example, the performance of a crew rowing a scull is dependent on each individual providing the same amount and type of physical thrust at precisely the same time. Synchronized swimmers must execute the same movements, in the same amount, at the same time. Similarly, the notion of team mental models is predicated on all team members sharing the same amount and type of knowledge (Klimoski & Mohammed, 1995). Ideal composition is also illustrated by theory and research on collective climate and collective efficacy. Group members' perceptions converge on the referent construct. Sharing is evaluated on the basis of consensus or consistency. Variability in elemental content and individual contributions is very low and uniform in distribution across members. Therefore, aggregation to the group mean eliminates the small amount of error variance and effectively represents the group on the higher-level construct.

Alternative subforms of this exemplar can be distinguished on the basis of the item referent used to create the emergent construct (Chan, 1998; Klein et al., 1998); that is, individual-level measures may reference the self ("how I perceive") or the group ("how I believe the group perceives"). The self-referenced-item form is described by Chan (1998) as "direct consensus," and the group-referenced form is described as "referent shift consensus." This latter form is regarded as being more consistent with the conceptual underpinnings of the higher-level construct (James, 1982; Klein et al., 1994; Rousseau, 1985). Some research suggests that the referent-shift form may enhance within-group agreement and between-group variability (Klein et al., 1998). In related fashion, DeShon et al. (1999) indicate that aggregated group-referenced measures are better predictors of group performance than aggregated individual-referenced measures of the same construct. Empirical findings are preliminary at this point. Sometimes the item referent (self or group) makes a difference; at other times it does not. Clearly, this is an important issue that can be resolved only with systematic research.

Pooled Constrained Emergence

This exemplar relaxes the assumptions for the amount of elemental contribution, but the type of content remains similar. The underlying model is based on the assumption that contextual factors and interaction processes shape emergence in such a way that some minimum amount of contribution is required of each individual. Therefore, there will be restricted variability within the group, yielding a pattern across individuals that is relatively uniform and moderate in dispersion. An additive or averaging model combines the elemental contributions.

Consider, for example, group sales performance for a district. Each salesperson makes an incremental, pooled contribution to group performance. The elemental contributions are similar in type but can vary in amount to some extent. Contextual constraints—such as incentives, competitiveness, leadership, and dismissal—are likely to restrict just how little can be contributed. All salespeople are not expected to contribute the same amount, but contributing too little will likely lead to turnover. Therefore, individual and group performance are not identical, but they are closely related.

Wittenbaum and Stasser (1996) provide a model of group discussion and consensus decision making consistent with this form of emergence. In their model, group members possess both unique and common information that must be discussed and combined to yield a group decision. Although individuals possess both similar and dissimilar types of elemental content (that is, common and unique information), groups have been found to focus virtually all of their discussion on sharing the common information. In effect, the nature of social interaction processes constrains emergence so that only common information is discussed and used for the decision. Although there is some variation in individual contribution, the dissimilar information plays no role in the team product. The group decision is essentially an average of the shared information.

Pooled Unconstrained Emergence

This exemplar fully relaxes the requirement on the amount of elemental contribution, but, as before, the type of content remains similar. Here, variation in the amount of elemental contribution can be quite high. For example, research demonstrates that performance in pooled tasks can be plagued by social loafing and free riding: some individuals contribute far less to the collective when the amount of their contributions cannot be identified (Harkins, Latane, & Williams, 1980). In such circumstances, the group product may be represented as a sum or mean. However, in contrast with the previous exemplar, the group representation and the individual contribution may be dramatically different. Similarly, one conceptualization of organizational climate is based on the assumption that within-group variation in climate perceptions is random measurement error (Glick, 1985, 1988). No restriction is placed on how much variability can be eliminated through averaging.

This exemplar is also frequently used for such group descriptive variables as absence, turnover, and accidents (e.g., Hofmann & Stetzer, 1996; Mathieu & Kohler, 1990). Unit rates are typically counts of the dichotomous presence or absence of some event: additive frequency counts, although sometimes these characteristics are summarized by means. Bliese (Chapter Eight, this volume) labels phenomena of this sort *fuzzy composition* because they lack the sharing that is the hallmark of composition. Other theorists have used group rates as examples of discontinuity (Rousseau, 1985), which is indicative of compilation. Therefore, these phenomena certainly represent fuzzy *something;* whether they are fuzzy composition or fuzzy compilation is not necessarily an important issue unless one is highly interested in classification. However, the fuzziness suggests that this exemplar captures a transition zone between the ideal types. Deeper conceptual digging may be useful for surfacing theoretical nuances that may help us better understand these differing forms of emergence.

One factor to consider in this deeper digging may be the base rate. In some instances, the elemental contribution can be spread across many (though not all) members of a unit—the incidence of stress, for example. In other instances, the rate is often predominantly influenced by the acts of just a few individuals—for example, serious accidents. Perhaps the first group of instances is more akin to fuzzy composition, and the second more akin to fuzzy compilation.

Minimum/Maximum Emergence

This exemplar represents a shift from linear combination rules (that is, additive models) to nonlinear rules. Elemental contribution is based on similar content, but the amount of contribution is qualitatively distinct. Contextual factors and interaction processes constrain emergence so that the pattern across individuals is discontinuous. The standing of one individual on the phenomenon in question determines the standing of the collective. Therefore, dispersion and uniformity are not directly applicable to the conceptualization of this exemplar.

This is a conjunctive (minimum) or disjunctive (maximum) model, in which the highest or lowest value for an individual in the group sets the value of the collective attribute (Steiner, 1972). Consider, for example, group cognitive ability for a tank crew (Tziner & Eden, 1985) or a football team. It is not the average level or dispersion of cognitive ability that is important, because the same sort of cognitive contribution may not be necessary for all members; as long as one person is high on cognitive ability and the rest of the team will take direction, the group as a whole can effectively assess the situation and execute the appropriate strategy. Therefore, the maximum individual-level standing on the attribute determines the standing of the collective. This emergence process is similar to the jury decision-making model, in which a lone holdout (minimum) can yield a hung jury and a mistrial (Davis, 1992), or to a mountain climbing team whose performance is determined by the slowest and weakest member of the team (e.g., Krakauer, 1997). Therefore, one individual can effectively determine the group-level outcome because the combination rule is nonlinear.

Variance Form of Emergence

Unlike the other exemplars, which focus on representative values to capture the emergent characteristic of the collective, this form of emergence represents the phenomenon as variability within the group. Conceptually, this form of emergence is related to heterogeneity (Klein et al., 1994), parts (Dansereau & Yammarino, Chapter Ten, this volume), and uniform dispersion (Brown & Kozlowski, 1997; Brown et al., 1996; Chan, 1998). The elemental contribution may be similar in type and amount (for example, norm crystallization) or different in type and amount (for example, demographic diversity). Therefore, individuals may make contributions that are similar or different, but the substantive focus is on the variance of contribution (Roberts et al., 1978). It is important to emphasize that this one form captures different types of emergence that may range from low dispersion to high dispersion.

For example, one form of creativity can be characterized by the diversity, or lack thereof, of the knowledge or perspectives that are brought to bear on a problem (Wiersema & Bantel, 1992). Demographic diversity captures the extent to which individual members of a unit differ in their demographic characteristics (Tsui, Egan, & O'Reilly, 1992; Jackson et al., 1995). Homogeneity of charisma (that is, the extent to which a leader has equally charismatic relationships with all of his or her subordinates; see Klein & House, 1995), norm crystallization (Jackson, 1975), and culture strength (Koene, Boone, & Soeters, 1997) are based on variability within a collective. Homogeneity, crystallization, and strength are predicated on low variance, whereas the absence of homogeneity, crystallization, and strength is indicated by high variance. Klein and colleagues (Chapter Six, this volume) explore the antecedents and consequences of variability in organizational boundary spanners' trust in and commitment to their organization's interorganizational partner. Variance, of course, is a key operationalization of variability. Variance can capture emergence that differs across groups, contexts, and time. Therefore, it represents a shift in conceptual focus, from the content of the phenomenon to the nature of emergence itself.

Patterned Emergence

This model is based on the widest variability in the type and amount of elemental contribution, and in the patterns by which those differences combine to represent emergent phenomena. This model incorporates the assumption that emergence may manifest itself as different forms, and it views nonuniform patterns of dispersion as meaningful substantive phenomena.

The variance form of emergence is based on uniform distributions of within-group dispersion, whereas the patterned or configural form is based on nonuniform distributions of within-group dispersion. The term *uniformity* refers to the pattern of the distribution. A uniform distribution is single-modal, indicating strong or weak *agreement*. A nonuniform distribution is highly skewed or multimodal, indicating strong or weak *disagreement* (that is, the formation of subgroup clusters). Indeed, this form is generally indicated by within-unit variance that exceeds what would be expected from purely random responding. Therefore, very high variance within a group may be indicative of polarized factions, or "faultlines," Lau and Murhighan's (1998) metaphor for the divisions that may erupt and split a group. In this sense, disagreement goes beyond lack of agreement; it is indicative of conflict or of opposing perspectives within the collective unit. It is in this respect that dispersion theory uses nonuniform patterns of subgroup bifurcation to capture such complex phenomena as conflict, polarization, competition, and coalition formation (Brown & Kozlowski, 1997, 1999).

In addition to patterns of subgroup bifurcation, this form of emergence includes configurations that attempt to capture networks of linkages. Consider, for example, the model of team compilation proposed by Kozlowski and colleagues (1999). The model specifies different types, amounts, and linking mechanisms to characterize performance contributions at the individual, dyad, and team levels. Adaptive team performance is represented as a configuration of compatible knowledge and actions across team members at different levels of analysis. Or consider notions of team mental models and transactive memory. Early notions of the team mental model concept assumed that all team members shared the same knowledge (e.g., Cannon-Bowers, Salas, & Converse, 1993; Klimoski & Mohammed, 1995). Therefore, early versions of this construct assumed isomorphic composition. As this concept has evolved in the literature, it has been reconceptualized as entailing different *compatible* knowledge

(Kozlowski, Gully, Salas, et al., 1996)—different knowledge across individuals that forms a congruent whole.

Similarly, Wegner (1995) proposes that individual group members may each have unique information essential to performing the group task. It is not necessary for individuals to share the same knowledge (that is, isomorphic assumptions); rather, one or more individuals simply need to know who possesses the unique information. The essential information can then be accessed, as necessary. In this model, group memory is a complex configuration of individual memory, distributed knowledge of the contents of individual memory, and the interaction process that links that information into an emergent whole.

Implications

We introduced this third and last section of the chapter with three intentions: to be inclusive and expansive in our consideration of alternative forms of emergence, to focus on building a theoretical foundation for different forms of emergence, and to use typology as a vehicle for explicating and elaborating on the theoretical underpinnings of emergence. We hope that we have, in some measure, accomplished these goals. We believe, as we shall describe, that our framework is largely consistent with other efforts to explore emergence. We also believe that our particular attention to the underlying processes and dynamics that shape different forms of emergence can enhance understanding of the moderator effects and boundary conditions affecting emergence. An appreciation of the influence of these processes will lead to more precise specification of the theory addressing emergent phenomena. We see our effort as a point of departure for guiding and pushing further theoretical elaboration.

It is interesting to us that when our effort was originally conceived, we viewed our focus on different forms of emergence, and on the processes that shape those forms, as novel. However, a number of other researchers, contemporaneous with the development of this chapter, have also started to explore emergence (Brown & Kozlowski, 1997, 1999; Brown et al., 1996; Chan, 1998; Kozlowski, 1998, 1999; Morgeson & Hofmann, 1999a, 1999b). Although this chapter is not intended as an integration of these efforts, we believe that our framework helps to make explicit the compatibilities across these apparently disparate efforts to explore emergence. For example, Brown and Kozlowski (1997, 1999) posit *dispersion theory*, which focuses on patterns of within-group variability or the dispersion of phenomena, as opposed to the more common focus on means or convergent points. In dispersion theory, uniform patterns that evidence low dispersion are consistent with composition processes, whereas subgroup bifurcation that creates nonuniform patterns of dispersion are consistent with compilation processes. Similarly, Morgeson and Hofmann (1999a, 1999b) have made a strong case for distinguishing construct *structure* and *function*. Structural and functional identity across levels is consistent with composition processes, and functional but not structural identity across levels is consistent with compilation processes.

Using examples from the literature, Chan (1998) has developed a typology to distinguish different types of "composition" or data-aggregation models. The typology includes additive models (e.g., Glick, 1985), direct-consensus models (e.g., James et al., 1984, 1993; Kozlowski & Hattrup, 1992), referent-shift-consensus models (e.g., James, 1982; Klein et al., 1994; Rousseau, 1985), dispersion models (e.g., Brown et al., 1996; Brown & Kozlowski, 1997), and process models (e.g., Kozlowski et al., 1994, 1999; Kozlowski, Gully, McHugh, et al., 1996). The direct-consensus, additive, and referent-shift-consensus models are consistent with composition processes, whereas the dispersion and process models are consistent with compilation processes.[8] Finally, our typology is also consistent with Steiner's (1972) typology of group performance. In many ways, Steiner's work is a precursor of all such typologies because it captures many of the basic combination rules that determine how individual characteristics, cognition, affect, and behavior can aggregate to represent higher-level, collective phenomena. We believe, as just discussed, that our framework is largely consistent with these other efforts. We also believe that our particular attention to the underlying processes and dynamics that shape different emergent forms enhances understanding of the moderator effects and boundary conditions affecting emergence. An appreciation of the influence of these processes will lead to more precise specification of theory addressing emergent phenomena.

We would be remiss if we did not note that there are also apparent inconsistencies between the contemporary treatments of emergence (just noted) and other treatments with a tradition in the literature. We see the treatments as compatible yet different efforts to understand the same general class of phenomena. For example, the varient paradigm (Dansereau et al., 1984) treats emergence as a relationship between variables that exists at a higher, collective level but that does not hold between similar variables at a lower level. Thus, for example, a relationship between two variables is said to emerge at the group level of analysis if the two variables are significantly related (both statistically and practically) at the group level of analysis but the relationship between the two variables is not significant at the individual level of analysis. The varient perspective on emergence and our perspective are related but distinct. Dansereau and his colleagues focus on the emergence of relationships between variables at higher unit levels and on the statistical detection of such relationships. In contrast, we have focused primarily on the emergence of higher-level constructs, endeavoring to show the variety of ways in which a higher-level construct may emerge from lower-level entities and interaction processes. Measurement and analysis are important but separable issues. Ultimately, specific theories that assume particular emergent forms will need to be tested empirically. The varient paradigm, other analytic approaches, and even new techniques will be useful in this process.

We believe that the theoretical issues surrounding emergence that we have explored here are critical to the development of our science. How individual cognition, affect, behavior, and other characteristics emerge to make contributions to group and organizational outcomes is largely an uncharted frontier. How theories, interventions, and tools from the fields of industrial/organizational (I/O) psychology and organizational behavior (OB) can enhance these contributions is largely an unanswered question. Like most researchers and practitioners in the field, we believe that I/O-OB theories and techniques make contributions to organizational effectiveness, but we cannot really substantiate that belief (Rousseau, Chapter Fourteen, this volume). The chapters in this volume that deal with theory begin to explore this missing link. The chapter on training effectiveness (Kozlowski et al., Chapter Four), in particular, uses the distinction between composition and compilation to draw implications for how training can influence higher-level outcomes. We are beginning to probe a critical issue, but there is much more to do.

We make no claim that our framework is all-encompassing and complete; it is a work in progress. Although our focus has been primarily conceptual, the alternative forms of emergence have implications for measurement and analysis. We have endeavored to address measurement and data representation where possible, but we readily admit that the more complex compilation forms of emergence do not have well-developed measurement methods and analytic models. We hope that our pushing theorists to consider more complex phenomena will lead to new developments in methods and analytic systems. We hope the theoretical framework and typology presented here will stimulate further efforts to expand the conceptualization of emergent phenomena in organizations.

Conclusion

As the next millennium approaches, we are poised to witness a renaissance in organizational theory and research. There is increasing recognition that the confines of single-level models—a legacy of primary disciplines that undergird organizational science—need to be broken. A meaningful understanding of the phenomena that comprise organizational behavior necessitates approaches that are more integrative, that cut across multiple levels, and that seek to understand phenomena from a combination of perspectives. There is a solid theoretical foundation for a broadly applicable levels perspective, for an expanding, empirically based research literature, and for progress toward the development of new and more powerful analytic tools. A levels perspective offers a paradigm that is distinctly organizational.

Our purposes in this chapter have been to review the conceptual foundations of the levels perspective in organizations, to synthesize principles for guiding theory development and research, and to elaborate neglected models of emergent phenomena. Our goal is to convince researchers that levels issues should be considered in the study of a broad range of phenomena that occur in organizations. We hope that this chapter will, in a small way, push researchers to use established frameworks and to explore new alternatives in their work.

The remaining chapters in this book apply a levels perspective to substantive topics, consider analytic methods, and reflect on the implications of the levels perspective for organizational science.

Several of the substantive topics were selected primarily because typical treatments of these topics in the industrial and organizational literature rarely consider the implications of levels, and yet levels issues are central. When the implications of a multilevel theory are considered, new and unexplored issues are surfaced. Prime examples of such topics include selection (Schneider et al., Chapter Two, this volume), performance appraisal (DeNisi, Chapter Three, this volume), training effectiveness (Kozlowski et al., Chapter Four, this volume), and human resource management (Ostroff & Bowen, Chapter Five, this volume).

Other topics were selected because they naturally embody a levels perspective, but a perspective that forces us to think beyond our current frameworks. Prime examples include cross-cultural (Chao, Chapter Seven, this volume) and interorganizational linkages (Klein et al., Chapter Six, this volume). Both chapters focus on the implications of individuals being representatives of the higher level collectivities to which they belong.

Next, there are chapters addressing each of the primary multilevel analytic methods and issues, including within-group agreement, non-independence, and reliability (Bliese, Chapter Eight, this volume); the cross-level operator and contextual analysis (James & Williams, Chapter Nine, this volume), within-and-between analysis (Dansereau & Yammarino, Chapter Ten, this volume); and hierarchical linear modeling (Hofmann et al., Chapter Eleven, this volume). In addition, we have endeavored to cut through to the heart of the assumptions, differences, and appropriate applications of these multilevel analytic techniques with a collaborative effort that combines our disparate knowledge and perspectives (Klein, Bliese et al., Chapter Twelve, this volume).

Finally, we close the book with reflective comments pertaining to the importance of the levels perspective to the deep historical roots of our science, and to the increasing centrality of levels theory in mainstream organizational theory and research (Brass, Chapter Thirteen, this volume). The multilevel perspective provides a means for us to unify our science, and creates a foundation for enhancing policy impact for the disciplines that study organizations (Rousseau, Chapter Fourteen, this volume). The authors of all these chapters have provided a wealth of ideas and actionable knowledge. We hope that these ideas, and this book, stimulates those, who like us, seek a more unified and impactful science of organizations.

Notes
1. Throughout this chapter, we use the term *multilevel* in a generic sense, to reference all types of models that entail more than one level of conceptualization and analysis. Therefore, our use of the term *multilevel* references composition and compilation forms of bottom-up emergence, cross-level models that address top-down contextual effects, and homologous multilevel models that address parallel constructs and processes occurring at multiple levels.
2. Any effort to briefly characterize the many and myriad contributions to multilevel theory in organizations is doomed from the outset to be incomplete. We recognize that there are other lines of theory and research that have contributed to multilevel theory; many are mentioned throughout this chapter. We have chosen, however, to focus on a very early, sustained, and reasonably coherent effort that spanned many decades and many contributors. Our apologies to all others.
3. We recognize that there are alternative perspectives on organizational culture that view it as a collective construct, one that cannot be decomposed to the individual level. However, research on organizational culture has become increasingly consistent with an emergent perspective (Denison, 1996).
4. Insofar as global, shared, and configural unit properties each describe a unit as a whole, they are "homogeneous constructs," as Klein and colleagues (1994) use the term; here, we elaborate on their typology, illuminating the variety of forms that homogeneous unit-level constructs may take.
5. Unit-level constructs may of course be compositional, as in situations where group members share identical values or the same attitudes, but we expect some characteristics, such as abilities and personality, to be more likely configural than shared.
6. We acknowledge that the conceptualization of phenomena *may* entail a universal form; for example, unit climate is often conceptualized as a unit property when it is shared and as an individual property when it is not (James, 1982).
7. Our definition of discontinuous phenomena is consistent with House and colleagues (1995). Note also that these authors propose three models of *relational* discontinuity, involving (a) magnitude, (b) relational patterns, and (c) behavior-outcome relations. We would characterize these models as top-down contextual models, not bottom-up emergent processes. These three models illustrate (a) cross-level direct effects,

(b) cross-level frog-pond relations, and (c) cross-level moderation, respectively. Our typology focuses on *discontinuity in emergence.*

8. We should clarify that Chan (1998) indicates that his additive, direct consensus, referent-shift consensus, and dispersion models are static, whereas the process model in his typology is more directly interested in the dynamics of emergence. We would argue that emergent process dynamics are relevant to *all* the categories in that such processes shape the emergent form and, therefore, should be an explicit part of the conceptualization.

References

Allport, F. H. (1954). The structuring of events: Outline of a general theory with applications to psychology. *Psychological Review, 61,* 281–303.

Ancona, D., & Chong, C. (1997). Entrainment: Pace, cycle, and rhythm in organizational behavior. In L. L. Cummings & B. Staw (Eds.), *Research in organizational behavior* (Vol. 18, pp. 251–284). Greenwich, CT: JAI Press.

Arthur, W. B. (1994). On the evolution of complexity. In G. Cowan, D. Pines, & D. Meltzer (Eds.), *Complexity: Metaphors, models, and reality* (pp. 65–77). Reading, MA: Addison-Wesley.

Ashby, W. R. (1952). *Design for a brain.* New York: Wiley.

Bliese, P. D. (2000). Within-group agreement, non-independence, and reliability: Implications for data aggregation and analysis. In K. J. Klein & S.W.J. Kozlowski (Eds.), *Multilevel theory, research, and methods in organizations* (pp. 349–381). San Francisco: Jossey-Bass.

Boulding, K. E. (1956). General systems theory: The skeleton of science. *General Systems, 1,* 1–17.

Bourgeois, V. W., & Pinder, C. C. (1983). Contrasting philosophical perspectives in administrative science: A reply to Morgan. *Administrative Science Quarterly, 28,* 608–613.

Brass, D. J. (1981). Structural relationships, job characteristics, and worker satisfaction and performance. *Administrative Science Quarterly, 26,* 331–348.

Brass, D. J. (1985). Technology and the structuring of jobs: Employee satisfaction, performance, and influence. *Organizational Behavior and Human Decision Processes, 35,* 216–240.

Brass, D. J. (1995). A social network perspective on human resources management. In G. R. Ferris (Ed.), *Research in personnel and human resources management* (Vol. 13, pp. 39–79). Greenwich, CT: JAI Press.

Brass, D. J. (2000). Networks and frog ponds: Trends in multilevel research. In K. J. Klein & S.W.J. Kozlowski (Eds.), *Multilevel theory, research, and methods in organizations* (pp. 557–571). San Francisco: Jossey-Bass.

Brown, K. G., & Kozlowski, S.W.J. (1997). Dispersion theory: A framework for emergent organizational phenomena. Unpublished paper, Department of Psychology, Michigan State University.

Brown, K. G., & Kozlowski, S.W.J. (1999, April). Toward an expanded conceptualization of emergent organizational phenomena: Dispersion theory. In F. P. Morgeson & D. A. Hofmann (Chairs), *New perspectives on higher-level phenomena in industrial/organizational psychology*. Symposium conducted at the 14th annual conference of the Society for Industrial and Organizational Psychology, Atlanta, GA.

Brown, K. G., Kozlowski, S.W.J., & Hattrup, K. (1996, August). Theory, issues, and recommendations in conceptualizing agreement as a construct in organizational research: The search for consensus regarding consensus. In S. Kozlowski & K. Klein (Chairs), *The meaning and measurement of within-group agreement in multi-level research*. Symposium conducted at the annual convention of the Academy of Management Association, Cincinnati, OH.

Bryk, A. S., & Raudenbush, S. W. (1992). *Hierarchical linear models: Applications and data analysis methods*. Thousand Oaks, CA: Sage.

Burstein, L. (1980). The analysis of multilevel data in educational research and evaluation. *Review of Research in Education, 8*, 158–233.

Campbell, D. T. (1955). The informant in qualitative research. *American Journal of Sociology, 60*, 339–342.

Campbell, D. T. (1958). Common fate, similarity, and other indices of the status of aggregates of persons as social entities. *Behavioral Science, 3*, 14–25.

Campion, M. A., Medsker, G. J., & Higgs, A. C. (1993). Relations between group characteristics and effectiveness: Implications for designing effective work groups. *Personnel Psychology, 46*, 823–850.

Cannon-Bowers, J. A., Salas, E., & Converse, S. A. (1993). Shared mental models in expert team decision-making. In N. J. Castellan, Jr. (Ed.), *Current issues in individual and group decision making* (pp. 221–246). Mahwah, NJ: Erlbaum.

Chan, D. (1998). Functional relations among constructs in the same content domain at different levels of analysis: A typology of composition models. *Journal of Applied Psychology, 83*, 234–246.

Chao, G. T. (2000). Multilevel issues and culture: An integrative view. In K. J. Klein & S.W.J. Kozlowski (Eds.), *Multilevel theory, research, and methods in organizations* (pp. 308–347). San Francisco: Jossey-Bass.

Cowan, G., Pines, D. & Meltzer, D. (1994). *Complexity: Metaphors, models, and reality*. Reading, MA: Addison-Wesley.

Crutchfield, J. P. (1994). Is anything ever new? Considering emergence. In G. Cowan, D. Pines, & D. Meltzer (Eds.), *Complexity: Metaphors, models, and reality* (pp. 515–533). Reading, MA: Addison-Wesley.

Dansereau, F., Alutto, J. A., & Yammarino, F. J. (1984). *Theory testing in organizational behavior: The varient approach.* Englewood Cliffs, NJ: Prentice Hall.

Dansereau, F., & Dumas, M. (1977). Pratfalls and pitfalls in drawing inferences about leadership behavior in organizations. In J. G. Hunt & L. L. Larson (Eds.), *Leadership: The cutting edge* (pp. 68–83). Carbondale: Southern Illinois University Press.

Dansereau, F., & Yammarino, F. J. (2000). Within and Between Analysis: The varient paradigm as an underlying approach to theory building and testing. In K. J. Klein & S.W.J. Kozlowski (Eds.), *Multilevel theory, research, and methods in organizations* (pp. 425–466). San Francisco: Jossey-Bass.

Dansereau, F., Yammarino, F. J., & Kohles, J. C. (1999). Multiple levels of analysis from a longitudinal perspective: Some implications for theory building. *Academy of Management Journal, 24,* 346–357.

Davis, J. H. (1992). Some compelling intuitions about group consensus decisions, theoretical and empirical research, and interpersonal aggregation phenomena: Selected examples, 1950–1990. *Organizational Behavior and Human Decision Processes, 52,* 3–38.

DeNisi, A. S. (2000). Performance appraisal and performance management: A multilevel analysis. In K. J. Klein & S.W.J. Kozlowski (Eds.), *Multilevel theory, research, and methods in organizations* (pp. 121–156). San Francisco: Jossey-Bass.

Denison, D. R. (1996). What IS the difference between organizational culture and organizational climate? A native's point of view on a decade of paradigm wars. *Academy of Management Review, 21,* 619–654.

DeShon, R. P., Milner, K. R., Kozlowski, S.W.J., Toney, R. J., Schmidt, A., Wiechmann, D., & Davis, C. (1999, April). The effects of team goal orientation on individual and team performance. In D. Steele-Johnson (Chair), *New directions in goal orientation research: Extending the construct, the nomological net, and analytic methods.* Symposium conducted at the fourteen annual conference of the Society for Industrial and Organizational Psychology, Atlanta, GA.

Emery, F. E., & Trist, E. L. (1960). Socio-technical systems. In *Management science models and techniques* (Vol. 2). London: Pergamon.

Firebaugh, G. (1979). Assessing group effects: A comparison of two methods. *Sociological Methods and Research, 7,* 384–395.

Fleishman, E. A., & Zaccaro, S. J. (1992). Toward a taxonomy of team performance functions. In R. W. Swezey & E. Salas (Eds.), *Teams: Their training and performance* (pp. 31–56). Norwood, NJ: Ablex.

Forehand, G. A., & Gilmer, B. H. (1964). Environmental variation in studies of organizational behavior. *Psychological Bulletin, 62,* 361–382.

Freeman, J. (1980). The unit problem in organizational research. In W. M. Evan (Ed.), *Frontiers in organization and management* (pp. 59–68). New York: Praeger.

Gell-Mann, M. (1994). Complex adaptive systems. In G. Cowan, D. Pines, & D. Meltzer (Eds.), *Complexity: Metaphors, models, and reality* (pp. 17–29). Reading, MA: Addison-Wesley.

George, J. M., & James, L. R. (1993). Personality, affect, and behavior in groups revisited: Comment on aggregation, levels of analysis, and a recent application of within and between analysis. *Journal of Applied Psychology, 78,* 798–804.

George, J. M., & James, L. R. (1994). Levels issues in theory development. *Academy of Management Review, 19,* 636–640.

Gersick, C.J.G., & Hackman, J. R. (1990). Habitual routines in task-performing groups. *Organizational Behavior and Human Decision Processes, 47,* 65–97.

Glick, W. H. (1985). Conceptualizing and measuring organizational and psychological climate: Pitfalls in multilevel research. *Academy of Management Review, 10,* 601–616.

Glick, W. H. (1988). Response: Organizations are not central tendencies: Shadowboxing in the dark, round 2. *Academy of Management Journal, 13,* 133–137.

Glick, W. H., & Roberts, K. (1984). Hypothesized interdependence, assumed independence. *Academy of Management Review, 9,* 722–735.

Graen, G. (1976). Role making processes within complex organizations. In M. D. Dunnette (Ed.), *Handbook of industrial and organizational psychology* (pp. 1201–1245). Skolie, IL: Rand McNally.

Griffin, M. A. (1997). Interaction between individuals and situations: Using HLM procedures to estimate reciprocal relationships. *Journal of Management, 23,* 759–773.

Hannan, M. T. (1991). *Aggregation and disaggregation in the social sciences.* San Francisco: New Lexington Press.

Harkins, S. G., Latane, B., & Williams, K. (1980). Social loafing: Allocating effort or taking it easy. *Journal of Experimental Social Psychology, 16,* 457–465.

Herman, J. B., & Hulin, C. L. (1972). Studying organizational attitudes from individual and organizational frames of reference. *Organizational Behavior and Human Performance, 8,* 81–108.

Hofmann, D. A., Griffin, M., & Gavin, M. (2000). The application of hierarchical linear modeling to organizational research. In K. J. Klein & S.W.J. Kozlowski (Eds.), *Multilevel theory, research, and methods in organizations* (pp. 467–511). San Francisco: Jossey-Bass.

Hofmann, D. A., & Stetzer, A. (1996). A cross-level investigation of factors influencing unsafe behaviors and accidents. *Personnel Psychology, 49,* 301–339.

Homans, G. C. (1950). *The human group.* Orlando, FL: Harcourt Brace.

House, R., Rousseau, D. M., & Thomas-Hunt, M. (1995). The meso paradigm: A framework for integration of micro and macro organizational. In L. L. Cummings & B. Staw (Eds.), *Research in organizational behavior* (Vol. 17, pp. 71–114). Greenwich, CT: JAI Press.

Huselid, M. A. (1995). The impact of human resource management practices on turnover, productivity, and corporate financial performance. *Academy of Management Journal, 38,* 635–672.

Indik, B. P. (1968). The scope of the problem and some suggestions toward a solution. In B. P. Indik & F. K. Berren (Eds.), *People, groups, and organizations* (pp. 3–30). New York: Teachers College Press.

Jackson, J. (1975). Normative power and conflict potential. *Sociological Methods and Research, 4,* 237–263.

Jackson, S. E., May, K. E., & Whitney, K. (1995). Understanding the dynamics of diversity in decision-making teams. In R. Guzzo, E. Salas, & Associates, *Team effectiveness and decision making in organizations* (pp. 204–261). San Francisco: Jossey-Bass.

James, L. R. (1982). Aggregation bias in estimates of perceptual agreement. *Journal of Applied Psychology, 67,* 219–229.

James, L. R., Demaree, R. G., & Wolf, G. (1984). Estimating within group interrater reliability with and without response bias. *Journal of Applied Psychology, 69,* 85–98.

James, L. R., Demaree, R. G., & Wolf, G. (1993). r_{wg}: An assessment of within-group interrater agreement. *Journal of Applied Psychology, 78,* 306–309.

James, L. R., & Jones, A. P. (1974). Organizational climate: A review of theory and research. *Psychological Bulletin, 81,* 1096–1112.

James, L. R., & Jones, A. P. (1976). Organizational structure: A review of structural dimensions and their conceptual relationships with individual attitudes and behavior. *Organizational Behavior and Human Performance, 16,* 74–113.

James, L. R., & Williams, L. J. (2000). The cross-level operator in regression, ANCOVA, and contextual analysis. In K. J. Klein & S.W.J. Kozlowski (Eds.), *Multilevel theory, research, and methods in organizations* (pp. 382–424). San Francisco: Jossey-Bass.

Jones, A. P., & James, L. R. (1979). Psychological climate: Dimensions and relationships of individual and aggregated work environment perceptions. *Organizational Behavior and Human Performance, 23,* 201–250.

Katz, D., & Kahn, R. L. (1966). *The social psychology of organizations.* New York: Wiley.

Kauffman, S. A. (1994). Whispers from Carnot: The origins of order and principles of adaptation in complex nonequilibrium systems. In

G. Cowan, D. Pines, & D. Meltzer (Eds.), *Complexity: Metaphors, models, and reality* (pp. 83–136). Reading, MA: Addison-Wesley.

Klein, K. J., Bliese, P. D., Kozlowski, S.W.J., Dansereau, F., Gavin, M. B., Griffin, M. A., Hofmann, D. A., James, L. R., Williams, L .J., Yammarino, F. J., & Bligh, M. C. (2000). Multilevel analytical techniques: Commonalities, differences, and continuing questions. In K. J. Klein & S.W.J. Kozlowski (Eds.), *Multilevel theory, research, and methods in organizations* (pp. 512–553). San Francisco: Jossey-Bass.

Klein, K. J., Conn, A. L., Smith, D. B, & Sorra, J. S. (1998). Is everyone in agreement? Exploring the determinants of within-group agreement in survey responses. Unpublished manuscript.

Klein, K. J., Dansereau, F., & Hall, R. J. (1994). Levels issues in theory development, data collection, and analysis. *Academy of Management Review, 19,* 195–229.

Klein, K. J., Dansereau, F., & Hall, R. J. (1995). On the level: Homogeneity, independence, heterogeneity, and interactions in organizational theory. *Academy of Management Review, 20,* 7–9.

Klein, K. J., & House, R. J. (1995). On fire: Charismatic leadership and levels of analysis. *Leadership Quarterly, 6,* 183–198.

Klein, K. J., Palmer, S. L., & Conn, A. B. (2000). Interorganizational relationships: A multilevel perspective. In K. J. Klein & S.W.J. Kozlowski (Eds.), *Multilevel theory, research, and methods in organizations* (pp. 267–307). San Francisco: Jossey-Bass.

Klimoski, R., & Mohammed, S. (1995). Team mental model: Construct or metaphor? *Journal of Management, 20,* 403–437.

Koene, B. A., Boone, C.A.J.J., & Soeters, J. L. (1997). Organizational factors influencing homogeneity and heterogeneity of organizational cultures. In S. A. Sackmann (Ed.), *Cultural complexity in organizations: Inherent contrasts and contradictions* (pp. 273–293). Thousand Oaks, CA: Sage.

Kozlowski, S.W.J. (1998, March). Extending and elaborating models of emergent phenomena. Presentation at MESO Organization Studies Group, Arizona State University, Tempe.

Kozlowski, S.W.J. (1999, April). A typology of emergence: Theoretical mechanisms undergirding bottom-up phenomena in organizations. In F. P. Morgeson & D. A. Hofmann (Chairs), *New perspectives on higher-level phenomenon in industrial/organizational psychology.* Symposium conducted at the fourteenth annual conference of the Society for Industrial and Organizational Psychology, Atlanta, GA.

Kozlowski, S.W.J., Brown, K. G., Weissbein, D. A., Cannon-Bowers, J. A., & Salas, E. (2000). A multilevel approach to training effectiveness:

Enhancing horizontal and vertical transfer. In K. J. Klein & S.W.J. Kozlowski (Eds.), *Multilevel theory, research, and methods in organizations* (pp. 157–210). San Francisco: Jossey-Bass.

Kozlowski, S.W.J., & Doherty, M. L. (1989). An integration of climate and leadership: Examination of a neglected issue. *Journal of Applied Psychology, 74,* 546–553.

Kozlowski, S.W.J., & Farr, J. L. (1988). An integrative model of updating and performance. *Human Performance, 1,* 5–29.

Kozlowski, S.W.J., Gully, S. M., McHugh, P. P., Salas, E., & Cannon-Bowers, J. A. (1996). A dynamic theory of leadership and team effectiveness: Developmental and task contingent leader roles. In G. R. Ferris (Ed.), *Research in personnel and human resource management* (Vol. 14, pp. 253–305). Greenwich, CT: JAI Press.

Kozlowski, S.W.J., Gully, S. M., Nason, E. R., Ford, J. K., Smith, E. M., Smith, M. R., & Futch, C. J. (1994, April). A composition theory of team development: Levels, content, process, and learning outcomes. In J. E. Mathieu (Chair), *Developmental views of team process and performance.* Symposium conducted at the ninth annual conference of the Society for Industrial and Organizational Psychology, Nashville, TN.

Kozlowski, S.W.J., Gully, S. M., Nason, E. R., & Smith, E. M. (1999). Developing adaptive teams: A theory of compilation and performance across levels and time. In D. R. Ilgen & E. D. Pulakos (Eds.), *The changing nature of work performance: Implications for staffing, personnel actions, and development.* San Francisco: Jossey-Bass.

Kozlowski, S.W.J., Gully, S. M., Salas, E., & Cannon-Bowers, J. A. (1996). Team leadership and development: Theory, principles, and guidelines for training leaders and teams. In M. Beyerlein, D. Johnson, & S. Beyerlein (Eds.), *Advances in interdisciplinary studies of work teams: Team leadership* (Vol. 3, pp. 251–289). Greenwich, CT: JAI Press.

Kozlowski, S.W.J., & Hattrup, K. (1992). A disagreement about within-group agreement: Disentangling issues of consistency versus consensus. *Journal of Applied Psychology, 77,* 161–167.

Kozlowski, S.W.J., & Hults, B. M. (1987). An exploration of climates for technical updating and performance. *Personnel Psychology, 40,* 539–563.

Kozlowski, S.W.J., & Salas, E. (1997). An organizational systems approach for the implementation and transfer of training. In J. K. Ford, S.W.J. Kozlowski, K. Kraiger, E. Salas, & M. Teachout (Eds.), *Improving training effectiveness in work organizations* (pp. 247–287). Mahwah, NJ: Erlbaum.

Krakauer, J. (1997). *Into thin air.* New York: Villard.

Kuhn, A., & Beam, R. D. (1982). *The logic of organization.* San Francisco: Jossey-Bass.

Lau, D. C., & Murhighan, J. K. (1998). Demographic diversity and fault-lines: The compositional dynamics of organizational groups. *Academy of Management Review, 23,* 325–340.

Levine, R. L., & Fitzgerald, H. E. (1992). *Analysis of dynamic psychological systems* (Vols. 1, 2). New York: Plenum.

Lewin, K. (1951). *Field theory in the social sciences.* New York: HarperCollins.

Lewin, K., Lippitt, R., & White, R. K. (1939). Patterns of aggressive behavior in experimentally created "social climates." *Journal of Social Psychology, 10,* 271–299.

Likert, R. (1961). *The human organization: Its management and value.* New York: McGraw-Hill.

Lindsley, D. H., Brass, D. J., & Thomas, J. B. (1995). Efficacy-performance spirals: A multilevel perspective. *Academy of Management Review, 20,* 645–678.

Louis, M. R. (1980). Surprise and sense-making: What newcomers experience in entering unfamiliar organizational settings. *Administrative Science Quarterly, 25,* 226–251.

Mathieu, J. E., & Kohler, S. S. (1990). A cross-level examination of group absence influences on individual absence. *Journal of Applied Psychology, 75,* 217–220.

McGrath, J. E. (1990). Time matters in groups. In J. Galegher, R. Krout, & C. C. Egido (Eds.), *Intellectual teamwork* (pp. 23–61). Mahwah, NJ: Erlbaum.

Meyer, A. D., Tsui, A. S., & Hinings, C. R. (1993). Guest co-editors' introduction: Configural approaches to organizational analysis. *Academy of Management Journal, 36,* 1175–1195.

Miller, J. G. (1978). *Living systems.* New York: McGraw-Hill.

Millikin, F. J., & Martins, L. L. (1996). Searching for common threads: Understanding the multiple effects of diversity in organizational groups. *Academy of Management Review, 21,* 402–433.

Moreland, R. L., & Levine, J. M. (1992). The composition of small groups. In E. E. Lawler III., B. Markovsky, C. Ridgeway, & H. Walker (Eds.), *Advances in group processes* (Vol. 9, pp. 237–280). Greenwich, CT: JAI Press.

Morgan, G. (1983). More on metaphor: Why we cannot control tropes in administrative science. *Administrative Science Quarterly, 28,* 601–607.

Morgeson, F. P., & Hofmann, D. A. (1999a, April). The structure and function of collective constructs. In F. P. Morgeson & D. A. Hofmann, (Chairs), *New perspectives on higher-level phenomena in industrial/ organizational psychology.* Symposium conducted at the Fourteenth

Annual Conference of the Society for Industrial and Organizational Psychology, Atlanta, GA.

Morgeson, F. P., & Hofmann, D. A. (1999b). The structure and function of collective constructs: Implications for multilevel research and theory development. *Academy of Management Review, 24,* 249–265.

Mossholder, K. W., & Bedeian, A. G. (1983). Cross-level inference and organizational research: Perspectives on interpretation and application. *Academy of Management Review, 8,* 547–558.

Muthen, B. (1994). Multilevel covariance structure analysis. *Sociological Methods and Research, 22,* 376–398.

Nicolis, G., & Prigogine, I. (1989). *Exploring complexity.* New York: Freeman.

Nonaka, I. (1994). A dynamic theory of knowledge creation. *Organizational Science, 5,* 14–37.

Oldham, G. R., & Hackman, J. R. (1981). Relationships between organizational structure and employee reactions: Comparing alternative frameworks. *Administrative Science Quarterly, 26,* 66–81.

Ostroff, C. (1993). Comparing correlations based on individual level and aggregate data. *Journal of Applied Psychology, 78,* 569–582.

Ostroff, C., & Bowen, D. E. (2000). Moving HR to a higher level: HR practices and organizational effectiveness. In K. J. Klein & S.W.J. Kozlowski (Eds.), *Multilevel theory, research, and methods in organizations* (pp. 211–266). San Francisco: Jossey-Bass.

Parsons, T. (1956). Suggestions for a sociological approach to the theory of organizations, I and II. *Administrative Science Quarterly, 1,* 225–239.

Parsons, T. (1960). *Structure and process in modern societies.* New York: Free Press.

Pinder, C. C., & Bourgeois, V. W. (1982). Controlling tropes in administrative science. *Administrative Science Quarterly, 27,* 641–652.

Prigogine, I., & Stengers, I. (1984). *Order out of chaos: Man's new dialogue with nature.* New York: Bantam.

Rentch, J. R. (1990). Climate and culture: Interaction and qualitative differences in organizational meanings. *Journal of Applied Psychology, 75,* 668–681.

Roberts, K. H., Hulin, C. L., & Rousseau, D. M. (1978). *Developing an interdisciplinary science of organizations.* San Francisco: Jossey-Bass.

Robinson, W. S. (1950). Ecological correlations and the behavior of individuals. *American Sociological Review, 15,* 351–357.

Roethlisberger, F. J., & Dickson, W. J. (1939). Human relations. In *Management and the worker.* Cambridge, MA: Harvard University Press.

Rouiller, J. Z., & Goldstein, I. L. (1993). The relationship between organizational transfer climate and positive transfer of training. *Human Resource Development Quarterly, 4,* 377–390.

Rousseau, D. M. (1978a). Characteristics of departments, positions, and individuals: Contexts for attitudes and behavior. *Administrative Science Quarterly, 23,* 521–540.

Rousseau, D. M. (1978b). Measures of technology as predictors of employee attitude. *Journal of Applied Psychology, 63,* 213–218.

Rousseau, D. M. (1985). Issues of level in organizational research: Multilevel and cross-level perspectives. In L. L. Cummings & B. Staw (Eds.), *Research in organizational behavior* (Vol. 7, pp. 1–37). Greenwich, CT: JAI Press.

Rousseau, D. M. (1988). The construction of climate in organizational research. In C. L. Cooper & I. Robertson (Eds.), *International review of industrial and organizational psychology* (pp. 139–158). New York: Wiley.

Rousseau, D. M. (2000). Multilevel competencies and missing linkages. In K. J. Klein & S.W.J. Kozlowski (Eds.), *Multilevel theory, research, and methods in organizations* (pp. 572–582). San Francisco: Jossey-Bass.

Schmidt, F. L., & Hunter, J. E. (1989). Interrater reliability coefficients cannot be computed when only one stimulus is rated. *Journal of Applied Psychology, 74,* 368–370.

Schmidt, F. L., Hunter, J. E., McKenzie, R. C., & Muldrow, T. W. (1979). The impact of valid selection procedures on work-force productivity. *Journal of Applied Psychology, 64,* 609–626.

Schneider, B. (1981). Work climates: An interactionist perspective. In N. Feimer & E. Geller (Eds.), *Environmental psychology: Directions and perspectives.* New York: Praeger.

Schneider, B., & Bowen, D. E. (1985). Employee and customer perceptions of service in banks: Replication and extension. *Journal of Applied Psychology, 70,* 423–433.

Schneider, B., & Reichers, A. E. (1983). On the etiology of climates. *Personnel Psychology, 36,* 19–39.

Schneider, B., Smith, D. B., & Sipe, W. P. Personnel selection psychology: Multilevel considerations. In K. J. Klein & S.W.J. Kozlowski (Eds.), *Multilevel theory, research, and methods in organizations* (pp. 91–120). San Francisco: Jossey-Bass.

Schriesheim, C. A. (1995). Multivariate and moderated within- and between-entity analysis (WABA) using hierarchical linear multiple regression. *Leadership Quarterly, 6,* 1–18.

Seidler, J. (1974). On using informants: A technique for collecting quantitative data and controlling measurement error in organizational analysis. *American Sociological Review, 39,* 816–831.

Simon, H. A. (1969). *The sciences of the artificial.* Cambridge, MA: MIT Press.

Simon, H. A. (1973). The organization of complex systems. In H. H. Pattee (Ed.), *Hierarchy theory* (pp. 1–27). New York: Braziller.

Staw, B., Sandelands, L. E., & Dutton, J. E. (1981). Threat-rigidity effects in organizational behavior: A multilevel analysis. *Administrative Science Quarterly, 26,* 501–524.

Steiner, I. D. (1972). *Group process and productivity.* Orlando, FL: Academic Press.

Terborg, J. R. (1981). Interactional psychology and research on behavior in organizations. *Academy of Management Review, 6,* 569–576.

Thompson, J. (1967). *Organizations in action.* New York: McGraw-Hill.

Thorndike, E. L. (1939). On the fallacy of imputing the correlations found for groups to the individuals or smaller groups composing them. *American Journal of Psychology, 52,* 122–124.

Tracy, L. (1989). *The living organization.* New York: Praeger.

Tsui, A. S., Egan, T. D., & O'Reilly, C. A. (1992). Being different: Relational demography and organizational attachment. *Administrative Science Quarterly, 37,* 547–579.

Tziner, A., & Eden, D. (1985). Effects of crew composition on crew performance: Does the whole equal the sum of its parts? *Journal of Applied Psychology, 70,* 85–93.

von Bertalanffy, L. (1968). *General systems theory.* New York: Braziller.

von Bertalanffy, L. (1972). The history and status of general systems theory. In G. J. Klir (Ed.), *Trends in general systems theory* (pp. 21–41). New York: Wiley.

Wegner, D. M. (1995). A computer network model of transactive memory. *Social Cognition, 13,* 319–339.

Weick, K. E. (1976). Educational organizations as loosely coupled systems. *Administrative Science Quarterly, 21,* 1–19.

Wiersema, M. F., & Bantel, K. A. (1992). Top management team demography and corporate strategic change. *Academy of Management Journal, 35,* 91–121.

Wittenbaum, G. M., & Stasser, G. (1996). Management of information in small groups. In J. L. Nye & A. M. Brower (Eds.), *What's social about social cognition: Research on socially shared cognition in small groups* (pp. 3–28). Thousand Oaks, CA: Sage.

Yammarino, F. J., & Markham, S. E. (1992). On the application of within and between analysis: Are absence and affect really group-based phenomena? *Journal of Applied Psychology, 77,* 168–176.

CHAPTER 2

Personnel Selection Psychology
Multilevel Considerations
Benjamin Schneider
D. Brent Smith
William P. Sipe

> *History shows that great . . . forces flow like a tide over*
> *communities only half-conscious of that which is befalling*
> *them. Wise statesmen foresee what time is thus bringing,*
> *and try to shape institutions and model men's thoughts*
> *and purposes in accordance with the change that is*
> *silently coming on.*
> JOHN STUART MILL

Industrial and organizational (I/O) psychology in general, and the subfield of personnel selection in particular, are experiencing a paradigm shift of which they may not be fully aware. The paradigm shift is from a focus on what Nord and Fox (1997) called the "essentialist individual" model of behavior to a newer focus on the organizational implications of personnel selection practices. From

Note: This chapter was prepared with the financial assistance of the Army Research Institute for the Behavioral and Social Sciences. The authors bear total responsibility for the content of the chapter; nothing in the chapter should be construed to represent positions of the U.S. Army and/or the Department of Defense.

its inception, personnel selection psychology has focused on individual differences as determinants of individual performance, assuming that individual performance translates neatly into organizational performance. This assumption remains the implicit justification for introducing new personnel selection practices into organizations. However, this assumption has not been the subject of strict empirical examination. Rather, our primary focus has jumped from a purely micro focus (on the relationship between individual differences and individual performance) to a purely macro focus (on the relationship between personnel selection practices and organizational performance), neglecting the intermediate, or meso, ground that examines the relationship between individual and organizational performance. Our primary suggestion is that personnel psychology, to advance as a field, must address the cross-level relationships between individual and organizational performance. The micro model ignores organizational issues and the macro model ignores individual differences.

The shift away from individual differences in understanding behavior in work organizations has been under way for three or more decades, since about 1960, and the accumulation of theory, research, and writing that focuses on the context of individual behavior has become overwhelming—overwhelming everywhere except in personnel selection. In personnel selection the focus remains on the "essentialist" individual (Nord & Fox, 1997). Guided by this model, researchers have concentrated on the cause of behavior as residing in the individual, considered the individual as the unit of theory and data so far as outcomes or criteria are concerned, and employed regression as the statistic of choice, with individuals as the unit of analysis for both predictor and criterion.

In the present chapter, we explore the history of the essentialist individual model in personnel selection and the potential for adding to that model issues concerning group and organizational behavior. In the first section, we show how the early study of individual differences, and the confluence of forces, or zeitgeist, from which that early study emerged, had a long-term impact on the subsequent theory and research carried out in that tradition. In the second section, we first review some early attempts by personnel selection researchers, to examine the contribution of personnel selection to organizational performance; we then provide a review of the literature, which suggests that the implementation of human resource management techniques (such as personnel selection) is actually related to organizational performance differences. In the last section, we provide a preliminary integration across these different levels of theory and data, to suggest the beginnings of a new agenda for personnel selection research.

It should be very clear at the outset that we write from an explicitly multilevel framework. This multilevel framework promotes the continued study of individual differences in attributes and behavior but adds to that focus the potential for contributions of individual attributes to group and organizational behavior, the potential for the contribution of group and organizational behavior to individual behavior, and the parsing of effects to different units of theory and data. We do not share the view of Dobbins, Cardy, and Carson (1991), who argue that individual differences account for such a small proportion of the variance in behavior as to be irrelevant to organizations. Our position is that there is reciprocal causation involved in the relationship between individuals and systems, and that this has been essentially ignored in organizational science research in general and personnel selection research in particular (Schneider, 1996). Because we also place great emphasis on the contributions of individual variability to the success of systems, it is appropriate to offer our conceptualization through the lens of personnel selection.

A Brief History of the Study of Individual Differences

In this section, we cite few references because the materials are generally known and represent a synthesis of readings from several sources: Bellows (1949), Boring (1950), Dennis (1948), Jenkins and Paterson (1961), and Viteles (1932). At any rate, as every informed psychologist knows (or should know), the history of the study of individual differences began in astronomy, when Bessel read in the 1820s about the 1796 firing of Kinnebrook by Maskelyne at the Greenwich Observatory. Bessel read that Maskelyne had dismissed Kinnebrook because the latter continued to obtain readings of the transit of stars that were different from those obtained by Maskelyne. Even then the boss was right, and Kinnebrook was gone. Bessel, however, was intrigued by Maskelyne's account of the firing and began to explore the degree to which different astronomers were obtaining similar readings when viewing stars. To make a long story short, Bessel discovered that there was considerable variability across astronomers in their readings. The research by Bessel prompted astronomers to calculate "personal equations" to equate their readings with those of other astronomers.

In the middle to late nineteenth century, as so frequently happens in science, a zeitgeist emerged as the confluence of the work of several noted scientists interested in the fundamental notion that people differ in reliable ways. For example, in England, Sir Francis Galton began his studies of hereditary intelligence and anthropometric testing, and in Germany, a brash young American named Cattell informed Wilhelm Wundt that he, Cattell, was Wundt's new research assistant. In Wundt's laboratory, Cattell began the study of individual differences in reaction time that served as a foundation for the later mental testing movement in the United States. In France, Binet and Simon conducted their "little experiments" designed to diagnose the mental age of children in the French school system—research that later contributed to the development of intelligence testing in the United States.

It is important to note that some of this work was predicated on Darwin's exploration and elaboration of evolution theory and his notion that random variability in species yields adaptation of the species to their environment or context. For Darwin, variability was the necessary ingredient for guaranteeing survival of the species. For Galton, too, variability in the species was a focus of interest, especially in the ways variability in attributes was reflected in variability in behavior. Adaptation and survival associated with variability in attributes is the philosophical theme uniting Darwin and Galton.

Darwin's work, of course, lies at the root of the school of psychology that came to be called *functionalism*. Members of this school of psychology studied the functional usefulness of individual attributes for coping with various environments, including schools and the workplace. From Dewey and Terman's work in the world of education to Cattell and Muensterburg's work in business and industry, functionalism in the United States emerged as the American version of survival of the fittest. Whereas for Darwin survival of the fittest was based on natural selection, in U.S. psychology it became survival of the fittest via personnel selection. Thus, by 1927, the central place of the study of individual differences in psychology was clear: "The fundamental fact of applied psychology is that the individual is the unit of action, and all advances in this science must rest upon a knowledge of the laws of individual behavior and the conditions which affect it" (Poffenberger, 1927, p. 16). In his masterly treatise on industrial psychology, Viteles made a similar observation: "Industrial psychology is based upon a study of *individual differences*—of human variability—the importance of which as an objective of scientific psychology seems to have first been definitely recognized and stressed by Sir Francis Galton" (Viteles, 1932, p. 29; emphasis in original).

By the time Viteles wrote his impressive survey of the field, Terman (1916) had revised the Binet-Simon scales for use in the United States, and the idea of testing groups of individuals had come to fruition in World War I. Indeed, by the late 1920s and early 1930s there was sufficient experience with what Cattell called "mental tests" as to provide a critical mass of knowledge. By 1928, Hull had summarized the literature then in existence, finding a validity coefficient of about .40 across studies for such procedures. (Sound familiar?) Hull had elaborated by then the basic formulation for conducting utility analysis to estimate the financial payoff of implementing personnel selection tests, estimating that in the typical job the best worker was two to three times as productive as the worst. Strong (1927) had already developed his Vocational Interest Blank, and Bingham and Moore (1931) had appropriately identified the problems with the typical employment interview (unreliability, lack of standardization of questions, and so forth). Until about 1960, the implicit model of human behavior, with the individual as the central focus, dominated not only personnel selection but much of applied psychology, too.

It is safe to say that by the end of World War II personnel selection research and application were essentially fixed. This is not to say that there have been no accomplishments since. For example, meta-analytic procedures have been found useful for summarizing results across studies; the validity of the assessment center method has been supported; we know more about the use of structured interviews; and the content validity model, underlying much of public sector personnel selection research in particular, has been well developed. But the fundamental focus on the assessment of individual differences in predictor and criterion domains has persisted, and it has persisted in spite of the paradigm shift that occurred around 1960, yielding modern organizational psychology and human resources management.

A paradigm shift occurred around 1960 (the zeitgeist changed) when psychology became entrenched in schools of business administration. Stimulated by the writings of Argyris (1957), McGregor (1960), and Likert (1961), organizations as systems became a focus of theory and research. The emphasis for these "organizational psychologists" moved from the explicit study of individual differences at the time of hire to the study of the effects of systems on people in the aggregate after they were hired, and to the effects of people in the aggregate on the performance of organizations. For example, Argyris (1957) proposed that the adult personality was thwarted by management techniques of the time because workers were being infantilized; the emphasis was on people in general. McGregor (1960), in his famous Theory Y, spoke of people striving for responsibility in the workplace and the inclination of people to view work as being natural as play. Likert (1961), too, took a systems approach, providing numerous explicit examples of the way organizations might be designed to capitalize on the attributes of the people in them. Some psychologists misinterpreted these theories and persisted in studying individual differences after people were hired. For example, ideas about systems and the effects of those systems on people and their performance were reinterpreted as studies of individual differences in satisfaction as correlates of individual differences in performance (Nord & Fox, 1997; Schneider, 1985). When Brayfield and Crockett (1955) and then Vroom (1964) showed that this relationship was very modest at best, many concluded, incorrectly, that satisfaction and performance are uncorrelated. Although it may very well be valid at the individual level of analysis, this conclusion is erroneous at the organizational level of analysis (Herzberg, 1966; Ostroff, 1992; Schneider, 1985).

But this paradigm shift that yielded the modern fields of organizational behavior and organizational psychology did not influence the work in personnel selection. Throughout much of the four decades that have passed since the birth of the more organizational foci for psychologists, personnel selection psychology has held steadfast in its concern for the individual as the unit of theory and data, both on the predictor side and on the criterion side. How job differences, in combination with individual differences in ability and personality, relate to performance has received little attention. How individual differences in ability and personality relate to organizational performance differences has not been studied. What has been studied recently is the ways in which organizational human resources management (HRM) practices (including personnel selection practices) may relate to organizational performance. In what follows, we first briefly review the literature on utility analysis because it demonstrates some inherent problems in cross-level inferences that can occur in attempts to generalize from studies accomplished at the individual level of analysis to organizational-level performance. Then, more extensively, we review the literature on the relationship between HRM practices and organizational performance and use it as a vehicle for introducing several additional levels-related issues relevant to personnel selection psychology research and practice.

Utility Analysis: Personnel Selection Researchers Attempt to "Go Organizational"

There have been some recent significant attempts by personnel selection researchers to "go organizational." What we mean by this is that researchers have tried to focus on the contributions of traditional personnel selection research to organizational performance. Recall that the typical personnel selection validity design is a demonstration that individual differences measured at time of hiring are related to later individual differences in individual performance. One approach advocated by personnel selection researchers to "go organizational" has been economic utility analysis.

The idea of utility analysis is to estimate the net financial benefits resulting from HRM interventions, including personnel selection procedures. The idea is to express the HRM intervention in terms of costs (recruitment, development of the intervention, administration of the intervention) and benefits (increased productivity compared to not using the intervention). Cascio (1991) has advocated this approach as a basis for influencing management about the effectiveness of the procedures we design, such as personnel selection. Indeed, the results of utility analyses conducted by researchers in economics, accounting, and industrial and organizational psychology suggest that adopting a valid selection procedure can raise the average level of individual performance and decrease the average level of turnover in organizations with concomitant economic benefits (Boudreau, 1992). Whether this results in improved organizational performance as has sometimes been claimed is another question.

While the purpose of utility analysis is to illustrate the monetary impact of a selection regimen on the organization, the data used for making these calculations are based on improvements in the productivity of individual employees and these improvements are within an organization. Using measures of individual performance to make inferences about outcomes at the organizational level of analysis raises several levels issues. For example, Cascio (1992) has acknowledged that utility analysis often overestimates organizational performance returns because researchers tend to oversimplify the complex set of issues that affect the utility of HRM practices. It is important to understand that increases in individual performance do not cumulate in simple additive ways to yield improvements in organizational performance. Several authors have suggested that it is not uncommon for an organizational intervention, whether it is an HRM policy or new technology, to increase the performance of individuals in the organization without improving organizational performance at all (e.g., Dansereau & Markham, 1987; Ruch, 1994; Schneider & Klein, 1994; Shea & Guzzo, 1987). This is due to the fact that organization-level outcomes are influenced by a variety of factors at various levels of analysis. Perhaps this oversimplification of the systems issues involved in relating individual differences to organizational performance is one of the reasons why management views these estimates with suspicion (Latham & Whyte, 1994). Not surprisingly, to our way of thinking, some of the most important issues that have been ignored in utility analyses are these levels-of-analysis issues.

The first issue concerns the fact that most research on the effectiveness of selection systems focuses on improved performance of individuals rather than on improvement in organizational outcomes. Several researchers (Huselid, 1995, Schmitt & Schneider, 1984; Terpstra & Rozelle, 1993) have noted the lack of research that directly examines the impact of a valid selection procedure on variables at the group or organizational level of analysis, such as turnover rates, new-product development, financial performance, and rate of production. Schmitt and Schneider (1984) suggested a number of years ago that researchers in personnel selection should address the question of how much a valid personnel selection procedure contributes to organizational performance by comparison with other strategies employed by organizations to enhance performance. Let us consider some of the reasons why utility analyses may overestimate the outcomes of implementing a personnel selection program.

When considering the impact of selection procedures on an organization, one must consider the influence that these procedures have on several levels of analysis simultaneously. Specifically, one should consider the effects that the selected individuals have on one another, the effects that the selected individuals and selected groups have on one another, and the effects that groups and organizations have on one another. Just as an example, consider the fact that an individual may be a very effective individual performer but may perform poorly as a member of a group (Wexley & Klimoski, 1984). Individual measures of productivity can be summed to obtain group-level performance measures if the individuals are working at independent, parallel jobs, but this is rarely the case. The more interdependent and differentiated the tasks, the larger the conceptual gap between cumulated individual performance and group performance. Therefore, because of the interaction between individuals and groups within organizations, the concept of effectiveness becomes more complex. When individuals form groups, the effects of a valid selection procedure can be nullified by any lack of cooperation within groups and by bottlenecks, shirking, and social loafing. Likewise, the effects can be intensified by the synergistic effects of cooperation and teamwork (Ruch, 1994).

In sum, utility analysis has been viewed with suspicion because it ignores all the systems- and levels-related issues that may intervene between increases in individual-level performance and organization-level performance. Utility analysis presumes that hiring more competent people through the use of a validated selection procedure produces more effective organizations, but there is little evidence to indicate that this is true. Further, there is no evidence to indicate that hiring more competent people on the basis of a validated personnel selection procedure will produce an organization that is competitively superior to organizations that do not use such procedures as a basis for hiring decisions. We will see later that such research designs are completely feasible and should be accomplished in the future. For now, we turn to another level of analysis—the systems level of analysis—and review a literature that does seem to show that using selection procedures, but without regard to the competence of the individuals selected (and other HRM procedures), is reflected in superior organizational performance.

HRM Practices and Organizational Performance

There is a growing body of evidence to indicate that organizations that employ more sophisticated human resources practices are superior performers, and the performance indicators have been quite variable—financial performance, turnover rates, and productivity. Terpstra and Rozelle (1993), for example, found a significant positive relationship between organizations' use of various selection techniques and recruitment strategies, on the one hand, and both annual profit and annual profit growth, on the other. In addition, Russell, Terborg, and Powers (1985) showed that the adoption of employee training programs is reflected in organizational financial performance. Linking valid performance appraisal systems with compensation has also been correlated with increased organizational performance (Gerhart & Milkovich, 1992).

Organizational financial performance is but one of the organization-level indices that have been studied as correlates of HRM practices. McEvoy and Cascio (1985) tested the impact of job enrichment and realistic job previews on turnover rates and found that these HRM practices were somewhat effective in reducing turnover. Bartel (1994) found a positive relationship between adoption of training programs and productivity growth. Holzer (1987) found a positive relationship between recruitment efforts and productivity. Gerhart and Milkovich (1992) demonstrated a link between compensation systems and productivity. Huselid (1995) notes that although these studies have found suggestive relationships between HR practices and organizational outcomes, the conclusion that the causal arrow is as hypothesized—from HR practices to organizational performance—must be tempered because all these studies were cross-sectional in nature. In addition, these studies examine only one or two HR practices at a time. Huselid (1995) proposes that HRM practices influence each other to such an extent that it would be difficult to attribute organizational performance to any one practice, arguing that the benefits of a particular HRM practice may be greatly enhanced or reduced by other HRM practices.

Indeed, several recent studies have been approached from this more systems-oriented perspective on HRM practices as correlates of organizational performance (Arthur, 1994; MacDuffie, 1995; Ichniowski, Shaw, & Prennushi, 1994). Results of these studies suggest that systems of HRM practices do have a positive impact on various organizational outcomes. From the vantage point of the present chapter, what is perhaps more interesting is that these studies suggest that examining the impact of a single HRM practice in isolation will lead to inflated estimates of the impact of that practice on organizational outcomes. This is true because organizations do not (or fail to) engage in only one of these practices; rather, each practice operates in the context of a larger number of HRM practices, and it is most likely true that the observed effect is multidetermined.

Other scholars have raised additional cautions about drawing firm conclusions from research on organizational consequences of HR practices. Historically, human resources management has been guided by the notion that there are "best practices" that apply universally across organizations. Once adopted, these "best practices" will improve individual productivity, decrease turnover, improve organizational financial performance, and so forth. However, recently some researchers have begun to question the acontextual nature of the universalistic perspective (Dyer, 1984; Jackson & Schuler, 1995). These researchers note that there are many factors, both inside and outside organizations, that may moderate the relationship between HR practices and organizational performance. One of the principal contextual factors hypothesized to moderate this relationship is the alignment of HR practices with the organization's governing strategic focus (Delery & Doty, 1996; Huselid, 1995; Schneider & Bowen, 1995). This perspective emerges from the strategic human resources management literature and is referred to as the contingency perspective; that is, the effectiveness of HR practices is contingent on corporate strategy.

Contingency theorists have noted that different strategic imperatives have different requirements with regard to human capital (individual knowledge, skills, and abilities). For example, an organization with a strategic imperative emphasizing quality requires HR practices that focus on the intellectual capital (cognitive ability) that is necessary to implement the quality-control programs consistent with a quality imperative (Youndt, Snell, Dean, & Lepak, 1996) or the personal qualities necessary to carry out a service-quality strategy (Schneider & Bowen, 1995). In this case, ideally, the firm's strategy has redefined the performance criteria for individual jobs and, subsequently, the individual-difference requirements for those jobs. We say "ideally" because, to our knowledge, there is no published research relating personnel selection strategies that fit the organization's market focus to organizational performance (for an exception, see Chung, 1996).

Nevertheless, researchers have found empirical support for both universalistic and contingency perspectives. Huselid (1995) has found that high-performance work practices were associated with both aggregate employee outcomes (productivity and turnover) and organizational financial performance in a sample of one thousand U.S. firms. This finding supports previous research by Terpstra and Rozelle (1993), Russell and colleagues (1985), and Gerhart and Milkovich (1992). Similarly, Youndt and colleagues (1996) have found support for the contingency perspective. In their research, HR practices that were aligned with a quality strategy had the greatest effect on manufacturing firms' financial performance. Youndt and colleagues (1996) argue that the contingency and universalistic perspectives are not mutually exclusive. There are, perhaps, some HR practices that may not be misaligned with any corporate strategy.

Strategic human resources management, particularly the contingency perspective, suggests the necessity of looking beyond even the organizational level of analysis and identifying environmental characteristics (in the form of market characteristics) that may constitute the boundary conditions under which specifically focused HR practices are likely to be reflected in organizational effectiveness—further complicating the levels-of-analysis issues. Chung

(1996), for example, showed that restaurants operating in the fast-food, diner, and upscale segments had more satisfied customers when their HRM practices (kinds of skills sought in people, skills trained, skills and abilities emphasized in appraisal and compensation) fit their respective market segments. For example, HRM practices that emphasized speed and reliability produced more satisfied customers in fast-food facilities, whereas HRM practices that emphasized empathy and responsiveness produced more satisfied customers in upscale facilities. Such research fits with other findings in the service-quality literature, suggesting that the facets of service quality have differential importance as a function of the market segment of the service organization (Sutton & Rafaeli, 1988). Of course, the notion that organizations must adapt to the larger environment to be effective is not new, having been demonstrated at least as early as 1961 by Burns and Stalker. What is new is the focus on HRM practices, rather than just a focus on structural arrangements, as the issues in the contingency framework. And, of course, it may very well be that there is a link between structural arrangements and HR practices!

In sum, we now have evidence that personnel selection strategies can yield the hiring of more competent people (the individual-differences approach). We also now have evidence to show that organizations that implement HRM practices, including personnel selection practices, seem to be organizations that perform more effectively on several different outcome measures. It is also quite clear that individuals reside in organizations that have different HRM practices, and that these organizations themselves are nested within larger market environments. What we lack are studies that cross these levels of analysis, and it is to this issue, with specific reference to the individual and organization levels of analyses, that we turn next.

Models of the Relationship Between Individual and Organizational Attributes and Performance

Now that we have sensitized the reader to the plethora of nestings to which personnel selection researchers might be sensitive, we turn to the issue of crossing the individual-differences model that characterizes personnel selection research with the contextual foci that characterize all other approaches to understanding behavior in and of organizations. The goal is to integrate the paradigms rather than promote one paradigm over the other, and to explicate research questions of potential interest and relevance to personnel selection researchers that have yet to receive the attention our thinking suggests they deserve.

Perhaps an introductory example will bound the issue. Suppose that validity-generalization (VG) analyses reveal that an aptitude test for programmers shows cross-situational consistency in validity (Schmidt, Gast-Rosenberg, & Hunter, 1980). A reasonable conclusion from such an analysis is that an organization would have superior programmers if it used this test as a basis for selection. But is it also a reasonable conclusion that organizations that differ in their use of this aptitude test will also differ in their organizational effectiveness, including their profitability? Hardly. This second conclusion is unreasonable because the use of a valid selection procedure tells us nothing about between-organization performance differences that may be due to myriad other causes of organizational performance. It might be thought that the conclusion of between-organization differences based on use of the test is reasonable because cross-situational consistency in validity indicates that contextual factors fail to moderate validity. The conclusion may not be reasonable, however, because the idea that situations may moderate validity is not the same as situations having a direct effect on performance; the former concerns slope differences in regression, the latter intercept differences. In what follows, we will be concerned primarily with intercept differences because it is likely that moderators will be difficult to find (Schmidt & Hunter, 1978; Schneider, 1978), but direct or main effects for situational variables and individual differences are likely to exist.

Jackson and Schuler (1995, p. 256) noted that industrial-organizational psychology is uniquely poised to contribute to the study of levels issues in HR when they stated:

> Through methodological contributions industrial-organizational psychology is in an excellent position to contribute to the advance of knowledge about HRM in context. Contributions will not come through research as usual, however. Several shifts in approach will be required: from treating organizational settings as sources of

error variance to attending as closely to them as we have traditionally attended to individual characteristics; from focusing on individuals to treating social systems as the target for study; from focusing on single practices or policies to adopting a holistic approach to conceptualizing HRM systems; from research conducted in single organizations at one point in time to research comparing multiple organizations and/or studying dynamic changes in organizations across times and places; and from a search for the "one best way" to a search for the fundamental features that characterize the many possible ways to design and maintain effective systems.

Jackson and Schuler (1995) correctly indicate that contributions will not come through "research as usual"; rather, we, as I/O psychologists, must drastically reconsider our approach to conducting organizational research, particularly validity research (Schneider, 1996; Schneider, Kristof, Goldstein, & Smith, 1997). Figure 2.1 shows a simple multilevel model explicating various linkages among individual differences, individual performance, organizational differences, and organizational performance. Although this model is intended only as a didactic example, it illustrates pictorially the hierarchically nested nature of organizations and the necessity of examining relationships at different levels of analysis to understand the complex determinants of organizational effectiveness—and variables at the group/team level of analysis and at the environment (market) level of analysis are not even shown! In what follows, we describe each linkage in Figure 2.1 and begin to identify in greater detail the analytical and methodological difficulties associated with them. We stress that this model is a simplification and is not intended to comprehensively model the complexities involved in individual and organizational linkages.

Linkage 1: Individual Differences/Individual Performance

Linkage 1 represents the traditional validity model so common in personnel selection research. We have little to say about this linkage, for it is the one linkage most familiar to selection researchers. One point we do want to make is that the typical personnel selection research validity study occurs in one organization at a time rather than across organizations. It must be noted in this context that validity-generalization studies, although they accumulate validity coefficients

Figure 2.1. Multilevel Model of Linkages.

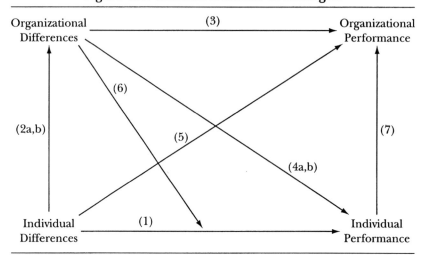

across organizations, do not study intercept differences across settings, and settings are treated only for their potential as moderators rather than as direct effects. Therefore, validity-generalization studies shed no light on the influence of organizational differences on individual differences in performance. It is with linkage 1 that personnel selection research typically begins and ends. As can seen in Figure 2.1, however, there are several other linkages relating individual and organizational differences and performance.

Linkage 2: Individual Differences/ Organizational Differences and Aggregated Individual Differences/Organizational Differences

Linkage 2a: Individual Differences/Organizational Differences
Perhaps an example concerning managerial and executive selection would clarify this linkage in Figure 2.1. It is painfully clear, when one looks at the published research on managerial or executive selection, that the range of predictors and criteria is very small indeed. For the most part, these areas of research have focused on the link between individual differences and individual performance. In the present chapter, we are less concerned with

specific predictors than with cross-level relationships in general. However, it is interesting to speculate, for example, about the kinds of criteria that might be of interest in validity studies for managers and executives.

If one thinks about linkage 2a in Figure 2.1, the criteria of interest in managerial and executive selection might become what we call *contextual criteria*. By this term we mean criteria that are concerned with the kinds of contexts or environments that managers and executives create and maintain for their organizations. The hypothesis is that managers who create and maintain these contexts or environments provide a basis for the organization to perform effectively. In contrast to the individual-level criteria that have characterized such research in the past (level achieved, for example, or compensation by comparison with cohort), organizationally relevant criteria could prove invaluable.

McGregor (1960) noted many years ago that managers, by their behavior, create a "managerial climate" in the organization, but where are the personnel selection studies that are validated against such criteria? For example, if we assume that innovation and change are the key issues with which contemporary organizations grapple, where are the personnel selection studies that use as criteria the creation of contexts for innovation and change? A book recently edited by Tushman and Anderson (1997) does a wonderful job of explicating the issues with which organizations struggle regarding innovation and change. The book contains numerous models of what managers and executives must do to effectively manage change and innovation—with not a single paper on the attributes of the managers and executives most likely to engage in those behaviors. The term *personnel selection* is nowhere to be found in the index, and competencies are indexed only under "core competencies"—which refer, of course, to the firm and not to the individuals in the firm. Another excellent book on change (Huber & Glick, 1993) presents some modest proposals for consideration of the attributes of managers in effectively making change, but the research support they are able to cite for their hypotheses is very slim (Huber, Sutcliffe, Miller, & Glick, 1993) because such research is essentially nonexistent (Herriot & Anderson, 1997).

In sum, if we knew that particular kinds of individuals are more likely than others to create climates for innovation and change, then such information would be valuable to organizations. Schein (1992), for example, speculates that the founders of organizations enact their personalities on organizations, creating the culture of those organizations. Miller and Droge (1986) have shown that the need for achievement is related to the kinds of structures executives create in their organizations. Such research, however, is rare indeed and would go far in promoting the potential importance of personnel selection to modern organizations and the challenges they face.

Linkage 2b: Aggregated Individual Differences/Organizational Differences

In linkage 2a, we suggested that certain individuals (for example, executives and founders), by directly affecting such organizational characteristics as climate, culture, strategy, and structure, can play a powerful role in shaping the context that others experience. Linkage 2b suggests that characteristics of the people in an organization (in the aggregate) can have similar effects on context. For instance, Holland (1997) has suggested that work environments are a function of the particular vocational personality characteristics of the people who inhabit them. Similarly, Schneider (1987; Schneider, Goldstein, & Smith, 1995) has suggested that organizational characteristics are direct reflections of the particular types of people who are attracted to and selected by, and who choose to remain with, particular organizations. Schneider refers to this model as the Attraction-Selection-Attrition, or ASA, model, and it directly posits a congruence between organizational characteristics and aggregated individual characteristics. There are many possible paths through which individual differences could affect organizational differences; we have provided only two as examples of linkages 2a and 2b. We do not intend these to be exhaustive.

Linkage 3: Organizational Differences/Organizational Performance

Earlier, we provided a brief review of the literature on organizational HRM practices as a way to conceptualize organizational differences and organizational performance; therefore, not much additional commentary is required here. We should note, of course, that HRM practices are not the only way to conceptualize organizational differences. Organizational researchers have frequently examined the relationship between other organizational characteristics and organizational performance. From culture (Denison, 1984; Kotter & Heskett, 1992) and climate (Schneider, White, & Paul, 1998) to structure (Galbraith, 1995; Nadler & Tushman, 1997) and change strategies (Huber & Glick, 1993), researchers have identified organizational characteristics that relate to organizational performance. As noted in the discussion of linkages 2a and 2b, a challenge for selection researchers is to identify the individual differences that might be related to the organizational differences, which in turn relate to organizational performance. We should note that we have made no attempt to delineate the construct of organizational differences. Some could argue that there is a distinction between somewhat objective organizational characteristics (structure, policy, process) and subjective organizational characteristics (climate, culture, strategy). We think it is important to recognize that different organizational characteristics imply very different processes with regard to the linkages described in Figure 2.1. Although we believe that most organizations are entropic entities, striving for a state of equilibrium or alignment between various characteristics, the model described in Figure 2.1 might have very different linkages if the organizational difference variable were, for example, organizational strategy as opposed to organizational climate.

One potential way to conceptualize organizational differences is that these differences are due to what might be called *tangible* or *universalistic attributes* of organizations. Such an attribute might be the structure or the culture of the organization. Another way to think about organizational differences might be to use the metaphor of "core competencies": what the organization is uniquely competent to do. Suppose we reconceptualized core competencies as the human resources competencies that exist in an organization and asked the following question: Are organizations that contain more competent people also organizations that are more effective? Such a question begins to introduce the attributes of individuals in the collective, and, therefore, linkage 2b into discussions of organizational differences that may in turn be reflected in organizational performance (linkage 3). Indeed, such a hypothesis is the implicit assumption (hope?) underlying traditional personnel selection validation research; that is, the assumption has been that if the organization contains more competent people in the aggregate (now an organizational difference), it will also be a competitively higher-performing organization. This is an interesting hypothesis, but to our knowledge there is no research to support it. Recall, in this context, that research on HRM practices and organizational performance has explored the degree to which organizations with HRM practices are more successful but has not explored whether a result of the implementation of those HRM practices is a more competent workforce; competence of the workforce is an intervening variable (unmeasured, so far as we know) in the relationship between differences in HRM practices and differences in organizational performance.

We have noted that organizations are inherently hierarchical, with people nested in organizations and organizations nested in environments. It is reasonable, then, to suspect that factors other than individual differences will affect individual performance. For example, cognitive ability may predict individual performance for a particular job, but it is also possible that the nature of the work individuals do (Bray, Campbell, & Grant, 1974; Kohn & Schooler, 1983), and the environment in which they do it (Lawler, 1993), also influence individual performance.

Organizational differences can have one of two kinds of effect with regard to individual performance: a direct effect on aggregate individual performance, or a combinatorial effect on individual performance that is independent of the effects of individual differences. (We deal later, in greater detail, with the issue of moderator variables; we also recognize that the construct of aggregate individual performance requires further explication than we give it here: the validity of the construct, we believe, can be determined only in situ and requires the elaboration of an adequate theory of composition.)

Linkage 4: Organizational Differences/ Aggregated Individual Performance and Organizational Differences/Individual Performance

Linkage 4a: Organizational Differences/
Aggregated Individual Performance
We believe that aggregate individual performance, rather than individual differences in performance, is the performance having to do with people that is of most concern to managers of organizations. Most managers of organizations are uninterested in which

of the people on the shop floor are superior; the concern is for the aggregate of the shop floor workers. This suggests a methodological issue that has not been well explored with regard to selection validity: alternatives to the individual-differences model of validation. As shown in Figure 2.1, linkage 4a would imply, for example, using an experimental or quasi-experimental design in which organizational differences in the use of HRM practices are related to differences in aggregated individual performance (Schneider et al., 1997).

In training evaluation, for example, validity is based on the degree to which those who receive training outperform, in the aggregate, those who do not receive training. By analogy, one could conceptualize personnel selection as an intervention and ask whether those selected with the new selection process outperform, in the aggregate (rather than the more traditional individual-differences approach), those selected in other ways (for example, through the old selection process, or through no selection process). Because the history of personnel selection research is grounded in individual differences, we rarely ask questions related to aggregated individual performance with respect to the validity of personnel selection procedures, and this is reminiscent of the two-disciplines argument of Cronbach (1957).

Linkage 4b: Organizational Differences/Individual Performance

We think it is absolutely imperative that personnel selection researchers begin to explore more fully the relative contribution of individual differences (linkage 1) and organizational differences (linkage 4b) to individual performance and the statistical models to enable such research that already exist. While there may be, in fact, organizational differences related to differences in individual performance, the chances of personnel selection researchers attending to such differences are not great. Nevertheless, combining linkage 1 and linkage 4b additively (intercept, not slope differences) makes sense and is possible.

Therefore, it is important to note that the proposal is to study the combined effects of individual differences and organizational differences on individual performance, not to study organizational differences as a moderator of the individual differences–individual performance link that is linkage 6, to be discussed later. In statistical terms, the issue is one of intercept differences, not slope differences, in the relationship between predictor and criterion. As noted earlier, in the literature on validity generalization the conclusion seems to be that situations do not matter. They may not matter, as far as validity coefficients are concerned (slope differences—and there is still debate over this; see James, Demaree, Mulaik, & Ladd, 1992), but they probably do matter as far as performance differences (intercept differences) are concerned. Indeed, it is safe to say (and/or we hypothesize) that organizational differences have more impact on individual performance than individual differences have on organizational performance.

In sum, linkages 4a and 4b are complex ones that have received little attention from selection researchers. This is true despite the importance of the two issues to which they refer: aggregate individual performance, and the contribution of situational effects to the understanding of differences in individual performance.

Linkage 5: Aggregated Individual Differences/Organizational Performance

In Figure 2.1, we did not draw a path between individual differences and organizational performance. To our way of thinking, the possibility of this relationship, positing individual differences as a cause of organizational performance, is at best far-fetched except for the individual differences associated with chief executive officers of firms. And even for this conceptualization of linkage 5, we hypothesize that the intervening variable in the linkage is revealed in linkage 2a, wherein individual differences result in organizational differences. There are simply too many issues that intervene between the personal characteristics and the performance of the organization for this relationship to be possible—and for this relationship to be studied (except, as noted, through the use of a combination of linkage 2a and linkage 3).

Whether individual differences in the aggregate are related to organizational performance may be a more meaningful question. This is true because so much of the logic of personnel selection rests on the assumption that organizational performance is enhanced when validated personnel selection procedures are in place. There are in fact two questions here. First, did the organization perform better this year than last year, having implemented personnel selection strategies? And, second, does organization A, which has validated personnel selection strategies, outperform organization B, which does not? As noted several times, we are unaware of any evidence to suggest that either of these possibilities exists.

It is intriguing to conceptualize a research strategy that might illuminate these questions. Consulting firms that design and implement personnel selection systems for organizations would be the logical source of data, given the need to use multiple organizations as the sample for testing between-organization differences. These firms might have samples of organizations with which they work. They might gather baseline organizational performance data on a sample (return on investment, return on equity, return on assets, financial analysts' ratings, customer satisfaction data, and so forth) and then roll out the selection procedures while tracking changes in each organization as well as the relative performance of the organizations.

In sum, it is our impression that linkage 5 is critical for selection researchers to study because it underpins the logic of personnel selection psychology. We believe that, except for the study of CEOs, the chances are minimal that there is any direct relationship between individual differences and organizational performance; and, even for CEOs as the individuals being studied, it is unlikely that differences between them will be reflected directly in organizational performance. Conversely, individual differences in the aggregate that might result from the application of validated personnel selection strategies could be reflected in differences in organizational performance, but the research on this possibility simply does not exist.

Linkage 6: Organizational Differences as Moderators of Linkage 1

Linkage 6 represents organizational differences as potential moderators of relationships connected with linkage 1. That is, linkage 6 proposes the following question: Do organizational differences moderate the validities of various selection strategies? As noted earlier, linkage 6 refers to the question of slope differences in the validity-generalization model. Research in the VG tradition finds no support for such moderation, although, as also noted earlier, the issue is far from settled (James, Demaree, Malaik, & Ladd, 1992). We do not engage this debate here except to note that research in the VG tradition has not explored organizational differences as main effects on individual performance, and so it is erroneous to conclude, on the basis of VG research, that organizations do not have an effect.

In connection with linkage 6, Schneider's review (1978) of the kind of research suggested by this linkage indicates that there are few such moderator effects. At the time of his review, Schneider hypothesized that the paucity of moderator effects in the field (he found some moderator effects in published laboratory research) was probably attributable to the fact that moderators, as interaction terms, require extremes, and that neither extremes of situations nor extremes of individual differences are likely to be found in the field. We conclude here that the hoped-for moderator effects of situation on the individual differences–individual performance relationship are unlikely, and that a potentially more fruitful approach is to focus on the additive combination suggested by combining linkage 1 and linkage 4b.

Linkage 7: Aggregated Individual Performance/Organizational Performance

The final linkage depicted in Figure 2.1 represents the primary assumption of the traditional validity model: that individual performance combines, in an almost mechanical way, to yield organizational performance. We have commented at length on the limitations of this assumption; and, now that the larger model has been elaborated, one can see the many issues that affect the relationship of individual performance to organizational performance.

Conclusion

The study of individual differences, and the application of that study to personnel selection psychology, represent an interesting and fruitful history. However, that very fruitfulness may have stifled further progress in understanding the full effects of personnel selection and individual differences in and on organizations. It is not unusual for success to stifle further success or, indeed, to promote failure. Miller (1990, p. 18), for example, in speaking about the decline of organizations over time, notes that "the very causes of success, when extended, may become the causes of failure." We propose that the early success of personnel selection techniques trapped researchers in a model that yielded success, but that, as the world around personnel selection psychology changed, it was slow to adapt. Being trapped by success is, then, a natural phenomenon that must be continuously battled. The first keys to winning this battle are to identify alternatives and take the risks inherent in the unknown, for the sake of the possible gains to be realized. We have shown that the individual-differences model, with the individual as the unit of theory and data on both the criterion side and the predictor side, limits the conclusions that can be reached with regard to organizational differences and organizational performance. The model's basic limitations are its failure to expand horizons on the criterion side and to study two specific relationships: the relationship between the individual manager and the organizational context, and the relationship between aggregate individual differences and criteria at the organizational level of analysis.

We have suggested several alternative research paradigms for conducting research that shows empathy for cross-level thinking. These suggestions by no means exhaust the possibilities, just as the linkages shown in Figure 2.1 do not exhaust the linkages that might have been presented; our goal was to be suggestive, not exhaustive.

There have been other attempts, of course, to integrate the focus on individual differences with these more organizational perspectives. In the general field of psychology, one attempt took the form of interactional psychology (Bowers, 1973); in I/O psychology, another attempt took the form of the person-environment fit paradigm (Kristof, 1996). In personnel selection, however, there has been no alternative to the individual-differences model. Indeed, continued pursuit of the individual-differences model as originally conceptualized by Galton and Cattell, even in the presence of so much evidence for the influence of situations on behavior, has led several commentators to conclude that the field of personnel selection is becoming increasingly marginalized. For example, in their introductory essay to the *International Handbook of Selection and Assessment* (Anderson & Herriot, 1997), Herriot and Anderson (1997, p. 1) boldly state, "Traditional personnel and selection psychology is in danger of terminal decline." Herriot and Anderson see many causes of this decline, but the fundamental one appears to be a failure to integrate the more situational and contextual facts of organizational life into the individual-differences tradition. We hope that our explication of what some of these integrated conceptualizations might look like will be helpful in extending the relevance of personnel selection psychology.

References

Anderson, N., & Herriot, P. (Eds.). (1997). *International handbook of selection and assessment.* New York: Wiley.

Argyris, C. (1957). *Personality and organization.* New York: HarperCollins.

Arthur, J. B. (1994). Effects of human resources systems on manufacturing performance and turnover. *Academy of Management Journal, 37,* 670–687.

Bartel, A. P. (1994). Productivity gains from the implementation of employee training programs. *Industrial Relations, 33,* 411–425.

Bellows, R. M. (1949). *Psychology of personnel in business and industry.* Englewood Cliffs, NJ: Prentice-Hall.

Bingham, W.V.D., & Moore, B. V. (1931). *How to interview.* New York: HarperCollins.

Boring, E. G. (1950). *History of experimental psychology* (2nd ed.). Englewood Cliffs, NJ: Appleton-Century-Crofts.

Boudreau, J. W. (1992). Utility analysis for decisions in human resources management. In M. D. Dunnette & L. M. Hough (Eds.), *Handbook of industrial and organizational psychology* (Vol. 2, 2nd ed., pp. 621–745). Palo Alto, CA: Consulting Psychologists Press.

Bowers, K. S. (1973). Situationism in psychology: An analysis and critique. *Psychological Review, 80,* 307–336.

Bray, D. B., Campbell, R. J., & Grant, D. L. (1974). *Formative years in business: A long-term AT&T study of managerial lives.* New York: Wiley.

Brayfield, A. H., & Crockett, W. H. (1955). Employee attitudes and employee performance. *Psychological Bulletin, 52,* 396–424.

Burns, T., & Stalker, G. M. (1961). *The management of innovation.* New York: Tavistock.

Cascio, W. F. (1991). *Costing human resources: The financial impact of behavior in organizations.* Boston: PWS-Kent.

Cascio, W. F. (1992). Assessing the utility of selection decisions: Theoretical and practical considerations. In N. Schmitt & W. C. Borman (Eds.), *Personnel selection in organizations* (pp. 310–340). San Francisco: Jossey-Bass.

Chung, B. G. (1996). Focusing HRM strategies towards service market segments: A three-factor model. Unpublished doctoral dissertation, University of Maryland.

Cronbach, L. J. (1957). The two disciplines of scientific psychology. *American Psychologist, 12,* 671–684.

Dansereau, F., & Markham, S. (1987). Levels of analysis in personnel and human resources management. In K. M. Rowland & G. R. Ferris (Eds.), *Research in personnel and human resources management* (Vol. 5, pp. 1–50). Greenwich, CT: JAI Press.

Delery, J. E., & Doty, D. H. (1996). Modes of theorizing in strategic human resources management: Tests of universalistic, contingency, and configurational performance predictions. *Academy of Management Journal, 39,* 802–835.

Denison, D. R. (1984). Bringing corporate culture to the bottom line. *Organizational Dynamics, 12,* 4–22.

Dennis, W. (Ed.). (1948). *Readings in the history of psychology.* Englewood Cliffs, NJ: Appleton-Century-Crofts.

Dobbins, G. H., Cardy, R. L., & Carson, K. P. (1991). Examining fundamental assumptions: A contrast of person and systems approaches to human resource management. In K. M. Rowland & G. R. Ferris (Eds.), *Research in personnel and human resources management* (Vol. 9, pp. 1–38). Greenwich, CT: JAI Press.

Dyer, L. (1984). Linking human resource and business strategies. *Human Resources Planning, 7,* 79–84.

Galbraith, J. R. (1995). *Designing organizations: An executive briefing on strategy, structure, and process.* San Francisco: Jossey-Bass.

Gerhart, B., & Milkovich, G. T. (1992). Organizational differences in managerial compensation and financial performance. *Academy of Management Journal, 33,* 663–691.

Herriot, P., & Anderson, N. (1997). Selecting for change: How will personnel selection psychology survive? In N. Anderson & P. Herriot (Eds.), *International handbook of selection and assessment.* New York: Wiley.

Herzberg, F. (1966). *Work and the nature of man.* Cleveland: World.

Holland, J. (1997). *Making vocational choices: A theory of vocational personalities and work environments.* Palo Alto, CA: Psychological Assessment Resources.

Holzer, H. J. (1987). Hiring procedures in the firm: Their economic determinants and outcomes. In M. M. Kleiner, R. N. Block, M. Roomkin, and S. W. Salsburg (Eds.), *Human resources and the performance of the firm.* Washington, DC: BNA Press.

Huber, G. P., & Glick, W. H. (Eds.) (1993). *Organizational change and redesign: Ideas and insights for improving performance.* New York: Oxford University Press.

Huber, G. P., Sutcliffe, K. M., Miller, C. C., & Glick, W. H. (1993). Understanding and predicting organizational change. In G. P. Huber &

W. H. Glick (Eds.), *Organizational change and redesign: Ideas and insights for improving performance* (pp. 215–268). New York: Oxford University Press.

Hull, C. L. (1928). *Aptitude testing.* Cleveland: World.

Huselid, M. A. (1995). The impact of human resources management practices on turnover, productivity, and corporate financial performance. *Academy of Management Journal, 38,* 635–672.

Ichniowski, C., Shaw, K., & Prennushi, G. (1994). The effects of human resource management practices on productivity. Unpublished paper, Graduate School of Business, Columbia University.

Jackson, S. E., & Schuler, R. S. (1995). Understanding human resource management in the context of organizations and their environments. *Annual Review of Psychology, 46,* 237–264.

James, L. R., Demaree, R. G., Mulaik, S. A., & Ladd, R. T. (1992). Validity generalization in the context of situational models. *Journal of Applied Psychology, 77,* 3–14.

Jenkins, J. J., & Paterson, D. G. (Eds.). (1961). *Studies in individual differences: The search for intelligence.* Englewood Cliffs, NJ: Appleton-Century-Crofts.

Kohn, M. L., & Schooler, C. (1983). *Work and personality: An inquiry into the impact of social stratification.* Norwood, NJ: Ablex.

Kotter, J. P., & Heskett, J. L. (1992). *Corporate culture and performance.* New York: Free Press.

Kristof, A. L. (1996). Person-organization fit: An integrative review of its conceptualization, measurement, and implications. *Personnel Psychology, 49,* 1–50.

Latham, G. P., & Whyte, G. (1994). The futility of utility analysis. *Personnel Psychology, 47,* 31–46.

Lawler, E. E. III (1993). Creating the high-involvement organization. In J. R. Galbraith & E. E. Lawler III (Eds.), *Organizing for the future: The new logic for managing complex organizations* (pp. 172–193). San Francisco: Jossey-Bass.

Likert, R. (1961). *New patterns of management.* New York: McGraw-Hill.

MacDuffie, J. P. (1995). Human resource bundles and manufacturing performance: Organizational logic and flexible production systems in the world auto industry. *Industrial and Labor Relations Review, 48,* 197–221.

McEvoy, G. M., & Cascio, W. F. (1985). Strategies for reducing employee turnover: A meta-analysis. *Journal of Applied Psychology, 70,* 312–353.

McGregor, D. M. (1960). *The human side of enterprise.* New York: McGraw-Hill.

Miller, D. (1990). *The Icarus paradox: How exceptional companies bring about their own downfall.* New York: HarperBusiness.

Miller, D., & Droge, C. (1986). Psychological and traditional determinants of structure. *Administrative Science Quarterly, 31,* 539–560.

Nadler, D. A., & Tushman, M. L. (1997). *Competing by design: The power of organizational architecture.* New York: Oxford University Press.

Nord, W. R., & Fox, S. (1997). The individual in organizational studies: The great disappearing act? In S. R. Clegg, C. Hardy, & W. R. Nord (Eds.), *Handbook of organizational studies* (177–183). Thousand Oaks, CA: Sage.

Ostroff, C. (1992). The relationship between satisfaction, attitudes, and performance. *Journal of Applied Psychology, 77,* 963–974.

Poffenberger, A. T. (1927). *Applied psychology.* Englewood Cliffs, NJ: Appleton-Century-Crofts.

Ruch, W. A. (1994). Measuring and managing individual productivity. In D. H. Harris (Ed.), *Organizational linkages: Understanding the productivity paradox* (pp. 105–130). Washington, DC: National Academy Press.

Russell, J. S., Terborg, J. R., & Powers, M. L. (1985). Organizational performance and organizational-level training and support. *Personnel Psychology, 38,* 849–863.

Schein, E. H. (1992). *Organizational culture and leadership* (2nd ed.). San Francisco: Jossey-Bass.

Schmidt, F. L., Gast-Rosenberg, I., & Hunter, J. E. (1980). Validity generalization results for computer programmers. *Journal of Applied Psychology, 65,* 643–661.

Schmidt, F. L., & Hunter, J. E. (1978). Moderator research and the law of small numbers. *Personnel Psychology, 31,* 215–231.

Schmitt, N., & Schneider, B. (1984). Current issues in personnel selection. In K. M. Rowland & G. R. Ferris (Eds.), *Research in personnel and human resources management* (Vol. 2, pp. 85–126). Greenwich, CT: JAI Press.

Schneider, B. (1978). Person-situation selection: A review of some ability-situation interaction research. *Personnel Psychology, 31,* 281–298.

Schneider, B. (1985). Organizational behavior. *Annual Review of Psychology, 36,* 573–611.

Schneider, B. (1987). The people make the place. *Personnel Psychology, 40,* 437–453.

Schneider, B. (1996). When individual differences aren't. In K. R. Murphy (Ed.), *Individual differences and behavior in organizations* (pp. 548–571). San Francisco: Jossey-Bass.

Schneider, B., & Bowen, D. E. (1995). *Winning the service game.* Boston: Harvard Business School Press.

Schneider, B., Goldstein, H. W., & Smith, D. B. (1995). The ASA framework: An Update. *Personnel Psychology, 48,* 747–773.

Schneider, B., & Klein, K. J. (1994). What is enough? A systems perspective on individual-organizational performance linkages. In D. H. Harris (Ed.), *Organizational linkages: Understanding the productivity paradox* (pp. 81–104). Washington, DC: National Academy Press.

Schneider, B., Kristof, A. L., Goldstein, H. W., & Smith, D. B. (1997). What is this thing called fit? In N. Anderson and P. Herriot (Eds.), *Handbook of selection and appraisal* (2nd ed., pp. 393–412). London: Wiley.

Schneider, B., White, S. S., & Paul, M. C. (1998). Linking service climate to customer perceptions of service quality: Test of a causal model. *Journal of Applied Psychology, 83,* 150–163.

Shea, G. P., & Guzzo, R. A. (1987). Groups as human resources. In K. M. Rowland & G. R. Ferris (Eds.), *Research in personnel and human resources management* (Vol. 5, pp. 289–322). Greenwich, CT: JAI Press.

Strong, E. K., Jr. (1927). Vocational interest test. *Educational Record, 8,* 107–121.

Sutton, R., & Rafaeli, A. (1988). Untangling the relationship between displayed emotions to organizational sales: The case of convenience stores. *Academy of Management Journal, 31,* 461–487.

Terman, L. M. (1916). *The measurement of intelligence.* Boston: Houghton Mifflin.

Terpstra, D. E., & Rozelle, E. J. (1993). The relationship of staffing practices to organizational-level measures of performance. *Personnel Psychology, 46,* 27–48.

Turban, D., & Keon, T. (1993). Organizational attractiveness: An interactionist perspective. *Journal of Applied Psychology, 78,* 184–193.

Tushman, M. L., & Anderson, P. (Eds.) (1997). *Managing strategic innovation and change: A collection of readings.* New York: Oxford University Press.

Viteles, M. S. (1932). *Industrial psychology.* New York: Norton.

Vroom, V. H. (1964). *Work and motivation.* New York: Wiley.

Wexley, K. N., & Klimoski, R. J. (1984). Performance appraisal: An update. In K. M. Rowland & G. R. Ferris (Eds.), *Research in personnel and human resources management* (Vol. 2, pp. 35–80). Greenwich, CT: JAI Press.

Youndt, M. A., Snell, S. A., Dean, J. W., Jr., & Lepak, D. P. (1996). Human resources management, manufacturing strategy and firm performance. *Academy of Management Journal, 34,* 836–866.

CHAPTER 3

Performance Appraisal and Performance Management
A Multilevel Analysis
Angelo S. DeNisi

Performance appraisals are used in most organizations as a means of providing feedback to employees about their performance on the job, and as the basis for making decisions about such things as pay increases and promotions. The term *performance appraisal* refers to the system whereby an organization assigns some "score" to indicate the level of performance of a target person or group. *Performance management* is somewhat different and refers to the range of activities engaged in by an organization to enhance the performance of a target person or group. The ultimate purpose of both activities, however, is to improve organizational effectiveness.

Given the central role these activities play in managing an organization's human resources, it is not surprising that a great deal of research has been directed to ways of improving the performance appraisal/management processes (see reviews by DeNisi, 1997; Landy & Farr, 1980; Murphy & Cleveland, 1995). What is not always clear from these reviews, however, is that the appraisal/management process is both a multilevel and a cross-level phenomenon; that is, appraisal and subsequent performance management activities take place at different levels of analysis, and many of the activities that occur at one level of analysis are assumed to have effects at other levels of analysis as well. The purpose of the present chapter is to more clearly delineate the multilevel and cross-level aspects of performance appraisals and to discuss some research issues that could grow out of this realization.

The recognition that these processes occur at multiple levels of analysis is not unique to this chapter. Models of the appraisal process have recognized this and included some reference to phenomena occurring at different levels of analysis (DeCotiis & Petit, 1978; DeNisi, Cafferty, & Meglino, 1984; Ilgen & Feldman, 1983; Landy & Farr, 1980), but studies based on these models have rarely made level-related issues an explicit part of their designs. Instead, these studies have been concerned with such issues as rating errors and rating accuracy, and the focus has been almost exclusively on the evaluation of performance at the level of the individual (but see Saal, Downey, & Lahey, 1980, for a discussion of problems arising from ignoring level-related issues).

Nevertheless, there has been increased concern about the problems associated with appraising the performance of groups or teams (e.g., Tesluk, Mathieu, Zaccaro, & Marks, 1997), although much of this concern has been confined to theorizing about how to conceptualize the performance of teams rather than considering how we would actually measure that performance. Furthermore, industrial-organizational (I/O) psychologists have recently been exhibiting more interest in performance at the level of the organization (e.g., Cascio, Young, & Morris, 1997).

A major step in the recognition of the multilevel nature of performance appraisal has come in a recent book by Murphy and Cleveland (1995). These authors discuss both proximal and distal contextual factors that influence performance appraisals, and their model makes the clearest statement to date about different levels of analysis and performance appraisal. Nevertheless, level-related issues are not the primary concern of the Murphy and Cleveland model. The present chapter represents an attempt to use an explicit level-related framework for thinking about performance appraisal and performance management.

To do so requires the acknowledgment that performance in organizations is always a multilevel phenomenon. Although relationships among levels of performance may vary, several statements seem to be typically true:

1. We measure and manage the performance of individual employees in the hope of ultimately influencing the performance of a team or of an entire organization.
2. Organizations do not "perform." Individuals or teams in an organization perform in ways that allow the organization to achieve outcomes we refer to as *organizational performance.*
3. Performance at a higher level of analysis is due, in part, to performance at lower levels, but it is often more than just the simple sum of performance at those lower levels. Therefore, changing individual performance is not always enough to change either a team's or a firm's performance.
4. Variables at higher levels of analysis (for example, organizational structure and strategy) serve as constraints on the performance of individuals and teams. Therefore, in order to completely understand (and ultimately change) the performance of a team or an individual, we must understand the organizational context in which this performance occurs.

Thus performance exists at the individual, group, and organizational levels. Although models for performance at each level are not identical, they are similar, a fact suggesting that performance is a multilevel construct. In addition, however, and as already noted, performance is also a cross-level construct because performance at one level of analysis influences performance at other levels of analysis. Furthermore, some of these effects are top-down effects whereas others are bottom-up effects. Finally, it should be clear that, despite tendencies to often think in these terms, performance appraisal and performance management are almost never concerned with single-level models.

In order to deal with these issues, the present chapter begins with a discussion of performance appraisals at different levels of analysis, noting issues associated with each (including some thoughts on the source of appraisals at different levels). The chapter then turns to performance management, focusing on the level of the desired performance change in any performance management intervention. This discussion is followed by a discussion of the links among performance at different levels, and of how performance at each level is constrained by and constrains performance at other levels. There follows a series of illustrative research questions proceeding from a levels-oriented perspective on performance appraisal, along with some concluding remarks.

The Multilevel Nature of Performance Appraisals

We begin with performance appraisal (because it is usually considered a precursor of the successful management of performance) and with the basic question of whose performance should be appraised. In the context of the present levels framework, this issue becomes a question of the level of analysis that should be the target of the appraisal.

Individual-Level Appraisals

Traditionally, appraisal research has focused on the evaluation of individual level performance. There is some logic to this focus because it is easiest for psychologists to conceptualize individual-level performance and because (as discussed later) it is easier to change individual-level performance. This would also be a case where we could consider performance appraisal as a single-level phenomenon only.

But this would not be completely correct. Even when the appraisal is focused at the level of the individual, other levels of phenomena may be considered, depending on the purpose of the appraisal. In fact, Cleveland, Murphy, and Williams (1989) found it useful to classify appraisal purposes into four categories. The purposes that were the most prevalent are termed *between-persons decisions,* and these are followed by *within-person decisions,* with *systems maintenance* and *documentation* purposes being the least prevalent. Of these, only within-person decisions result in appraisals that exist only at the individual level of analysis, for these are concerned with identifying the strengths and weaknesses of a given individual (and even these appraisals may not be totally independent of performance at other levels of analysis).

In the case of between-persons decisions (which include such decisions as who should be promoted or receive the merit pay increase), the real focus is at the level of the work group. Clearly, a person's performance may not be outstanding, and that person may still receive a promotion if no one else in the group has a performance as good. Therefore, between-persons decisions can more correctly be characterized as examples of frog-pond models of cross-level effects. Here, the performance of the other work group members serves as a contextual variable that is part of the decision about whether an individual is tapped for a promotion.

The other two categories of use for appraisals described by Cleveland and colleagues (1989) deal more clearly with phenomena that go across levels of analysis (the different nature of such models is discussed in more detail in Chapter One of this volume). These authors' "systems maintenance" purposes include manpower planning and assessment of organizational effectiveness. When individual performance is rated for these purposes, we assume that individual-level performance has an effect on higher levels of performance (a bottom-up model) and, possibly, that the global factor (organizational effectiveness) is simply a function of the aggregation of that individual-level performance. The authors' "documentation" purposes include using ratings as criteria for validation research. Here, the configural property of the relationship between scores on a selection technique and individual performance on the job would be used to assess the selection systems used throughout the organization.

Team-Level Appraisals

The nature of work is changing. Many tasks traditionally carried out by individuals are now done by work groups or work teams (see reviews by Gully, in press; Sundstrom, DeMeuse, & Futrell, 1990), with resulting concern over how we appraise the performance of a team as opposed to that of an individual (Cannon-Bowers & Salas, 1997; Hallam & Campbell, 1997). It may be reasonable, in some cases, to obtain information about team performance by simply appraising the performance of individual members and then aggregating this information at the team level. In such a case, team performance may be nothing more than the sum of individual-level performance.

Such a situation is not often likely to appear, however. Research on work teams has indicated that the nature of performance in a team or group is dependent on such factors as the nature of the technology involved (Goodman, 1986), group performance strategies (Hackman, Brousseau, & Weiss, 1976), and the nature of the task (Saavedra, Earley, & Van Dyne, 1993). Others (e.g., Ancona & Caldwell, 1988) have suggested that interpersonal relationships among group members are extremely important factors for team effectiveness. Still others have gone so far as to suggest that critical behaviors for team effectiveness include such things as willingness to pitch in, "backup" behavior, and communication among group members (Murphy & Cleveland, 1995, p. 359). All of this suggests that team performance is determined by a complex set of factors, and that appraisals focused at the level of the group must do more than simply combine individual-level appraisals.

In cases where team performance must be assessed at the team level rather than at the individual level, we are focusing on a measure of performance that is a property of a team rather than a property of an individual. Measures such as decision accuracy, team productivity, teamwork processes, and team cohesiveness would be examples of performance indices that have meaning only at the team level of analysis, and the rater should probably be some "expert."

Another issue associated with team-level performance measures is the proper role for individual-level performance assessment in the group. There is no reason why we could not assess both individual- and team-level performance and, in many cases, such a multilevel conceptualization of performance might make sense. Alternatively, there are a number of potential problems associated with using multiple-level measures of performance. For example, Ilgen, Major, Hollenbeck, and Sego (1993) note that if an organization emphasizes the importance of team or group efforts, and if it appraises performance at the individual level, group members may well focus on the competition implied in individual appraisal systems and thus work counter to the group-oriented goals of the organization.

Alternatively, including individual-level appraisals with team-level appraisals might help combat a different problem. In almost any work group, some individual members will perceive themselves as providing greater inputs than other members provide. This perception may well be accurate because working in groups does often lead to social loafing (e.g., Latane, Williams, & Harkins, 1979).

This phenomenon occurs when individual group members exert less effort because they believe that the slack will be picked up by other members (but see Erez & Somech, 1996, for a discussion of some cultural limitations).

The exact nature of the relationship between individual- and team-level appraisals (and performance itself) depends largely on the nature of the task facing the team. Although team-level performance should always be the focus of appraisals in settings where employees work in teams, some measures of team performance are more closely linked than others to measures of individual performance. For example, in the case of what can be called simple teams (Kozlowski, Gully, Nason, & Smith, 1999), team performance is nothing more than the sum or the average of the performance of the individual team members. Such teams include any type of committee or jury, as well as situations represented, in golf, by scoring in the Ryder Cup, wherein the team score is a direct function of individual members' scores, or, in tennis, by the Davis Cup, where team performance is a function of the win/loss records of team members. These cases are characterized as cases of pooled interdependence (Van De Ven, Delbecq, & Koenig, 1976): performance is assessed first at the individual level and is then aggregated to form a measure of team performance.

The team settings studied by Hollenbeck and his associates (Hollenbeck et al., 1995) seem more closely related to situations of sequential interdependence (Van De Ven et al., 1976). Here, individual team members make judgments and then feed these to the leader, who must integrate the information and make decisions. In these settings, both individual-level and team-level performance should be assessed, although the team's performance becomes a function of the leader's ability to integrate and compile the information from the team members. Nevertheless, if the individual team members make poor decisions at their level, the leader's input will be poor, and so any decision made on the basis of this input will suffer as well.

A more typical team setting relies on either the reciprocal interdependence model or the team dependence model (Van De Ven et al., 1976). Here, the performance of one team member is dependent on the performance and behavior of other team members, as when the output of one team member is the input for a different member. In these settings, it makes less sense to consider individual-level performance appraisals; in fact, these are settings where such appraisals could actually be damaging. Here, too, behaviors that we might commonly characterize as "teamwork" (which include communicating with and supporting other team members and generally instilling a team spirit) are essential for the team to perform well. These process variables exist at the level of the team and represent either shared (emerging from individuals' common perceptions) or configural (reflecting some pattern or array of individual perceptions) properties of teams, and so they need to be evaluated by outside experts.

It would seem, therefore, that appraisals focusing on the team level are rather complex. Depending on the nature of the tasks involved (and the nature of the reward system and other contextual variables), we must decide if the team's performance should be assessed through a focus on aggregated individual-level performance or through a focus on team-level performance only. The choice of level also has clear implications for who should be relied on to conduct the appraisal (see Cannon-Bowers & Salas, 1997, for a more detailed discussion of the relationship between level of focus and choice of rating sources). As we move more toward team models of performance on the job, it will become more critical to understand the nature of team performance so that we can know better how to appraise it.

Organization-Level Appraisals

Most settings where we conduct performance appraisals will be focused on either the individual level or the team level, or on both. But there are also situations where our focus is on the organizational level, and so we must evaluate organization-level performance. Furthermore, it should be noted that whenever we focus on appraisals at lower levels of analysis, we do so with the ultimate hope of affecting performance at the organizational level as well.

Appraisals involving departments, plants, business units, or even entire organizations are usually not the purview of HR managers but are typically considered in the appraisal of the top management team; that is, someone interested in evaluating the performance of a company's CEO often focuses, for information, on performance measures obtained at the organizational level. Thus, although the nominal level of analysis is the individual, the appraisal is actually focused at the organizational level. It is assumed (sometimes implicitly) that the CEO (or another top manager) can affect these measures of performance at the organizational level, and so he or she becomes responsible for performance measured at this level.

These appraisals are rarely expressed in terms of processes or behaviors but rely instead on more "objective" measures of performance, such as sales, output, accounting, and finance-based measures (return on equity, return on assets) or stock prices (see Miller & Bromiley, 1990, for a discussion of these different measures). Such measures are derived from records or archival data, and so "experts" who have access to these records typically do the appraisals.

Of course, individual- and team-level performance will influence organization-level performance, but it is generally assumed that these effects operate through the behavior of a top manager who is responsible for translating performance at lower levels into performance at the organizational level. However, since it is difficult to determine what critical behaviors a manager should engage in to be successful (but see Mintzberg, 1980), it is also difficult to understand why a single person (or top management team) should be assessed through reliance on measures of organization-level performance.

In fact, some scholars of top management have noted that environmental constraints (operating at a yet higher level of analysis) limit the impact any CEO can have on the firm's performance (referred to as "managerial discretion"; see Finkelstein & Hambrick, 1990; Hambrick & Finkelstein, 1987). Other scholars argue that organizational performance and survival have very little to do with managerial performance; specifically, these "population ecologists" argue that the conditions existing at the time the firm was founded, and the ease with which firms can enter and exit markets, are the true determinants of the firm's long-term performance (see Amburgey & Rao, 1996, for an excellent overview of the population ecology perspective).

Nevertheless, performance at the level of the organization is often seen as an indicator of the performance of the top management team. Yet, as will be discussed in more detail, efforts to improve individual-level performance are undertaken in the hope that these efforts will eventually lead to improvement in firm-level performance. Therefore, we must assume an unstated belief that the top management team's personnel improve the firm's performance, at least to some extent, by the actions they take to manage the performance of employees and teams in the organization. The relative importance of these actions, as opposed to more strategic decisions made by top management personnel, is unknown, but a focus on employee- and team-oriented activities, versus strategic decisions on the part of top managers, is one of the points that distinguish I/O psychologists from scholars of strategic management.

In sum, perhaps the most basic levels-of-analysis issue for performance appraisal relates to the decision to focus appraisal efforts at the level of the individual, the group or team, or the organization. When we focus appraisal efforts at the level of either the individual or the organization, the choice of performance measures and methods is relatively simple. In the case of work groups or teams, however, the relative emphasis on team-level versus aggregated individual-level performance measures should depend on the nature of the task involved.

Managing Performance at Different Levels

The ultimate goal of performance appraisal in most organizations is to improve performance; that is, we hope that if we communicate where an individual, team, or even an organization stands in terms of performance, and if we provide feedback about strengths and weaknesses, there will be a willingness to exert effort to improve performance. This is the heart of the performance management process.

But a willingness to exert that effort depends, in part, on perceived reward contingencies; that is, the target of the performance management process must believe that performance improvements are associated with obtaining some desired outcomes. Within the present framework, however, this means that there must be some correspondence between the level of performance targeted for change and the level of the rewards available. In addition, as already mentioned, the ultimate goal, regardless of the level at which the appraisal is focused, is to influence performance at the organizational level. Therefore, we must also be concerned with the links between the level of analysis for performance appraisals and the level of the desired performance change.

The situation is relatively simple when superiors conduct appraisals of their subordinates at the individual level, and when the organization provides incentive pay tied to improved individual-level performance (measured as a function of improved appraisals), with no concern about changes in performance at higher levels. A more complex (and more common) situation arises when individual team members evaluate performance at the team level, and when incentives are tied to corporate earnings. Let us begin with the most basic question associated with performance management efforts.

Level of Performance Targeted for Change

All performance in organizations, regardless of the level of analysis, must ultimately be a function of individual-level behavior. Although we use such terms as *organizational behavior* and *corporate performance,* these are really still a function of coordinated efforts by individuals. Therefore, regardless of the level at which we want to influence performance, we must do so by influencing the behavior of individuals. Yet, as noted earlier, it is insufficient in almost all organization to change performance at the level of the individual. Unless those changes can translate into changes in performance at the organizational level, they will be considered to have limited success. It is for this reason that management scholars have attempted to demonstrate that practices targeted at the individual or team level are in fact related to improved organization-level performance (Jackson & Schuler, 1995).

Most performance management systems include (or claim to include) systematic evaluations, with face-to-face feedback, some type of goal setting, and a reward system that reinforces the behaviors specified in the goals that are set. Just as performance appraisals can be focused at any one of several levels within the organization, feedback and change efforts can also be focused at different levels; that is, if we focus our evaluation at the individual level, feedback is most readily available at the individual level as well. In a similar fashion, appraisals focused at the team level will result in feedback being most readily available at the team level. But because we can directly affect only the behavior of an individual, when appraisals and subsequent feedback are available only at the team level, we must translate this team-level feedback into goals and objectives for the individual.

The information needed to accomplish this is not necessarily available from the team appraisal, however. For example, if a manager evaluates the performance of an individual within a team or group and finds that the ratee does not cooperate well with co-workers, a manager can feed this information back to the ratee and discuss with the ratee ways in which cooperative behaviors could be fostered. If the individual ratee's behavior is monitored, if feedback is continued, and if there are rewards associated with improved cooperation, then it is not unreasonable to expect that the ratee will become more "cooperative" in the future. Presumably, if each team member received similar feedback and was the target of similar performance management efforts, the overall level of cooperation within the team would improve. But if the same manager focuses an evaluation at the team level, believes that the team level of cooperation and coordination are not what they should be, and provides feedback of this nature to the team, the situation is more complex. Team members may have little insight into what they should do to improve cooperation and coordination, or into who is responsible for the problem. The manager might spend time discussing the problem with the team, but it will essentially be up to the team members to manage the behavior and performance of other members (and themselves) in order to improve cooperation and coordination. The team members may in fact decide on a strategy for improving cooperation and coordination and set in place a performance management effort of their own, but this will require an extra step by comparison with efforts aimed only at the individual level.

In either case, the ultimate goal of the performance management effort is not simply to improve cooperation and coordination but to improve team effectiveness. When appraisal and performance management efforts are focused at the individual level, it may be possible for the individual to change his or her behavior, become more cooperative, and be rewarded for these changes while the team still fails to become more effective. When the focus of the appraisal and performance management efforts is on the team level, however, team members are rewarded only when the team becomes more effective. Therefore, focusing on the individual level of performance is more likely to get desired changes in behavior more quickly, but there is no guarantee that these changes will result in improved team performance. Focusing instead on the team level may make it more difficult to obtain desired changes in behavior, but any rewards that come to team members are more likely to come only when team effectiveness is improved.

It is important to appreciate that this trade-off is part of any performance management system. The further away from the individual level the desired behavior, the more complex the links are between changing the individual behavior and obtaining the desired changes in performance. Furthermore, as the targeted performance moves to higher levels, we also require some strategy for how to change individual behavior in such a way that the larger group's performance will be affected. Therefore, if we focus our efforts on any level below that of the organization, we first need to evaluate the current state of organization-level performance and diagnose the cause for performance being lower than desired. We must then identify individual- and, eventually, group-level behaviors that might change that performance, and we must implement a program whereby the efforts of individuals and groups are all integrated, with an eye toward corporate performance goals. However, while these efforts are being carried out, their impact is being limited by organizational and environmental constraints on organization-level performance (for example, the market is too competitive), team-level performance (the organization cannot devote the resources needed to obtain the best people and equipment for the teams), and individual-level performance (the organization does not provide adequate training for individual employees). Clearly, this is a much more complex problem than simply trying to get one individual to cooperate with a co-worker, and yet all performance management efforts are ultimately aimed at changing performance at this highest level.

Nature of Desired Changes in Behavior

The challenges in changing performance at the organizational level become even more daunting when we realize that it is possible to change behavior at a lower level of analysis in such a way that it actually reduces performance at a higher level; that is, we can easily create a situation where individual employees are actually working counter to the higher-level organizational goals. What is truly disturbing about this is that we can create these situations through our own efforts to change individual-level behavior in a way that will improve organization-level performance.

For example, let us return to the case of the team that needs its members' cooperation in order to meet its deadlines, with cooperation as the focus of the performance management process. If we conduct evaluations, provide feedback, and reward employees at the individual level only, individuals may see it as in their best interests to engage in behaviors that lead away from cooperation and from desired group-level behavior; that is, an individual may see that the best way to maximize individual-level performance is to keep all information closely guarded, not communicate openly with other group members, and, in fact, never help another group member to improve performance. If the organization rewards individuals for improved performance at the individual level, these behaviors would be reinforced, even though they would lead to decreased cooperation and, presumably, to more missed deadlines in the future.

The seemingly obvious nature of this problem might suggest that organizations would rarely fall into the trap just outlined, and yet they do, with some frequency. For example, an engineering firm that managed major construction projects (such as shopping malls and highway improvements) would bid on these projects. Although the firm was still rather small, it had been fairly successful and had enjoyed rapid growth over the years. A consulting firm was hired when the CEO grew concerned about his ability to manage the growing company, and the consultants' report emphasized the importance of focusing on corporate earnings by increasing "billable hours." A reward system was designed to encourage employees to engage in activities that generated fees, as is done in most law firms. Employees immediately began focusing on client-service activities that could be billed, and earnings grew. In this environment, however, there was no incentive for anyone to write proposals for new projects, because no one could be billed for the time spent in writing a proposal unless the project was eventually awarded to the firm. After two years, the firm began reducing the number of its employees because of the slow decline in the number of new projects, and earnings began to slip as well. The performance management system rewarded individuals for behaviors that generated earnings, but it failed to consider that, in the long run, the firm's existence depended on generating new business, which required efforts that maximized organizational goals rather than individual goals.

Therefore, it is critical, if an organization is interested in performance at a level higher than that of the individual, to develop goals for individual performance and behavior that will lead to those higher-level performance goals. It is especially critical that the organization not reward efforts that are counter to those higher-level goals. If an organization focuses its performance management efforts on the right behaviors and can tie rewards to performance improvements at the desired level, it is reasonable to expect that efforts aimed at changing individual-level performance will eventually result in improvements in organization-level performance as well. This is likely to be the case, even considering the various constraints imposed by higher levels on performance at lower levels of analysis. Nevertheless, this statement raises another set of problems associated with crossing levels of performance management and rewards.

Levels of Performance Change Desired and Levels of Rewards

Earlier, we saw that organizations interested in managing team-level performance often make matters more complicated by focusing appraisals at the individual level. In such cases, if rewards are associated with performance at the individual level, employees may well engage in behaviors designed to maximize their own individual outcomes, at a cost to team outcomes. An obvious example might be an employee's unwillingness to share information with another team member if there are rewards associated with individual-level performance.

We have also seen that the ultimate target of any performance management effort must be improved performance at the organizational level, and that it is important for organizations to design goals for individuals that will lead to changes in performance at that higher level. But higher-level goals can introduce some additional problems. Underlying all of them is the fact that the individual may not have much impact on the attainment of organization-level performance goals. For example, any number of accounting and financial indices that might be used to measure corporate performance can often be improved on if costs are reduced. In addition, individually targeted programs for cost reduction may be easy to implement, and these efforts would presumably lead to more favorable earnings ratios. And yet successful earnings also depend on a coherent and effective corporate strategy (although the relationship between corporate strategy and firm performance is also not simple; see Miller & Friesen, 1986; White, 1986).

As a result, if the organization seeks to reduce costs without implementing any other procedures, there is little chance that financial performance will increase appreciably. If an individual's incentives are based on these corporate performance measures (because these are the ultimate target of performance management), the individual may see his or her personal cost-reduction efforts being successful and yet receive no rewards, because these lower-level successes are not being translated into higher-level success. Over time, this will result in the individual employee's reducing his or her cost-saving efforts because there is no reward for those efforts, and the entire effort will fail. Other indices of performance at the organizational level, such as stock prices, surely must rely more heavily on factors other than individual effort if they are to be improved. As a result, even if we can identify individual behaviors that will lead to improved performance at a higher level, and even if we reward those behaviors properly, there are mitigating factors that may make it difficult for the individual employee to see the relationship between individual effort and organizational performance that will lead to rewards.

Most theories or models of motivation suggest that an individual is most likely to exert effort if there is a clear link between his or her effort and the possibility of obtaining rewards, but if an organization tries to manage corporate performance by using an index like stock prices, these links become very tenuous. The individual can do all that is asked, and the required behaviors may even be those that should lead to higher stock prices, but if a competitor comes to the market with a new product, the firm's own stock prices are likely to fall, regardless of how successful individual efforts have been. Everything we know about individual motivation suggests that as the link between effort and performance becomes weaker, the individual will grow less interested in exerting efforts that may not be rewarded.

It should be clear, then, that performance management is much more difficult as the organization moves away from individual-level performance and toward group- or corporate-level performance as the target of the management efforts. It is interesting to note, therefore, the growing interest in the relationship between human resource management programs and such criteria as firm performance (e.g., Becker & Gerhart, 1996: Jackson & Schuler, 1995). This research has suggested that firms engaging in more advanced HR practices, such as goal-based performance management, tend to be more successful (on the basis of a variety of financial indices) than firms not engaging in these practices. But such a relationship suggests that tying individual-level performance appraisals to organization-level outcomes is not very complicated. In fact, it would simply be a matter of putting improved systems for appraisal and performance management (or other HR systems) in place (this is commonly referred to as a "best practices" approach; see Pfeffer, 1994; Applebaum & Batt, 1994). It should be noted, though, that the scholars who report such relationships often do not specify why HR practices should relate to firm performance (although Huselid, 1995, notes that reduced turnover and increased individual productivity play a role). Perhaps more important, most scholars do not specify how these would be linked. (Various contingency factors have been proposed: see Delery & Doty, 1996; Snell & Youndt, 1995; Wright, Smart, & McMahan, 1995; Ostroff & Bowen, Chapter Five, this volume.)

The fact that such relationships exist at all is encouraging, but it may also be misleading. The preceding discussion has attempted to explain how and why it is difficult to relate individual-level performance appraisals to higher-level performance outcomes in a performance management system, and we will return to this issue a bit later. For now, though, it is safe to say that the mere presence of more advanced systems cannot guarantee higher organization-level performance.

Unfortunately, little is known at this time about the processes that link individual-level practices to firm-level outcomes. Among the various authors just cited, various proposals have been made.

Most involve the general notion that if individual employees are knowledgeable about their jobs and their organization, committed to their organization and its goals, and empowered to make changes as they see fit, the organization will prosper. The assumption, then, is that the different HR practices, focused at the individual level and implemented as a set, will result in the right employees being hired and in their being sufficiently motivated and empowered to make the necessary changes. For now, this assumption remains untested.

In summary, several points seem clear:

1. Regardless of the initial level of focus, performance management efforts are ultimately aimed at changing performance at the organizational level.
2. It is almost impossible to change the "behavior" of an organization, whereas it is relatively straightforward to change the behavior of an individual.
3. Most performance management efforts are focused at the level of the individual, and we must find ways to enable the changes at this level that are needed to influence changes at higher levels (that is, at the team and organizational levels).

It is critical, therefore, that we identify ways for changes that occur at the level of the individual to influence higher-level changes as well. As noted, performance at the organizational level is also constrained by various environmental influences at even higher levels (the industry, the nation), and so organization-level change is always difficult to accomplish. Furthermore, the absence of data (along with a plethora of speculation) means that we have few real guidelines to help this bottom-up process of influence along. Nevertheless, we do have some ideas and data with respect to performance in connection with the nature of the relationships among the different levels in an organization. These relationships can provide some insights into how we ultimately change performance at the level of the organization.

Linking Performance at Different Levels

Clearly, organizations need to understand how to move from performance appraisals and performance management at the level of the individual to performance at the level of the organization.

There are some notions of how performance at a higher level in an organization constrains performance at a lower level, but there are no obvious models of how lower-level changes in performance translate into changes at a higher level. Such cross-level effects can be considered as emergent or aggregate effects (because the domain of the effect remains the same at each level), and there have been some suggestions for how these effects might be accomplished.

Bottom-Up Emergent Effects

Two interesting perspectives on organizational interventions designed to increase organizational productivity provide insights into what needs to be done and make clearer the complexity of relationships among performance at different levels. The first perspective is that of Schneider and Klein (1994), who note that many an intervention that is designed to affect organizational productivity, but that is aimed at individual performance, fails because the organization fails to take a systems perspective in designing the intervention: even if the organization is able to improve individual performance (and these authors note that such interventions rarely operate exactly as intended), it is unlikely that organizational productivity will improve as well. They note that organizational productivity is determined by a variety of factors, such as organizational norms and strategy, and that unless these systems change as well, problems with productivity are likely to remain. Furthermore, they note that some interventions may simply not be appropriate for the organization and so may lose effectiveness.

The latter point is especially relevant in the context of the present discussion, especially in discussing possible shifts from individual-level to group- or team-level appraisals. In many U.S. corporations, there is a strong value placed on the individual and on individual efforts. In such organizations, employees are quite comfortable when individual performance is evaluated and when rewards are based on individual performance. They become somewhat uncomfortable, however, when their rewards depend on the performance of others, as is the case with group-level ratings and/or group-based incentives. Imposing such a change is therefore likely to meet with resistance and is not likely to have the desired impact, even if a group-level performance management system is exactly what would seem to be required.

For example, an HR executive from a large engineering firm recently said that his organization had moved to an appraisal system wherein team members rated each other, in addition to having the more traditional supervisor-based appraisals. He said it was because the company operated on a project-team basis, and that because these teams were formed, reconfigured, and dissolved, it seemed important to get fellow team members' perspective on the performance of any one individual. The company also believed in incentive pay systems. When the executive was asked how incentives were determined, especially in cases where supervisors and peers might have different views of an individual's performance, the answer was simple: only the supervisor's evaluation was used for compensation decisions. This may seem strange in light of the strong team orientation, but the executive explained that it would be counter the organization's culture for the rating of any peer to have the ability to "hurt" another. Whether or not this is right for the organization, it is useful for the organization to be aware of what the culture will and will not accept. In this case, the company's culture will have to be changed before an intervention designed to improve productivity can be implemented.

Schneider and Klein (1994) argue that organizational efforts to implement this type of bottom-up performance effect will always be risky. However, they also make clear that an organization must take a larger, systems perspective and give full consideration to any contextual factors that might be operating if it is to have any chance of obtaining those effects. Of course, including these consideration still does not guarantee that the effect will be successful.

The second perspective on bottom-up performance effects is that of Goodman, Lerch, and Mukhopadhyay (1994). These authors propose and discuss a series of factors that can either facilitate or inhibit the impact of individual-level performance on organization-level productivity. They note, for example, that when jobs are linked so that the output from one job is used as the input for another job, increasing productivity in the first job will not have an effect on organizational productivity unless performance in the second job is improved as well. They also note that interventions that improve individual performance but allow organizational slack to increase are unlikely to improve organizational productivity. Further, they discuss processes that can enhance the link between individual and organizational productivity, and they conclude with the following proposal:

> Individual productivity contributes to organizational productivity when (1) the five processes of coordination, problem solving, focus of attention [processes that make certain outcomes and the paths to those outcomes salient], organizational evolution [where changes are introduced as part of a continuous cycle of change], and motivation are operative and (2) the processes are congruent and reinforcing [Goodman, Lerch, & Mukhopadhyay, 1994, p. 66].

Both these theoretical perspectives reinforce the idea that relationships between individual- and higher-level performance are complex. But both perspectives also provide insights into what an organization might do to facilitate the transfer from individual-level to organization-level performance. Again, there are still many other contextual constraints, but at least these perspectives provide some ideas about what to include (or what to avoid) in trying to manage performance at the organizational level.

A proposed model of team effectiveness (Kozlowski et al., 1999) provides yet another perspective on how an organization might translate individual-level performance management into organization-level performance. These authors argue that teams are more than just aggregates of individuals. Individuals are clearly the basis of all teams. Teams go beyond the individual, however, as they become adaptive networks and learn how to integrate individual-level and team-level goals.

Theirs is a developmental model, which begins with team members learning about their teams and each other and how to "think like a team" (the team development phase). Team members then begin to focus on individual-level performance and work to master their specific tasks within the team. This phase, which the authors call the "task compilation phase," requires self-regulation as well as self-efficacy. The team next moves to the "role compilation phase," where team members learn how to coordinate their performance with the performance of others, but the focus is primarily at the level of the dyad. Finally, at the "team compilation phase," the adaptive network begins to form; team members begin to recognize the indirect links among their tasks, monitor the performance of other team members, and provide feedback, trying to improve team effectiveness.

It is at this final stage that it becomes possible to integrate individual-level performance goals with team performance goals. Although there are no specific recommendations about how this should be accomplished (and the authors point out that there is very little research addressing this step), the important implication here is that we cannot decide between individual-level and team-level performance; both are important. Only when individual performance is managed in such a way that communication, coordination, monitoring, and feedback among team members are encouraged, along with individual performance, can a team be truly effective. We can then take the Kozlowski and colleagues (1999) model to one higher level of analysis and suggest that the goals set for teams must be managed in a way that maximizes the chances for improved performance at the organizational level. Therefore, we can suggest the need for compilation at the organizational level, where the goals of the organization are considered simultaneously with the goals of the team, which are already integrated with individual-level goals.

All of this suggests that managing performance at the organizational level requires both top-down and bottom-up processes to be in place. Beginning at the organizational level, goals and performance expectations must be set for teams (or other types of work groups) that reflect the higher-level organizational goals. In other words, if the team meets its goals, this will help move the organization toward meeting its goals. The same thing must then cascade down to the individual level, so that the goals that are driving performance at each level are aimed at supporting performance goals at the next highest level. Meanwhile, beginning at the level of the individual, team members, through compilation processes, must work at integrating their own personal goals with the goals of the team. Presumably, this can be done with better networking, mutual performance monitoring, and mutual feedback. The teams must then presumably go through a similar process and integrate their goals with those at the organizational level. Thus it seems clear that performance management efforts must proceed from both directions if we hope to improve organization-level performance via the efforts made at the level of the individual.

Top-Down Cross-Level Effects

The Kozlowski and colleagues (1999) model goes beyond looking at bottom-up effects and argues for coordination between top-down and bottom-up efforts. In addition, though, there are other cross-level links that are more top-down in nature and that also need to be discussed. Quite often we think about higher-level performance effects (or other factors) acting to constrain performance at lower levels, but higher-level performance effects can also facilitate performance at lower levels.

If we focus on performance at the organizational level, we can find examples of both types of cross-level effects. For example, when rewards are based on success at the organizational level, such success can provide rewards that can also be used for individuals who achieve their own performance goals. But when the organization is not as successful at it would like, and when such performance indices as profits decline, there will generally be less money available for any type of performance-based reward. Therefore, even if performance goals are being met at the team and/or individual levels, it may not be possible to reward anyone for that performance. Higher levels of performance may persist for a while in the absence of any rewards, but we would expect it to eventually decline if there is no formal recognition. Thus, in the long (or even intermediate) run, the level of organizational profitability will serve as a constraint on the team and individual levels of performance.

Success at the level of the organization can also provide the funds and flexibility needed to allow an organization to implement performance management systems that can affect individual-level performance. This is a situation that should be recognizable to many academicians: successful colleges and universities find it easier to attract better faculty, and they make it easier for those faculty members to be successful because of the support that can be offered. Thus, whereas it is surely possible to have a strong academic department in a university that is not particularly effective, it is easier to have strong departments in a strong university.

It is interesting to note that researchers interested in the relationship between HR practices and organizational performance have also acknowledged this potential symbiosis (e.g., Huselid, 1995); that is, they have recognized that part of the explanation for a relationship between organizational performance and HR practices is perhaps that successful firms have the slack and foresight to implement better HR practices. Furthermore, it is conceivable that this relationship is due to the fact that successful firms do everything better than less successful firms, including the implementation of better HR systems. Likewise, firms that manage higher levels of performance successfully may have the expertise to effectively manage performance at lower levels as well.

Similar arguments could be made for the constraining effects of performance at the team level, as well as for the facilitating effects of performance at this level on performance at the level of the individual (that is, there will be more or fewer rewards available). In addition, though, a team that does not exhibit a high level of teamwork behavior, even if individuals are performing effectively, may not be successful. Moreover, this team-level construct (teamwork) will reduce the ability of individual-level performance to translate into team-level performance (compare the concept of "process loss"; see Steiner, 1972). Although this more complex cross-level moderating effect is clearest at the levels of the team and the individual, one could also argue that poor organizational planning and strategy will limit the ability of team-level performance to influence organization-level performance.

Of course, strategies, structures, and policies at each level will serve to constrain lower-level performance effects as well. Organizations that value internal equity in their pay policies may well constrain performance at the team and individual levels because performance-based rewards may be limited so as to not violate internal equity considerations. In fact, too much concern over internal equity could erode an organization's competitive position relative to external equity, which would result in higher levels of turnover, especially among individuals with more market appeal (that is, high performers). This, in turn, would seriously dampen the success of any attempts to improve performance at any level.

Thus it seems clear that performance at one level can have an influence on performance at other levels. The fact of this relationship makes managing performance somewhat more complicated, but it also suggests that even if an organization focuses on the "wrong" level of performance, it may still influence the desired level of performance because of the interdependencies involved. Therefore, it is to be hoped that evaluating and managing team-level performance will influence performance at that level, but this success is also likely to have an influence on individual-level performance. Exhibit 3.1 helps illustrate some of this interdependence.

It is necessary to note, however, that although there are clearly relationships among different levels of performance, it is not always simple to change performance at one level and have it influence other, especially higher, levels of performance. It is also clear that it is critical to coordinate goals and goal-setting efforts at different levels, but these activities are not always enough to effect the desired changes. There is at present no clear set of steps to guarantee that individual-level performance will translate into organization-level performance, but several theoretical perspectives offer some insights into things an organization can do to increase the probability of the desired cross-level effects:

1. Keep a systems perspective, and pay attention to contextual factors that influence performance at each level of analysis.
2. Ensure that efforts aimed at coordination, problem solving, focus of attention, motivation, and evolution are congruent and mutually reinforcing across levels.
3. Recognize that team effectiveness and organizational effectiveness develop over time, so that we ensure that earlier phases of development have been completed before we try to get individuals (and eventually teams) to develop the kinds of mutual networks they need to translate their efforts into performance at a higher level.

Finally, considering the appraisal and performance management processes from a levels perspective leads to a number of research questions that might help guide research designed to better enable organizations to manage performance at the level desired. In addition, this perspective leads to some other research questions that simply may not arise without the use of this perspective.

Issues for Future Research

A number of proposed models of the appraisal process are already available, and each one has the potential to generate a number of

Exhibit 3.1. Conceptual Framework
of Cross-Level Influences on Performance.

Conditions at higher levels of analysis can influence performance at lower levels so that such factors as

- The external environment
- Strategy
- Structure

can constrain *organization-level* performance for reasons such as

- A weak economy, which dampens performance and profits for all firms
- A corporate strategy that focuses on the long-term customer base rather than on short-term profits
- Strong performance in some units that is offset by weak performance in other units of the same firm

and this can constrain *team performance* for reasons such as

- Poor organizational performance that limits the available resources
- Poor organizational performance that lowers morale
- Poor organizational performance that reduces rewards available

and this in turn can constrain *individual-level performance* for reasons such as

- Poor team performance that reduces morale and motivation
- Poor team performance that serves as a ceiling for individual performance
- Poorly performing teams that do not attract effective managers or employees

but performance at lower levels can influence performance at higher levels as well so that individual-level performance can influence higher level performance for reasons such as

- Individual-level performance that influences team-level performance because high-performing individuals contribute to team-level productivity
- Individual-level performance that influences organization-level performance because low levels of motivation will always depress performance, even in the presence of effective corporate-level strategies

Exhibit 3.1. Conceptual Framework
of Cross-Level Influences on Performance, Cont'd.

- Individual-level performance that influences external factors because low levels of individual-level performance can make it more difficult to attract the new employees needed to carry out a high-growth strategy

and team-level performance can likewise influence performance at higher levels for reasons such as

- Team-level performance that influences organization-level performance because poorly performing teams can depress corporate profits
- Team-level performance that influences external factors because variance in performance across teams can necessitate closer controls, which in turn require a shift in both corporate strategy and organizational structure

research questions. The present framework for the discussion of appraisals and performance management is less of a formal model, but it, too, has the potential to help direct future research. A simple illustration of this framework is presented in Exhibit 3.1, and is based on the assumption that performance at each level of analysis is influenced by and simultaneously influences performance at other levels.

From an applied perspective, as noted earlier, the most critical issue arising from a levels framework deals with how an organization can translate changes in behavior at the level of the individual to changes in performance at the level of the organization. This remains the key, not only to fully implementing a performance model based on a levels framework but also to understanding the bottom-line payoff of any organizational intervention that is focused at the level of the individual. The work relating HR systems to firm performance, discussed in several places throughout this volume, is a perfect place to begin exploring this relationship (Schneider, Smith, & Sipe, Chapter Two, and Ostroff & Bowen, Chapter Five).

As noted, there is a growing body of literature that has demonstrated that specific HR practices (for example, using standardized selection procedures) can result in higher levels of organizational performance (for example, greater profitability). Furthermore, there is a debate within this literature about whether the same HR practices produce higher levels of organizational performance in all cases or whether the specific practices leading to higher organizational performance are dependent on the strategy used by the firm to compete. The fact that support is claimed for both views suggests that we really do not understand the process by which HR practices can result in organizational performance. Do more enlightened practices (which would probably be invariant across strategies) cause employees to feel more valued and therefore more committed to the organization? Does this commitment then translate to working smarter as well as harder so that organizational performance improves as a result? Alternatively, do specific HR practices help align the efforts of the individuals with the goals of the organization (so that these would be dependent on the specific strategy employed), with the result of better organizational performance?

Is it possible that better HR practices simply result in the selection and rewarding of better people for behaviors truly related to organizational goals, and that when we implement these practices (assuming we recognize constraints and interrelationships) we always improve performance at all levels of analysis—that, in other words, hiring smarter people and rewarding them properly is the key to success at all levels? It is unlikely that things are this simple, but it is interesting to note that this last possibility focuses our attention more on the basics of I/O psychology than on any strategic orientation toward human resource management. In any case, a critical research issue for the future will be how to change individual-level performance in such a way that it translates into organization-level performance.

In addition to this general question, there are a number of more specific research questions that grow out of a levels perspective on performance appraisal. Some of these stem from simply recognizing that performance is a construct that can be conceptualized at a number of levels. Many of these questions focus on comparing effects of appraisal- and performance management–related variables, occurring at different levels, on outcomes of interest. Other research questions are derived from the recognition that performance at any given level can influence performance at other levels. These questions tend to focus on constraints (or facilitating factors) on performance at one level, stemming from performance at a different level. Finally, a levels perspective can generate research questions concerning processes underlying performance and performance appraisal. Some of these research questions are discussed in the following sections.

Performance at Different Levels

Two research questions flow from the recognition that performance can be conceptualized at different levels. They concern the level at which we should direct performance feedback in order for it to be most effective, and how ratees react to performance ratings and feedback provided at different levels.

These two questions are clearly related. The first follows from a recent paper (Kluger & DeNisi, 1996) suggesting that in some cases performance feedback may actually hurt subsequent performance because it focuses the target's attention on processes other than task performance. These authors argue that feedback that is comparative in nature, or more personalized, is more likely to cause problems, and these conditions are most likely to occur when feedback is provided at the level of the individual or (to a lesser extent) at the level of the team. Yet it is probably easier to set goals at the individual level, and so future research might focus on potential trade-offs among the different levels of feedback.

The broader question of reactions to ratings and feedback at different levels is also worth pursuing. In addition to affective reactions, ratees may differ in terms of motivation to change behavior as a function of the level of the ratings provided. Perceptions of potential bias may be stronger at the individual level, and the rater's motivation to distort ratings (Murphy & Cleveland, 1995) is likely to be greater for ratings at this level. Therefore, ratees may prefer ratings at higher levels of analysis, even though their behavior may be more affected by ratings focused at lower levels.

Cross-Level Effects

Performance appraisal research has not often paid attention to constraints on performance imposed by performance at some higher level, yet such constraints are typically present. From this there may follow the research question of how raters consider higher-level situational constraints on performance when making performance ratings. For example, Murphy and Cleveland (1995) suggest that the level of organizational performance may affect a rater's definition of good and poor performance at a lower level. Furthermore, Kane's (1982) Performance Distribution Assessment model explicitly includes the role of constraints from higher levels as part of the procedure for rating of performance. But whereas the more general research on situational constraints is fairly well accepted (for example, O'Connor et al., 1984), we clearly need to know more about how raters consider this information when they are making rating decisions.

Underlying Processes

One final area that requires further research attention relates to raters' mental models of performance at different levels. Such models are seen as important for guiding evaluations focused at the individual level, and such models seem to be developed and used by raters at this level (Borman, 1991).

Can performance models be developed and used for performance at the team or organizational level? For example, at the individual level, there is evidence that nonperformance factors (such as citizenship behavior) are important, both for the mental models of performance (Borman, White, Pulakos, & Oppler, 1991) and for the appraisals themselves (Werner, 1994). Do such factors play a role in higher-level evaluations as well? In the case of teams, it would even be interesting to know exactly what kinds of behaviors would be considered nonperformance factors, because behaviors that could be considered teamwork are considered important for team effectiveness. At the organizational level, it would be interesting to know if corporate social performance is really part of the mental model of an "excellent" organization, and, if so, to know exactly how information about social performance influences evaluations of overall corporate performance.

Conclusion

The research questions just posed are not meant to be an exhaustive list but are meant instead to be suggestive of the kinds of research questions can that grow out of a recognition of the multilevel nature of performance appraisals and performance management. The purpose of this chapter is not to be exhaustive but to make explicit the implicit assumption that performance in organizations does take place at multiple levels, and that performance at each level can influence and is influenced by performance at other levels. Furthermore, this chapter can be seen as suggesting why this explicit consideration of levels issues is important for appraisal research.

Traditionally, performance appraisal and management research in I/O psychology have focused on the individual level of analysis. Although we have occasionally ventured onto the level of the team or the group (and are increasingly moving in that direction), we have not paid much attention to organization-level performance. As a result, most of our research has focused on such things as rater errors, rating bias, rating-scale format, and rater-memory issues. This chapter has referred throughout to the work of scholars in our field who, recognizing that this focus was too narrow, have called for recognition of the constraints placed on lower levels of performance by performance occurring at higher levels of analysis, and they have suggested ways of translating performance at lower levels to performance at higher levels.

I/O psychologists may have been guilty of focusing too much on individual-level performance and the psychological processes underlying that performance, but they are not alone in ignoring the whole picture. Scholars interested in performance at higher levels of analysis, especially at the level of the organization, have been equally guilty of ignoring the importance of performance at lower levels and the importance of understanding relationships among performance at different levels of analysis. It is not enough simply to state that organizations implementing certain HR programs will perform better than those who do not, unless we can understand how and why those programs result in performance at each level of analysis and, eventually, at the level of the organization. It is hoped that this chapter can help I/O psychologists to consider how their models of individual performance might translate into performance at higher levels of analysis. Perhaps it can also help macro-level scholars give more thought to how HR programs aimed at individuals can lead to team-level and, ultimately, corporate-level performance. Only when we appreciate the multiple-level nature of performance can we hope to successfully implement programs that can improve performance at all levels of analysis.

References

Amburgey, T. L., & Rao, H. (1996). Organizational ecology: past, present, and future directions. *Academy of Management Journal, 5,* 1265–1286.

Ancona, D. G., & Caldwell, D. F. (1988). Beyond task maintenance: Defining external functions in groups. *Group and Organizational Studies, 13,* 468–494.

Applebaum, E., & Batt, R. (1994). *The new American workplace: Transforming work systems in the U.S.* Ithaca, NY: ILR Press.

Becker, B., & Gerhart, B. (1996). The impact of human resource management on organizational performance: Progress and prospects. *Academy of Management Journal, 39,* 779–801.

Borman, W. C. (1991). Job behavior, performance, and effectiveness. In M. D. Dunnette & L. M. Hough (Eds.), *Handbook of industrial and organizational psychology* (Vol. 2, 2nd ed., pp. 271–326). Palo Alto, CA: Consulting Psychologists Press.

Borman, W. C., White, L. A., Pulakos, E. D., & Oppler, S. H. (1991). Models of supervisory job performance ratings. *Journal of Applied Psychology, 76,* 863–872.

Cannon-Bowers, J. A., & Salas, E. (1997). A framework for developing team performance measures in training. In M. Brannick, E. Salas, & C. Prince (Eds.), *Team performance, assessment, and measurement: Theory, methods, and applications* (pp. 45–62). Mahwah, NJ: Erlbaum.

Cascio, W. F., Young, C. E., & Morris, J. R. (1997). Financial consequences of employment change decisions in major U.S. corporations. *Academy of Management Journal, 40,* 1175–1189.

Cleveland, J. N., Murphy, K. R., & Williams, R. E. (1989). Multiple uses of performance appraisal: Prevalence and correlates. *Journal of Applied Psychology, 74,* 130–135.

DeCotiis, T. A., & Petit, A. (1978). The performance appraisal process: A model and some testable hypotheses. *Academy of Management Review, 21,* 635–646.

Delery, J. E., & Doty, D. H. (1996). Modes of theorizing in strategic human resource management: Tests of universalistic, contingency, and configurational performance predictions. *Academy of Management Journal, 39,* 802–835.

DeNisi, A. S. (1997). *Cognitive processes in performance appraisal: A research agenda with implications for practice.* London: Routledge.

DeNisi, A. S., Cafferty, T. P., & Meglino, B. M. (1984). A cognitive view of the performance appraisal process: A model and research propositions. *Organizational Behavior and Human Performance, 33,* 360–396.

Erez, M., & Somech, A. (1996). Is group productivity loss the rule or the exception? Effects of culture- and group-based motivation. *Academy of Management Journal, 39,* 1513–1537.

Finkelstein, S., & Hambrick, D. C. (1990). Top-management-team tenure and organizational outcomes: The moderating role of managerial discretion. *Administrative Science Quarterly, 35,* 484–503.

Goodman, P. S. (1986). Impact of task and technology on group performance. In P. S. Goodman (Ed.), *Designing effective work groups* (pp. 120–167). San Francisco: Jossey-Bass.

Goodman, P. S., Lerch, F. J., & Mukhopadhyay, T. (1994). Individual and organizational productivity: Linkages and processes. In D. H. Harris (Ed.), *Organizational linkages: Understanding the productivity paradox* (pp. 55–80). Washington, DC: National Academy Press.

Gully, S. M. (in press). Work team research since 1985: Recent findings and future trends. In M. Beyerlein (Ed.), *Work teams: Past, present, and future.* Norwell, MA: Kluwer.

Hackman, J. R., Brousseau, K. R., & Weiss, J. (1976). The interaction of task design and group strategies in determining group effectiveness. *Organizational Behavior and Human Performance, 16,* 350–365.

Hallam, G., & Campbell, D. (1997). The measurement of team performance with a standardized survey. In M. Brannick, E. Salas, & C. Prince (Eds.), *Team performance, assessment, and measurement: Theory, methods, and applications* (pp. 155–171). Mahwah, NJ: Erlbaum.

Hambrick, D. C., & Finkelstein, S. (1987). Managerial discretion: A bridge between polar views on organizations. In L. L. Cummings & B. M. Staw (Eds.), *Research in organizational behavior* (Vol. 9, pp. 369–406). Greenwich, CT: JAI Press.

Hollenbeck, J. R., Ilgen, D. R., Sego, D. J., Hedlund, J., Major, D. A., & Phillips, J. (1995). Multilevel theory of team decision making:

Decision making in teams incorporating distributed expertise. *Journal of Applied Psychology, 80,* 292–316.

Huselid, M. A. (1995). The impact of human resource practices on turnover, productivity, and corporate financial performance. *Academy of Management Journal, 38,* 635–672.

Ilgen, D. R., & Feldman, J. M. (1983). Performance appraisal: A process focus. In B. Staw and L. L. Cummings (Eds.), *Research in organizational behavior* (Vol. 5). Greenwich, CT: JAI Press.

Ilgen, D. R., Major, D. A., Hollenbeck, J. R., & Sego, D. J. (1993). Team research in the 1990s. In M. Chemers & R. Ayman (Eds.), *Leadership theory and research* (pp. 245–270). Orlando, FL: Academic Press.

Jackson, S. E., & Schuler, R. S. (1995). Understanding human resource management in the context of organizations and their environments. *Annual Review of Psychology, 46,* 237–264.

Kane, J. S. (1982). *Rethinking the problem of measuring performance: Some new conclusions and a new appraisal method to fit them.* Paper presented at the fourth Johns Hopkins University National Symposium on Educational Research.

Kluger, A. N., & DeNisi, A. S. (1996). The effects of feedback interventions on performance: Historical review, meta-analysis, and a preliminary feedback intervention theory. *Psychological Bulletin, 119,* 254–284.

Kozlowski, S.W.J., Gully, S. M., Nason, E. R., & Smith, E. M. (1999). Developing adaptive teams: A theory of compilation and performance across levels and time. In D. R. Ilgen & E. D. Pulakos (Eds.), *The changing nature of work and performance: Implications for staffing, personnel actions, and development* (pp. 240–292). San Francisco: Jossey-Bass.

Landy, F. J., & Farr, J. L. (1980). Performance rating. *Psychological Bulletin, 87,* 72–102.

Latane, B., Williams, K., & Harkins, S. (1979). Many hands make light the work: The causes and consequences of social loafing. *Journal of Personality and Social Psychology, 37,* 822–832.

Miller, D., & Friesen, P. (1986). Porter's (1980) generic strategies and performance: An empirical examination with American data. *Organization Studies, 7,* 37–55.

Miller, K. D., & Bromiley, P. (1990). Strategic risk and corporate performance: An analysis of alternative risk measures. *Academy of Management Journal, 33,* 756–779.

Mintzberg, H. (1980). *The nature of managerial work.* Englewood Cliffs, NJ: Prentice Hall.

Murphy, K. R., & Cleveland, J. N. (1995). *Understanding performance appraisal: Social, organizational, and goal-based perspectives.* Thousand Oaks, CA: Sage.

O'Connor, E. J., Peters, L. H., Pooyan, A., Weekley, J., Frank, B., & Erenkrantz, B. (1984). Situational constraint effects on performance, affective reactions, and turnover: A field replication and extension. *Journal of Applied Psychology, 69,* 663–672.

Organ, D. W. (1988). *Organizational citizenship behavior: The good-soldier syndrome.* San Francisco: New Lexington Press.

Ostroff, C., & Bowen, D. E. (2000). Moving HR to a higher level: HR practices and organizational effectiveness. In K. J. Klein & S.W.J. Kozlowski (Eds.), *Multilevel theory, research, and methods in organizations* (pp. 211–266). San Francisco: Jossey-Bass.

Pfeffer, J. (1994). *Competitive advantage through people.* Cambridge, MA: Harvard University Press.

Saal, F. E., Downey, R. G., & Lahey, M. (1980). Rating the ratings: Assessing the quality of ratings data. *Psychological Bulletin, 88,* 413–428.

Saavedra, R., Earley, P. C., & Van Dyne, L. (1993). Complex interdependence in task-performing groups. *Journal of Applied Psychology, 78,* 61–72.

Schneider, B., & Klein, K. J. (1994). What is enough? A systems perspective on individual-organizational performance links. In D. H. Harris (Ed.), *Organizational linkages: Understanding the productivity paradox* (pp. 81–104). Washington, DC: National Academy Press.

Schneider, B., Smith, D. B., & Sipe, W. P. (2000). Personnel selection psychology: Multilevel considerations. In K. J. Klein & S.W.J. Kozlowski (Eds.), *Multilevel theory, research, and methods in organizations* (pp. 91–120). San Francisco: Jossey-Bass.

Snell, S. A., & Youndt, M. (1995). Human resource management and firm performance: Testing a contingency model of executive controls. *Journal of Management, 21,* 711–737.

Steiner, I. D. (1972). *Group process and productivity.* Orlando, FL: Academic Press.

Sundstrom, E., DeMeuse, K. P., & Futrell, D. (1990). Work teams: Applications and effectiveness. *American Psychologist, 45,* 120–133.

Tesluk, P., Mathieu, J. E., Zaccaro, S. J., & Marks, M. (1997). Task and aggregation issues in the analysis and assessment of team performance. In M. Brannick, E. Salas, & C. Prince (Eds.), *Team performance, assessment, and measurement: Theory, methods, and applications* (pp. 197–224). Mahwah, NJ: Erlbaum.

Van De Ven, A. H., Delbecq, A., & Koenig, R. (1976). Determinants of coordination modes within organizations. *American Sociological Review, 41,* 322–338.

Werner, J. M. (1994). Dimensions that make a difference: Examining the impact of in-role and extra-role behaviors on supervisory ratings. *Journal of Applied Psychology, 79,* 98–107.

White, R. (1986). Generic business strategies, organizational context, and performance: An empirical analysis. *Strategic Management Journal, 7,* 217–231.

Wright, P. M., Smart, D., & McMahan, G. C. (1995). Matches between human resources and strategy among NCAA basketball teams. *Academy of Management Journal, 38,* 301–326.

CHAPTER 4

A Multilevel Approach to Training Effectiveness

Enhancing Horizontal and Vertical Transfer

Steve W. J. Kozlowski
Kenneth G. Brown
Daniel A. Weissbein
Janis A. Cannon-Bowers
Eduardo Salas

Over a quarter-century ago, Terreberry (1968) predicted that organizational environments were evolving to become increasingly complex, dynamic, and uncertain. As we approach the next millennium, that prediction has become reality. Organizations are increasingly pressured by technological, political, economic, social, and cultural changes that are global in scope and impact. Although change is often incremental, it is also frequently rapid and unpredictable.

Note: We would like to thank Irv Goldstein, Katherine Klein, John Mathieu, Scott Tannenbaum, and Shelly Zedeck for their helpful comments on earlier drafts of this chapter. The views, opinions, and findings expressed in this chapter are those of the authors and do not necessarily reflect the views of any organization. Please address correspondence to Steve W. J. Kozlowski, Department of Psychology, Michigan State University, East Lansing, MI 48824–1117; (517) 353–8924 (voice), (517) 353–4873 (fax); stevekoz@msu.edu.

These dynamics drive a need for continuous improvement and adaptive capabilities across all levels of the organization.

Virtually all approaches to organizational improvement and development are based on enhancing the knowledge, skills, and attitudes (KSAs) or abilities of the workforce. This may be accomplished through recruitment, selection, and replacement of the workforce as one means to import upgraded abilities. Often improvement is accomplished through training to develop workforce KSAs. Organizations in the United States invest a remarkable $55.3 billion annually in training and development activities (Bassi & Van Buren, 1998). The presumption is that this sizable investment is warranted because training improves the organization's ability to accomplish key objectives. *From this perspective, training is effective to the extent that it directly contributes to the strategy, objectives, or outcomes central to organizational effectiveness* (Jackson & Schuler, 1990).

Pressures for continuous improvement and adaptability place renewed emphasis on this presumed link between training outcomes and organizational effectiveness. This link spans multiple levels in that training effectiveness is inherently macro, and yet it is rooted in micro-level processes. Interestingly, although the contribution of training to organizational effectiveness is assumed in training models (Goldstein, 1993; McGehee & Thayer, 1961), the specific nature of this linkage is not well articulated. Moreover, this critical linkage has received relatively little research attention. The best current efforts to establish training effectiveness end with demonstrating transfer of individual-level training outcomes to the job context. There is a presumption that individual-level training outcomes aggregate and emerge to create valued outcomes at higher levels, but there is little theoretical guidance as to how to conceptualize and model these effects. Hence, there have been few efforts to do so.

This situation creates a levels paradox. The primary goal of training is to enhance organizational effectiveness. That is, training is predicated on contributing to higher-level group and organizational objectives, outcomes, and results, yet the models, methods, and tools of training are focused on the individual level. Training needs are derived for individual-level KSAs, training programs are delivered to individuals, and training effectiveness is evaluated for individual-level outcomes and transfer. The organizational context, its effects on training, and the means by which training effectiveness will affect organizational objectives are not adequately addressed in current models. *Thus there is a levels gap between theoretical models of training needs assessment, design, and evaluation, on the one hand, and, on the other, the higher levels at which training must have an impact if it is to contribute to organizational effectiveness* (Kozlowski & Salas, 1997).

Overview

The purpose of this chapter is to explicate a multilevel model that bridges this gap. We focus on training transfer because it is the primary leverage point by which training can influence organizational effectiveness. Levels issues are embedded in two distinct transfer foci: horizontal transfer and vertical transfer. *Horizontal transfer* (Kozlowski & Salas, 1997) is transfer across different settings or contexts at the same level. Horizontal transfer has been the primary focus in traditional models of training effectiveness. *Vertical transfer* (Kozlowski & Salas, 1997) is upward transfer across different levels of the organizational system. Vertical transfer is concerned with the link between individual-level training outcomes and outcomes or results at higher levels of the organizational system.

Qualitatively distinct levels issues are relevant to each of these transfer foci. One issue concerns *top-down* contextual effects (Kozlowski & Klein, Chapter One, this volume) that facilitate or inhibit individual learning and transfer. Top-down contextual effects are group and organizational factors that have direct and moderating effects on learning and transfer. These effects have been the source of recent theory and research addressing the influence of organizational factors on motivation to learn, transfer, and training effectiveness at the individual level of analysis. Top-down effects are relevant to horizontal transfer. The second issue concerns *bottom-up* emergent processes (Kozlowski & Klein, Chapter One, this volume) that influence the contribution of individual-level training outcomes to higher-level group and organizational outcomes. This second issue is concerned with strengthening the linkage between training and organizational effectiveness. The processes by which individual-level training outcomes combine and emerge, bottom-up, to manifest as higher-level outcomes have been largely neglected in training theory and research. We acknowledge that experienced practitioners may consider vertical transfer processes, at least implicitly. However, the link between individual-and higher-level training outcomes has been neglected in formal research and practice models. Bottom-up effects are relevant to vertical transfer. *In our view, vertical transfer is a key leverage point for strengthening the link between training and organizational effectiveness.*

An example may be useful for illustrating the importance of both transfer foci. Consider total-quality management (TQM) programs that are intended to contribute to organizational objectives of continually improving processes, products, and services. In many instances, TQM training is the primary intervention for accomplishing these organizational objectives, and yet, even if individuals learn the trained knowledge and skills, there are often many incongruent contextual factors in the job setting that are not addressed as part of the development effort. Top-down contextual factors, such as leadership, structure, job design, rewards, climate, and so forth, can inhibit the horizontal transfer of outcomes when they are not aligned with the content of training. When there is no support from one's leader or peers, insufficient opportunity to practice new skills, no rewards, and a climate that is inconsistent with the trained skills, horizontal transfer of the trained knowledge and skills to the work setting is unlikely. In the absence of horizontal transfer, training cannot contribute to organizational effectiveness.

Furthermore, the typical TQM program is designed to deliver the same training content to virtually every member of the organization. Everyone is responsible for quality, and everyone is exposed to identical content. With respect to vertical transfer as an emergent process, the implicit assumption of this approach is that improving the "quality" of organizational products, processes, and services is an additive function of similar individual outcomes or contributions: each individual contribution sums together to yield higher-level impacts. Training will contribute to organizational effectiveness when this assumption holds; that is, when quality really is a sum of incremental contributions, this approach will have impacts on quality outcomes at higher levels in the system. Yet in many (if not most) organizations, improving quality for higher-level objectives is not consistent with a simple additive model.

Rather, quality is a complex combination of different contributions across individuals and across different levels of the organization. When this more complex model holds, the typical approach to TQM training will be, at best, inefficient; more likely, it will be ineffective. The distinctive knowledge and skills needed for different individuals and different levels, and the integration of these skills, will be neglected by training. If training is to meet its promise of improving the organization's capability to learn, adapt, and improve, these level-related gaps must be bridged.

We address both levels issues in this chapter. First we consider top-down contextual influences on horizontal transfer. We assert that the foundation of theory, methods, and research findings is sufficiently well developed such that top-down contextual effects should be explicitly incorporated in training research and practice. We review this foundation and use it to specify basic levels *principles;* that is, we regard the principles as established knowledge. These principles are intended to promote state-of-the-art research and practice that enhances the horizontal transfer as one aspect of training effectiveness.

Second, we assert that neglected bottom-up processes should be the focal point for theory development and new research to elaborate the linkage between training and emergent outcomes at higher levels in the organizational system. This is intended to bridge the gap between training outcomes and organizational effectiveness. We present a theoretical framework to guide new research on vertical transfer. The framework distinguishes two distinctive forms of emergence—composition and compilation—that characterize different types of vertical transfer processes. We describe distinguishing characteristics and present examples to illustrate different types of emergent effects. The model is then used to posit theory-based *propositions* regarding vertical transfer that have implications for training needs assessment, design and delivery, and evaluation. In other words, the propositions represent theoretical assertions in need of research evaluation. Our intent is to promote conceptual development, influence training research, and suggest potential implications for practice. By doing so, we hope to stimulate research on vertical transfer, a neglected and yet critical aspect of training effectiveness.

Multilevel Issues in Training Effectiveness

The training literature identifies two critical foci for training effectiveness (Goldstein, 1993; McGehee & Thayer, 1961): first, individuals have to learn trained knowledge and skills and transfer them to the work context; and, second, transferred learning has to yield intended individual, group, or organizational objectives. From a traditional perspective, the first focus is accomplished through appropriate training design, which entails the application of classic learning and instructional design principles to enhance learning in the training environment, as well as the replication of trained KSAs in the work setting, which translate into measurable training outcomes (that is, improved individual performance). We characterize this critical focus of training effectiveness as *horizontal transfer.*

From a traditional perspective, the second focus is accomplished through appropriate needs assessment. Organizational objectives serve as a point of departure for the needs assessment process. The derivation of individual KSAs, which drive the content of training, are presumably decomposed from organizational objectives, although the method of decomposition is not well specified. There is a presumption that if KSAs are learned and transferred, organizational objectives will be accomplished. We characterize this focus of training effectiveness as *vertical transfer.* Interestingly, a direct link between transferred knowledge and skills at the individual level and the accomplishment of higher-level objectives is never addressed in traditional models, but levels issues are central to a better elaboration of both these traditional foci of training effectiveness. We will now address each of these critical foci—horizontal and vertical transfer—and consider their implications for research and practice.

Horizontal Transfer: Contextual Influences on Training Effectiveness

Learning and Transfer

Goldstein (1993) defines training effectiveness with respect to improvements in trainee KSAs (that is, learning) that yield improved performance in the work context (that is, transfer). Both aspects, learning and transfer, are considered to be essential to training effectiveness (Cannon-Bowers, Salas, Tannenbaum, & Mathieu, 1995; Mathieu & Martineau, 1997). Learning is a psychological phenomenon; it is axiomatic that learning occurs at the individual level. Thus the individual level is an appropriate focus for training and instructional design.[1] Transfer refers to the reproduction, persistence, and generalization of learned KSAs across different contexts (Baldwin & Ford, 1988; Tesluk, Farr, Mathieu, & Vance, 1995). Although the traditional perspective considers transfer at the individual level, alternatives recognize that training and transfer can be targeted at higher-levels, such as groups or subunits (Kozlowski & Salas, 1997). Nevertheless, virtually all models of training effectiveness conceptualize transfer as horizontal linkages across different settings or contexts that are at the same level (typically the individual level).

Contemporary models of training effectiveness differ from their traditional counterparts in that they explicitly conceptualize training in an organizational context that can have multiple influences on the training process (Cannon-Bowers et al., 1995; Kozlowski, 1998; Kozlowski & Salas, 1997; Mathieu, Tannenbaum, & Salas, 1992). Traditional models, such as the widely used instructional system design (ISD) model, are program-focused; that is, they are self-contained systems that focus on reciprocal linkages among needs assessment, training design and delivery, and evaluation. Training effectiveness is completely represented by the evaluation of transfer. Linkages to a broader organizational context are represented as a portion of the needs assessment process (that is, organizational analysis). This bounded conceptualization provides a limited consideration of the many and varied influences that higher-level contexts—group, subunit, and organization—can exert on training effectiveness (Baldwin & Ford, 1988; Campbell, 1988, 1989; Tannenbaum & Yukl, 1992).

More recent work takes a broader perspective on training effectiveness (Cannon-Bowers et al., 1995). It goes beyond simple evaluation ("Did training work?") in an effort to understand the effects of training ("Why did training work?") on a multifaceted array of outcomes (Kraiger, Ford, & Salas, 1993). The effects of organizational-context factors are central to this contemporary perspective. Theory and research indicate three types of effects through which higher-level contextual factors influence training effectiveness as a process of horizontal transfer (Kozlowski & Salas, 1997; Mathieu & Martineau, 1997):

1. Contextual factors can affect pretraining motivation so that learning is either enhanced or inhibited. As the critical first step in the chain, a failure of the trainee to learn requisite KSAs precludes training effectiveness.

2. Contextual factors can moderate the extent to which learning during training is translated into new job behavior and performance outcomes. Learning in the absence of transfer also precludes training effectiveness.

3. Contextual factors can exert direct effects to facilitate retention and maintenance of trained KSAs in the job setting. Training effectiveness is predicated on the persistence of trained KSAs back on the job.

These three effects are illustrated in Figure 4.1. A variety of contextual factors have been identified that influence these effects, many of which are not unique and operate through multiple linkages in the model. The discussion that follows provides a selective review within this perspective of training effectiveness. It focuses on these three types of top-down contextual effects and their influence on horizontal transfer.

Figure 4.1. Cross-Level Organizational-Context Effects on Horizontal Transfer.

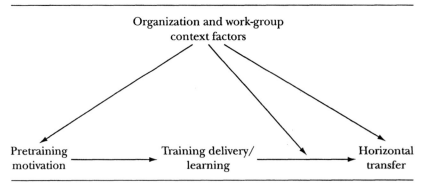

Contextual Effects on Learning

Several models have focused on the way in which contextual factors influence pretraining motivation with direct effects on learning, the link between training motivation and learning having been well established (Hicks & Klimoski, 1987). This line of inquiry was sparked by Noe and Schmitt (1986), who posited that pretraining motivation would be a critical antecedent of learning and transfer. Research on pretraining motivation has focused on individual differences (Noe, 1986; Tannenbaum, Mathieu, Salas, & Cannon-Bowers, 1991), contextual factors (Baldwin & Magjuka, 1997; Quiñones, 1995), and the joint effects of individual and contextual factors (Cannon-Bowers et al., 1995; Mathieu & Martineau, 1997; Mathieu et al., 1992). Our focus in this chapter is on contextual effects.

Contextual effects have generally been conceptualized in two ways: as tangible *situational constraints* that affect motivation and learning, or as *perceptions* of organizational features, events, and processes that convey meaning about the importance and relevance of training, which in turn influence motivation and learning. For example, Mathieu and Martineau (1997) suggest that situational constraints such as insufficient job information, equipment, supplies, money, and time (Peters & O'Connor, 1980) hinder motivation to learn. Salinger (1973) indicates that insufficient time makes participation in training a penalty. Mathieu, Tannenbaum, and Salas (1992) and Mathieu, Martineau, and Tannenbaum (1993) report that situational constraints negatively affect indicators of trainee motivation during training. Noe and Wilk (1993) have shown that situational constraints negatively affect voluntary participation in managerial development. This and other research supports the view that situational constraints can directly inhibit motivation and learning during training.

Other work has focused on what may be regarded as contextual effects that occur through mediating perceptions; that is, organizational features and events surrounding training are perceived and interpreted by trainees. The interpretation and meaning ascribed to the training are what determine trainee motivation and learning (Quiñones, 1997). For example, Baldwin and Magjuka (1997) conceptualize training as a series of socially constructed, episodic experiences. Their perspective focuses on the symbolism trainees attach to the various events that surround the announcement and implementation of a training program. In other words, what the training is about, how it is introduced, who is selected and how, and organizational support (or lack thereof) for training influence the significance trainees attach to it. Within this perspective, the culture and climate of the organization, the climate for transfer, and interpersonal support from leaders and peers signify the importance of training and affect trainee motivation and learning (Cannon-Bowers et al., 1995; Mathieu et al., 1992; Quiñones, 1995).

Contextual Effects on Transfer

Recent models of training effectiveness consider the direct and moderating effects of higher-level contexts on individual-level transfer (see Figure 4.1). For example, Kozlowski and Salas (1997) view the organization as a multilevel system where training is deeply embedded in structure and process. The model emphasizes the necessity for congruence or alignment between the target of training and higher-level contextual factors in the work setting as a condition for horizontal transfer. Cross-level alignment can assume different forms of relationship, including direct or moderated effects. Direct cross-level effects, for instance, occur when the organization's climate for innovation supports individual skill updating and continuous learning. When the climate is more supportive of innovation, individuals are more likely to keep their skills on the cutting edge. Cross-level moderation can be illustrated by the influence of unit structure on the link between empowerment training and individual initiative. When structure is rigid, empowerment is misaligned with the context, and initiative behaviors are less likely to occur. In contrast, when structure is flexible there are more opportunities for individual initiative, and thus the training-transfer link should be stronger.

A fairly substantial theoretical and research base has developed that supports the direct effects of contextual factors on horizontal transfer. For example, it has long been noted that organizational support for training, in the form of policies, practices, and procedures, and social support from supervisors and peers are likely to improve training transfer. Some research has focused on self-reports of transfer. Social support from leaders and peers has been related to greater reports of transfer following training (Baumgartel & Jean-pierre, 1972; Baumgartel, Reynolds, & Pathan, 1984; Huczynski & Lewis, 1980).

More rigorous research has focused on independent assessments of transfer behavior or job performance. Perhaps the earliest observation of this effect was offered by Fleishman (1953), who indicated that the transfer of trained leadership behavior was affected by the support provided by trainees' leaders. More recently, several studies have shown that climates indicative of alignment between the organizational context and training yield improved performance on the job. For example, Kozlowski and Farr (1988) indicate that perceptions of a positive climate for updating and innovation (that is, supportive contextual factors) predict participation in development activities and better job performance. Similarly, Kozlowski and Hults (1987) demonstrate that climate factors predict higher supervisory ratings of involvement in professional training, as well as higher job performance. Moreover, Kozlowski and Hults have demonstrated an increase, over a one-year time lag, in the strength of the climate–job performance relationship. Taking a different approach, Rouiller and Goldstein (1993) have shown that a climate for transfer (that is, a climate specifically focused on training-transfer factors) predicted job performance above and beyond that accounted for by learning and unit performance. Tracey, Tannenbaum, and Kavanaugh (1995) have also shown that the climate for transfer and a culture for continuous learning contribute to transfer. Taken together, all this research has rather consistently demonstrated a direct cross-level effect of organizational-context factors on horizontal transfer.

Some models view contextual factors as specifically exerting moderating effects on the link between training outcomes and work behaviors (Cannon-Bowers et al., 1995; Mathieu & Martineau, 1997; Tracey et al., 1995). Support for this moderating effect has been more elusive. Although there is good theoretical support for this proposed moderating effect, the empirical support is primarily for direct effects. For example, Tracey and colleagues (1995) explicitly examine this relationship for transfer climate and continuous-learning culture. Although both contextual factors had direct effects on transfer, hypothesized moderating relations were not supported. An exception is described by Ford, Quiñones, Sego, and

Sorra (1992) who report on a situation in which contextual factors affected the opportunity to perform trained skills, which in turn moderated the learning-to-transfer link.

Contextual Effects: Implications for Research and Practice

Conceptual Issues

Recent theory and research on training effectiveness reflect a greater appreciation of the extent to which training is embedded in a broader, unfolding organizational context. Contextual influences are pervasive, with pretraining, training, and posttraining effects. Moreover, training is not merely a single isolated event. It typically comprises a series of experiences to which trainees attach meaning over time (Baldwin & Magjuka, 1997; Kozlowski, 1998). Thus training activities are subject to the same sensemaking processes that apply to other salient organizational practices, and they must be understood with these effects in mind.

Research support for direct, cross-level contextual effects on pretraining and posttraining processes is compelling. Support for hypothesized moderating effects on the learning-to-transfer linkage is more equivocal, although the lack of consistent support may be due to restricted sampling variability on contextual factors; that is, much of this research is conducted in single organizations, a situation that of necessity restricts contextual variance. Therefore, although this is a relatively new research area, results support its relevance for enhancing our understanding of horizontal transfer and training effectiveness.

In our view, there is a sufficiently well developed theoretical and research foundation to specify principles to guide state-of-the-art theory, research, and practice addressing the effects of contextual factors on horizontal transfer. There are several implications for training research. At a minimum, research should incorporate contextual factors that are likely to influence pretraining motivation constructs (for example, self-efficacy, training attitudes, expectations) and facilitate posttraining transfer. The literature previously reviewed provides a foundation for identifying likely contextual influences. Given the demonstrated effects of contextual factors, a failure to include them in research can be expected to yield underspecified models of training effectiveness.

PRINCIPLE 1: *Research on training effectiveness should explicitly model the direct, cross-level effects of relevant contextual factors on pretraining motivation and on facilitation of transfer, retention, and maintenance.*

In addition, further attention to potential moderating effects on the learning-to-transfer linkage is warranted. However, we believe that such research must be more sensitive to the levels at which constructs are conceptualized, sampled, assessed, and aggregated, because these issues determine the likelihood of detecting cross-level moderation. The problem is that contextual factors are often conceptualized at the organizational level, sampled within a single organization, assessed at the individual level, and aggregated to the unit level (e.g., Tracey et al., 1995). Because the units are all embedded in the same organization, such practices are likely to yield restricted variance on the contextual moderator, thereby limiting the ability to detect potential moderation (Kozlowski & Klein, Chapter One, this volume). Although this discussion focuses on moderation, the same issues are relevant for examining all three contextual effects: pretraining, cross-level direct, or cross-level moderation.

PRINCIPLE 2: *Research on training effectiveness should model, where appropriate, potential moderation of the learning-to-transfer linkage.*

Research in this area would also benefit from a more consistent and integrated conceptual framework that clusters contextual factors and effects. Currently there is little consistency in the literature with respect to what types of factors are likely to have what types of effects. Climate constructs are perhaps most problematic in that they are variously hypothesized to influence each of the three types of contextual effects illustrated in Figure 4.1. From a global perspective, this may be so; presumably, however, a more differentiated framework can be constructed. To date there have been few efforts to develop such integrated yet specific models. Work by Cannon-Bowers and colleagues (1995) and by Mathieu and Martineau (1997), described in this section, represents a point of departure for integration and distinction. More theoretical work to build on and elaborate this foundation is warranted.

PRINCIPLE 3: *Training-effectiveness models should specify contextual factors and make explicit the expected type of contextual effect: pretraining, moderation, or posttraining.*

· Any effort to elaborate an integrated framework needs to distinguish features of the organizational environment from perceptions of those features. For example, Mathieu and Martineau (1997) distinguish tangible situational characteristics from social-psychological influences. Similarly, Kozlowski and Salas (1997) distinguish tangible technostructural factors from less tangible enabling factors that are primarily the result of social interaction and perceptual processes. Tangible factors may often operate through perceptions—in the sense that climate perceptions represent an interpretation of policies, practices, and procedures—but tangible factors may serve as direct constraints. If time and resources for training are insufficient, development cannot occur (Noe & Wilk, 1993). If there is no opportunity to apply trained skills on the job, transfer cannot occur (Ford et al., 1992). These differing factors and mechanisms need to be carefully distinguished and modeled.

PRINCIPLE 4: *Training-effectiveness models should distinguish tangible situational constraints from social psychological processes and interpretive perceptions.*

On the perceptual side, we need to be more thoughtful in our conceptualization and treatment of climate constructs. Some researchers have exhibited a tendency to treat content-specific climates (that is, a climate supportive of the specific content of training) and climate for transfer (that is, a general climate supporting the on-the-job application of trained skills) as identical constructs. Although they both reference climate as a broad construct domain, these are distinguishable conceptualizations. The dimensions for transfer climate (Rouiller & Goldstein, 1993) are based on a model of behavior modification that distinguishes proximal environmental stimuli or cues (goal, social, task, structure, and self-control cues) and individual consequences (positive, negative, and no feedback; punishment) relevant to applying trained behaviors. This conceptualization emphasizes the instrumental aspects of trained behaviors to the individual and has been shown to be predictive of individual-level transfer (Rouiller & Goldstein, 1993). Its content is general and has the potential to be applicable across many training content domains and different organizational settings.

In contrast, content-specific climates are generally conceptualized at the organizational or work-group level, with the content focus specified by the phenomenon of interest; climates are *for* something (Schneider, 1981). In this conceptualization, climate is viewed as an interpretation of organizational or work-group features, events, and processes relevant to the specific content area. Therefore, content that is relevant will vary with the nature of training rather than being generally applicable. However, while specific content may vary by training situation (for example, climate for updating, climate for safety), the underlying contextual foci to which the content applies are less variable. Even a cursory examination across this literature suggests consistency for the importance of leader and peer encouragement, open communications, policies to support internal or external training, challenging and flexible work, and adequate resources (Kozlowski & Farr, 1988; Kozlowski & Hults, 1987; Mathieu & Martineau, 1997) as focal referents for content-specific climates that support training. The content-specific climate approach has enabled researchers to effectively predict important outcomes like job performance, training participation, and other job-relevant behaviors.

Research indicates that these differing conceptualizations of climate are distinct, and that both are relevant and add value to our understanding of horizontal transfer. For example, Tracey and colleagues (1995) have found that climate for transfer and a content-specific climate for continuous learning are empirically distinct, and that they make independent contributions to transfer. In our view, with appropriate design and sampling, climate for transfer is more likely to operate as a contextual moderator because it focuses on proximal stimuli and consequences that are instrumental to trained behaviors. Content-specific climates are more likely to have direct effects on pretraining motivation and the facilitation of posttraining transfer because of their higher-level focus and broad implications for interpretation and meaning construction. This latter assertion, of course, is a more speculative research proposition.

PRINCIPLE 5: *Contextually based perceptions should distinguish a climate for transfer from climates specific to the phenomenon; these different conceptualizations are likely to have distinct influences on horizontal transfer.*

Issues in Research Design

Taking a levels approach to training effectiveness entails attention to several critical issues in research design that are often neglected in training research. The levels of the contextual constructs must be consistent with the levels inherent in sampling design, measurement, aggregation, and analysis. Contextual factors at the organizational level should implicate overarching characteristics applicable to the entire organization, such as its culture, climate, or strategic focus. They necessitate multiple organizational samples and analyses that represent the constructs at the organizational level (e.g., Kozlowski & Hults, 1987). Studies in single organizations are advised to conceptualize contextual characteristics at the unit level; otherwise, there is no reason to anticipate substantial across-unit variance (Kozlowski & Klein, Chapter One, this volume). Unit-level contextual factors should implicate constructs that shift across unit boundaries. Contextual factors that focus on unit technology, structure, and work flow, or on more constrained climate perceptions that implicate leaders, co-workers, and social interaction, are more proximal to the unit, more likely to be relevant, and more likely to vary across units.

PRINCIPLE 6: *The theoretical level of contextual factors should have a consistent representation in the research sampling design, measurement, aggregation procedure, and analysis.*

PRINCIPLE 7: *Examination of contextual effects necessitates sampling across distinct organizational contexts to ensure variance on the contextual factors of interest.*

Researchers have classified situational factors (Mathieu & Martineau, 1997; Peters & O'Connor, 1980) and social psychological factors (Mathieu & Martineau, 1997) that can serve as the raw material for identifying contextual factors likely to influence the effectiveness of horizontal transfer. Kozlowski and Salas (1997) provide a multilevel model that identifies contextual characteristics relevant to different content (technostructural versus enabling processes) at different levels (individual, unit, and organization) of the organizational system that can serve as a guide for this specification process; that is, the construction of a model that specifies which factors comprise the context at different levels of the organizational system. Thus there is a sufficient foundation in place to facilitate research that defines, refines, and extends our knowledge of the influence of top-down contextual effects on horizontal transfer.

Vertical Transfer: Training Effectiveness as an Emergent Process

Training Outcomes and Organizational Objectives

Virtually all models of training assume the achievement of organizational goals or objectives via training as a critical aspect of effectiveness (e.g., Goldstein, 1993; McGehee & Thayer, 1961). Kirkpatrick's (1974) well-known taxonomy of training evaluation criteria may be as responsible as anything else for this assumed link between training outcomes and organizational objectives. The taxonomy presents four categories of criteria to evaluate the effectiveness of training: affective reactions, learning, on-the-job behavior, and organizational results. Alliger and Janak (1989) identify three presumptions attributed to the taxonomy that are without theoretical or empirical foundation: that the criteria are arranged in hierarchical order of increasing informativeness, are causally linked, and are positively intercorrelated. In the absence of both theoretical and empirical support for these assumptions, the widely presumed link between training effectiveness and organizational impact becomes tenuous.

Issues of level, augmenting the limitations identified by Alliger and Janak, also undermine this assumed linkage. The presumed effects of training beyond the individual level (at the group, unit, or organizational levels) are based on three implicit assumptions:

that individual-level learning occurs, that cross-context (horizontal) transfer of KSAs takes place, and that the effects of individual on-the-job behaviors emerge to yield outcomes at higher levels. The first two assumptions are related to issues identified by Alliger and Janak (1989) and to the previous section of this chapter on horizontal transfer. The third assumption directly implicates emergence. Exactly how training interventions, which focus on individual outcomes, will yield higher-level outcomes has been largely neglected. To understand the process that links training effectiveness at the individual level with higher-level objectives, we need to formulate theoretical models that address these assumptions explicitly and explain how this emergent process links different levels of the organizational system.

To distinguish this emergence from the more common focus on horizontal links within a level across contexts, Kozlowski and Salas (1997) describe it as a process of vertical transfer that aggregates upward across levels. Recognizing that training is generally delivered to individuals but often targets higher-level outcomes, their model addresses factors that influence the extent to which lower-level training can contribute to higher-level objectives. The essence of their argument is that training conducted at a lower level has to be congruent with the contextual content of the higher-level target. This congruence helps to ensure that training delivered at the individual level will propagate upward across levels to influence organizational objectives. Their theory specifies propositions with regard to training delivery and contextual alignment to facilitate this emergent process.

A distinguishing feature of their framework concerns the nature of work-flow interdependencies that bind individual performance to group products, or subunit performance to organizational outcomes. For example, these authors propose that training must be congruent with the underlying composition model that maps the linkage between individual and group performance. They posit that pooled coordination mechanisms at the group level or higher levels implicate additive processes, whereas sequential and reciprocal coordination mechanisms at the group level or higher levels implicate more complex vertical transfer processes. This is consistent with the TQM example offered at the beginning of this chapter. When the higher-level TQM outcome is the result of many similar individual actions, vertical transfer will be based on simple linear models. However, when the higher-level TQM outcome is a complex combination of different interdependent individual actions, vertical transfer will be based on nonlinear processes.

The critical implication of their framework is that the nature of the linkage—the model of vertical transfer—between the lower-level targets of training, on the one hand, and the desired higher-level outcomes, on the other, must drive training if it is to be effective. Although this framework provides a good point of departure, there is a need to elaborate more precisely the nature of the emergent processes that underlie training effectiveness and to articulate the implications of different vertical transfer processes for training needs assessment, design, and evaluation.

Vertical Transfer: Composition and Compilation Forms of Emergence

We assert that conceptualizations or training effectiveness must be expanded beyond current views of transfer as a horizontal linkage across environmental settings. Models of training effectiveness must explicitly address how individual-level learning and transfer emerge to yield effects at the work-group, unit, and organizational levels. Kozlowski and Klein (Chapter One, this volume) note that the levels literature has focused almost exclusively on composition as the primary conceptual tool for addressing emergent phenomena in organizations; our goal is to elaborate the conceptualization of emergent organizational phenomena beyond a single model. Therefore, we contrast composition, as one model of emergence, with compilation, which anchors the other end of a range of emergence models. For purposes of the current discussion, key features distinguishing composition and compilation forms of emergence are illustrated in Table 4.1.

Composition processes are based on the concept of *isomorphism,* which references essentially the same construct at different levels of analysis. Composition is predicated on generalizing the same construct across different levels. Composition assumes similarity in content, in the nomological networks, and in the meaning of the constructs at the different levels. Data combination or aggregation rules for composition indicate the manner in which higher-level

Table 4.1. Emergence Models for Vertical Transfer.

1. Emergent process	Composition	Compilation
2. Theoretical basis	Isomorphism	Discontinuity
3. Lower-level content	Same: x, x, x	Different: x, y, z
4. Combination	Simple: Average Addictive	Complex: Disjunctive Conjunctive Multiplicative Configural
5. Functional equivalence (lower-higher level)	Equivalent	Equivalent

phenomena are represented by lower-level indicators. Additive or mean-aggregation are common combination rules for composition-based models.

Compilation forms of emergence are based on the concept of *discontinuity* in the manifestation of a phenomenon across levels. Discontinuity is defined as different manifestations of related constructs that occur at different levels (House, Rousseau, & Thomas-Hunt, 1995; Rousseau, 1985). Compilation addresses emergence in a common, functionally equivalent construct domain but recognizes that specific lower-level contributions may be diverse rather than similar. For example, individual and team performance represent a common, functionally equivalent construct domain, yet the nature of individual performance, and the myriad ways that individuals contribute to team performance, can be quite different (Kozlowski, Gully, Nason, & Smith, 1999).

There have been relatively few efforts to conceptualize discontinuity-based emergence, and there is some inconsistency in the literature with respect to definitions and exemplars (compare House et al., 1995; Kozlowski & Klein, Chapter One, this volume). Our conceptualization of discontinuity is directly tied to its definition: different manifestations of similar phenomena across levels. There are two key features for distinguishing these different forms of emergence. One feature that distinguishes discontinuity from isomorphism is the diversity in lower-level content that comprises the higher-level phenomenon. If the content of the phenomenon or construct domain is similar when one looks across the lower-level contributors within a unit, emergence is isomorphic. If the content of the phenomenon or construct domain is different when one looks across the lower-level contributors within a unit, emergence is discontinuous. A second distinguishing feature is the combination rule. Combination rules for isomorphic phenomena are generally based on additive or averaging models that combine similar content contributions. Combination rules for discontinuous phenomena are more complex, entailing the combination of the different content via distributive, disjunctive, conjunctive, multiplicative, or other configural models (Kozlowski & Klein, Chapter One, this volume).

An example may help illustrate the differences between composition and compilation forms of emergence. Job performance is a focal criterion for training. This outcome is conceptualized at the individual level but is presumed to be the foundation for higher-level organizational outcomes. This is a complex construct or, more correctly, construct domain. Job performance for a specific role is typically conceptualized as multidimensional, entailing many distinct constructs referencing different content areas. In addition, although we often talk about the "performance construct" as a universal of some sort, specific multidimensional performance constructs vary as a function of the job in question. Therefore, performance for a set of jobs is a domain composed of many specific constructs referencing different content; it is not a unitary construct.

Individual-level performance and team-level performance exhibit composition when their theoretical relationship is isomorphic—that is, when they involve essentially the same content and meaning. When team performance is based on a pooled form of coordination (Thompson, 1967), each member of the team contributes the same performance content to the group product. In other words, the same multidimensional constructs comprise performance at the individual and group levels. In a typing pool, for example, individual contributions are additive and compensatory (Steiner, 1972). Individuals may vary in their amounts of contribution, but the contributions are of the same content. The construct domains are isomorphic, and the combination rule (aggregation) of the composition model would specify the sum of individual contributions (Kozlowski & Salas, 1997).

Individual-level performance and team-level performance exhibit compilation when their theoretical relationship is discontinuous (Kozlowski et al., 1999). When team performance is based on reciprocal interdependencies (Thompson, 1967), each member of the team contributes different performance content to the team product. In other words, the set of multidimensional performance constructs is different across the individuals who make up the team. In a surgical team, for example, the individual performance contributions of the surgeon, the nurse, and the anesthesiologist are distinctively different, comprising different KSAs and different performance content. Moreover, in this example, the combination of the individual contributions to team performance is conjunctive (Steiner, 1972): a failure on the part of any one specialist will jeopardize the team's performance—and the patient's well-being. Therefore, the conceptual meaning of the job performance construct domain is similar across levels, but the content that constitutes the individual contributions is diverse, and the linkage of those contributions to the higher level is discontinuous rather than isomorphic. The combination rule would specify pooled minimum contributions or multiplicative relations (Kozlowski & Klein, Chapter One this volume). Yet, although the individual content that makes up team performance is diverse, the meaning of the domains as representations of performance, and their role in causal models at each level, are essentially analogous. In other words, individual and team performance are functionally equivalent though discontinuous.

Emergence: Implications for Training Research and Practice

What are the implications of these different forms of emergence for training effectiveness? Current models of training effectiveness, while cognizant of contextual influences, do not explicitly consider how individual learning and transfer link to the organizational objectives on which training is predicated. The implicit assumption regarding this link is essentially based on composition forms of emergence. It is assumed that individual transfer of trained skills will have an additive, cumulative aggregation that translates into higher-level outcomes. This assumption will yield effectiveness when composition is the appropriate model of vertical transfer. However, it will yield ineffectiveness when compilation is the appropriate model. We assert that compilation is frequently the appropriate model for vertical transfer. Therefore, the nature of vertical transfer emergence has implications for training needs assessment, design and delivery, and evaluation.

PROPOSITION 1: *Composition and compilation represent fundamentally different forms of vertical transfer that require appropriate alignments in training needs assessment, design and delivery, and evaluation.*

We contend that training-effectiveness theory and research must explicitly address vertical transfer as an emergent process. A failure to do so will impede efforts to demonstrate that training contributes to organizational effectiveness. Moreover, a failure to consider the form or type of vertical transfer is likely to lead to training that is inefficient or ineffective at higher levels. Trained skills or delivery systems that are not aligned with the vertical transfer process will not combine appropriately across individuals to emerge as group-level and higher-level outcomes. A failure to attend to the higher-level objective of training, and to map emergent combination rules onto that objective, is likely to lead to training that targets the wrong KSAs, the wrong individuals, or the wrong level. This will reduce the influence that training can have on higher-level organizational objectives.

PROPOSITION 2: *Training effectiveness will be enhanced to the extent that the training system is aligned with the form of vertical transfer as a composition or compilation process. Misalignments will yield inefficiency or ineffectiveness.*

We believe that training can play a central role in creating effective organizations. However, in order for training to play that crucial role, the nature of the contribution of training to organizational objectives must guide training activities. In the remainder of this chapter, we assume horizontal transfer so that we can focus on the implications of vertical transfer. From this perspective, our conceptualization of training effectiveness as an emergent *macro* phenomenon necessitates a reconceptualization of the classic training system: needs assessment, training design and delivery, and evaluation. For each of these activities, we elaborate the implications of our model by contrasting the assumptions of the composition process with those of the compilation process. We use examples to illustrate key distinctions between these different vertical transfer processes. Theoretical propositions with implications for each aspect of the training system—needs assessment, training design and delivery, and evaluation—are discussed in the relevant sections. The propositions are intended to highlight those issues most in need of further elaboration and research attention. Before presenting the implications of vertical transfer for training, however, it is necessary to discuss further how composition and compilation processes typically exist in organizations.

Background Assumptions: Vertical Transfer and Organizational Outcomes

It is typical in the world of work psychology to think in terms of jobs, and so the initial tendency may be to analyze the job in order to consider whether a process involves composition or compilation. However, that is not the appropriate focus. Instead, we argue that, depending on the outcomes involved, composition and compilation processes can exist simultaneously within the same individual, subteam, team, department, or organization. Therefore, we argue, it is essential to understand the nature of the outcomes desired by an organization to determine what type of vertical transfer is relevant.

Even the simplest organizations are multifaceted, seeking to accomplish several desired outcomes simultaneously. In fact, typical organizations desire to accomplish multiple outcomes that may be related to one another in complex ways. For example, a hospital seeks to maximize patient health while making an acceptable profit. Subordinate goals might include reducing administrative costs and keeping the facilities clean. Each of these outcomes, although they are all related, may actually represent a different kind of work process. For example, the outcome related to patient care involves compilation: a number of dissimilar processes (in terms of jobs, people, and skills) must combine in a complex configuration to accomplish this outcome. However, the outcome related to cleanliness may be better conceptualized as composition: many similar cleanliness behaviors may combine in a fairly straightforward, additive manner to accomplish the goal.

It is also important to note that both types of processes can exist not only within the same organization or subunit but also within the same job. To continue the hospital example, consider that a nurse might contribute certain behaviors that combine in a complex manner to support the health of patients, but in an additive way to facilitate cleanliness. Thus the same job contributes to outcomes that involve both composition and compilation processes. This fact has implications for the manner in which vertical transfer processes affect training.

PROPOSITION 3: *Organizational outcomes involve both composition and compilation processes of vertical transfer. For each outcome of interest, modeling and analysis are required to extract the precise nature and form as well as the associated vertical transfer processes.*

Given that the nature of organizational outcomes determines the type of vertical transfer, we propose that it is important to analyze outcomes so that the implications for training and other activities can be determined; that is, it is necessary to determine which types of vertical transfer processes exist for critical outcomes within an organization, and which jobs/roles are involved in accomplishing each of them. As a point of departure, the following questions are offered as a means to begin accomplishing this analysis. These questions are meant to stimulate thinking about the nature of higher-level outcomes; more formal multilevel outcome analysis procedures, discussed in subsequent sections, require further development.

- What is the nature and form of the organization's desired outcomes?
- Are the outcomes unidimensional or multidimensional?
- How can overall or aggregate outcomes be broken down into subordinate or component outcomes?
- Who (that is, which units, teams, and/or individuals) will contribute to the outcome?

- What is the nature of the contribution made by each unit, team, and/or individual?
- What is the nature of the process (in terms of tasks, jobs, and roles) that leads to outcomes?
- How do units combine to obtain desired outcomes? How is this process mapped? Is the nature of the combination simple (additive), suggesting a composition process, or more complex, suggesting a compilation process?
- Can relationships (dependencies) among outcomes be modeled conceptually? graphically?

Our contention is that by considering these questions, it will be possible to build a more complete understanding of the vertical transfer processes in an organization. This type of analysis can be used as a precursor to more traditional procedures for training needs analysis, which typically do not consider vertical transfer (Ostroff & Ford, 1989). With this background, we now turn to the needs assessment process and its relationship to vertical transfer.

Needs Assessment

The needs assessment process contains three major steps: organizational analysis, task and requirements analysis, and person analysis (Goldstein, 1993; Wexley & Latham, 1981). Organizational analysis focuses on organizational goals and resources and on whether training is the appropriate intervention to accomplish the objective. Task and requirements analysis is used to determine the nature of the task faced by trainees, as well as the required knowledge and skills to effectively perform that task. Person analysis is used to determine, on the basis of current knowledge and skills, which individuals need what parts of training.

Researchers have noted that these needs assessment procedures are insensitive to a number of critical levels-related issues (Ostroff & Ford, 1989), including linkages among training outcomes at different levels. More specifically, these procedures do not offer an explicit means to link higher-level objectives, goals, or outcomes (for example, bringing a product to market more quickly, raising the level of plant safety, or increasing customer satisfaction) to individual training needs. Articulating these linkages is essential to achieving training effectiveness as a multilevel process.

Composition

The traditional method of assessing training needs assumes that higher-level objectives can be achieved by improving individual-level KSAs and, consequently, improving individual-level outcomes such as performance, satisfaction, retention, and so on. This assumption will hold when vertical transfer occurs through a composition process so that individual and higher-level outcomes are isomorphic. Needs assessment can focus on the individual because vertical transfer will occur through a simple additive or averaged combination of individual-level outcomes.

To ensure that training is effective, task and requirements analysis should determine the knowledge and skills that are critical for improving individual-level outcomes. Person analysis should then be used to determine the proficiency of relevant organizational members and, consequently, who should receive what portions of training. Organizational analysis can be used to determine the context in which these individuals perform, so that training can be modified or supplemented with follow-up to increase the probability of horizontal transfer.

PROPOSITION 4: *Needs assessment for composition-based higher-level outcomes can rely on traditional individual-level techniques. Individual-level KSAs, behavior, and performance will compose (additively or on average) higher-level outcomes.*

An example of composition-based vertical transfer is offered by current work on customer satisfaction in the service industry. The assumption is that customer satisfaction is in large part derived from the individual-level service behaviors of employees, whether generated by individual characteristics (Anselmi & Zemanek, 1997) or facilitated by a positive climate for service (Schneider & Bowen, 1985). Research supports the existence of a causal link between server friendliness and the satisfaction of their customers. A study by Brown and Sulzer-Azaroff (1994) showed that bank tellers' greetings were positively related to customers' satisfaction with interactions. Furthermore, there is evidence that service training is related to service quality and customer satisfaction (Johnson, 1996; Schneider, Wheeler, & Cox, 1992). When global customer satisfaction is determined by the treatment customers receive from individual providers, individual-level service behavior will link to aggregate customer satisfaction.

Compilation

When vertical transfer is based on a compilation process, individual and higher-level outcomes are discontinuous. As a result, it is necessary to consider not only the nature of individual tasks but also the means by which individual outcomes combine to influence a higher-level objective. This suggests that task and requirements analysis must use both traditional individual-level analysis (primarily job analysis tools from selection) and higher-level tools, such as team task analysis. Team task analysis uses observation and assessment tools to understand the process by which groups create complex products or services, such as with flight operations for major airlines or medical surgery (Bowers, Baker, & Salas, 1994). Although considerable research has focused on individual task analysis (for example, Harvey, 1991), there is far less research on team task analysis (Cannon-Bowers & Salas, 1997).

PROPOSITION 5: *Needs assessment for compilation-based higher-level outcomes necessitates new techniques to map linkages of individual, dyadic, and team outcomes across levels. The contribution of individual KSAs, behaviors, and performance to work flow is the focus for a model of the compilation process.*

Consider the needs assessment process that is followed by the commercial airline industry to reduce human error in flight operations. After several reports that human error had played a critical role in aviation disasters, commercial airlines began investigating crew performance to determine what caused problems in crew coordination. This assessment involved detailed observation of individual positions and of coordinated crew behavior (Helmreich & Foushee, 1993). The result of this detailed analysis was a model explaining how interpersonal and technical skills combine to influence crew performance. Similar analyses have also been applied in other performance contexts (e.g., Bowers et al., 1994; Cannon-Bowers & Salas, 1998; Prince & Salas, 1993).

The goal of these efforts was to determine training needs for teams. Teamwork behaviors identified during this research were added to the training of individual technical skills in what became known as crew resource management (CRM) training (Weiner, Kanki, & Helmreich, 1993). An understanding of the crew's task, and of the process that led to the crew's performance, indicated that different skills and behaviors had to combine across positions in the cockpit. Effective crews had assertive members who voiced concerns, as well as pilots who accepted or even encouraged such communication (for a review, see Kanki & Palmer, 1993).

Research Implications

Research is needed to develop and evaluate methods for analyzing higher-level tasks. Current knowledge of team task analysis and other forms of higher-level task assessment is limited and leaves a great deal to be learned about the effectiveness of different approaches (Cannon-Bowers & Salas, 1997). Researchers are beginning to focus on this issue. For example, Levine and Baker (1991) have outlined a method for analyzing interdependent tasks; their method involves a series of procedural steps resulting in a task inventory. Similarly, Campion (1994) has developed a listing of teamwork-related skills that, he suggests, should be used in efforts aimed at teamwork job analysis. These approaches, however, focus primarily on the individual level.

There is also a significant literature addressing team performance (Fleishman & Zaccaro, 1992). Although this work is also focused on the individual level, it is more explicitly oriented to individual behaviors that are *directly linked* to team-level outcomes. In addition, there are techniques, better suited to the multilevel nature of compilation processes, that focus on the work-flow interdependencies among members of an integrated work unit. Many of these techniques are derivative of Thompson's model (1967) of work flow (e.g., Van De Ven, Delbecq, & Koenig, 1976). In a recent training application, this conceptual tool was used to characterize the task interdependencies among hospital employees (Tesluk, Mathieu, Zaccaro, & Marks, 1997). Examining team interdependencies in a nuclear power plant, Mathieu and Day (1997) have illustrated how an analysis of team functions could be linked with generalizability analysis as a method to diagnose within- and between-team processes. Coovert and Craiger (1997) suggest that petri net analysis, whereby each step of a process is mapped graphically, can be used to determine the knowledge and skill requirements of an interdependent task. Other approaches have suggested the use of network analysis to map dyadic role-to-role and team-level network configurations that are dynamic over time (Kozlowski et al., 1999). All these techniques entail methods for linking desired team-level outcomes to knowledge, skill, and performance requirements for individuals, including technical, task-related skills and the coordination behaviors that enable individual contributions to combine to yield team-level outcomes.

In our view, the various work-flow models represent prime research opportunities for developing and operationalizing compilation-based models of vertical transfer. Kozlowski and Klein (Chapter One, this volume) provide a typology of emergence that can be used to structure compilation models. Such models should be studied for their effectiveness in linking critical KSAs, behaviors, and performance indicators, as well as their combination rules, to higher-level outcomes. Research is also necessary to generalize techniques of team task analysis to higher-level units, departments, and organizations. In addition, the effectiveness of incorporating individual-level teamwork skill inventories into job analysis should be investigated. At the very least, these approaches provide a point of departure for the development of more sophisticated models of compilation.

Design and Delivery

The nature of vertical transfer as a composition or compilation process has implications for training design and delivery, which involve choices that trainers make regarding the learning environment and the instructional stimuli to which trainees are exposed. Design and delivery involve selecting appropriate media, learning principles, sequencing, training content, and participants to achieve training objectives (Goldstein, 1993; Baldwin & Ford, 1988), although there is little research guiding trainers to make choices that optimize learning and transfer. According to Goldstein (1993,

p. 225), "At a molar level, basic knowledge helps specify the appropriate technique for particular behaviors . . . unfortunately, there has been no advancement beyond molar generalities." As a result, practical considerations have tended to drive the way in which training is designed and delivered.

The concept of vertical transfer can provide guidance in making some of these decisions. For example, two choices that must be made about training are the target level of training and the sequence of delivery. The target level of training involves deciding whether training will be delivered to individuals or to intact groups. The sequence of training involves decisions about who gets trained on what, and when. The type of vertical transfer process (composition or compilation) is an important factor guiding what level of target and what sequence of activities will be effective in accomplishing higher-level outcomes (Kozlowski & Salas, 1997).

Composition

Training can focus on individuals as the target of training for composition-based outcomes because changes at the individual level have a simple, direct influence on higher-level outcomes. Composition-based outcomes do not require individuals to coordinate or combine capabilities in complex ways, and so group members can be trained individually. In fact, the training of intact work groups may require the use of additional resources (for example, trainers' time, materials, time off work, and so on), with no added benefit. Furthermore, the order in which the individuals are trained is not necessarily critical for composition-based outcomes. Because members work independently, the performance of one member may not influence the performance of other members. Therefore, the trainer can build the skills of unit members in whatever order is most practical or convenient.

PROPOSITION 6: *Training design and delivery for composition-based higher-level outcomes should focus on the individual level. It is not beneficial to train intact groups or teams.*

PROPOSITION 7: *Under composition, the sequence in which individuals are trained will not be critical to achieving higher-level outcomes.*

As an example of a composition-based outcome, consider sales performance for an insurance unit. There is a direct, additive influence from individual sales performance to unit performance. Across sales territories, the requisite sales skills are generally the same because each sales agent performs a similar job (e.g., Behrens & Halverson, 1991). Anything that improves the sales of one member improves unit sales. Training for such a unit should focus on similar content, such as interpersonal skills and intensity (Anselmi & Zemanek, 1997) and should focus on each sales agent individually. There is no inherent need to take everyone off his or her sales route at the same time for training; in fact, doing so may be impractical and detrimental to unit performance. Likewise, unit members can also be trained in any order without an adverse effect on other members. Because salespeople in this type of unit do not depend on one another for critical inputs, and because there is no need for skill integration, trainees do not have to wait until others are trained before applying their newly acquired skills. Other factors, such as performance, can determine the sequence of training. Assuming the problem is skill deficiency, training the lowest-performing members of a unit may be the most efficient use of training resources. Higher-performing members may gain less from training and, consequently, provide less gain with regard to the higher-level outcome.

Compilation

Compilation processes involve complex interactions among individuals and integration of their unique skills in order to bring about higher-level outcomes. Under compilation, training must focus not only on the individual but also on the fit and distinctive contribution of that individual to the higher-level outcome. Individuals must be trained on skills unique to their roles. Moreover, groups must also be trained to ensure the integration of essential skills. Practice as an intact unit in the performance context will likely be beneficial to enhancing vertical transfer (Kozlowski, 1998). The target of training for units in compilation situations is therefore both the individual (for task-specific skills) and the intact unit (for integration).

Training for intact work groups or teams requires more than just having team members practice together. Kozlowski, Gully, McHugh, Salas, and Cannon-Bowers (1996) have proposed a model of team development that discusses the importance of leadership roles for building successful teams. For composition outcomes, the leader serves primarily as a coach and as a source of motivation for individuals. However, for teams whose efforts result in compilation outcomes, the leader's role as trainer is more complex. Kozlowski and colleagues suggest that leaders need to sequence training and practice experiences to build individual competency, later shifting to skill integration for the team. The model describes how leaders or trainers need to sequence instructional content, the target level (individual versus team), and the nature of practice experiences (for example, mastery-oriented versus performance-oriented) as team members progress. Thus the nature and sequence of training and practice are important elements in helping leaders build coherent, adaptive, self-managing teams.

PROPOSITION 8: *For compilation-based outcomes, training design and delivery should focus on skill integration for achieving higher-level outcomes. This necessitates attention to the unique contribution of individual outcomes to team outcomes.*

PROPOSITION 9: *For compilation-based outcomes, the sequencing of training content and experiences is central to skill integration and vertical transfer.*

Consider an operating room (OR) team in which individual performance is determined by how well team members (anesthesiologist, surgical assistants, surgeon) execute their particular functions, but the team also has such outcomes as the length of the surgery and the success of the operation. Higher-level outcomes are achieved through compilation processes. Members must each perform effectively as individuals and must integrate their performance to attain the higher-level outcomes. By contrast with the results of composition outcomes, the results of compilation processes are not compensatory: if the surgeon and the surgical assistants do their jobs effectively but the anesthesiologist fails, the outcome is failure for the team.

From a training standpoint, each member must possess the requisite skills for his or her role in the team (the individual level), but team members must also learn to function together as a whole. Research using simulated anesthesiology crises in surgical OR teams, where the entire team is present, demonstrates that team members must be able to perform their particular roles and integrate their skills successfully. Botney and colleagues (Botney, Gaba, & Howard, 1993; Botney, Gaba, Howard, & Jump, 1993; Gaba, 1994) have found OR problems frequently to have been due to faulty interactions among team members and to faulty integration processes involving communication, workload management, and leadership problems. Critical mistakes have been made because of ambiguous commands and because people did not realize they were being addressed, anesthesiologists did not use nurses and surgeons as resources to help in patient management, surgeons were not informed of relevant problems, no one assumed command, decisions were made by committee in the absence of any attempt to unify the team's mental model, and less experienced personnel took over during crises from more experienced personnel. These findings are similar to those noted for aircrews (Orasanu, 1990) and other interdependent teams.

Training an intact team allows the members to identify skill-integration problems, learn the requirements and preferences of other members, reduce the amount of communication needed, and develop a common mental model, which in turn leads to anticipatory activity whereby members provide what is needed before or as the needs of other members arise (Kleinman & Serfaty, 1989). This contributes to effective team performance, particularly in emergencies (Kleinman & Serfaty, 1989; Orasanu, 1990). In a sample of thirty hospital emergency units, Argote (1989) found that agreement about norms within and across interacting groups was associated with better performance in terms of the promptness and quality of care. Therefore, emerging models of team performance emphasize the necessity of creating shared or compatible systems of knowledge at the team level, in addition to specific knowledge unique to differentiated roles (Kozlowski et al., 1996, 1999).

Research Implications

Research is needed in a number of areas to better inform trainers how to design training for composition and compilation outcomes.

We suggest that compilation outcomes may sometimes require individual skill training and sometimes training of intact units. Research is needed to determine how best to strike a balance between individual training and training of intact groups in order for training to be effective. Which skills are best learned individually, and which are best learned by an intact unit? When should training shift from a focus on the individual to a focus on the team? Some skills (such as teamwork skills) can be learned only if people work together as an intact unit, whereas other, more difficult or complex role-specific skills may best be learned individually. Compilation models of team performance that begin to address these issues have been proposed (Kozlowski et al., 1996, 1999), but little empirical research has been conducted so far.

In addition, research is needed to determine effective ways of delivering training to intact units. Merely training people together does not yield effective unit or team training. Training research must focus on how to foster unit outcomes by establishing roles and norms and creating common mental models. Some methods (such as cross-training, work simulations, and crew-coordination training) are being investigated and used in high-performance work environments (the military, the nuclear power industry, the field of anesthesiology), but it is important for researchers to refine these methods for application to more common work settings.

Furthermore, the range of design tools for group-level training should be expanded; that is, research is needed to find effective methods of training the people in a unit to work together to achieve compilation-based outcomes. Compilation creates pressure to push training out of the classroom and into the workplace because it places emphasis on context, work flow, and behavior integration—characteristics best realized in work settings or well-designed simulations. Research is needed to translate emerging theory into tools and techniques that enable leaders to be effective instructors (Kozlowski et al., 1996), use models of performance compilation to drive training design and developmental experiences (Kozlowski et al., 1999), and embed training and practice opportunities into the existing work context and process (Kozlowski, 1998; Kozlowski et al., in press).

Finally, compilation and composition processes may suggest different ways that individual skills should be trained. Anderson (1987) suggests that at the final stage of skill acquisition—automatization—performance is smooth and error-free, and few cognitive resources are required. However, once a skill has been automatized, it is difficult to alter its execution. Because composition-based outcomes do not require skill integration, it may be appropriate to train to the point of automaticity. Compilation-based outcomes, however, may necessitate a degree of flexibility or adaptability on the part of individuals; people may need to change their skill execution to integrate with others and adapt to dynamic conditions, and if they are trained to the point of automaticity, these changes may be difficult to make. This suggests that individuals trained for such a situation might be better off trained initially to the point of proceduralization, with people's skills automatized together at the group level. Research is needed to understand the degree to which this type of adaptability is needed for compilation and compo-sition outcomes, and to find other means by which adaptability can be trained (e.g., Kozlowski et al., in press; Smith, Ford, & Kozlowski, 1997).

Evaluation

The distinction between composition and compilation processes of vertical transfer has implications for training evaluation. Traditional training evaluation focuses on changes in the learner as a result of training (e.g., Kirkpatrick, 1974; Kraiger et al., 1993; Jonassen & Tessmer, 1996/1997), and horizontal transfer from the training to the performance context (e.g., Baldwin & Ford, 1988). We emphasize the importance and necessity of these preconditions, but we focus our attention on the evaluative implications of vertical transfer.

Vertical transfer addresses the issue of how individual-level outcomes are linked to higher-level outcomes. Higher-level outcomes may be regarded as a combination of what have been called "behavior and results criteria" in the evaluation framework of Kirkpatrick (1974). Kirkpatrick's concept of level III evaluation focuses on individuals' behavior in the organizational context. Level IV evaluation focuses on organizationally relevant results or outcomes.

Unfortunately, the framework does not address how individual behaviors are linked to organizational outcomes. Kirkpatrick states,
"There are so many complicating factors that it is extremely difficult, if not impossible, to evaluate certain kinds of programs in
terms of results" (1974, p. 18). A focus on vertical transfer offers a
means of understanding many of these complicating factors. Our
model of vertical transfer has several implications for training evaluation research, including attention to issues of measurement, research design, and statistical techniques.

Composition
For composition outcomes, the link between individual behavior
and higher-level outcomes is clear. When individual-level and higher-
level outcomes are isomorphic, evaluation efforts should focus on
changes in the individual. Averaged or additive unit aggregates provide a straightforward assessment of lower-level contributions to
higher-level outcomes. For the most part, this is consistent with conventional assumptions and models of training evaluation.

One new issue raised by a composition view of vertical transfer concerns a sensitivity to within-unit dispersion (e.g., Brown &
Kozlowski, 1997; Brown, Kozlowski, & Hattrup, 1996). Alliger &
Katzman (1997) suggest that dispersion of individual outcomes
should be studied, and they present a model that discusses how
dispersion can increase or decrease as a result of training. For
composition-based unit outcomes, changes in dispersion are critical. For example, safety training that raised mean levels of safety
behavior while also creating greater dispersion would probably
not be preferred over training that provided smaller mean increases in safety behavior and less dispersion.

The apparent paradox in the preceding example is due to a frequently neglected trade-off between central tendency and dispersion. In the example, dispersion might have a stronger impact on
the probability of an accident than the mean of safety behaviors.
Behavioral consistency or homogeneity should allow unit members
to anticipate one another's behavior, even where it may be "unsafe."
This may lead to fewer accidents than a situation in which the overall mean is higher but in which increased variance makes anticipa-
tion more difficult. An increase in accidents will result. Therefore,
reducing dispersion that results from unpredictable behavior may

be more important than raising the overall level of safety behavior. Ultimately, the nature of the training, along with its relationship to the higher-level outcome of interest, will determine the consequences of these trade-offs. Vertical transfer, as a composition process, necessitates evaluation designs that explicitly consider dispersion in addition to changes in means or additive aggregates.

PROPOSITION 10: *Vertical transfer as a composition process can model higher-level outcomes on the basis of mean or additive individual-level change. However, composition also necessitates explicit attention to outcome dispersion or variance, and to its implications for emergence of the higher-level outcome.*

A pooled work setting provides a situation in which to explore evaluation models for composition-based outcomes. Consider, for example, evaluation of a training intervention designed to enhance sewing proficiency in a sewing pool, such as those interventions studied by Deadrick and colleagues (Deadrick & Gardner, 1997; Deadrick & Madigan, 1990). The effects of training on factory output (that is, unit productivity) are entirely mediated by increases in individual-level performance; that is, unit performance is an aggregate of individual contributions. Therefore, evaluation should focus on the mean level of individual improvement. This focus is consistent with conventional evaluation models.

However, composition also necessitates explicit consideration of changes in the dispersion of individual sewing skill and output. For example, did organizational output increase through the incremental productivity of most members, or was it primarily due to large increases of a few members (which would also lead to an increase in dispersion)? This type of evaluation provides information regarding whether an organizationally relevant training objective was achieved, and it provides diagnostic information. Dispersion is an indication of the potential for enhancing the higher-level outcome. The key is to identify what factors are limiting some individual-level transfer, and to intervene. Thus dispersion indicates to what extent further improvements are possible by increasing the uniformity of individual contributions. Follow-up training interventions would try to push lagging individuals closer to the performance maximum.

Compilation

In compilation settings, the evaluation picture becomes more complex. The discontinuity of individual-level and higher-level outcomes means that individual outcomes can no longer be added or averaged to represent the higher-level unit. Different types of outcomes must be assessed across individuals, and the change in these skills must be modeled for their influence on higher-level outcomes; that is, evaluation of outcomes that form through compilation should include empirical validation of the content and combination rules that define vertical transfer.

There are both conceptual and statistical challenges to evaluating the link between individual-level and higher-level constructs when the higher-level construct is defined by compilation. Conceptually, compilation outcomes necessitate longer time frames than composition outcomes. Because compilation outcomes are created through the interactions and nonlinear configural combination of outcomes from individuals, the time frames needed for individual outcomes to unfold and for group outcomes to emerge are different (Indik, 1968; Simon, 1973). This, coupled with the fact that individual-level and higher-level outcomes are not isomorphic, indicates that it will be necessary to assess both individual-level and higher-level outcomes in order to develop and validate compilation models. In other words, an evaluation model will require an independent measure of the higher-level outcome in addition to individual-level outcomes. Once validated, however, such a model can be used to synthesize or predict higher-level outcomes from lower-level contributions.

Validation of the compilation model will require the following elements:

- A reliable measure of the higher-level outcome
- Measures of relevant individual-level outcomes, which will vary in content across individuals
- Models or equations that reflect the combination rules

The role of the researcher is to collect the appropriate measures and test whether hypothesized content and combination rules account for greater variance in higher-level outcomes than different content and/or simpler combination rules. Content and combination rules could be tested independently, but in practice this may prove difficult. Without the use of appropriate combination rules, the predictive efficiency of individual outcomes (content) may be underestimated.

PROPOSITION 11: *Under compilation-based vertical transfer, evaluation should focus on both individual-level and higher-level outcomes.*

PROPOSITION 12: *Under compilation-based vertical transfer, evaluation should explicitly model the content and combination rules presumed to determine higher-level outcomes.*

An example of evaluation for a compilation outcome is provided by product manufacturing, where the quality of outputs is a result of inputs and interactions among many people. Improving quality would require changing different skills across different employees, depending on how the worker interacts with or contributes to the final product. The nature of task-related training to improve the quality of work outcomes would differ according to the work performed. Assuming that training had been properly targeted and delivered, how could its effectiveness be gauged? An overall measure of product quality would be important to this process, but it would also be necessary to map individual contributions onto this outcome; that is, the real issue for evaluation of vertical transfer is to link individual changes in knowledge and skill to changes in product quality. Assuming that trainees learned quality-improvement skills and were able to apply them to their jobs with resulting improvements in work performance, evaluation of vertical transfer would require linking individual outcomes of work quality to end-product quality.

The ideal situation for studying this would be one in which there were not only multiple groups that had received different amounts or types of training but also quality indicators for products created by each group. This type of design would allow for a comparison of group quality that resulted from different types of training. Alternatively, a pre-post design could be used to study changes in each group's product quality after training. In either case, the researcher should control for differences in non–training-related influences (for example, age of machines, quality of input materials) on group-product quality and should model the effects of individual outcomes on group-level quality, using the content and combination rules unveiled in the analysis of vertical transfer. This type of analysis empirically validates the content and combination rules. More important, it also allows the researcher to understand the process by which training did or did not have its intended effects.

Research Implications

Composition and compilation models of vertical transfer entail very different assumptions regarding the linkage between individual-level and higher-level outcomes. Implications of these assumptions for composition relative to compilation, respectively, include the following issues:

- Measurement issues: individual versus individual and unit levels
- Time sampling in research designs: static versus time series
- Analysis issues: individual-level versus multilevel repeated measures, multilevel random-coefficient modeling (for example, hierarchical linear modeling, or HLM), and configural analysis techniques

Compilation-based higher-level outcomes necessitate assessments of individual-level and higher-level outcomes, whereas composition outcomes can be assessed at the individual level. Once a model of the compilation process is validated (see implications for needs assessment), it is possible to predict higher-level outcomes from lower-level data. However, initial efforts to construct such models will necessitate assessments of phenomena at both levels. In other words, independent measures at both levels are essential for validating compilation models.

Time is a critical factor to consider in the evaluation of compilation. The linkage of composition outcomes from the individual level to higher levels occurs in relatively shorter time frames. Therefore, evaluation designs can be relatively more static. The compilation of individual skills and behaviors into higher-level outcomes, however, is an emergent, developmental process (Kozlowski et al., 1999). Lower-level changes occur at faster rates, and they take time to emerge or link to the higher level (Kozlowski & Klein,

Chapter One, this volume). As a result, compilation outcomes are more likely to require longer time frames to manifest, necessitating longitudinal evaluation designs. This issue is critically important in determining the design and temporal sampling strategy for an evaluation study. Evaluation for compilation must incorporate appropriate time lags for the intervention to have effects at the higher level. Sampling must also be sensitive to critical phases in the compilation process, when phenomena may shift to higher levels. This necessitates a much stronger reliance on a theory of emergence for compilation outcomes (Kozlowski & Klein, Chapter One, this volume) and on explicit modeling of the combination rules for the higher-level outcome. Ultimately, research will be needed to understand the time lags that occur with different types of compilation outcomes.

Finally, research is needed to clarify how existing statistical techniques can be adapted to verify content and combination rules. Compilation models necessitate multilevel repeated-measures analyses, multilevel random-coefficient modeling (for example, HLM), and other techniques suited to analyzing nonlinear configural relationships (for example, multidimensional scaling, profile, and network analyses). Although these analytic techniques have the potential to be useful for capturing compilation processes, to our knowledge there are no direct applications to the kinds of phenomena described by our model. Therefore, basic research is needed to develop appropriate assessment and analytic methodologies for compilation processes.

Summary and Implications

The goal of this chapter is to expand and extend the perspective of training effectiveness in organizations. In particular, we argue that multilevel issues must become more central in theory and research if training is to contribute to organizational effectiveness. We contend that training effectiveness, with few exceptions, has been conceptualized and researched at the individual level, and yet training effectiveness is ultimately determined by the degree to which training contributes to strategic organizational objectives that manifest at higher levels. This makes training effectiveness an inherently multilevel phenomenon: it has roots at the individual level but implications that span multiple levels of the organizational system. This link—between individual-level training outcomes and emergent outcomes at higher levels in the organization—has been neglected. As a result, there is a levels gap between current models of training and the higher levels to which training must contribute if it is to be effective.

Our perspective is predicated on two fundamental principles, the first with implications for horizontal transfer and the second with implications for vertical transfer. First, training effectiveness is not isolated as a self-contained system; rather, training is embedded in a broader organizational context, and so models of training effectiveness must be sensitive to the multiple, top-down linkages that training has with that context, and to its implications for the effectiveness of horizontal transfer. Second, training effectiveness is not solely a micro phenomenon based on individual-level transfer, retention, and maintenance; rather, training effectiveness involves the linkage between micro training outcomes and macro objectives at higher organizational levels. Training effectiveness is also a bottom-up process that emerges vertically across levels. Therefore, multilevel issues related to both horizontal and vertical transfer must be considered in concert if training is to realize its potential impact on organizational effectiveness.

Horizontal Transfer: Multiple Influences of the Organizational Context

One focus of our multilevel perspective—that trained skills are acquired and transferred horizontally to the performance setting— addresses the ways in which the embedding organizational context can influence the effectiveness of training within a level. Because training is most often delivered at the individual level, this has constituted our focus. We have reviewed the relatively recent theory and research pertaining to contextual effects and their influence on processes related to horizontal transfer, identifying three types of effects (Kozlowski & Salas, 1997; Mathieu & Martineau, 1997). First, contextual factors can affect pretraining motivation; failure to learn requisite KSAs precludes training effectiveness. Second, contextual factors can moderate whether skills acquired during training are translated into new job behavior; learning in the absence of transfer precludes training effectiveness. Third, contextual factors can exert direct effects that facilitate retention and maintenance of trained KSAs in the job setting; early evidence of transfer in the absence of persistence precludes training effectiveness.

We argue that theory and research on the effects of contextual characteristics on training effectiveness are well enough developed to offer a basis from which principles can be derived. By *principles* we mean established issues that are grounded in theory and have empirical support. Therefore, they should guide state-of-the-art training research and practice. For example, researchers and practitioners need to specify important contextual factors as well as the types of effects that those contextual factors will have on training—direct effects on pretraining motivation or posttraining transfer, or moderating effects on the training-to-transfer linkage. Moreover, researchers need to shift from examining basic questions (Does the context influence training effectiveness?) to a more precise mapping of contextual influences. There needs to be more precise treatment of constructs. Transfer climates and content-specific or strategically focused climates are not the same. There is evidence that they have independent influences, and we think they have the potential to exhibit different types of linkages. Finally, future research in this area needs to be more sensitive to the demands that levels issues place on research designs and analyses (Kozlowski & Klein, Chapter One, this volume). We believe there is a solid foundation to begin developing better-elaborated, more integrated, and more rigorous models of contextual influences on the effectiveness of horizontal transfer.

Vertical Transfer: Emergent Outcomes

In our explication of the processes of vertical transfer, we have addressed the linkage between training outcomes at the individual level and emergent outcomes at higher organizational levels. It is important to recognize that vertical transfer processes are outcome-focused rather than job-focused; that is, the form of emergence for a particular outcome drives the process. Jobs make contributions to higher-level outcomes that entail both composition and compilation forms of emergence. Therefore, vertical transfer is targeted on outcomes, not on jobs.

· We contrasted two different forms of emergence: composition (based on the combination of similar contributions across trained individuals) and compilation (based on the combination of dissimilar contributions to the whole; see Kozlowski & Klein, Chapter One, this volume). These two different forms of emergence were then used to pose theoretical propositions for vertical transfer. By *propositions* we mean theoretically based assertions that are in need of empirical confirmation. Where principles are established guidelines, propositions provide new avenues for research and the development of formal models to guide practice. Implications of both forms of vertical transfer were posited for needs assessment, training design/delivery, and evaluation. In this regard, compilation outcomes provide the greatest challenges for training research and practice.

Compilation forms of vertical transfer have several implications for training needs assessment. The primary concern is one of mapping the links among individual, dyadic, team, and more macro outcomes across levels. Efforts to develop techniques and methods for conducting such mapping models are in their infancy. We have identified several promising approaches targeted at the individual level, including team task inventories (Levine & Baker, 1991), teamwork KSAs (Campion, 1994), and team performance dimensions (Fleishman & Zaccaro, 1992). Team-level approaches focus on work flows, including task interdependencies (Tesluk et al., 1997), petri nets (Coovert & Craiger, 1997), and network configurations (Kozlowski et al., 1999). These and other new techniques need continued development and refinement to supplement more traditional approaches to training needs assessment.

Compilation forms of vertical transfer have several implications for training design and delivery. Here, the primary concern is the need to accomplish individual-level and unit-level skill integration (Kozlowski, 1998; Kozlowski & Salas, 1997): What skills are delivered to individuals? to intact units? What is the sequence of training content and experiences across units? The need, inherent in compilation, for complex forms of skill integration creates an impetus to push training out of the classroom and into the workplace. Research is needed to translate recent theory into techniques and methods enabling leaders to be effective instructors (Kozlowski et al., 1996), to use models of performance compilation in driving training design and developmental experiences (Kozlowski et al., 1999), and to embed training and practice opportunities in work technology and processes (Kozlowski, 1998; Kozlowski et al., in press).

Compilation forms of vertical transfer have several implications for training evaluation. A primary concern is the need to explicitly validate well-specified models linking individual-level outcomes to higher-level outcomes. This has implications for measurement, research design, and analysis. Measures of individual-level and higher-level outcomes are needed initially to validate compilation models. Validated combination rules will allow applications to predict higher-level effects from lower-level measures. Compilation forms of emergence unfold over time, necessitating longitudinal evaluation designs and the adaptation of sophisticated multilevel analytic systems. This area represents a challenging frontier for the development of new techniques for multilevel measurement and analysis.

Conclusion

Many challenges—to theory, research, and practice—are inherent in our multilevel approach to training effectiveness. However, we believe that this broadening of perspective will enhance the ability of training to play a more central role in organizational strategy and in the meeting of critical organizational objectives. This is clearly where the field of training and development is headed (e.g., Jackson & Schuler, 1990; Schuler & Jackson, 1987). Our field needs to provide the foundation of theory, empirical validation, and applications for supporting this enhanced role of training in organizational effectiveness.

The primary contribution of our framework is its effort to articulate models for the implicitly assumed linkage between individual-level skills, behavior, and performance and higher-level organizational outcomes. Indeed, the conceptual issues we address, although focused on training, are relevant to the link between all human resource interventions (selection, performance assessment and management, reward systems, and so on) and organizational effectiveness. There is a research base indicating that training contributes to individual effectiveness. There is also more recent research indicating a link between human resource policies (such as training) and organizational effectiveness (Huselid, 1995; Huselid, Jackson, & Schuler, 1997). Our framework represents a point of departure for the development of theoretical detail that is missing from work like Huselid's, which shows links between human resources policy and organizational effectiveness but does not address the foundation, explanation, or means by which effects occur. Our model begins to lay that missing conceptual foundation. We emphasize the need for a well-developed and well-aligned organizational infrastructure (context) that supports the training system. This enhances horizontal transfer. Vertical transfer focuses attention on the micro-to-macro link. It makes salient the need to consider how individuals contribute to organizational outcomes, the need to model how those contributions combine, and the need to apply that knowledge to the development of an integrated training system—a system predicated on influencing organizational effectiveness. For us, that is the essence of training effectiveness.

Note
1. We also acknowledge higher-level phenomena of group and organizational learning, but we agree with others—e.g., Rousseau, 1985—that these higher-level manifestations are different and complex phenomena, and they are beyond the scope of this chapter. We will not address links among individual, group, and organizational learning in this chapter; that would be another chapter.

References
Alliger, G. M., & Janak, E. A. (1989). Kirkpatrick's levels of training criteria: Thirty years later. *Personnel Psychology, 42,* 331–342.

Alliger, G. M., & Katzman, S. (1997). Reconsidering training evaluation: Heterogeneity of variances as a training effect. In J. K. Ford & Associates (Eds.), *Improving training effectiveness in work organizations* (pp. 223–246). Mahwah, NJ: Erlbaum.

Anderson, J. R. (1987). Skill acquisition: Compilation of weak-method problem solutions. *Psychological Review, 94,* 129–210.

Anselmi, K., & Zemanek, J. E. (1997). Relationship selling: How personal characteristics of salespeople affect buyer satisfaction. *Journal of Social Behavior and Personality, 12,* 539–550.

Argote, L. (1989). Agreement about norms and work-unit effectiveness: Evidence from the field. *Basic and Applied Social Psychology, 10,* 131–140.

Baldwin, T. T., & Ford, J. K. (1988). Transfer of training: A review and directions for future research. *Personnel Psychology, 41,* 63–105.

Baldwin, T. T., & Magjuka, R. J. (1997). Organizational context and training effectiveness. In J. K. Ford, S.W.J. Kozlowski, K. Kraiger, E. Salas, & M. Teachout (Eds.), *Improving training effectiveness in work organizations* (pp. 99–128). Mahwah, NJ: Erlbaum.

Bassi, L. J., & Van Buren, M. E. (1998). *The 1998 ASTD state of the industry report.* [http://www.astd.org]

Baumgartel, H., & Jeanpierre, F. (1972). Applying new knowledge in the back-home setting: A study of Indian managers' adoptive efforts. *Journal of Applied Behavioral Science, 8,* 674–694.

Baumgartel, H. J., Reynolds, M.J.I., & Pathan, R. Z. (1984). How personality and organizational climate variables moderate the effectiveness of management development programmes: A review and some recent research findings. *Management and Labour Studies, 9,* 1–16.

Behrens, G. M., & Halverson, R. R. (1991). Predicting successful territory sales performance. *Journal of Business and Psychology, 6,* 273–277.

Botney, R., Gaba, D. M., & Howard, S. (1993). Anesthesiologist performance during a simulated loss of pipeline oxygen. *Anesthesiology, 79,* A11118.

Botney, R., Gaba, D. M., Howard, S., & Jump, B. (1993). The role of fixation error in preventing the detection and correction of a simulated volatile anesthetic overdose. *Anesthesiology, 79,* A11115.

Bowers, C. A., Baker, D. P., & Salas, E. (1994). Measuring the importance of teamwork: The reliability and validity of job/task analysis indices for team-training designs. *Military Psychology, 6,* 205–214.

Brown, C. S., & Sulzer-Azaroff, B. (1994). An assessment of the relationship between customer satisfaction and service friendliness. *Journal of Organizational Behavior Management, 14,* 55–75.

Brown, K. G., & Kozlowski, S.W.J. (1997). *Dispersion theory: A framework for emergent organizational phenomena.* Unpublished paper, Department of Psychology, Michigan State University.

Brown, K. G., Kozlowski, S.W.J., & Hattrup, K. (1996, August). *Theory, issues, and recommendations in conceptualizing agreement as a construct in organizational research: The search for consensus regarding consensus.* Paper presented at the annual convention of the Academy of Management Association, Cincinnati, OH.

Campbell, J. P. (1988). Training design for performance improvement. In J. P. Campbell, R. J. Campbell, & Associates, *Productivity in organizations* (pp. 177–215). San Francisco: Jossey-Bass.

Campbell, J. P. (1989). The agenda for theory and research. In I. L. Goldstein (Ed.), *Training and development in organizations* (pp. 469–486). San Francisco: Jossey-Bass.

Campion, M. A. (1994). Job analysis for the future. In M. G. Rumsey, C. B. Walker, & J. H. Harris (Eds.), *Personnel selection and classification* (pp. 1–12). Mahwah, NJ: Erlbaum.

Cannon-Bowers, J. A., & Salas, E. (1997). A framework for developing team performance measures in training. In M. Brannick, E. Salas, & C. Prince (Eds.), *Team performance, assessment, and measurement: Theory, methods, and applications* (pp. 45–62). Mahwah, NJ: Erlbaum.

Cannon-Bowers, J. A., & Salas, E. (1998). *Decision making under stress: Implications for training and simulation.* Washington, DC: APA Books.

Cannon-Bowers, J. A., Salas, E., Tannenbaum, S. I., & Mathieu, J. E. (1995). Toward theoretically based principles of training effectiveness: A model and initial empirical investigation. *Military Psychology, 7,* 141–164.

Coovert, M., & Craiger, J. P. (1997). Performance modeling for training effectiveness. In J. K. Ford, S.W.J. Kozlowski, K. Kraiger, E. Salas, & M. Teachout (Eds.), *Improving training effectiveness in work organizations* (pp. 47–72). Mahwah, NJ: Erlbaum.

Deadrick, D. L., & Gardner, D. G. (1997). Distributional ratings of performance levels and variability. *Group and Organization Management, 22,* 317–342.

Deadrick, D. L., & Madigan, R. M. (1990). Dynamic criteria revisited: A longitudinal study of performance stability and predictive validity. *Personnel Psychology, 43,* 717–744.

Fleishman, E. (1953). Leadership climate, human relations training, and supervisory behavior. *Personnel Psychology, 6,* 205–222.

Fleishman, E. A., & Zaccaro, S. J. (1992). Toward a taxonomy of team performance functions. In R. W. Swezey & E. Salas (Eds.), *Teams: Their training and performance* (pp. 31–56). Norwood, NJ: Ablex.

Ford, J. K., Quiñones, M. A., Sego, D. J., & Sorra, J. S. (1992). Factors affecting the opportunity to perform trained tasks on the job. *Personnel Psychology, 45,* 511–527.

Gaba, D. M. (1994). Human error in dynamic medical domains. In M. S. Bogner (Ed.), *Human error in medicine* (pp. 197–221). Mahwah, NJ: Erlbaum.

Goldstein, I. L. (1993). *Training in organizations: Needs assessment, development, and evaluation.* Pacific Grove, CA: Brooks/Cole.

Harvey, R. J. (1991). Job analysis. In M. D. Dunnette & L. M. Hough (Eds.), *Handbook of industrial and organizational psychology* (Vol. 1, 2nd ed., pp. 71–163). Palo Alto, CA: Consulting Psychologists Press.

Helmreich, R., & Foushee, H. C. (1993). Why crew resource management? Empirical and theoretical bases of human factors in aviation. In E. L. Weiner, B. Kanki, & R. Helmreich (Eds.) *Cockpit resource management* (pp. 3–45). Orlando, FL: Academic Press.

Hicks, W. D., and Klimoski, R. J. (1987). Entry into training programs and its effects on training outcomes: A field experiment. *Academy of Management Journal, 30,* 542–552.

House, R., Rousseau, D. M., & Thomas-Hunt, M. (1995). The meso paradigm: A framework for the integration of micro and macro organizational behavior. In L. L. Cummings & B. M. Staw (Eds.), *Research in organizational behavior* (Vol. 16, pp. 71–114). Greenwich, CT: JAI Press.

Huczynski, A. A., & Lewis, J. W. (1980). An empirical study into the learning transfer process in management training. *Journal of Management Studies, 17,* 227–240.

Huselid, M. A. (1995). The impact of human resource management practices on turnover, productivity, and corporate financial performance. *Academy of Management Journal, 38,* 635–672.

Huselid, M. A., Jackson, S. E., & Schuler, R. S. (1997). Technical and strategic human resource management effectiveness as determinants of firm performance. *Academy of Management Journal, 40,* 171–188.

Indik, B. P. (1968). The scope of the problem and some suggestions toward a solution. In B. P. Indik & F. K. Berren (Eds.), *People, groups, and organizations* (pp. 3–30). New York: Teachers College Press.

Jackson, S. E., & Schuler, R. S. (1990). Human resource planning: Challenges for industrial/organizational psychologists. *American Psychologist, 45,* 223–239.

Johnson, J. W. (1996). Linking employee perceptions of service climate to customer satisfaction. *Personnel Psychology, 49,* 831–851.

Jonassen, D., & Tessmer, D. (1996/1997). An outcomes-based taxonomy for instructional systems design, evaluation, and research. *Training Research Journal, 2,* 11–46.

Kanki, B., & Palmer, M. T. (1993). Communication and crew resource management. In E. L. Weiner, B. Kanki, & R. Helmreich (Eds.) *Cockpit resource management* (pp. 99–136). Orlando, FL: Academic Press.

Kirkpatrick, D. L. (1974). Evaluation of training. In R. L. Craig (Ed.), *Training and development handbook* (2nd ed., Chapter 18). New York: McGraw-Hill.

Kleinman, D. L., & Serfaty, D. (1989). Team performance assessment in distributed decision making. *Proceedings of the Symposium on Interactive Networked Simulation for Training.* Orlando: University of Central Florida.

Kozlowski, S.W.J. (1998). Training and developing adaptive teams: Theory, principles, and research. In J. A. Cannon-Bowers & E. Salas

(Eds.), *Decision making under stress: Implications for training and simulation* (pp. 115–153). Washington, DC: APA Books.

Kozlowski, S.W.J., & Farr, J. L. (1988). An integrative model of updating and performance. *Human Performance, 1,* 5–29.

Kozlowski, S.W.J., Gully, S. M., McHugh, P. P., Salas, E., & Cannon-Bowers, J. A. (1996). A dynamic theory of leadership and team effectiveness: Developmental and task-contingent leader roles. In G. R. Ferris (Ed.), *Research in personnel and human resource management* (Vol. 14, pp. 253–305). Greenwich, CT: JAI Press.

Kozlowski, S.W.J., Gully, S. M., Nason, E. R., & Smith, E. M. (1999). Team compilation: Development, performance, and effectiveness across levels and time. In D. R. Ilgen & E. D. Pulakos (Eds.), *The changing nature of work performance: Implications for staffing, personnel actions, and development* (pp. 240–292). San Francisco: Jossey-Bass.

Kozlowski, S.W.J., & Hults, B. M. (1987). An exploration of climates for technical updating and performance. *Personnel Psychology, 40,* 539–563.

Kozlowski, S.W.J., & Klein, K. J. (2000). A multilevel approach to theory and research in organizations: Contextual, temporal, and emergent processes. In K. J. Klein & S.W.J. Kozlowski (Eds.), *Multilevel theory, research, and methods in organizations* (pp. 3–90). San Francisco: Jossey-Bass.

Kozlowski, S.W.J., & Salas, E. (1997). An organizational systems approach for the implementation and transfer of training. In J. K. Ford, S.W.J. Kozlowski, K. Kraiger, E. Salas, & M. Teachout (Eds.), *Improving training effectiveness in work organizations* (pp. 247–287). Mahwah, NJ: Erlbaum.

Kozlowski, S.W.J., Toney, R. J., Mullins, M. E., Weissbein, D. A., Brown, K. G., & Bell, B. S. (in press). Developing adaptability: A theory for the design of integrated-embedded training systems. In E. Salas (Ed.), *Human/technology interaction in complex systems* (Vol. 10). Greenwich, CT: JAI Press.

Kraiger, K., Ford, J. K., & Salas, E. (1993). Application of cognitive, skill-based, and affective theories of learning outcomes to new methods of training evaluation. *Journal of Applied Psychology, 78,* 311–328.

Levine, E. L., & Baker, C. V. (1991, April). *Team task analysis: A procedural guide and test of the methodology.* Paper presented at the sixth annual conference of the Society for Industrial and Organizational Psychology, St. Louis, MO.

Mathieu, J. E., & Day, D. V. (1997). Assessing processes within and between organizational teams: A nuclear power plant example. In M. Brannick, E. Salas, & C. Prince (Eds.), *Team performance, assessment, and measurement: Theory, methods, and applications* (pp. 173–195). Mahwah, NJ: Erlbaum.

Mathieu, J. E., & Martineau, J. W. (1997). Individual and situational influences on training motivation. In J. K. Ford, S.W.J. Kozlowski, K. Kraiger, E. Salas, & M. Teachout (Eds.), *Improving training effectiveness in work organizations* (pp. 193–222). Mahwah, NJ: Erlbaum.

Mathieu, J. E., Martineau, J. W., & Tannenbaum, S. I. (1993). Individual and situational influences on the development of self-efficacy: Implications for training effectiveness. *Personnel Psychology, 46,* 125–147.

Mathieu, J. E., Tannenbaum, S. I., & Salas, E. (1992). Influences of individual and situational characteristics on measures of training effectiveness. *Academy of Management Journal, 35,* 828–847.

McGehee, W., & Thayer, P. W. (1961). *Training in business and industry.* New York: Wiley.

Noe, R. A. (1986). Trainees' attributes and attitudes: Neglected influences on training effectiveness. *Academy of Management Review, 11,* 736–749.

Noe, R. A., & Schmitt, N. (1986). The influence of trainee attitudes on training effectiveness: Test of a model. *Personnel Psychology, 39,* 497–523.

Noe, R. A., & Wilk, S. L. (1993). Investigation of factors that influence employees' participation in development activities. *Journal of Applied Psychology, 78,* 291–302.

Orasanu, J. (1990). *Shared mental models and crew performance.* Paper presented at 34th annual meeting of the Human Factors Society, Orlando, FL.

Ostroff, C., & Ford, J. K. (1989). Assessing training needs: Critical levels of analysis. In I. L. Goldstein (Ed.), *Training and development in organizations* (pp. 25–62). San Francisco: Jossey-Bass.

Peters, L. H., & O'Connor, E. J. (1980). Situational constraints and work outcomes: The influences of a frequently overlooked construct. *Academy of Management Review, 5,* 391–397.

Prince, C., & Salas, E. (1993). Training and research for teamwork in the military aircrew. In E. L. Weiner, B. Kanki, & R. Helmreich (Eds.) *Cockpit resource management* (pp. 337–366). Orlando, FL: Academic Press.

Quiñones, M. A. (1995). Pretraining context effects: Training assignment as feedback. *Journal of Applied Psychology, 80,* 226–238.

Quiñones, M. A. (1997). Contextual influences on training effectiveness. In M. A. Quiñones & A. Dudda (Eds.), *Training for a rapidly changing workplace: Application of psychological research* (pp. 177–199). Washington, DC: APA Books.

Rouiller, J. Z., & Goldstein, I. L. (1993). The relationship between organizational transfer climate and positive transfer of training. *Human Resource Development Quarterly, 4*, 377–390.

Rousseau, D. M. (1985). Issues of level in organizational research: Multilevel and cross-level perspectives. In L. L. Cummings & B. Staw (Eds.), *Research in organizational behavior* (Vol. 7, pp. 1–37). Greenwich, CT: JAI Press.

Salinger, R. D. (1973). *Disincentives to effective employee training and development.* Washington, DC: U.S. Civil Service Commission, Bureau of Training.

Schneider, B. (1981). Work climates: An interactionist perspective. In N. W. Feimer & E. S. Geller (Eds.), *Environmental psychology: Directions and perspectives* (pp. 106–128). New York: Praeger.

Schneider, B., & Bowen, D. E. (1985). Employee and customer perceptions of service in banks: Replication and extension. *Journal of Applied Psychology, 70*, 423–433.

Schneider, B., Wheeler, J. K, & Cox, J. F. (1992). A passion for service: Using content analysis to explicate service climate themes. *Journal of Applied Psychology, 77*, 705–716.

Schuler, R. S., & Jackson, S. E. (1987). Linking human resource practices with competitive strategies. *Academy of Management Executive, 1*, 207–219.

Simon, H. A. (1973). The organization of complex systems. In H. H. Pattee (Ed.), *Hierarchy theory* (pp. 1–27). New York: Braziller.

Smith, E. M., Ford, J. K., & Kozlowski, S.W.J. (1997). Building adaptive expertise: Implications for training design. In M. A. Quiñones & A. Dudda (Eds.), *Training for a rapidly changing workplace: Applications of psychological research* (pp. 89–118). Washington, DC: APA Books.

Steiner, I. D. (1972). *Group process and productivity.* Orlando, FL: Academic Press.

Tannenbaum, S. I., Mathieu, J. E., Salas, E., & Cannon-Bowers, J. A. (1991). Meeting trainees' expectations: The influence of training fulfillment on the development of commitment, self-efficacy, and motivation. *Journal of Applied Psychology, 76*, 759–769.

Tannenbaum, S. I., and Yukl, G. (1992). Training and development in work organizations. *Annual Review of Psychology, 43*, 474–483.

Terreberry, S. (1968). The evolution of organizational environments. *Administrative Science Quarterly, 12*, 590–613.

Tesluk, P. E., Farr, J. L., Mathieu, J. E., and Vance, R. J. (1995). Generalization of employee involvement training to the job setting: Individual and situational effects. *Personnel Psychology, 48*, 607–632.

Tesluk, P., Mathieu, J. E., Zaccaro, S. J., & Marks, M. (1997). Task and aggregation issues in the analysis and assessment of team performance. In M. Brannick, E. Salas, & C. Prince (Eds.), *Team performance, assessment, and measurement: Theory, methods, and applications* (pp. 197–224). Mahwah, NJ: Erlbaum.

Thompson, J. (1967). *Organizations in action: Social science bases of administrative theory.* New York: McGraw-Hill.

Tracey, J. B., Tannenbaum, S. I., & Kavanaugh, M. J. (1995). Applying trained skills to the job: The importance of the work environment. *Journal of Applied Psychology, 80,* 239–252.

Van De Ven, A. H., Delbecq, A. L., & Koenig, R. (1976). Determinants of coordination modes within organizations. *American Sociological Review, 41,* 322–338.

Weiner, E. L., Kanki, B., & Helmreich, R. (1993). *Cockpit resource management.* Orlando, FL: Academic Press.

Wexley, K. N., & Latham, G. P. (1981). *Developing and training human resources in organizations.* Glenview, IL: Scott, Foresman.

CHAPTER 5

Moving HR to a Higher Level
HR Practices and Organizational Effectiveness

Cheri Ostroff
David E. Bowen

Psychologists, sociologists, and organizational theorists have long recognized that multiple, interdependent levels in organizations exist and that understanding the interrelations within and between levels is critical to understanding organizations and organizational behavior (e.g., Klein, Danserau, & Hall, 1994; Roberts, Hulin, & Rousseau, 1978). However, research and theory have lagged behind this thinking. The past twenty-five years of research in organizational phenomena can be largely characterized by a split along the two extremes in the macro-micro continuum (Staw & Sutton, 1992; Schneider, Goldstein, & Smith, 1995). On the one hand, we have had a micro focus aimed at understanding such individual-level issues as ability, motivation, performance, and attitudes, often studied without regard to the organizational context in which these processes occur. On the other hand, we have had a macro focus aimed at understanding such organization-level phenomena as structure, strategy, culture, and effectiveness and the linkages among these factors, with little regard given to the human processes in organizations.

The dichotomy between micro and macro research and the need for integration from multiple levels and perspectives is particularly evident in the area of human resources (HR). For many years, researchers and practitioners have asserted that a key to organizational effectiveness is human resources (e.g., Gross & Etzioni, 1985; Levering, Moskowitz, & Katz, 1985; Likert, 1961; Mayo, 1933; McGregor, 1960). Attention to human resources and adherence to technically superior HR practices are believed to result in more productive, motivated, satisfied, and committed employees, who in turn promote a more effective firm. This assumption is based on multilevel issues. First, there is an underlying premise of a macro or organization-level linkage between HR practices and firm effectiveness. Second, there is an individual-level premise that HR practices influence individual behavior and attitudes in organizations. Third, there is an underlying cross-level and multilevel premise that there is a collective influence of individual attitudes and behaviors on organizational effectiveness. Yet a multilevel perspective has not been applied to understanding linkages between HR and firm effectiveness.

Traditional research in HR has been conducted through the gathering of data from individuals, often within a single firm, and the examination of relationships to individual-level performance, behavior, and attitudes in organizations. On the basis of these individual-level results, organization-level inferences about firm performance have been offered. It is not clear that results gleaned from studies of individual differences translate into organizational effectiveness. In recent years, a few studies have adopted an organization-level approach, empirically testing linkages between HR practices and firm performance (e.g., Arthur, 1992; Huselid, 1995; Ichniowski, Shaw, & Prennushi, 1997; MacDuffie, 1995). Other researchers have adopted a multilevel approach, examining linkages between the collective influence of individual attitudes and behavior and their relationships to measures of firm effectiveness (e.g., Ostroff, 1992; Ryan, Schmit, & Johnson, 1996; Schneider & Bowen, 1985) and between HR attributes at the job level and individual behavior and attitudes (e.g., Tsui, Pearce, Porter, & Tripoli, 1997). The growing body of evidence from individual-level, organization-level, and multilevel approaches begins to support some of the implicit linkages between HR practices, employee attitudes and behaviors, and organizational performance. What is needed is a guiding theoretical framework that builds linkages among HR practices, employee characteristics, and effectiveness across multiple levels.

Our goal is to integrate the three primary streams of research—individual-level, organization-level, and cross- or multilevel approaches—into a cohesive multilevel framework. We propose a meso paradigm (House, Rousseau, & Thomas-Hunt, 1995) for understanding linkages between HR practices and firm performance. Meso theory and research concern the simultaneous study of organizational and individual- or group-level processes and delineate the processes by which the levels are related in the form of linking mechanisms. Both micro-level and macro-level variables are needed to theoretically explain and account for the relationship between HR practices and organizational performance. Like others (e.g., Heneman, Schwab, Fossum, & Dyer, 1989; Huselid, 1995; Ichniowski, Kochan, Levine, Olson, & Strauss, 1996), we adopt the perspective that HR practices have their impact through two primary means. First, HR practices shape the skills, attitudes, and behaviors of an organization's workforce, and these skills, attitudes, and behaviors in turn influence organizational performance. Second, HR practices can have a direct impact on firm performance by creating structural and operational efficiencies. Building on this notion, we explore how HR practices shape employee characteristics through organizational climate and normative contracts at the organizational level and through psychological climate and contracts at the individual level; that is, the set of HR practices fosters coordination and interactions among individuals by creating shared perceptions across individuals. We also argue that the type of climate and the system of HR practices must be aligned with each another and must be aligned with key organizational contextual variables, such as business strategy. Further, we adopt a multidimensional view whereby there are multiple configurations of HR practices that drive climates and contracts, multiple climates and contracts that guide the behaviors and attitudes of the workforce, and multiple dimensions of firm performance and effectiveness.

Current State of Research on HR Practices and Firm Performance

A number of theoretical treatises have addressed why HR practices matter for firm performance (e.g., Lado & Wilson, 1994; Ulrich, 1987; Ulrich & Lake, 1991; Wright, McMahan, & McWilliams, 1994). A firm's resource capability (a concept founded on the resource-based approach; see Barney, 1991) is believed to be directly linked to the skills, abilities, and attributes of the employees who comprise the firm's pool of human capital (Lado & Wilson, 1994; Wright et al., 1994). HR practices represent investments in human capital. These practices contribute to firm performance because such practices as selecting and training ensure that employees have the skills and abilities to perform activities required to achieve organizational goals. Further, such HR practices as rewards or incentives motivate employees to apply their skills and abilities and encourage employees to work harder and improve the work process. Therefore, HR practices increase the quality of the human capital pool and elicit valuable behaviors from employees, both of which lead to a condition whereby the firm has a unique combination of human capital that is not easily imitated by other firms and is more difficult to substitute for with other means, such as financial capital (Wright et al., 1994).

A growing number of studies have attempted to empirically test the relationship between HR practices and firm performance. This literature can be characterized by three basic approaches: a universalistic approach, a configural approach, and a contingency approach. Researchers adopting a universalistic approach test the notion that some HR practices are appropriate for all firms. For example, significant relationships to plant or firm performance have been found for training (Bartel, 1994; Russell, Terborg, & Powers, 1985), staffing practices (Terpstra & Rozell, 1993), compensation practices and systems (Abowd, 1990; Banker, Lee, Potter, & Srinivasan, 1996; Gerhart & Milkovich, 1990; Kruse, 1993), labor relations (Katz, Kochan, & Weber, 1985), teams (Banker, Field, Schroeder, & Sinha, 1996), and quality of work life (Katz, Kochan, & Gobeille, 1983). However, examining practices separately carries the implicit assumption that the effects of HR decisions are additive. And yet HR practices are interrelated and should interact or work together in achieving their effects; therefore, investigation of the effects of individual HR practices is incomplete, and erroneous conclusions may be drawn (Ichniowski et al., 1997). Research emphasizing a single "best" practice should not be interpreted to suggest that implementation of this practice will have a strategic impact on firm performance (Becker & Gerhart, 1996).

A second approach to examining HR-performance relationships has focused on combinations of sets of practices. Those adopting a configural approach focus on how the pattern of multiple HR practices is related to firm performance. The total effect of HR practices is not equal to the sum of the effects of the individual practices; rather, sets of mutually reinforcing practices offer performance advantages for firms (Delery & Doty, 1996; Dunlop & Weil, 1996; Ichniowski et al., 1997; MacDuffie, 1995; Milgrom & Roberts, 1995; Pil & MacDuffie, 1996).

Some researchers adopting a configural approach have attempted to identify the set of HR practices that is superior for all firms. Most work in this area has focused on high-involvement or high-performance work systems (Arthur, 1992; Huselid, 1995; Lawler, Mohrman, & Ledford, 1995; Pfeffer, 1994). In general, a system of high-performance work practices is founded on employee involvement, participation, and empowerment. HR practices supporting this system include teams, expanded job duties, employee ownership, performance-sensitive pay, and rewards based on unit performance. Studies investigating the degree to which firms use high-performance work systems have found positive relationships to productivity and financial performance (Huselid, 1995; Ichniowski et al., 1997; Lawler et al., 1995). However, a true configural approach to HR systems (Delery & Doty, 1996) requires the identification of unique patterns of practices that are believed to be maximally effective, rather than a focus on a single system. Multiple unique configurations can result in performance advantages (Doty & Glick, 1994). In some studies, high-performance work systems have been favorably compared to more traditional, control-oriented systems, which include tightly defined jobs, job-based pay, employee monitoring, supervisory appraisals of performance, and management's retention of decision making (Arthur, 1992; Dunlop & Weil, 1996; Ichniowski et al., 1997; MacDuffie, 1995; Youndt, Snell, Dean, & Lepak, 1996). Other researchers have delineated a wider range of different types of HR systems. For example, Delery and Doty (1996) examined three types of systems, and Ostroff (1995) identified five types of HR systems. In both cases, multiple systems were found to be effective under different conditions.

Finally, some researchers have adopted a contingency view of HR systems. The contingent view of HR presumes that the impact of HR systems or practices depends on key contextual features, such as strategy, technology, and environmental stability (e.g., Bowen &

Lawler, 1992; Delery & Doty, 1996; Dyer & Holder, 1988; Schuler & Jackson, 1995). Some recent evidence suggests that the effectiveness of different types of HR systems depends on firm size (Kelley, 1996), the type of customer-oriented information system (Dunlop & Weil, 1996), manufacturing policies and systems (MacDuffie, 1995; Pil & MacDuffie, 1996), top management philosophies about HR (Ostroff, 1995), and business strategy (MacDuffie, 1995; Youndt et al., 1996; Ostroff, 1995).

Little theory prescribes the sets of HR practices that are reinforcing and complementary (Ichniowski et al., 1996), and what theoretical work has been done is inconsistent in defining the HR practices that make up different types of HR systems. A variety of empirical methods have been employed to identify systems of HR practices, including cluster analysis, factor analysis, and combining (additively) a number of practices into a smaller number of indices. The result has been inconsistent delineation of which practices go together to represent different types of HR systems. Further, with the exception of Ostroff (1995), only a relatively small number of HR practices have been investigated out of the many available. To complicate matters further, there is little theoretical guidance pertaining to which contextual features are most critical for alignment with different HR systems.

An additional complication is that a variety of measures for examining organizational performance and effectiveness have been offered. For example, performance measures have included return on investment, return on equity, sales growth, market-book value, rate of new-product development, productivity, efficiency, quality results, customer satisfaction, efficiency, attainment of objectives, employee satisfaction, loyalty, and communication (Campbell, 1977; Lewin & Minton, 1986; Meyer & Gupta, 1994). One reason for the diversity of performance measures is the persistent finding that organizational effectiveness is multidimensional (Meyer & Gupta, 1994). Therefore, researchers and theorists have suggested that investigations of organizational performance should include multiple criteria (e.g., Cameron, 1986; Campbell, 1977; Meyer & Gupta, 1994).

Organizations operate in many domains and may perform well only in a limited number of them (Cameron, 1978). For example, the multiple-constituency perspective proposes that an organization is effective to the extent that it satisfies the interests of one or more constituencies (Tsui, 1990). This viewpoint implies that organizations must accommodate diverse interests and that, as a consequence, multiple performance measures should be expected (Meyer & Gupta, 1994). Further, there may be trade-offs between different performance dimensions (Mahoney, 1988). For example, an organization attempting to achieve operational efficiency to provide a low-cost product or service may develop problems with attention to customer service. Progression along one performance dimension may entail regression along another (Kopelman, Brief, & Guzzo, 1990). Given this multidimensional view of performance, different patterns or configurations among various organizational attributes should emerge as determinants of performance. If so, we expect different patterns of HR practices to be relevant to different measures of organizational effectiveness.

How, then, can we make sense of the relationship between HR practices and organizational effectiveness? An HR system is believed to be a complex set of practices designed to influence employees' skills, behavior, motivation, satisfaction, and commitment. These employee attributes are purported to be the mediating mechanism that links HR practices and firm performance. Unfortunately, empirical attempts to investigate relationships among HR practices, systems, and firm performance have largely ignored employee attributes. For a fuller understanding of these relationships, several issues must be addressed. Do collective employee attributes influence firm performance? If so, which attributes are most critical? How do individual attributes interact and accumulate to influence organizational effectiveness? How do HR practices shape these employee attributes?

A General Framework

Figure 5.1 places the construct of HR systems within a conceptual framework that drives our discussion of linkages between HR systems and firm performance. Starting in the upper left of the figure, general organizational theory holds that structural features of an organization should fit the demands of the environment and technology (e.g., Burns & Stalker, 1961; Galbraith, 1974; Lawrence & Lorsch, 1967). However, organizational design alone will not ensure

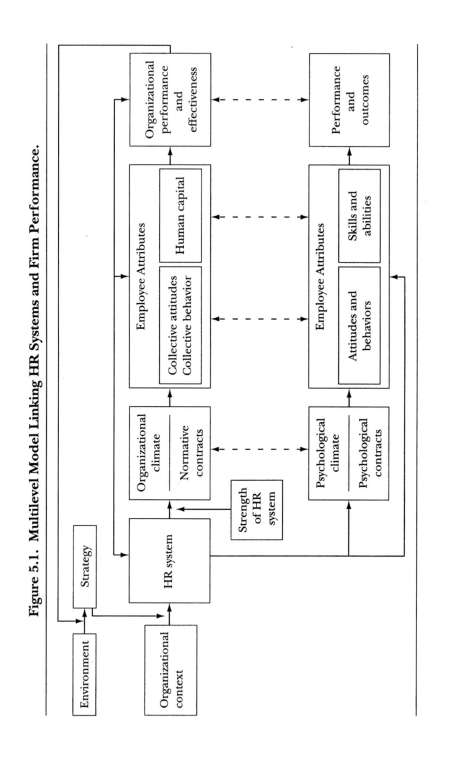

Figure 5.1. Multilevel Model Linking HR Systems and Firm Performance.

organizational effectiveness; the members of the organization must behave in a manner supportive of organizational goals (Angle & Perry, 1981). Employees who are satisfied, committed, and well adjusted will be more willing to work toward organizational objectives, hence promoting organizational performance (Ostroff, 1992; Likert 1961; Argyris, 1964; Kopelman et al., 1990). We focus on HR practices as a critical determinant in eliciting employees to behave in ways supportive of organizational goals. HR practices are the means through which employee perceptions, attitudes, and behavior are shaped (Wright et al., 1994).

At the organizational level, we propose that the HR system influences the organizational climate and normative contracts that shape human capital development (workforce skills and abilities) and collective attitudes and behaviors. These in turn influence organizational performance. Further, the HR system of an organization can have a direct impact on organizational performance by creating efficiencies through job structure and operational processes (Ichniowski et al., 1996).

How do organizational climate and normative contracts develop? HR practices shape individuals' perceptions of what the organization is like (psychological climate) and shape expectations about the exchange between employees and employers (psychological contract). When these are shared across employees within an organization, we have the emergence of organizational climate and normative contracts. The dashed arrows in Figure 5.1 indicate the multilevel nature of these constructs and symbolize how the organization-level constructs emerge from individual-level constructs. Further, we create a distinction between the content of the HR system (the specific practices used by a firm) and the process by which HR is enacted in the organization. Therefore, we also propose that shared climate perceptions and shared contract expectations will occur only when the process of the HR system is strong (for example, visible, clear, and internally consistent). A strong system communicates clear and direct signals to employees about norms, expectations, and what the organization is like. A weak system will result in more idiosyncratic perceptions within an organization, which will produce wide variability in perceptions of climate and contracts within an organization. This will subsequently result in wide variability in attitudes and human capital development within an organization, diminishing the relationship to organizational performance. Finally, we include a feedback loop to denote that this process linking HR to firm performance occurs over time.

We also note that there are reciprocal relationships between levels for the perceptual variables (climate and contracts) and employee attributes. Individual perceptions of the work environment are subject to contextual and social influences (Jones & James, 1979). Therefore, both individual-level climate and contract perceptions will be influenced in part by the existing organizational climate and normative contracts. Similarly, individual attitudes and behaviors will be influenced in part by collective attitudes and behaviors. It is important to note that we did not include all possible linkages, based on theory and research, between constructs in Figure 5.1; rather, our purpose was to highlight those relationships that are most critical for explaining relationships between the systems and firm performance from multiple levels of analysis. We begin by discussing what role HR plays in influencing the individual employee attributes (lower-middle box) as well as aspects of the work process. We then describe how individual effects translate into collective attitudes and behaviors and human capital (upper-middle box), which in turn affect organizational performance. Central to this discussion is a consideration of how the HR system has its effects on collective attitudes and behaviors, largely via organizational and psychological climates and contracts. We then describe the characteristics of a strong HR system and how it can moderate HR effects. Finally, we discuss what form these variables would assume in pursuit of different specific business strategies.

HR Effects on Individual Employee Attributes and Work Process

A key premise in meso theory is that organizations affect individual attitudes and behaviors (House et al., 1995). A number of studies have clearly demonstrated that features of the organizational context (for example, technology, structure, structural characteristics, size) affect individual behaviors, affective responses, motives, and attitudes (Newman, 1975; Kozlowski & Farr, 1988; Oldham & Hackman, 1981). We focus on HR practices and examine how they affect firm performance by influencing such employee attributes as motivation, attitudes, and abilities and by influencing job structure and work processes. An enormous amount of research has been devoted to examining impacts of HR practices on employee behavior and attitudes, particularly at the individual level. Rather than review the vast literature in this area, we highlight our views of the differential impact of HR practices on employees. In Table 5.1, for any given attitude or attitude we identify the HR practices that should have the most direct or salient impact on that outcome.

HR practices can have an impact on the collective knowledge and skills (human capital) of the firm. This effect can be brought about by attention to recruiting and selecting employees of high ability. Employee knowledge and skills can be developed through formal and informal training and development activities. Appraisals of performance, accompanied by developmental feedback, can aid skill acquisition and development. Expanding job duties through team structures and/or job enrichment requires employees to develop new sets of technical and interpersonal skills. Skill-based pay programs directly influence skill acquisition by rewarding employees for the skills they possess. Finally, firms with strong internal labor markets provide opportunities for career development and advancement.

Some HR practices can increase employees' identification with and commitment to the organization. For example, organization-based pay programs, such as employee stock option plans or profit sharing, tie employees' rewards to those of the firm, thereby increasing their identification with the firm. Internal labor markets can increase commitment as employees see potential for their own advancement and development. Firms that offer job security and attempt to minimize the threat of layoffs can encourage commitment because employees see the firm as taking care of them. Positive relations among diverse sets of employees and good relations between union and management can promote identification and commitment because employees can feel a sense of belonging and a lack of conflict.

Satisfaction of employees can be influenced by a wide variety of practices. In general, practices that provide employees with a positive work environment and that allow employees to have voice, participation, autonomy, and decision-making power are positive influences on satisfaction.

Table 5.1. Impact of HR Practices.

HR Practice	Knowledge and Skills	Identification/ Commitment	Satisfaction	Intrinsic Motivation	Reward Motivation	Citizenship Collaboration	Flexibility	Monitoring and Control
Recruiting and selectivity	X		X				X	
Training and development	X			X			X	
Job analysis: narrow jobs								X
Supervisory appraisal	X							X
360° appraisal	X					X		
Job-based pay					X	X		X
Merit-based pay					X			
Organization-based pay		X			X	X		
Unit-based pay					X	X		
Pay leader in market					X			
Contingent pay					X			
Skill-based pay	X			X	X		X	

Teams	X	X	X		
Job enrichment	X	X	X	X	
Empowerment and voice		X	X	X	
Participation in decision making		X	X		
Employee assistance/welfare	X	X			
Internal labor market	X	X	X		
Due process		X	X		X
Job security	X	X			
Contingent workforce				X	
Legal compliance					X
Promotion of diversity	X	X		X	
Union relations	X	X			X
Safety in workplace	X	X			X

Intrinsic motivation is influenced by opportunities for enjoyment and fulfillment at work and for gaining a sense of accomplishment from work itself. Such practices as training and development and use of skill-based pay, teams, job enrichment, empowerment, and participation should directly influence feelings of intrinsic motivation and personal achievement. Reward motivation is driven primarily through such reward systems as merit-based pay, organization-based pay, contingent pay, and advancement opportunities available within the company. Such practices can influence outcome expectancies for employees.

Citizenship behaviors and collaboration can be encouraged with pay programs based on unit and organizational performance and through the use of team structures. Such behaviors may also be encouraged when they are directly specified in appraisal systems.

The affective and motivation variables are interrelated. For example, satisfaction has been shown to be a consistent predictor of citizenship behaviors (Brief & Motowidlo, 1986; Organ, 1988). Further, satisfaction is related consistently to commitment and is negatively related to turnover and absenteeism (e.g., Tett & Meyer, 1993), which can signify lack of commitment and lack of identification with the organization.

In addition to influencing attributes, attitudes, motivation, and behaviors of employees, some HR practices can enhance the structural and operational aspects of the work, such as adaptability of the workforce and control of employee behaviors. These processes can improve operating efficiencies.

A flexible, adaptive workforce that can respond quickly to changing technologies, customer demands, or other organizational needs can be enhanced by selective hiring of employees who are flexible and innovative. Such practices as formal and informal training and development and use of teams, skill-based pay, and job enrichment encourage employees to possess a broader range of skills, and this promotes flexibility. Further, a diverse workforce can provide a broader range of opinions and ideas, and these can enhance the flexibility and adaptability of the organization. Such practices can make organizational structures more efficient. Organizations that rely on contingent workers, particularly for noncore jobs, may increase flexibility in that they have the ability to add or subtract from the organization more quickly and easily as different circumstances arise. Teams, empowerment, and participation in decision making can reduce the number of supervisors and middle managers required.

Finally, HR practices that monitor and control employee behavior can help standardize processes and work procedures and ensure that workers behave in job-related ways to promote achievement of organizational goals. For example, narrowly defined jobs, supervisory appraisals of performance, pay structures based on the job, due process and grievance procedures, legal compliance, and promotion of safe workplace practices all have components of monitoring or controlling how employees behave in the workplace. When employee behavior is controlled and standardized, operating efficiencies can emerge. Further, worker and union involvement in decision making can reduce grievances and conflict, thereby improving operating efficiencies (Ichniowski et al., 1996).

It is clear that HR practices can have a variety of impacts (see Table 5.1). We support the notion that HR practices have a direct impact on the knowledge and skills of employees, which in turn influence firm performance. Some practices promote flexibility in the workforce; others provide monitoring and control functions. Although these may have some impact on employee attitudes and behaviors, their most direct impact is on the creation of structural and operational processes that enhance firm performance. Finally, HR practices have an impact on attitudes, motivation, and citizenship. This impact is mediated through cognitive and perceptual processes of climate and contracts, which are elucidated in a later section of this chapter.

Collective Employee Attributes and Firm Performance

Employee attributes are believed to be a mediating mechanism linking HR practices and firm performance. A meso perspective includes the notion that individual-level processes affect organizations (House et al., 1995). The aggregate activities, attributes, and motives of individuals have important impacts on macro variables (Schneider, 1987; Staw & Sutton, 1992). We argue that three interrelated sets of employee attributes influence firm performance: collective attitudes (for example, satisfaction and identification) and motivation, collective behaviors (for example, citizenship behaviors and performance-related behaviors), and human capital (collective skills and abilities). Our model suggests that HR practices do not have a direct impact on collective attitudes and behaviors; rather, HR practices are perceptually filtered by employees. Employees interpret practices to determine what the organization is like and to define the nature of the mutual expectations between employer and employee. (This perceptual mediation is discussed in a later section.) Our model also suggests that HR practices can have a direct impact on human capital, independent of their effect through climate and contracts (discussed later).

Collective Attitudes and Behaviors

The notion that satisfaction, motivation, and employee attitudes are related to performance has intrigued organizational researchers for many years. At the individual level, relationships between individual attitudes and performance have been consistently weak (e.g., Iaffaldano & Muchinsky, 1985). However, collective attitudes may be more strongly related to firm performance (Ostroff, 1992; Schneider & Schmitt, 1986).

A few studies have addressed relationships between the collective influence of employee attributes and firm performance. Ostroff (1992) has demonstrated significant differences between organizations in collective attitudes (the average satisfaction and commitment across organizational members) and has found that relationships between aggregate satisfaction and commitment and various measures of organizational performance in nonprofit organizations are stronger than those typically found at the individual level. In addition, relationships between employee attitudes, organizational unit performance, customer satisfaction, and turnover have been demonstrated (Ryan et al., 1996). Commitment of employees has been related to turnover intentions at the organizational level but not to organizational efficiency (Angle & Perry, 1981). Employee satisfaction and attitudes have been related to perceptions of customer service (Schneider & Bowen, 1985).

Despite the paucity of empirical work on these relationships, it has been consistently theorized that satisfaction, motivation, and attitudes of employees are key factors in determining appropriate employee behavior and responses at work, which ultimately contribute to organizational effectiveness. A number of theorists (e.g., Likert, 1961; Mayo, 1933; McGregor, 1960) have suggested that organizational productivity is achieved through employee satisfaction and attention to workers' physical and emotional needs. The extent to which an employee will give his or her services wholeheartedly to the organization and perform up to potential largely depends on the way the worker feels about the job, fellow workers, and supervisors (Likert, 1961). Employee satisfaction and attitudes influence the development of routine patterns of interaction. Employees develop relationships at work through daily associations with others, and these patterns prescribe behavioral expectations and influence behaviors. Positive attitudes result in patterns that are directed toward achieving the organization's objectives (Roethlisberger, 1959).

The satisfaction, motivation, and well-being of employees can result in organizational effectiveness because they foster salient productivity-related behaviors. Three pertinent categories of behavior are performance, attachment, and citizenship (Kopelman et al., 1990). Performance behaviors include job-related tasks and activities comprising the employee's formal organizational role. Although performance behaviors can be largely influenced by skills and abilities (addressed more fully later), employees who are motivated and satisfied are more likely to work to their potential and use their skills and abilities in fulfilling job-related tasks. Attachment behaviors include attending to and staying in the organization. Conversely, lack of attachment results in turnover and absenteeism, which can be costly to the organization. Citizenship or prosocial behaviors include cooperation and collaborative effort. It is likely that any single occurrence of citizenship behavior has a modest or trivial impact (Organ, 1988); however, across multiple acts of citizenship from a single employee, and across multiple employees, the aggregate impact should be more substantial. Collaborative effort that is directed toward the organization's goals is necessary for achievement of the organization's objectives. Unhappy employees cannot effectively participate in such efforts (Likert, 1961; Roethlisberger, 1959), whereas satisfied employees will be more likely to engage in collaborative effort, attend to and stay in the organization, put forth effort in performing job-related tasks, and accept organizational goals. Dissatisfied employees may fail to work collaboratively or may work collaboratively but divert effort away from the achievement of the organization's goals (Ostroff, 1992).

The relationships among any one individual's satisfaction, attitudes, motives, and performance may be difficult to predict (Iaffaldano & Muchinsky, 1985). Lower performance is only one possible response to dissatisfaction. A dissatisfied employee could file a grievance, engage in sabotage, ask for a transfer, try to improve performance, or fail to pass on important information (Locke, 1984). In contrast, a satisfied employee could work harder, engage in more citizenship behaviors, improve skills, or make suggestions for improvements in work procedures. Although the relationship between individual-level attributes and performance may be weak, collective effects can be much stronger because of the cumulative impacts of the behaviors and responses of satisfied or dissatisfied employees in general (Ostroff, 1992).

Therefore, satisfaction and attitudes influence individuals' behaviors, which in turn influence organizational performance. Measures of organizational performance most likely reflect an interaction of salient employee behaviors and responses. That is, organizational performance is not a simple sum of individual or unit performance (Mahoney, 1988). Instead, because of interactions and dependencies in the work process, organizational performance can be more (in the case of positive collaboration and interactions) or less (in the case of negative collaboration) than the sum of the parts. For example, citizenship behaviors can be productivity-enhancing behaviors because they help maintain contributions of attachment and performance behaviors. Without such extrarole behaviors and cooperation, productivity would slowly deteriorate (Kopelman et al., 1990). Other studies have shown that such aggregate behaviors as unit-level absenteeism have effects independent of individual-level absenteeism (Mathieu & Kohler, 1990), indicating that cumulative responses create an additional effect. Therefore, measures of organizational effectiveness can reflect the cumulative responses and interactions among employees. It may be difficult to predict the relationship between any one individual's satisfaction or attitudes and that individual's behavior and performance, but organization-level relationships should be stronger because of cumulative interactions (Ostroff, 1992). From a levels perspective, this suggests a bottom-up process whereby individuals' attitudes and behaviors combine to emerge into a collective effect that is greater than the simple additive effect across individuals (Kozlowski & Klein, Chapter One, this volume).

Human Capital

As already noted, one of the key productivity-related behaviors of employees is performance. Although performance behaviors are a direct way in which employees can work toward achieving the organization's goals, employees must have the skills and competencies required to exhibit these behaviors (Wright et al., 1994). Therefore, in addition to collective attitudes and behavior, the collective knowledge, skills, and abilities of employees should influence firm performance.

Consistently positive findings have been demonstrated between skills or ability (particularly cognitive ability) and job performance at the individual level (e.g., Hunter & Hunter, 1984; Schmidt, Hunter, Pearlman, & Shane, 1979). At the collective level, the overall knowledge and skill level of employees is purported to relate to firm performance (Huselid, 1995; Ichniowski et al., 1996; Wright et al., 1994) but has not been directly tested. Some work on the relationship between training and organizational performance (e.g., Bartel, 1994) suggests that greater skill development of employees relates to better performance. Certainly, a great deal of attention, particularly in the practitioner literature and the popular press, has recently been devoted to the competitive advantages of creating a "learning" organization and developing the collective "brainpower" of the workforce (e.g., Senge, 1990).

Our model suggests that HR practices have a direct link to development of human capital. Higher levels of human capital can be achieved through such practices as recruiting, selection, performance appraisal, and training. These practices can have an impact on both general and firm-specific human capital. Higher-ability employees, or employees whose skill sets match the firm's needs, can be recruited and selected. After selection, new employees are observed and monitored. Supervisors can make posthire appraisals of the new employees' skills and learning capacity, evaluating the potential for enhanced productivity through future training and development. Only workers judged to possess higher ability are likely to be retained in the firm's workforce (Knoke & Kallenberg, 1996). Training and development may focus on developing general skills of employees, which are transportable to other types of jobs, or training and development opportunities can focus on developing firm-specific skills, which should increase the productivity of workers only within the firm that provides the training and development (Becker, 1964). Arguments have made for the importance of both types of human capital development in creating a competitive advantage for firms. Wright and colleagues (1994) propose that higher ability levels in general create value for the firm, are relatively rare, are difficult for other firms to imitate over time as the workforce is developed, and are not easily substituted for with other resources. For example, firms that have acquired and/or developed the general skill level of employees should have employees whose skills are transferable across a wide variety of technologies, products, and markets so that the firm can be more flexible and respond more quickly to changes. Similarly, productivity can be increased as a firm develops unique skills in its workforce that are not easily transferable to other firms. In addition to productivity increases, employees should remain with the firm longer, given that their skills are not easily portable to other firms (Becker, 1964). Although it is difficult to obtain distinct measures of firm-specific and general human capital (Knoke & Kallenberg, 1996), it is likely that a firm in which both general and specific skills of workers are developed will have better performance than a firm in which only general skills of workers are developed.

Relationships among attitudes, behaviors, and firm performance can be explained through two mechanisms: the social environment, and exchange relationships. Satisfaction and positive attitudes can be achieved through maintenance of a positive social environment, such as through good communication, participation, autonomy, and mutual trust (Argyris, 1964; Likert, 1961). HR practices create the social environment by fostering climates. Organizational climate influences attitudes and prescribes behavioral expectations, influencing behaviors in the direction of organizational objectives. Further, the attitude-performance relationship can be explained by a social exchange in which employees accorded some manner of social gift would experience satisfaction and feel an obligation to reciprocate, perhaps in the form of increased productivity (Organ, 1977). HR practices also foster psychologically based contracts (Rousseau, 1995).

HR Practices and Collective Perceptions

Theorists from the sociotechnical school of organizational theory (Emery & Trist, 1960) posit that organizational effectiveness depends on both the technical structure and the social structure of the organization. Some social and psychological structures may be superior to others, both for employee satisfaction and productivity. We propose that organizational climate and normative contracts are defining aspects of the social structure that link HR practices to human capital, collective attitudes and behaviors, and, subsequently, to organizational performance. With climate, employees develop a perception of what the organization is really like. With contracts, HR practices signal what is expected of employees and what employees can expect in return from the organization.

HR and Climate Across Levels

An important distinction has been made between *psychological climate* and *organizational climate* (James & Jones, 1974). Psychological climate is based on individuals' perceptions of aspects of the work environment and can be idiosyncratic; organizational climate is a shared or summary perception that people attach to particular features of the work setting (Schneider & Reichers, 1983). As noted by Schneider (1990), perceptions of what the organization is like, in terms of its routines, practices, procedures, and rewards, come from individuals. However, when individuals in the same focal unit or organization agree or share their perceptions, organizational climate emerges from individual perceptions. These climate perceptions shape employees' inferences about what the organization is like in terms of how the organization goes about its daily business and the goals that the organization pursues (Schneider, Brief, & Guzzo, 1996). Therefore, one way to view climate is as a molar concept that is indicative of the organization's goals and of the appropriate means of goal attainment (Reichers & Schneider, 1990).

The study of organizational climate over the years has increasingly moved from this molar, general perspective to a more strategic focus linking climate perceptions to a specific criterion of interest (for example, service or innovation; Schneider, 1990). Rather than treating climate as an abstract concept that includes everything that occurs in an organization, climate is treated as a strategic concept linking shared perceptions to a particular strategic goal. The research interest, from this strategic perspective, is to specify the routines, rewards, and so forth, that are related to a particular strategic focus. For example, if the organization espouses a service focus, to what extent do organization members perceive the organization to be enacting this focus? These climate perceptions give employees direction and orientation with respect to where they should focus their skills, attitudes, and behaviors (Schneider, Gunnarson, & Niles-Jolly, 1994). The strategic-focus perspective indicates that, in order to create the strategic climate of interest, all subsystems of an organization must be targeted effectively on the strategic goal (Schneider, 1990).

The practices of the HR subsystem represent a set of salient and universal practices that can form organizational climates. The HR practices create the foundation for particular types of climate to develop (Schneider, 1990). Further, climate is a cumulative construct. It suggests that an organization's practices and policies for a particular type of climate should be evaluated as a comprehensive, interdependent whole, and that they may be more predictive of organizational outcomes than a focus on the determinants of the climate would be. Particular climates of equal strength could ensue from different combinations of HR practices (Klein & Sorra, 1996). For example, to foster a learning orientation, one organization might focus largely on formal training, career development, and promotions, whereas another organization might focus on skill-based pay systems, developmental performance appraisal, and job enrichment. Studies of psychological climate have shown that individuals' perceptions of climate (psychological climate) affect their satisfaction and performance (e.g., Friedlander & Marguiles, 1969; Lawler, Hall, & Oldham, 1974; Pritchard & Karasick, 1973); perceptions that the environment is participative, warm, and social, for instance, are related to individual satisfaction. Other studies have demonstrated that an organizational climate for a specific outcome influences employees' behaviors regarding that outcome (Klein & Sorra, 1996). Examples include relationships between climate for safety and factory safety (Hofmann & Stetzer, 1996; Zohar, 1980), climate for innovation and technological breakthroughs (Abbey & Dickson, 1983), and climate for innovation and updating and engineers' performance (Kozlowski and Hults, 1987). Climates for a specific focus (for example, innovation or quality) should encourage employees to respond and behave in ways that support that focus.

HR and Contracts Across Levels

Psychological contracts are exchange agreements between employees and employers. They represent beliefs that individuals hold about promises made, accepted, and relied on between themselves and the organization. *Normative contracts* are shared psychological contracts that emerge when members of an organization or a unit hold similar beliefs about the exchange agreement.

Two interdependent components of contracts are noteworthy: *transactions* and *relations*. Transactional contracts are explicit and of limited duration; they feature well-specified performance terms and well-specified expectations of employees, actions, and responses in exchange for well-specified rewards. Relational contracts are more abstract; they are long-term agreements, with incomplete performance requirements, and they concern such issues as respect, opportunities for growth, and promises of future rewards in exchange for hard work and citizenship behaviors (Rousseau, 1995). Most contracts contain both transactional and relational terms, to varying extents (Guzzo & Noonan, 1994).

HR practices and events signal the intentions and expectations that lead to contract development. HR practices can communicate promises and future intents in the name of the organization through types of hiring practices, reward practices, and developmental activities. Individuals commonly view these practices as forms of contracts and act according to the commitments conveyed and behaviors cued (Rousseau, 1995). Therefore, HR practices are the major means through which workers and the organization contract by sending messages regarding what the organization expects of employees and what rewards employees expect in return. Relational aspects of the contract are primarily formed by practices that manifest identification, commitment, and loyalty and through skill development (particularly firm-specific skills). Transactional aspects of the contract are primarily manifested through contingent reward practices. Common situational conditions provide the basis for normative or shared contracts (Rousseau, 1995). Thus, if individuals in an organization are exposed to a salient set of HR practices, shared expectations and normative contracts should emerge.

Contracts are important influences on employee responses. Fulfillment of a contract is related to such attitudes as satisfaction and commitment (Guzzo & Noonan, 1994; Rousseau, 1995; Schein, 1980). Less favorable assessments of the degree to which a contract has been fulfilled lead to less favorable attitudes and behaviors, such as absenteeism and turnover (Guzzo & Noonan, 1994). For example, employees may be willing to accept job transfers and to learn firm-specific skills because they expect job security and future growth with the company. Because of this implied contract, employees are willing to learn and develop. If the contract is perceived as being met along the way, positive attitudes will continue. However, if the contract is violated in some way, such as through failure of the organization to offer the expected career opportunities, negative attitudes and behavior will result. In addition, belief in shared obligations can also create social pressures to adhere to these commitments (Rousseau, 1995).

A recent study by Tsui and colleagues (1997) illustrates the importance of these relationships. These authors focused on employee-organization relationships to capture employers' expectations about specific contributions desired from employees and the inducements used to effect the desired contributions. HR practices were the primary means through which employers defined the employment relationship between organization and employee. Employee contributions were denoted by the extent to which employers encouraged employees, through human resource practices, to focus attention on work units in addition to performance in their own jobs. Employer investment was based on the extent to which employers provided training and job security. Employee performance, commitment, citizenship, and trust were higher in organizations where the relationship was balanced and focused on mutual investment; with transaction-based relationships, employee performance and attitudes were lowest.

It is also important to note that HR practices influence the effects of both climate and contracts because these practices have an impact on employee-organization fit. A great deal of theory and research has addressed the notion that it is necessary to match the characteristics of the person to the situation in order to provide the most productive environment in which to work (e.g., Aronoff & Wilson, 1985; Bowen, Ledford, & Nathan, 1991; Chatman, 1991). Therefore, the greatest effects on employee responses will occur when there is a good fit between the particular type of climate and the personality, values, and attributes of the employee. Similarly, when the expectations of the organization match what the employee desires and is willing to offer, stronger employee responses should occur. As an illustration, Klein and Sorra (1996) hypothesize that a strong climate for innovation results in opposition and resistance if there is a poor fit between employees' values regarding innovation and the climate for innovation. Key mechanisms for achieving good fit are the attraction-selection-attrition process (Schneider & Reichers, 1983) and the use of HR practices. Realistic job previews shape employee perceptions about the exchange agreement (Rousseau & Greller, 1994) and lead to initial perceptions of the climate. Employees who do not agree with the perceived terms of the exchange, or who do not believe the climate will be a good fit, will be less likely to accept a job if one is offered. Selectivity in hiring can lead to good fit if employees are hired whose attributes fit with the climate. Further, the socialization of organizational members can result in changes in members' values or personalities in the direction of organizational values (Fisher, 1986) and can provide further signaling about the exchange agreement (Rousseau, 1995). Through the socialization process, newcomers' perceptions are thought to converge over time with the perceptions of others (Kozlowski, Gully, McHugh, Salas, & Cannon-Bowers, 1996). Individuals who do not fit into the organizational environment are likely to leave if misinterpretation and misinformation occur during attraction, selection, and socialization.

Strength of the HR System

A fundamental assumption of interactional psychology is that it is impossible to understand behavior in organizations without understanding the interactions between features of the context and characteristics of the individuals operating within the context (Pfeffer & Salancik, 1978; Schneider, 1983). In addition, the relative effects of the situation and person factors are dependent of the strength of the situation. The term *situational strength* essentially refers to the degree of ambiguity presented in the context. Situational strength is a moderator of the relationship between the situation and individual outcomes and moderates the degree to which individual responses are expressed (Mischel, 1973).

In this section, we develop a new construct of HR system strength. A strong HR system is one in which HR practices create a situation, a social structure, in which there is little ambiguity concerning what the organization is like in terms of organizational goals and routines (that is, climate perceptions) and in terms of the exchange between employee and employer (that is, contract beliefs). We propose that the strength of the HR system will determine whether organizational climate and normative contracts will emerge from psychological climate and contracts; that is, the strength of the HR system moderates whether shared meanings are evoked. Therefore, the construct of HR strength can offer insights into the processes and mechanisms by which individual and organizational levels are linked.

The strength of the HR system will be associated with how effectively HR practices communicate the strategic focus of the organization. A strong HR system unambiguously creates the foundation for a particular type of climate to develop (for example, a climate of innovation or service). In turn, this indicates what attitudes, behaviors, skills, and abilities are thought to be most critical to performance.

There really is no research on the strength of the HR system per se, but we can speculate that its strength would be a function of several characteristics. *Visibility* refers to whether the processes and outcomes of HR practices are shared with those employees covered by them. For example, "pay secrecy" is the norm in many organizations, cloaking the reward-motivation messages that the pay system is intended to convey. *Clarity* refers to whether available and visible information about HR practices is easily understandable by employees. For example, benefit plans are often poorly comprehended by those who are supposed to feel rewarded by them. *Acceptability* of the practices refers to employees' willingness to contribute resources (time, data) to the design and implementation of HR practices and to use the output of HR practices (data, feedback) to influence their own attitudes and behavior. Waldman and Bowen (1998) have described the critical role that acceptability plays in the success or failure of 360-degree appraisal programs.

Consistency of administration refers to the uniform application of the practices across employees and across time. For example, do recruiters and selection decision makers consistently apply the same criteria, sending uniform messages about the right type of person for the organization? Consistent application of HR practices builds shared perceptions of "procedural justice" (Folger, 1987), which in turn have been shown to enhance commitment, satisfaction, and citizenship behaviors. *Effectiveness of administration* involves whether the HR practice actually does what it was designed to do. *Validity,* then, is one obvious element of effectiveness; that is, do selection instruments effectively screen on desired KSAs, thereby making intended contributions to human capital and at the same time signaling to employees what KSAs are valued in the setting by adding more employees with specified skills to the workforce? A less-obvious aspect of effective administration involves how experienced the HR staff is in delivering HR practices. This is particularly relevant with more state-of-the-art practices, such as peer hiring and performance appraisal, team-based pay, and so on. In this vein, Lawler (1992) has suggested that "new" HR systems/ configurations may display weaker empirical relationships with performance than do more conventional configurations, not because of any intrinsic inferiority but because of errors in implementation. In effect, the HR staff may be doing the right thing the wrong way. *Internal consistency* of HR practices will affect the strength of the HR system; that is, if employee risk taking, for example, is a desired individual outcome in a setting, do all the practices help build and reinforce that behavior?

Intensity of the HR system refers to the effort required to implement practices, the range of different practices in use, and the number of employees affected by them. A firm that uses certain practices (such as job security and organization-based pay) to a great extent in order to promote identification with the organization, and that uses other HR practices minimally, would be a low-intensity system. In contrast, a firm that adopts a wide range of practices that foster involvement, flexibility, intrinsic motivation, and development of knowledge and skills would be an intensive system, enhancing the strength of the HR system.

Weak HR systems create weak situations for employees. Weak situations are ambiguous and provide little guidance to individuals about what is appropriate behavior. Because individuals are uncertain about the appropriate response, variability or dispersion of responses should be large (Mischel, 1973). Here, individual-level processes can have macro-level effects. Less powerful individuals can have substantial influence on the implementation of top management directives and informal activities of organizational members (Staw & Sutton, 1992). To the extent that the HR situation is weak, expectations are ambiguous and subject to individual interpretation. Individuals can then construct their own versions of reality (House et al., 1995) or their own versions of the appropriate behaviors and responses desired from the HR system, and they can enforce their own interpretations of the implementation of HR practices. In such a case, variables at the individual level are likely to show strong relationships; that is, within an organization, individual climate perceptions and psychological contracts will have a strong relationship to individual responses. By contrast, strong situations lead all individuals to construe events in a similar way and foster uniform expectations about appropriate behaviors and responses. Hence, with a strong situation, variability in perceptions will be small within an organization but will differ across organizations, and it is these differences in organizational climates and normative contracts that influence attitudes and responses at work. Therefore, the impact of organization-level practices is moderated by the strength of the situation so that individuals will use more discretion in the execution of policies in weak situations than in strong situations (House et al., 1995).

The strength of the HR system is also related to inclusion. *Inclusiveness* is a key isomorphic construct in organizations and refers to the extent of involvement of one unit with another unit (House et al., 1995). Inclusiveness creates homogeneity at the unit level when all members are exposed to the same unit-level characteristics, such as incentive systems or other HR practices. For example, for part-time or contingent workers, work motivation and attitudes should be better predicted by individual factors than by organizational features. However, full-time employees in organizations with clear and consistent rewards are more likely to be affected by the situational context than by individual attributes (House et al., 1995). Similarly, we propose that inclusion is stronger when the set of HR practices is internally consistent, salient, and communicated strongly. This produces homogeneity among the individual organizational members, giving rise to shared perceptions and contracts, and homogeneity in attitudes and behaviors. When the HR system is weak, inclusion effects are weaker, giving rise to more idiosyncratic perceptions and psychological contracts. In such a case, homogeneity is not produced, and individuals within the organization differ in their attitudes and behaviors.

The strength and consistency with which particular HR practices are used can also influence whether shared climates or contracts will emerge. For example, when a selection system is strong (that is, when the organization is highly selective in recruiting and selecting people who fit the organization in terms of both their skills and their personal attributes), similar types of individuals will be selected, and a shared sense of what the organization is like continues. However, when the selection system is weak, within-organization heterogeneity will occur (House et al., 1995; Klein et al., 1994), and weak norms, weak expectations, and a lack of shared climate perceptions will occur (unless other consistently administered practices, such as socialization, reward programs, and training are in place to create shared perceptions). Similarly, a well-designed training and development system that is consistently administered to employees should increase the human capital of the organization. However, when the training system is weak or poorly designed, learning is more likely to be influenced by individual attributes, such as motivation and personality. Some individuals will increase their KSAs, but others will not. Greater variability in learning will occur, manifesting greater dispersion in human capital and decreasing relationships to firm performance. Therefore, strong and well-designed HR practices produce greater homogeneity of perceptions, attitudes, and behaviors within the organization. This greater homogeneity gives rise to shared meaning in terms of organizational climate and normative contracts and has larger effects on individual attitudes, behaviors, and skills than such individual attributes as personality. With poorly designed or poorly administered practices, individual behavior and attitudes are more likely to be influenced by individual-level variables, such as psychological climate, psychological contracts, perceptions, and personality. Shared climate and contract perceptions are less likely to develop.

Because the strength of the HR system will have an impact on the dispersion of individual perceptions within an organization, it is not sufficient to focus only on an aggregate measure of climate or contract. Two organizations could have the same aggregate or mean score across individuals within the organization but could differ dramatically in extent of shared meaning. Therefore, variability or dispersion of responses (Brown, Kozlowski, & Hattrup, 1996; Chan, 1998) is also a critical factor that must be accounted for in studying the relationships proposed in Figure 5.1.

A final observation is that strong HR systems are likely to require a strong top management philosophy that values HR. The success of HR systems is likely to depend largely on top management support, including top management beliefs about the importance of people, investment in human resources, and involvement of HR professionals in business planning processes (Ostroff, 1995). HR systems that are reciprocally integrated with their management and strategic suprasystems should achieve longer-lasting performance relative to firms that lack such an integration (Lado & Wilson, 1994). Consider this relative to our "intensity" characteristic of a strong HR system, for example. The optimal implementation of intensive HR practices cannot be accomplished without strong support from top management. Some evidence suggests that, with a low regard for the importance of human resources, firm performance is lowest when intensive sets of HR practices are used. In contrast, firm performance is higher when intensive sets of HR practices are used in combination with top management support and valuing of human resources (Ostroff, 1995). These findings imply that intensive HR systems are related to firm performance, but only when top management values human resources and sees them as a source of competitive advantage. With intensive HR systems and strong top management valuing of human resources, we are likely to see the relationships depicted in Figure 5.1. With low intensity HR coupled with low top management support for human resources, the relationships depicted are likely to be weak, and the firm can use means other than human resources (for example, technology and resources) to compete. Similarly, firm performance is affected not only by the technical expertise of practices but also by the effectiveness of the HR staff (Huselid, Jackson, & Schuler, 1997).

Organizational Context, HR Systems, Climate, and Performance

As alluded to in the beginning of our discussion, organizations operate in multiple domains, and different configurations of organizational attributes will be relevant to different effectiveness criteria. Much work is needed to fully elucidate the clusters or combinations of HR practices that form HR systems. Some empirical evidence indicates that a wide variety of different combinations of HR practices will be used in organizations, with no single dominant cluster of practices (e.g., Cappelli et al., 1997; Ostroff, 1995). The key issue is to determine which sets of practices ultimately result in a sustained competitive advantage. We propose that for any given domain of effectiveness, the establishment of an organizational climate for that particular outcome will be the key factor that establishes whether people in the organization will enable the organization to achieve a competitive advantage.

Some researchers and theorists have suggested that a single set of practices is equally effective for all firms. In particular, researchers have proposed the adoption of a high-performance work system, which promotes employee development, involvement, and a sense of achievement through such practices as use of teams, job enrichment, participation in decision making, and contingent rewards (e.g., Lawler, 1992; Arthur, 1992; Huselid, 1995; MacDuffie, 1995; Pfeffer, 1994). This viewpoint ignores the organizational context in which HR operates. Some recent evidence suggests that the effectiveness of this system depends on contextual variables, such as organizational size, manufacturing, and production systems (e.g., Kelley, 1996; MacDuffie, 1995; Pil & MacDuffie, 1996). One of the most salient contextual features is organizational strategy. In recent years, a number of researchers have argued that HR practices must be aligned with one another in order to achieve the firm's chosen strategy, and that the set of HR practices must be aligned with the firm's strategy (e.g., Dyer & Holder, 1988; Miles & Snow, 1994; Schuler & Jackson, 1987, 1995; Wright & Snell, 1991).

Empirical studies examining differential sets of HR practices for different strategies have yielded mixed results (e.g., Bennett & Schultz, 1995; Jackson, Schuler, & Rivero, 1989; Schuler & Jackson, 1987). In general, small differences in HR practices by strategic type have been found. Although the weak findings may indicate that strategy does not drive HR systems, it is likely that firms with different strategies may not consistently adopt the most appropriate practices for achieving their strategic objectives. Attention to this issue is relatively recent, and the most appropriate HR systems for different strategies of firms may not yet be fully developed. It is more important to examine the relationships among strategy, HR, and firm performance, not just strategy as a driver of HR, to elucidate the appropriate coordination between HR and strategy for achieving performance advantages.

As a basis for beginning to examine how configurations of strategy, climate, and HR practices influence performance, we first focus on identifying relevant performance domains. On the basis of the results of a study of a wide variety of criteria of organizational performance, Quinn and Rohrbaugh (1983) have proposed a fourfold competing-values framework. The four approaches to performance are defined by two underlying value dimensions. The first dimension contrasts an internal versus an external organizational focus. The internal focus emphasizes the well-being and development of people in the organization, whereas the external focus emphasizes the well-being of the organization itself, with an emphasis on task accomplishment. The second dimension contrasts stability and control with flexibility and change. Control focuses on order and standardization, whereas flexibility focuses on innovation, adaptation, and change. Further, a distinction is also drawn between the process or means to organizational outcomes and the outcomes or ends themselves. Figure 5.2 is a modified version of this framework (Quinn & Rohrbaugh, 1983), showing the dimensions, means, and ends encompassing each of the four performance models. The boxes in the figure represent organizational ends or criteria reflecting organizational outcomes. The ovals represent primary means to achieving these ends. The effectiveness measure of quality of outputs was not found to fit any particular model and probably encompasses aspects of all models.

Figure 5.2. Spatial Model of Organizational Effectiveness.

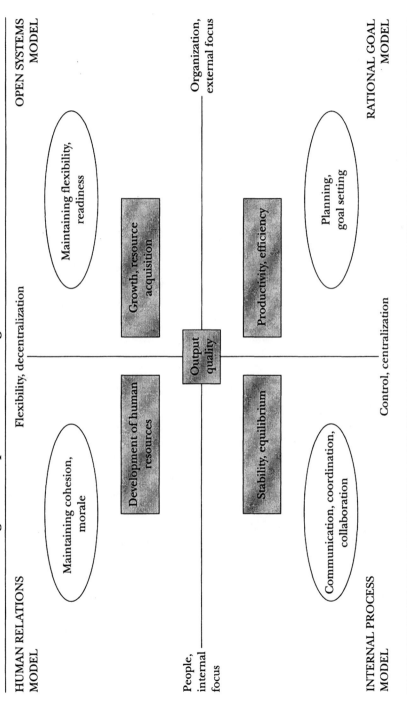

Source: Quinn & Rohrbaugh, 1983.

We propose that the achievement of the different effectiveness outcomes identified in Quinn and Rohrbaugh's framework requires different employee attributes. Growth and resource-acquisition outcomes require flexibility and adaptability from employees. Productivity and efficiency outcomes primarily require monitoring and control of employee behaviors. Stability and equilibrium outcomes require identification with and commitment to the organization, as well as monitoring and controlling of employee behaviors. For the development of human resource outcomes, relevant employee attributes include knowledge and skill development, satisfaction, intrinsic motivation, and citizenship. Earlier (see Table 5.1), we identified these attributes and the relevant HR practices that promote them. Given this link between effectiveness outcomes and employee attributes, we can now focus on how different business strategies, coupled with relevant climate and sets of HR practices, contribute to achieving the different categories of effectiveness criteria.

A number of typologies of generic business strategy have been offered (e.g., Porter, 1980; Miles & Snow, 1984). Although labels and specific definitions vary somewhat by researcher, we will focus on three strategies to illustrate our points: the innovative-prospector strategy, the quality-enhancer strategy, and the cost-defender strategy.

Firms employing an innovative-prospector strategy seek out new markets, and they produce new and innovative products at a reasonable cost and quality. Effectiveness criteria for such firms can include growth, resource acquisition, adaptation to the environment, customer service, and increased market share (see upper-right quadrant of Figure 5.2). Firms seeking innovation are associated with decentralized structures and an external focus (Quinn & Rohrbaugh, 1983). Flexibility and adaptability of the workforce are key attributes necessary for innovation. In order to elicit these employee behaviors, attitudes, and attributes, a climate for innovation is necessary. A climate for innovation ensures employee skill in innovation use, provides incentives for innovation use and disincentives for innovation avoidance, and removes obstacles to innovation use (Klein & Sorra, 1996). Flexibility and innovation in organizations also require heterogeneity and diversity among employees in order to foster multiple viewpoints, which enhance innovation (Kanter, 1989; Cox, 1993). Because of the focus on flexibility and the decentralization of structure, these organizations should develop HR systems containing practices that promote flexibility in the workforce and that give employees authority and control (see Table 5.1). Developing workforce skills for innovation, as well as incorporating such practices as promotion of diversity, use of teams, empowerment of employees, use of contingent pay, and job enrichment, can enhance the flexibility and adaptability of the workforce.

Firms employing a quality-enhancer strategy are customer-oriented. They focus on continuous improvement and on producing high-quality goods or services. An emphasis on the strategic outcome of output quality requires a balance between control and flexibility and between internal and external focus (Quinn & Rohrbaugh, 1983). The emphasis on customer service indicates that some degree of empowerment, voice, and participation in decision making is important (Schneider & Bowen, 1995). For example, to ensure that quality standards are met, consistency in producing products or in dealing with customers is required. To ensure such consistency, some degree of monitoring and control of employee behavior is warranted, perhaps through careful observation and appraisal of employee behaviors or through specialized training in statistical process control or service delivery. A climate for quality would be created by the types of HR practices that have been specified in the growing literature on total-quality management, or TQM (e.g., Dean & Bowen, 1994), and service quality (e.g., Schneider & Bowen, 1995). In both TQM and service quality, employee satisfaction is emphasized as necessary to support both continuous improvement and, in particular, customer satisfaction. The latter interest stems from research that documents the relationship between employee satisfaction and customer satisfaction (e.g., Schneider & Bowen, 1985; Schneider, Parkington, & Buxton, 1980). In service organizations, the "climate for service" appears evident not only to employees but also to customers. This climate for service—or, more broadly, quality—is created through HR practices that increase knowledge and skills (see Table 5.1), such as training employees to be able to deliver high quality and developing expectations of high quality in employees through selection and reward systems (Schneider et al., 1996). There is also increasing emphasis on organizational commitment via such practices as promises of job security (see Table 5.1), in the belief that longer-tenured employees are more capable of delivering value to customers, thereby increasing customer loyalty and profitability (Reichheld, 1996; Heskett, Sasser, & Schlesinger, 1997). Quality-focused climates can be characterized by flexibility, control, or both. HR practices associated with TQM have been characterized as emphasizing more employee empowerment and voice (Dean & Evans, 1994), on the one hand, and, on the other, relying on peer pressure for oppressive control (Boje, 1993) and work simplification (Lawler, 1994). Professional service firms often use empowerment practices to create flexibility, whereas some standardized consumer organizations (for example, fast-food restaurants) have narrow jobs and a focus on control (this latter focus is the cost focus discussed in the following passage). Both strategic orientations—and climates—can be effective, given differences in their environments (for example, in terms of customer expectations; Bowen & Lawler, 1992, 1995).

Firms using a cost-defender strategy focus on operational excellence, efficient use of assets, and production at a relatively low market cost. Relevant performance criteria for an organization with a strategic objective of cost would include productivity, efficiency, cost minimization, profitability, and return on investment (lower-right quadrant of Figure 5.2). Planning and division of labor are important factors (Quinn & Rohrbaugh, 1983). HR practices that should support this model are primarily those that emphasize monitoring and control of employee behaviors (see Table 5.1). However, because practices that increase flexibility (see Table 5.1) can also improve operating efficiencies, the use of such practices may also be relevant. Typically, though, a climate for cost is created by HR practices that provide management the means to closely monitor and control the activities of employees. The HR practices that have been suggested as useful include relatively fixed and stable job descriptions that allow little employee discretion; narrowly designed jobs and career paths that encourage specialization, expertise, and efficiency; short-term, results-oriented performance appraisals; close monitoring of market pay levels for use in making compensation decisions; and minimal levels of employee training and development (Schuler & Jackson, 1987). These HR practices create the skills, knowledge, motivation, and attitudes that are consistent with a cost-leadership strategy.

We have been focusing here on a limited number of generic strategies and strategic performance outcomes. Our primary purpose is to illustrate how an internally consistent set of organizational attributes and HR practices can be developed to create a specific climate for a given performance outcome. A multidimensional view of performance implies different relationships between organizational performance and its determinants (Cameron, 1978; Lewin & Minton, 1986; Tsui, 1990). When the organization is primarily focused on one strategic performance outcome, we are likely to see different patterns of organizational attributes (different patterns of contextual features and HR practices) that are relevant to different organizational performance domains. Nevertheless, we recognize that we have not discussed other domains of organizational effectiveness, such as speed, stability, and organizational learning, each of which, for a particular objective, may require a different climate (derived from HR practices) in order to elicit the employee attributes appropriate to the achievement of that objective. Similarly, some organizations have quite different objectives for different divisions or units. Therefore, a consistent HR system at the organizational level may not be feasible, and two different sets of HR systems and different climates (for example, one for cost and one for innovation) may be appropriate at different divisional or functional units.

Further, it is important to note that at any given time there are likely to be trade-offs between effectiveness criteria (Quinn & Rohrbaugh, 1983). Some evidence has shown that the most effective organizations are those that can achieve a balance among the different organizational characteristics associated with different domains (Lawrence & Lorsch, 1967; Ostroff & Schmitt, 1993). Given this evidence, there may be a wider variety of different configurations for equally effective HR practices than has typically been assumed. Some evidence for this notion is beginning to emerge (e.g., Delery & Doty, 1996; Ostroff, 1995).

It is important to note that, although some strategic objectives may appear to be opposites, they may be complementary and are not necessarily empirical opposites (Quinn & Rohrbaugh, 1983). This is the inherent paradox in organizations: competing values can be complementary (Cameron, 1986). For example, efficient and cost-focused organizations may best be represented by a climate that enhances control and monitoring, but these organizations may also possess characteristics of other organizational climates and HR systems. Some cost defenders may also value stability and so use practices that promote coordination, communication, citizenship, and collaboration, and practices that promote identification and commitment to the organization because they should lead to a more stable workforce (see Table 5.1).

We also propose that employee attitudes, motivation, and human capital are critical to all organizational performance domains. These employee attributes are most clearly linked to internal effectiveness criteria, such as morale and cohesion. However, in keeping with the inherent paradox of competing values in organizations, we propose that employee attributes are also critical to achieving performance across domains. Productivity can be achieved through worker satisfaction and through people. Therefore, it appears, HR practices that develop employees can also increase productivity and efficiency. Training in such areas as problem solving or statistical process control can increase the benefits of new technologies. HR practices that provide workers with a sense of achievement and involvement in the work (for example, use of teams, job enrichment, and empowerment) may also lead workers to be more efficient as they share ideas and redesign their jobs to better coordinate their efforts (Ichniowski et al., 1996).

There is relatively little research that simultaneously investigates strategy, HR systems, and effectiveness (Huselid, 1995; Delery & Doty, 1996; MacDuffie, 1995; Ostroff, 1995; Youndt et al., 1996). Most studies have investigated relatively few HR practices and systems, and so findings are limited. Ostroff (1995) has investigated a wide range of practices and found stronger strategy effects so that effectiveness depended on the coupling of HR systems with strategy. For example, productivity was highest for cost defenders that had a balance of practices and for quality enhancers that had practices promoting involvement, flexibility, identification, and achievement. When an externally focused measure of market-based performance was considered, performance was highest for innovators that used practices enhancing flexibility, achievement, intrinsic motivation, and employee attitudes (as in high-performance work systems). These results are consistent with the notion of competing values. Cost defenders should place an emphasis on HR practices that monitor and control employee behavior, and yet the fact that a balance of practices was found to be superior represents the inherent paradox in organizations: that competing values can indeed be complementary. Attention to workers' sense of personal achievement can also promote productivity. Similarly, an externally focused criterion of effectiveness (market-based performance) is consistent with innovation, and innovative strategies coupled with HR practices that promote flexibility have been found to be superior.

Environment, Context, HR, and Relationships over Time

Our model represents a snapshot of relationships at a single point in time. In our model, we view the organizational context and HR systems as influences on individual-level processes as well as on organization-level processes. However, we also believe that these processes are active over time, are reciprocal and interdependent, and are often simultaneous. People not only react to organizational contexts but also create or enact them (Terborg, 1981; Weick, 1979).

Our orientation has focused on context as the driving force for HR. At any given time, and when organizational practices and policies have been institutionalized, contextual variables should influence the appropriate HR system. However, when changes in organizational design, structure, strategy, culture, and so forth, are required, changes in HR can be the driving force for inducing changes in the organizational context. For example, HR practices can be key to moving from a centralized to a decentralized structure. Implementing practices (such as the use of teams, job enrichment, contingent rewards, and empowerment) forces employees to reconceptualize and recreate their sense of the organization. Different expectations and beliefs are created. Over time, these shared beliefs create a different climate and different contractual expectations.

In response to the organizational context, as well as to the HR system of practices, patterns of attitudes emerge, and workers come to interpret events in ways similar to those of their peers (Pfeffer & Salancik, 1978). We have proposed that these shared interpretations are manifested in organizational climate and normative contracts. Such shared meanings, once developed, remain largely tacit until exceptions arise, or until the meanings are no longer adequate for the particular situation. At that time, meanings are renegotiated (Louis, 1980). Therefore, a change in any of the HR practices will lead to a redefinition of what the organization is like and what is expected of employees. HR practices can bring about changes in organizational performance largely through their effect on climate (Kopelman et al., 1990).

In a growing organization, in an organization undergoing change, or in an organization seeking innovation, individual-level beliefs, attitudes, motives, and behaviors will have an impact on the HR system, the organizational climate, and normative contracts. Under more stable organizational conditions, such as when there is a stable environment and when there are institutionalized practices in the organization, the organizational context will have a stronger influence on the beliefs, attitudes, motives, and behaviors of individuals in the organization. House and colleagues (1995) propose an example of such a process by focusing on selection effects. The types of people selected to work in an organization shape the climate, culture, and practices of that organization. Through careful screening, the heterogeneity of organizational members is often reduced. The result is that the people in the organization have the same basic personalities, attitudes, and attributes. During growth, however, newly hired employees introduce new behaviors, norms, expectations, and values before the growing organization has stabilized and institutionalized its practices. Further, organizations may purposely select members with different attributes in order to stimulate innovation. Although this produces initial heterogeneity in the organization, over time these individuals can introduce substantial changes in the organization's climate and practices. This suggests that the environmental and contextual features of the organization will influence the types and strength of the HR practices employed. In conditions of change, turbulence, or growth, the organization can use HR practices (for example, hiring different types of employees, introducing flexible work arrangements, or empowering employees) to produce needed organizational changes. The initial effect will be to produce heterogeneity in the organization. However, over time, new behaviors and attitudes will be introduced and ultimately will "make the place"

(Schneider, 1987) and result in stabilized and institutionalized practices.

Perceptual interpretations of HR practices are likely to remain stable, and employees are unlikely to consider them actively and regularly unless a change in practices is made. Changes in practices stimulate active evaluation and systematic processing of information in the context (Guzzo & Noonan, 1994). This can lead to changes in climate perceptions. Some employees may leave if they perceive the new situation to be a poor fit with their needs, and other employees whose attributes fit the new situation may take their place. Over time, this process will create a new collective sense of the organization.

Environmental and organizational contextual features are also related to the strength of the HR system. When the organizational environment is turbulent, when an organization is young, or when organizational practices and policies have not been institutionalized, ambiguity is introduced and the result is a weak situation (House et al., 1995). In changing conditions or conditions of growth, the content of the HR system is unlikely to be well specified, and the "process" is likely to be weak. Similarly, a smaller organization is less likely to have a well-developed system of HR practices, and the result will be a weak situation. In these conditions, the mediating effect of perceptual processes and employee attributes is likely to be small in the relationship between HR systems and firm performance.

Contextual features of the organization also constrain the range and types of HR practices. For example, such features as centralization and formalization make monitoring and control appropriate but empowerment inappropriate. Likewise, it can be argued that HR affects organizational contextual features. Again, the process is likely to be reciprocal. In a stable or mature organization, the organizational context is likely to drive the HR system. Key decision makers, powerful individuals, and leaders have made choices about the context. The HR function has traditionally played a subordinate role in organizations, attempting to develop practices that fit the context and are appropriate to it. Only recently have we witnessed the involvement of HR in the processes of strategic planning and goal setting. Therefore, the HR system should be chosen to be consistent with or fit the context.

Conclusions, Implications, and Future Directions

We have argued that HR makes three types of contributions to organizations. First, HR practices can make a contribution to operations. Some HR practices promote flexibility in the workforce and provide monitoring and control functions, which can create structural and operational efficiencies that directly enhance firm performance. Second, HR can make a substantive contribution through human capital development. Some practices, such as selection and training, have a direct impact on the knowledge and skills of employees, which in turn influence firm performance. Third, HR provides a signaling and messaging function about the attitudes and behaviors that are valued. When these signals are centered on certain strategic outcomes, such as those involving quality, cost, or innovation, corresponding climates for these strategic outcomes emerge, sending strong messages to employees about appropriate ways to behave in order to achieve the organization's goals.

The influence of an HR system on a firm's performance occurs in large part through the establishment of an organizational climate and a normative contract that has an impact on collective attitudes and behaviors. Shared perceptions of climates and contracts, as well as collective employee attributes, emerge from lower-level phenomena. These constructs are compositional in that they have similar meanings across levels (Rousseau, 1985); however, the processes across levels are not entirely isomorphic. The term *isomorphism* refers to the degree to which the variables in the process are similar across levels. In our model, we have identified the key components that are similar across levels and have specified how individual phenomena interact and accumulate to influence organizational effectiveness. However, since our focus was primarily on organizational relationships between firm performance and the organization-level variables of HR systems, we did not specify all the individual-level variables that influence individual-level performance and outcomes. Other key individual-level constructs are likely to influence relationships at the individual level. Therefore, we do not assert that the same set of variables or the same network of variables explains both relationships between HR systems and individual-level performance and between HR systems and firm performance.

Clearly, more research is needed to test the proposed linkages among HR systems, collective attitudes, ability, and firm performance. A key issue for our model is the notion of collective perceptions and collective responses. This notion is based on the premise that different processes often operate at different levels of analysis (Klein et al., 1994; Ostroff, 1993). In order for such effects to be found, differences on these variables must exist among organizations. There is evidence for mean organizational or unit-level differences and differences in correlations across levels in many areas, including satisfaction (Ostroff, 1992), commitment (Angle & Perry, 1981), goals (Vancouver & Schmitt, 1991), affect (George, 1990), service perceptions (Schneider & Bowen, 1985), and climate perceptions (Jones & James, 1979). Schneider (1987) supports the notion that there will be mean differences across organizations in individuals' attitudes and behaviors because individuals are attracted to, are selected by, and remain in organizations that have characteristics similar to their own (Schneider, Smith, Taylor, & Fleenor, 1998). In addition, organizations with strong HR systems may attempt to constrain the work behavior, responses, and performance of their members; therefore, performance variation within an organization may be restricted but may be accompanied by large variation between organizations (Johns, 1991).

From a methodological standpoint, several key factors must be considered in testing relationships in this research domain or in other multilevel models:

1. If global measures of constructs are not available (typically the case for attitudes), data must be gathered from multiple employees within a firm, and from multiple firms.
2. Rationales for aggregating individual-level measures to represent an organization-level construct must be provided. For employee attributes, rationales were provided earlier, in terms of interactions and dependencies among workers.
3. In establishing attitude, ability, and performance linkages, between-organization differences must be shown to exist in such measures; that is, when aggregated measures of some attitude, for example, are used, significant differences must exist between organizations for meaningful relationships to organizational performance to be detected.

4. A researcher must determine the type of composition model that is of interest, such as a simple additive model whereby variability within an organization is not an issue, or a direct consensus model in which within-organization agreement must be demonstrated to justify aggregation (Chan, 1998; Morgeson & Hofmann, 1999; Kozlowski & Klein, Chapter One, this volume).

5. Even when within-organization agreement is sufficiently high, there is likely to be variation at the individual level. A researcher must determine whether this individual-level variation should be considered "error" or should be accounted for in examining organization-level relationships among aggregated variables. For example, a researcher could control for dispersion in responses (Chan, 1998; Kozlowski and Klein, Chapter One, this volume) in examining relationships between aggregate climate perceptions and aggregate satisfaction. At the individual level, this variation in responses allows for examining within-organization individual-level relationships in these same variables.

6. A range of organizational performance and organizational effectiveness criteria should be included. Multiple internal and external criteria are needed for a more comprehensive evaluation of organizations (e.g., Cameron, 1986; Connolly, Conlon, & Deutsch, 1980).

We argue that HR practices will not reach their maximum potential for enhancing firm performance unless they are coupled with appropriate contextual features. Multiple types of HR systems can be equally effective according to the environment, the organizational context, the strength and intensity of the HR system, and the performance domain. Little research has addressed this.

It appears that different sets of practices will be differentially effective depending on contextual variables, such as strategy. Although prescriptive models of HR systems have been offered for different contexts and different business strategies (e.g., Dyer & Holder, 1988; Miles & Snow, 1994; Schuler & Jackson, 1987), they are often contradictory. Clearly, work is needed in defining HR systems. We suggest some mechanisms to begin building HR systems for investigation. It is important to elucidate key variables pertaining to organizational effectiveness and performance. Different orientations are more relevant to some types of effectiveness outcomes than to others (for example, flexibility is important to customer satisfaction, whereas control is important to efficiency). Once a researcher has identified the relevant performance goal (for example, quality of outputs, or growth and acquisition) and the employee attributes (for example, knowledge, citizenship, or satisfaction) required to achieve that goal, the researcher can use Table 5.1 to derive the sets of HR practices (for example, use of teams, contingent rewards, empowerment to promote flexibility) that should promote the desired outcomes. At the same time, the organizational contextual variables must be taken into account. For example, decentralized structures should be coupled with HR practices that promote flexibility. Such an approach could yield useful insights into the feasible sets of consistent configurations for organization-level attributes. In addition, case studies across a range of types of organizations and industries could provide evidence for appropriate sets of HR practices. Future work is also needed to elucidate the investigation of multiple organizational goals or outcomes simultaneously. To the extent that an organization pursues multiple goals, all of which are important and all of which are quite distinct, it seems unlikely that an effective set of HR practices can be developed. However, for an organization pursuing fewer, more molar, compatible goals, the range of relevant climates would be smaller, and a consistent set of HR practices could be developed. Future work could focus on identifying which sets of organizational goals are compatible and consistent, thereby fostering a situation whereby a clear climate and a clear HR system could be developed to promote goal attainment.

An alternative is to focus on climates as opposed to focusing directly on HR practices. Climates of equal strength may emerge from quite different sets of HR practices and policies. For example, a climate for the implementation of innovation may be driven by the training of employees in innovation skills, or by the motivation of employees through rewards, or by the selection of employees who are skilled in innovation use, or by some combination of these practices (Klein & Sorra, 1996). In promoting the particular type of climate, a practice may be critical to one organization but not to another. Therefore, specific types of HR practices may show little consistent relationship to a specific type of outcome across organizations. Climate, however, can demonstrate the cumulative influence of the HR practices (Klein & Sorra, 1996) and may be a more readily identifiable means of determining relationships to firm performance. Therefore, for a given strategic outcome, such as innovation, it may be more useful to focus on the relevant climate (in this case, a climate of innovation) that can foster the types of employee behaviors and responses necessary to the achievement of that strategic outcome. Alternative sets of HR practices for creating the innovation climate can be explored.

The relationships proposed are complex and dynamic. Longitudinal research is needed to test the causal linkages highlighted in our model. It is highly likely that there is a time lag between adoption of HR practices and their ultimate effects on firm performance (Huselid & Becker, 1996). Further, performance may deteriorate initially and then improve (Pil & MacDuffie, 1996). Longitudinal research is also critical to the determination of whether appropriate HR systems lead to higher performance or whether strongly performing firms then pay attention to their HR systems.

Finally, we argue that a multilevel perspective for examining relationships between HR practices and firm performance is critical if we are to advance our understanding in this area. At the organizational level, any type of subsystem of the organization (in our case, the HR system) is likely to have a strong impact on how people perceive their work environment and on the types of responses elicited from employees. It is impossible to fully understand how the HR system influences firm performance without considering the mechanisms through which that influence occurs (that is, climates, contracts, and employee attributes). HR systems have clear impacts on how people perceive their work environment and, ultimately, on the behaviors and responses of employees in the organizations. Only by considering the impacts of these practices at both the individual level and the organizational level will we be able to elucidate which types of HR systems are effective for which types of strategic goals. The collective perceptions of individuals and the collective attributes of employees emerge from these individual-level processes, enabling interactions and interdependencies to operate among workers to fulfill the organization's goals.

References

Abbey, A., & Dickson, J. W. (1983). R&D work climate and innovation in semi-conductors. *Academy of Management Journal, 26,* 362–368.

Abowd, J. M. (1990). Does performance-based managerial compensation affect corporate performance? *Industrial and Labor Relations Review, 43,* 52–73.

Angle, H. L., & Perry, J. L. (1981). An empirical assessment of organizational commitment and organizational effectiveness. *Administrative Science Quarterly, 26,* 1–13.

Argyris, C. (1964). *Integrating the individual and the organization.* New York: Wiley.

Aronoff, J., & Wilson, J. P. (1985). *Personality in the social process.* Mahwah, NJ: Erlbaum.

Arthur, J. B. (1992). The link between business strategy and industrial relations systems in American steel minimills. *Industrial and Labor Relations Review, 45,* 488–506.

Banker, R. D., Field, J. M., Schroeder, R. G., & Sinha, K. (1996). Impact of work teams on manufacturing performance: A longitudinal field study. *Academy of Management Journal, 39,* 867–890.

Banker, R. D., Lee, S., Potter, G., & Srinivasan, D. (1996). Contextual analysis of performance impacts of outcome-based incentive compensation. *Academy of Management Journal, 39,* 920–949.

Barney, J. (1991). Firm resources and sustained competitive advantage. *Journal of Management, 17,* 99–120.

Bartel, A. P. (1994). Productivity gains from the implementation of employee training programs. *Industrial Relations, 33,* 411–425.

Becker, B., & Gerhart, B. (1996). The impact of human resource management on organizational performance: Progress and prospects. *Academy of Management Journal, 39,* 779–801.

Becker, G. S. (1964). *Human capital: A theoretical and empirical analysis with special reference to education.* New York: National Bureau of Economic Research.

Bennett, N., and Schultz, E. B. (1995). *Is anyone listening? An empirical test of prescribed relationships between human resource management and strategic type.* Paper presented at the Academy of Management Conference, Vancouver.

Boje, D. M. (1993). *Toyota: Deconstructing our 21st-century organizations.* Paper presented at the annual meeting of the International Academy of Business Disciplines, New Orleans.

Bowen, D. E., & Lawler, E. E. III (1992). The empowerment of service workers: What, why, how, and when. *Sloan Management Review, 33,* 31–39.

Bowen, D. E., & Lawler, E. E. III (1995). Empowering service employees. *Sloan Management Review, 36,* 73–84.

Bowen, D. E., Ledford, G. E., & Nathan, B. R. (1991). Hiring for the organization, not the job. *Academy of Management Executive, 5,* 35–51.

Brief, A. P., & Motowidlo, S. J. (1986). Prosocial organizational behaviors. *Academy of Management Review, 11,* 710–725.

Brown, K. G., Kozlowski, S.W.J., & Hattrup, K. (1996, August). *Theory, issues, and recommendations in conceptualizing agreement as a construct in organizational research: The search for consensus regarding consensus.* Paper presented at the annual convention of the Academy of Management Association, Cincinnati, OH.

Burns, T., & Stalker, G. M. (1961). *The management of innovation.* London: Tavistock.

Cameron, K. (1978). Measuring organizational effectiveness in institutes of higher education. *Administrative Science Quarterly, 23,* 604–632.

Cameron, K. (1981). Domains of organizational effectiveness in college and universities. *Academy of Management Journal, 24,* 25–47.

Cameron, K. (1986). Effectiveness as paradox: Consensus and conflict in conceptions of organizational effectiveness. *Management Science, 32,* 539–553.

Campbell, J. P. (1977). On the nature of effectiveness. In P. S. Goodman & J. M. Pennings (Eds.), *New perspectives on organizational effectiveness* (pp. 13–55). San Francisco: Jossey-Bass.

Cappelli, P., Bassi, L., Katz, H., Knoke, D., Osterman, P., & Useem, M. (1997). *Change at work.* New York: Oxford University Press.

Chan, D. (1998). Functional relations among constructs in the same content domain at different levels of analysis: A typology of composition models. *Journal of Applied Psychology, 83,* 234–246.

Chatman, J. A. (1991). Matching people and organizations: Selection and socialization in public accounting firms. *Administrative Science Quarterly, 36,* 459–484.

Connolly, T., Conlon, E. M., & Deutsch, S. J. (1980). Organizational effectiveness: A multiple constituency approach. *Academy of Management Review, 5,* 211–218.

Cox, T. H. (1993). *Cultural diversity in organizations.* San Francisco: Jossey-Bass.

Dean, J. W., Jr., & Bowen, D. E. (1994). Defining quality: Alternatives and implications. *Academy of Management Review, 19,* 392–418.

Dean, J. W., Jr., & Evans, J. R. (1994). *Total quality: Management, organization, and strategy.* St. Paul, MN: West.

Delery, J. E., & Doty, D. H. (1996). Modes of theorizing in strategic human resource management: Tests of universalistic, contingency, and configural performance predictions. *Academy of Management Journal, 39,* 802–835.

Doty, D. H., & Glick, W. H. (1994). Typologies as a unique form of theory building: Toward improved understanding and modeling. *Academy of Management Review, 19,* 230–251.

Dunlop, J. T., & Weil, D. (1996). Diffusion and performance of modular production in the U.S. apparel industry. *Industrial Relations, 35,* 334–355.

Dyer, L., & Holder, G. W. (1988). A strategic perspective of human resource management. In L. Dyer (Ed.), *Human resource management: Evolving roles and responsibilities* (pp. 1–45). Washington, DC: Bureau of National Affairs.

Emery, R. E., & Trist, E. L. (1960). Socio-technical systems. In C. W. Churchman & M. Verhulst (Eds.), *Management science models and techniques* (pp. 83–97). New York: Pergamon.

Fisher, C. D. (1986). Organizational socialization: An integrative review. *Research in Personnel and Human Resource Management, 4,* 101–145.

Folger, R. (1987). Distributive and procedural justice. *Social Justice Research, 1,* 143–159.

Friedlander, F., & Marguiles, N. (1969). Multiple impacts of organizational climate and individual value systems upon job satisfaction. *Personnel Psychology, 22,* 171–183.

Galbraith, J. R. (1974). Organizational design: An information processing view. *Interfaces, 4,* 28–36.

George, J. M. (1990). Personality, affect, and behavior in groups. *Journal of Applied Psychology, 75,* 107–116.

Gerhart, B., & Milkovich, G. T. (1990). Organizational differences in managerial compensation and financial performance. *Academy of Management Journal, 33,* 663–691.

Gross, E., & Etzioni, A. (1985). *Organizations in society.* New York: Macmillan.

Guzzo, R. A., & Noonan, K. A. (1994). Human resource practices as communications of the psychological contract. *Human Resource Management, 33,* 447–462.

Heneman, H. G. III, Schwab, D. P., Fossum, J. A., & Dyer, L. D. (1989). *Personnel/human resource management.* Burr Ridge, IL: Irwin.

Heskett, J. L., Sasser, E. W., Jr., & Schlesinger, L. A. (1997). *The service profit chain.* New York: Free Press.

Hofmann, D. A., and Stetzer, A. (1996). A cross-level investigation of factors influencing unsafe behaviors and accidents. *Personnel Psychology, 49,* 307–339.

House, R., Rousseau, D. M., & Thomas-Hunt, M. (1995). The meso paradigm: A framework for the integration of micro and macro organizational behavior. *Research in Organizational Behavior, 17,* 41–114.

Hunter, J. E., & Hunter, R. F. (1984). Validity and utility of alternative predictors of job performance. *Psychological Bulletin, 96,* 72–98.

Huselid, M. A. (1995). The impact of human resource management practices on turnover, productivity, and corporate financial performance. *Academy of Management Journal, 38,* 635–672.

Huselid, M. A., and Becker, B. E. (1996). Methodological issues in cross-sectional and panel estimates of the human resource firm performance link. *Industrial Relations, 35,* 400–422.

Huselid, M. A., Jackson, S. E., & Schuler, R. S. (1997). Technical and strategic human resource management effectiveness as determinants of firm performance. *Academy of Management Journal, 40,* 171–188.

Iaffaldano, M. T., & Muchinksy, P. M. (1985). Job satisfaction and job performance: A meta-analysis. *Psychological Bulletin, 97,* 251–273.

Ichniowski, C., Kochan, T., Levine, D., Olson, C., & Strauss, G. (1996). What works at work: Overview and Assessment. *Industrial Relations, 35,* 299–333.

Ichniowski, C., Shaw, K., & Prennushi, G. (1997). The effect of human resource management practices on productivity. *American Economic Review, 87,* 291–313.

Jackson, S. E., Schuler, R. S., & Rivero, J. C. (1989). Organizational characteristics as predictors of personnel practices. *Personnel Psychology, 42,* 727–786.

James, L. R., & Jones, A. P. (1974). Organizational climate: A review of theory and research. *Psychological Bulletin, 81,* 1096–1112.

Johns, G. (1991). Substantive and methodological constraints on behavior and attitudes in organizational research. *Organizational Behavior and Human Decision Processes, 49,* 80–104.

Jones, A. P., & James, L. R. (1979). Psychological climate: Dimensions and relationships of individual and aggregated work environment perceptions. *Organizational Behavior and Human Decision Processes, 23,* 201–250.

Kanter, R. M. (1989). *When giants learn to dance.* New York: Simon & Schuster.

Katz, H. C., Kochan, T. A., & Gobeille, K. R. (1983). Industrial relations performance, economic performance, and QWL programs: An interplant analysis. *Industrial and Labor Relations Review, 37,* 3–17.

Katz, H. C., Kochan, T. A., & Weber, M. R. (1985). Assessing the effects of industrial relations systems and efforts to improve the quality of working life on organizational effectiveness. *Academy of Management Journal, 28,* 509–526.

Kelley, M. R. (1996). Participative bureaucracy and productivity in the machined products sector. *Industrial Relations, 35,* 374–399.

Klein, K. J., Dansereau, F., & Hall, R. J. (1994). Levels issues in theory development, data collection, and analysis. *Academy of Management Review, 19,* 195–229.

Klein, K. J. & Sorra, J. S. (1996). The challenge of innovation implementation. *Academy of Management Review, 21,* 1055–1080.

Knoke, D., & Kallenberg, A. L. (1996). Job training in U.S. organizations. In A. L. Kallenberg, D. Knoke, P. V. Marsden, & J. L. Spaeth (Eds.), *Organizations in America.* Thousand Oaks, CA: Sage.

Kopelman, R. E., Brief, A. P., & Guzzo, R. A. (1990). The role of climate and culture in productivity. In B. Schneider (Ed.), *Organizational climate and culture* (pp. 282–318). San Francisco: Jossey-Bass.

Kozlowski, S.W.J., & Farr, J. L. (1988). An integrative model of updating and performance. *Human Performance, 1,* 5–29.

Kozlowski, S.W.J., Gully, S. M., McHugh, P. P., Salas, E., & Cannon-Bowers, J. A. (1996). A dynamic theory of leadership and team effectiveness: Developmental and task-contingent leader roles. *Research in Personnel and Human Resource Management, 14,* 253–305.

Kozlowski, S.W.J., & Hults, B. M. (1987). An exploration of climates for technical updating and performance. *Personnel Psychology, 40,* 539–563.

Kozlowski, S.W.J., & Klein, K. J. (2000). A multilevel approach to theory and research in organizations: Contextual, temporal, and emergent processes. In K. J. Klein & S.W.J. Kozlowski (Eds.), *Multilevel theory, research, and methods in organizations* (pp. 3–90). San Francisco: Jossey-Bass.

Kruse, D. L. (1993). *Profit sharing.* Kalamazoo, MI: W. E. Upjohn Institute.

Lado, A. A., & Wilson, M. C. (1994). Human resource systems and sustained competitive advantage: A competency-based perspective. *Academy of Management Review, 19,* 699–727.

Lawler, E. E. III (1992). *The ultimate advantage: Creating the high-involvement organization.* San Francisco: Jossey-Bass.

Lawler, E. E. III (1994). Total quality management and employee involvement: Are they compatible? *Academy of Management Executive, 8,* 68–76.

Lawler, E. E. III, Hall, D. T., & Oldham, G. R. (1974). Organizational climate: Relationships to organizational structure, process and performance. *Organizational Behavior and Human Performance, 11,* 139–155.

Lawler, E. E. III, Mohrman, S. A., & Ledford, G. E., Jr. (1995). *Creating high-performance organizations.* San Francisco: Jossey-Bass.

Lawrence, P. R., & Lorsch, J. W. (1967). *Organization and environment: Managing differentiation and innovation.* Cambridge, MA: Harvard University Press.

Levering, R., Moskowitz, M., & Katz, M. (1985). *The 100 best companies to work for in America.* Reading, MA: Addison-Wesley.

Lewin, A. Y., & Minton, J. W. (1986). Determining organizational effectiveness: Another look, and an agenda for research. *Management Science, 32,* 514–538.

Likert, R. L. (1961). *The human organization.* New York: McGraw-Hill.

Locke, E. A. (1984). Job satisfaction. In M. Gruneberg & T. Wall (Eds.), *Social psychology and organizational behavior* (pp. 93–117). New York: Wiley.

Louis, M. R. (1980). Surprise and sense making: What newcomers experience in entering unfamiliar organizational settings. *Administrative Science Quarterly, 25,* 226–251.

MacDuffie, J. P. (1995). Human resource bundles and manufacturing performance: Organizational logic and flexible production systems in the world auto industry. *Industrial and Labor Relations Review, 48,* 199–221.

Mahoney, T. A. (1988). Productivity defined: The relativity of efficiency, effectiveness, and change. In J. P. Campbell & R. J. Campbell (Eds.), *Productivity in organizations* (pp. 13–39). San Francisco: Jossey-Bass.

Mathieu, J. E., & Kohler, S. S. (1990). A cross-level examination of group absence influence on individual absence. *Journal of Applied Psychology, 75,* 217–220.

Mayo, E. (1933). *The human problems of industrial civilization.* New York: Macmillan.

McGregor, D. (1960). *The human side of enterprise.* New York: McGraw-Hill.

Meyer, M. W., & Gupta, V. (1994). The performance paradox. *Research in Organizational Behavior, 16,* 309–369.

Miles, R. E. & Snow, C. C. (1984). Designing strategic human resources systems. *Organizational Dynamics, 13,* 36–52.

Miles, R. E., & Snow, C. C. (1994). *Fit, failure and the hall of fame.* New York: Free Press.

Milgrom, P., & Roberts, J. (1995). Complementarities and fit: Strategy, structure, and organizational change in manufacturing. *Journal of Accounting and Economics, 19,* 179–208.

Mischel, W. (1973). Toward a cognitive social learning reconceptualization of personality. *Psychological Review, 80,* 252–283.

Morgeson, F. P., & Hofmann, D. A. (1999). The structure and function of collective constructs: Implications for multilevel research and theory development. *Academy of Management Review, 24,* 249–265.

Newman, J. E. (1975). Understanding the organization structure—job attitude relationship through perceptions of the work environment. *Organizational Behavior and Human Performance, 14,* 371–397.

Oldham, G. R., & Hackman, J. R. (1981). Relationships between organizational structures and employee reactions: Comparing alternative frameworks. *Administrative Science Quarterly, 22,* 203–219.

Organ, D. W. (1977). A reappraisal and reinterpretation of the satisfaction-causes-performance hypothesis. *Academy of Management Review, 2,* 46–53.

Organ, D. W. (1988). *Organizational citizenship behavior: The good-solider syndrome.* San Francisco: New Lexington Books.

Ostroff, C. (1992). The relationship between satisfaction, attitudes, and performance: An organizational-level analysis. *Journal of Applied Psychology, 77,* 693–974.

Ostroff, C. (1993). Comparing correlations based on individual-level and aggregated data. *Journal of Applied Psychology, 78,* 569–582.

Ostroff, C. (1995). SHRM/CCH survey. *Human Resources Management, 356,* 1–12.

Ostroff, C., & Schmitt, N. (1993). Configurations of organizational effectiveness and efficiency. *Academy of Management Journal, 36,* 1345–1361.

Pil, F. K., & MacDuffie, J. P. (1996). The adoption of high-involvement work practices. *Industrial Relations, 35,* 423–455.

Pfeffer, J. (1994). *Competitive advantage through people.* Boston: Harvard Business School Press.

Pfeffer, J., & Salancik, G. R. (1978). *The external control of organizations: A resource-dependence perspective.* New York: HarperCollins.

Porter, M. E. (1980). *Competitive strategy.* New York: Free Press.

Pritchard, R. D., & Karasick, B. W. (1973). The effects of organizational climate on managerial job performance and job satisfaction. *Organizational Behavior and Human Performance, 9,* 126–146.

Quinn, R. E., & Rohrbaugh, J. (1983). A spatial model of effectiveness criteria: Towards a competing-values approach to organizational analysis. *Management Science, 29,* 363–377.

Reichers, A. E., & Schneider, B. (1990). Climate and culture: An evolution of constructs. In B. Schneider (Ed.), *Organizational climate and culture* (pp. 5–39). San Francisco: Jossey-Bass.

Reichheld, F. (1996). *The loyalty effect.* Boston: Harvard Business School Press.

Roberts, K. H., Hulin, C. L., & Rousseau, D. M. (1978). *Developing an interdisciplinary science of organizations.* San Francisco: Jossey-Bass.

Roethlisberger, F. J. (1959). *Management and morale.* Cambridge, MA: Harvard University Press.

Rousseau, D. M. (1995). *Psychological contracts in organizations.* Thousand Oaks, CA: Sage.

Rousseau, D. M., & Greller, M. M. (1994). Human resource practices: Administrative contract makers. *Human Resource Management, 33,* 385–402.

Russell, J. S., Terborg, J. R., & Powers, M. L. (1985). Organizational performance and organizational-level training and support. *Personnel Psychology, 38,* 849–863.

Ryan, A. M., Schmit, M. J. & Johnson, R. (1996). Attitudes and effectiveness: Examining relations at an organizational level. *Personnel Psychology, 49,* 853–882.

Schein, E. H. (1980). *Organizational psychology* (3rd ed.). Englewood Cliffs, NJ: Prentice Hall.

Schmidt, F. L., Hunter, J. E., Pearlman, K., & Shane, G. S. (1979). Further tests of the Schmidt-Hunter Bayesian validity generalization procedure. *Personnel Psychology, 32,* 257–381.

Schneider, B. (1983). Interactional psychology and organizational behavior. *Research in Organizational Behavior, 5,* 1–31.

Schneider, B. (1987). The people make the place. *Personnel Psychology, 40,* 437–453.

Schneider, B. (1990). The climate for service: An application of the climate construct. In B. Schneider (Ed.), *Organizational climate and culture* (pp. 384–412). San Francisco: Jossey-Bass.

Schneider, B., & Bowen, D. E. (1985). Employee and customer perceptions of services in banks: Replication and extension. *Journal of Applied Psychology, 7,* 423–433.

Schneider, B., & Bowen, D. E. (1995). *Winning the service game.* Cambridge, MA: Harvard University Press.

Schneider, B., Brief, A. P., & Guzzo, R. A. (1996). Creating a climate and culture for sustainable organizational culture. *Organizational Dynamics, 24,* 7–19.

Schneider, B., Goldstein, H. W., & Smith, D. B. (1995). The ASA framework: An update. *Personnel Psychology, 48,* 747–773.

Schneider, B., Gunnarson, S. K., & Niles-Jolly, K. (1994). Creating the climate and culture of success. *Organizational Dynamics, 23,* 17–29.

Schneider, B., Parkington, J. J., & Buxton, V. M. (1980). Employee and customer perceptions of service in banks. *Administrative Science Quarterly, 25,* 252–267.

Schneider, B., & Reichers, A. (1983). On the etiology of climates. *Personnel Psychology, 36,* 19–40.

Schneider, B., & Schmitt, N. (1986). *Staffing organizations.* Glenview, IL: Scott, Foresman.

Schneider, B., Smith, D. B., Taylor, S. & Fleenor, J. (1998). Personality and organizations: A test of the homogeneity of personality hypothesis. *Journal of Applied Psychology, 83,* 462–470.

Schuler, R. S., & Jackson, S. E. (1987). Linking competitive strategy and human resource management practices. *Academy of Management Executive, 3,* 207–219.

Schuler, R. S., & Jackson, S. E. (1995). Understanding human resource management in the context of organizations and their environments. *Annual Review of Psychology, 46,* 237–264.

Senge, P. M. (1990). *The fifth discipline: The art and practice of the learning organization.* New York: Doubleday.

Staw, B. M., & Sutton, R. I. (1992). Macro organizational psychology. In J. K. Murnighan (Ed.), *Social psychology in organizations: Advances in theory and research.* Englewood Cliffs, NJ: Prentice Hall.

Terborg, J. (1981). Interactional psychology and research on human behavior in organizations. *Academy of Management Review, 6,* 569–576.

Terpstra, D. E., & Rozell, E. J. (1993). The relationship of staffing practices to organizational-level measures of performance. *Personnel Psychology, 46,* 27–48.

Tett, R. P., & Meyer, J. P. (1993). Job satisfaction, organizational commitment, turnover intention, and turnover: Path analyses based on meta-analytic findings. *Personnel Psychology, 46,* 259–293.

Tsui, A. S. (1990). A multiple-constituency model of effectiveness: An empirical examination at the human resource subunit level. *Administrative Science Quarterly, 35,* 458–483.

Tsui, A. S., Pearce, J. L., Porter, L. W. & Tripoli, A. M. (1997). Alternative approaches to employee-organization relationship: Does investment in employees pay off? *Academy of Management Journal, 40,* 1089–1121.

Ulrich, D. (1987). Organizational capability as a competitive advantage: Human resource professionals as strategic partners. *Human Resource Planning, 10,* 169–184.

Ulrich, D., & Lake, D. (1991). Organizational capability: Creating competitive advantage. *Academy of Management Executive, 5,* 77–91.

Vancouver, J., & Schmitt, N. (1991). An exploratory examination of person-organization fit: Organizational goal congruence. *Personnel Psychology, 44,* 333–352.

Waldman, D. A., & Bowen, D. E. (1998). The acceptability of 360-degree appraisals: A customer-supplier relationship perspective. *Human Resource Management, 37,* 117–130.

Weick, K. E. (1979). *The social psychology of organizing.* Reading, MA: Addison-Wesley.

Wright, P. M., McMahan, G. C., & McWilliams, A. (1994). Human resources and sustained competitive advantage: A resource-based perspective. *International Journal of Human Resource Management, 5,* 301–326.

Wright, P. M., & Snell, S. A. (1991). Toward an integrative view of strategic human resource management. *Human Resource Management Review, 1,* 203–225.

Youndt, M. A., Snell, S. A., Dean, J. W., Jr., & Lepak, D. P. (1996). Human resource management, manufacturing strategy, and firm performance. *Academy of Management Journal, 39,* 836–866.

Zohar, S. (1980). Safety climate in industrial organizations: Theoretical and applied implications. *Journal of Applied Psychology, 65,* 96–102.

CHAPTER 6

Interorganizational Relationships
A Multilevel Perspective

Katherine J. Klein
Shannon L. Palmer
Amy Buhl Conn

During the past decade, both research and theory regarding collaborative interorganizational relationships (IORs) have burgeoned. The increase in such theory and research reflects the recent rise in the number of organizations forming IORs—that is, the rise in the number of organizations creating relatively enduring formal and informal arrangements with other organizations to transfer, exchange, share, codevelop, or produce information, raw materials, technologies, and products (Auster, 1994; Gulati, 1995b; Oliver, 1990). Although the study of interorganizational relationships is still young, theorists and researchers have assembled a rich and impressive body of work. Theorists and researchers have explored, for example, the reasons why organizations form IORs (Eisenhardt & Schoonhoven, 1996; Gulati, 1995b), differing types of IORs (Oliver, 1990; Sheppard & Tuchinsky, 1996), the role of interorganizational trust and cooperation in fostering IOR success (Gulati, 1995a; Smith, Carroll, & Ashford, 1995), and the influence of key boundary spanners during the formation and maintenance of IORs (Currall & Judge, 1995; Seabright, Levinthal, & Fichman, 1992).

There is a sense of excitement—of discovery and import—in writings on interorganizational relationships. This excitement reflects, in part, the potential influence of such work on organizational practice, effectiveness, and survival. Researchers, theorists, and practitioners alike extol the virtues of interorganizational relationships, suggesting that organizations participating in IORs may gain knowledge and resources critical for long-term organizational survival (Powell, 1990; Uzzi, 1997), improve time to market for new products and innovations (Powell, Koput, & Smith-Doerr, 1996), and undertake otherwise prohibitively costly and risky research, development, and production activities (Powell, 1990; Powell et al., 1996). In sum, interorganizational relationships may allow firms to reduce market uncertainty and vulnerability and to meet strategic needs with greater flexibility and ease (Day, 1995; Dyer & Singh, 1998; Eisenhardt & Schoonhoven, 1996).

The sense of excitement in IOR writings stems as well from the challenge that IOR theory and research present to the strictest tenets of transaction-cost economics (TCE). TCE theory suggests, in essence, that the risks of opportunism (cheating, self-interest, guile) are so great, and that transaction costs (for example, interorganizational monitoring) are so high, that the production of goods and services may take place within just two basic types of entities: *markets,* in which buyers contract formally, and for a very limited period, with limited risk as well as trust, to pay sellers for their goods and services; and *hierarchies,* in which owners rely on internal controls and formalized monitoring to produce goods and perform necessary services to support the organization (Williamson, 1975, 1985). The existence and effective performance of IORs—in which rules of interorganizational coordination are loose, monitoring is informal, and trust is high—call key assumptions of transaction-cost economics into some question (Larson, 1992; Uzzi, 1997; Powell, 1990): IORs are neither pure markets nor pure hierarchies; rather, they are relatively interdependent, collaborative, enduring relationships between firms.

The sense of excitement in IOR theory and research stems, finally, from the diversity of perspectives and methods represented in this work. Research and theory range from macro (for example, studies of the performance of interorganizational networks) to micro (for example, studies of the characteristics of individual boundary spanners). Further, research methods in this area include longitudinal and network analyses using archival data (Gulati,

1995a), in-depth qualitative case studies (Larson, 1992; Uzzi, 1997), and surveys of key informants (Currall & Judge, 1995). One can find in the IOR literature a number of diverse scholars applying diverse perspectives and methods to the study of an important and topical issue.

Although the IOR literature is vibrant and rapidly growing, there looms within it a levels-related muddle. IORs are inherently and inescapably multilevel: individuals are nested within organizations, which are nested within dyadic interorganizational relationships, which are nested within networks of organizations, which are nested within industries and national economies and cultures. Further, as we have noted, the IOR literature is young and characterized by a great diversity of perspectives. The youth of the literature, the existence of numerous vantage points from which to study IORs, and the multilevel complexity of the IOR phenomenon lend both richness and levels-related confusion to IOR theory and research. Although some IOR theorists and researchers (Auster, 1994; Day, 1995; Weitz & Jap, 1995) note the numerous levels of analysis at which IORs may be conceptualized and studied, many do not specify explicitly their focal level(s) of theory and research.

Our goal in this chapter is to explore the levels of IOR theory and research. By making explicit the assumptions on which rests work at different levels of analysis, and in some cases by challenging these assumptions, we hope to increase the conceptual clarity of the IOR literature and to inspire multilevel studies of IORs. We seek not to criticize the existing literature but to identify ways in which multilevel research and theory can complement, elaborate, and extend the conclusions of current IOR theory and research. IOR research and theory are increasingly prominent in the macro organizational literature. We hope that our exploration of issues and assumptions largely overlooked in the existing IOR literature will suggest new avenues of research and theory building to macro scholars already familiar with the IOR literature. At the same time, we hope that our work will encourage more micro organizational scholars to take an interest in this important topic. Because the topic may be new to some readers, we have included in this chapter many quotations from IOR theory and research, as a means of familiarizing readers with the literature.

In the first section of the chapter, we outline numerous levels of analysis that are potentially relevant to the conceptualization and study of interorganizational relationships. In the second and third sections of the chapter, we highlight, respectively, the two levels that have received the greatest attention in the IOR literature: the interorganizational dyad as a homogeneous whole, and the organization as a homogeneous whole. In the second section we examine the implications—the benefits and drawbacks—of assuming homogeneity within the IOR dyad, and in the third section we examine the implications of assuming homogeneity within the organization. Our exploration of homogeneity continues in the fourth section of the chapter. We challenge the common assumption in the IOR literature that an organization's boundary spanners are homogeneous in their attitudes about and behaviors toward their organization's IOR(s). We argue that in some organizations boundary spanners may be united in their trust in and commitment to their organization's IOR partner, but that in other organizations boundary spanners may vary in their trust and commitment to the IOR. We provide a preliminary model of possible antecedents and consequences of within-organization variability in boundary spanners' trust in and commitment to the IOR. The chapter concludes with a brief summary of our key points and a call for multilevel research on interorganizational relationships.

Levels of Analysis and Interorganizational Relationships: The Potential Array

In considering the potential levels of analysis at which IORs may be studied and conceptualized, we have drawn on Klein, Dansereau, and Hall's (1994) conceptualization of levels-of-analysis issues in the organizational sciences. The choice of a level or levels of theory and analysis, as Klein and her colleagues have emphasized, has a profound influence on the entities on which a researcher or theorist focuses, the assumptions he or she makes, the questions he or she addresses, and the practical conclusions he or she draws. They propose that, in choosing or specifying the level of a theoretical construct, one implicitly or explicitly predicts that members of a group are *homogeneous, independent,* or *heterogeneous* with respect to the construct of interest. Homogeneous constructs include units' global properties, shared or consensus properties, and dispersion or configural properties (Chan, 1998; Kozlowski & Klein, Chapter One, this volume). In specifying that the level of a construct is a *homogeneous* unit or group, "a theorist predicts that group [or unit] members are sufficiently similar with respect to the construct in question that they may be characterized as a whole" (Klein et al., 1994, p. 199). The theorist's primary goal is thus to identify the sources or consequences of variability between whole units or groups. In specifying that the level of a construct is an *independent* individual (or unit), a theorist suggests that individuals (or units), with respect to the construct of interest, are substantially or fully independent of the larger contextual environment. The theorist's primary interest is thus in examining the sources or consequences of variability between individuals or units. Finally, in specifying that the level of a construct is *heterogeneous* (a frog-pond effect), the theorist suggests that unit members are neither homogeneous within the unit nor independent of the unit; rather, unit members vary with respect to the construct of interest, but the effects of such variability depend on the unit context: "Within one context, a given X value may be relatively large. Within a second context, the same X value may be relatively small. Relative, not absolute, value is predictive" (Klein et al., 1994, p. 201). Here we use Klein, Dansereau, and Hall's framework as a prism through which to examine the potential levels of IOR theory and research. Later in the chapter we draw more explicitly on other discussions of levels-related issues (Chan, 1998; House, Rousseau, & Thomas-Hunt, 1995; Kozlowski & Klein, Chapter One, this volume). To summarize our discussion in this section, Table 6.1 lists the many different levels of analysis at which IORs can be conceptualized and studied.

We begin our exploration of potential levels of IOR theory and research at the most macro, or global, end of the continuum. In the IOR literature, the most macro studies and conceptual models focus neither on single organizations nor on dyadic relationships between two organizations but rather on *interorganizational networks*. An interorganizational network describes the pattern of relationships linking an entire array of organizations in a single industrial sector or locality. Uzzi (1997), for example, conducted an ethnographic field study of the relationships among twenty-three

Table 6.1. Interorganizational Relationships and Levels of Analysis: Potential Array.

Level of Analysis	Likely Focus of Theory and Research	Example[a]
Interorganizational network as a homogeneous whole	The characteristics and actions of an entire network of organizations	Uzzi (1997)
Interorganizational dyad within the network	How the relationship between two organizations is affected by the relationships among other organizations in the network	Gulati (1995b)
Interorganizational dyad as a homogeneous whole	The effects of characteristics of the IOR relationship on the dynamics, longevity, or outcomes of the IOR relationship	Wilson (1995)
The organization within the interorganizational dyad	The effects of an IOR on one organization, given the organization's standing relative to its IOR partner	Oliver (1990)
The organization as a homogeneous whole	The influence of the characteristics of an organization on the organization's interorganizational relationships	Eisenhardt and Schoonhoven (1996)
Individuals and groups	The influence of individual or group characteristics on individuals' or groups' perceptions of and behavior toward their organization's interorganizational relationship(s)	Zaheer, McEvily, and Perrone (1998)

[a]The references cited as examples of the differing levels of analysis may illustrate just the level of analysis noted or may illustrate that level of analysis as well as other levels of analysis.

women's better-dress firms in the New York City apparel industry. On the basis of his research, Uzzi (1997) developed several propositions regarding single organizations, dyadic interorganizational relationships, and—most relevant to the current discussion—whole networks of organizations. For example, Uzzi proposes (p. 58) that "the loss of a core organization in a network will have a large negative effect on the viability of the network as a whole."

A somewhat less macro conceptualization focuses on the *interorganizational dyad in the network*. Rather than assuming the homogeneity of the interorganizational network, researchers and theorists considering the interorganizational dyad in the network attempt to capture network heterogeneity. The focus at this level of analysis is the extent to which the relationship between two organizations may be influenced by the relationships of other organizations in the network. Thus, for example, the consequences of a close relationship between two organizations may differ according to the number of other organizations in the network that have such close ties. Few researchers and theorists have espoused this level of analysis. Gulati (1995b, p. 646), however, hints at this level of analysis in observing that "today's choice of an alliance partner can affect tomorrow's alliance choices. This historical effect is further complicated by the fact that the underlying social network is modified by the prior alliance decisions of other firms. Hence, both a firm's own past alliances and those of other firms in a network influence its future actions."

At a still less macro level of analysis, theorists and researchers examine the *interorganizational dyad as a homogeneous whole*, making little or no reference to the larger interorganizational network in which the relationship occurs. In focusing on the IOR dyad as the unit of theory and analysis, a theorist or researcher suggests implicitly or explicitly that, for the constructs of interest, the respective experiences or perspectives of each individual organization in the IOR are sufficiently similar that the dyadic relationship per se is the appropriate focus of theory and analysis. This level of theory and analysis is quite common in the IOR literature. Van de Ven (1976, p. 25) writes that "many activities in an [interorganizational relationship] cannot be explained simply by analyzing the behavior of member organizations. Collective events arise out of the actions of the social system and are formally a property of the [IOR] itself." In a similar vein, Wilson (1995, p. 337) comments that "the atmosphere of the [interorganizational] relationship can be thought of as a hybrid culture that develops between the buying and selling firms and reflects elements of both firms' cultures but is different from either firm's culture."

Continuing along the macro-to-micro continuum, researchers and theorists may adopt a heterogeneous conceptualization of *the organization within the interorganizational dyad.* Here, the theorist or researcher attempts to capture one organization's experiences or standing relative to its IOR partner. The assumption underlying this perspective is that the organizations that make up an IOR differ with respect to key constructs of interest. Further, the theorist posits a compensatory, complementary, or compositional quality (Kozlowski & Klein, Chapter One, this volume) to the construct(s) of interest: the parties are interdependent but not homogeneous. This level of theory is not common in the IOR literature except perhaps in work that draws on a resource-dependency model of the firm (Pfeffer & Salancik, 1978). For example, Oliver (1990, pp. 243–244) notes that an organization may be prompted to form an IOR "by the potential to exercise power or control over another organization or its resources . . . [A] power approach to explaining IORs suggests that resource scarcity prompts organizations to attempt to exert power, influence, or control over organizations that possess the required scarce resources." Some theoretical models of the determinants of IOR formation also examine the experience of the organization within the dyadic IOR. For example, Weitz and Jap (1995, p. 312) posit that "a channel member will seek to develop relationships with firms offering synergistic capabilities that it does not possess."

Less macro still is the organizational level of analysis. In this case, the theorist focuses on the *organization as a homogeneous whole.* This level of analysis is quite common in the IOR literature. Thus, for example, Alexander (1995, p. 16) comments, "Some organizational characteristics seem to predispose organizations towards IOC [interorganizational coordination]. . . . Outward looking organizations are likely to be more ready to undertake coordinated efforts with other organizations. . . . In terms of organizational culture, this means a cosmopolitan and pluralist world-view, rather than a narrow one focused on local concerns." In their study of strategic alliance formation, Eisenhardt and Schoonhoven (1996) adopt the organizational level of analysis. They hypothesize and find that the greater the number of a firm's competitors, and the more innovative its strategy, the more likely the firm is to form strategic alliances.

Still further along the continuum, IOR theory and research may focus on the *individuals and groups* that compose the organizations within an IOR. Theorists and researchers might examine, for example, the extent to which individuals in an organization involved in an IOR are indeed homogeneous in their attitudes and behaviors toward the IOR. In this vein, Day (1995, p. 299) comments, "The foundation of mutual commitment is a recognition by each partner [in an IOR] that the other partner brings assets and capabilities that will enable the alliance to accomplish what neither can do alone. This belief must be diffused through all levels of the two organizations . . . rather than be restricted to the top managers who consummated the relationship." In general, however, IOR theorists and researchers have devoted very little attention to the individuals (other than the respective organizations' CEOs) who may be involved in creating, developing, and maintaining an IOR. In research focusing specifically on interorganizational trust, Zaheer, McEvily, and Perrone (1998) lament the dearth of attention to the multiple individuals involved in an IOR, noting that "not clearly specifying how trust translates from the individual to the organization level leads to theoretical confusion about who is trusting whom because it is *individuals* as members of organizations, rather than the organizations themselves, who trust."

Our brief review has described the variety of levels of analysis at which IORs can be conceptualized and studied. Each level of analysis is valid, we believe; no single level of analysis is necessarily more correct or appropriate than any other. Consideration of the array of levels, however, reveals possible contradictions among theories and studies focused on different levels of analysis. The interorganizational-network level of analysis suggests that the network operates as a homogeneous whole; thus, by definition, events that affect the network as a whole should affect each organizational member of the network in the same way. Research and theory focusing on the interorganizational dyad within the network, however, contradict this assertion, suggesting instead that some IOR dyads in a network may experience different consequences of network events than other IOR dyads. Therefore, work at these two levels of analysis may be difficult to reconcile and integrate—difficult, but not impossible. The challenge is to specify the boundary conditions for work at each level of analysis. When, in what ways, and with respect to what constructs is an interorganizational network a homogeneous whole? When, in what ways, and with respect to what constructs do IOR dyads differ as a function of other IOR dyads in the network? The answers to these questions—and to comparable questions regarding other levels of analysis—will facilitate the synthesis and further development of IOR theory and research.

The Interorganizational Dyad as a Whole: Implications of Assuming Homogeneity in the IOR Dyad

In the preceding section, we outlined the array of units of analysis on which IOR theorists and researchers focus. Two units of analysis are, however, most common in the IOR literature: the dyadic interorganizational relationship as a homogeneous whole, and the organization as a homogeneous whole. In this section, we review in more detail examples of theory and research regarding the IOR dyad. Further, we highlight the benefits and drawbacks ensuing from the assumption of homogeneity in the IOR dyad. In the following section, we consider IOR theory and research regarding the organization as a whole, and we explore the benefits and drawbacks of assuming homogeneity in the organization.

Theory and Research at This Level of Analysis: Examples

Researchers and theorists who focus on the dyadic IOR as a homogeneous whole often examine either the stages through which an IOR may progress or differing types of IORs. For example,

Dwyer, Schurr, and Oh (1987, p. 15) suggest that interorganizational buyer-seller relationships evolve through five stages:

1. Awareness
2. Exploration
3. Expansion
4. Commitment
5. Dissolution

The names of these phases make the dynamics of each phase rather clear. Thus, for example, "expansion refers to the continual increase in benefits obtained by exchange partners and to their increasing interdependence . . . The critical distinction is that the rudiments of trust and joint satisfactions established in the exploration stage now lead to increased risk taking within the dyad" (Dwyer et al., 1987, p. 18). Ring and Van de Ven (1994, pp. 96–97) offer a more complex conceptualization of the stages of an IOR, suggesting that "the development and evolution of a cooperative IOR [consist of] a repetitive sequence of negotiation, commitment, and execution stages, each of which is assessed in terms of efficiency and equity." Aspects of the two models dovetail as, for example, Ring and Van De Ven (1994, p. 105) suggest that "informal psychological contracts increasingly compensate . . . for formal contractual safeguards as reliance on trust among parties increases over time."

Several authors have catalogued the differing forms that IORs may take. Oliver's (1990) typology is a prominent one. She distinguishes among trade associations, voluntary agency federations, joint ventures, joint programs, corporate-financial interlocks, and agency-sponsor linkages. Adopting a very different approach, Sheppard and his colleagues build on work by Fiske (1990, 1992) to describe differing forms of buyer-seller relationships (Sheppard & Tuchinsky, 1996) and four different kinds of trust (Sheppard & Sherman, 1998). At one end of the continuum are relationships characterized by what Fiske (1990, 1992) has called market pricing: relationships in which "standard purchase and delivery terms prevail. . . . There is little consideration of past or future; the supplier is self-contained and the customer is free to shop elsewhere"

(Sheppard & Tuchinsky, 1996, p. 346). In such relationships, risks are low and interparty trust is limited (Sheppard & Sherman, 1998). At the other end of the continuum are relationships characterized by what Fiske (1990) terms "communal sharing." When firms are engaged in communal sharing, "one member's needs become the other's. The futures of the two firms become deeply intertwined. . . . [Each firm hopes to derive] long-term benefit from a deep relationship with the best customer or supplier" (Sheppard & Tuchinsky, 1996, pp. 352–353). In relationships of communal sharing, risks are high and trust is deep (Sheppard & Sherman, 1998). Sheppard and his colleagues' work bears an obvious relationship to stage models of IORs; the longer two organizations have shared an IOR, the more likely their relationship is to be characterized by interdependence, trust, and mutual consideration.

Benefits of Assuming Homogeneity in the IOR Dyad

In describing the dyadic interorganizational relationship as a homogeneous whole, researchers and theorists focus on experiences and characteristics shared by both organizations that comprise the IOR. The risk of this approach, as we shall discuss in more detail, is that the experiences and characteristics of both organizations may in fact not be shared; the homogeneity implicitly or explicitly assumed in research and theory at this level of analysis may be a misrepresentation.

And yet researchers and theorists achieve important benefits in focusing on the shared characteristics and experiences of both parties in an IOR. Parsimony is a considerable benefit. In focusing on the interorganizational relationship, researchers and theorists eschew the complexity of considering the interaction of two organizations differing in attitudes, behaviors, experiences, and motives. But perhaps even more beneficial is the ability of researchers and theorists espousing this level of theory to draw on research and theory regarding other forms of social relationships, and to thereby build multilevel models. Multilevel models (House et al., 1995; Klein et al., 1994; Kozlowski & Klein, Chapter One, this volume) suggest that the relationship between two or more variables holds at multiple levels of analysis.

Multilevel IOR models posit that hypotheses and findings linking two or more variables apply both to interpersonal relationships and to interorganizational relationships. In some cases, multilevel models are relatively simple and even metaphorical. Many theorists (for example, Dwyer et al., 1987; Powell, 1990) liken the IOR to a marriage. Building on this metaphor, Weitz and Jap (1995, p. 316) propose that "communication that helps to maintain the [IOR] over time involves increased interaction and time spent together relative to the early stages of the relationship. Topics of discussion are of a wider variety and deeper level than earlier in the relationship."

Other multilevel models are more complex. For example, Sheppard and Sherman (1998) propose that "type and depth of interdependence are qualities of relationships that are similar among entities of different scale and features. Thus, for example, deep dependence between children and parents, employees and companies, franchisees and franchisers, and citizens and government is much alike." Sheppard and Sherman's discussion (1998) of "quadratic trust" (Fiske, 1990) provides a particularly compelling example of the explanatory power of isomorphic constructs. When entities share a relationship of deep dependence or communal sharing, "people with social links to the primary parties have a duty to react when the primary parties fail to meet their obligations—they must modify their social relationships with the primary parties in suitable ways" (Fiske, 1990, p. 171). Anticipating such displays of quadratic trust, individuals and organizations alike may conform to the norms of a deep dependence relationship. Larson's ethnographic study (1992) of the interorganizational alliances of seven high-growth firms provides an example of organizational quadratic trust. Although Larson does not use the term quadratic trust, she does (p. 85) note its powerful effects: "If affiliation with a respected organization enhanced a second firm's reputation by earning it legitimacy and credibility, then the failure of a relationship could have a serious impact on reputation and status and, subsequently, on business." In a similar vein, Gulati (1995a, p. 93) notes that "untrustworthy behavior by a partner can lead to costly sanctions [including loss of reputation] that exceed any potential benefits that opportunistic behavior may provide."

Although multilevel constructs—that is, compositional or compilation constructs (Kozlowski & Klein, Chapter One, this volume) such as trust, risk, dependence, reputation, and communication—dot the IOR literature, few IOR scholars have developed detailed and thoroughly researched multilevel models. Sheppard and his colleagues (Sheppard & Sherman, 1998; Sheppard & Tuchinsky, 1996) provide an exception; they have drawn relatively explicitly and thoroughly on Fiske's (1990) research and theory in developing their theoretical models. But the growing psychological literature on marital and other interpersonal relationships (Berscheid & Reis, 1998; Gabarro, 1987; Gottman, 1993, 1994; Karney & Bradbury, 1995) may provide the basis for the development of creative, detailed, and empirically grounded multilevel models of the relationships of individuals and of organizations. If IOR researchers and theorists move beyond the consideration of marriage as a mere metaphor to the consideration of research on marriage (and other interpersonal relationships) as the basis for IOR theory building and research, then IOR scholars may gain further benefits from adopting the interorganizational dyad as the unit of analysis. Klein and Kozlowski (Chapter One, this volume) offer guidelines for multilevel theory development and research of this type.

Drawbacks of Assuming Homogeneity in the IOR Dyad

A focus on the dyadic interorganizational relationship as a homogeneous whole offers considerable benefits, but it also raises the possibility of three substantial drawbacks. First and foremost, the organizations in an IOR may not be homogeneous; they may differ greatly in their characteristics, behaviors, and experiences of the IOR. Theory and research (described in the following section) focusing on the organization as a homogeneous unit, rather than on the interorganizational dyad as a homogeneous unit, suggest that both an organization's motivation to form an IOR and its behavior within an IOR may be shaped by the organization's strategy, resources, history, and culture and by the values and reputation of its senior personnel (Wilkof, Brown, & Selsky, 1995). Given that two organizations involved in an IOR are very unlikely to be identical with respect to these characteristics, this body of theory calls into question assumptions of homogeneity in the interorganizational dyad. Thus, challenging assumptions of dyadic homogeneity, an organization may be highly committed to maintaining a cooperative relationship with its partner organization, but the partner organization may be ready to dissolve the relationship. Further, one organization may be highly dependent on its IOR, whereas its IOR partner is not. In short, interorganizational stages, communication, commitment, trust, risk, and dependence—assumed, in the bulk of theory and research already discussed here, to be homogeneous within the IOR—may or may not actually be shared.

This possibility has received very little attention in the IOR literature. Indeed, we know of only one study in which researchers have assessed the extent to which organizational representatives agree in their assessment of the interorganizational relationship. Currall and Judge (1995) surveyed 152 pairs of school superintendents and union presidents regarding their relationship and found that superintendents and presidents agreed substantially in their ratings of the extent to which they trusted each other; within-dyad variance in the survey responses was significantly less than between-dyad variance. Note, however, that whereas school superintendents and union presidents certainly share a boundary-spanning *interpersonal* relationship, their relationship may or may not truly represent an *interorganizational* relationship.

Thus the IOR literature provides very little empirical data either to support or to refute the claim that organizations in a dyadic IOR are homogeneous in their experience of interorganizational stages, trust, dependence, communication, and benefits. The magnitude of interorganizational homogeneity in these constructs is worthy of theoretical and empirical attention. If IOR dyads are not homogeneous with respect to these constructs, then research measures that are based on the assumption of such homogeneity mask potentially important variability in IOR dyads. Perhaps homogeneity within an IOR dyad is itself predictive of the success of the interorganizational relationship. If so, then homogeneity is not a constant that may be assumed but is instead a predictor to be assessed. An IOR may be most likely to survive if the IOR is beneficial to both of the firms that make up the IOR *and* if both firms are similar in their assessments of interorganizational trust, communication, dependence, risk, and so on. Whetten (1987, p. 249) proposes that organizational partners, ideally, should share "some common background, so that they can relate to one another, form a trusting relationship, and establish a common language for discussing their common objectives. In addition, participating organizations should have comparable resources and reputations, so that the power bases of their representatives will be similar."

A second drawback of theory and research focused on the homogeneous interorganizational dyad is that this focus may introduce a positive bias in the literature. Theory and research at this level of analysis typically examine surviving IORs. Out of the picture, typically, are IORs that never quite came to fruition and IORs that disintegrated in conflict or neglect and died (Auster, 1994). Perhaps not surprisingly, then, many theoretical models (Powell, 1990) and qualitative analyses (Larson, 1992) are very positive in their assessments of the benefits of IORs, noting only in passing, or not at all, the time-consuming conflicts and disruptions that a troubled IOR may cause its member organizations. (For an exception, see Whetten, 1987, who offers a discussion of the possible negative consequences of IORs.)

A third drawback of research and theory focused on the homogeneous interorganizational dyad is that such work presupposes not only interorganizational homogeneity but also intraorganizational homogeneity. That is, if two organizations are homogeneous in their experience of interorganizational stages, trust, dependence, communication, and benefits, then the boundary-spanning members of each organization must be homogeneous with respect to these experiences and characteristics, as well. This assumption of intraorganizational homogeneity, as we shall suggest, may be untenable in many instances.

Summary Comments

The assumption of dyadic interorganizational homogeneity offers both benefits and drawbacks for IOR theory and research. Models and analyses based on assumptions of dyadic IOR homogeneity are parsimonious and may benefit from the insights of multilevel models of interpersonal relationships. If, however, the assumption of dyadic IOR homogeneity is incorrect, then models and analyses based on this assumption overestimate both the similarity of the member organizations and the benefits to be gained from an IOR. Our hope is that by drawing attention to the assumptions undergirding IOR theory and research at this level of analysis, we may help IOR theorists and researchers gain the potential benefits and avoid the potential drawbacks associated with this level of analysis.

The Organization as a Whole: Implications of Assuming Organizational Homogeneity

Theory and Research at This Level of Analysis: Examples

IOR researchers and theorists who focus on the organization as a homogeneous whole commonly examine the characteristics that predispose an organization to form and maintain interorganizational relationships. Key organizational characteristics identified in the IOR literature include organizational culture, structure, and strategy and the characteristics of an organization's chief executive officer or top management team. For example, Whetten (1987) suggests that an organization is most likely to form an IOR if its executives or administrators have a positive attitude toward interorganizational coordination, recognize a need for such coordination, and are aware of potential coordination partners. Alexander (1995) proposes that organizations low in centralization, high in task complexity, accessible to other organizations through voluntary associations and informal contacts, and characterized by outward-looking, cosmopolitan, and trusting cultures are most likely to form IORs. Larson (1992, p. 99) concludes, on the basis of her ethnographic research, that firms are most likely to form IORs if they have "a history of prior personal relations," "reputational knowledge that provides a receptive context for the initiation and evolution of economic exchange," and "a capacity to commit to a mutual orientation." Studying semiconductor firms, Eisenhardt and Schoonhoven (1996) hypothesized and found that firms were most likely to form interorganizational alliances if they operated in a highly competitive market, employed technically innovative strategies, and had large founding top management teams whose members had previously worked for many semiconductor firms in high management positions.

Benefits of Assuming Organizational Homogeneity

IOR researchers and theorists who adopt this level of analysis focus on the organization as a whole, devoting relatively little explicit attention to more macro or more micro levels of analysis. Research and theory at this level of analysis suggest, implicitly or explicitly, that an organization may be studied as an independent actor, with little regard to its organizational partner in the IOR; the organization, not the organizational dyad, is the unit of analysis. Research and theory at this level of analysis suggest as well that the organizational boundary spanners who enact the organization's interorganizational relationship(s) are homogeneous with respect to the constructs of interest. The organization may be characterized as a whole, without regard to the perceptions and experiences of individual boundary spanners.

This level of analysis, like the dyadic organizational level of analysis, offers substantial benefits to the theorist or researcher. The primary benefits are parsimony, isomorphism, and practicality. The theorist or researcher focusing solely on the organization as a whole eschews the complexity of also considering levels of analysis higher and/or lower than the organizational level. Moreover, because the IOR literature is still young, there remains much to be learned about the correlates of an organization's pursuit and maintenance of interorganizational relationships. IOR research at the organizational level of analysis (Eisenhardt & Schoonhoven, 1996; Larson, 1992) has yielded important insights.

Further, IOR theorists and researchers working at this level of analysis may develop and test multilevel models. Interdependence theory (Kelley & Thibaut, 1969, 1978; Rusbult & Van Lange, 1996), a social psychological theory of interpersonal processes, provides a rich foundation for the development of organization-level IOR theory. For example, a key construct in this theory—the comparison level for alternatives (CL-alt)—is applicable to individuals and to organizations. The CL-alt is the standard an individual uses "in deciding whether to remain in or to leave the relationship" (Thibaut & Kelley, 1959, p. 21). The greater the number of attractive possible alternatives to a current relationship partner an individual perceives, the more he or she is likely to demand of his or her relationship partner. If the individual is not satisfied with his or her current partner, he or she can go elsewhere. Wilson (1995) proposes that the same principle applies to buyer-seller relationships. Interdependence theory suggests as well that "as a consequence of their unique histories, individuals acquire *interpersonal dispositions*" (Rusbult & Van Lange, 1996, p. 582) to approach or avoid interdependence, to trust or to distrust, to compete or to cooperate, and so on. This construct, too, appears isomorphic, manifested at the organizational level of analysis in an organization's "culture of trust" (Alexander, 1995, p. 16).

A final benefit of IOR research at the organizational level of analysis is practicality. Many researchers studying IORs at the organizational level of analysis (Eisenhardt & Schoonhoven, 1996) conceptualize and operationalize their variables as global measures (Kozlowski & Klein, Chapter One, this volume), gathering survey data from just one respondent per organization. Other researchers studying IORs at this level of analysis (Gulati, 1995a) rely on archival measures to operationalize their constructs. Both strategies are, of course, far less time-consuming than gathering data from multiple individual respondents in each organization participating in an IOR.

Drawbacks of Assuming Organizational Homogeneity

IOR research and theory at the organizational level of analysis offer substantial advantages, as we have noted, but substantial drawbacks as well. A first drawback is that researchers and theorists, in adopting the homogeneous organizational level of analysis, may overlook, sometimes just temporarily, the larger context of the IOR—the focal organization's partner in the interorganizational relationship, as well as the larger organizational network. A great deal of organization-level IOR theory and research has focused on the characteristics that predispose an organization to form and maintain interorganizational relationships, but the determinants of IOR formation and maintenance transcend a single organization. For example, the success and longevity of an IOR may depend on the match between the focal organization's culture and the culture of its partner organization (Wilkof et al., 1995). Further, the likelihood that an organization will form an alliance with another firm is influenced in part by the larger social network of firms in an organization's niche; "previously unconnected firms are more likely to enter an alliance if they have common partners" (Gulati, 1995b, p. 644).

A second drawback is that organization-level IOR theory and research may create the erroneous if inadvertent impression that a given organization is likely to form similar IORs with multiple organizations. Consider, for example, the finding that organizations with "a capacity to commit to a mutual orientation" (Larson, 1992, p. 99) are particularly likely to form highly cooperative, trusting interfirm alliances. This finding may create the impression that an organization with such a capacity will have highly cooperative, trusting relationships with all its organizational partners, but IOR research has documented that a given organization is likely to have both embedded (close, collaborative, trusting) ties to some organizations and arm's-length (formal, time-limited, transactional) ties to other organizations. As Uzzi (1997, p. 42) reports, "stringent assumptions about individuals being either innately self-interested or cooperative are too simplistic, because the same individuals simultaneously [act] 'selfishly' and cooperatively with different actors in their network—an orientation . . . shown to be an emergent property of the quality of the social tie and the structure of the network in which the actors [are] embedded." By definition, pure organization-level models focus on between-organization differences in predictors (for example, organizational structure, culture, and strategy) as well as in outcomes (for example, IOR formation, maintenance, and longevity). Accordingly, these models cannot explain variability in the nature of a single organization's relationships with different organizations.

A third potential drawback of IOR theory and research focused at the organizational level of analysis is that such work may blur the distinction between an organization and its CEO. Statistically, this blurring of the distinction between the organization and its CEO is not necessarily problematic because there is, of course, just one CEO per company; therefore, the number of CEOs in a sample equals the number of companies. Conceptually, however, this blurring of the distinction between the CEO and the organization can be confusing: Is the theorist's focus the CEO or the organization as a whole? For example, in describing "the capacity to commit to a mutual orientation," Larson (1992, p. 99) writes, "The mutual orientation requires sufficient commitment of resources and time to develop knowledge of the prospective partner's business and respect for the other's interests through a learning and adaptation process." But who is making the commitment of resources and time? Is it the CEO or the organization as a whole? For scholars hoping to build on Larson's impressive qualitative research, this is not a tangential question; rather, it has important implications for measurement and data collection.

A fourth and fundamental drawback of research and theory at the organizational level of analysis is that the underlying assumption of organizational homogeneity may not be tenable; the members of a single organization may differ in their experiences and perceptions of a given IOR. Fichman and Goodman (1996, p. 315) note that diverse organization members (company executives, sales personnel, service personnel, billing personnel) are involved at different times, and in different ways, in the relationship between a buyer firm and a seller firm. Wilson (1995, p. 341) comments, "If the buyer-seller [IOR] team has developed strong mutual goals, trust and social bonding, they will want their firm to commit appropriate resources to complete the task. As the team fights for resources to do this, resource negotiation will take place not only between the partner firms but also between the firm's hybrid team members and their colleagues." This description underscores the point that organization members may not all view the IOR in identical fashion: those most involved in the IOR may be highly committed to the interfirm alliance, whereas those less involved may view the IOR as a risky investment and a financial drain.

Summary Comments

The organizational level of analysis offers important benefits for IOR theory and research. Theory at this level of analysis may be parsimonious, building on isomorphic constructs. Further, research at this level of analysis has proved both practical and fruitful. But there are drawbacks to this level of analysis. IOR theorists and researchers, in assuming organizational homogeneity, may underestimate the influence of other organizations on the focal organization's interorganizational relationships; the variability among a focal organization's interorganizational relationships; the role of individuals other than the CEO in developing and maintaining the organization's IORs; and the extent to which organization members vary in their experience and perceptions of the IOR.

Antecedents and Consequences of Variability in Trust and Commitment: Preliminary Model

The assumption of within-organization homogeneity of boundary spanners' trust in and commitment to an IOR partner bears conceptual and empirical scrutiny, as we have already suggested. Before presenting our model of the possible consequences and antecedents of such homogeneity, we discuss errors of measurement and conceptual limitations that may arise if the common assumption of organizational homogeneity in boundary spanners' trust and commitment is inaccurate. Further, we comment on the identity of organization members, beyond the CEO, who may serve as IOR boundary spanners.

Homogeneity: An Assumption Worth Testing

The vast majority of the IOR literature rests on the tacit assumption of within-organization homogeneity in perceptions and experiences of the IOR and in behavior toward the organization's IOR partner. This tacit assumption is manifest in IOR researchers' and theorists' discussions and analyses of organizational trust, for example, without regard to the specific individuals who trust (Zaheer et al., 1998). It is manifest in IOR researchers' and theorists' equation of the CEO and the organization, without regard to the other organization members who may participate in the IOR and who may differ from the CEO in their perceptions, experiences, and behaviors. It is manifest as well in IOR researchers' and theorists' broad discussions of the individuals who participate in an IOR, discussions with little specificity regarding who the individuals are, how they participate in the IOR, and whether and why they agree or disagree in their perceptions and experiences of, and behaviors within, the IOR. Moreover, the assumption of within-organization homogeneity is implicit in higher-level theories; by assuming homogeneity of organizations within the interorganizational dyad or the interorganizational network, researchers implicitly assume homogeneity of individuals within organizations.

But what if this assumption of within-organization homogeneity is incorrect? What if the members of an organization who span their organization's boundary do not all feel equally trustful of, interdependent with, committed to, or willing to collaborate with their firm's interorganizational partner? If the assumption of within-organization homogeneity is erroneous, then research scholarship based on this assumption is, as we have suggested, at best incomplete, lacking in potentially important complexities and nuances. The researcher who assumes within-organization homogeneity in his or her measures is unlikely to gather the data necessary to assess the extent of within-organization, between-individual variability in the measures. Instead, the researcher is likely to rely on interview or survey responses of a key informant, or on archival data, to measure his or her constructs. If, however, boundary-spanning organization members in fact vary in, for example, their feelings of trust and their skills in collaboration, then global, organizational measures misrepresent the organizational reality. In the presence of substantial within-organization variability, the construct validity of a global organization-level measure is limited (Klein et al., 1994; Kozlowski & Klein, Chapter One, this volume).

The problem is not only one of measurement error, however, but also one of interpretation and counsel. Theoretical models and studies that rest on erroneous assumptions of within-organization homogeneity obscure potentially important intra-and interorganizational dynamics. Suppose, for example, that top managers and day-to-day boundary spanners differ in their assessments of the long-term benefits of an IOR. How do managers convince employees on the front lines of the IOR of the wisdom of their views? How do day-to-day boundary spanners alert managers to problems in, or to the unexplored potential of, an IOR? How do boundary spanners manage their involvement in the IOR, in the absence of full managerial support for their views? Further, how do the individuals in the partner organization respond to the mixed signals emanating from their organizational partner? In assuming within-organization homogeneity, theorists and researchers ignore these issues and thus can offer little or no advice to managers struggling with these challenges. Accordingly, further study is warranted of the extent to which an organization's boundary spanners are united in their perceptions, experiences, and behaviors.

Variability Among Whom?
Identity of Organizational Boundary Spanners

Unfortunately, the IOR literature as a whole sheds little light on the identity of the employees who span the organizational boundary and represent their organization in its interactions with other organizations. Qualitative case studies (Larson, 1992; Uzzi, 1997) offer rich descriptions of the dynamics of interorganizational coordination and trust but relatively few specifics regarding the status or titles of the individuals who in fact coordinate, communicate, and trust across organizational lines. Ring and Van De Ven (1994, p. 95) emphasize that IORs "only emerge, evolve, grow, and dissolve over time as a consequence of individual activities." Nevertheless, Ring and Van de Ven describe the individuals involved in an IOR obliquely, referring to them simply as "parties" (p. 101) or as "individuals assigned to a cooperative IOR" (p. 103). As already noted, Fichman and Goodman (1996) describe in some detail the diverse personnel involved in an interorganizational buyer-seller relationship. Still, their description is brief; it offers scant illumination of individual roles and relationships.

In sum, although many authors (e.g., Eisenhardt & Schoonhoven, 1996) highlight the role of the company founder, CEO, or top management team in forming IORs, and although many authors (e.g., Ring & Van de Ven, 1994) suggest implicitly or explicitly that other organization members are involved in the day-to-day boundary-spanning coordination of an IOR, the available literature sheds little light on the actions and interactions that occur in an organization as it negotiates and maintains an IOR. Surely a mature IOR involves many individuals—R&D personnel, sales personnel, and/or production personnel, for example—in addition to the executive who may have initiated and approved the deal. But the IOR literature has scarcely documented how the boundary-spanning members of an organization interact with one another nor how they interact with their counterparts across the organizational boundary. Of necessity, then, our discussion of these individuals, their interactions, and the extent to which they are united in their perceptions of and behaviors toward individuals across the organizational boundary is speculative.

Possible Consequences of Variability in Trust and Commitment

In this section, we focus on the possible consequences of variability in the extent to which an organization's multiple boundary spanners trust, are committed to, perceive that their organization is interdependent with, and collaborate with their organization's IOR partner firm. We focus on these attitudes and behaviors, hereafter referred to simply as "boundary-spanner IOR trust and commitment," because they are the defining characteristics of IORs; that is, the existing literature describes IORs as relatively trusting, interdependent, committed, and collaborative relationships between firms—relationships that differ markedly from firms' more common, arm's-length, market relationships (Powell, 1990; Larson, 1992; Ring & Van de Ven, 1994; Uzzi, 1997). We note, however, that boundary-spanner IOR trust and commitment are likely to vary not only within firms but also between them. Therefore, the average level of boundary-spanner IOR trust and commitment may be higher in some organizations than in others. Further, the relationship between the average level of boundary spanner IOR trust and commitment, on the one hand, and the benefits of the IOR to the organization, on the other, is uncertain. Much of the IOR literature, implicitly or explicitly, suggests that IORs distinguished by high boundary-spanner trust and commitment are the ones most likely to yield organizational benefits (e.g., Day, 1995; Kumar, 1996; Powell et al., 1996); nevertheless, it is certainly possible to imagine that in some circumstances IORs characterized by relatively low trust and commitment are still quite beneficial to the organizational partners. We will now focus on the consequences of within-organization (as opposed to between-organization) variability in boundary-spanner IOR trust and commitment. Figure 6.1 depicts our model of the likely consequences and antecedents of variability in boundary-spanner IOR trust and commitment. We begin by discussing the consequences rather than the antecedents of variability because the antecedents of variability are important only if

Figure 6.1. Possible Antecedents and Consequences of Variability in Boundary Spanners' IOR Trust and Commitment.

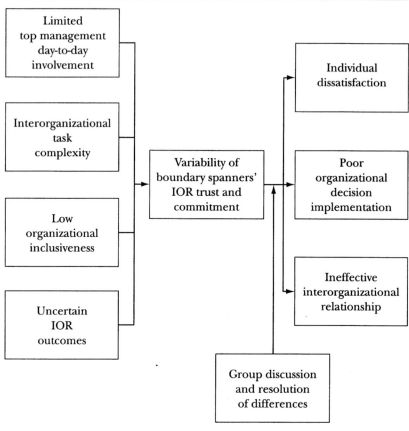

the consequences of variability are potentially substantial, as we believe they are.

Variability in Trust and Commitment: A Dispersion Construct

Variability is, of course, the opposite of homogeneity. Within-organization variability in boundary-spanner IOR trust and commitment is a dispersion (Chan, 1998) or configural construct (Kozlowski & Klein, Chapter One, this volume). Chan (1998, p. 239) notes that "dispersion is by definition a group-level characteristic . . . because it refers to the variability within a group and a variance statistic is indexing an attribute of a group as opposed to an attribute of any individual-level response." Elaborating on Chan (1998), we may differentiate organizations on the basis of their high, medium, or low variability in boundary-spanner IOR trust and commitment. When variability is high, organization members who are directly or indirectly involved in an IOR differ a great deal in the extent to which they trust the partner firm, are committed to maintaining a relationship with the partner firm, perceive that their organization is interdependent with the partner firm, and are inclined to collaborate with the partner firm. Note that variability in boundary-spanner IOR trust and commitment may itself vary within a firm; that is, an organization's boundary spanners may vary a great deal in their trust in and commitment to one of their firm's partners, but the same organization's boundary spanners may vary little—may be homogeneous—in their trust in and commitment to one of their firm's *other* organizational partners. Complicating the picture still further, in a single organization the individual boundary spanners who are involved in the organization's relationship with one organizational partner (firm A) may differ from the individual boundary spanners who are involved in the organization's relationship with another partner (firm B). In discussing within-organization variability in boundary-spanner IOR trust and commitment, we have set these nuances and complications aside while nevertheless recognizing that they merit additional attention in subsequent theoretical and empirical analyses.

Dispersion constructs such as variability in boundary-spanner IOR trust and commitment are receiving increasing attention but are still rare in organizational theory and research. Perhaps the most common example of a dispersion variable in the empirical organizational literature is demographic heterogeneity—a measure of the variability among unit members' with respect to age, gender, race, tenure, educational background, and other characteristics. In the past decade, many studies (e.g., Chatman, Polzer, Barsade, & Neale, 1998; Harrison, Price, and Bell, 1998; Tsui, Egan, & O'Reilly, 1992) have examined the correlates of demographic heterogeneity. More rarely have researchers examined the correlates of variability in unit members' perceptions, attitudes, and behaviors (trust and commitment, for example). Bliese and Halverson (1998), however, hypothesized and found that the greater the variability in unit members' perceptions of their unit's leadership climate and peer relations, the lower the group members' average psychological well-being.

Dispersion constructs are increasingly common in the theoretical literature. Klein and House (1995), for example, explored the homogeneity of charisma (a dispersion construct), arguing that a leader may have charismatic relationships with all, some, or none of his or her followers. Hambrick (1994) has examined top management team members' paradigm homogeneity—the extent to which team members have a vocabulary in common, reach consensus on strategic means and ends, and share perceptions of the environment, the organization's strategic position, and its prospects. Other recent examples of dispersion include Waldman and Yammarino's discussion (1999) of culture strength, Kostova's discussion (1999) of the degree of compatibility between the values of a parent company and its subsidiaries, and Drazin, Glynn, and Kazanjian's discussion (1999) of the extent to which diverse occupational groups have a common creative frame of reference.

Intriguingly, a common thread unites studies and conceptual analyses of dispersion. Across topic areas, organizational scholars have proposed and increasingly documented that dispersion within a group—dispersion of demographic variables, attitudes, perceptions, or values—is positively related to group creativity but negatively related to social integration within the group, cohesion, speed of decision making, and ease of decision implementation (Bliese & Halverson 1998; Drazin et al., 1999; Hambrick, 1994; Harrison et al., 1998; Jackson, May, & Whitney, 1995; Klein & House, 1995; Kostova, 1999; Pelled 1996; Williams & O'Reilly, 1998). In their review of the literature on organizational demography, for example, Williams & O'Reilly (1998, p. 88) note that "diversity in the composition of the group is proposed to increase the information available for problem solving and, in turn, enhance the ability of the group to generate correct or creative solutions to problems." Yet diversity is also proposed, as Williams and O'Reilly (1998, p. 88) note, "to result in increased conflict, factionalism, and communication difficulties." Pelled (1996, p. 625) links the two outcomes—creative problem solving and conflict—and suggests that "substantive conflict allows group members to test their ideas by exposing them to criticism. Exploration of opposing positions can help them gather new data, delve into issues more deeply, and develop a more complete understanding of problems and alternative solutions." Pelled's formulation rests, however, on the assumption that group members have the time and inclination to air and resolve their conflicting views.

Potentially Negative Consequences of Variability in IOR Trust and Commitment

Research and theory on within-group dispersion, broadly defined, thus suggests that in ideal circumstances organizational boundary spanners who vary in their IOR trust and commitment are likely to make thoughtful and well-reasoned decisions regarding their organization's involvement with a current or prospective IOR partner; that is, in ideal circumstances, boundary spanners will come together openly to air and resolve their differing views of the extent to which their firm should trust, be committed to, and collaborate with an IOR partner. After they have carefully weighed the available evidence regarding the trustworthiness of their current or prospective IOR partner and the strategic significance of the IOR, the organization's boundary spanners reach a sound and informed decision.

But ideal circumstances may not prevail. An organization's boundary spanners are likely to vary in hierarchical level and function, and so they may have little opportunity or inclination to openly air their differing views. R&D personnel, for example, may hesitate to tell the director of R&D or the CEO that they do not share the R&D director's or CEO's enthusiasm for a given IOR, but the R&D personnel may drag their feet in implementing the IOR. They may withhold information from their organization's IOR partner. They may respond slowly, if at all, to the requests of their organization's IOR partner. They may covertly block their firm's coordination and communication with its IOR partner.

Accordingly, we suspect that variability in boundary spanners' IOR trust and commitment is likely, in most cases, to yield individual dissatisfaction, poor organizational decision implementation, inadequate intraorganizational coordination, and, ultimately, an ineffective interorganizational alliance. The potential negative consequences of variability in boundary-spanner IOR trust and commitment thus span three levels of analysis. At the individual level of analysis, individual boundary spanners whose trust in and commitment to an IOR differ from other boundary spanners' trust and commitment to the IOR may feel out of step with their organization and frustrated that the merits of their position are not apparent to other boundary spanners in the organization. At the organizational level of analysis, variability in boundary spanners' trust in and commitment to an IOR may lead to poor decision implementation: boundary spanners who question the wisdom of their top management's decisions regarding a current or prospective IOR partner may subvert those decisions, carrying out top management's directives minimally, slowly, or not at all. Further, boundary spanners may find it difficult to coordinate their efforts with colleagues who differ in their trust in and commitment to the organization's IOR partner. Finally, at the IOR dyadic level of analysis, variability in boundary spanners' trust in and commitment to the IOR may damage the quality of the interorganizational relationship as a whole. When the boundary-spanning members of firm A send firm B a mixed message regarding firm A's trust in and commitment to working with firm B, the boundary-spanning members of firm B may pull back from the IOR, finding firm A an inconsistent and unpredictable IOR partner. Further, variability in firm A's trust in and commitment to working with firm B may prove contagious: experiencing differing treatment from firm A boundary spanners, firm B boundary spanners may come to differ in their own trust in and commitment to working with firm A. Slow and incomplete decision implementation on the part of one or both organizational partners, and variability in the trust and commitment of one or both organizations' boundary spanners with respect to their partner organization, are likely to jeopardize the viability of the firms' IOR.

In sum, we suspect that in many circumstances variability in the extent to which an organization's IOR boundary spanners trust in and are committed to one of their firm's IOR partners will have quite negative consequences. In ideal circumstances, however, variability in boundary-spanner IOR trust and commitment may lead not to negative outcomes but rather to an open discussion of differences of opinion, followed by a resolution of differences and effective decision implementation. We caution that our discussion of the consequences of variability in boundary spanners' trust and commitment is tentative. Dispersion constructs remain rare in the organizational literature; to our knowledge, dispersion of boundary spanners' trust and commitment has not been discussed or studied previously. Finally, we emphasize that we have focused on one type of dispersion among boundary spanners: dispersion of boundary spanners' trust in and commitment to an IOR. Other forms of dispersion—for example, dispersion of boundary spanners' skills, abilities, or roles—may have quite different, even positive, consequences.

Possible Antecedents of Variability in Boundary Spanners' Trust and Commitment

The IOR literature suggests a number of factors that may influence the extent to which organizational boundary spanners are homogeneous in their trust in and commitment to the IOR.

Top Management's Involvement

Top managers are shapers of opinion and culture in the organization (Schein, 1992), influencing their immediate and more distal subordinates' views of complex and ambiguous stimuli, such as an interorganizational relationship. Accordingly, the more actively top managers are involved in the day-to-day interactions between their firm and its IOR partner, the more likely organizational boundary spanners are to be homogeneous in their trust in and commitment to the IOR. When top managers provide hands-on oversight of their organization's IOR, organizational boundary spanners are likely to follow top managers' lead—trusting in, committing themselves to, and collaborating with their firm's IOR partner in the way their top managers demonstrate.

Although much of the IOR literature gives the impression that top executives are deeply involved in the day-to-day interactions between their firm and its IOR partner, we suspect that top management's involvement in the IOR lessens over time as the interorganizational relationship is routinized. When two organizations share a relatively long-standing relationship, employees lower in the organizational hierarchy may interact more frequently and directly with their firm's IOR partner than do senior executives. If the interorganizational relationship is stable, boundary spanners' trust in and commitment to the IOR may remain stable as well, and therefore quite homogeneous. If, however, the nature of the IOR changes over time but top managers remain removed from the day-to-day interactions between their firm and its IOR partner, then organizational homogeneity of IOR trust and commitment may diminish.

Nature of IOR Interaction: Task Complexity

Some interorganizational relationships are relatively simple and routine; in the context of these IORs, individuals' interactions across organizational boundaries are of limited duration, frequency, and complexity. Other interorganizational relationships are, of course, more complex and nonroutine; individuals interact across organizational boundaries at greater length, and with greater frequency, in attempting to accomplish tasks of greater uncertainty. IOR theorists and researchers have discussed the nature of interorganizational interactions very little. Sheppard and Sherman's typology (1998) seems somewhat relevant: relationships of "shallow dependence" seem likely to be more simple and routine than relationships of "deep interdependence." Still, these researchers' typology does not specify the nature of individuals' interactions in these different types of relationships. Accordingly, in this section we define interorganizational task complexity and explore the implications of interorganizational task complexity for the homogeneity of boundary spanners' IOR trust and commitment.

The notion of interorganizational task complexity describes the nature of the interactions between the members of two organizations. Interorganizational task complexity, we propose, is a function of several factors:

- The number of individuals in each organization who interact with each other across organizational boundaries
- The frequency of individuals' interactions across organizational boundaries
- The duration of individuals' interactions across organizational boundaries
- The routineness of individuals' boundary-spanning tasks

In defining the routineness of interactions across organizational boundaries, we borrow Perrow's definition (1970) of "routineness" of work tasks. Perrow proposes two dimensions to characterize work tasks. The first, *variety*, refers to the frequency with which employees experience novel, unexpected events, demands, and problems requiring their response. The second, *analyzability*, describes the extent to which employees rely on standardized procedures (a manual, a computer, or even a clerk) in responding to novel and unexpected events, demands, and problems. When employees can rely on standardized procedures, task analyzability is high. When, by contrast, employees must rely not on standardized procedures but on "experience, judgment, knack, wisdom, intuition" (Perrow, 1970, p. 76), analyzability is low. Perrow combines these two dimensions, suggesting that tasks low in variety and high in analyzability are routine, whereas tasks high in variety and low in analyzability are nonroutine. Routine tasks are readily planned, close-ended, and concrete. Accordingly, routine interactions across organizational boundaries are low in variety and high in analyzability; organization members perform the same tasks repeatedly, experiencing few novel exceptions. Further, problems are readily solved if standard operating procedures are followed. In contrast, nonroutine tasks are "hectic, open-ended, and uncertain" (Perrow, 1970, p. 83). Employees working on nonroutine tasks across organizational boundaries must rely on experience, judgment, and intuition to resolve work quandaries.

To summarize these dimensions, we propose that interorganizational task complexity is lowest when just a few individuals interact across organizational boundaries and do so rarely, for a limited amount of time, and in the interest of completing routine tasks. Thus, for example, when an organization occasionally buys made-to-stock (not custom or made-to-order) supplies from a seller organization, the interaction of the two organizations is low in complexity (simple). In contrast, when a large number of individuals from one organization interact with a large number of individuals from another organization and do so frequently, for long periods of time, and in the interest of completing nonroutine tasks, the interaction of the two organizations is complex.

The greater the interorganizational task complexity, we propose, the more likely boundary spanners are to vary in their trust in and commitment to the IOR. When the nature of the interaction between two organizations is relatively simple, few people cross organizational boundaries. This in and of itself fosters homogeneity.

Further, individuals' interorganizational tasks are rare, time-limited, and straightforward. Accordingly, boundary spanners are unlikely to develop idiosyncratic perceptions of the trustworthiness of their firm's IOR partner or of the merits of the interorganizational relationship. In contrast, when interorganizational complexity is high, a relatively large number of boundary-spanning individuals interact with great frequency and duration to perform challenging, novel, ill-defined tasks. Some of these individuals may consider the interorganizational relationship a stimulating challenge and a great opportunity for their organization. Others may consider the same interorganizational relationship an unwarranted risk for their organization and a drain on important resources.

Organizational Characteristics Fostering Inclusiveness

A number of organizational characteristics may foster "inclusiveness" (House et al., 1995, pp. 89–90): involvement, interaction, and interdependence of organization members in an organization or unit. Inclusiveness fosters homogeneity of attitudes and actions among organization members (House et al., 1995) and thus homogeneity among the specific boundary-spanning members of the organization. For example, organization members are likely to be relatively homogeneous in attitudes and actions when their organization is small and young. In a small or young organization, the founder and other top managers are likely to have a particularly strong influence on the organization's cultural values and norms and thus over employee attitudes and behaviors (Schein, 1992). Organizations with strong cultures breed homogeneity of attitudes and behaviors among employees (O'Reilly & Chatman, 1996; House et al., 1995). Further, organizational structures and human resources practices may foster homogeneity of employee attitudes and behaviors. Thus a highly centralized organization, an organization with a strong reward system, or an organization dominated by a single occupational group (for example, lawyers or scientists) may engender substantial within-organization homogeneity of employee attitudes and behaviors. When organization members are united in their norms, values, attitudes, and behaviors, whether as a function of the organization's size or of its age, culture, structure, and/or management practices, organization members are likely, we propose, also to be united in their trust in and commitment to their company's IORs. Conversely, low organizational inclusiveness may foster variability of boundary-spanner IOR trust and commitment.

Certainty of IOR Outcomes

An IOR may, of course, prove advantageous or disadvantageous for the organizational partners. When the benefits of involvement in an IOR are clearly positive for an organization, or clearly negative, boundary spanners are likely to be united in their perceptions, attitudes, and behaviors; homogeneity is likely to be high. When, however, the benefits of IOR involvement are more uncertain or ambiguous, boundary spanners are more likely to be divided in their characterizations of the IOR. Ambiguous stimuli, by their very nature, invite a diversity of interpretations (House et al., 1995). Thus, when the immediate benefits of IOR involvement are mixed, or when the long-term benefits of IOR involvement are questionable, boundary spanners may differ in their trust in and commitment to the IOR. Top managers, for example, having negotiated the IOR, may be optimistic about the long-term benefits of IOR involvement, whereas boundary-spanning individuals at lower levels of the organizational hierarchy may question the merits of involvement.

Summary Comments and Future Research Directions

An organization's boundary spanners are likely to be most homogeneous in their perceptions, attitudes, and actions regarding an IOR, we have proposed, in the following circumstances:

- When top managers are actively involved in day-to-day interorganizational interactions
- When interorganizational task complexity is low and stable
- When the focal organization is highly inclusive
- When, with respect to the focal organization, the benefits or drawbacks of the IOR are unequivocal

In these conditions, the tacit assumption of organizational homogeneity, which underlies a great deal of IOR theory and research, is most likely to be valid. Conversely, when managers are but little involved in day-to-day IOR interactions, when interorganizational tasks are complex, when the focal organization is low in inclusiveness, and when the benefits of participation in the IOR are uncertain, individual boundary spanners may differ in their trust in and commitment to the IOR. We have proposed that such intraorganizational variability in boundary-spanner IOR trust and commitment is likely, in most circumstances, to lead to negative outcomes at multiple levels of analysis.

We caution, again, that our discussion of the antecedents and consequences of boundary-spanner homogeneity of trust and commitment is speculative and incomplete. A great deal of research and further theory building are needed to refine, test, and extend our preliminary conceptualization. Thus, for example, exploratory qualitative studies describing the individual boundary spanners involved in the day-to-day management of interorganizational relationships would be instructive. Who are these individuals? What is the nature of their interactions in and across organizational boundaries? How and to what extent do top managers shape lower-level boundary spanners' perceptions of and interactions with their organization's IOR partner?

Also needed in the IOR literature are empirical studies of the extent, antecedents, and multilevel consequences of within-organization variability in IOR trust and commitment. These studies will be both time-and labor-intensive, requiring researchers to gather data from multiple individuals in each of multiple organizations. This, indeed, is the common challenge of multilevel research. But the challenges of multilevel IOR research may be unusually complex because interorganizational relationships, by definition, cross organizational lines, because each firm may have interorganizational relationships with a number of different partners, and because interorganizational relationships develop over time. We recognize that the prevalence of multilevel IOR research will therefore grow slowly. We hope it will grow steadily.

Conclusion

In this chapter, we have examined the levels of analysis at which IORs are conceptualized and studied. We have emphasized the profound implications of choosing a level of analysis—the assumptions made and the questions examined and unexamined because of this choice. We have noted the benefits and the drawbacks of assuming homogeneity in the IOR dyad and in the organization as a whole. The assumptions of intra-and interorganizational homogeneity are worth testing, we have argued, because these assumptions may mask meaningful intra-and interorganizational variability in boundary spanners' perceptions, attitudes, and behaviors. Finally, we have proposed a preliminary model of possible antecedents and consequences of variability in boundary spanners' IOR trust and commitment.

In the past decade, research and theory have yielded important and interesting insights regarding the nature and consequences of interorganizational relationships, but the existing IOR literature reveals little about the intraorganizational dynamics of interorganizational relationships. Multilevel research—research examining the extent and correlates of variability in boundary spanners' IOR perceptions, attitudes, and behaviors—will begin to illuminate these dynamics. The result, we believe, will be a richer, more detailed and rigorous, and ultimately more practical understanding of interorganizational relationships.

References

Alexander, E. R. (1995). *How organizations act together: interorganizational coordination in theory and practice.* Newark, NJ: Gordon & Breach.

Auster, E. R. (1994). Macro and strategic perspectives on interorganizational linkages: A comparative analysis and review with suggestions for reorientation. In P. Srhivastava, A. Huff, and J. Dutton (Eds.), *Advances in strategic management* (Vol. 10B). Greenwich, CT: JAI Press.

Berscheid, E., & Reis, H. T. (1998). Attraction and close relationships. In D. T. Gilbert, S. T. Fiske, & G. Lindzey (Eds.), *The handbook of social psychology* (Vol. 2, 4th ed., pp. 193–281). New York: McGraw-Hill.

Bliese, P. D., & Halverson, R. R. (1998). Group consensus and psychological well-being: A large field study. *Journal of Applied Social Psychology, 28,* 563–580.

Chan, D. (1998). Functional relations among constructs in the same content domain at different levels of analysis: A typology of composition models. *Journal of Applied Psychology, 83,* 234–246.

Chatman, J. A., Polzer, J. T., Barsade, S. G., & Neale, M. A. (1998). Being different yet feeling similar: The influence of demographic composition on work processes and outcomes. *Administrative Science Quarterly, 43,* 749–780.

Currall, S. C., & Judge, T. A. (1995). Measuring trust between organizational boundary role persons. *Organizational Behavior and Human Decision Processes, 64,* 151–170.

Day, G. S. (1995). Advantageous alliances. *Journal of the Academy of Marketing Science, 23,* 297–300.

Drazin, R., Glynn, M., & Kazanjian, R. (1999). Multilevel theorizing about creativity in organizations: A sensemaking perspective. *Academy of Management Review, 24,* 286–307.

Dwyer, F. R., Schurr, P. H., & Oh, S. (1987). Developing buyer-seller relationships. *Journal of Marketing, 51,* 11–27.

Dyer, J. H., & Singh, H. (1998). The relational view: Cooperative strategy and sources of interorganizational competitive advantage. *Academy of Management Review, 23,* 660–679.

Eisenhardt, K. M., & Schoonhoven, E. B. (1996). Resource-based view of strategic alliance formation: Strategic and social effects in entrepreneurial firms. *Organization Science, 7,* 136–150.

Fichman, M., & Goodman, P. (1996). Customer-supplier ties in interorganizational relations. In L. L. Cummings & B. M. Staw (Eds.), *Research in organizational behavior* (Vol. 18, pp. 285–329). Greenwich, CT: JAI Press.

Fiske, A. P. (1990). Relativity in Moose culture: Four incommensurable models of social relationships. *Ethos, 18,* 180–204.

Fiske, A. P. (1992). The four elementary forms of sociality: Framework for a unified theory of social relations. *Psychological Review, 99,* 689–723.

Gabarro, J. J. (1987). The development of working relationships. In J. W. Lorsch (Ed.), *Handbook of organizational behavior* (pp. 172–189). Englewood Cliffs, NJ: Prentice Hall.

Gottman, J. M. (1993). The roles of conflict engagement, escalation, and avoidance in marital interaction: A longitudinal view of five types of couples. *Journal of Consulting and Clinical Psychology, 61,* 6–15.

Gottman, J. M. (1994). *What predicts divorce? The relationship between marital processes and marital outcomes.* Mahwah, NJ: Erlbaum.

Gulati, R. (1995a). Does familiarity breed trust? The implications of repeated ties for contractual choice in alliances. *Academy of Management Journal, 38,* 85–112.

Gulati, R. (1995b). Social structure and alliance formation patterns: A longitudinal analysis. *Administrative Science Quarterly, 40,* 619–652.

Hambrick, D. C. (1994). Top management groups: A conceptual integration and reconsideration of the "team" label. *Research in Organizational Behavior, 16,* 171–213.

Harrison, D. A., Price, K. H., & Bell, M. P. (1998). Beyond relational demography: Time and the effects of surface- and deep-level diversity on work group cohesion. *Academy of Management Journal, 41,* 55–67.

House, R., Rousseau, D. M., & Thomas-Hunt, M. (1995). The meso paradigm: A framework for the integration of micro and macro organizational behavior. In L. L. Cummings & B. M. Staw (Eds.), *Research in organizational behavior* (Vol. 17, 71–114). Greenwich, CT: JAI Press.

Jackson, S. E., May, K. E., & Whitney, K. (1995). Understanding the dynamics of diversity in decision-making teams. In R. A. Guzzo & E. A. Salas (Eds.), *Team effectiveness and decision making in organizations* (pp. 204–261). San Francisco: Jossey-Bass.

Karney, B. R., & Bradbury, T. N. (1995). The longitudinal course of marital quality and stability: A review of theory, research, and method. *Psychological Bulletin, 118,* 3–34.

Kelley, H. H., & Thibaut, J. W. (1969). Group problem solving. In G. Lindzey and E. Aronson (Eds.), *Handbook of social psychology* (Vol. 4, 2nd ed., pp. 1–101). Reading, MA: Addison-Wesley.

Kelley, H. H., & Thibaut, J. W. (1978). *Interpersonal relations: A theory of interdependence.* New York: Wiley.

Klein, K. J., Dansereau, F., & Hall, R. J. (1994). Levels issues in theory development, data collection, and analysis. *Academy of Management Review, 19,* 195–229.

Klein, K. J., & House, R. J. (1995). On fire: Charismatic leadership and levels of analysis. *Leadership Quarterly, 6,* 183–198.

Kostova, T. (1999). Transnational transfer of strategic organizational practices: A contextual perspective. *Academy of Management Review, 24,* 308–324.

Kozlowski, S.W.J., & Klein, K. J. (2000). A multilevel approach to theory and research in organizations: Contextual, temporal, and emergent processes. In K. J. Klein & S.W.J. Kozlowski (Eds.), *Multilevel theory, research, and methods in organizations* (pp. 3–90). San Francisco: Jossey-Bass.

Kumar, N. (1996). The power of trust in manufacturer-retailer relationships. *Harvard Business Review, 74*(6), 92–106.

Larson, A. (1992). Network dyads in entrepreneurial settings: A study of the governance of exchange relationships. *Administrative Science Quarterly, 37,* 76–104.

Oliver, C. (1990). Determinants of interorganizational relationships: Integration and future directions. *Academy of Management Review, 15,* 241–265.

O'Reilly, C. A., & Chatman, J. A. (1996). Culture as social control: Corporations, cults, and commitment. In L. L. Cummings & B. M. Staw (Eds.), *Research in organizational behavior* (Vol. 18, pp. 157–200). Greenwich, CT: JAI Press.

Pelled, L. (1996). Demographic diversity, conflict, and work group outcomes: An intervening process theory. *Organization Science, 7,* 615–631.

Perrow, C. B. (1970). *Organizational analysis: A sociological view.* Belmont, CA: Wadsworth.

Pfeffer, J., & Salancik, G. R. (1978). *The external control of organizations: A resource-dependence perspective.* New York: HarperCollins.

Powell, W. W. (1990). Neither market nor hierarchy: Network forms of organization. In L. L. Cummings & B. M. Staw (Eds.), *Research in organizational behavior* (Vol. 12, pp. 295–336). Greenwich, CT: JAI Press.

Powell, W. W., Koput, K. W., & Smith-Doerr, L. (1996). Interorganizational collaboration and the locus of innovation: Networks of learning in biotechnology. *Administrative Science Quarterly, 41,* 116–145.

Ring, P. S., & Van De Ven, A. H. (1994). Developmental processes of cooperative interorganizational relationships. *Academy of Management Review, 19,* 90–118.

Rusbult, C. E., & Van Lange, P.A.M. (1996). Interdependence processes. In E. T. Higgins & A. W. Kruglanski (Eds.), *Social psychology: Handbook of basic principles* (pp. 564–596). New York: Guilford Press.

Seabright, M. A., Levinthal, D. A., & Fichman, M. (1992). Role of individual attachments in the dissolution of interorganizational relationships. *Academy of Management Journal, 35,* 122–160.

Schein, E. H. (1992). *Organizational culture and leadership.* San Francisco: Jossey-Bass.

Sheppard, B. H., & Sherman, D. M. (1998). Initial trust formation in new organizational relationship. *Academy of Management Review, 23,* 473–490.

Sheppard, B. H., & Tuchinsky, M. (1996). Interfirm relationships: A grammar of pairs. In L. L. Cummings & B. M. Staw (Eds.), *Research in organizational behavior* (Vol 18, pp. 331–373). Greenwich, CT: JAI Press.

Smith, K. G., Carroll, S. J., & Ashford, S. J. (1995). Intra- and interorganizational cooperation: Toward a research agenda. *Academy of Management Journal, 38,* 7–23.

Thibaut, J. W., & Kelley, H. H. (1959). *The social psychology of groups.* New York: Wiley.

Tsui, A., Egan, T., & O'Reilly, C. (1992). Being different: Relational demography and organizational attachment. *Administrative Science Quarterly, 37,* 549–579.

Van de Ven, A. H. (1976). On the nature, formation, and maintenance of relations among organizations. *Academy of Management Review, 1,* 24–35.

Uzzi, B. (1997). Social structure and competition in interfirm networks: The paradox of embeddedness. *Administrative Science Quarterly, 42,* 35–67.

Waldman, D. A., & Yammarino, F. J. (1999). CEO charismatic leadership: Levels-of-management and levels-of-analysis effects. *Academy of Management Review, 24,* 266–285.

Weitz, B. A., & Jap, S. D. (1995). Relationship marketing and distribution channels. *Journal of the Academy of Marketing Science, 23,* 305–320.

Whetten, D. A. (1987). Interorganizational relations. In J. W. Lorsch (Ed.), *Handbook of organizational behavior.* Englewood Cliffs, NJ: Prentice Hall.

Wilkof, M. V., Brown, D. W., & Selsky, J. W. (1995). When the stories are different: The influence of corporate culture mismatches on interorganizational relations. *Journal of Applied Behavioral Science, 31,* 373–388.

Williams, K. Y., & O'Reilly, C. A. III (1998). Demography and diversity in organizations: A review of 40 years of research. In B. M. Staw & L. L. Cummings, *Research in organizational behavior* (Vol. 20). Greenwich, CT: JAI Press, 70–140.

Williamson, O. E. (1975). *Markets and hierarchies: Analysis and antitrust implications.* New York: Free Press.

Williamson, O. E. (1985). *The economic institutions of capitalism.* New York: Free Press.

Wilson, D. T. (1995). An integrated model of buyer-seller relationships. *Journal of the Academy of Marketing Science, 23,* 335–345.

Zaheer, A., McEvily, B., & Perrone, V. (1998). Does trust matter? Exploring the effects of interorganizational and interpersonal trust on performance. *Organization Science, 9,* 141–159.

CHAPTER 7

Multilevel Issues and Culture
An Integrative View
Georgia T. Chao

International expansions in many organizations have prompted increased attention to and research on issues related to international industrial/organizational (I/O) psychology. Shadowing the proliferation of cultural studies in applied psychology is a growing concern that research adequately identify appropriate levels of theory, measurement, and analysis when drawing conclusions about individuals, groups, organizations, or cultures. Addressing levels issues is a fundamental part of any research in I/O psychology (Klein, Dansereau, & Hall, 1994; Rousseau, 1985). Many constructs in organizational behavior are neatly nested in hierarchical levels, commonly described by individual, group, and organizational steps. Indeed, most of the chapters in this volume assume nested hierarchies in the development of composition theories (Kozlowski & Klein, Chapter One, this volume) and in analytic systems, such as hierarchical linear modeling (HLM) and within-and-between analysis (Dansereau & Yammarino, Chapter Ten, this volume; Hofmann, Griffin, & Gavin, Chapter Eleven, this volume). However, cultural research may require new ways of conceptualizing culture at multiple levels of analysis: individual, group, organizational, national, and/or regional.

A review of the quality of several prominent studies in cross-cultural research has revealed several weaknesses, among them level-of-analysis problems. Roberts and Boyacigiller (1984) note that some variables, such as technology (Hickson & McMillan, 1981), are difficult to measure across countries, and a level-of-analysis problem arises when technology is interpreted in different ways at various organizational levels. Hofstede (1984) describes ecological fallacy as an error when researchers interpret ecological correlations as meaningful descriptions of individuals. He recognizes this as a levels problem in cultural research, yet he commits this error when he discusses how his research findings at the cultural level can explain why Austrian and American motivation theories for individual behavior might differ. This shortcoming is not exclusive to researchers. Bond (1997) criticizes readers of Hofstede's research, noting that many misinterpret his data analyses and commit the ecological fallacy of using nation-level data to describe individuals. Thus the conduct of cultural research and the understanding or interpretation of that research will require knowledge about the level of the constructs and the relationships among constructs at multiple levels.

My purpose in this chapter is to present a conceptualization of culture as a multilevel construct. Given the many ways in which culture has been researched, I briefly review how culture is defined and viewed from different levels. Against this background, the multilevel nature of culture is examined in two domains of international research.

First, *cross-cultural* research compares psychological constructs and relationships between and among two or more cultures. Traditionally, most psychological studies on culture have been cross-cultural, with the focus on comparisons between and among two or more cultures and not on how these cultures interact with one another. This research generally acknowledges national and global levels through discussions of emic and etic perspectives, but a detailed integration of these perspectives and levels issues is needed. I extend current discussions of emic and etic relationships in cross-cultural research by examining how they might differ across levels. Thus a new layer of complexity is recognized when researchers move beyond simple comparisons between two countries and identify appropriate levels of constructs and relationships that make comparisons theoretically meaningful. The second domain of international research has received more recent attention because of the globalization of many organizations. *Intercultural* research examines how people from two or more cultures interact. There is currently a gap between developments within the levels literature and current research examining culture in organizations. A multilevel model of intercultural organizational behavior is presented to illustrate how levels interact as they affect individual behavior. I examine how different levels of culture are needed to understand organizational behavior, and I provide guidelines for future research. Although cross-cultural and intercultural research streams are distinguished by their emphases on comparative studies across cultures and the interaction of cultures, respectively, the two are subsumed under the general rubric of *cultural research.*

Defining Culture and Its Levels

There are many definitions of culture. In 1952, Kroeber and Kluckhohn listed 164 definitions of culture. More recently, Munroe and Munroe (1997) have noted that definitions of culture have evolved from a construct at the supraindividual level to a more internalized system of ideas within people. Some of the more widely cited definitions are as follows:

> Culture consists of patterns, explicit and implicit, of and for behavior acquired and transmitted by symbols, constituting the distinctive achievements of human groups, including their embodiments in artifacts; the essential core of culture consists of traditional (i.e., historically derived and selected) ideas and especially their attached values; culture systems may, on the one hand, be considered as products of action, on the other as conditioning influences upon further action [Kluckhohn, 1962, p. 73].

> I treat culture as "the collective programming of the mind which distinguishes the members of one human group from another.". . . Culture, in this sense, includes systems of values; and values are among the building blocks of culture. Culture is to a human collectivity what personality is to an individual [Hofstede, 1984, p. 21].

> Culture is a set of human-made objective and subjective elements that in the past have increased the probability of survival and resulted in satisfaction for the participants in an ecological niche,

and thus became shared among those who could communicate with each other because they had a common language and lived in the same time and place [Triandis, Kurowski, & Gelfand, 1994, p. 778]. Culture is to society what memory is to individuals [Triandis, 1995, p. 4].

By these definitions, culture is a group-level construct because it seeks to describe a collectivity of people. However, there are research questions and methodologies that treat culture as an individual-level construct, whereas others define a group's culture at higher levels, including, most typically, the nation level. For this chapter, there are two reasons why my discussion of culture will focus on value systems that differentiate groups of people with a common language, a communal arena for interaction, and shared experiences. First, most definitions of culture used in the study of organizational behavior embody a value component. Second, most of the empirical research on cultural values aggregates value ratings or rankings that were collected at the individual level. Schwartz (1994) notes that individual values are jointly determined by shared cultural forces and unique individual experiences. Thus definitions and measurements of culture, as a given collective's values, have traditionally involved multiple levels. My focus on values retains the breadth of culture from individual-level values to collective, shared systems of values. Implications for a multilevel conceptualization of culture are discussed in what follows.

Traditional and New Approaches to Culture

Traditionally, most level issues in organizational research describe a hierarchy of levels, whereby lower levels are nested within the domains of higher levels (Rousseau, 1985). As Figure 7.1a depicts, individuals may work in groups that function within departments that in turn make up parts of an organization operating within a larger environment or culture.

Research on national cultural values (Hofstede, 1984; Schwartz, 1994) reports nation-level means that describe environments for organizations. National cultural values are typically measured by aggregating responses to questionnaires administered to employees working in their own countries. Hofstede (1983) has plotted the

Figure 7.1. Traditional and Multilevel Conceptualizations of Culture.

(a) Culture traditionally conceptualized at the highest level

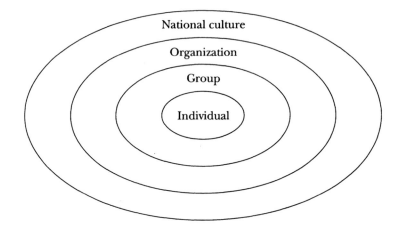

(b) Multilevel conceptualization of culture

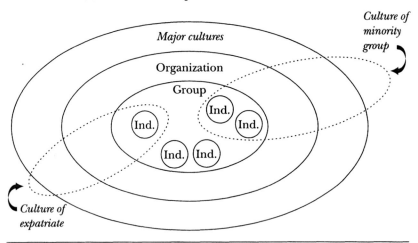

Note: Ind. = Individual.

relative positions of fifty countries on his four cultural dimensions and discussed how these national differences can explain different views on leadership, organizational structure, and motivation. Smith, Dugan, and Trompenaars (1996) have also aggregated data at the nation level and found links between country values and preferences for particular organizational behaviors.

However, since culture may be conceptualized as an individual- or group-level phenomenon, it may not always fit as an overarching canopy at the top of a levels hierarchy. The increased mobility of people across organizations and national boundaries creates cultural mixes that do not conform to nesting. These cultural mixes necessitate that culture be viewed as a multilevel construct, with different levels poised to address different research questions. As Figure 7.1b illustrates, a multilevel view of culture acknowledges that different cultures within a geographical location may be relevant to organizational members and their behavior. Furthermore, individuals from a diversity of cultural backgrounds, who may also differ from the geographically based cultures, bring cultural elements that shape their behavior. For example, I worked with a German manager who headed a department that included Indonesian, American, and Australian specialists for an American company operating in Singapore. The Singaporean staff had to accommodate a number of different foreigners with higher organizational rank. The American company had a strong organizational culture rooted in the Midwest. Outside the company's walls, Singapore's multicultural environment included significant British and Chinese components that shaped political and social practices. All these cultural sources influenced how we worked with one another. The key point of this example is that a detailed understanding of cultural effects on organizational behavior must include knowledge of culture at different levels.

Particularly when one is interested in examining how two or more cultures interact, defining the level of the cultural construct becomes complicated. Is one culture nested within another, as when an expatriate is working in a foreign land? Are there a dominant or majority culture and several minority cultures, as in the case of most diverse workforces in the United States? Do two cultures interact as roughly equal partners, as may be the case in an international joint venture? In these examples, culture may be conceptualized at the individual level when one tries to predict behavioral outcomes from intercultural negotiations between two people. Conversely, culture may be conceptualized at the group level when one tries to predict the success of an international joint venture that comprises different nationalities. Figure 7.1b also illustrates how the research focus can help specify the level of a culture construct. If the focus is on the individual, cultural levels of measurement and analyses should also be at the individual level lest the researcher risk committing an ecological fallacy. By contrast with what is shown in Figure 7.1a, culture is not neatly nested in a simple hierarchy; it may involve partial inclusion in a hierarchy and is likely to be polymorphic. Thus the construct of culture differs from many concepts in organizational behavior because it has been defined and measured at a number of different levels. As in the Indian parable of the blind men who touch different parts of an elephant and come up with different descriptions of the animal, the different level perspectives on culture also yield partially true yet incomplete pictures of what culture is and how it affects individuals and groups.

James and Jones (1974) advocate the use of different terms to denote similar constructs that are conceptualized at multiple levels. Their distinction between *organizational climate* and *psychological climate* is one example of separating climate constructs at the organizational and individual levels, respectively. In the general culture literature, Triandis (1995) also uses different terms to recognize distinct levels. *Idiocentrism* and *allocentrism* are the individual-level terms for the more common cultural-level constructs of individualism and collectivism, respectively. However, despite Triandis's efforts to separate the levels with different terms, most researchers ignore this distinction and use the more common terms *individualism* and *collectivism* to describe both levels (Kagitçibasi, 1997). Although common labels may be preferred for simplification, the distinctions must be at least tacitly maintained in order to preserve and track level effects and cross-level relationships.

An introduction to culture, as construed at the individual and collective levels, is presented here to provide the background for an examination of emic and etic approaches to culture research. How culture is conceptualized at different levels can shed light on whether cultural aspects are universal or confined to particular collectives of people.

Cultural Research at the Individual Level

Earley and Randel (1997, p. 63) define culture as "individual-level manifestations of shared meaning systems which are learned from other members of the society." By emphasizing an individual-level perspective on culture, Earley and Randel argue that micro-organizational behavior research will benefit from this direct connection between culture and behavior. In fact, they explicitly state, "Contrary to most views of culture, we advocate that culture is best thought of as a psychological experience of individuals and not a collective phenomenon, group characteristic, or the like" (p. 64). Their approach to culture is tailored to the study of micro-level theory in organizational behavior.

If the purpose of the research is to predict individual behavior, then cultural perceptions at the individual level would serve as important predictors of behavior rather than aggregating individual data to a group level. Constraining cultural perceptions at the individual level retains both the shared cultural and the unique psychological components of values. Both components are important predictors of individual behavior. Earley (1994) examined relationships between individualism-collectivism (IC) and training interventions on performance for Chinese and American subjects. He found significant interactions showing higher performance when individualists were trained with an individual (versus group) focus and when collectivists were trained with a group (versus individual) focus. IC was measured at two levels: the group level aggregated data for each country, and the individual level was a difference score between a subject's IC score and his or her country's mean, calculated without that subject's score.[1] Stronger interactions were found when IC was measured at the individual level than when it was measured at the group level. In keeping the level of analysis at the individual level, Earley recognized that some Chinese subjects may be more individualist and some American subjects may be more collectivist than their respective national cultural stereotypes. Of course, the stronger relationship between variables at the individual level may simply reflect the fact that those data were measured and analyzed at one level; however, Earley also found that the group-level measure of IC significantly moderated the relationship between training focus and performance. He concluded that the dual-level assessment of IC revealed parallel constructs, and that both were valuable in understanding culturally influenced behavior.

Certainly, relationships between an individual's cultural values and performance should be examined at the individual level. In fact, one might argue that this kind of research is single-level research because all the data are collected and analyzed at one level. However, because the definition of culture embodies a group construct or shared meaning across people, cultural research at the individual level will still have group implications. An individual's cultural values reflect the interaction between the collective's shared meanings and that individual's unique personality. The extent to which individual cultural values are shared among people will help define the cultural boundaries of a collective. There are many research questions that benefit from examination and measurement of culture at the individual level. For example, research examining expatriates' adjustment to new work environments often mentions intercultural problems as a frequent reason for expatriates' failure (Chao & Sun, 1997; Tung, 1981). Key to an expatriate's adjustment would be the cultural perceptions he or she holds about the host country. The more negative these perceptions are, or the more incompatible they are with the expatriate's own cultural values, the more likely this expatriate is to experience difficulty adjusting to the host country's culture. In this example, it is the individual's perceptions of another culture, not the shared meaning among that culture's members, that may be the key to organizational behavior adjustment. As in the previous example, the key dependent variable—individual adjustment—is at the individual level. Thus some research questions are framed to examine culture as an individual-level construct.

Cultural Research at the Collective Level

Cultural research is fragmented at levels above the individual level. Researchers from two primary disciplines, psychology and anthropology, have developed parallel literatures on organizational climate and culture, respectively. There is a great deal of conceptual overlap between organizational climate and culture, and both have been examined at the individual, group, and organization levels (Reichers & Schneider, 1990). James and Jones (1974) originally made distinctions between the terms *organizational climate* and *psychological climate* by specifying organizations as the unit of theory for the first construct and individuals as the unit of theory for the second. From a levels perspective, Glick (1985) and Dansereau and Alutto (1990) have examined organizational climate/culture theory and methodology. In the organizational culture literature, Glick notes that terms for individual or group cultural phenomena are not well developed; clearly, however, there is a need to recognize multiple levels of organizational culture and to understand their cross-level effects. Dansereau and Alutto (1990) focus on level-of-analysis issues in organizational climate and culture. Like Glick, and a central point in this chapter, they describe multiple-level frameworks that can conceptualize culture at more than one level. However, the examples and level applications developed in organizational climate and culture research have limited generalizability to international studies of culture. They are mentioned here only to show how culture and levels issues have been discussed together. To return to Figure 7.1b, multinational organizations and their subunits are likely to be composed of different mixes of employees from a variety of cultures. Consequently, international cultures, unlike organizational climate and culture, are not neatly nested in hierarchical levels. Furthermore, aspects of organizational climate, although assumed to have equivalent meanings for all employees, may vary greatly in terms of relevance and interpretation for particular nations or ethnic groups. Thus an important distinction to keep in mind is that the theoretical underpinnings of organizational climate/culture may not generalize to research on international cultures.

Much of the current literature in cross-cultural I/O psychology focuses on geopolitical groups, equating, in particular, a cultural group with a nation state (Boyacigiller, Kleinberg, Phillips, & Sackmann, 1996). Although many researchers caution against this practice, the simplicity of this classification holds wide appeal. Boyacigiller et al. (1996) have traced the tendency to equate cultures with nation-states to early managerial research conducted after World War II. In that research, a main goal was to identify how U.S. management practices worked in foreign political and economic environments. Furthermore, cross-national differences were viewed as key independent variables in understanding competitive advantages among countries vying for shares of a global market. Governments can serve as a constant historical and political factor for all of their citizens; therefore, a common cultural base for an entire nation may be evident. However, regional differences often lead to the identification of subcultures (Ralston et al., 1996; Schwartz & Ros, 1995), and common cultural values may be observed that cross national borders to constitute country clusters (Ronen & Shenkar, 1985).

Perhaps the best way to identify a culture's boundaries is to examine the extent to which people share particular cultural values. Triandis (1994, p. 115) states, "We should not assume that nation, race, religion, or other natural aggregates of individuals necessarily constitute a culture until we have evidence that the individuals share points of view, unstated assumptions, meanings, or other elements of subjective culture." Thus, if culture is to be considered a collective-level construct, the boundaries for a collective are partly determined by the level of agreement that members have about their perceptions of their culture. Lytle, Brett, Barsness, Tinsley, and Janssens (1995) emphasize that sharedness of values is an underlying component of culture.

There can be dramatic differences between research conclusions drawn at the individual level and those drawn at the group level. Hofstede, Neuijen, Ohayv, and Sanders (1990), in order to measure organizational culture, analyzed data on work values and managerial practices at the organizational-unit level. Hofstede, Bond and Luk (1993) reanalyzed those data to examine individual-level relationships. Comparison of results from factor analyses at the unit level and the individual level revealed different factor structures. They conclude, "The dramatic difference in results, depending on whether we analyze the same data at the ecological or at the individual level, should be a caution to look very carefully at the methods of analysis used when comparing the results of different studies" (p. 501).

In summary, theories of organizational behavior and organizational performance should define the level at which culture affects these phenomena and recognize that more than one level may be required to fully capture cultural effects. Munroe and Munroe (1997) observe that current research on cultural psychology generally employs culture in two ways: to identify contexts and antecedents for behavior. In identifying general cultural contexts, higher levels (represented by different ethnic groups, organizational cultures, and national and geopolitical collectives) are suitable for cross-cultural comparisons of these contexts and for discovery of universal phenomena. These levels, generally measured through aggregation of individual responses, would also be appropriate for examinations of cultural effects on organizational performance. In contrast, when culture is examined as a specific context from an individual's perspective, or when individual behavior is the dependent variable, lower levels (represented by individuals and groups) are more appropriate. These levels retain information on values that are shaped by shared cultural and unique psychological forces relevant to individual behavior. Both forces act as filters for individuals to perceive, make sense of, and act on their environments. Examination of culture at the individual level not only will allow cross-cultural comparisons but also will enable researchers to study within-culture variations.

To date, most of the international literature on organizational behavior has paid little attention to level issues. Discussions on etic and emic research perspectives roughly capture levels, but they are not well integrated into level terminology and measurement issues. A discussion of etic and emic perspectives and their links to level issues follows, to provide this integration.

Level Issues and Cross-Cultural Psychology: Etic and Emic Perspectives

Historically, researchers in cross-cultural psychology have treated levels issues in terms of etic and emic distinctions, where emic perspectives are confined to the nation level and etic perspectives are raised to the global level. Pike (1967) coined the terms *etic* and *emic* to differentiate two basic research perspectives. The etic approach provides a broad perspective and studies behavior without much regard for the context of that behavior. Research from an etic perspective seeks to identify and understand universal cultural factors that are relevant and meaningful to all people, regardless of nationality or cultural group. Culture and context are not viewed as important conditions in shaping construct identification, definition, or theory. For example, IC constructs are believed to be universal, and an etic approach examines them across all groups. In contrast, the emic approach takes a narrower perspective by focusing on behavior in a specific context. This focus allows an in-depth examination of historical developments, individual differences, cultural characteristics, situational constraints, and their combined effects on behavior. Research from an emic perspective seeks to identify factors unique to a particular culture, such as Confucian dynamism (Chinese Culture Connection, 1987). Pike stresses that both etic and emic research approaches are valuable and should not be viewed as mutually exclusive. He draws an analogy between etic/emic viewpoints and stereographic pictures. Two stereographs are viewed through an optical instrument, or stereoscope, to produce one three-dimensional image. Superficially, each stereograph looks like the other, but they are actually pictures taken from different points of view. Moreover, when they are viewed through a stereoscope, the three-dimensional effect provides a more lifelike picture than either stereograph alone. Likewise, "three-dimensional understanding" may be gained when data are viewed from both etic and emic perspectives. Berry (1989, p. 729) notes that in cross-cultural psychology "we cannot be 'cultural' without some notion like emic; and we cannot be 'cross' without some notion like etic."

The terms *etic* and *emic* have been extended beyond a description of research approaches to describe universal and unique factors and relationships. Examining etic and emic relationships across levels highlights a complexity in cultural research. If constructs have equal meanings across all cultures, then an etic approach is appropriate, *but only for the level(s) in which the constructs are conceptualized and measured.* Generalizations to other levels would impose an etic approach and may not be merited. If constructs are uniquely defined or relevant to a collective, an emic approach, or at least a combined etic/emic approach, is warranted. When relationships among psychological constructs vary by culture, these differences can be identified from etic-based research, but an in-depth understanding of unique cultural factors is achieved only with an emic approach. Thus, in order to accommodate level issues, research in cultural psychology must examine the suitability of etic and emic frames within the levels of the research design. This does not mean that all cultural research should have a combination of etic and emic perspectives. The main point here is that a sound design for cultural research should include a clear specification of the levels involved and an examination of how etic and/or emic approaches can best address the questions and hypotheses posed in the study. Examples of different etic and emic relationships are presented here to illustrate how phenomena observed across all individuals may differ when examined within a particular cultural context (see Figure 7.2).

Figure 7.2 illustrates examples of different etic and emic relationships. Each solid-line ellipse represents one culture's scatterplot area, or relationship between two variables. In these examples, the unit of analysis for culture is unimportant—cultures may be defined by politics, ethnicity, religion, work unit, and so on. The dotted line that encircles all the solid-line ellipses represents the relationship between two variables across all cultures, or the relationship at the individual level. Leung and Bond (1989) define strong etic relationships when similar relationships are found at multiple levels. Figure 7.2a depicts a strong etic relationship. The positive relationship between the two variables found for each culture is also found for all cultures combined (regression lines for each culture and for all subjects combined would show similar slopes). Berry and Dasen (1974), testing for these relationships, used the term *subsystem validation* to describe hypotheses that are tested at the individual and cultural levels (that is, the intracultural and cross-cultural levels). Outside the emic/etic nomenclature, Figure 7.2a illustrates a homology (Ostroff, 1993), or an isomorphic model (Klein, Tosi, & Cannella, 1999), generally defined when constructs and a relationship at one level are observed at another.

An example of an individual-level etic relationship, or what Leung and Bond (1989) term a "weak etic," is depicted in Figure 7.2b. Here, the positive relationship from data analyzed at the individual level is shown by the large dotted-line ellipse that encircles all the data. Intracultural analyses run separate analyses for each culture. Figure 7.2b illustrates a positive relationship from an individual analysis, with intracultural analyses that show zero relationships. However, a more accurate interpretation of this figure would move toward the conclusion that the positive correlation

Figure 7.2. Examples of
Different Etic and Emic Relationships.

(a) Strong etic effect

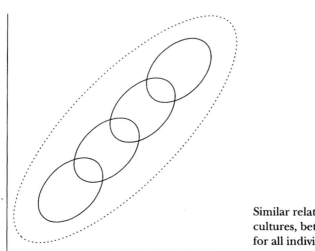

Similar relationship within all
cultures, between cultures, and
for all individuals

(b) Example of weak positive etic relationship at the individual level

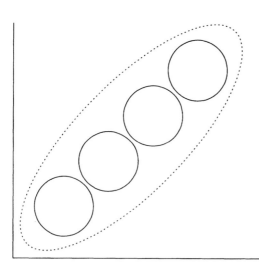

Relationship observed
from individual
analysis is not matched
by intracultural
analyses

Figure 7.2. Examples of
Different Etic and Emic Relationships, Cont'd.

(c) Example of weak positive etic relationship at the culture level

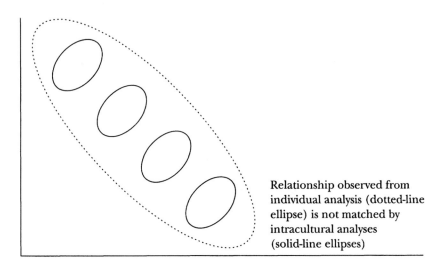

Relationship observed from individual analysis (dotted-line ellipse) is not matched by intracultural analyses (solid-line ellipses)

(d) Example of emic relationships

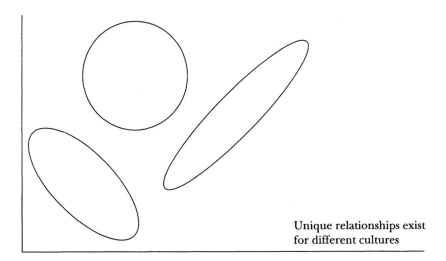

Unique relationships exist for different cultures

from the individual-level analysis is entirely due to the between-culture covariance of the two variables. Thus, although there is no significant relationship between the independent and dependent variables within each culture, there is a cultural effect because culture restricts the range of responses for a given group. Although I could not find a single study to serve as an example, findings from case studies can illustrate these results in a hypothetical study.

Suppose a researcher is interested in examining the relationship between a cultural value—power distance—and organizational control over nonwork behavior. High power distance is generally defined by Hofstede (1984) as sanctioned unequal distributions of power. Thus, in high power-distance cultures, people expect some people to be more powerful than others, and they accept these differences. In contrast, low power-distance cultures are characterized by intolerance for unequal power distributions and by a preference for equal treatment. The United Kingdom, for example, is generally described as a country with low power distance, and Sharpe (1997) describes a case study of a Japanese manufacturing organization operating in the United Kingdom. On one occasion, a Japanese expatriate suggested that one work group work overtime on Saturday. His suggestion was shouted down by the British employees, and the group members voted on their overtime preferences. In contrast, South Korea is generally described as moderately high on power distance. Jang and Chung (1997) describe a new management program at Samsung that includes elements of moral and social management. Not only are appropriate employee attitudes and behaviors toward supervisors and subordinates measured, but appropriate attitudes and behaviors toward parents, spouses, neighbors, and the nation are also included. Finally, China is generally described as high on power distance. I have found that organizations can exercise a great deal of control over their Chinese employees' nonwork behavior. Choice of housing and medical care are often controlled by organizations, particularly state-owned enterprises, and an employee must get organizational approval to have a child. Data across these three cultures can show a positive relationship between power distance and organizational control over nonwork behaviors. The variability of the dependent and independent variables is maximized when data are pooled across all groups and analyzed at the individual level. In HLM terms, there are significant mean differences in the independent variable and significant intercept differences in the dependent variable, but there are no slope differences within groups; therefore, the relationship is found only at the individual level. Figure 7.2b illustrates the importance of levels in cross-cultural research. If a researcher observed a zero correlation between two variables in one culture and replicated these findings in other cultures only by conducting parallel intracultural analyses, then those conclusions would reveal only a partial picture. By analyzing the data at the individual level, the researcher would observe a positive relationship and understand how that relationship is a function of between-culture variability.

Triandis et al. (1993) describe "cultural factors that do not describe individuals" when factors from ecological factor analyses (analyses at the culture level, aggregating individual data within each culture) are not matched by factors from an individual analysis. Given Leung and Bond's (1989) restriction of identifying etic factors at the individual level, these cultural factors would not qualify as etics. However, they are consistent with Pike's original description (1967) of etic viewpoints, and because they are culture-general, they may be considered etic factors at the cultural level. The distinction among results generated from different analyses and the discovery of etic factors or etic relationships reflects the levels perspective of the researcher. At the individual level, etics are identified from individual analyses; at the cultural level, etics are identified from ecological analyses or through comparisons across intracultural analyses.

Within cultures, a weak etic relationship is illustrated in Figure 7.2c. Here, the positive relationship observed within each culture is not replicated by the individual analysis. Weak etic relationships are universal across cultures at one level but not at another. For example, a positive relationship holds for all individuals within a culture but not across cultures. Weak etic relationships are not homologous. Van de Vijver and Leung (1997) posit that weak etics are likely due to different processes operating at the two levels or to different meanings that the construct takes from one level to the other. Note that the focus of these examples is on a positive relationship between two variables. If the focus were shifted to examine the negative relationship in Figure 7.2c, we would also shift from the within-culture level to the individual level. Consequently,

Figure 7.2c can illustrate a positive, weak etic relationship within a culture or a negative, weak etic relationship at the individual level.

Incidentally, a negative relationship between groups and a positive relationship within groups, shown in Figure 7.2c, is also known as a *reversal paradox* (Messick & van de Geer, 1981). As an example, Lincoln and Zeitz (1980) found a positive correlation between professional status and administrative duties for employees in human service agencies: the higher an individual's professional status, the more likely that individual was to supervise others. However, when data were aggregated and analyzed at the organizational-unit level, a negative correlation was found: more professional units reduced the organization's likelihood of generating supervisory duties. Thus reversal paradoxes have been found in field studies, although it remains to be seen if they are evident with culture variables.

Finally, emic factors are identified when solutions from intracultural analyses are not comparable. Here, unique factors from different cultures would indicate that an a priori set of items may not have common meanings across cultures. In this case, emic research approaches are needed to better understand the particular cultural context that helps define relevant constructs. Figure 7.2d illustrates emic relationships such that the relationship between two variables in one culture is unique. Although this cannot be illustrated, additional emic issues arise when measured variables are inappropriate to a particular culture and when unmeasured variables are more pertinent to the research question. Intracultural analyses are needed to detect specific emic relationships. Studies that have examined data from both etic and emic perspectives include Triandis et al. (1993) and Hofstede et al. (1993).

The examples shown in Figure 7.2 are intended as clear illustrations of etic and emic relationships. Real data are more complicated, with overlapping distributions and polymorphic relationships among cultures. Ostroff (1993) provides a statistical explanation for different relationships between individual and aggregate correlations. When higher-level constructs are based on aggregated data collected at the individual level, the degree to which individual and aggregated correlations are similar may reflect statistical artifacts or meaningful differences. Of course, higher-level constructs are not always based on aggregated data, and the conceptual arguments made here for strong and weak etic and emic relationships would hold, regardless of how the constructs were operationalized.

In summary, cross-cultural research generally compares different countries on specific constructs or relationships that are of interest to researchers. Data from different countries are collected independently and are often aggregates of individual-level data for each country. With regard to level issues, this research and future efforts should (1) examine the appropriate level(s) in which culture ought to be conceptualized, (2) draw theoretically appropriate boundaries for the culture constructs that complement identified levels, and (3) specify the level(s) of the constructs and relationships that are hypothesized to be etic or emic. These efforts will help define cultural comparisons of organizational behavior. However, the extension of cultural research into studies of cultural interaction becomes more complicated when two or more cultures are interacting with one another, representing different levels and operating across levels. A multilevel model of intercultural effects on organizational behavior is presented here, to integrate cultural psychology and level issues in this growing field of research.

A Multilevel Model of Intercultural Effects on Organizational Behavior

Erez and Earley (1993), having reviewed several cultural models from anthropology, sociology, psychology, and organizational behavior, describe their own cultural self-representation theory. The frameworks they reviewed take different perspectives—examining culture as shared cognitive structures, values, self-concept, and so forth—yet none of the frameworks explicitly describes how level issues can affect behavior. Cultural effects on human behavior are most salient when individuals from different cultures interact with each other. Interactions are partially influenced by perceptions of each participant's national culture, organizational culture, group memberships, and individual personality. Furthermore, these interactions become more complex when individuals assume leadership roles, representing groups, organizations, and/or nations. The term *plenipotentiary* defines an individual who is vested with full power to transact business on behalf of an organization or government. Interactions with such individuals simultaneously involve interactions at the individual level and at the higher levels that a plenipotentiary represents. Future interactions would be strongly influenced by the extent to which past individual actions represent higher levels. Schein (1992) describes how the values of an organization's founding leader establish a culture for other organizational members to operate within. Thus higher-level cultural issues may have a profound impact on lower-level phenomena even if the higher level is fully represented by one individual.

Organizations involved in international operations are inherently described by cross-level models. Phenomena at one level are influenced by phenomena at another. For example, like plenipotentiaries, business executives make individual decisions that represent organizational actions. Home-country nationals view an expatriate's behavior as representative of that expatriate's culture. Cultural stereotypes influence how a manager works with a particular group of people. These common examples illustrate how different levels interact in an intercultural context. Given the increase in international business activities, researchers in organizational behavior are challenged to better understand intercultural psychology and how level issues contribute to this understanding. Toward this end, I have proposed a multilevel model of intercultural effects on organizational behavior. The model is presented in Figure 7.3 and was designed for two purposes: to highlight multilevel issues in an international study of organizational behavior, and to stimulate future research in this area.

The model is a heuristic to illustrate how intercultural interactions at the individual level are shaped by intercultural interactions at higher levels. From left to right, the model describes three major processes:

1. Antecedents of culture and perceptions of other cultures
2. The influence of higher-level intercultural relationships on lower-level interactions
3. The subsequent sensemaking of these multilevel relationships

Details of the model are presented here, but with one caveat: throughout the model, I have used traditional terms like *national level* or *organizational level* to describe higher levels, and *group level*

Figure 7.3. Multilevel Model of Intercultural Organizational Behavior.

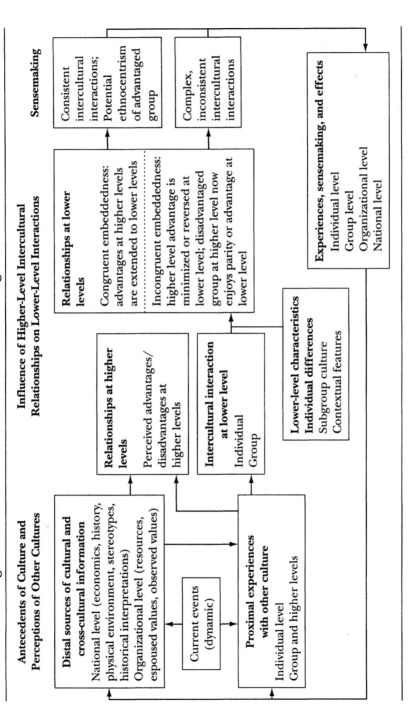

or *individual level* to describe lower levels. Obviously, what is a higher or lower level really depends on a specific reference level that is best determined by a researcher's focus. Therefore, the reader is cautioned that my examples for higher and lower levels are for descriptive purposes only, and that other conceptualizations (for example, organizational consortia, geographic region within a country, multinational pacts, and so on) may be more appropriate.

Antecedents of Culture and Perceptions of Other Cultures

Triandis (1972), in his theoretical framework of subjective culture, identifies two types of antecedents: distal and proximal. My model employs these antecedents both as determining components of one's own culture and as information sources to shape perceptions of another culture. Triandis describes distal antecedents of subjective culture as physical environmental characteristics and historical events that shape proximal antecedents tapping language, religion, social situations, and occupations. Distal antecedents can be identified as objective or subjective sources of cultural information. Objective sources include such factors as historical events, law, geographic features and resources (for example, fertile land supports agrarian lifestyles, whereas drought conditions support competition for scarce resources), and formal organizational principles and procedures. Subjective sources are more informal and include such factors as cultural stereotypes, interpretations of historical events, and informal organizational practices. Implicitly, these distal antecedents describe phenomena at organizational or national levels that affect large groups of people and shape perceptions of the relative advantages or disadvantages that these organizations or nations have with respect to one another. Futhermore, given the dynamic nature of culture and of international relationships, current events can dramatically change perceptions of one's own culture, of another culture, and of their relative standings. These current events may be distal (for example, governmental actions that do not directly affect a particular individual) or proximal (for example, organizational actions that demand individual adjustments).

In addition to distal antecedents of culture, an individual's own culture is strongly influenced by that person's own experiences, and perceptions of another culture are strongly influenced by that person's interactions with members of the other culture. Initially, these proximal experiences can be shaped by cultural information that was gained from distal sources. Direct interactions can reinforce preconceived notions of culture or they can dispel learned prejudices when personal contacts render stereotypes inaccurate. Proximal experiences generally occur at lower levels, with individuals representing only themselves or small groups. However, there are instances when an individual's actions represent higher levels, such as when business executives negotiate. If these individuals are empowered to represent groups/organizations, their relationship also translates into perceived advantages or disadvantages at the higher levels. In addition, current events involving two nations and/or two organizations interject a dynamic component into the model, reminding us that culture is not static but evolves over time.

Given the objective nature of some distal antecedents, members from two cultures can share perceptions of advantages or disadvantages that one group may have over the other. For example, Americans and Russians agree that most Americans have a higher standard of living than most Russians. Chinese and Japanese acknowledge that Japan lost World War II. However, the subjective nature of some distal antecedents may be further shaped or refined by proximal experiences an individual has with another culture. Thus cultural explanations for why Americans have a high standard of living, or why Japan lost World War II, are likely to vary. These experiences are subject to an individual's own sensemaking, viewed through that person's own cultural lens, and can also lead to perceived advantages and disadvantages between two cultures. In summary, the first multilevel process can be described by the following propositions:

P1. *Culture is determined by information, experiences, and events that occur on different levels at different times.*

P2. *Higher-level events and distal information provide a foundation for the interpretation of proximal experiences.*

P3. *Current events can alter perceptions of culture at any time.*

The Influence of Higher-Level
Intercultural Relationships
on Lower-Level Interactions

Cross-level intercultural relationships represent the second major process in my model. Key to these processes is Alderfer and Smith's (1982) concept of embedded intergroup relations that highlight the importance of level issues in intergroup dynamics. These authors argue that intergroup relationships are affected by specific group identities and their relative standings in larger groups and environments. The way a particular group is embedded in a larger context can dramatically affect how other groups react to it, even if the interaction occurs at the individual level. Thus negotiations between an Arab and a Jew are affected by these cultural identities and by the relative standings of these groups, as shaped by current and historical events. To complicate matters, more than one group identity, at different levels, may be salient. In an organizational context, an individual can be linked to group identities associated with internal organizational characteristics like function and rank, with external attributes like organizational status and power, and with stereotypes associated with the individual's nationality, age, gender, and race. To refer again to Figure 7.1b, the multiple levels in which culture can be conceptualized are an indication that there are different ways to study effects on intercultural dynamics. Rarely would two interacting groups represent different cultures equally in a neutral environment. More realistically, one culture dominates another by providing the geographical/cultural locale or the specific context for interactions, or through the sheer number of its people. Thus research on intercultural organizational behavior might have to accommodate and integrate individual-level cultural measures of a lone expatriate, group-level cultural measures of a prominent minority or microclimate group, and general cultural measures of the majority collective. Using different levels to describe cultural measures presents unique challenges for researchers.

Alderfer and Smith's (1982) concept of embedded intergroup relations not only acknowledges higher-level group identities of individuals but also recognizes the importance of the relative standings of these higher-level groups. Power differences between groups at the subsystem, system, and suprasystem levels can affect how individuals perceive their relative group advantages and disadvantages. As Alderfer and Smith wrote, "Intergroup dynamics operate at multiple levels, and the perceptions of groups at any particular level tend to be shaped by phenomena at higher levels, such that perceived disadvantage at a higher level tends toward denial of advantage at lower levels" (p. 60). Their research on different racial groups clearly demonstrates that local group interactions were shaped by each group's perceptions of its relative standing in a larger context. Specifically, both black managers and white managers viewed their own groups as being disadvantaged in promotion decisions. White managers acknowledged that they constituted a majority group within the organization, but they also noted that the external environment favored affirmative action policies, thus favoring black candidates for promotion. Black managers viewed the white majority in the corporation, and in the larger environment, as offering more approval for white candidates. Thus individual perceptions about group interactions at higher levels can shape perceptions, attitudes, and behaviors at lower levels.

In an intercultural interaction, perceived advantages at higher levels will prompt a group to extend the advantages to lower levels. For example, many First World countries maintain controlling interests in international joint ventures with Third World partners. The dominant partner's personnel are placed in positions with more power and status, thus filtering down the same power differential from national and organizational levels to group and individual levels. Alderfer and Smith (1982) describe *congruent* embeddedness when power differentials between two groups at one level are reinforced by similar power differentials at sub- and supralevels. Congruent embeddedness is also observed when a perceived disadvantage between two groups generalizes from higher to lower levels. For example, many Third World countries accept the fact that they are less technologically developed than most Western countries. Individuals and groups from the disadvantaged culture may subordinate themselves in order to learn as much as they can from the other culture. When one culture's advantages are congruent across levels, the resulting intercultural interactions are relatively simple, with consistent dominance of one culture and, perhaps, the exhibition of ethnocentric tendencies.

In contrast, perceived disadvantages at higher levels can lead to *incongruent* embeddedness when the disadvantaged group seeks to reverse this differential at lower levels. In my interviews of American expatriates working in China and with Chinese managers, it was clear that both groups recognized American partners as having more financial resources than their Chinese partners. Americans came to China to build a market there and to take advantage of low labor costs. Yet the Chinese often expressed the view that the Americans should be more generous with their pay scales because America is rich and China is poor. Thus one group's advantage at the national or organizational level can lead to conflicting expectations at lower levels. Incongruent embeddedness will lead to more complex intercultural interactions because the power differentials at different levels are inconsistent.

The preceding examples of congruent and incongruent embeddedness raise a simple question: What factors determine congruent versus incongruent embeddedness? I propose that the relationship between higher- and lower-level intercultural actions is moderated by lower-level characteristics. If the lower-level focus is at the individual level, then individual differences will moderate the extent to which higher-level power differentials are reinforced, reduced, or reversed at the individual level. My model does not explicitly identify specific individual differences because the nature of the cultural comparison will likely determine the relevance of individual personality, value, and demographic characteristics. An individual might accept the fact that another culture is economically and technologically superior, but that individual's own ethnocentrism can help determine the extent to which the power differential will generalize to that individual's own interactions with members of the target culture. To illustrate, in a multinational organization operating in China, several of the Chinese employees recounted the same critical incident (Chao & Sun, 1997). It was a common organizational practice to book different travel arrangements for Chinese and foreign employees who were making the same business trip. Expatriates were generally given first-class air tickets, whereas the Chinese employees were booked in coach class. An American expatriate was scheduled to make a trip with three Chinese employees. When the American discovered the difference in travel arrangements, he asked the secretary to upgrade the Chinese reservations. When he discovered that there were not enough first-class seats available to accommodate the entire party, he exchanged his first-class ticket for coach class and sat with his colleagues. Applying this example back to the model, characteristics associated with this American could be pivotal for the resulting incongruent embeddedness. The actions of this individual resulted in higher-level advantages, set by organizational practices, to be converted to a more egalitarian kind of intercultural behavior. One can only speculate that the American's low ethnocentrism, high initiative, conscientiousness, belief in equality, or all of the above were factors guiding his interactions with his Chinese colleagues. Although incongruent embeddedness produces a more complicated pattern for intercultural interactions, for this particular American it resulted in personal gains. The Chinese interviewees recounted this incident with great fondness, and the American's reputation and ability to work with the Chinese were enhanced.

The same phenomenon can be observed at the group level. While on vacation in Guilin, China, I was among a few hundred tourists from all over the world who were scheduled to take a river cruise. It was a very hot August day, and there were dozens of tourist boats to accommodate the crowds, but only two had air conditioning. My party was lucky enough to be escorted onto an air-conditioned boat, and it quickly filled up with an international mix of small groups, each with its own tour guide. There was an unexplained delay in our departure; most of the other boats had launched. Some of the tour guides and tourists on my boat discovered that the captain was notified that a large Japanese tour group was on its way to the dock. At that time, the Japanese enjoyed the reputation of being the most affluent tourists and were often accorded the best accommodations. The captain was informed that he should wait for this group and move his current passengers to another boat, one without air conditioning. The tourists, informed of this plan, expressed outrage at the prospect. All the tour guides quickly formed a very cohesive group and informed the captain that they would protect the interests of their clients, the tourists who were already on board. Some of the guides also appealed to the captain's sense of fairness and to the efficiency of the operation. Finally, the captain decided to leave with his current passengers; the Japanese group would have to settle for a boat without air conditioning. The tour guides' shared concern for their clients, and their own group cohesiveness, were deciding factors in persuading the captain to ignore an upper-management directive. Contextual features, such as the inability of the Japanese tour guides to rebut the onboard guides' arguments to the captain, may have also contributed to the outcome. Many interpretations of these events could be made (for example, that the onboard tour guides may have been acting in their own interests only, and that they themselves did not want to leave air-conditioned comfort), but the arguments presented by the group of tour guides can illustrate incongruent embeddedness. Higher-level acknowledgment of Japanese affluence and influence were rejected in favor of lower-level actions reflecting egalitarian values. The situational context (delayed departure, upset passengers, only one communication from the Japanese group, and so on), the cohesiveness of the group of tour guides, and the values espoused moderated the relationship between higher- and lower-level congruence. Unlike the American in the preceding example, the captain probably did not enjoy many benefits from his actions. Thus the consequences of incongruent embeddedness are complex.

Results from congruent and incongruent embeddedness have implications for units at all levels. Congruent embeddedness offers simplicity and consistency, with one culture at an advantage over another at all levels. This uniformity can create shared expectations from both cultures that can facilitate negotiations in future interactions. However, potential problems may ferment. Ethnocentric values developed or reinforced by the advantaged culture might demand greater concessions from the disadvantaged culture and/or provoke disadvantaged individuals and groups to seek redress. Forces for or against change will vary within and across levels. In summary, the second multilevel process is described by the following propositions:

P4. *Intercultural relationships at higher levels influence intercultural relationships at lower levels. Embedded intergroup relations would predict that power differentials between two cultures at higher levels tend to be extended at lower levels.*

P5. *The relationship between the relative standings of two cultures at higher and lower levels is moderated by lower-level characteristics.*

Sensemaking of Multilevel Relationships

The nature of intercultural interactions, and the embeddedness of intercultural interactions at higher or lower levels, serve as critical information for individuals to make sense of these interactions and to add this information and its effects to an existing body of knowledge that will shape future interactions. When an individual or group from one culture engages in the sensemaking of behaviors observed from another culture, the analyses can include individual-, group-, or nation-level interpretations. Sensemaking at different levels will become a critical source of information for future intercultural interactions and highlights the dynamic component of the model.

Weick (1995) describes seven properties of sensemaking: (1) It is an ongoing process; (2) it is social; (3) it is grounded in identity constructions; (4) it is retrospective, examining past interactions with current situational filters, a process that in turn affects future events; (5) it is shaped by particular environmental cues that we focus on and extract; (6) it is shaped by our own actions that define a situation; and (7) it is shaped by plausible reasoning that need not be accurate. Within these properties of sensemaking, cultural levels can shift dramatically. An individual's sensemaking may represent an organization's perspective and subsequent actions, if that individual is vested with organizational power and authority. The ongoing sensemaking can focus on one level or it can shift to higher or lower levels in order to derive plausible explanations for behavior. To return to the example of the Chinese boat captain, sensemaking of his decision to sail with his current passengers, rather than wait for the Japanese group, can be made at a number of levels. At the individual level, the captain may have been highly influenced by the group of tour guides who were personally pleading with him. At the group level, the captain may have been following a group norm for captains to run efficient operations. At the national or political level, the captain may have been enacting Communist values of egalitarianism and rejection of preferential treatment for anyone. Relevant environmental cues may come from distal, higher-level sources (for example, Communist values), or there may be a shift to proximal, lower-level cues (for example, the pleading of the tour guides). Therefore, one challenge for researchers is to examine how sensemaking is directed at different levels and their subsequent effects. This can be a formidable challenge when one considers how the knowledge generated from sensemaking, and the subsequent adjustments that people make, can be tacit and nonconscious (Chao, 1997). In summary, the third multilevel process is described by the following propositions:

P6. *Incongruent embeddedness will lead to more complex, inconsistent intercultural interactions than congruent embeddedness.*

P7. *Sensemaking of intercultural experiences will have multilevel implications. An individual's conclusions with respect to these experiences are tied to particular individuals, groups, organizations, and/or nations and serve as new information for the individual to update his or her cultural assessments.*

The multilevel model serves as a heuristic to describe the impact that cultural variables from one level may have on other levels. The level specification of any component in the model will depend on the specific research context. One study's higher-level constructs may be another study's lower-level constructs. Likewise, the specific level of potential moderators of higher- and lower-level relationships must complement the levels specified in the focal relationships. Furthermore, as with the complex level issues raised in cross-cultural research, culture can be conceptualized at a number of levels within a single study. For example, governmental actions can provide critical information that defines higher-level intercultural relationships; organizations can set policies; organizational units can define climates that support or refute formal policies; and individuals can accept or reject group norms. Referring back to Figure 7.1b, the level at which individuals, groups, organizations, and geographic environments define cultures relevant to a study on intercultural organizational behavior will vary.

Level Lessons for Cultural Psychology and Organizational Behavior

In cultural psychology, level issues may not be neatly nested within a traditional hierarchy. Instead of being viewed as an overarching level that defines an environment for organizations, culture might be better conceptualized as group-level and/or individual-level constructs that can be meaningful predictors for organizational behavior. Relationships between constructs that are conceptualized at multiple levels can vary within and across levels. Similar relationships are termed *strong etics* when cultures are involved, or (in the nomenclature of levels) *homologies*. In contrast, relationships across all cultures that are not replicated within a particular culture are described as *weak etics,* and significantly dissimilar relationships within cultures are termed *emic relationships*. Strong and weak etics and emic relationships clearly show that levels-related issues are important to cross-cultural research.

When cultures interact, level issues are further complicated. Apart from the fact that there are multiple levels of defining and measuring culture, perceptions and reactions at lower levels are likely to be influenced by higher-level knowledge bases. This chapter has presented a heuristic model of multilevel effects on intercultural psychology, both to illustrate how multiple levels of culture interact with one another and to show the subsequent sensemaking that also ensues at multiple levels. Sensemaking of another culture can be attributed to a number of cultural identities of the perceiving unit, the target unit, and interactions between the two. Moreover, the ramifications of this sensemaking can shape future interactions with the same target level or can generalize to higher levels. Finally, an iterative process of sensemaking and intercultural interactions can lead to higher-level changes. For example, a subject's own culture can change when common lessons are learned by a number of other members in the cultural collective.

Moreover, apart from the fact that there are multilevel ways of conceptualizing and measuring culture, the context for cultural comparisons and the dynamic nature of culture also have multilevel implications. For instance, the degree to which people from one culture view another culture as similar to their own may depend on the experiences that these people have with a variety of other cultures. As with frog-pond effects (Firebaugh, 1980), relatively objective comparisons between two cultures may be viewed against a backdrop of comparisons with all other cultures. One comparison may be perceived as more similar if all other comparisons with other cultures are judged to be very different. Thus comparisons between two cultures may be made relative to parallel comparisons with other cultures. Given Weick's (1995) notion that sensemaking involves pragmatic reasoning, comparisons with other cultures may take place at different levels. Historical events at the geopolitical, organizational, group, and individual levels can affect relationships between culture and organizational behavior. International political events can influence intercultural exchanges at the individual level, and individual cultural values of key players can set or change organizational values and strategies.

For example, DiBella (1996) describes reorganization efforts at an international organization's Latin American and South Asian operations. The reorganization required more interactions among field offices and between national and regional staffs. Field offices in the Latin American locations were far more culturally homogeneous than were the offices in South Asia. In the Latin American region, a common language and similar cultures allowed these staff members direct communication, and they shared training materials. Although there were distinct cultural identities among the Latin American countries, they could be viewed as similar by comparison to other countries where the global organization was doing business. The common language and the similarity of cultures may have rendered national borders inappropriate as a cultural boundary for this region, and so communication among the Latin American locations might have been better described as intracultural than intercultural. In the South Asian region, different languages and historical cultural hostilities posed special barriers for the reorganization. National staff members in Nepal and Sri Lanka were unreceptive to Indian staff members from regional offices. Although DiBella does not elaborate on what caused the problems in South Asia, my multilevel model offers a vehicle for explaining the observed behavior. According to the model, nation-level hostilities among Nepal, Sri Lanka, and India generally gave India the advantage (Dunung, 1995). Furthermore, the Indians' regional-office power may have entailed an advantage over the Nepalese and Sri Lankan local national offices. The observed coolness of the Nepalese and the Sri Lankans toward the Indians may have reflected attempts to minimize higher-level advantages, given the nationalistic pride of these individuals.

In this way, individual differences (such as nationalism or ethnocentrism) may be key moderators in the extent to which national/organizational advantages extend to interactions at the individual level. This incongruent embeddedness would interfere in the organization's restructuring attempts. Thus, intercultural relationships at higher levels can have an impact on how individuals will interact in an organizational context.

Future research must define appropriate levels in theoretical development and research design. Berry (1989) describes a general methodology for cross-cultural research. Initial domestic research would reflect an emic approach because the research methodology implicitly incorporates the cultural values of the researchers and subjects. If those researchers try to extend their findings to other cultures, an imposed etic is applied when research methods developed in one culture are blindly applied to another. Observed differences can be further examined with an emic exploration of a study's constructs and relationships, to identify the relevance and suitability of these constructs to the new culture. Finally, comparisons of results from the original emic study and from the refined emic study in the new culture can yield similarities that would be termed *derived etics*.

Although this chapter has focused on a conceptual discussion of level issues, as opposed to methodology and measurement issues, one point is raised here: an in-depth emic perspective on culture is most likely to require aggregation of data collected from individuals. Observations and global data (that is, higher-level data that are indivisible, such as the percentage of left-handed people as a measure of a culture's conformity) may only tap artifacts and espoused values of culture and not the basic underlying assumptions or unconscious, taken-for-granted beliefs, perceptions, thoughts, and feelings that best capture culture (Schein, 1992). Triandis (1996) suggests that cultural syndromes, or patterns of attitudes and values that are centered on a theme, can be identified to measure culture. Using data from individuals, and setting up rules for agreement, he provides examples of how cultural responses can be identified from individuals and small groups. Within a work context or theme, cultural syndromes can be identified to capture those aspects of culture that are most relevant to issues in organizational behavior. Thus, although culture is inherently a construct applied to a collective of people, measures of its complexity and depth are likely to come from data gathered at the individual level, centered on cultural syndromes.

Segall, Lonner, and Berry (1998) note that psychology in general has typically ignored the role of culture in human behavior. Schein (1996) echoes this sentiment when he criticizes much of the research in organizational behavior for ignoring cultural influences. Their plea for the development of cross-cultural psychology as a scholarly discipline is partially answered by I/O psychologists who work in global organizations. The competitive advantage of any global organization is often seen as that organization's ability to integrate the cultural backgrounds of the firm's employees into an effective and efficient workforce (Hofstede, 1983). Understanding how culture is conceptualized at different levels, how they might be compared with one another, and how they interact is a fundamental building block of knowledge for competitive global firms. Understanding how level issues help to unlock this knowledge is an important key for researchers.

Note

1. Earley describes the difference score between a subject's IC score and the country mean as representative of the individual level of analysis. However, data derived from individual *and* aggregated measures are more accurately described as cross-level. His study is presented here to illustrate how cultural measures from individuals are better predictors of individual behavior than purely aggregated measures at the nation level.

References

Alderfer, C. P., & Smith, K. K. (1982). Studying intergroup relations embedded in organizations. *Administrative Science Quarterly, 27,* 35–65.

Berry, J. W. (1989). Imposed etics-emics–derived etics: The operationalization of a compelling idea. *International Journal of Psychology, 24,* 721–735.

Berry, J. W., & Dasen, P. R. (1974). *Culture and cognition: Readings in cross-cultural psychology.* London: Methuen.

Bond, M. H. (1997). Adding value to the cross-cultural study of organizational behavior: *Reculer pour mieux sauter.* In P. C. Earley & M. Erez (Eds.), *New perspectives on international industrial/organizational psychology* (pp. 256–275). San Francisco: New Lexington Press.

Boyacigiller, N. A., Kleinberg, M. J., Phillips, M. E., & Sackmann, S. A. (1996). Conceptualizing culture. In B. J. Punnett & O. Shenkar (Eds.), *Handbook for international management research* (pp. 157–208). Cambridge, MA: Blackwell.

Chao, G. T. (1997). Organizational socialization in multinational corporations: The role of implicit learning. In C. L. Cooper & S. Jackson (Eds.), *Creating tomorrow's organizations* (pp. 43–57). New York: Wiley.

Chao, G. T., & Sun, Y. J. (1997). Training needs for expatriate adjustment in the People's Republic of China. In Z. Aycan (Ed.), *New approaches to employee management* (Vol. 4, pp. 205–224). Greenwich, CT: JAI Press.

Chinese Culture Connection. (1987). Chinese values and the search for culture-free dimensions of culture. *Journal of Cross-Cultural Psychology, 18,* 143–164.

Dansereau, F., Jr., & Alutto, J. A. (1990). Level-of-analysis issues in climate and culture research. In B. Schneider (Ed.), *Organizational climate and culture* (pp. 193–236). San Francisco: Jossey-Bass.

Dansereau, F., & Yammarino, F. J. (2000). Within and Between Analysis: The varient paradigm as an underlying approach to theory building and testing. In K. J. Klein & S.W.J. Kozlowski (Eds.), *Multilevel theory, research, and methods in organizations* (pp. 425–466). San Francisco: Jossey-Bass.

DiBella, A. J. (1996). Culture and planned change in an international organization: A multi-level predicament. *International Journal of Organizational Analysis, 4,* 352–372.

Dunung, S. P. (1995). *Doing business in Asia: The complete guide.* San Francisco: New Lexington Press.

Earley, P. C. (1994). Self or group? Cultural effects of training on self-efficacy and performance. *Administrative Science Quarterly, 39,* 89–117.

Earley, P. C., & Randel, A. E. (1997). Culture without borders: An individual-level approach to cross-cultural research in organizational behavior. In C. L. Cooper & S. Jackson (Eds.), *Creating tomorrow's organizations* (pp. 59–73). New York: Wiley.

Erez, M., & Earley, P. C. (1993). *Culture, self-identity, and work.* New York: Oxford University Press.

Firebaugh, G. (1980). Groups as contexts and frog ponds. In K. H. Roberts & L. Burstein (Eds.), *Issues in aggregation.* New Directions for Methodology of Social and Behavioral Science, no. 6. San Francisco: Jossey-Bass.

Glick, W. (1985). Conceptualizing and measuring organizational and psychological climate: Pitfalls in multilevel research. *Academy of Management Review, 10(3),* 601–616.

Hickson, D. J., & McMillan, C. J. (1981). *Organization and nation: The Aston programme IV.* Westmead, England: Gower.

Hofmann, D. A., Griffin, M., & Gavin, M. (2000). The application of hierarchical linear modeling to organizational research. In K. J. Klein & S.W.J. Kozlowski (Eds.), *Multilevel theory, research, and methods in organizations* (pp. 467–511). San Francisco: Jossey-Bass.

Hofstede, G. (1983). The cultural relativity of organizational practices and theories. *Journal of International Business Studies, 14,* 75–89.

Hofstede, G. (1984). *Culture's consequences.* Thousand Oaks, CA: Sage.

Hofstede, G., Bond, M. H., & Luk, C. (1993). Individual perceptions of organizational cultures: A methodological treatise on levels of analysis. *Organizational Studies, 14(4),* 483–503.

Hofstede, G., Neuijen, B., Ohayv, D. D. & Sanders, G. (1990). Measuring organizational cultures: A qualitative and quantitative study across twenty cases. *Administrative Science Quarterly, 35,* 286–316.

James, L. R., & Jones, A. P. (1974). Organizational climate: A review of theory and research. *Psychological Bulletin, 81,* 1096–1112.

Jang, S., & Chung, M. (1997). Discursive contradiction of tradition and modernity in Korean management practices. In S. A. Sackmann (Ed.), *Cultural complexity in organizations: Inherent contrasts and contradictions.* Thousand Oaks, CA: Sage.

Kagitçibasi, C. (1997). Individualism and collectivism. In J. W. Berry, M. H. Segall, & C. Kagitçibasi (Eds.), *Handbook of cross-cultural psychology, Vol. 3: Social behavior and applications* (pp. 1–49). Needham Heights, MA: Allyn & Bacon.

Klein, K. J., Dansereau, F., & Hall, R. J. (1994). Levels issues in theory development, data collection, and analysis. *Academy of Management Review, 19,* 195–229.

Klein, K. J., Tosi, H., & Cannella, A. A., Jr. (1999). Multilevel theory building: Benefits, barriers, and new developments. *Academy of Management Review, 24,* 243–248.

Kluckhohn, C. (1962). *Culture and behavior.* New York: Free Press.

Kozlowski, S.W.J., & Klein, K. J. (2000). A multilevel approach to theory and research in organizations: Contextual, temporal, and emergent processes. In K. J. Klein & S.W.J. Kozlowski (Eds.), *Multilevel theory, research, and methods in organizations* (pp. 3–90). San Francisco: Jossey-Bass.

Kroeber, A. L., & Kluckhohn, C. (1952). *Culture: A critical review of concepts and definitions.* Papers of the Peabody Museum of American Archaeology and Ethnology, Harvard University, vol. 47, no. 1. Cambridge, MA: Peabody Museum.

Leung, K., & Bond, M. H. (1989). On the empirical identification of dimensions for cross-cultural comparisons. *Journal of Cross-Cultural Psychology, 20(2),* 133–151.

Lincoln, J. R., & Zeitz, G. (1980). Organizational properties from aggregate data: Separating individual and structural effects. *American Sociological Review, 45,* 391–408.

Lytle, A. L., Brett, J. M., Barsness, Z. I., Tinsley, C. H., & Janssens, M. (1995). A paradigm for confirmatory cross-cultural research in organizational behavior. In L. L. Cummings & B. M. Staw (Eds.), *Research in organizational behavior* (Vol. 17, pp. 167–214). Greenwich, CT: JAI Press.

Messick, D. M., & van de Geer, J. P. (1981). A reversal paradox. *Psychological Bulletin, 90,* 582–593.

Munroe, R. L., & Munroe, R. H. (1997). A comparative anthropological perspective. In J. W. Berry, Y. H. Poortinga, & J. Pandey (Eds.), *Handbook of cross-cultural psychology: Theory and method* (Vol. 1, pp. 171–213). Needham Heights, MA: Allyn & Bacon.

Ostroff, C. (1993). Comparing correlations based on individual-level and aggregated data. *Journal of Applied Psychology, 78,* 569–582.

Pike, K. L. (1967). *Language in relation to a unified theory of the structure of human behaviour.* Hawthorne, NY: Mouton de Gruyter.

Ralston, D. A., Yu, K., Wang, X., Terpstra, R. H., Gustafson, D. J., & He, W. (1996). The cosmopolitan Chinese manager: Findings of a study on managerial values across the six regions of China. *Journal of International Management, 2,* 79–109.

Reichers, A. E., & Schneider, B. (1990). Climate and culture: An evolution of constructs. In B. Schneider (Ed.), *Organizational climate and culture* (pp. 5–39). San Francisco: Jossey-Bass.

Roberts, K. H., & Boyacigiller, N. A. (1984). Cross-national organizational research: The grasp of the blind men. In L. L. Cummings & B. M. Staw (Eds.), *Research in organizational behavior* (Vol. 6, pp. 423–475). Greenwich, CT: JAI Press.

Ronen, S., & Shenkar, O. (1985). Clustering countries on attitudinal dimensions: A review and synthesis. *Academy of Management Review, 10(3),* 435–454.

Rousseau, D. M. (1985). Issues of level in organizational research: Multilevel and cross-level perspectives. In L. L. Cummings & B. M. Staw (Eds.), *Research in organizational behavior* (Vol. 7, pp. 1–37). Greenwich, CT: JAI Press.

Schein, E. H. (1992). *Organizational culture and leadership* (2nd ed.). San Francisco: Jossey-Bass.

Schein, E. H. (1996). Culture: The missing concept in organization studies. *Administrative Science Quarterly, 41,* 229–240.

Schwartz, S. H. (1994). Beyond individualism/collectivism: New cultural dimensions of values. In U. Kim, H. C. Triandis, C. Kagitçibasi, S. Choi, & G. Yoon (Eds.) *Individualism and collectivism: Theory, method, and applications* (Vol. 18, pp. 85–119). Thousand Oaks, CA: Sage.

Schwartz, S. H., & Ros, M. (1995). Values in the West: A theoretical and empirical challenge to the individualism-collectivism cultural dimension. *World Psychology, 1,* 91–122.

Segall, M. H., Lonner, W. J., & Berry, J. W. (1998). Cross-cultural psychology as a scholarly discipline. *American Psychologist, 53,* 1101–1110.

Sharpe, D. R. (1997). Managerial control strategies and subcultural processes: On the shop floor in a Japanese manufacturing organization in the United Kingdom. In S. A. Sackmann (Ed.), *Cultural complexity in organizations: Inherent contrasts and contradictions* (pp. 228–251). Thousand Oaks, CA: Sage.

Smith, P. B., Dugan, S., & Trompenaars, F. (1996). National culture and the values of organizational employees: A dimensional analysis across 43 nations. *Journal of Cross-Cultural Psychology, 27,* 231–264.

Triandis, H. C. (1972). *The analysis of subjective culture.* New York: Wiley.

Triandis, H. C. (1994). *Culture and social behavior.* New York: McGraw-Hill.

Triandis, H. C. (1995). *Individualism and collectivism.* Boulder, CO: Westview.

Triandis, H. C. (1996). The psychological measurement of cultural syndromes. *American Psychologist, 51(4),* 407–415.

Triandis, H. C., Kurowski, L. L., & Gelfand, M. J. (1994). Workplace diversity. In H. C. Triandis, M. D. Dunnette, & L. M. Hough (Eds.), *Handbook of industrial and organizational psychology* (Vol. 4, 2nd ed., pp. 769–827). Palo Alto, CA: Consulting Psychologists Press.

Triandis, H. C., McCusker, C., Betancourt, H., Iwao, S., Leung, K., Salazar, J. M., Setiadi, B., Sinha, J.B.P., Touzard, H., & Zaleski, Z. (1993). An etic-emic analysis of individualism and collectivism. *Journal of Cross-Cultural Psychology, 24(3),* 366–383.

Tung, R. L. (1981). Selection and training of personnel for overseas assignments. *Columbia Journal of World Business, 16(1),* 68–78.

Van de Vijver, F., & Leung, K. (1997). *Methods and data analysis for cross-cultural research.* Thousand Oaks, CA: Sage.

Weick, K. E. (1995). *Sensemaking in organizations.* Thousand Oaks, CA: Sage.

PART 2

Analyzing Multilevel Data

CHAPTER 8

Within-Group Agreement, Non-Independence, and Reliability
Implications for Data Aggregation and Analysis
Paul D. Bliese

Issues surrounding within-group agreement, non-independence, and group-mean reliability have important theoretical and practical implications for organizational researchers. Unfortunately, the interpretation of agreement, non-independence, and reliability indices tends to be one of the more controversial issues in organizational multilevel research (see Dansereau and Alutto, 1990; George & James, 1993; Glick, 1985, 1988; James, 1982; James, Demaree, & Wolf, 1984, 1993; James, Joyce, & Slocum, 1988; Joyce & Slocum, 1984; Klein, Dansereau, & Hall, 1994; Kozlowski & Hattrup, 1992; Schmidt & Hunter, 1989; Yammarino & Markham, 1992). This chapter was written to serve two purposes. The first purpose is to differentiate among the most commonly used indices of agreement, reliability, and non-independence and to provide an overview of what each measure reveals about the group-level properties of one's data. Particular attention is devoted to the concept of non-independence and to the relationship between one form of the intraclass correlation coefficient (ICC)—the ICC(1)—and eta-squared. These issues have important implications for conducting and interpreting organizational multilevel research but have received relatively little attention in the organizational literature. The second purpose of this chapter is to extend the discussion of agreement, reliability, and non-independence from an exclusive focus on validating one's measurement model to a broader focus that includes testing substantive models and detecting emergent phenomena. It is widely recognized that the various agreement and reliability indices are important for theoretical reasons related to the establishment of construct validity in one's measurement model; I suggest, however, that reliability indices are also important for practical reasons related to testing substantive models and detecting emergent phenomena. My discussion of these issues is organized around the notions of top-down and bottom-up processes (Kozlowski & Klein, Chapter One, this volume). In the discussion of bottom-up processes, particular attention is paid to a category that I define as "fuzzy" composition processes.

Within-Group Agreement, Reliability, and Non-Independence

At first glance, it would appear to be easy to show that group members agree about some construct of interest. To establish agreement, one merely needs to demonstrate that responses from group members are more similar to each other than would be expected by chance (Klein et al., 1994). What ultimately makes the task of establishing agreement controversial revolves around how one defines "greater than chance similarity." There are two basic ways to define it. One approach is to contrast observed group variances to some theoretical expected random variance. In essence, one calculates group members' variance surrounding some construct of interest and determines whether the observed group variance is "small" (high agreement) or "large" (low agreement) relative to the theoretical random variance. This approach is generally adopted in estimates of agreement. The second approach is to contrast within-group variance to between-group variance, using traditional analysis-of-variance (ANOVA) designs. Equal between-group and within-group variances suggest chance similarity among group members, whereas small within-group variance relative to between-group variance indicates greater than chance similarity among group members. This approach is generally used in the calculation of reliability and non-independence measures. As will be discussed in more detail later, both reliability and non-independence are frequently estimated by means of the ICC(1); consequently, the ICC(1), an ANOVA-based measure, can be interpreted as either a reliability index or as a measure of non-independence according to the context. What is important to notice is that agreement and reliability indices are conceptually and mathematically distinct; that is, they are based on completely different ideas about what constitutes greater than chance similarity. Nevertheless, both types of measures reveal important information about the group-level properties of one's data, and so I consider both in the following sections.

Within-Group Agreement

The term *within-group agreement* refers to the degree to which ratings from individuals are interchangeable; that is, agreement reflects the degree to which raters provide essentially the same rating (Kozlowski & Hattrup, 1992; Tinsley & Weiss, 1975). The most frequently encountered measure of within-group agreement in the organizational literature is the r_{wg} or $r_{wg(j)}$ (James et al., 1984, 1993). The former is designed for single items, and the latter is designed for multiple-item scales; for brevity, however, in this chapter I refer to both indices as the r_{wg}. The r_{wg} is calculated by comparing an observed group variance to an expected random variance. James and colleagues (1984) propose that one option for the expected random variance would be the variance that would be observed if responses from group members formed a uniform (that is, rectangular) distribution (see also Finn, 1970). The uniform distribution is the distribution that would emerge if group members provided the same number of responses for each response category—for example, if group members provided an equal number of 1s, 2s, 3s, 4s, and 5s on a 5-point scale. Clearly, there are theoretical problems with assuming that the uniform distribution is always the best choice to represent a random distribution. For one thing, the uniform distribution assumes no response bias, yet it is likely that some degree of response bias will be present in many of the data collected in organizations. Under conditions of response bias, the uniform distribution is a poor choice to use for a random distribution. This is because response bias typically results in respondents' using a restricted part of the response range. For example, under a positive response bias, individuals will be inclined to use neutral or positive response options (for example, 3s, 4s, and 5s). This restricted use of the response range will reduce within-group variance (relative to the variance from a uniform distribution) and make it appear that group members agree. James and colleagues (1984) recognize this potential flaw, and one of their major contributions is to have provided several alternatives for use as a random distribution. Nevertheless, the task of choosing an appropriate random distribution for a specific sample falls to the researcher. There are at least two options available in choosing this distribution. First, Kozlowski and Hults (1987) recommend examining the response distribution in an independent data set to establish alternative random distributions. The response distribution from the independent data can be used to set a lower bound for r_{wg}. That is, in using this distribution, one makes the extreme assumption that the response distribution is solely due to bias. In contrast, using the rectangular distribution provides the upper bound for r_{wg}. True agreement can be expected to be somewhere in between the two conditions. The second promising alternative is to employ resampling approaches (Efron & Tibshirani, 1993) to estimate the expected random distribution, using an approach that we refer to as *random group resampling* (RGR) (Bliese & Halverson, 1996, 1998a, 1999; Bliese, Halverson, & Rothberg, 1994). RGR capitalizes on the widespread availability of computer power to create a response distribution on a parameter of interest from numerous pseudo groups. The parameter of interest estimated from the pseudo groups could be within-group variances, group means, group medians, or any number of other statistical parameters. Results from the pseudo group response distribution are then compared to results from the actual groups. When one uses RGR to test for within-group agreement, one sets up the algorithm to calculate variances from numerous pseudo groups. In other words, one randomly assigns individuals to pseudo groups matching the size characteristics of the actual groups, and for each of the pseudo groups one calculates a variance. For instance, one might calculate the variance of pseudo group members' perceptions of leadership. The distribution of the pseudo group variances is used to determine whether actual group variances are significantly smaller than or larger than pseudo group variances, either on a case-by-case basis or for the groups as a whole (Bliese et al., 1994). Evidence that actual group variances are significantly smaller than pseudo group variances is strong support for the idea that within-group agreement exists. It would be reasonable to use the average pseudo group variance as an estimate of the expected random variance in the calculation of the r_{wg}. An advantage of doing so is that the average pseudo group variance should correct for any individual-level response biases. One should note, however, that this strategy (like the strategy proposed by Kozlowski & Hults) is likely to produce r_{wg} values that are substantially smaller than values using the uniform rectangular distribution as the expected random variance. S-PLUS (Statistical Sciences, 1997) algorithms for using RGR to calculate agreement are available from the author.

Before the discussion of RGR concludes, it is worth noting that using RGR to estimate agreement blurs the line between agreement-based measures and reliability-based measures (discussed in detail in the following section). That is because the pseudo group estimate of the random expected variance depends, in part, on the degree of between-group variability. For example, when all group members from all groups have provided the same score, the pseudo group variance will equal zero. Consequently, the r_{wg}, based on the pseudo group variance, would also be zero. In contrast, if one felt that it was reasonable to use a uniform, rectangular distribution as the basis for the random variance, and if one used this variance in the calculation of r_{wg}, one would get very high r_{wg} values.

In any event, researchers should be encouraged to consider alternative options to the uniform rectangular distribution in the calculation of the r_{wg}. All too often, researchers appear to rely solely on the uniform rectangular distribution as the expected random distribution for the random variance without considering alternatives. This overreliance on the use of the uniform rectangular distribution is likely to result in systematic overestimates of within-group agreement. Despite this potential problem, there are still theoretical and practical reasons why one may elect to calculate the r_{wg}. These reasons center on two facts: the magnitude of the r_{wg} is not dependent on between-group variance (except when RGR routines are used to estimate the expected random distribution); and the r_{wg} provides a measure of agreement for each group rather than an omnibus measure for the groups as a whole. This can be important if one needs to identify whether or not specific groups show agreement.

Reliability

Reliability can be considered a measure assessing the relative consistency of responses among raters (Kozlowski & Hattrup, 1992). It is the degree to which ratings are consistent "when expressed as deviations from their means" (Tinsley & Weiss, 1975, p. 359). One can have high reliability in cases where agreement is low. For example, if rater A uses only 1, 2, and 3 on a 5-point scale while rater B uses only 3, 4, and 5, then across ratees a rating of 3 from rater A will be equivalent to a rating of 5 from rater B. Agreement will be low because 3 is different from 5, but reliability will be high because the responses are proportionally consistent.

In the multilevel organizational literature, reliability is commonly assessed by means of one or both of the two major forms of the intraclass correlation coefficient: the ICC(1) and the ICC(2) (Bartko, 1976; James, 1982). Both forms of the ICC are calculated from a one-way random-effects ANOVA where the variable of interest is the dependent variable (that is, the ratings), and group membership is the independent variable. For example, if one wanted to calculate ICCs on individuals' reports of satisfaction, one would estimate an ANOVA model with individual ratings of satisfaction as the dependent variable and group membership as the independent variable. This model is equivalent to a regression model in which satisfaction is the dependent variable and group membership is coded by means of $N-1$ contrast codes representing group membership.

The first form of the ICC is the ICC(1) (Bartko, 1976; James, 1982: McGraw & Wong, 1996) also known as the ICC (Bryk & Raudenbush, 1982), and the ICC(1,1) (Shrout & Fleiss, 1979). While the ICC(1) represents a form of proportional consistency, it has been defined in several slightly different ways. Bryk and Raudenbush (1982) interpret it as the proportion of the total variance that can be explained by group membership. For example, an ICC(1) of .10 on a leadership variable indicates that 10 percent of the variability in an individual's ratings of leadership could be explained by or is related to group membership. James (1982) interprets the ICC(1) as the degree of reliability associated with a single assessment of the group mean. That is, he interprets the ICC(1) as an index of interrater reliability (the extent to which raters are substitutable), which is why he recommends using it as a criterion for aggregating.

Mathematically, the ratio of between-group variance to total variance is calculated in order to estimate the ICC(1). Random-coefficient models, such as hierarchical linear modeling, or HLM (Bryk & Raudenbush, 1992), lme for S-PLUS (Statistical Sciences, 1997), and MLn (Kreft & DeLeeuw, 1998), provide variance estimates of the between-group and the within-group components. Consequently, the ICC(1) is easily calculated as $\tau_{00}/(\tau_{00}+\sigma^2)$ where τ_{00} represents the between-group variance and σ^2 represents the within-group variance.

From a one-way random-effects ANOVA model, ICC(1) can be calculated with the Bartko (1976) formula:

$$ICC(1) = \frac{MSB-MSW}{MSB+[(k-1)*MSW]}.$$

In the Bartko formula, *MSB* is the between-group mean square, *MSW* is the within-group mean square, and *k* is the group size. This formula is simply a way of estimating and contrasting the between-group and within-group variance components from the ANOVA model (McGraw & Wong, 1996). Note that in most cases one can use average group size for *k* if group sizes differ. Blalock (1972) provides a formula for *k* that can be used when group sizes differ dramatically; that formula is reproduced in Bliese and Halverson (1998b).

There is one important difference between the ICC(1) calculated from a random-coefficient model and an ICC(1) calculated from an ANOVA model. This difference is that the range of the ICC(1) in the ANOVA model is from −1 to +1, whereas in the random-coefficient model it is from 0 to +1. In other words, negative ICC(1) values are possible in ANOVA models but not in random-coefficient models.

Negative values occur in the ANOVA model when the within-group variance is smaller than the between-group variance (that is, when MSB is smaller than MSW). For instance, a value of −1 occurs when group means are identical (that is, when MSB is zero) but individual variability exists within groups (that is, when MSW is nonzero). By contrast, in the random-coefficient model the minimum value for τ_{00} is zero because a zero τ_{00} value indicates no between-group variability in the intercept (that is, the mean). It is obvious from the formula above that when τ_{00} is zero, the ICC(1) must also be zero. Negative ICC(1) values are of theoretical interest because they provide evidence of within-group or frog-pond situations (Dansereau, Alutto, & Yammarino, 1984). In other words, they suggest that individual variability, relative to a group mean, is an important source of variability. A good example where one might expect to find a frog-pond effect would be with pay satisfaction. One might expect the main predictor of pay satisfaction to be an individual's pay relative to the average pay of his or her work group.

The second form of the ICC commonly encountered in organizational research is the ICC(2) (Bartko, 1976; James, 1982). The ICC(2) provides an estimate of the reliability of the group means (Bartko, 1976; James, 1982; McGraw & Wong, 1996; Shrout & Fleiss, 1979). ICC(2) has been referred to as the ICC(1,k) by Shrout and Fleiss (1979) and as the ICC(k) by McGraw and Wong (1996). In cases where group sizes are equal, the ICC(2) is equivalent to the overall sample-mean reliability estimate, $\hat{\lambda}$, discussed by Bryk and Raudenbush (1992, p. 63). The ICC(2) is typically estimated with the use of mean squares from a one-way random-effects ANOVA in the following formula:

$$ICC(2) = \frac{MSB - MSW}{MSB}.$$

ICC(1) and ICC(2) are related to each other as a function of group size (Bliese, 1998; Glick, 1985; Shrout & Fleiss, 1979). The relationship among ICC(1), ICC(2), and group size can be described as follows: ICC(1) may be considered a measure of the reliability associated with a single assessment of the group mean (James, 1982). When ICC(1) is large, a single rating from an individual is likely to provide a relatively reliable rating of the group mean; when ICC(1) is small, multiple ratings are necessary to provide reliable estimates of the group mean.

If we assume that ICC(1) represents the reliability of a single assessment of a group-level property, and if we know the group size, then we can use the Spearman-Brown formula, following Shrout and Fleiss (1979), to predict the reliability of the group mean, ICC(2), as shown here in equation 1:

$$ICC(2) = \frac{k(ICC(1))}{1+(k-1)ICC(1)} \qquad (1)$$

where k represents the group size. Note that Bliese (1998) has shown that the Spearman-Brown formula using ICC(1) and group size does not exactly match the ICC(2) estimate of group-mean reliability; rather, reliability estimates based on the Spearman-Brown formula asymptotically approach the ICC(2) as group sizes increase. For an example showing the utility of equation 1, consider Ostroff (1992), who reports an ICC(1) of .26 for a teachers' satisfaction scale. The average number of teachers per group was 40.67. If 40.67 is used for k and .26 is used for ICC(1) in equation 1, the expected ICC(2) value is .93. This matches the ICC(2) value reported by Ostroff and presumably calculated using MSB – MSW/MSB.

Non-Independence

The term *non-independence* is not frequently encountered in the organizational literature, but it refers to the degree to which responses from individuals in the same group are influenced by, depend on, or cluster by group (Kenny & Judd, 1986, 1996). Non-independence can occur for numerous reasons; according to Kenny and Judd (1996, p. 138), "observations may be dependent, for instance, because they share some common feature, come from some common source, are affected by social interaction, or are arranged spatially or sequentially in time."

There are several ways to estimate non-independence, depending on which form of non-independence one expects to find. For example, in longitudinal data there is likely to be sequential non-independence in the form of a first-order autoregressive model or a first-order moving-average model. If one suspects these forms of non-independence, there are tests to determine whether autocorrelation differs from zero (see Kenny & Judd, 1986). In cases where non-independence due to group membership is expected, the most commonly used test is the ICC(1) (see Bryk & Raudenbush, 1992; Kenny & Judd, 1986; Kreft & DeLeeuw, 1998). A nonzero ICC(1) value indicates that group membership affects or is related to lower-level observations.

The concept of non-independence is relevant to multilevel analysts even in cases where the analyst is not interested in establishing criteria for aggregation. This is because non-independence plays a critical role in the analysis and interpretation of results from grouped data (Bryk & Raudenbush, 1992; Kenny & Judd, 1986; Kreft & DeLeeuw, 1998; Singer, 1998) and because non-independence is ubiquitous in organizational data. The role of non-independence in data analysis will be addressed in the discussion of top-down processes, later in the chapter. In this section, I will focus on the widespread presence of non-independence.

Although one typically expects clustering to occur when individuals are rating shared unit properties such as organizational climate, it is important to note that clustering is often evident for constructs that do not necessarily measure attributes of a higher-level unit. That is, there are logical reasons to believe that many of the variables of interest to organizational researchers cluster by group membership even if the variable of interest makes no reference to the group. For instance, in U.S. Army data we have found that individual-level constructs, such as self-reports of work hours and psychological well-being, often cluster as a function of army company membership (Bliese & Halverson, 1996). To take other examples, Ostroff (1992) has found that teachers' reports of job satisfaction, commitment, adjustment, and stress clustered by school; moreover, Barrick, Stewart, Neubert, and Mount (1998) and Schneider, Smith, Taylor, and Fleenor (1998) report evidence to suggest that "personality" clusters by groups and organizations. The fact that non-independence is present in these cases indicates that group membership is related to constructs that are typically considered to be individual-level constructs.

It may be somewhat confusing that ICC(1) can be considered both a measure of reliability and a measure of non-independence. One way to help clarify this distinction is to note that when ICC(1) is calculated on the dependent variable, it is generally considered a measure of non-independence (Bryk & Raudenbush, 1992; Kreft &

DeLeeuw, 1998). One is estimating ICC(1) to answer the question "Is my outcome variable affected by or related to group membership?" In contrast, when ICC(1) is calculated on an independent variable, it is generally being used as a measure of reliability. In this case, one is typically attempting to answer the question "Can I aggregate this variable and analyze it as a group mean?" In short, ICC(1) can be used either as a measure of reliability or as a measure of non-independence; how one interprets the index depends on the research question one is asking.

It is important to distinguish between reliability and non-independence because there are cases in which organizational researchers would have no theoretical reason to want to estimate reliability; that is, a researcher might not be faced with questions about whether it is appropriate to aggregate a variable. Even in these cases, however, the nested nature of organizational data often makes it important to know whether group membership plays a role in the interrelationships among variables (Kreft & DeLeeuw, 1998). Therefore, there is often a need to estimate non-independence in cases where there is no need to estimate reliability. (I discuss this issue in more detail in a later section.)

Eta-Squared

In concluding the discussion of agreement, reliability, and non-independence, it is necessary to mention eta-squared. In the organizational literature, eta-squared is occasionally equated to the ICC(1) (Drexler, 1977; James, 1982; Glick, 1985), and it is also a central component of inferences drawn with E-tests in WABA I (Dansereau & Alutto, 1990; Dansereau et al., 1984; Yammarino & Markham, 1992). Eta-squared, like ICC(1), is calculated from a one-way random-effects ANOVA, where group membership is the independent variable and the construct of interest (for example, job satisfaction) is the dependent variable. The eta-squared value is equivalent to the R-squared from a regression model in which the variable of interest is the dependent variable and group membership is coded into $N-1$ dummy variables.

The magnitude of eta-squared is highly dependent on the size of the groups in the sample (Bliese & Halverson, 1998b). When group sizes are large, eta-squared values are equivalent to ICC(1) values; however, when group sizes are small, eta-squared values show significant inflation relative to the ICC(1). In the extreme case of dyads, for example, eta-squared values will be .50 even if there are absolutely no group-level properties associated with the data. That is, if one uses a random-number generator to create a vector of numbers, arbitrarily assigns dyad membership to the numbers, and calculates eta-squared values, then one will observe that eta-squared values are .50. Table 8.1 shows the relationship between ICC(1) values and eta-squared values using simulated data. In the simulation, data were created to have ICC(1) values of .01, .10, and .25 in groups with two, four, ten, and twenty-five members (additional information on the simulation algorithms can be found in Bliese, 1998; Bliese & Halverson, 1998b). In each iteration of the simulation, a data set with a targeted ICC(1) value and a known group size was created, and the ICC(1) value and eta-squared values for the specific data set were calculated with conventional formulas. This process was repeated a thousand times for each ICC(1) and group-size condition. Table 8.1 provides the average ICC(1) and eta-squared values for each condition.

Table 8.1. Comparison of Eta-Squared and ICC(1) Values.

Group Size	Targeted ICC(1) Value	Observed ICC(1) Value	Observed η^2 Value	Bias $[\eta^2 - ICC(1)]$
2	.010	.015	.505	.490
	.100	.100	.547	.447
	.250	.247	.621	.374
4	.101	.006	.253	.247
	.100	.099	.322	.223
	.250	.249	.434	.185
10	.010	.011	.109	.098
	.100	.099	.188	.089
	.250	.247	.320	.073
25	.010	.009	.049	.040
	.100	.099	.134	.035
	.250	.250	.278	.028

Notice that ICC(1) values and eta-squared values differ dramatically even though they are estimated on the same data. Differences are particularly apparent in cases where group sizes are small and/or targeted ICC(1) values are small. The last column of Table 8.1 provides an estimate of bias associated with eta-squared. From this column it is obvious that eta-squared values asymptotically approach ICC(1) values as group sizes increase. Notice, though, that even with groups simulated to have twenty-five members, eta-squared values provide significantly biased estimates of group effects.

Attempts to interpret eta-squared without considering group size could lead to considerable confusion in the organizational literature. Researchers could struggle to explain why studies with small groups have eta-squared values of .50, whereas other studies, which seem equally sound yet have larger group sizes, barely manage to have eta-squared values of .10 (for a case where this is relevant, see Yammarino & Markham, 1992). If one contrasted eta-squared values from dyads with eta-squared values from groups larger than dyads, but without considering group-size effects, one could easily conclude that the appropriate level of analysis was the dyad. This conclusion would seemingly be supported by the large eta-squared values from dyads; in reality, however, these results would be merely artifacts of group size.

Equating eta-squared and ICC(1) values has probably led to overestimates of "typical" group-level properties associated with data. For example, James (1982, p. 224) reviewed a number of studies and found that ICC(1) values ranged from .00 to .50, and that the median value was .12. However, James equated eta-squared and ICC(1); consequently, both the range and the median value were probably overestimated. In my own experience with U.S. Army data from numerous deployment and garrison environments, I have never encountered ICC(1) values greater than .30; I typically see values between .05 and .20. It is possible that this represents restriction of range and homogeneity of groups in our samples; nevertheless, I would be surprised to find ICC(1) values greater than .30 in most applied field research. (Note that one could easily obtain eta-squared values greater than .30 by arbitrarily reducing group size.) In short, it seems prudent to compare eta-squared values across studies only if the group sizes of the studies are identical.

An alternative is to correct eta-squared values for group-size differences; Bliese and Halverson (1998b) provide one such correction. The relationship between group size and eta-squared values further suggests that E-tests in WABA (Dansereau et al., 1984) should be used only if one is examining dyads; applying E-tests to groups larger than dyads is problematic because the E-tests will become increasingly stringent as group size increases. In short, researchers are probably best advised simply to avoid using and interpreting eta-squared values, particularly because ICC(1) values are easily estimated. (However, see Dansereau & Yammarino, Chapter Ten, this volume, for a different view of the merits of conducting E-tests within WABA.)

Summary

The first part of this chapter has provided definitions of *within-group agreement, group reliability,* and *non-independence.* At this point, it should be clear that measures of within-group agreement and measures of reliability are conceptually and mathematically distinct. Recall that it is possible for variables to be simultaneously high on one dimension (for example, agreement) while low the other (for example, reliability). For a good example of a situation where agreement and reliability do not coincide, see Tinsley and Weiss (1975). Recall that reliability can be high and agreement low if raters are proportionally consistent in ratings, even if absolute rating values are inconsistent. That is, one rater might tend to use 1, 2, and 3; another might tend to use 3, 4, and 5; and a final rater might tend to use 5, 6, and 7. In this case, individuals with low ratings would be rated 1, 3, and 5; individuals with medium ratings would be rated 2, 4, and 6; and individuals with high ratings would receive 3, 5, and 7. This scheme would result in low agreement but high reliability. In contrast, agreement would be high but reliability low if raters tended to use a restricted range of the item responses— that is, if all raters used 3, 4, and 5 on a 9-point scale.

At this point in the chapter, it should also be clear that non-independence and reliability are conceptually distinct, although both can be measured with the ICC(1). Again, the term *non-independence* refers to the degree to which lower-level (individual) responses are affected by or related to higher-level (group) factors.

The issue of non-independence is generally brought up in the context of the dependent variable (e.g., Kreft & DeLeeuw, 1998). In the following sections, I will return to the importance of non-independence in model estimation. In contrast, reliability is typically an issue in terms of the independent variable and refers to the degree to which an individual rating can be considered a reliable assessment of a group-level construct. Let us now consider the methodological and conceptual importance of within-group agreement, group reliability, and non-independence in the context of top-down and bottom-up processes.

Top-Down Processes

There are strong theoretical reasons to believe that higher-level processes have an impact on lower-level entities: organizations implement policies that affect organizational members; groups have leaders who vary in degree of competence and consideration; physical work environments vary across groups. Presumably, these higher-level factors affect lower-level variables both directly and indirectly.

Top-down effects either can be integral to one's theoretical model (Hofmann & Stetzer, 1996; Jex & Bliese, 1999; Mathieu & Kohler, 1990) or can be nuisance factors (Bryk & Raudenbush, 1992; Kenny & Judd, 1986; Kreft & DeLeeuw, 1998; Singer, 1998). In the first case, for example, one may propose that such group-level variables as climate for safety, collective efficacy, or average absenteeism are related to individual actions, attitudes and/or behaviors. Essentially, one is proposing that higher-level factors (that is, contextual effects) have an impact on lower-level relationships.

It is equally important, however, to recognize that top-down effects can be a nuisance factor. Nuisance effects occur in cases where one is interested in examining data that have a hierarchical nature. For example, one might be interested in examining the relationship between individual job satisfaction and individual job performance by using data collected from individuals who are nested within work groups. In testing one's hypothesis, caution must be exercised because work-group membership may be related to individual performance; that is, work-group membership may exhibit a top-down process effect on individual performance. In cases where higher-level variables are related to lower-level outcomes, one cannot simply ignore the higher-level factor; to do so leads to biases in one's model (Bryk & Raudenbush, 1992; Kenny & Judd, 1986; Kreft & DeLeeuw, 1998). Even a very small degree of non-independence due to group membership in the dependent variable can significantly bias statistical models (Barcikowski, 1981, cited in Kreft & DeLeeuw, 1998). This bias occurs because a fundamental assumption underlying commonly used analytic techniques, such as regression and ANOVA, is that the data are independent (Bryk & Raudenbush, 1992; Kenny & Judd, 1986). If non-independence is present but not accounted for, it causes bias in standard errors in such traditional ordinary least squares procedures as regression and ANOVA.

One can think about this in the following way: when one calculates parameter estimates using individual-level data taken from a thousand independent observations, the thousand observations are used to calculate standard errors. A large number of independent observations means stable parameter estimates and results in small standard errors. If one has a thousand observations, but if they are not independent, one essentially has fewer than a thousand observations. This occurs because respondents are providing overlapping information. Thus, for example, an ICC(1) of .20 might translate into having the equivalent of eight hundred independent observations instead of a thousand (this is only an illustrative example; one needs to consider group size to get an exact estimate). Failure to make adjustments for non-independence causes standard errors to be based on the full sample size and results in standard errors that are too small. Thus researchers might think that they are testing a hypothesis at $p < .05$, but in reality they are testing it at $p < .15$.

Consequently, even in cases where researchers are interested only in individual-level relationships, the estimation of non-independence is important if the data have been collected from hierarchically nested entities. In cases where non-independence is present, appropriate statistical analyses need to be used to control for the degree of non-independence. In general, this is accomplished by incorporating the effects of group membership into one's statistical models. One of the reasons why multilevel random-coefficient models (Bryk & Raudenbush, 1992; Kreft & DeLeeuw, 1998; Longford, 1995) have gained popularity in educational and organizational research is because of their flexibility in including group membership in statistical models, thereby providing tests of individual-level relationships that correct for non-independence.

Regardless of whether top-down processes are an integral part of one's theoretical model, or whether they are nuisance factors, measures of non-independence in the dependent variable reveal important information about one's data. When the purpose of the research is to determine the degree to which higher-level factors have direct impacts on lower-level entities, the ICC(1) provides an estimate of the amount of lower-level variance that can be accounted for by the higher-level entity (Bryk & Raudenbush, 1992; Kreft & DeLeeuw, 1998). In other words, the ICC(1) provides information about the degree to which contextual factors influence lower-level data. For instance, an ICC(1) of .10 indicates that a maximum of 10 percent of the lower-level variance can be accounted for by contextual factors such as collective efficacy, cohesion, climate for safety, and so on.

In contrast, when one suspects that higher-level entities are a nuisance factor, estimates of non-independence in the dependent variable provide a way of determining the degree to which lower-level relationships will be biased if higher-level effects are not adequately controlled for. In summary, non-independence needs to be calculated as a matter of "good" science in dealing with hierarchically nested data, regardless of whether or not one is explicitly interested in modeling contextual effects. In cases where one is not particularly interested in modeling contextual effects, bias will occur if one does not account for the influence of higher-order effects. In contrast, in cases where one is specifically interested in contextual effects, non-independence is important because it provides information about the possible magnitude of impact that contextual effects can be expected to have.

Bottom-Up Processes

Agreement and reliability indices also play an important role in issues of construct validity related to bottom-up processes. The mathematical foundations of many organization-level constructs are in data collected from individuals. The fundamental assumption underlying bottom-up processes is that lower-level data can be combined to represent phenomena at higher levels. Kozlowski and

Klein (Chapter One, this volume) identify two ideal forms of bottom-up processes: composition and compilation. *Composition processes* are rooted in a theoretical model of isomorphism, where lower-level data are assumed to be similar to each other and to the higher-level constructs. In contrast, *compilation processes* are rooted in a theoretical model of discontinuity, where lower-level data points are considered to be dissimilar to each other and to the higher-level construct. The two processes represent two ends of a continuum, with the majority of bottom-up processes occurring in the area between the two end points.

In this section, I explore the importance of agreement and reliability indices as they pertain to issues of construct validity in bottom-up processes. Construct validity will be discussed as it relates to the establishment of the measurement model, and to evaluations of the substantive theoretical model. I will address these issues as they pertain to compilation processes, to composition processes, and to a class of processes that I refer to as "fuzzy" composition processes.

Compilation Processes

Compilation processes are based on the premise that phenomena constitute a common domain area across levels, but that there are distinct differences between aggregated and nonaggregated data (Kozlowski & Klein, Chapter One, this volume). In compilation models, lower-level data are expected to vary within groups, yet when the data are aggregated, the aggregate variable is expected to measure some phenomenon not evident at the lower level. In pure compilation process models, there is no theoretical need to establish "agreement" about the aggregate variable. The logic behind establishing agreement is to demonstrate that lower-level entities share key similarities with each other; in compilation process models, however, similarity is not a prerequisite for creating an aggregate variable; in fact, the aggregate variable is often based on the notion of dissimilarity (Kozlowski & Klein, Chapter One, this volume). Thus, in compilation processes, agreement measures have little if any importance in terms of establishing the construct validity of the measurement model.

For an example, consider diversity research (Jackson et al., 1991; Milliken & Martins, 1996). In research of this nature, one creates an aggregate variable from lower-level observable attributes, such as demographics, or from lower-level underlying attributes, such as values and personality (Milliken & Martins, 1996). Some groups have considerable diversity, whereas other groups have a high degree of homogeneity. One expects the level of diversity in the group to be related to various group and/or individual outcomes. It is important to emphasize, however, that the aggregate variable in this line of research is theoretically distinct from its lower-level counterpart (see also Chan, 1998). For instance, the gender of the individuals in a group may be used to create an aggregate variable reflecting the homogeneity of gender in the group. The aggregate variable, however, is technically a measure of group diversity, whereas the individual-level variable remains a measure of gender. Or, to take another example, one might create an aggregate variable that measures the degree to which there is consensus among group members about some construct (such as quality of group leadership) and use consensus as a predictor of group outcomes (Bliese & Halverson, 1998a). Again, the aggregate measure is theoretically distinct from the individual-level measure. In both cases, it is clear that in pure compilation process models one does not need to establish agreement to support the construct validity of the measurement model.

In compilation models, measures of reliability and non-independence will also tend to be irrelevant. This is because reliability-based measures provide estimates of the reliability of a single assessment of the group mean, ICC(1), or an estimate of the reliability of the group means, ICC(2). Diversity research, however, does not model group means except as potential covariates (Bliese & Halverson, 1998a), and so the issue of group-mean reliability is not important to one's conceptual model. In summary, one does not generally have to be concerned about establishing agreement or about demonstrating group-mean reliability to establish the construct validity of compilation-based aggregate measures.

Composition Processes

Composition process models, in contrast to compilation process models, are based on the premise that lower-level phenomena are isomorphic with each other and with the higher-level construct (see Kozlowski & Klein, Chapter One, this volume). Stated another way, aggregated variables in composition process models are assumed to be essentially identical to lower-level constructs in both form and function. In the ideal case of isomorphism, every member of a group would provide exactly the same score on a measure of climate, cognition, behavior, and so forth. In this ideal case, individual responses would be completely interchangeable. This emphasis on interchangeability suggests that when one's theoretical model is based on a composition process, within-group agreement is the appropriate index to use in establishing the validity of the measurement model. For example, by demonstrating agreement, individual reports of psychological climate might be aggregated to create an organizational-climate variable (James & Jones, 1974). In the absence of within-group agreement, one's measurement model would be unsupported.

In pure composition process situations, measures of reliability are unimportant. This is because in cases of pure isomorphism, measures of reliability either are 1.0 or cannot be estimated. If individuals in each group provide the same score and groups differ, then ICC(1) will be 1.0. If individuals in each group provide the same score but groups do not differ, then it will be impossible to estimate ICC(1) and ICC(2) because there will be no between-group variance; attempts to calculate ICC values in this later case will result in a mathematical attempt to divide zero by zero.

Although within-group agreement may be used to establish the construct validity of the measurement model in composition models, it is important to acknowledge that agreement reveals little about one's ability to test substantive theoretical models. If individual responses do not differ within groups and do not differ between groups, then there is no variability to analyze. Conversely, if individuals are identical within groups and if groups differ, one can learn just as much from studying one person from each group as one can from studying all individuals from all groups.

Despite the widespread theoretical reliance on composition models in organizational research, true isomorphism is probably quite rare. Even in the presence of very high within-group agreement, aggregate variables probably measure contextual factors not detected at the lower level of analysis. Firebaugh (1978, p. 560) recognizes the nonisomorphic nature of much aggregated data when he states, "The demystification of cross-level bias begins with the recognition that an aggregate variable often measures a different construct than its namesake at the individual level." Thus it is somewhat surprising that isomorphic bottom-up process models have so dominated the field of organizational psychology. This sentiment is apparently shared by others who have raised critical questions about an overreliance on isomorphic models (House, Rousseau, & Thomas, 1995; Rousseau, 1985; Kozlowski & Klein, Chapter One, this volume). I believe there is low probability of a researcher's encountering truly isomorphic bottom-up processes. Instead, researchers are much more likely to encounter partial isomorphism—a situation in which the aggregate variable maintains conceptual links to the lower-level variable, but in which the aggregate variable is also quite distinct. I discuss this situation in the following section.

Fuzzy Composition Processes

In bottom-up composition processes, the aggregation of lower-level constructs into higher-level variables is likely to create an aggregate-level variable that is simultaneously related to and different from its lower-level counterpart (Firebaugh, 1978). In this chapter, I label these partially isomorphic situations "fuzzy" composition processes.

In both fuzzy composition processes and compilation processes, the aggregate variable is considered nonisomorphic with its lower-level counterpart. Nevertheless, fuzzy composition processes and compilation processes are quite different from each other. In compilation processes, the aggregate is qualitatively different from its lower-level counterpart (for example, group gender diversity versus gender). That is, the aggregate variable differs to such an extent from its lower-level counterpart that the two constructs can be considered distinct—the concept of diversity is much different from the concept of gender. In fuzzy composition processes, by contrast, the aggregate maintains close links to its lower-level counterpart but nevertheless differs in subtle and important ways. The differences between higher- and lower-level manifestations of the variable, and the implications of these differences for detecting emergent relationships, are the topic of this section of the chapter.

The main difference between a lower-level and an aggregate-level variable in fuzzy composition models is that the aggregate variable contains higher-level contextual influences that are not captured by the lower-level construct (Firebaugh, 1978). The degree to which the lower-level variable and the aggregate-level variable differ (that is, the fuzziness of the composition process) is largely influenced by the magnitude of the ICC(1).

Interestingly, there are two conditions where aggregate-level variables and lower-level variables can be considered equivalent. One is where ICC(1) values for the variables of interest are zero. The other is where ICC(1) values for the variables are equal to one. In both cases, the aggregate-level variable is equivalent to the lower-level variable. It is easy to see why lower- and higher-level variables are identical when ICC(1) is equal to one: this is a case of true isomorphism. It may not be immediately evident, however, why lower- and higher-level variables are identical when ICC(1) values are zero.

To clarify why group-level and individual-level relationships are identical when ICC(1) values are zero, consider the case where one has two correlated vectors (X and Y) and arbitrarily assigns group identifiers to the vectors to make aggregate variables. For instance, in a simulation I used the *mvnorm* function in SPLUS to create two columns, each of which contained one thousand normally distributed random numbers. The two columns were created to be correlated, and in this case the correlation between X and Y was .524. An arbitrary grouping variable was created to generate groups of two, five, and ten. Because this grouping variable was arbitrary, the ICC(1) value for both X and Y was zero. Using these data, I calculated the covariance theorem (WABA) equation and recorded the between-group and within-group correlations. For stability, I reassigned the arbitrary grouping factor and recalculated the correlations one hundred times. Table 8.2 shows the average correlation results.

Table 8.2. Correlations When ICC(1) Values Are Zero.

Group Size	Raw Correlation	Between-Group Correlation	Within-Group Correlation
2	0.524	0.524	0.522
5	0.524	0.523	0.524
10	0.524	0.524	0.523

Notice that in all group-size conditions the raw correlation, the between-group correlation, and the within-group correlations are equal. That is, despite the fact that there were absolutely no group-level properties associated with these data, the group-level correlation was significant. Results of this nature (equal raw, between-group, and within-group correlations) represent a classic "equivocal" situation in WABA, one that Dansereau and colleagues (1984) rightly recommend be interpreted only in terms of the raw correlation. The simulation in Table 8.2 shows that the magnitude of aggregate-level relationships is identical to the magnitude of lower-level relationships in cases where ICC(1) values are zero. In these cases, contextual effects are absent, and aggregate-level variables are equivalent to lower-level variables. As stated previously, it is my opinion that this type of situation generally exists only in simulations. In practice, ICC(1) values are frequently larger than zero in all types of organizational data. Therefore, in the remainder of this section I will examine the implications of situations where ICC(1) values are greater than zero but less than one—the implications of dealing with fuzzy composition processes.

One consequence of dealing with fuzzy composition processes is that analyses involving higher-level constructs are likely to reveal relationships that differ from those at lower levels. For example, studies by Schmitt, Colligan, and Fitzgerald (1980) and Bliese and Halverson (1996) have found that relationships between aggregated work-hour scores and aggregated well-being scores had emergent properties. Specifically, the relationship between individuals' reports of work hours and individuals' reports of well-being were substantially smaller than results based on average work hours and average well-being levels for groups. In the study reported by Bliese and Halverson, for instance, the raw correlation was −.16, whereas the weighted aggregate correlation based on ninety-nine group means was −.71. Magnitude differences of this degree have important theoretical and practical significance, particularly when the level of inference is the group (see Bliese and Jex, 1999)—that is, when one is using group-level results to make informed decisions about groups.

As an aside, when group-level correlations differ substantially from individual-level correlations (as in the preceding example), questions arise about aggregation bias. The term *aggregation bias* refers to the fact that group-level results are biased estimates of individual-level relationships (Thorndike, 1939; Robinson, 1950). For example, the group-level correlation of −.71, discussed in the preceding paragraph, is a biased estimate of the individual-level relationship (which we know to be −.16). It is equally important to understand, however, that −.16 is a biased estimate of the group-level relationship (which we know to be −.71). In short, neither raw nor aggregate-level results are biased in and of themselves; they become biased only when results at one level are used to make inferences at another.

To return to my main argument, one of the strengths of fuzzy composition process models is that they potentially allow one to detect emergent aggregate-level relationships that might not be evident in analyses of lower-level data. It is therefore important to understand some of the properties of fuzzy composition processes that lead to the detection of emergent relationships in bottom-up models.

Clearly, non-independence/reliability will play an important role in the "fuzziness" of the composition process and in one's ability to detect emergent aggregate-level relationships (Bliese, 1998; Glick & Roberts, 1984; Ostroff, 1993). To a certain degree, the relationship between non-independence/reliability and the equivalence of lower- and higher-level variables has been clouded by the use of eta-squared as an estimate of non-independence/reliability. For example, Glick and Roberts (1984) and Ostroff (1993) discuss emergent relationships between lower-level and higher-level constructs, using formulas based on eta-squared. One shortcoming of this approach, however, is that nonzero eta-squared values can be the result of small group sizes rather than of actual group-level properties, and so these approaches confound non-independence/reliability effects with group-size effects. Nevertheless, both Glick and Roberts (1984) and Ostroff (1993) convincingly demonstrate that the degree of non-independence/reliability in the variables plays an important role in one's ability to detect emergent relationships. Bliese (1998) extends work by Glick and Roberts (1984) and Ostroff (1993) and discusses emergent relationships in terms of ICC(1), group size, and ICC(2). The advantage of this approach is that it clearly separates group-size effects from non-independence/reliability effects. With this approach, it becomes clear that very powerful emergent aggregate-level relationships can be detected in cases where ICC(1) values for the dependent and independent variables are quite weak (Bliese, 1998). For instance, one can simulate conditions where only 1 percent of the variance in a lower-level response is shared among group members, and yet this shared variance can still allow one to detect strong aggregate relationships that are not evident in lower-level data. The key to detecting emergent relationships is to have groups large enough to produce reliable group-mean values—that is, high ICC(2) values. With large groups, in other words, one's aggregate-level variable can reliably measure phenomena that are almost undetectable in lower-level variables.

The fact that group size plays such an important role in the ability to detect emergent relationships is somewhat problematic because it potentially makes it difficult to compare results across studies (given that studies rarely have identical group sizes). For example, Ostroff (1992) provides aggregate-level correlations between average satisfaction and average turnover intentions, using data collected from 13,808 teachers from about 350 schools. In this research, the aggregate-level variables were based on groups with an average size of 40.67. A replication of Ostroff's study, using a sample in which group sizes were smaller, would find smaller group-level correlations even if all other factors where identical. One way to conduct comparisons across studies with groups of different sizes would be to correct the observed aggregate (r_{XY}) correlation for the unreliability of the group means—that is, the ICC(2) values. This would essentially correct for group-size differences. The formula for this correction is provide in Bliese (1998):

$$\rho_{XY} = \frac{r_{XY}}{\sqrt{ICC(2)_X * ICC(2)_Y}}. \tag{2}$$

In this formula, ρ_{XY} represents the "corrected" group-level correlation. Using simulations, I have shown that this correction provides accurate estimates of actual aggregate-level relationships across a wide variety of conditions. By comparing "corrected" group-level correlations, one could determine whether correlational differences between two studies were simply caused by group size or whether they represented more fundamental differences.

Perhaps the largest difficulty with fuzzy composition models revolves around how one interprets the aggregate variable. Consequently, I will devote the remainder of this section to a discussion of the interpretation of aggregate fuzzy composition variables. Let us begin with a simple situation: in cases where a lower-level construct makes reference to a higher-level unit, it is logical to assume that the aggregate-level variable is simply providing a more reliable measure of the construct of interest than is its lower-level counterpart (Paunonen & Gardner, 1991). For instance, one could assess collective efficacy by having each group member rate the level of collective efficacy in the group. Any single group member's perception of collective efficacy might be unreliable because of individual differences in perceptions, but it is logical to presume that the average perceptions of numerous group members would provide a more reliable measure of the group's collective efficacy than would any single member's rating. Therefore, a potential strength associated with calculating and using aggregate measures on variables reflecting shared unit properties is that aggregate measures may increase one's ability to measure subtle group phenomena. (It seems likely that many differences among groups in organizations are likely to be subtle—organizations, after all, actively manage groups to minimize large differences on many factors that are likely to be of interest to researchers.) Note that in cases involving shared unit properties, the aggregate measure is still a fuzzy representation of the lower-level variable; that is, the aggregate and lower-level variables are similar but not identical. They are not identical because the aggregate variable presumably benefits from having multiple ratings of the group-level phenomena.

When the variable of interest does not reference shared unit properties, it is difficult to consider the aggregate measure as being a more reliable manifestation of its lower-level counterpart. In such a case, the aggregate variable is measuring something different from its lower-level form, and yet it retains a nomological link to the lower-level form. For example, when an individual measure, such as absenteeism, has an ICC(1) value larger than zero, this indicates that an aggregate variable (average group absenteeism) will partially reflect common environmental factors. As a consequence of these common environmental factors, the aggregate measure (average absenteeism) is no longer isomorphic with its lower-level form. In this case, however, it is difficult to think of the aggregate measure as a more "reliable" manifestation of its lower-level counterpart. Instead, it is probably best conceptualized as a largely separate construct.

Without doubt, the meaning of the aggregate variable becomes complicated when the lower-level variable does not reference shared higher-level phenomena. In such a case, it is critical that the researcher have a clear theoretical foundation for defining the aggregate variable. Again using the example of absenteeism, Mathieu and Kohler (1990) have defined aggregated group absenteeism as "absence culture," and they present a strong theoretical basis for why absence culture exists and how it differs from individual-level absenteeism. As another example, Bliese and Halverson (1996) argue that average group work hours provide a measure of externally mandated group work requirements, whereas individual work hours measure the work hours of a single individual. Again, the higher- and lower-level variables are related (fuzzy representations of each other), but there are theoretical reasons to believe that they measure different constructs.

Note that one's theoretical conceptualization of the meaning of the aggregate variable also sets the stage for determining whether one needs to estimate agreement. In fuzzy composition processes that involve perceptions of shared unit properties, it is probably important to demonstrate agreement. This is because agreement helps establish the construct validity of the aggregate variable. For instance, one can argue that it is important to demonstrate agreement on an attribute such as the group's collective efficacy, because this is something that group members should be able to agree about. The need to establish agreement, however, is not universal for all fuzzy composition process variables. One would not necessarily expect group members to agree about other group members' level of satisfaction, well-being, absenteeism, and so on, yet there may be strong theoretical reasons why each of these variables might be aggregated to the group level.

In contrast to my position on within-group agreement, I maintain that estimating group-mean reliability—ICC(2)—is always important in fuzzy composition models. Regardless of the type of variable being aggregated, groups need to have reliably different mean values on the construct of interest if one hopes to detect emergent relationships.

In summary, in this section I have argued that researchers are more likely to encounter fuzzy composition models than pure composition models when they examine bottom-up processes. The characteristics of the fuzzy composition models are that aggregate constructs are related to but not isomorphic with their lower-level counterparts. This is because aggregate variables reflect the influences of contextual effects that are not reflected in lower-level variables (Firebaugh, 1978). The ability to detect emergent relationships in fuzzy composition models has been shown here to be a function of the reliability/non-independence associated with the measures, and of the group sizes used in the studies.

Conclusion

Issues surrounding the calculation of within-group agreement, non-independence, and group-mean reliability are important because in many cases they help establish the construct validity of one's measurement model. I hope this chapter has also demonstrated that these indices have considerable relevance in testing substantive models and in allowing one to detect emergent relationships in bottom-up models.

I conclude this chapter by noting that emergent relationships often appear to be treated with mistrust. In discussing the interpretation of aggregate-level results, Cohen (1994, p. 765) has written that epidemiological theory is based on "circumstantial evidence," and he laments the "all-too-common position" taken by epidemiologists that aggregate-level studies provide meaningless results. The bias Cohen notes is that epidemiologists often approach a problem with the assumption that individual-level results are correct and that aggregate results are incorrect (see also Schwartz, 1994). Too often, I think, organizational psychologists are willing to make the same error. One of the potential strengths of multilevel studies is that they allow a researcher to model contextual effects and emergent relationships: when ICC(1) values are greater than zero contextual effects are present, and one's aggregate-level constructs are no longer directly equivalent to one's lower-level constructs; that is, one is dealing with a situation in which the aggregate-level construct is a fuzzy representation of the lower-level construct. Rather than dismiss aggregate-level effects and aggregate-level variables as flawed,

I believe that analyses involving aggregate-level variables may be quite valuable in furthering our understanding of organizational behavior. In addition, from a pragmatic perspective, the analysis of fuzzy composition process models and the detection of emergent aggregate-level relationships may have considerable utility in organizational psychology. This is because organizational researchers often implement group-level interventions (that is, interventions that target groups). When groups are targeted for interventions, it is important to estimate the impact of the intervention by examining relationships based on group-level data (Bliese & Jex, 1999; Diez-Roux, 1998). Using results based on lower-level data to estimate the impact of group-level interventions constitutes committing an "atomistic" fallacy (Diez-Roux, 1998). All too often, I believe, organizational researchers are cognizant of the ecological fallacy (using aggregate-level results to make individual-level inferences) but may unknowingly commit the atomistic fallacy. Recognizing the prevalence of fuzzy composition processes in organizational data emphasizes the need to pay attention to both atomistic and ecological fallacies. If this is done, care can be taken to match the level of analysis with the level of inference. In the long run, this is likely to benefit organizational research.

References

Barrick, M. R., Stewart, G. L., Neubert, M. J., & Mount, M. K. (1998). Relating member ability and personality to work-team processes and team effectiveness. *Journal of Applied Psychology, 83,* 377–391.

Bartko, J. J. (1976). On various intraclass correlation reliability coefficients. *Psychological Bulletin, 83,* 762–765.

Blalock, H. M., Jr. (1972). *Social statistics* (2nd ed.). New York: McGraw-Hill.

Bliese, P. D. (1998). Group size, ICC values and group-level correlations: A simulation. *Organizational Research Methods, 1,* 355–373.

Bliese, P. D., & Halverson, R. R. (1996). Individual and nomothetic models of job stress: An examination of work hours, cohesion, and well-being. *Journal of Applied Social Psychology, 26,* 1171–1189.

Bliese, P. D., & Halverson, R. R. (1998a). Group consensus and psychological well-being: A large field study. *Journal of Applied Social Psychology, 28,* 563–580.

Bliese, P. D., & Halverson, R. R. (1998b). Group size and measures of group-level properties: An examination of eta-squared and ICC values. *Journal of Management, 24,* 157–172.

Bliese, P. D., & Halverson, R. R. (1999). *Using random group resampling in multilevel research.* Unpublished manuscript.

Bliese, P. D., Halverson, R. R., & Rothberg, J. M. (1994). Within-group agreement scores: Using resampling procedures to estimate expected variance. *Academy of Management Best Paper Proceedings, 303–307.*

Bliese, P. D., & Jex S. M. (1999). Incorporating multiple levels of analysis into occupational-stress research. *Work and Stress, 13,* 1–6.

Bryk, A. S., & Raudenbush, S. W. (1992). *Hierarchical linear models.* Thousand Oaks, CA: Sage.

Chan, D. (1998). Functional relations among constructs in the same content domain at different levels of analysis: A typology of composition models. *Journal of Applied Psychology, 83,* 234–246.

Cohen, B. L. (1994). Invited commentary: In defense of ecologic studies for testing a linear-no threshold theory. *American Journal of Epidemiology, 139,* 765–768.

Dansereau, F., & Alutto, J. A. (1990). Level-of-analysis issues in climate and culture research. In B. Schneider (Ed.), *Organizational climate and culture.* San Francisco: Jossey-Bass.

Dansereau, F., Alutto, J. A., & Yammarino, F. J. (1984). *Theory testing in organizational behavior: The varient approach.* Englewood Cliffs, NJ: Prentice Hall.

Dansereau, F., & Yammarino, F. J. (2000). Within and Between Analysis: The varient paradigm as an underlying approach to theory building and testing. In K. J. Klein & S.W.J. Kozlowski (Eds.), *Multilevel theory, research, and methods in organizations* (pp. 425–466). San Francisco: Jossey-Bass.

Diez-Roux, A. V. (1998). Bringing context back into epidemiology: Variables and fallacies in multilevel analyses. *American Journal of Public Health, 88,* 216–222.

Drexler, J. A., Jr. (1977). Organizational climate: Its homogeneity within organizations. *Journal of Applied Psychology, 62,* 38–42.

Efron, B., & Tibshirani, R. (1993). *An introduction to the bootstrap.* New York: Chapman & Hall.

Finn, R. H. (1970). A note on estimating the reliability of categorical data. *Educational and Psychological Measurement, 10,* 3–31.

Firebaugh, G. (1978). A rule for inferring individual-level relationships from aggregate data. *American Sociological Review, 43,* 557–572.

George, J. M., & James, L. R. (1993). Personality, affect, and behavior in groups revisited: Comment on aggregation, levels of analysis, and a recent application of within and between analysis. *Journal of Applied Psychology, 78,* 798–804.

Glick, W. H. (1985). Conceptualizing and measuring organizational and psychological climate: Pitfalls in multilevel research. *Academy of Management Review, 10,* 601–616.

Glick, W. H. (1988). Organizations are not central tendencies: Shadowboxing in the dark, round 2. *Academy of Management Review, 13,* 133–137.

Glick, W. H., & Roberts, K. H. (1984). Hypothesized interdependence, assumed independence. *Academy of Management Review, 9,* 722–735.

Hofmann, D. A., & Stetzer, A. (1996). A cross-level investigation of factors influencing unsafe behaviors and accidents. *Personnel Psychology, 49,* 301–339.

House, R., Rousseau, D. M., & Thomas, M. (1995). The meso paradigm: The integration of micro and macro organizational behavior. In L. L. Cummings & B. M. Staw (Eds.), *Research in organizational behavior,* vol. 17. Greenwich, CT: JAI Press.

Jackson, S. E., Brett, J. F., Sessa, V. I., Cooper, D. M., Julin, J. A., & Peyronnin, K. (1991). Some differences make a difference: Individual dissimilarity and group heterogeneity as correlates of recruitment, promotions, and turnover. *Journal of Applied Psychology, 76,* 675–689.

James, L. R. (1982). Aggregation bias in estimates of perceptual agreement. *Journal of Applied Psychology, 67,* 219–229.

James, L. R., Demaree, R. J., & Wolf, G. (1984). Estimating within-group interrater reliability with and without response bias. *Journal of Applied Psychology, 69,* 85–98.

James, L. R., Demaree, R. J., & Wolf, G. (1993). r_{wg}: An assessment of within-group interrater agreement. *Journal of Applied Psychology, 78,* 306–309.

James, L. R., & Jones, A. P. (1974). Organizational climate: A review of theory and research. *Psychological Bulletin, 81,* 1096–1112.

James, L. R., Joyce, W. F., & Slocum, J. W., Jr. (1988). Comment: Organizations do not cognize. *Academy of Management Review, 9,* 722–735.

Jex, S. M., & Bliese, P. D. (1999). Efficacy beliefs as a moderator of the impact of work-related stressors: A multi-level study. *Journal of Applied Psychology, 84,* 349–361.

Joyce, W. F., & Slocum, J. W., Jr. (1984). Collective climate: Agreement as a basis for defining aggregate climates in organizations. *Academy of Management Journal, 27,* 721–742.

Kenny, D. A., & Judd, C. M. (1986). Consequences of violating the independence assumption in analysis of variance. *Psychological Bulletin, 99,* 422–431.

Kenny, D. A., & Judd, C. M. (1996). A general procedure for the estimation of interdependence. *Psychological Bulletin, 119,* 138–148.

Klein, K. J., Dansereau, F., & Hall, R. J. (1994). Levels issues in theory development, data collection, and analysis. *Academy of Management Review, 19,* 195–229.

Kozlowski, S.W.J., & Hattrup, K. (1992). A disagreement about within-group agreement: Disentangling issues of consistency versus consensus. *Journal of Applied Psychology, 77,* 161–167.

Kozlowski, S. W., & Hults, B. M. (1987). An exploration of climates for technical updating and performance. *Personnel Psychology, 40,* 539–563.

Kozlowski, S.W.J., & Klein, K. J. (2000). A multilevel approach to theory and research in organizations: Contextual, temporal, and emergent processes. In K. J. Klein & S.W.J. Kozlowski (Eds.), *Multilevel theory, research, and methods in organizations* (pp. 3–90). San Francisco: Jossey-Bass.

Kreft, I., & DeLeeuw, J. (1998). *Introducing multilevel modeling.* Thousand Oaks, CA: Sage.

Longford, N. T. (1995). Random coefficient models. In G. Arminger, C. C. Clogg, & M. E. Sobel (Eds.), *Handbook of statistical modeling for the social and behavioral sciences* (pp. 519–577). New York: Plenum.

Mathieu, J. E., & Kohler, S. S. (1990). A cross-level examination of group absence influences on individual absence. *Journal of Applied Psychology, 75,* 217–220.

McGraw, K. O., & Wong, S. P. (1996). Forming inferences about some intraclass correlation coefficients. *Psychological Methods, 1,* 30–46.

Milliken, F. J., & Martins, L. L. (1996). Searching for common threads: Understanding the multiple effects of diversity in organizational groups. *Academy of Management Review, 21,* 402–433.

Ostroff, C. (1992). The relationship between satisfaction, attitudes and performance: An organizational-level analysis. *Journal of Applied Psychology, 77,* 963–974.

Ostroff, C. (1993). Comparing correlations based on individual-level and aggregated data. *Journal of Applied Psychology, 78,* 569–582.

Paunonen, S. V., & Gardner, R. C. (1991). Biases resulting from the use of aggregated variables in psychology. *Psychological Bulletin, 109,* 520–523.

Robinson, W. S. (1950). Ecological correlations and the behavior of individuals. *American Sociological Review, 15,* 351–357.

Rousseau, D. M. (1985). Issues of level in organizational research: Multilevel and cross-level perspectives. In L. L. Cummings & B. Staw (Eds.), *Research in organizational behavior* (Vol. 7). Greenwich, CT: JAI Press.

Schmidt, F. L., & Hunter, J. E. (1989). Interrater reliability coefficients cannot be computed when only one stimulus is rated. *Journal of Applied Psychology, 74,* 368–370.

Schmitt, N., Colligan, M. J., & Fitzgerald, M. (1980). Unexplained physical symptoms in eight organizations: Industrial and organizational analyses. *Journal of Occupational Psychology, 53,* 305–317.

Schneider, B., Smith, D. B., Taylor, S., & Fleenor J. (1998). Personality and organizations: A test of the homogeneity of personality hypothesis. *Journal of Applied Psychology, 83,* 462–470.

Schwartz, S. (1994). The fallacy of the ecological fallacy: The potential misuse of a concept and the consequences. *American Journal of Public Health, 84,* 819–824.

Shrout, P. E., & Fleiss, J. L. (1979). Intraclass correlations: Uses in assessing rater reliability. *Psychological Bulletin, 86,* 420–428.

Singer, J. D. (1998). Using SAS PROC MIXED to fit multilevel models, hierarchical models, and individual growth models. *Journal of Educational and Behavioral Statistics, 24,* 323–355.

Statistical Sciences (1997). *S-PLUS 4.0 guide to statistics.* Seattle: Mathsoft.

Thorndike, E. L. (1939). On the fallacy of imputing the correlations found for groups to the individuals or smaller groups composing them. *American Journal of Psychology, 52,* 122–124.

Tinsley, H.E.A., & Weiss, D. J. (1975). Interrater reliability and agreement of subjective judgments. *Journal of Counseling Psychology, 22,* 358–376.

Yammarino, F. J., & Markham, S. E. (1992). On the application of within and between analysis: Are absence and affect really group-based phenomena? *Journal of Applied Psychology, 77,* 168–176.

CHAPTER 9

The Cross-Level Operator in Regression, ANCOVA, and Contextual Analysis

Lawrence R. James
Larry J. Williams

Many chapters in this book discuss new statistical techniques. This chapter focuses primarily on old but venerable statistical techniques. The emphases of this chapter are thus somewhat different from those of other chapters. Our energy is devoted not to introducing a new technique but to promoting understanding of several old techniques. Basically, we focus on what happens statistically and substantively when situations and situational variables are related to individual variables, using various applications of the general linear model.

How situational attributes relate to individual attributes has been the subject of many thousands of experiments, interventions, manipulations, natural field experiments, and correlational studies. Yet, substantive and statistical understanding of the process by which situational variables connect with individual variables remains shrouded in confusion; the epitome of puzzlement is seen when research involves an individual variable (for example, aggressiveness in the work situation) and a situational variable (for example, extent of the organization's use of monitoring systems). To relate the variables, it is not uncommon for investigators to agonize over whether to aggregate aggressiveness over individuals in each organization and correlate the aggregates with organizational monitoring on the sample of organizations, or to assign organizational monitoring scores to individuals in organizations and correlate the assigned scores with individuals' aggressiveness on the sample of individuals.

Which is the more appropriate procedure is conditioned on what one wishes to know. If the goal is to ascertain whether organizations that install monitoring systems can expect greater frequency of aggressive acts, as assessed by (mean) number of aggressive acts per organization, then one is concerned with the first option (that is, aggregating aggressiveness over individuals in each organization and correlating the aggregates with organizational monitoring on the sample of organizations), and this chapter will be of little benefit. However, if the objective is to determine whether installing a monitoring system acts as a triggering mechanism that stimulates individuals to commit aggressive acts, then one is concerned with the second option (that is, assigning organizational monitoring scores to individuals in organizations and correlating the assigned scores with individuals' aggressiveness on the sample of individuals). Analyses based on procedures analogous to the latter one are the substance of this chapter.

Data generated by this procedure have been analyzed with the general linear model (particularly using regression, ANOVA, and ANCOVA) in countless studies. We assume that readers have already amassed as much knowledge as they wish to possess about the history of regression, ANOVA, and ANCOVA. (Contextual analysis is a possible exception, but it has a short and easily encapsulated history.) We further assume that readers have been introduced to these topics in statistics courses and have read scores of articles that have used them (contextual analysis again being the exception). Therefore, we shall not dwell on history and shall go instead directly to the heart of the matter.

This chapter discusses very basic issues pertaining to *cross-level inference,* defined as a hypothesis about how variation in situations is related to variations among individuals. It is an inferred relationship that crosses from the situational to the individual level of analysis. In the first part of the chapter, we delve rather intensely into the question of how one crosses levels of analysis. The idea of a cross-level operator is introduced, discussed, and illustrated. Statistical analyses that engage cross-level operators are then addressed.

These, in effect, are tests of cross-level inferences based on the general linear model. The primary topics receiving attention are ANOVA, regression, analysis of covariance, and contextual analysis. An analytic rationale for each topic is presented and is followed by an empirical illustration.

The Fundamental Cross-Level Relationship

Theoretical Overview and Organizational Applications

Cross-level inference is encountered most directly in experimentation. For example, different leadership styles, different types of reinforcement systems, or different job designs constitute the treatment. Subjects are then randomly sampled into treatments, the experiment is conducted, and measurements are taken on an individual-level–dependent variable, such as performance, motivation, or satisfaction. The cross-level inference pertains to how the treatment has affected individual outcomes. We could focus our attention here or on quasi-experimental studies (where interventions are made in field settings). However, most of the literature on cross-level inference in organizational research deals with non-experimental research designs. Therefore, we shall focus on non-experimental designs. However, we wish to note that a large experimental literature does exist. Interestingly, the puzzlement mentioned earlier, about how to analyze cross-level data, occurs only infrequently in this experimental literature.

The basic problem in cross-level inference that we address here begins with individuals who are nested in different work situations. Variation in some aspects of work situations—differences in pay, stress, cultural norms, or technological requirements of jobs, for example—is suspected of engendering or at least covarying with variation on an individual construct or on a person variable (such as motivation, performance, or satisfaction). Suspicion breeds a *cross-level inference*, or a hypothesis that an association or perhaps even a functional relationship exists between variations in the work situations and variations in the person variable. This is often as simple as proposing that people whose companies pay them at the level of the norm for their occupations are likely to be more satisfied with their jobs, or at least with their pay, than people who work for more miserly organizations.

Estimates of the degree to which differences in work situations (for example, pay) are associated with variations in a person variable (for example, pay satisfaction) involve *between-groups analyses*. Connection to (or "group membership" in) a particular situation (involving, for example, job type, work group, functional specialty, or organization) is used as the independent variable, and scores on the person variable (PV) are employed as the dependent variable. By means of various forms of the general linear model (soon to be described), estimates of variance accounted for in the PV by group membership are reported in the form of an eta-square, omega-square, intraclass correlation, or squared multiple correlation. The term *group* is a generic statistical indicator used to identify a category of subjects (for example, a team, or people who report to the same vice president, or people with the same job type or functional specialty, or people who work in the same organization).

Let us begin by addressing several sources of potential confusion in cross-level inference. First, the term *between-groups analysis* does not connote that the analysis is based exclusively on group scores; rather, it denotes that the objective of the analysis is to determine how much of the variation on the PV (for example, variation among individuals in pay satisfaction), as measured on individuals, is associated with or can be accounted for by differences among groups (for example, differences among organizations). This association will be high when (a) large differences exist among groups on a correlate of the PV, such as large differences among groups in pay levels when the PV is pay satisfaction; (b) the group means on the PV vary in a manner commensurate with differences in the correlate; and (c) little variation in the PV scores exists among individuals in the same group.

Second, the term *cross-level inference* has several meanings. Pedhazur (1997), for example, uses this term to refer to the use of statistics computed at one level of analysis (for example, a correlation based on group means) to infer what statistics would be at a different level of analysis (for example, a correlation based on individuals' scores). This is not what we mean by the term. The term *cross-level inference* for us (and thus for this chapter) refers to a hypothesis regarding how variations in a situational attribute are thought to be associated with variations in an individual attribute. The level of explanation in our treatment of cross-level inference is the individual (or the lowest level in the hierarchy, which will always be the individual in this chapter).

Cross-level inference is often confusing statistically because one must understand (or explain) how a group-level score is mapped onto the individual level of analysis. A reason for this confusion is that the statistical literature has spent little time describing what we shall refer to here as the *cross-level operator*. Our intent in this section of the chapter is to attempt to explain how, statistically, a group attribute is mapped onto the individual level of analysis. We shall go to the heart of cross-level analysis and shall demonstrate, by using simple one-way ANOVA, how one crosses levels so that a group score influences (is associated with) an individual's score. The rationale for why the individual is the statistical and logical level of explanation for cross-level inference is an integral part of this discussion. After the presentation of ANOVA-based cross-level inference, we shall proceed to its regression analog.

Later, we shall turn to contextual analysis, which has a short history and narrow scope (see Firebaugh, 1979; Pedhazur, 1997). Contextual analysis is a technique that evolved primarily in several areas of the social sciences (for example, education and sociology) to test for "the effects of groups independent of the personal attributes of the individuals comprising the groups" (Firebaugh, 1979, p. 384). The technique initially regresses an individual-level dependent variable (for example, job satisfaction) on an individual-level independent variable (for example, dispositional negative affect). The sample consists of multiple individuals nested within each of a set of groups (organizations). Group means on the independent variable are added to the regression equation (the mean score for each group is assigned to all the members of that group). If the addition of group means to the regression equation significantly enhances prediction, then a "group effect," somehow traceable to the group-level aggregates on the independent variable, is considered viable.

We discuss contextual analysis from the perspective of cross-level inference because the group means may indicate a cross-level effect. We suggest that contextual analysis is useful as an exploratory test to assess whether group-level predictors should be considered in an analysis. If a group effect is indicated, however, we strongly recommend that its interpretation not be limited to group-level interpretations of the individual-level independent variable, because the group means may serve simply as a surrogate for other situational constructs with which these means are correlated (Pedhazur, 1997).

An ANOVA-Based Perspective on Cross-Level Inference

Suppose that we have five organizations, or statistical groups, which are identified by $g_1, g_2, g_3, g_4,$ and g_5 (the general case being g_i, where I varies from $1, ..., k = 5$ groups). We believe that g_1 has a very benevolent pay structure, g_2 has a modestly benevolent pay structure, g_3 is neither particularly benevolent nor stingy, g_4 is somewhat stingy, and g_5 is very stingy. Our hypothesis (cross-level inference), based on this belief, is that the employees in g_1 will be very highly satisfied with their pay, employees in g_2 will be highly satisfied, employees in g_3 will be moderately satisfied, employees in g_4 will be modestly dissatisfied, and employees in g_5 will be very dissatisfied. To test our hypothesis, we first randomly sample ten employees from each group. (The statistical processes illustrated here are easily extended to larger ns per group, as well as to more groups.) We then give each sample a pay-satisfaction questionnaire, which has a scale that varies from 0 ("terminally unhappy") to 60 ("forever grateful").

The scores for the ten members of each group are reported in Table 9.1. Also reported in this table are the sum of scores and the mean on pay satisfaction for each group. Note that the values of the means correspond to our inference about the effects of pay structure on pay satisfaction. This suggests that we could use planned comparisons to test the patterning of means. However, we have different fish to fry here, and so we will forgo this more powerful statistical procedure in favor of an omnibus ANOVA analysis.

Between-Groups Analysis

The two key components of an ANOVA for the data in Table 9.1 are presented in Table 9.2. Section A of this table presents a between-groups analysis. As already noted, the objective of a between-groups analysis is to determine how much of the variation among individuals in pay satisfaction can be accounted for by differences among groups. To compute this statistic, we first assign the group mean for each group, or $\bar{Y}_i$, to all ten members of that group. For

Table 9.1. Job Satisfaction Scores
for Ten Employees in Each of Five Organizations.

	Organizations				
	g_1	g_2	g_3	g_4	g_5
	160	150	140	130	120
	155	145	135	125	115
	150	140	130	120	110
	145	135	125	115	105
	140	130	120	110	100
	135	125	115	105	95
	130	120	110	100	90
	125	115	105	95	85
	120	110	100	90	80
	115	105	95	85	75
Group Means	137.5	127.5	117.5	107.5	97.5
Grand Mean:	117.5				

example, the ten members of g_1 are assigned the value for $\bar{Y}_1$, or 137.5, as shown in Table 9.2. It is this assignment of the group mean to the individuals in a group that lies at the heart of cross-level analysis and inference. This is because the assignment of a group mean to an individual is how one "crosses levels" from the group to the individual in ANOVA. We shall use the term *cross-level operator* in connection with this assignment (there are also other types of cross-level operators).

The assigned group mean for each individual indexes the effect of the group on the PV (pay satisfaction) for all of the individuals in that group. Inasmuch as the assumed basis for this effect, benevolence of pay structure, is constant for all individuals in a group, the group effect on pay satisfaction is assumed to be constant for all individuals in the group. This is why the group mean on pay satisfaction is assigned to everyone in the group; it denotes that the effect of pay structure is uniform for all group members.

Table 9.2. Within-Group and Between-Group Sums of Squares.

Between-group sums of squares (SS_B)

	g_1	g_2	g_3	g_4	g_5
Subject 1	$(137.5-117.5)^2$	$(127.5-117.5)^2$	$(117.5-117.5)^2$	$(107.5-117.5)^2$	$(97.5-117.5)^2$
Subject 2	$(137.5-117.5)^2$	$(127.5-117.5)^2$	$(117.5-117.5)^2$	$(107.5-117.5)^2$	$(97.5-117.5)^2$
Subject j	$(137.5-117.5)^2$	$(127.5-117.5)^2$	$(117.5-117.5)^2$	$(107.5-117.5)^2$	$(97.5-117.5)^2$
Subject 10	$(137.5-117.5)^2$	$(127.5-117.5)^2$	$(117.5-117.5)^2$	$(107.5-117.5)^2$	$(97.5-117.5)^2$
Sum	4000	1000	0	1000	4000

$$SS_B = 10{,}000$$

Within-group sums of squares (SS_W)

	g_1	g_2	g_3	g_4	g_5
Subject 1	$(160-137.5)^2$	$(150-127.5)^2$	$(140-117.5)^2$	$(130-107.5)^2$	$(120-97.5)^2$
Subject 2	$(155-137.5)^2$	$(145-127.5)^2$	$(135-117.5)^2$	$(135-107.5)^2$	$(115-97.5)^2$
Subject 10	$(115-137.5)^2$	$(105-127.5)^2$	$(95-117.5)^2$	$(85-107.5)^2$	$(75-97.5)^2$
Sum	2062.51	2062.51	2062.51	2062.51	2062.51

$$SS_W = 10{,}312.5$$

To estimate the effects of group differences on individuals' pay satisfaction, we first subtract the grand or overall mean for pay satisfaction $\bar{Y}_G = 117.5$) from the group mean assigned to each individual. These deviations are then squared and summed over the members of each group. A statistical shortcut is to compute the squared deviation for one member of a group and then multiply this value by the number of group members, or n_i, to obtain the sum of squared deviations for a group. The sum of squared deviations for each group indexes the effects of group differences on pay satisfaction for the individuals in that group. Note that both the level of analysis and the level of explanation is the individual, even though means are what is being contrasted. The key is that the means are contrasted only after we have crossed from the group to the individual level of analysis/explanation by assigning the group mean score on pay satisfaction to all individuals in the group.

After computing the sum of squared deviations for each group, we sum these values over the three groups to obtain the *between-groups sum of squares,* or SS_B. As shown in Table 9.2, SS_B is equal to 10,000.

Within-Groups Analysis

Section B of Table 9.2 shows the within-groups analysis. This analysis addresses the question of how much error we make if we use only differences among groups to account for differences in individuals' pay satisfaction. For example, if differences in groups' pay structures were the only cause of variation in individuals' pay satisfaction, then all variation in individuals' pay satisfaction would occur between groups, which means that all observed scores on pay satisfaction would be the same within a group. Variation among scores on pay satisfaction within a group indicates that attitudes toward pay have nongroup-related causes (in addition, perhaps, to some measurement error in the instrument assessing pay satisfaction). Statistically speaking, these unspecified causes are sources of "error" in the model. We need to estimate the magnitudes of these errors in order to determine the strength of the effect of group differences on individuals' pay satisfaction. We shall also use estimates of error to determine sampling error, or the degree to which the $\bar{Y}_i$ could be expected to vary by chance when there is actually no effect of the group on individuals' pay satisfaction.

Error is estimated within each group by subtracting the mean assigned to each individual in the group ($\bar{Y_i}$) from each individual's raw or observed score (Y_{ij}), where j indicates each subject within a group and varies from 1 to 10. Each of these deviation scores is squared, and the resulting values are summed over the members of each group. The sums of the squared deviations for the groups are then summed over the three groups, to furnish an overall or "pooled" measure of error. This measure is generally referred to as the *within-groups sum of squares,* or SS_W. The term *error sum of squares* is also applied to this statistic. As shown in Table 9.2, SS_W is equal to 10,312.5.

Test of the Cross-Level Inference

The cross-level inference (hypothesis) that differences in groups (for example, differences in pay structure) account for variation in individuals' pay satisfaction may now be assessed in several ways. A simple ANOVA can be conducted by dividing SS_B and SS_W by their respective degrees of freedom and computing an F-test. The resulting F, with 4 and 45 degrees of freedom, is $(10000/4)/(10312.5/45) = 10.91$, which is highly significant. Eta-squared, or η^2, computed by $(SS_B) / (SS_B + SS_W)$, is equal to $(10000)/(10000 + 10312.5) = .492$. This estimator suggests that approximately 49 percent of the variance in individuals' satisfaction with pay is accounted for by differences in groups.

As before, we believe that the explanatory group-level variable is benevolence of organizational pay structure. However, pay structure was not measured and, more important, any variable that correlates with organizational pay structure could be partially or totally responsible for the between-group variation in pay satisfaction. Included here are group-level variables (such as opportunities for advancement) and PVs that vary across groups in a manner similar to pay satisfaction (for example, groups vary in regard to education/experience of employees). Thus our cross-level inference that individual differences in pay satisfaction can be accounted for by group differences has been confirmed. It appears helpful to use differences in pay structure to explain these results, but we cannot rule out alternative causal explanations (see James, Mulaik, and Brett, 1982).

The Regression Analog to ANOVA and Cross-Level Inference

The ANOVA displayed above can also be framed in terms of the general linear model and a multiple-regression analysis. The regression equation takes the form shown in equation 1:

$$Y_{im} = A + B_1 G_1 + B_2 G_2 + B_3 G_3 + B_4 G_4 + e_{ij} \qquad (1)$$

where Y_{ij} is the pay satisfaction score for person j in group i, G_1 through G_4 are nominally scaled variables that uniquely define group membership for each individual, and e_{ij} is the error term (that part of Y_{ij} that cannot be predicted by group membership). If we use "dummy coding" for nominal scaling purposes, then the following statements are true:

1. Individuals in g_1 would receive a score of 1 on G_1 and a score of 0 on G_2, G_3, and G_4 (see Cohen and Cohen, 1983; Pedhazur, 1997).
2. Individuals in g_2 would receive a score of 0 on G_1, G_3, and G_4 and a score of 1 on G_2.
3. Individuals in g_3 would receive a score of 0 on G_1, G_2, and G_4 and a score of 1 on G_3.
4. Individuals in g_4 would receive a score of 0 on G_1, G_2, and G_3 and a score of 1 on G_4.
5. Individuals in g_5 would receive a score of 0 on G_1, G_2, G_3, and G_4.

G_1 through G_4 are the independent or predictor variables that will be used to determine how much of the variance in the Y_{ij} can be attributed to group membership. B_1 through B_4 are the unstandardized regression weights that determine the salience of these predictors. A regression analysis based on equation 1 furnishes a significant R^2 of .492, which is identical to the η^2 reported in the ANOVA analysis and is interpreted in an identical manner.

In sum, use of the term *cross-level inference* generally connotes that group-level attributes will be used to infer how, why, or when individual-level attitudes and/or behaviors occur. The individual is both the level of explanation and the level of analysis. To cross levels from the group to the individual, we must map the group-level attribute onto the individual level of analysis. This mapping or crossing process is accomplished via the cross-level operator, the use of which consists of assigning the statistical index for the group (the group mean on the PV, in this case) to each individual in the group. The crossing process is made less obtuse, perhaps even clear, when we use actual situational variables, as the following discussion attempts to demonstrate.

Cross-Level Inference with a Specific Situational Variable

The omnibus ANOVA/regression analysis has informed us that approximately 49 percent of the variance in the PV (individuals' satisfaction with pay) is associated with between-group differences. We know also that these groups vary in terms of pay structure in a manner consistent with the group differences in pay satisfaction. A reasonable cross-level inference is that differences in individuals' pay satisfaction are associated with differences in organizational pay structure. It is not reasonable, however, to infer that 49 percent of the variance in pay satisfaction is associated with differences in pay structure. This is because group-level variables other than pay structure may be partially responsible for variation in pay satisfaction (an example of such a variable might be largess of the organizational benefit system).

Suppose that we wish to estimate the magnitude of the association between the PV (individuals' pay satisfaction) and a specific situational variable, such as organizational pay structure. We begin by measuring organizational pay structure (for example, the organization's relative standing on average pay in a normative sample of comparable organizations) for our sample of five organizations. We retain our sample of ten individuals nested in each of these organizations. Then, using the methods to be described here, we correlate group-level pay structure with individuals' pay satisfaction.

The key to estimating the relationship between a specific situational variable measured on groups and a PV measured on individuals is to apply a cross-level operator whose use is analogous to the assignment of group means to individuals in the ANOVA. In the present case, the operator that allows us to cross levels from groups to individuals is assignment of the score on the situational variable for a group to all individuals in that group. This process and the estimation procedure will be described here; the discussion is based on James, Demaree, and Hater (1980).

To begin, several points are noteworthy. First, it is assumed that the score on the situational variable is homogeneous for all individuals in a particular group (see Roberts, Hulin, and Rousseau, 1978, pp. 106–107, for a discussion of homogeneity). Second, use of a specific situational variable for prediction is likely to result in a loss of predictive power by comparison with the between-groups procedure, which employs only group membership as the predictor. This is because the between-groups procedure identifies *all* reliable variation in a PV that is associated with between-group differences, whereas the use of a specific situational variable generally involves only one of a subset of the variables that are associated with between-group differences in the PV. This stimulates the following question: How much reliable between-group variance in a PV remains to be accounted for after the variance attributable to a specific situational variable has been estimated? Alternatively, we might ask the following question: What proportion of the total possible variation in a PV that is attributable to between-group differences is accounted for by this specific situational variable? Answers to these questions are provided in the discussion that follows.

Statistical Rationale for Relating a Situational Variable to a Person Variable

For illustrative purposes, the following conditions are assumed:

1. S_i is a continuously distributed situational variable (for example, organizational pay structure, technological complexity) on which each of k groups (for example, job types, work groups, departments, divisions, organizations) has a unique score ($i = 1, 2, \ldots, k$). Some groups may have the same score as other groups. All individual members of the same group are assigned the same value of S_i for that group. The designation S_i is used for the assigned scores, where j represents the jth individual in a group comprising n_i individuals ($j = 1, 2, \ldots, n_i$). It is assumed that an S_i is homogeneous for each group, which is to say that the S_{ij} scores are the same for all n_i individuals.

2. Y_{ij} is the jth individual's score in the ith group on the PV. Note that the Y_{ij} are not constrained to be equal for all n_i individuals in the ith group.

It will simplify matters to express the S_{ij} and Y_{ij} in the form of a grand-mean deviation. This denotes that the mean on the S_{ij} for all individuals across all groups—the grand mean—is subtracted from each S_{ij} to provide a deviation score, which is labeled s_{ij}. Similarly, the mean on the Y_{ij} for all individuals across all groups—the grand mean $\bar{Y}_G$—is subtracted from each Y_{ij} to provide a deviation score, which is labeled y_{ij}. By means of the grand-mean deviations, the correlation between the S_{ij} and the Y_{ij} or, analogously, the s_{ij} and the y_{ij}, can be expressed as shown in equation 2:

$$r_{ys} = \left(\sum_i \sum_j y_{ij} s_{ij} \right) / N \left[\frac{1}{N} \left(\sum_i \sum_j y_{ij}^2 \right) \right]^{\frac{1}{2}} \left[\frac{1}{N} \left(\sum_i \sum_j s_{ij}^2 \right) \right]^{\frac{1}{2}} \tag{2}$$

where $N = \sum_i n_i$. Equation 2 may be expressed in a form that clarifies the cross-level operator by noting that $\sum_j s_{ij} = n_i s_i$ (and $\sum_j s_{ij}^2 = n_i s_i^2$), and that $\sum_j y_{ij} = n_i \bar{y}_i$. It follows, as shown in equation 3, that

$$r_{ys} = \left(\sum_i n_i \bar{y}_i s_i \right) / N \left[\frac{1}{N} \left(\sum_i \sum_j y_{ij}^2 \right) \right]^{\frac{1}{2}} \left[\frac{1}{N} \left(\sum_i n_i s_i^2 \right) \right]^{\frac{1}{2}}$$

$$= \sigma y_i s_i / \left(\sigma y_{ij} \sigma s_i \right) \tag{3}$$

where the σ's represent variances and covariances (see James, Demaree, and Hater, 1980 for more extensive presentations of equations).

Equations 2 and 3 present a correlation that estimates the cross-level relationship between a specific situational variable and a PV. This correlation is designated r_{ys}. Inspection of equation 2 shows that r_{ys} operates at the individual levels of analysis and explanation. The simplifying algebraic identities underlying equation 3 show that r_{ys} is a function of the covariance between the weighted group means on the PV and each group's score on the situational variable, relative to the standard deviations of the PV and the situational variable on the total individual sample.

Of interest are the facts that r_{ys} will attain absolute values greater than zero only when variation exists among the scores over groups on the S_{ij} (that is, when the variance of the S_i is nonzero), when there is comparatively more between-group variation in the Y_{ij} than within-group variation, and when the (weighted) group means on the Y_{ij} covary with the S_i. The differential weighting due to different n_i may become a confounding factor if the group n_i's are substantially different (that is, larger groups will have stronger effects on r_{ys}), and so caution should be used when analyses employ groups with large differences in group sample sizes.

In regard to our illustrative data, a scale varying from 1 (stingy) to 10 (extremely benevolent) was developed to index organizational pay structure. A score of 6 was given to the first organization (g_1), a score of 8 was given to the second organization (g_2), a score of 10 was given to g_3, a score of 2 was given to g_4, and a score of 4 was given to g_5. The score on the situational variable for each respective organization was assigned to all ten individuals in that organization. For example, all ten individuals in the first organization (g_1) were assigned a score of 6. The process constitutes the cross-level operator.

After situational scores had been assigned to individuals, the assigned scores were correlated with scores on the PV. The analysis was conducted on the fifty individuals in the sample and provided a value for r_{ys}. This value is .35. If we square .35, which provides .12, we have an estimate for how much of the total variance in pay satisfaction is associated with the benevolence-of-pay situational variable. Note that 49 percent of the variance in pay satisfaction was associated with between-group differences, but only 12 percent of this same variance was associated with between-group differences in benevolence of pay. Whereas the 12 percent is significant, it appears that benevolence of pay structure is not the only situational antecedent of individuals' pay satisfaction. This stimulates the following discussion.

A salient question for research is the degree to which r_{ys}^2 approaches the maximum variation in the PV that is associated with between-group differences. To answer this question, it is necessary to determine both the total amount of variation in the PV that is associated with between-group differences and that portion of this total variation that is associated with differences in the S_i. Estimations of these values are attained by first deriving an equation for the correlation between the S_i and the weighted group means on Y_{ij}. As shown in equation 4, this correlation, designated $r_{\bar{y}s}$, is as follows:

$$r_{\bar{y}s} = \left(\sum_i n_i \bar{y}_i s_i\right) / N \left[\frac{1}{N}\left(\sum_i n\bar{y}_i^2\right)\right]^{\frac{1}{2}}\left[\frac{1}{N}\left(\sum_i n_i s_i^2\right)\right]^{\frac{1}{2}} \tag{4}$$

$$= \sigma_{\bar{y}_i s_i} / \left(\sigma_{\bar{y}_i}\sigma_{s_i}\right)$$

If equations 3 and 4 are each solved for the covariance terms, and if the solutions set equal to each other, we have the following:

$$r_{ys}\sigma_{y_{ij}}\sigma_{s_i} = r_{\bar{y}s}\sigma_{\bar{y}_i}\sigma_{s_i}$$

which, after solving for $r_{\bar{y}s}$ and squaring all terms, is as shown in equation 5:

$$r_{ys}^2 = (\sigma_{\bar{y}_i}^2/\sigma_{y_i}^2)\, r_{\bar{y}s}^2, \tag{5}$$

Furthermore, $(\sigma_{\bar{y}_i}^2/\sigma_{y_{ij}}^2)$ is η_y^2, the squared correlation ratio (eta square) of y_{ij} on group membership. Thus equation 5 becomes, as shown in equation 6,

$$r_{ys}^2 = \eta_y^2\, r_{\bar{y}s}^2, \tag{6}$$

where r_{ys}^2 is the proportion of the variance in a PV associated with situational variable S_i; η_y^2 is the *total* amount of variation in the PV associated with between-group differences; and $r_{\bar{y}s}^2$ is the variance in the weighted group-mean PV scores that is associated with differences in the situational variable S_i.

Viewed from another perspective, η_y^2 is the maximum possible variation in the PV that is associated with between-group differences; r_{ys}^2 will be equal to η_y^2 only in the condition that $r_{\bar{y}s}^2 = 1.0$, which can be seen in equation 6; $r_{\bar{y}s}^2$ will be less than 1.0, and therefore $r_{ys}^2 < \eta_y^2$, when the relationship between the $\bar{y}_i$ and s_i is nonlinear, and/or between-group variation exists in the $\bar{y}_i$ that is not associated with the s_i (see equation 4). Assuming relationships to be *linear*, an assumption that can be checked empirically, we see that $r_{\bar{y}s}^2$ represents the proportion of variation in η_y^2 that is included in r_{ys}^2. In other words, $r_{\bar{y}s}^2$ indicates the degree to which the obtained r_{ys}^2 approaches η_y^2, which is the maximum possible variation in a PV associated with between-group differences. This can be seen by converting equation 6 to what is shown here in equation 7:

$$r_{\bar{y}s}^2 = r_{ys}^2 / \eta_y^2 \qquad (7)$$

These points can be illustrated with our data. We know that the total amount of variation in individuals' pay satisfaction associated with between-group differences is .49 (that is, $\eta_y^2 = 49$). We also know that r_{ys}^2 is .12, which indicates that 12 percent of the variation in individuals' pay satisfaction is associated with between-group differences in the situational variable benevolence of pay. Applying equation 7, we find that $r_{\bar{y}s}^2$ (= .12/.49) is equal to .25. This result suggests that situational variation in benevolence of pay accounts for 25 percent of the variance in individuals' pay satisfaction that is associated with between-group differences.

It is noteworthy that meaningful interpretation of $r_{\bar{y}s}^2$ requires careful attention to the values of r_{ys}^2 and η_y^2 inasmuch as $r_{\bar{y}s}^2$ may assume high values that are essentially meaningless. To illustrate, if $r_{ys}^2 = .010$ and $\eta_y^2 = .011$, then $r_{\bar{y}s}^2 = .909$. The value of .909 suggests that r_{ys}^2 did in fact approach the maximum possible variation in the Y_{ij} associated with between-group differences (η_y^2). However, an η_y^2 of .011 indicates that essentially none of the variation in the variable Y was associated with between-group differences in the first place. That is, the variance on Y is almost exclusively *within-group variance*, and all that the $r_{\bar{y}s}^2$ of .909 indicates is that the investigator has accounted for approximately 91 percent of, in effect, nothing.

Nevertheless, η_y^2 (and r_{ys}^2) may assume reasonably high values, in which case the information provided by equation 7 is salient. A straightforward use of this information would be to ascertain whether additional situational variables should be added to a study, in the interest of accounting for reliable variance that still remains between groups—that is, $1 - r_{\bar{y}s}^2$ indicates the proportion of between-group variation in the PV that is *not* accounted for by the situational variable S. If $1 - r_{\bar{y}s}^2$ is not equal to zero, then the suggestion is that additional situational variables are needed in the analysis. For example, $1 - r_{ys}^2 = 1 - .25 = .75$, for our illustrative data. This result indicates that 75 percent of the variance in individuals' pay satisfaction that is associated with between-group differences remains unclaimed.

There is also the possibility that a portion of the between-group differences in a PV is a product of differences among the types of individuals who are attracted to and/or selected by certain types of groups (see Schneider, 1987). If tenable, this alternative hypothesis expands our analysis into an analysis of covariance (ANCOVA will be discussed shortly). First, however, we shall briefly address extension of this discussion to multiple situational variables.

Cross-Level Inference with Multiple Situational Variables

In the preceding illustration, η_y^2 is reasonably large and suggests the 49 percent of the variance in the PV is related to between-group differences. However, on the basis of a single situational variable, S, r_{ys}^2 is only .12, and $1 - r_{ys}^2$ is .75, indicating that 75 percent of the variance in Y attributable to between-group differences is unaccounted for by the single S, benevolence of pay. In an attempt to uncloak situational correlates for this accounted-for but undefined between-group variance, more situational variables could be added to the analysis. Inasmuch as we would now have more than one situational predictor, we would have to add a subscript to S to represent "variable." The designator p is employed for this purpose, where p varies from 1 to q variables. The value on the pth situational variable, measured on the ith group, will thus be S_{pi}. When the value of S_{pi} is assigned to all members of the ith group, the jth member's score is S_{pij}, which in grand-mean deviation form is s_{pij}.

Adding situational variables to an analysis indicates that the bivariate-regression analysis, described in the previous section, will be replaced with a multiple-regression analysis. The transfer to a multiple-regression paradigm is easily achieved; the preceding logic extends directly to multiple-correlation analyses based on two or more situational variables, given that the values on these variables for each group have been assigned to all members of that group. The same basic cross-level operator is thus applied for each variable. To illustrate, suppose that we add two situational variables to the analysis in which we previously regressed the PV "satisfaction with pay" on the situational variable "benevolence of organizational pay structure." These new variables are "opportunity to engage in profit sharing" and "benevolence of benefit package." We effect the cross-level operator separately for each of what are now three specific situational variables.

The resulting regression equation for the *individual* level of analysis is shown in equation 8:

$$Y_{ij} = A + B_1 S_{1ij} + B_2 S_{2ij} + B_3 S_{3ij} + e_{ij} \tag{8}$$

where Y_{ij} is the observed score of the jth individual in the ith group on the PV; A is the intercept; S_{1ij} is the score of the jth individual in the ith group on organizational pay structure, S_{2ij} is the score of this same individual on "profit sharing," and S_{3ij} is the score of this individual on "benefits"; B_1, B_2, and B_3 are unstandardized regression weights estimated by ordinary least squares (OLS) or multiple regression; and e_{ij} is the error score for this individual.

Derivations analogous to the bivariate case will show that the squared multiple correlation associated with equation 8, or R_y^2, can be expressed as $R_y^2 = \eta_y^2 R_{\bar{y}}^2$. Using the same logic as before, $R_{\bar{y}}^2$, the squared multiple correlation between the weighted group means on the PV and the situational variables, indicates the degree to which R_y^2 from equation 8 approaches the maximum variation in the PV that is associated with between-group differences, as indicated by η_y^2. Thus, for example, if $R_y^2 = .33$, then, given the value of .49 for η_y^2, we will find that $R_{\bar{y}}^2 = .67$. This denotes that 67 percent of the variance in individuals' pay satisfaction that is accounted for by between-group differences is attributable (statistically but not necessarily causally) to group differences in pay structure, profit sharing, and benefits.

A third of the variance in individuals' pay satisfaction associated with between-group differences still remains unaccounted for. That is, $1 - (R_{\bar{y}}^2 = .67) = .33$. We may decide to add more situational variables to the analysis to account for this outstanding variance. Suppose, however, that we suspect that some portion of the between-group variation represented in the value of .33 might not be attributable to strictly situational attributes. For example, a part of the between-group variation in individuals' pay satisfaction might reflect *group* differences in one or more individual difference variables (such as age, education, experience, or socioeconomic status).

It follows from the preceding analysis that R_y^2 might not achieve a value of 1.0 by adding exclusively situational variables to the analysis. Moreover, we might account for some portion of the .33 statistic by adding one or more individual-difference variables to the analysis. The term *covariate* is often applied to an individual-difference variable that is added to a cross-level analysis for the purpose of accounting for, or statistically controlling for, between-group (as well as within-group) variance in a PV. The statistical procedure that uses between-group variation in an individual difference variable to account for and control between-group variation in a PV is analysis of covariance, or ANCOVA. We turn now to this subject.

Cross-Level Inference with Individual-Level Covariates

One can approach this problem from several different perspectives. In the preceding scenarios, we investigated situational antecedents of between-group differences in individuals' pay satisfaction before turning to the present quest for individual-level covariates. We might just as well have started with an attempt to ascertain whether group differences on one or more covariates accounted for between-group variation in the PV before attempting to unshroud between-group variation with specific situational variables. In the latter case, the covariates are generally thought of as "controlling for" variation they share with the PV.

Basically, the term *controlling* or *covarying* denotes that variation in the PV that can be predicted by variation in the covariate is removed from the analysis. As part of this process, scores on the PV that are associated with group differences in individuals' scores on the covariate are removed. This removal of variance is often conveyed statistically by saying that group means on the PV have been "adjusted" for differences in the covariate. In addition, controlling for between-group variation in the PV via a covariate also removes from consideration variation shared between a covariate and a specific situational variable. This includes variance jointly shared by the covariate and the situational variable with the PV. It follows that when the covariate is correlated with the situational variable, controlling for the covariate will likely diminish the level of prediction enjoyed by the situational variable in regard to the PV.

Controlling for a covariate also removes from analysis the variation in a PV that is not associated with between-group variation. Statistically, this is that part of the association between the covariate and the PV that is referred to as the *within-group component*. Partitioning covariation into between-group and within-group components is treated extensively in other chapters of this book; we will not take that discussion up here other than to say that removal of within-group covariation from the cross-level analysis serves to enhance the precision of the analysis (that is, by statistically controlling for irrelevant or confounding variables, one removes undesired variance from the PV). The net effect is that the PV has been made more predictable, and the statistical tests more powerful.

Suppose we return to our illustrative data, in which individuals' pay satisfaction has been associated both with between-organization differences ($\eta_y^2 = .49$) and with benevolence of organizational pay structure ($r_{ys}^2 = .12$). We decide to add the covariate "education" to our analysis. The idea is that groups in our sample differ with respect to the types of individuals who are attracted to them and/or who are formally selected by them (see Schneider, 1987). Some groups attract or select individuals with greater education. We suspect that groups comprising more-educated individuals will have a higher overall pay level, and therefore greater pay satisfaction on the average.

The preceding discussion suggests that at least some of the between-group variance in individuals' pay satisfaction that is related to benevolence of pay structure has its roots in between-group differences in education and experience. It is also likely that more-educated employees receive more benefits and share in more profits, factors that in turn engender greater pay satisfaction. The intent of a covariance analysis is to control for between-group variation in pay satisfaction that is explained by the simple expedient that more-educated employees are paid more. Correlation that is left over between individuals' pay satisfaction and benevolence of group pay structure could then be more clearly attributed to situational factors, such as concern of the organization for the well-being of its employees.

Technically, what follows is not a formal ANCOVA, because ANCOVA deals only with groups and not with specific situational variables. We will present a formal ANCOVA later. What follows is a quasi-ANCOVA, by which we mean an ANCOVA based on specific situational variables. We will, however, continue to use the term *ANCOVA*.

To conduct an ANCOVA, we first regress pay satisfaction on the covariate, using the entire multiorganizational sample of fifty individuals (Cohen and Cohen, 1983; Pedhazur, 1997). The equation is, as shown in equation 9,

$$Y_{ij} = A + B_1 X_{ij} + e_{ij} \qquad (9)$$

where X_{ij} is the score of the jth individual in the ith group on education. Estimation of the unstandardized regression weight B_1 by OLS provides a squared multiple correlation, R_1^2, which informs us of the proportion of the total variance in the PV that is associated with education.

For illustrative purposes, the correlation between education and the PV, pay satisfaction, was set equal to .30 ($p < .05$). The unstandardized regression weight, B_1 in equation 9, is 4.96 (the standardized regression weight is equal to the correlation of .30). These results are based on a scale for education that varies from 1 = less than high school education to 5 = graduate work or graduate degree.

The next step in ANCOVA is to add the situational variable, benevolence of pay structure, to the analysis. The result, as shown in equation 10, is

$$Y_{ij} = A + B_1 X_{ij} + B_2 S_{ij} + e_{ij} \qquad (10)$$

Equation 10 is a combination of equations 8 and 9. The order of variables in equation 10 corresponds to the step in which each variable—covariate and specific situational variable—is added to the analysis. The levels of analysis and explanation for equation 10 remain the individual.

Estimation of the two unstandardized regression weights by OLS provides a squared multiple correlation, R_2^2, which informs us of the proportion of the total variance in the Y_{ij} that is associated with variation in the covariate and variation in the assigned scores on the specific situational variable. Estimation of the B's takes into account covariation between scores on the covariate and the assigned scores on the situational variable. The R_2^2, based on equation 10 for our illustrative data, is .195. Both B_1 and B_2 are significant. B_1 is equal to 4.51, whereas B_2 is equal to 2.34. The standardized regression weights, or beta-weights, are .268 and .329, respectively.

The next step in the ANCOVA is to subtract R_1^2 from R_2^2. Subtraction of R_1^2 from R_2^2 partials or covaries (hence the term *covariance*) the contribution of the covariate from the prediction of the Y_{ij}. Specifically, $R_2^2 - R_1^2$ is the proportion of variance in the Y_{ij} that is accounted for by the covariate and specific situational variable, including prediction that obtains from the joint association between scores on the covariate and the assigned situational scores, minus the proportion of variance in the Y_{ij} that is accounted for by the covariate, which includes prediction that obtains from the joint association between scores on the covariate and the assigned situational scores. This is equal to the proportion of variance in the Y_{ij} that is attributable to the specific situational variable, sans prediction engendered by variation in education.

The strategy just described is often referred to as a *hierarchical regression analysis* (Cohen and Cohen, 1983; Pedhazur, 1997). The term *hierarchical* conveys the idea that predictor variables are added to the analysis in a predetermined sequence. In ANCOVA as applied to cross-level inference, this sequence is designed so that we may, through subtraction of R^2's, statistically remove from prediction the between-group variance in a PV that is associated with between-group variation in the covariate. Thus $R_2^2 - R_1^2$ statistically controls for between-group variation in pay satisfaction that is explained by the fact that groups composed of more-educated employees have greater rates of pay. For our illustrative data, $R_2^2 - R_1^2 = .195 - .09 = .105$, which is significant. We may thus conclude that cross-level associations between pay satisfaction and benevolence of pay structure are not simply attributable to the fact that more-educated people receive greater pay.

If the difference produced by $R_2^2 - R_1^2$ is nonsignificant, then we may infer that cross-level associations between the PV and the specific situational variable are quite likely explained by the simple expedient that more-educated people receive better rewards.

However, if $R_2^2 - R_1^2$ is significant, then we may infer that cross-level associations between the PV and the specific situational variable are not simply due to the fact that more-educated people receive better rewards.

It is noteworthy that the preceding analyses and interpretations are conditional. The condition is that one cannot add or subtract R^2's unless the covariate and specific situational variable combine additively. The additivity assumption is usually stated statistically as "the within-group regressions of the PV on the covariate are assumed to be homogeneous over situations." In other words, before we can effect controls for the covariate, we must show that the covariate and situational variable do not interact.

Testing for interactions between covariates and situational variables constitutes the third step of the ANCOVA. We add a regression equation to the ANCOVA that allows us to test for additivity (or for the lack of interaction). As shown in equation 11, the regression equation is

$$Y_{ij} = A + B_1 X + B_2 S + B_3 XS + e \qquad (11)$$

Equation 11 is equation 10 after dropping subscripts for individuals and groups, to conserve space, and adding one two-way interaction, to capture the covariate by situational-variable interaction. Unstandardized regression weight B_3 carries the interaction. Estimation of these and the other weights in equation 11 by OLS provides R_3^2, which estimates the combined additive and nonadditive (that is, interactive) contributions to the prediction of the PV.

Subtraction of R_3^2 from R_2^2 takes the symbolic form

(additive + interactive contributions) − (additive contributions)
= (interactive contributions)

A statistical test of the difference $R_3^2 - R_2^2$ is analogous to a test of the significance of the covariate by situational-variable interaction. If nonsignificant, then one returns to the covariance analysis and proceeds to interpret the results of analyses provided by equations 9 and 10. If significant, then ANCOVA is not legitimate with these data. One may proceed to investigate the data from the perspective of person-by-situation interactions. Fortunately, the test for nonadditivity or interaction was nonsignificant for our illustrative data. R_3^2 was equal to .198, which did not represent a significant increase over $R_2^2 = .195$. Thus the covariance analysis can be interpreted.

We proceed now to several additional subjects pertinent to AN-COVA. These include non-quasi or formal ANCOVA, cross-level inference with group means on the covariates, and contextual analysis.

Formal ANCOVA

The formal use of ANCOVA in cross-level inference involves, as before, one or more individual-difference variables as covariates. However, situations are now represented by groups coded as dummy variables—that is, the nominally coded dummy variables identify group membership of individuals. The situational component is thus analogous to equation 1, where we employed dummy variables to represent group membership and to assess differences in a PV attributable to omnibus differences in situations (see Pedhazur, 1997). The analytic aspects of ANCOVA are similar to those previously outlined for a specific situational variable, only now one uses nominally coded variables to represent group membership in place of a specific situational variable. To illustrate principal points, let us return to our prior use of five groups, designated g_1 through g_5, to symbolize group membership. Four independent variables defined earlier as G_1 through G_4 will again be used to nominally code the four groups (the same dummy-variable coding is employed). To G_1 through G_4 we add the covariate "education," X.

Equations 12. 13, and 14, which comprise the formal AN-COVA, are as follows:

$$Y = A + B_1 X + e \tag{12}$$

$$Y = A + B_1 X + B_2 G_1 + B_3 G_2 + B_4 G_3 + B_5 G_4 + e \tag{13}$$

$$Y = A + B_1 X + B_2 G_1 + B_3 G_2 + B_4 G_3 + B_5 G_4 + B_6 X G_1 + B_7 X G_2 + B_8 X G_3 + B_9 X G_4 + e \tag{14}$$

Equations 12, 13, and 14 are analogous to equations 9, 10, and 11 from the quasi-ANCOVA. The subscripts for group and individual are deleted, to conserve space. Estimation of the B's in each of the three equations by OLS provides a basis for estimating a multiple correlation for each equation—namely, as before, R_1^2, R_2^2, and R_3^2.

R_1^2 again informs us of the proportion of the total variance in the PV that is associated with the covariate "education." R_2^2 estimates the proportion of variance in the Y_{ij} that is associated with variation in the covariate and variation in situations (that is, the five organizations). Unlike equation 10, which estimated variance in the PV associated with only one specific situational variable, equation 13 estimates the total amount of variation in the PV that is accounted for by situations. Estimation of the B's takes into account covariation between scores on the covariate and the dummy variables.

The objective of the ANCOVA is to determine whether controlling for the covariate erases the relationship between group differences and the PV. This determination is made by subtracting R_1^2 from R_2^2. Following our previous discussion, $R_2^2 - R_1^2$ is the proportion of variance in the Y_{ij} that is accounted for jointly by the covariate and group differences, minus the proportion of variance in the Y_{ij} that is accounted for by the covariate, which includes prediction that obtains from the joint association between scores on the covariate and group differences. This is equal to the proportion of variance in the Y_{ij} that is attributable to group differences, sans prediction engendered by variation in education. If the difference produced by $R_2^2 - R_1^2$ is significant, then we may infer that controlling for the variation over (as well as within) groups in education did not erase the cross-level relationship between the PV and group membership. In other words, group differences still account for a significant proportion of the variance in the Y_{ij} after difference among groups in education is controlled. This appears to be the case for our illustrative data. As previously, $R_1^2 = .09$. $R_2^2 = .496$, which corresponds to our prior knowledge that group membership accounts for approximately one-fifth of the variance in satisfaction with pay. $R_2^2 - R_1^2 = .406$, which is highly significant.

As in quasi-ANCOVA, the preceding analyses and interpretations are conditional on additivity, or the lack of interaction between the covariate and groups coded as dummy variables. Indeed, the within-group regressions of the PV on the covariate are expected to be homogeneous (that is, parallel) over the three groups. We must therefore show that the covariate does not interact with the group variables in order to interpret the results of equations 12 and 13. Equation 14 carries the interactions via B_6 through B_9, and the squared multiple correlation associated with this equation, R_3^2, estimates the combined additive and interactive contributions to the prediction of the PV. The difference between R_2^2 and R_3^2 estimates the contribution of the interactions. If the difference $R_3^2 - R_2^2$ is nonsignificant, as it is with the illustrative data (that is, $R_3^2 = .55$, which is not significantly greater than $R_2^2 = .496$), then the results of the ANCOVA are interpretable. Had this difference been significant, then the results of equations 12 and 13 could not have been interpreted as an ANCOVA.

Extension to Multiple Covariates and Specific Situational Variables

Prior to the discussion of ANCOVA, we described how one might regress a PV on multiple specific situational variables. Our example was based on the three specific situational variables of pay structure, profit sharing, and benefits. Equation 8 was

$$Y_{ij} = A + B_1 S_{1ij} + B_2 S_{2ij} + B_3 S_{3ij} + e_{ij}$$

We noted that the squared multiple correlation for Y, or R_y^2, had the form: $R_y^2 = \eta_y^2 R_{\bar{y}}^2$. The ratio R_y^2/η_y^2, which is equal to $R_{\bar{y}}^2$, estimates the degree to which R_y^2 from equation 8 approaches η_y^2, which is the maximum variation in the PV associated with between-group differences. An example was offered in which $R_y^2 = .33$, $\eta_y^2 = .49$, and $R_{\bar{y}}^2 = R_y^2/\eta_y^2 = .67$. These data indicate that 49 percent of the variance in individuals' pay satisfaction is attributable to between group differences, and that 67 percent of the variance in pay satisfaction that is attributable to group differences is accounted for by differences in benevolence of pay structure, profit sharing, and benefits. Thus we accounted for 67 percent of the 49 percent of the variance in the PV that is associated with between-group differences. It follows that one-third of the variance in individuals' pay satisfaction that is associated with between-group differences still remains unaccounted for; that is, $1 - (R_{\bar{y}}^2 = .67) = .33$.

We might now decide to check whether some portion of this outstanding variance might be attributable to between-group differences in multiple individual-level covariates. Our illustration here will be carried out on education and experience. We shall ask the following question: Did we account for all of the outstanding between-group variation in the PV by adding multiple covariates and specific situational variables to the analysis? The following hierarchy of analyses (equations 15, 16, and 17) is designed to answer this question. (The three specific situational variables can be dropped from the analysis in order to illustrate the case for multiple covariates. Also, we shall assume additivity, but this assumption is testable via the hierarchical regression procedures presented earlier.)

$$Y_{ij} = A + B_1 X_{1ij} + B_2 X_{2ij} + e_{ij} \tag{15}$$

$$Y_{ij} = A + B_1 X_{1ij} + B_2 X_{2ij} + B_3 S_{1ij} + B_4 S_{2ij} + B_5 S_{3ij} + e_{ij} \tag{16}$$

$$Y = B_1 X_1 + B_2 X_2 + B_3 S_1 + B_4 S_2 + B_5 S_3 + B_6 G_1 + B_7 G_2 + B_8 G_3 + B_9 G_4 + e \tag{17}$$

Equation 15 begins with the covariates "education" (X_1) and "experience" (X_2). The associated squared multiple correlation, which is R_1^2 in this sequence of equations, informs us of how much variation in the PV is accounted for by the two covariates. Equation 16 adds the specific situational variables to the analysis. The squared multiple correlation associated with this equation, or R_2^2, tells us how much of the variation in Y is accounted for by both the S's and the covariates. If the difference $R_2^2 - R_1^2$ is significant, then we know that addition of the specific situational variables to the analysis has contributed significantly to prediction of Y. Alternatively, the covariates do not account for all the cross-level relations between the situational variables and the PV.

The addition of equation 17 to the analysis is designed to ascertain whether the combination of covariates and specific situational variables accounts for all of the between-group variation in Y (subscripts i and j are deleted from this equation for reasons of space). The R^2 for this equation, or R_3^2, will be greater than R_2^2 if the addition of the nominally coded group variables G_1 through G_4 add significantly to prediction. Thus, if $R_3^2 - R_2^2$ is significant, then between-group variation remains in Y that has not been accounted for by the S's and X's. However, if $R_3^2 - R_2^2$ is nonsignificant, then we may infer that we accounted for all between-group variation in Y via the X's and S's.

It is, of course, unlikely that the X's and S's will account for all of the between-group variation in Y, although the addition of the covariates may account for some of the $1-(R_{\bar{y}}^2 = .67) = .33$, already described. Unfortunately, the analysis based on equations 15–17 does not offer the precision of being able to estimate how much of the unattributed between-group variation in Y (the .33 value) was accounted for by the addition of the covariates to the analysis. At present, we are not aware of equations that would allow us to make this determination if the covariates remain in individual-difference form.

Contextual Analysis and Effects

Contextual analysis is the designation given to an area of analysis in which the cross-level operator is the group mean on an individual variable (for example, $\bar{X}_i$). A *contextual effect* is the contribution these group means make to prediction of a PV (for example, Y_{ij}) after controls are effected for the individual-level scores on the individual-difference variable (that is, the X_{ij}). A theoretical scenario is employed to describe the primary approach to contextual analysis and estimation of contextual effects.

Suppose that we have two schools. In the first school, students' IQs vary from 85 to 115, with a mean of 100. In the second school, students' IQs vary from 100 to 130, with a mean of 115. Clearly, individuals' scores on IQ vary significantly by school. Students in school 2 tend, on the average, to have higher IQs than students in school 1.

Now suppose that we find that scores on academic achievement tests are higher in school 2 than in school 1. Some investigators hypothesize that these differences are nothing more than reflections of the known differences in individuals' IQs between the two schools. We can conduct an ANCOVA to test this hypothesis. The covariance analysis consists of equations 18 and 19, two regression equations (additivity is assumed, and the subscripts for i and j are deleted):

$$AA = I + B_1 IQ + e \tag{18}$$

$$AA = I + B_1 IQ + B_2 G + e \tag{19}$$

where AA is academic achievement, I is the intercept, G represents school (scored 1 if a member of school 1 and 2 if a member of school 2), the B's and e's are estimated by OLS, and the equations are operationalized at the individual level of analysis.

The first equation controls for variation in academic achievement that is attributable to within-school variation in individuals' IQ scores and to between-school variation in individuals' IQ scores. The second equation adds a dummy variable for school. If the squared multiple correlation for the second equation is not significantly greater than that for the first, then we conclude that differences in individual IQ account for all of the between-school variation in individual academic achievement. However, if the squared multiple correlation for the second equation is significantly greater than that for the first, then we conclude that covarying IQ out of academic achievement does not remove all of the between-school variation in individual academic achievement scores. Let's assume that this is so.

The question now is what it is about the schools—namely, the differences between the schools—that is responsible for the remaining differences between the schools in academic achievement. In our previous discussion, we introduced specific situational variables to address this question. We could do the same here. Consider, for example, the hypothesis that students with higher IQ scores create a culture that values education, hard study, and academic excellence. This suggests that students who attend school in academic cultures composed of, on the average, students with high IQ scores will experience pressure to respect the educational experience and will attempt to excel academically. In contrast, students who attend school in academic cultures composed of students with lower IQ scores will experience less intense pressure to perform academically.

The crux of the hypothesis is that the IQ score–based composition of the student body has a main effect on the academic values and study habits of the students. This main effect should influence individuals' academic achievement independently of the individual IQ scores of the students; that is, individuals who attend a school with a stronger intellectual culture or composition should have higher academic test scores than students who attend a school with a weaker intellectual culture or composition, irrespective of each student's intelligence.

To test this hypothesis, we measure the intellectual composition of a school by the mean IQ for that school. We then assign the mean IQ for a school to every student in that school. Note that we are now treating mean IQ as a specific situational variable—namely, as a measure of intellectual composition—and are applying the cross-level operator to it. Note further that our intent is to capture variance in academic achievement that is not attributable to (which is to say, that has not already been captured by) between-school variation in individuals' IQ scores. This point is made clear by equations 20 and 21, a set of contextual analysis equations:

$$AA = I + B_1 IQ + e \qquad (20)$$

$$AA = I + B_1 IQ + B_2 \overline{IQ} + e \qquad (21)$$

where $\overline{IQ}$ refers to mean school IQ following application of the cross-level operator.

The first equation in this set is the same as the first equation in the ANCOVA (that is, equation 18). This equation again controls for variation in academic achievement that is attributable to within-school variation in individuals' IQ scores and to between-school variation in individuals' IQ scores. The second equation adds mean IQ as a specific situational variable—namely as a "contextual variable" or a "compositional variable" (see Coleman et al., 1966; Pedhazur, 1997) to the cross-level analysis. If the squared multiple correlation for the second equation is significantly greater than that for the first, then we infer that the intellectual compositions of the schools have a contextual effect on individuals' academic achievement. A contextual effect is defined as a cross-level relation between individual attitudes/performance on a criterion and assigned group means on an individual-difference variable (often a covariate), after controlling for the effects of the individual-difference variable (see Alwin, 1976; Firebaugh, 1979, 1980; Pedhazur, 1997; Werts, Linn, and Joreskog, 1971). Statistically, perhaps the best way to think of a contextual effect is to envision a condition in which a subset of individuals has the same score on individual-difference variable X (there may be many such subsets), these individuals belong to different groups, the groups have different means on X—that is, the $\overline{X}_i$'s vary), and the $\overline{X}_{ij}$'s (group means assigned to group members) correlate significantly with the Y_{ij}'s. This is the condition in which the $\overline{X}_{ij}$'s are most likely to be correlated with the Y_{ij}'s after controls are put in place for the X_{ij}'s (that is, the X_{ij}'s are partialed from the $\overline{X}_{ij}$). The key is that people with the same individual scores belong to groups with different means, and the means have a unique effect on the Y_{ij}'s.

We can complete our illustrative contextual analysis by asking whether the mean IQ scores account for all the remaining be-tween-group variance in academic achievement. One approach to answering this question is to add the dummy variable for school to the contextual analysis via the equation 22:

$$AA = I + B_1 IQ + B_2 \overline{IQ} + B_3 G + e \qquad (22)$$

If by adding this term we account for a significant increment in the variance of academic achievement, then we may infer that adding mean IQ to individual IQ has not exhausted the between-school variance in academic achievement. Alternatively, if adding the dummy variable for school to the analysis fails to increase variance accounted for, then we may conclude that the statistical task of ex-plaining between-school variance in academic achievement has been completed.

It would be an error to conclude that the explanatory task has been concluded. The primary reason for this caveat is that we have yet to establish the construct validity of mean IQ. We have hy-pothesized that it is an indicator of the intellectual composition of the student body and serves as a surrogate for such things as the value placed on receiving an education, motivation to study, and the desirability of academic excellence. The problem for construct validity and causal explanation is that mean IQ may serve as a sur-rogate for a number of other variables (Firebaugh, 1979, 1980), such as quality of teachers, quality of educational facilities, diets of students, and size of classes. Basically, any variable that is reason-ably correlated with mean IQ has the potential to offer an alterna-tive explanation for the contextual effect of mean IQ on academic achievement.

Ruling out possible alternative explanations requires that we measure variables representing alternative constructs and control for them in the contextual analysis. This brings us to the use of other specific situational variables in conjunction with mean IQ. Suppose, for example, that we measure the specific situational vari-able "#comps," which stands for number of computers per class-room. We shall also add a random selection of more schools and students (nested in schools) to the analysis, for statistical purposes. Our hierarchical regression analysis would now take form of equa-tions 23, 24, and 25:

$$AA = I + B_1 IQ + e \tag{23}$$

$$AA = I + B_1 IQ + B_2 \overline{IQ} + e \tag{24}$$

$$AA = I + B_1 IQ + B_2 \overline{IQ} + B_3 \#comps + e \tag{25}$$

If the regression weight for mean IQ in equation 25 falls to non-significance with the addition of *#comps* to the equation, then we have an alternative explanation for the contextual analysis; that is, perhaps it is technology rather than composition of student body that explains differences in academic achievement. There are, of course, other possibilities, such as that B_2 and B_3 are both significant in equation 25. In this case, we would likely infer that both intellectual composition of the student body and enhanced technology contribute to individuals' academic performance.

Empirical Illustration

We will conclude the treatment of contextual analysis with a brief return to the illustrative data involving the PV "pay satisfaction" and the covariate "education." We know from the results of the formal ANCOVA that partialing individuals' scores on education (X_{ij}) from their scores on pay satisfaction (the PV or the Y_{ij}) does not remove all the between-group variation in individuals' pay satisfaction. Moreover, on the basis of the quasi-ANCOVA, we know that some of this outstanding between-group variation in the PV is related to the specific situational variable "benevolence of pay structure." However, even after accounting for the increment in between-group variation attributed to the specific situational variable, we still have significant between-group variance in the Y_{ij}.

Now let us consider the potential for a contextual effect based on the covariate "education." We suspect a contextual effect might be engendered by social-influence processes. For example, being better paid on the average, groups composed of more-educated people might create a culture that views the organizational reward system as equitable. A member of one of those groups that, relatively speaking, are less educated than the average would encounter social pressure to view the organization as equitable, which in turn would serve to encourage a more positive attitude about pay than would be the case if the attitude were contingent simply on this person's own education. In contrast, groups composed of less highly educated individuals might be less prone to frame the organizational reward system as equitable. Indeed, perceptions of inequity might exist. An individual with the same education as the illustrative individual either would not encounter social pressure to frame the organization and his or her pay positively or perhaps would be encouraged to see the organization as inequitable, with an accompanying deleterious effect on pay satisfaction.

We now have a condition in which individuals with the same education are members of groups that differ with respect to mean education. This creates a situation that is conducive to a contextual effect in which groups' means on education, after having been assigned to group members (the cross-level operator $\overline{X}_{ij}$), contribute significantly to the prediction of the Y_{ij} after controls are in place for X_{ij}. The basic hypothesis is that groups composed of more-educated individuals create cultures that view pay as more equitable than groups composed of less highly educated individuals.

To test this hypothesis, we conduct a contextual analysis using equations 26 and 27:

$$Y_{ij} = A + B_1 X_{ij} + e_{ij} \tag{26}$$

$$Y_{ij} = A + B_1 X_{ij} + B_2 \overline{X}_{ij} + e_{ij} \tag{27}$$

Equation 26 controls for variation in the PV that is attributable to within-group variation in individuals' education scores and to between-group variation in individuals' education scores. Equation 27 adds mean education as a contextual variable to the cross-level analysis. If the weight for this variable is significant (or the squared multiple correlation for equation 27 is significantly greater than that for equation 26), then we infer that a contextual effect has occurred on individuals' pay satisfaction.

Results of the contextual analysis are as presented here. Estimates of parameters for equations 26 and 27, and accompanying R^2's, are reported. Asterisks indicate significance ($p < .05$).

Estimates for equation 26:

$$Y_{ij} = 103.30 + 4.96^* X_{ij} + e_{ij} \tag{28}$$

$$R_1^2 = .087^*$$

Estimates for equation 27:

$$Y_{ij} = 56.17 + 1.154 X_{ij} + 20.30 * \overline{X}_{.j} + e_{ij} \qquad (29)$$

$$R_2^2 = .31*$$

Test for contextual effect:

$$R_2^2 - R_1^2 = (.31 - .087) = .223* \qquad (30)$$

Simply put, group mean education added significantly to the prediction of pay satisfaction after the controls were effected for individual-level education. We also added the dummy variables for groups to equation 29 and found that the R^2 increased significantly. This result indicates that the contextual effect contributed by mean education did not account for all the between-group variation in pay satisfaction.

Whether the contextual effect is due to social-influence processes and emergent perceptions of organizational equity has yet to be verified. We could now attempt to assess the viability of specific explanations by measuring the relevant variables and including them as specific situational variables in the cross-level analysis. We might, for example, attempt to assess group equity as a specific situational variable and redo the analyses with this variable included. We would also want to include measures that capture variables offering alternative explanations for the contextual effect in our analyses.

We should note that we have assumed additivity throughout this treatment. We also have not considered statistical problems that may occur, chief among which is multicollinearity. These remain thorny issues for contextual analysis (see Pedhazur, 1997). Nevertheless, contextual analysis is a legitimate component of cross-level analysis. Our recommendation is to conduct a contextual analysis if a group composition effect appears plausible. If a contextual effect is found, then engage in further research to measure the specific situational variables that are considered responsible for the contextual effect, and test for the presumed influences.

Include in such tests variables that form the basis for alternative explanations.

Breadth of Application of the General Linear Model to Study of Cross-Level Inference

This chapter has focused on very basic issues pertaining to how one crosses levels of analysis so as to make inferences about how variation in situations is related to variation among individuals. We have emphasized the cross-level operator as the statistical process that allows one to infer relationships that cross from the situational to the individual level of analysis. Cross-level operators were defined and illustrated for ANOVA, regression, analysis of covariance (both quasi and formal), and contextual analysis. We hope that this treatment of cross-level operators helps clarify what is happening, both conceptually and statistically, as the researcher engages in cross-level inference.

The discussion of cross-level operators focused on nonexperimental applications. The statistical and substantive processes for relating situational attributes to individual attributes are basically the same for experimental and quasi-experimental applications (although differences may occur in formal statistical models used for hypothesis testing, an issue treated in statistical treatments of the general linear model). The discussion accompanying Tables 9.1 and 9.2 applies directly to the use of ANOVA and regression to test for experimental effects of a situational treatment on individual outcomes.

The extension of cross-level operators to include experimental and quasi-experimental studies suggests that cross-level inference, as described in this chapter, applies to hundreds of studies. Experimental and quasi-experimental manipulations of leadership styles, reward structures, goals, task designs, performance standards, power distributions, selection procedures, training approaches, communication structures, team-building strategies, and working conditions have served as situational variables in numerous organizational studies. The cross-level influences of these situational variables on individual attributes have been examined for such things as performance, motivation, satisfaction, anxiety, aggressiveness, conscientiousness, health, accidents, commitment, attendance, career choices, physical comfort, participation in team activities, goal setting, expectancies, and perceptions of situational attributes.

Of course, the number of cross-level inference studies increases geometrically if we broaden our set to include studies from such areas as social psychology, economics, political science, marketing, personality, and medicine. In many if not the vast majority of such investigations, some form of the general linear model is used for analytic purposes. When the independent variables are composed of discrete interventions (treatments, manipulations), styles, or types into which subjects have been randomly (or perhaps not so randomly) sampled, ANOVA is generally employed, with ANCOVA entering as soon as a covariate is identified and measured. Multiple dependent variables engender use of multivariate analogs of the techniques described here. When situational variables are random variables—where, for example, attributes (such as size) of existing situations are assessed on continuous scales—then regression procedures are invoked after assignment of situational scores to individuals. Covariance typically takes the form of the use of control variables in a hierarchical regression. And, of course, interaction analyses are available in all forms of analyses. We suspect also that contextual analysis will be used to explore for the possibility of group effects as organizational investigators become familiar with this technique.

In sum, the history of the use of the general linear model to study cross-level inference is extensive. We suspect that the popularity of the general linear model in this capacity will continue for some time. Yet the general approach, as described here, is limited in many respects. There is no attempt to ascertain how group means on the individual variable are correlated with the (group-level) situational scores. When two or more individual-level variables are involved (as in contextual analysis), no attention is given to decomposing the covariances between the variables into "within" and "between" components. These and other missing analyses are provided by newer techniques, particularly hierarchical linear modeling (HLM) and within-and-between analysis (WABA). A more specific discussion of the interplay between the techniques described here and both HLM and WABA completes this chapter.

Cross-Level Inference in Relation to Hierarchical Linear Modeling and Within and Between Analysis

The statistical relationships of primary concern exist between contextual analysis and WABA, and regression approaches to cross-level inference (including ANOVA, regression, and ANCOVA) and HLM. As in preceding discussions, we shall focus on naturally occurring data, wherein individuals are nested in existing groups.

Contextual Analysis and WABA

This relationship is simple and direct. The regression of an individual-level dependent variable (for example, academic achievement, or AA) on an individual-level independent variable (for example, intelligence, or IQ) for students nested in schools is a function of two different regression coefficients. The first coefficient is the pooled within-groups coefficient (b_w). To estimate a value for b_w, one regresses AA on IQ in each of the groups (schools). The regression coefficient associated with each school is the within-group regression coefficient. If we average these coefficients over schools, weighting by school size, we have (approximately) the pooled (across-school) within-groups regression coefficient, or b_w.

The second coefficient is the between-groups coefficient, or b_b. To estimate this coefficient, we compute the mean AA and the mean IQ for each school. We then assign the school means for a school to all individuals in the school. Finally, we regress the assigned mean AA on the assigned mean IQs. This is b_b, and it is equivalent to regressing the school mean AA scores on the school mean IQ scores, using the sample of schools but weighting each set of means from a school for school size.

Functions of b_w, including b_w itself, are used to index how much of the correlation between AA and IQ is attributable to individual differences, independent of differences among groups. We use b_b and its functions to index how much of the correlation between AA and IQ is due to differences among groups independent of differences among individuals in the same group. Further, b_w and b_b have direct ties to contextual analysis; for example, see equation 21 from the discussion of contextual analysis. To review briefly, the objective is to determine whether school means on *IQ* add significantly to prediction of *AA* when individual differences in *IQ* are already in the equation.

As described by Pedhazur (1997), B_1 in equation 21 is equivalent to b_w in WABA. Moreover, B_2 in equation 21 is equal to $b_b - b_w$. Therefore, a direct link exists between contextual analysis and WABA. The pooled within-groups coefficient is output for both analyses. Incremental variance added by between-groups regression coefficients is addressed in both analytic procedures. Indeed, both analytic procedures place considerable emphasis on $b_b - b_w$, or B_2. Thus the two approaches appear complementary. Given the greater breadth and depth of information provided by WABA, we recommend that those interested in contextual analysis also consider WABA. For WABA enthusiasts, we suggest consideration of cross-level inferences between group means on the independent variable and individual differences on the dependent variable.

Cross-Level Inference and HLM

We began this chapter by suggesting that investigators often agonize over how to deal with a design that involves an individual-level variable (for example, aggressiveness in the work situation) and a situation-level variable (for example, the extent of the organization's use of monitoring systems). Does one aggregate aggressiveness over individuals in each organization and correlate the aggregates with organizational monitoring on the sample of organizations? Or does one assign organizational monitoring scores to individuals within organizations and correlate the assigned scores with individuals' aggressiveness on the sample of individuals? We have suggested that what one wishes to know determines how one answers this question.

The focal point of this chapter has been questions that call for the second of the two analytic options just described. This analysis addresses the question of whether installing a monitoring system acts as a triggering mechanism that provokes individuals to commit aggressive acts. This is a cross-level-inference issue that asks whether individuals' aggressiveness tends to be enhanced by increased surveillance, supervision, and control, perhaps some of which is surreptitious. (It is also likely the case that the installation of a monitoring system acts as a trigger for aggression primarily for those individuals who have a disposition to respond aggressively to frustration and anger.)

Suppose, however, that an investigator is concerned with testing whether the presence or pervasiveness of monitoring systems is associated with greater frequency of aggressive acts. This question is addressed by the first of the two analytic options just described, because frequency of aggressive acts is an organizational-level variable and because frequency of aggressive acts can be assessed via a function of an aggregate of individual aggressive acts per organization (perhaps adjusted for organizational size). The procedure for cross-level inference that has been described in this chapter does not focus on relationships between aggregates of individual-level variables and situational variables.

Assessment of relationships between aggregates of individual-level variables and situational variables can be dealt with in a number of ways. These include regression analyses in which (weighted) aggregates of individuals' scores are regressed on situational variables via ordinary least squares. However, the most sophisticated method for addressing this issue at the present time is considered by many to be HLM (Bryk & Raudenbush, 1992). An HLM analysis would consist of an ANOVA-type analysis to estimate how much of the variance in individuals' aggression is explained by differences in organizations. Assuming this value is significantly greater than zero, the mean of individuals' aggression scores per organization would be calculated. In our terms, these means are aggregates. A means-as-outcomes or level 2 conditional analysis would then follow, in which the means (aggregate aggression scores per organization) would be regressed on the situational variable (monitoring). Output from the situational analysis would include the following elements:

1. The unstandardized regression weight for the regression of mean aggression scores on monitoring, via the sample of organizations (call this the b_A)
2. The proportion of variance in the mean aggression scores that is explained by differences in monitoring
3. The unstandardized regression weight for the regression of individuals' aggression scores on monitoring, via the sample of individuals (call this b_I)

4. The proportion of variance in individuals' aggression scores that is explained by monitoring

The association between the frequency of aggressive acts and the extent of organizational monitoring is addressed in outputs 1 and 2. Results reported in outputs 3 and 4 are analogous to those presented by the cross-level operator; that is, they address the association between monitoring and individuals' acts of aggression.

Cross-level results are obtained via algebraic substitution of level 2 equations into level 1 equations and the use of a full-information estimator (that is, all parameters in all equations are estimated simultaneously). It is noteworthy that if all equations are well specified (for example, they contain no unmeasured-variables problems, they have the correct causal order, and the influences are unidirectional), if the variables are reliable, and if samples are large, then the full-information estimator is a more efficient system than regression (OLS is a single-equation estimator). Moreover—again, if the equations are well-specified, if the variables are reliable, and if samples are large—HLM provides more accurate estimates of error terms than regression does (Bryk & Raudenbush, 1992).

It would seem that HLM is the preferred procedure for estimating associations, both between a situational attribute and an individual attribute and between a situational attribute and aggregates of individuals' scores on an attribute. The traditional statistical methods described in this chapter would give way to the new and more sophisticated methodology. (The substantive explications of cross-level operators would remain, however.) Actually, we are happy to recommend the use of HLM for these purposes. However, our enthusiasm for HLM is not unbridled, and we offer the following caveats.

- We have spent many years dealing with full-information estimators in structural-equation modeling. We have learned that engaging in such techniques with poorly specified equations (for example, unmeasured variables), poorly measured variables, and/or small samples can be problematic. Results may not replicate, and specification errors in one equation may be spread throughout the entire model. Sometimes less sophisticated procedures, such as OLS, are preferable because they are more stable and bound specification errors to those equations in which they occur.

• The unstandardized regression weights b_A and b_I will generally be of similar if not the same magnitude in HLM analysis (Bryk & Raudenbush, 1992). This is technically correct because these weights index the amount of change in mean aggression associated with a unit of change in monitoring at both the individual and organizational levels of analysis. However, similarity of b_A and b_I can be misleading because it suggests a homology for strengths of association at both the individual and organizational levels of analysis. This suggestion is misleading because the reduction in uncertainty, degree of prediction, and proportion of variance explained in the dependent variable are typically quite different for the individual level of analysis versus aggregate levels of analysis. For example, the correlation between individuals' aggression and monitoring (on the sample of individuals) would typically be lower than the correlation between rate of aggression and monitoring (on the organizational sample).

• The variance-explained statistics reported in outputs 2 and 4 will more accurately reflect the fact that organizational monitoring will probably explain more variance in mean aggression than in individuals' aggression. These statistics offer a more useful basis for comparing differences in associations between the individual and aggregate levels of analysis. Unfortunately, Bryk and Raudenbush (1992, p. 95) recommend variance explained in aggregates over variance explained in individuals' scores as the clearest evidence for making judgments about the importance of situational variables. In other words, according to the key authors in this area, output 2 provides clearer evidence about the effects of monitoring on aggression than does output 4. We disagree. Neither statistic is to be preferred over the other. As already discussed, variance explained in individual manifestations of aggression and variance-explained rates of aggression answer different questions. It is up to the investigator to decide, in the context of her or his research objectives, which (if either) is the more relevant question.

In sum, HLM is a powerful and sophisticated new methodology. When samples are large, when equations are well specified, and when variables are reliable, HLM provides more efficient estimation of parameters and more accurate estimation of errors than the regression-based statistics discussed in this chapter. Nevertheless, if one or more of these conditions is not satisfied, then regression may be preferable: simpler is sometimes better.

References

Alwin, D. F. (1976). Assessing school effects: Some identities. *Sociology of Education, 49,* 294–303.

Bryk, A. S., & Raudenbush, S. W. (1992). *Hierarchical linear models.* Thousand Oaks, CA: Sage.

Cohen, J., & Cohen, P. (1983). *Applied multiple regression/correlation analysis for the behavioral sciences* (2nd ed.). Mahwah, NJ: Erlbaum.

Coleman, J. S., Campbell, E. Q., Hobson, C. J., McPartland, J., Mood, A. M., Weinfeld, F. D., & York, R. L. (1966). *Equality of educational opportunity.* Washington, DC: U.S. Government Printing Office.

Firebaugh, G. (1979). Assessing group effects: A comparison of two methods. *Sociological Methods and Research, 7,* 384–395.

Firebaugh, G. (1980). Assessing group effects: A comparison of two methods. In E. F. Borgatta & D. J. Jacksons (Eds.), *Aggregate data: Analysis and interpretation.* Thousand Oaks, CA: Sage.

James, L. R., Demaree, R. G., & Hater, J. J. (1980). A statistical rationale for relating situational variables and individual differences. *Organizational Behavior and Human Performance, 25,* 354–364.

James, L. R., Mulaik, S. A., & Brett, J. M. (1982). *Causal analysis: Assumptions, models, and data.* Thousand Oaks, CA: Sage.

Pedhazur, E. J. (1997). *Multiple regression in behavioral research* (3rd ed.). Orlando, FL: Klein.

Roberts, K. H., Hulin, C. L., & Rousseau, D. M. (1978). *Developing an interdisciplinary science of organizations.* San Francisco: Jossey-Bass.

Schneider, B. (1987). The people make the place. *Personnel Psychology, 40,* 437–453.

Werts, C. E., Linn, R. L., & Joreskog, K. G. (1971). Estimating the parameters of path models involving unmeasured variables. In H. M. Blalock, Jr. (Ed.), *Causal models in the social sciences.* Hawthorne, NY: Aldine de Gruyter.

CHAPTER 10

Within and Between Analysis

The Varient Paradigm as an Underlying Approach to Theory Building and Testing

Fred Dansereau
Francis J. Yammarino

In this chapter, we describe the types of problems that gave rise to the varient paradigm, an approach for formulating and testing theories that includes multiple levels of analysis. On the basis of the conceptualization that underlies the varient paradigm, we describe the basic logic of the multiple-level data-analytic technique called within and between analysis, or WABA, that is part of the paradigm. We also illustrate the types of questions that WABA does and does not address and present illustrations of the technique from journal articles; these illustrations provide justification for the technique's use. Finally, we focus on the criticisms and limitations of the technique and provide some suggestions regarding ways that WABA can complement other approaches.

Impetus for the Technique

As described by Dansereau (1995), the critical question that gave rise to WABA was this: What are the reasons why a leader may develop

Note: The authors would like to thank Michelle Bligh, Jeffrey Kohles, and Chester A. Schriesheim for their comments on an earlier draft of this chapter.

close relationships with some individuals (followers or people who behave in ways that satisfy the leader) but not with others (people who behave in ways that do not satisfy the leader)? Basically, to address this simple question required an ability to address four questions that pertain to the following topics:

1. Single-level analysis
2. Multiple-level analysis
3. Multiple-variable analysis
4. Multiple-relationship analysis

Throughout this chapter we focus on four key issues:

1. How to conceptualize each of several levels of analysis
2. How to combine levels of analysis
3. How to associate different formulations of variables with each of several levels of analysis
4. How to identify conditions under which higher levels of analysis (for example, the collective level) moderate the development of lower levels of analysis (for example, groups)

Single-Level Analysis

Wholes View

In the early 1970s, the time of the beginning of WABA, the field of leadership study focused mainly on the individual differences or styles of leaders. This focus implied that an individual displayed a consistent style over time and across people. The central question in the literature concerned the nature of the relationship of the differences between *superiors* with differences between the *work groups* that they supervised. Although the focus was on superiors and subordinates separately, it implied a multiple-level approach in that each superior was viewed as a whole entity displaying person-level individual differences, and each group was viewed as a group composed of essentially homogeneous followers. Klein, Dansereau, and Hall (1994) called such a view *homogeneous*. Dansereau, Alutto, and Yammarino (1984) called this view a *wholes* condition. Another way to think about this idea is in terms of similarity; that is, group members are presumed to be highly similar. Examples of

this approach are studies at the time that correlated the consideration of a superior (one score for each superior) with a whole work
group's (one score for each group) performance (e.g., Stogdill and
Coons, 1957).

Parts View

Although individual differences were and continue to be of major
significance, it seemed likely that individuals (superiors) could also
differentiate among the individuals (subordinates) who reported
to them. For example, a superior could delegate supervisory-type
tasks to the relatively more competent subordinates and delegate
only nonsupervisory-type tasks to less competent peers in the same
group. This notion, which was not recognized in the study of leadership, focuses on the way in which individuals (superiors) differentiate among a set of individuals (subordinates), as well as on the
differentiation that occurs within work groups. This is called a *heterogeneous* view by Klein and colleagues (1994) and a *parts* condition by Dansereau and colleagues (1984). It is a frog-pond effect
in that how a superior treats one subordinate depends on how the
superior treats another subordinate (Firebaugh, 1980). It is a com-
plementarity notion; that is, group members are conceptualized
as complementary but not similar. An example of this approach is
a study by Schriesheim, Neider, and Scandura (1998) that focuses
on delegation and performance within groups. Earlier examples
of this idea can be found in Dansereau, Graen, and Haga (1975)
and Dansereau and Dumas (1977). Although this idea is often expressed by subtracting an individual's score from the group average, the subtraction procedure actually produces a set of relative
scores for all the individuals in the group. It is a way to represent
all individuals relative to each other.

Equivocal View

The focus on differences within individuals (person parts) and within
work groups (group parts) contains a relativistic notion, which does
not reflect the possibility that a superior can treat individuals independently of each other. To allow for this condition, another view of
superiors and subordinates had to be created. It is called the *individualized leadership* approach (Dansereau &Yammarino, 1998a,
1998b). In this approach, a focal individual (superior) views other

individuals (subordinates) as independent of each other. Likewise, a set of individuals (subordinates) remains as a set of individuals and does not form into a group in which people are interdependent (that is, similar or complementary). This is called an *equivocal* view at the group level by Dansereau and colleagues (1984) and a case of "independence" by Klein and colleagues (1994). A good example of a study of this type is one by Dansereau, Yammarino, Markham, Alutto, and colleagues (1995), who report that superiors provide a sense of self-worth to subordinates as individuals in exchange for subordinates performing in ways that satisfy the superior (such as by increasing the quality of their performance).

Summary

The ability to decide among these alternatives—wholes, parts, and equivocal condition—involves the question of *single-level analysis.* Specifically, the question is this: When we examine the relationship between superiors and their subordinates, which of the three views (wholes, parts, or equivocal) is hypothesized? These alternatives have been fully described and developed in a variety of articles (Avolio & Bass, 1995; Dansereau & Alutto, 1991; Dansereau & Markham, 1987a, 1987b; Dansereau, Yammarino, & Markham, 1995; Dansereau, Yammarino, Markham, Alutto, et al., 1995; Klein & House, 1995; Markham, 1988; Markham & McKee, 1991, 1995; Schriesheim, Cogliser, and Neider, 1995; Yammarino, 1990, 1998, in press; Yammarino & Dubinsky, 1992, 1994; Yammarino, Dubinsky, Comer, & Jolson, 1997; Yammarino & Markham, 1992) and books (Dansereau et al., 1984; Dansereau & Yammarino, 1998a, 1998b). Moreover, what is very clear from this line of work is that the views of wholes and parts and the equivocal view are not limited to the realm of superior-subordinate relationships; the three alternatives are relevant to a vast number of constructs and domains in the field.

Multiple-Variable Analysis

To permit and not prohibit any one of the three alternative views, it was necessary to allow for the possibility that different variables, or sets of variables, at any one level of analysis might be considered in terms of wholes, parts, or equivocal views. Specifically, one set of variables might refer to wholes (for example, consideration of the supervisor's and the work group's performance). A second set of variables might refer to parts (for example, delegation and performance in the work group). A third set of variables might refer to the equivocal view (for example, giving a sense of self-worth to and receiving performance from an individual). This creates a complex set of possibilities; for example, we can have the following six variables, which are related in pairs but independent of one another:

Wholes superior consideration (x_1) $\leftrightarrow$ work group performance (y_1)

Parts superior delegation (x_2) $\leftrightarrow$ performance within work groups (y_2)

Equivocal condition superior provides self-worth (x_3) $\leftrightarrow$ satisfying performance by subordinate as preferred by superior (y_3)

In addition, x_1 and y_1 are independent of x_2 and y_2, all of which are independent of x_3 and y_3. Thus there is the notion of independence among the variables. It was necessary to be able to identify formulations of variables of this type when variables were more unrelated than related. In this way, different variables could be viewed as associated with different levels of analysis. A focus on this type of question is called *multiple-variable analysis*. This analysis answers the following question: What are the relationships among an entire set of variables at multiple levels: are they related, unrelated, or something in between? In the preceding case, for example, with six variables that are related only in pairs, there are only three nonzero relationships. The remaining twelve correlations are near zero. Thus the variables, as a set, are generally unrelated.

Multiple-Level Analysis

It is, of course, not sufficient to consider superiors and work groups in isolation. It is also necessary to consider the context in which the superiors and work groups are embedded. For example, Pfeffer (1977) suggests that what a superior does may be a reflection of organizational and structural characteristics rather than of the superior as a person. This possibility requires more than just recognition that supervisors and their groups are embedded in higher-level units called *collectives* (for example, departments); rather, these higher-level units serve as alternative explanations of leadership for any differences that one observes between superiors. Such differences would not reflect leadership per se or the relationship between superiors and subordinates as persons; rather, they would reflect the structural characteristics in the particular setting. Therefore, *multiple-level* analysis is required.

This possibility creates two issues that must be addressed. First, any level of analysis can be considered in any of the three views (wholes, parts, or equivocal); and, second, when levels are nested (for example, groups within collectives), it is necessary to allow for all alternatives at each level. Accordingly, the effects at a higher level (collective level) may apply at a lower level. In this case, where effects generalize up one level (to the collective), leadership per se is not asserted because leadership focuses on the individual and the group and not on the collective. Alternatively, the effects at a higher level may not apply at a lower level (the equivocal condition). In the latter case, leadership, but not collective-level effects, would be asserted because the results would involve leaders as individuals and their work groups. This is a critical issue because it goes to the heart of what leadership is and is not.

To illustrate the point, consider the following simple chart, where *yes* means acceptance of a level and *no* means rejection of that level of analysis:[1]

	Not Just Leadership (Cross-Level)	Leadership (Level-Specific)	System (Emergent)	No Effects (Null)
Collective level	Yes	No	Yes	No
Group level	Yes	Yes	No	No

In the first case ("Not Just Leadership"), there are not only leadership effects but also collective-level effects. For example, a leader may behave as everyone else does in the department (collective), which is a structural and not purely individual-level leadership effect. In the second case ("Leadership"), the leadership variable does not aggregate to the higher level. Accordingly, only leadership is asserted. In the third case ("System"), there are collective-level effects that do not disaggregate to the lower (group) level. This is not leadership but system-level effects. A fourth case ("No

Effects"), as the heading of the column implies, permits no effects in terms of the focal levels of analysis. Thus the varient approach was developed as a way of being able to ascertain whether a leadership effect at one level of analysis (person and group) was actually a reflection of an effect at a higher (collective) level. The multiple-level question is this: Does a set of variables apply to one or several levels of analysis?

Multiple-Relationship Analysis

Finally, it was necessary to allow for the possibility that one view (for example, wholes) may serve as a boundary condition for or interact with another view (for example, parts). For example, consideration at the group level may serve as a boundary on the degree to which superiors delegate differentially to subordinates within groups. In addition, the degree to which superiors delegate (group-parts view) may serve as a boundary on the degree to which superiors provide self-worth to individuals (individual-level view). As a specific example, one may need to receive delegation before one can develop a sense of self-worth at the individual level. This is called *multiple-relationship* analysis because it focuses on the same relationships among variables under different conditions.

It is important to recognize that multiple-relationship analysis also applies to multiple levels of analysis. For example, subsystems in organizations may be more or less conducive to the development of leadership relationships. To be more specific, in more loosely coupled systems (Weick, 1976) leadership may be more likely to occur than it is in tightly coupled systems. In this approach, a relationship between variables does not hold at a particular level (a traditional moderator effect), and the variance of the variable also indicates that the "leadership" level does not hold in a tightly coupled system. Instead, a relationship may hold at the individual (nongroup) level but be equivocal at the dyad and group levels in a tightly coupled systems. It is also critical to note that the issue here is not the identification of a moderator variable at one level of analysis. For example, consider the case of how the interaction of consideration and structure influences performance. This latter type of interaction or contingency approach is straightforward with the use of traditional approaches. The point of the varient approach is that variables at a *higher* level of analysis moderate the "existence" of *lower* levels of analysis. Finally, this notion of multiple-relationship analysis also implies that, to examine a moderator, one needs to have variables at a higher level of analysis that are different from variables at the lower level of analysis. Again, it is important to keep in mind that multiple-relationship analysis focuses on identifying conditions where different levels occur, and that this approach goes beyond the moderation of relationships among variables at one level of analysis.

Summary of the Impetus for the Technique

Table 10.1 summarizes, on the basis of the reasons why the paradigm was created, the various purposes of the varient paradigm and WABA. Essentially, the varient paradigm was created both to allow for multiple-level theorizing and to test for the viability of a theorist's assertions. A theorist asserts different variables and relationships among them for multiple levels (individual, group, collective) and from the different perspectives (wholes, parts, equivocal). Whether variables are viewed as independent or correlated depends on the theory. Variables can represent different dimensions at different levels, or they can represent the same dimension at different levels. In addition to direct interdependence among variables, an interaction across levels can be specified, where higher levels influence effects at lower levels. The varient paradigm was developed to allow for theories about these types of multiple variables, single levels, multiple levels, multiple relationships, and cross-level effects and multiple-level interactions. These points are summarized in Table 10.1 for the four analyses.

Theoretical Issues and Assumptions

The varient paradigm deals with all the issues shown in Table 10.1. In addition, the paradigm was designed to allow multiple alternatives to be considered simultaneously in developing and testing a theory. One assumption underlying the paradigm is that one "tests" a theory by ruling out equally plausible alternatives. The four analyses contained in the paradigm, which correspond to the four key questions in Table 10.1, make the assumptions listed in the following sections.

Table 10.1. Purpose of Varient Paradigm and WABA.

Purpose	Alternatives	Name of Analysis
Allow and test for three views at one level of analysis	Wholes (homogeneous) Equivocal (independence) Parts (heterogeneous)	Single-level analysis
Allow and test for higher levels of analysis to be or not to be the basis of effects at lower levels of analysis	Cross-level Level-specific Emergent	Multiple-level analysis
Allow for different variables and relationships to associate with different levels or views of one level; allow for groups, persons within groups, and collective effects	Related Generally related Generally unrelated Unrelated	Multiple-variable analysis
Allow for higher-level variables to serve as contingencies for lower levels of analysis	Contingent Noncontingent (multiplexed)	Multiple-relationship analysis

Single-Level Analysis

An example should illustrate the assumptions of the varient approach at one level of analysis. Imagine five groups, each composed of three individuals. The varient approach suggests that the individual group members may display four alternative configurations in their groups.

First, the groups may comprise homogeneous members: all individuals do the same thing. In this way, the individuals are positively correlated on a particular variable: a wholes perspective in each group (r = 1.0).

Second, the three persons in each group may form groups in which individuals are interdependent so that what one individual does, another person does not do (r = −1.0). In this way, there is a negative relationship between individuals in the group: a parts perspective. These two alternative views illustrate one assumption that underlies this approach:

1a.   *The wholes and parts views of groups are at two ends of a continuum.*

At the wholes end of the continuum, groups are composed of homogeneous individuals (no within-groups focus), and the groups differ from one another (a between-groups focus). In contrast, at the other end of the continuum all groups are the same (no differences between groups) in that each is differentiated in a similar, relativistic way (a within-groups focus). Along the continuum, there are a number of points. Nevertheless, at the wholes endpoint, all individuals are positively related in the sense that the scores in the group remain the same so that if one individual increases his or her score, the others do the same (r = +). At the parts endpoint, the individuals are negatively related in the sense that the scores are individually related so that if one individual increases his or her score, another decreases his or her score (r = −).

In addition to the wholes and parts alternatives, there is a midpoint (between +1 and −1) where there are differences both between and within groups. This zero point is the case in which individuals are not interdependent but rather independent (r = 0). This would be the case in our example of groups of three individuals when the individuals do not form a group but remain as individuals. One view of these conditions is that the zero value represents individual differences among individuals. This point illustrates a second assumption of the approach:

1b.   *Between the wholes and parts conditions are nonaggregatable points that represent independence among individuals in the group. There are two ways to view these nonaggregatable points: the within-group differences and between-group differences are both error, or they are both valid. In the former case, the lower-level nonaggregated variables are error. In the latter case, the lower-level nonaggregatable variables are valid representations at the lower level.*

A third assumption of this approach is as follows:

1c. *There are two alternative views of one level of analysis (wholes or parts)
and two alternative views that suggest a rejection of that level of analysis (equivocal and null).*

The upper portion of Table 10.2 summarizes these conceptually based points in terms of how each alternative is conceptualized
via differences between units and within units or entities. Another
way to summarize all the assumptions is in terms of the following
continuum:

Endpoint	Midpoint	Endpoint
Wholes	Equivocal	Parts
$(r = +1)$	$(r = 0)$	$(r = -1)$

This shows that WABA assumes basically that correlations run from
+1 to −1, which includes a value of zero at the midpoint in the range.
This continuum shows the need to develop decision points along
the continuum so that one can infer which of the three alternatives

Table 10.2. Plausible Alternatives for
Single-Level Analysis and Empirical Representations.

Alternatives	Focus Between Units (e.g., Groups)	Focus Within Units (e.g., Groups)
Wholes	Valid	Error
Parts	Error	Valid
Equivocal	Valid	Valid
Inexplicable	Error	Error

Empirical Representation	Between		Within	Difference
Wholes	r_B	>	r_W	+
Equivocal	$r_B = +$	=	$r_W = +$	0
Null	$r_B = 0$	=	$r_W = 0$	0
Parts	r_B	<	r_W	−

seems more likely. Of course, the question of which alternative to choose must be based on theory as well as on data. Before we turn to this empirical issue, it is necessary to focus on multiple levels rather than on just one level of analysis.

Multiple-Level Analysis

To illustrate the assumptions for multiple-level analysis, an example may be helpful. Let us say at the group level that we have selected wholes. This means, by definition, that we have rejected the parts, equivocal, and null conditions given in the continuum. Now we can focus on whole groups embedded within collectives (for example, departments or organizations). There are again four alternatives at the collective level. The groups can be homogenized into collectives and can differ between collectives: the wholes ($r = +1$) alternative. The groups can be negatively interdependent within the collectives in that the more of something one group does, the less of it the others do ($r = -1$). Or the groups can remain groups ($r = 0$) and not be influenced by the higher level of analysis. The first example we call a *cross-level* effect because it applies both to groups and collectives. The second example is also a *cross-level* effect in that whole groups become parts of collectives. The third example we call *level-specific* in that the group does not aggregate to the higher (collective) level. This illustration is limited by the assertion that whole groups apply at the lower level. Therefore, it is necessary to develop a very different alternative case. In this alternative case, we do not begin with groups; rather, we argue that only the collective level is viable. In this case, the lower-level groups fail to serve as the basis for the collective level. This is called an *emergent* effect (that is, a nonreducible higher-level effect).

These alternatives illustrate the assumptions that underlie the varient approach to multiple levels of analysis:

2a. *For any two levels of analysis, effects may hold at (1) both levels, (2) only the higher level, (3) only the lower level, or (4) neither level.*

The upper portion of Table 10.3 summarizes these alternatives, using the ideas from Table 10.2. Essentially, any level can be viewed as contained in another level (that is, cross-level), not contained in the higher level (that is, level-specific), or not based on a lower level (that is, emergent). Thus an additional assumption is as follows:

2b. *Any number of levels of analysis can be considered if the focus is on two levels of analysis at a time.*

Of course, the decision to select one of these alternative views for a set of levels of analysis should be based on both theory and data. Before we consider this empirical issue, it is necessary to consider multiple variables.

Multiple-Variable Analysis

One of the unique features of the varient approach is that different variables may associate with different combinations of levels of analysis. For example, some variables may reflect whole persons, whole groups, and whole collectives, whereas others may reflect only whole groups and not persons or collectives. Therefore, the assumption is as follows:

3a. *Different variables can associate with different levels of analysis or combinations of levels of analysis.*

Table 10.3. Plausible Alternatives for Multiple-Level Analysis.

Alternatives	Lower Level	Higher Level
Cross-level	Valid	Valid
Level-specific	Valid	Error
Emergent	Error	Valid
Null	Error	Error

Empirical Representation	Lower Level	Higher Level
Cross-level	Wholes	Wholes
	Wholes	Parts
Level-specific	Wholes	Equivocal
	Parts	Null
Emergent	Equivocal or independence	Wholes
	Equivocal or independence	Parts

This allows one to state a specific number of the alternative theoretical formulations implied by any one theoretical position. For example, suppose we are interested in supervisory consideration as a whole-person concept (x_1) and its relationship to a whole-work-group variable, such as group performance (y_1). But suppose at the same time that we are interested in delegation within groups (x_2) and within-group performance (y_2)—a parts formulation. Given the way wholes and parts are defined, one would expect relationships between x_1 and y_1 as well as between x_2 and y_2, but not between the two sets of variables (that is, x_1 and y_1 would not be related to x_2 and y_2). To state this differently, we expect to find two significant relationships, and all the other relationships between these variables will be near zero. Multiple-variable analysis places such a formulation (that is, x_1 and y_1 are related, and x_2 and y_2 are related, but all other correlations are near zero) in a context of alternative ways to formulate relationships among a set of variables. For example, the formulation just described is very different from a multiple-regression type of formulation, such as $x_1 + x_2 = y_1$ in which x_1 and x_2, although unrelated, would, given some relationship, both relate to y_1. The upper portion of Table 10.4 illustrates these alternatives. Again, of course, the selection of alternatives is based on both theory and data. Before we turn to such empirical issues, we need to consider the set of alternatives and assumptions included in multiple-relationship analysis.

Multiple-Relationship Analysis

A final concern of the varient approach is that the existence of lower levels of analysis may be contingent on higher levels of analysis, and vice versa. We are not talking about interactions among variables, such as those that can be considered with multiple-variable or multiple-regression analyses, nor are we talking about finding different or similar slopes of relationships among variables inside different entities, as can be done with hierarchical linear modeling (HLM). Here the focus is on how the actual emergence of one level of analysis depends on effects or variables at a higher level of analysis. This includes the variance and covariance of the variables. For example, in organizations that are more loosely coupled (whole organization–level effects), leadership effects at the

Table 10.4. Plausible Alternatives for Multiple-Variable Analysis.

Alternatives	Characteristics
Related	All variables related
Generally related	More variables related than unrelated
Mixed	Variables equally related and unrelated
Generally unrelated	More variables unrelated than related
Unrelated	All variables unrelated

Empirical Representation	Characteristics
Related	x, y, z all related
Generally related	$x \perp y$, $x \leftrightarrow z$, $y \leftrightarrow z$
Mixed	none
Generally unrelated	$x \perp z$, $y \perp z$, $x \leftrightarrow y$
Unrelated	x, y, z all unrelated

group level may be more likely to occur, whereas in less loosely coupled organizations, only individual-level effects may be found. Obviously, the organization level of analysis may depend on leadership effects as well. The assumption underlying this element of the varient approach is as follows:

4a. *Effects or levels of analysis may or may not influence the very existence of (effects at) other levels of analysis.*

Table 10.5 summarizes the alternatives in this analysis. The decision about whether there are no effects of lower and higher levels on each other—a level-of-analysis type of interaction—is based on theoretical as well as empirical issues. We now turn to such empirical issues for all the analyses.

Basic Logic of the Technique

The following example illustrates the basic logic of the varient paradigm and the WABA technique. Let us say one hypothesizes that superiors' treatment of their subordinates varies from superior to

Table 10.5. Plausible Alternatives for Multiple-Relationship Analysis.

Alternatives	Meaning	
Contingent	Effects at one level moderate effects at other levels and the existence of the other level	
Multiplexed	Simultaneous effects at different levels	

Empirical Representatives	One Condition	Other Condition
Multiplexed	Wholes	Wholes
Multiplexed	Parts	Parts
Contingent	Wholes	Null or equivocal
Contingent	Parts	Null or equivocal

superior, and that this variation relates to the performance of whole groups of subordinates. Such a statement can be converted to the following set of testable assertions:

Single-level analysis: Select a focus on differences between whole groups for subordinates, and between whole persons for superiors. This is selected instead of a focus within groups or within superiors (a parts view).

Multiple-level analysis: For superiors, select a level-specific formulation in that superiors' behaviors reflect their personal styles, not collective-level effects. For subordinates, select cross-level effects in that group performance is viewed as an aggregate of individual performance. Also select level-specific because groups are not viewed as embedded in collectives for this set of variables.

Multiple-variable analysis: Select the related-variables case (consideration and performance are related).

Multiple-relationship analysis: Select the multiplexed view that group-level effects occur simultaneously with and are not contingent on other effects at higher levels of analysis.

This theoretical specification is relatively simple. It is in the empirical testing that the varient approach presents challenges in analyzing data. To illustrate, given the preceding selections, suppose a researcher decides to take an assumptive approach and aggregates individual reports about the same superior, uses the average for each group, and does the same with the performance measure. This procedure is in line with the specifications of single-level analysis and theory. Likewise, on the basis of multiple-level analysis, because the researcher did not expect differences to be due to levels above the work group (for example, the collective level), the researcher assumes that this holds, and he or she samples only work groups, giving no consideration to the collectives in which the whole groups are embedded. Moreover, on the basis of multiple-variable analysis, the researcher might examine only the relationship between performance and leadership style because that is assumed to be the relationship of interest. Finally, on the basis of multiple-relationship analysis, these results are expected to hold regardless of the setting. Therefore, the researcher assumes that this holds, and he or she samples across different kinds of settings (for example, across organizations).

The preceding example precludes the use of the varient approach by *assuming* that the theory is correct (except perhaps for the question of whether the two variables—consideration and performance—are related). From a varient perspective, the following problems arise:

1. In terms of single-level analysis, the use of averages may not be justifiable, because averages often reflect only individual differences rather than whole-work-group effects. In the latter case, averages would be group performance scores; in the former case, averages would just be individual differences and would not reflect group differences. The point, of course, is that averages can have two meanings (an issue of single-level analysis).
2. Failure to give empirical consideration to the levels in which a focal level (work group) may embed prohibits testing for the possibility that obtained results may reflect differences between collectives rather than solely differences between individuals and groups (an issue of multiple-level analysis).
3. The choice to examine only two variables fails to allow for the establishment of convergent and discriminant validity (an issue of multiple-variable analysis).

4. Failure to consider the different conditions in the data makes it unclear when or if the results will replicate across settings (an issue of multiple-relationship analysis).

The reason why the illustrative strategy selected by this assumptive (nonvarient) approach fails, from the varient perspective, is that the alternatives selected on the basis of theory are not tested relative to other alternatives, which are viewed as equally plausible in the varient approach. Instead, the alternatives are assumed not to be applicable. In our view, it makes sense to assert or select, on the basis of theory, one set of alternatives as the focal set of hypotheses for empirical testing, but it seems to us inadequate and less rigorous to test only one set of alternatives in isolation, or without comparing them to other viable alternatives. Therefore, we will now illustrate the logic that underlies each analysis used in the varient paradigm to compare and test these alternative formulations.

Single-Level Analysis

Basic Logic

In single-level analysis, as shown in Table 10.2, differences between and within units at the level of interest discriminate among the four alternatives. In WABA, the question is whether there is validity or error within or between units. In terms of between variance (BV) and within variance (WV), we can say the following:

Wholes	$BV > WV$
Equivocal	$BV = WV > 0$
Parts	$BV < WV$
Null	$BV = WV \approx 0$

In this case, (1) greater variance between groups than within groups indicates wholes, (2) equal variance between and within groups indicates equivocal, and (3) greater variance within than between groups indicates parts. The F-ratio of the one-way analysis of variance (ANOVA) provides a test of the statistical significance as follows:

Wholes	$F > 1$
Equivocal	$F \approx 1$
Parts	$F < 1$

In addition, we can estimate between-and-within variance on the basis of eta correlations. For example, the between eta correlation of η_{BX} is the correlation of a raw score (x) with the average for the group ($\bar{x}$). The within-group eta correlation (η_{WX}) is the correlation of the raw score with deviations from the group average (x − $\bar{x}$). The intervals range from "mainly within groups" to "mainly between groups" and can be represented in terms of *variance* as follows:

Wholes	$\eta_B > 66$ percent	$\eta_W < 33$ percent
Equivocal	33 percent $< \eta_B < 66$ percent	33 percent $< \eta_W < 66$ percent
Parts	$\eta_B < 33$ percent	$\eta_W > 66$ percent

Dansereau and colleagues (1984) base the decision points not just on variance but also on geometric properties called the 15° and 30° tests. The 15° values approximate the case where one-third of the possible results are distributed to each alternative (wholes, equivocal, parts). The idea, of course, is to try and decide whether there is

More variation between groups = wholes

Equal variation between and within groups = independence

More variation within groups = parts

In this procedure, significantly less variation between groups than within groups is assumed to indicate error between groups. Likewise, significantly less variation within groups than between groups is assumed to indicate error within groups.

A second factor, beyond variance, that we can use to assess whether there is validity or error is covariance. If we use correlations based on averages (r_{BXY}) and correlations based on within-group scores (r_{WXY}), we can then decide among the alternatives as follows:

Wholes	$r_{BXY} > r_{WXY}$	Difference
Equivocal	$r_{BXY} = r_{WXY} > 0$	No Difference
Parts	$r_{BXY} < r_{WXY}$	Difference
Inexplicable	$r_{BXY} = r_{WXY} = 0$	No Difference

Tests of the differences between the correlations, called the A-test and the Z-test, are used to decide which condition (wholes, parts, equivocal, or null) fits with the data.

Finally, a critical aspect of the WABA approach is that any correlation—say, between individual reports of consideration and performance—can actually be broken down into a between-group component and a within-group component. The between-group component equals the between eta correlations for x and for y multiplied by the between-group correlation. The within-group component equals the within eta correlations for x and for y multiplied by the within-group correlation. These components form the WABA equation:

$$\text{Total correlation} = \text{between component (BC)}$$
$$+ \text{within component (WC)}$$
$$r_{XY} = \eta_{BX}\, \eta_{BY}\, r_{BXY} + \eta_{WX}\, \eta_{WY}\, r_{WXY}$$

Because the components are determined by the etas and the correlations, the tests just described determine the results of the inference process. Specifically,

Wholes	$BC > WC$
Equivocal	$BC = WC > 0$
Parts	$BC < WC$
Null	$BC = WC = 0$

These points are summarized in the lower portion of Table 10.2.

Comparison to Other Analytical Strategies

Proponents of the within-group agreement approach have at times criticized WABA (e.g., George & James, 1993; James, 1998). But as Schriesheim, Cogliser, and Neider (1998) point out, WABA and the within-group agreement approach can complement each other. If one were to find differences between groups, James's approach (r_{wg}) could be used to test whether the scores within *all* groups are indeed very similar. In other words, WABA can be viewed as a kind of pretest to ensure that there are group-level effects or differences between groups across a set of groups. In contrast, r_{wg} is an indicator of the agreement for *each* group separately.

Other researchers use ANOVA to test for between-group effects and use r_{wg} to examine within-group agreement, but these approaches do not consider the eta correlations.

Multiple-Level Analysis

Basic Logic

Once they have been identified at one level of analysis, it is possible to consider the between-group scores (averages), if wholes are inferred, and examine the data at a higher level of analysis (for example, the collective level), using the same decision process as described for single-level analysis. Clearly, wholes at the lower level ($\bar{x}_J$) may be parts ($\bar{x}_J - \bar{x}_K$), wholes ($\bar{x}_K$), or equivocal ($\bar{x}_J$) at the next highest level (where J represents groups and K represents collectives). Interestingly, if parts are inferred at a (lower) level, the differences between groups at that level are error, by definition. Therefore, at the next highest level, parts will not hold, because there are no valid differences between groups. This means that parts remain parts for one set of variables across levels.

It is of particular importance that multiple-level analysis allows for an inference of equivocal at a lower-level analysis and then an examination of the between-groups scores at the higher level. The notion is that the variable at the lower level may not be valid. However, by taking the average of the lower-level scores and examining the data at the next highest level, parts or wholes may emerge. These points are summarized in the lower part of Table 10.3.

Comparison to Other Approaches

The point of WABA is to test which of any number of levels may apply for a particular set of variables. No attempt is made to assess how much of the variance or covariance can be attributed to one level of analysis rather than another. After an identification that a particular set of variables (say, x_1 and x_2) shows wholes at the group level and the individual level, we could examine, using hierarchical linear modeling (HLM), whether the set of (independent) variables at the group level relates to a second (dependent) variable (y) at the individual level. For example, we could consider whether the consideration and the structure (x_1 and x_2) of the leader at the group level relate to individual (y) performance. All that WABA attempts to do is to decide whether it is reasonable to assert a particular level or combination of levels will be appropriate for a particular set of variables—for example, a set of variables at the group level (x_1 and x_2) and one at the individual level (y). After this decision is made, HLM (Raudenbush, 1995) or structural equation modeling (SEM) can be used. (See Dansereau, Yammarino, Markham, Alutto, et al., 1995, for an example of the use of SEM.) One can then use WABA as an initial screening approach, which indicates the validity of assertions that certain levels may apply. There is nothing inherently contradictory between WABA and HLM or SEM. Each analysis provides a different piece of information. As should be apparent, it depends on the theoretical question of interest.

Multiple-Variable Analysis

Basic Logic

Multiple-variable analysis takes all the variables in a theoretically specified set and considers three variables at a time to assess the structure of the relationships among all the variables. For example, one can ask whether all the variables are about equally correlated. If so, this is the related-variables case. Are all the variables unrelated? If so, then this is the unrelated-variables case. Are the variables related more than not related? If yes, then this is the generally-related-variables case. If it is the opposite, then it is the generally-unrelated-variables case. This analysis uses Hotelling's t-test and an A-test to select among the alternatives. These ideas are summarized in the lower portion of Table 10.4.

Comparison to Other Approaches

Multiple-variable analysis examines the simple bivariate correlations among variables. A multiple-regression formulation is viewed as only one plausible condition—for example, if the independent variables correlate more strongly with the dependent variable than with each other, then a multiple-regression type formulation is suggested. In other cases, the analysis may identify two networks of variables that are not related. In this latter case, a multiple-regression formulation would not be viewed as appropriate.

Schriesheim (1995) has extended WABA so that one can examine multiple regressions rather than bivariate correlations. Essentially, one can think of the independent variables, when weighted by their beta weights, as one variable. The dependent variable is the second variable. Accordingly, one can use all WABA procedures with multiple regression. Therefore, multiple-variable analysis and multiple regression are quite compatible within WABA. In cases where the degrees of freedom for the variables in a regression equation are not equal but definable with WABA, HLM can be used as a form of regression. It is important to note that, unlike multiple-relationship analysis (described later), HLM does *not* allow that lower levels may *not* be applicable within higher levels; that is to say, HLM *assumes* that particular levels apply (a higher and a lower level). For example, HLM may consider the differences in slopes among individual-level reports separately, depending on the collective within which the individuals embed. In contrast, multiple-relationship analysis, to which we now turn, tests which levels hold within other levels. In other words, multiple-relationship analysis allows for the possibility that only individual-level effects may hold in one organization, and that individual-level and group-level effects may hold in another organization.

Multiple-Relationship Analysis

Basic Logic

Multiple-relationship analysis is, by default, a part of any WABA analysis. Any set of data is viewed as potentially embedded within a particular condition. A data set may or may not contain such conditions, but every data analysis is assumed in WABA as collected under one condition. Multiple-relationship analysis compares the level-of-analysis results in one condition with the results in any number of other conditions. Let us say that wholes are asserted for one set of variables in two conditions, and that parts are asserted for a second set of variables in only one of the two conditions. This is a situation in which two different views of the one level (parts and wholes) apply to different variables. But it is also the case that there are marked differences between the two conditions. In one condition, there are wholes and parts, whereas in the other condition the level is wholes with *no* parts. One can perform a complete WABA for any number of correlations within any number of conditions and compare the results for each condition. Such analyses test for the differences between the conditions in terms of levels of analysis, using A and Z tests as well as an assessment of variance in each condition. The lower portion of Table 10.5 illustrates this approach.

Comparison to Other Approaches

Multiple-relationship analysis is unique in comparison with other approaches because the level of analysis, not the relationship among variables, is viewed as changing according to conditions. Therefore, it really has no comparable analytical analog. Although it is possible to use Schriesheim's (1995) multivariate approach, the degrees of freedom are not clear for the interaction term for variables at different levels. The general idea is that variables and their relationships may apply at different levels of analysis according to the conditions specified.

Questions Addressable and Not Addressable with the Technique

The varient approach is both a deductive and an inductive approach to developing and testing theories. As such, it does not fit with approaches that are only inductive or only deductive in nature.

Comparison to Inductive Approaches

A key inductive approach is cluster analysis, which is an alternative to WABA. In this approach, the user provides only variables, and the groups are then generated on the basis of the data. In WABA, one has to specify the levels (for example, groups) before the analysis, and WABA tests this assertion about levels. One reason why cluster analysis can perform this task is that, unlike WABA, it often ensures that within-group variation is minimized in forming clusters (a wholes view for single-level analysis). Moreover, usually one level is found with cluster analyses (a level-specific assumption for multiple-level analysis), and the variables are assumed to be independent (a generally unrelated case for multiple-variable analysis). Moreover, there is no expectation of any condition that would indicate a lack of groups (a multiplexed condition for multiple-relationship analysis). Once all these factors are regarded as given in cluster analysis, the procedure will faithfully generate groups.

Network analysis is another variation of the same mainly inductive approach. It uses a set of definitions and analyzes nominations or evaluations of individuals by other individuals. It then constructs a within-group picture of the individuals represented in the sample. Here again, there is no initial specification of levels of analysis; rather, a series of simplifying assumptions is used to derive a network. To state this idea differently, if one wants to analyze data and derive the definition of a group without asserting any groups (or levels) in advance, then WABA does not apply. WABA is not a purely inductive approach.

This is not to say that WABA does not have an inductive component. It clearly does. Let us say that a researcher theorizes that two variables (for example, support for self-worth and performance) are related, on the basis of a superior's providing support for self-worth to the group as a whole (a whole-person and whole-group formulation). Moreover, a researcher asserts that this notion has nothing to do with collective-level effects (multiple-level analysis). In addition, theoretically, the researcher believes that such effects do not depend on the conditions in which they are measured (multiple-relationship analysis). Actual data using WABA may show that the results do not reflect the style of the leader but rather the individualized leadership relationship of each subordinate with the leader (an equivocal result at the person level for superiors and at the group level for subordinates). This would be an inductive finding. Let us say the remaining assertions hold in that the collective level is not appropriate and effects hold across conditions. This would be a deductive finding.

When results such as those just described do not correspond with an original theoretical assertion, and when another, equally likely alternative is suggested, WABA provides "inductive" information that can be useful in later deductive research. To return to the preceding example, the researcher might now begin to hypothesize about why superiors view each subordinate as a unique individual independent of other individuals, and about why subordinates remain individuals and do not form a group. This would create the hypothesis of a purely dyadic interpersonal relationship (Dansereau, Yammarino, Markham, Alutto, et al., 1995). The approach does not work, however, without the specification of variables as well as entities or levels of analysis. In contrast, cluster and network analyses require the specification of only variables.

Comparison to Deductive Approaches

There are a variety of purely deductive approaches that take a perspective different from that of WABA and the varient paradigm. The most obvious position is one in which a theorist predicts a certain set of alternatives and then looks at only those alternatives, ignoring all the equally plausible ones that have been implicitly rejected in the approach (see Tables 10.2, 10.3, 10.4, and 10.5). As an example, a theorist may select as follows:

Single-level analysis	Whole groups
Multiple-level analysis:	Level-specific and emergent
Multiple-variable analysis:	A multiple-regression formulation with an interaction term
Multiple-relationship analysis:	No contingencies based on level differences

This is a popular deductive approach. Using the preceding assertions as assumptions, a theorist might obtain scores for groups and focus only on groups (no single-level or multiple-level analysis). The theorist might use a regression equation (no multiple-variable analysis) and assume that the same level of analysis applies across all conditions (no multiple-relationship analysis).

The work of Huselid (1995) that focuses on the interesting relationship between an organization's human resources practices and organization-level performance is an example of this type of research. There is little consideration, theoretically or empirically, of other ways to disaggregate below the organization level, nor is there theoretical discussion of the basis for the aggregation of data to the organization level. There is also little consideration of how these factors may apply at lower levels of analysis. There is little consideration of the possibility that different human resources practices may operate at different levels, nor is there much consideration of whether the levels of analysis of interest may vary across different conditions. In such a purely deductive strategy, there is no place for WABA. The questions that WABA addresses are considered irrelevant, known, given by a theory, or perhaps important to study only at some later time. This means that various assumptions are taken to be "true," at least tacitly. By contrast, the varient approach argues that such an assertion should be tested and considered on both a theoretical and an empirical basis. This would allow for an extension of Huselid's (1995) work.

The purely deductive approach (as illustrated by the work of Huselid, 1995) is not limited to approaches that assert wholes. For example, one can take a purely deductive approach and argue that individuals are the unit of analysis, and that there are also between-group and within-group effects. Thus individual differences are sampled, and within-group indicators (for example, variance) and between-group indicators (for example, means) are examined. This approach assumes that there are group effects. From a varient perspective, this approach makes it impossible to argue that there is *not* a group effect. There is, by assumption, some type of group effect on individuals that allows for the examination of means and variances. According to this approach, the only way to reject group-level effects is if there are null results. In contrast, the varient approach requires more than the simple rejection of a null hypothesis. It requires the rejection of the *equally likely* plausible alternatives implied by a particular theoretical specification about levels. Proponents of the purely deductive approach may view this testing requirement for levels of WABA as "awkward" because one cannot directly ensure group-level effects and variance but instead must test them. Nevertheless, additional tests are required because the varient approach does not assume that any theoretical assertion about levels is correct.

Deductive and Inductive Approaches

Between the extreme deductive and the extreme inductive positions reside different degrees of incorporation of various combinations of the two approaches relative to the varient approach. For example, consider a zero-degree test (Dansereau et al., 1984), which means that on the continuum from "between groups (wholes)" to "within groups (parts)" there are really only two categories: between groups and within groups. Thus there is no interval for the equivocal condition, only one point. In this case, as is common, the idea is that there is only a wholes condition (between-group variation is valid and within-group variation is error) and a null condition. Compare this to the view shown in Table 10.2 that describes four conditions and permits intervals for the wholes, parts, and equivocal conditions. The analysis performed by Yammarino and Markham (1992) illustrates how there are no group effects when all three, rather than only two, intervals are allowed. When one does not allow for all the conditions shown in Tables 10.2 to 10.5, the researcher is using only selected elements of WABA.

In the traditional ANOVA framework, within-cell (or within-group) variance is viewed as error. In WABA, by contrast, within-group variance is viewed as potentially valid, as noted by Hays (1985). Thus, although the F-ratio from a one-way ANOVA is used in WABA, it is viewed as a necessary but not sufficient test. In WABA, the F-ratio is used in conjunction with an E-test.

In a somewhat similar fashion, James (1998) describes the use of r_{wg} to test for agreement in groups. We believe that, after using WABA to demonstrate variation between groups, researchers can use r_{wg} to test how much agreement is within each group, after the fashion of Schriesheim and his colleagues (1995), which answers a different question from the one involved in WABA. By contrast, James (1998) seems to argue that only r_{wg} should be used, because inherent range restriction can result. According to James (1998), when range restriction occurs, there is lack of between-group differences even though there is substantial within-group agreement. This is a different model from the one involved in WABA. WABA assumes that if a researcher wants to assess a variable that varies mainly between groups, the researcher will try to obtain between-group variability in the variable of interest, in alignment with the theory. The WABA position is simple: when we find significant between-group variation, we can look at r_{wg}; when the between-group and within-group variations are comparable, there is a failure to obtain a group effect. Accordingly, James's procedure may convert equivocal effects found in WABA into group effects using r_{wg} (Schriesheim et al., 1995). This will tend to occur at times because James's approach views parts as nonexistent or as error.

As Schriesheim, Cogliser, and Neider (1998, p. 70) point out in response to James (1998), "The one apparent point where James (1998) wishes to take issue with our presentation concerns our recommendation that when WABA and r_{wg} disagree, WABA results should be given greater weight in drawing conclusions." They go on to say:

> Thus, what we were arguing is not that WABA I is a better indicator of within-group agreement than is r_{wg}, but that if WABA I between-groups variance is small, large between-groups WABA II effects cannot be obtained. This, of course, does not address the issue of whether one can rightfully conclude that groups "exist"—it addresses only the issue of whether groups "matter." James is therefore entirely correct in that computed r_{wg} statistics will speak to the former issue better than will WABA I when range restriction exists in group means. We, however, felt that the latter issue was of generally greater interest to researchers and so that, when conflict in WABA–r_{wg} findings [is] obtained, the WABA results will be more useful overall [p. 70].

In a similar way, HLM assumes that the levels for a particular variable are known. For example, there are districts, schools, and student-level variables. When HLM is used in this way, single-and multiple-level analyses are assumed to hold in data, in a particular way. Levels are assumed to be known. Likewise, in the HLM multiple-regression formulation, levels do not change under various conditions, and the empirical portions of multiple-variable and multiple-relationship analyses are also not necessary, because the levels are assumed to hold. WABA makes none of these assumptions; rather, it tests them. The assumption that variables tend to vary on the basis of differences between whole units at different levels becomes instead an empirical question in WABA. In contrast to WABA, HLM estimates the similarity of the slopes of lines within units. WABA does not do so, nor is it intended to. Once the levels are shown to be viable, such questions can clearly be examined with HLM.

Published Illustrations of the Technique

Most of the published illustrations of the varient/WABA approach have focused on single-level and multiple-level analyses. These are very important studies because they provide empirical validation that the various key conditions in the varient approach are indeed plausible for different variables and across studies. After a brief discussion of these studies, the existing illustrations of multiple-variable and multiple-relationship analyses will be highlighted.

Single-Level and Multiple-Level Analyses

In terms of single-level analysis, there are at least four published illustrations that provide multiple examples of the key alternatives described in Table 10.2:

1. Dansereau, Yammarino, Markham, Alutto, and colleagues (1995), in seven studies of self-worth provided by a leader to a subordinate, provide multiple examples of wholes—mainly between-groups variation and covariation using two-person groups.
2. Schriesheim, Neider, and Scandura (1998), in a study of leader-member exchange and power, provide multiple examples of parts—mainly within-groups variation and covariation.
3. Schriesheim and colleagues (1995), in a study of the consideration and structuring of the leader, provide multiple empirical examples of similar variation within groups and between group—the equivocal alternative.
4. Yammarino and Markham (1992), in a study of positive affect, reanalyze data from George (1990) and provide numerous examples of null results.

As shown in Table 10.6, these studies, as a set, demonstrate that although mainly one of the conditions was found in each data set, any one of the four conditions is plausible for any one data set. This is the case because in each study the data were free to vary mainly between or within groups, or neither between nor within groups, or both between and within groups. To illustrate this point, Table 10.6 presents the within-groups and between-groups components and total correlations from each study. In the actual studies, the elements that make up the two components are tested against each other and the conclusion is reached that between-groups or within-groups variation and covariation are larger or the same. The point, however, is that all four alternatives have been illustrated in the literature.

In terms of multiple-level analysis, Dansereau and colleagues (1984) provide an illustration of whole effects that apply at the group and collective levels (a cross-level case). Yammarino and Dubinsky (1992) provide evidence for a case in which a lower-level

Table 10.6. Alternative Conditions in Previous Studies.

Alternative	Variables	Between Component	Within Component	Total Correlation	Source
Wholes (groups)	Support for self-worth by superior and satisfying performance by subordinate (across studies)	.46	.10	.56	Dansereau and others (1995), Table 13 (average of all values)
Parts (groups)	Delegation by superior and performance by subordinate	.00	.38	.38	Schriesheim, Neider, and Scandura (1998), Table 5
Equivocal (groups)	Consideration (C) + role clarity (R) + (C) (R) = satisfaction	.26	.27	.53	Schriesheim, Cogliser, and Neider (1995, 1998), Table 6
Null (groups)	Positive affect and absence	−.06	−.02	−.08	Yammarino and Markham (1992), Table 6

dyad effect becomes equivocal at the higher group level (a level-specific case). Finally, Dansereau, Yammarino, Markham, Alutto, and colleagues (1995) show that superiors, when they describe their subordinates, show neither mainly between-superior variation nor mainly within-superior variation; indeed, the descriptions occur independent of other individuals. This results in a rejection of the superior as the appropriate level of analysis. The independent evaluations of subordinates cannot be explained at the superior level. Instead, they form one of the elements in the dyad. In this way, the dyad effects cannot be reduced to the level of the superior as a person. This is an illustration of the *emergent* condition. Table 10.7, then, shows that cross-level, level-specific, and emergent alternatives have appeared in different published studies. This also illustrates that at the beginning of any one of the studies, any of the multiple-level alternatives could have occurred because the data collected were free to vary between groups and/or within groups and collectives. Only with data analysis does the more likely alternative become apparent.

Multiple-Variable and Multiple-Relationship Analyses

Although they have received less attention so far in the literature, multiple-variable and multiple-relationship analyses are described in Dansereau and colleagues (1984). Yammarino (1998), using data from John Mathieu, shows that the following three alternatives result from the analysis of the data set (where SUPP indicates supportive leadership, INST indicates instrumental leadership, SAT indicates satisfaction, ES indicates early socialization, and REM indicates intention to remain):

Related case $r_{(SUPP)\ (INST)} = .61$, $r_{(SUPP)\ (SAT)} = .48$, $r_{(INST)\ (SAT)} = .47$

Generally related case $r_{(SAT)\ (REM)} = .33$, $r_{(SUPP)\ (SAT)} = .48$, $r_{(SUPP)\ (REM)} = .10$

Generally unrelated case $r_{(SUPP)\ (INST)} = .61$, $r_{(SUPP)\ (ES)} = -.07$, $r_{(INST)\ (ES)} = -.03$

Table 10.7. Alternative Views of Two Levels of Analysis in Previous Studies.

Alternatives	Variables at All Levels	Between Component	Within Component	Total	Source
Cross-Level					
Whole collectives	Education and freedom from machines	.38	.15	.53[a]	Dansereau and others (1984), Table 9.8 (collective) and Table 9.5 (group)
Whole groups		.33	.07	.40	
Level-Specific					
Equivocal at the group level	Attention by superior and satisfaction with performance	.26	.32	.58[a]	Yammarino and Dubinsky (1992), Table III (dyad) and Table V (group)
Whole dyads		.44	−.01	.43	
Emergent					
Whole dyads	Support for self-worth and satisfying performance	.41	.10	.51[a]	Dansereau and others (1995, 1998), Table 13 (dyad) and Table 7 (person)
Equivocal at the person level (across 7 studies)		.23	.31	.54	

[a]The total correlation at the higher level of analysis is the between-groups correlation from the lower level of analysis.

The correlations illustrate that these alternatives simply reflect the number of significant and near-zero correlations based on difference tests.

Finally, multiple-relationship analysis is illustrated in Dansereau and colleagues (1984) and Yammarino (1998). Yammarino's example (1998) provides a relatively simple illustration of the contingent and multiplexed alternatives.

Criticisms and Limitations of the Technique

The main school of thought that seems quite antithetical to WABA is represented by the work by Bliese and Halverson (1998). As pointed out previously, we regard the approaches of James (1998) (r_{wg}) and Bryk and Raudenbush (1992) (HLM) as potentially valuable after WABA has been used to analyze data and test for hypothesized levels. In contrast, the work of Bliese and Halverson (1998) is in some ways in direct opposition to WABA.

We believe that the essence of the Bliese and Halverson (1998) position is as follows:

1. The magnitude of the eta-squared from a one-way ANOVA is partially a function of group size.
2. WABA uses eta-squared to interpret the magnitude of group effects.
3. The F-test from eta-squared is not biased by group size.
4. WABA does, however, use the F-test and the E-test of practical significance to infer the strength of group effects (wholes, parts, or equivocal).
5. Therefore, "if tests of practical significance are considered important in WABA, the tests should be based on measures that provide estimates of the group properties of the data that are not biased by group size" (Bliese & Halverson, 1998, p. 166).

We agree with the portion of their position that says that we should use F-ratios to test for statistical significance. WABA uses F-ratios, and there is apparently no quarrel with this test.

We strongly disagree that we should not use the E-ratio in addition to the F-ratio to examine practical significance. In our view, the E-ratio refers to the strength of an effect predicted, regardless of any statistical effects. The same indicator, called "f" by Cohen (1988), is used and described in some detail by him (pp. 273–406). Also relevant is the work of Hays (1981), Cohen (1965, pp. 104–105), Cohen and Cohen (1983, pp. 196–198), and Friedman (1968, 1982), as well as Hays's review (1985) of the varient approach. This general approach, using "f" or "E," attempts to develop a consistent way to assess the strength of effects that can be defined independently of sample size across various analyses.

Thus the E-ratio comes from a particular tradition in statistics that concerns the strength of effects. The E-ratio (or "f," in Cohen's work) varies from zero to infinity (Cohen, 1988, Table 8.22). The equivalence of the E in WABA and the f in Cohen's work is obvious if we define η^2_{BX} as the between-eta squared, and if we define the within-eta squared as η^2_{WX}. It is known that $\eta^2_{BX} + \eta^2_{WX} = 1$ (see Dansereau et al., 1984, for a proof). Therefore, $1 - \eta^2_{BX} = \eta^2_{WX}$. Cohen (1988, p. 284) has defined f as

$$f = \frac{\eta^2_{BX}}{1 - \eta^2_{BX}}$$

by simple algebraic substitution:

$$f = \frac{\eta^2_{BX}}{\eta^2_{WX}} = E$$

which is the E-ratio of Dansereau and colleagues (1984).

Cohen (1988) goes on to define intervals for the strength of effects for f (E-ratio). His intervals are as follows:

Small-effect f = .10

Medium-effect f = .25

Large-effect f = .40

Cohen's approach (1988) is focused on a one-way ANOVA, where within-groups variance is by definition error. For levels work, we take the view that the interval from between variance to within variance should have three equal intervals (wholes, parts, and equivocal). Obviously, different intervals can be used. For the 30° test, the intervals are as follows:

Wholes	E > 1.73	$\eta_B^2 > 75$ percent
Equivocal	.58 < E < 1.73	$\eta_B^2 \approx 50$ percent
Parts	E < .58	$\eta_B^2 < 25$ percent

For the 15° test, the intervals are as follows:

Wholes	E > 1.30	$\eta_B^2 > 63$ percent
Equivocal	.77 < E < 1.30	$\eta_B^2 \approx 50$ percent
Parts	E < .77	$\eta_B^2 < 37$ percent

In the case of the 15° test, there are approximately equal intervals in terms of variance. In the case of the 30° test, however, there are equal intervals in terms of angles. Another way to show the equal intervals in terms of variance for the 15° test is as follows:

Wholes	100 percent to 63 percent variance between groups
Equivocal	62 percent to 38 percent between groups
Parts	0 percent to 37 percent between groups

The E-ratio also has a particularly useful characteristic that reflects the approach used in the varient paradigm. Specifically, it allows for a score to be represented in one of three ways: as a between-group effect, as a within-group effect, or as both. The intervals are equally likely. A close examination of the traditional intraclass correlation reveals that it includes eta-squared, as well as degrees of freedom. We want an indicator that is not based on degrees of freedom, but that is based instead solely on the scores, to use in conjunction with the indicator that is based both on degrees of freedom and on scores. The F-ratio and intraclass correlations use degrees of freedom in their calculation. The E-ratio is a geometric indicator without degrees of freedom.

What is not debatable is the notion that if data are random, then the number of individuals in the groups, as well as the number of groups, will influence the value of eta-squared. This hypothesis is tested with an F-ratio. What is obvious, if the data are random, is that if one has ten groups with one hundred individuals in each, then it will be harder to find variation between groups than if one has ten groups with two individuals in each. If the data are not random and the effects are clear, then the size of the sample should not matter, and an E-value should hold (see also Cohen, 1988). We believe, as does Cohen (1988), that effect sizes should be specified in advance and tested. We recognize, however, that the question of the exact intervals to use in inferring wholes, parts, or equivocal effects, on the basis of effect sizes, is open to debate. We believe the best response to this question has been given by Cohen (1988, p. 12):

> The behavior scientist who comes to statistical power analysis may [grapple] with the problem of what [effect size] to posit as an alternate to the null hypothesis, or, more simply, how to answer the question "How large an effect do I expect exists in the population?" [The scientist] may initially find it difficult to answer the question even in general terms, that is, "small" or "large," let alone in terms of the specific [effect size] index demanded. Being forced to think in more exact terms than demanded by the Fisherian alternative ([effect size] is any nonzero value) is likely to prove salutary.

There will be debate about what values to use in defining whether there are wholes, equivocal, or parts effects. These will need to be resolved on the basis of one's specific theory (as House, 1987, has pointed out in his review of the varient paradigm). We do not believe that the answer lies in adjusting eta-squared values by degrees of freedom, as the intraclass correlation does. The answer lies in deciding what value is of significance. We prefer the 15° and 30° intervals because they give geometrically equal intervals for the alternatives.

Essentially, given eta-squared values and degrees of freedom, one can calculate various indicators of effect size. Because researchers may disagree about effect sizes and the indicators (intraclass correlation), we advocate that researchers simply report the strength of effects in such a way that individuals with different perspectives can evaluate and interpret these effects according to their views. We believe this involves reporting not only F-ratios but also eta-squared values or the E (or f) value in addition to statistical significance tests.

Conclusion

In this chapter, we have described the impetus for assumptions underlying WABA, as well as the basic logic of WABA. We have emphasized that WABA is designed to balance inductive and deductive approaches. Some may argue that WABA requires too much theory. Others may argue that WABA is not sufficiently dominated by theory. WABA is not an approach that will just let the data speak without theory. WABA is also not a means of forcing data to conform with theory. In WABA, the attempt is to give each alternative a fair chance despite one's theoretical preference for one alternative over another (for example, one's inclination toward whole groups). The object, of course, is to end up with better alignment between theory and data. We believe that WABA accomplishes this alignment by focusing simultaneously on both theory formulation (deductive logic) and empirical testing (inductive logic).

As an approach to theory testing, WABA allows a researcher to test whether a particular level of analysis or set of levels of analysis, as asserted, underlies the variance and covariance in a set of variables. Various formulations of variables can be associated and tested. Accordingly, some variables may apply to one level and others to different levels. Finally, the conditions that may be necessary for a particular level of analysis to hold can be asserted and tested. All these ideas, of course, become even more useful, in our opinion, when the concept of time is added to the approach (Dansereau, Yammarino, & Kohles, 1999).

We have also positioned the approach so that once the varient paradigm is used, various other approaches are very useful. These include HLM, SEM, and James's r_{wg}. Interestingly, one can ask whether the same groups arise with cluster or network analysis as arise from WABA-based tests for levels of analysis. Moreover, one can examine the multiple responses of individuals to assess whether individuals tend to rate other individuals as individuals (equivocal) or according to their own views (wholes) or in relativistic terms (parts). This would be very useful to know before we attempted to perform various forms of network or cluster analyses. In a sense, the varient paradigm and WABA are a method of testing various tacit assumptions that underlie many analyses. It is after these varient-based tests, we believe, that various assumptions underlying analyses can be relied on to hold as empirically demonstrated. We hope that others, when it comes to understanding multiple levels of analysis, will be encouraged by this chapter to develop approaches that are deductive as well as inductive. We also hope that their approaches will also consider the fundamental assumptions that underlie various views of multiple levels of analyses.

Note

1. We use the term *cross-level* here following the notion from Miller (1978). In the varient approach, *cross-level* means that variables and effects hold at a higher and a lower level of analysis, or at each of multiple levels of analysis. Rousseau (1985) uses the term *cross-level* to refer to the case, for example, in which a group-level variable (x) relates to an individual-level variable (y). In the varient approach, a cross-level effect occurs if the variables (x and y) relate at each of several levels of analysis and therefore, by definition, from one level to another. Rousseau uses another term, *multilevel*, to indicate that one effect (effect A) holds at only one level of analysis but that a different effect (effect B), including the same variables but defined differently, holds at another level. In the varient approach, this means that one effect would be emergent and level-specific and another version of the same variables would also be emergent and level-specific at a different level of analysis. These are two views of how variables at one level may relate to variables at a lower level.

References

Avolio, B. J., & Bass, B. M. (1995). Individualized consideration viewed at multiple levels of analysis: A multi-level framework for examining the diffusion of transformational leadership. *Leadership Quarterly, 6,* 199–218.

Bliese, P. D., & Halverson, R. R. (1998). Group size and measures of group-level properties: An examination of eta-squared and ICC values. *Journal of Management, 24,* 157–172.

Bryk, A. J., & Raudenbush, S. W. (1992). *Hierarchical linear models: Applications and data analysis methods.* Thousand Oaks, CA: Sage.

Cohen, J. (1965). Some statistical issues in psychological research. In B. B. Wolman (Ed.), *Handbook of clinical psychology* (pp. 95–121). New York: McGraw-Hill.

Cohen, J. (1988). *Statistical power analysis for the behavioral sciences.* Hillsdale, NJ: Lawrence Erlbaum Associates.

Cohen, J., & Cohen, P. (1983). *Applied multiple regression/correlation analysis for the behavioral sciences.* Mahwah, NJ: Erlbaum.

Dansereau, F. (1995). A dyadic approach to leadership: Creating and nurturing this approach under fire. *Leadership Quarterly, 6,* 479–498.

Dansereau, F., & Alutto, J. A. (1991). Levels of analysis issues in climate and culture research. In B. Schneider (Ed.), *Climate and culture in organizations* (pp. 193–239). San Francisco: Jossey-Bass.

Dansereau, F., Alutto, J., & Yammarino, F. (1984). *Theory testing in organizational behavior: The varient approach.* Englewood Cliffs, NJ: Prentice Hall.

Dansereau, F., & Dumas, M. (1977). Pratfalls and pitfalls in drawing inferences about leadership behavior in organizations. In J. G. Hunt & L. L. Larson (Eds.), *Leadership: The cutting edge* (pp. 68–83). Carbondale: Southern Illinois University Press.

Dansereau, F., Jr., Graen, G., & Haga, J. (1975). A vertical dyad linkage approach to leadership within formal organizations: A longitudinal investigation of the role making process. *Organizational Behavior and Human Performance, 13,* 46–78.

Dansereau, F., & Markham, S. E. (1987a). Levels of analysis in personnel and human resources management. In K. Rowland & G. Ferris (Eds.), *Research in personnel and human resources management* (Vol. 5, pp. 1–50). Greenwich, CT: JAI Press.

Dansereau, F., & Markham, S. E. (1987b). Superior-subordinate communication. In F. Jablin, L. Putnam, K. Roberts, & L. Porter (Eds.), *Handbook of organizational communication* (pp. 343–388). Thousand Oaks, CA: Sage.

Dansereau, F., & Yammarino, F. J. (1998a). *Leadership: The multiple-level approaches. Part A: Classical and new wave.* Greenwich, CT: JAI Press.

Dansereau, F., & Yammarino, F. J. (1998b). *Leadership: The multiple-level approaches. Part B: Contemporary and alternative.* Greenwich, CT: JAI Press.

Dansereau, F., Yammarino, F. J. & Kohles, J. (1999). Multiple levels of analysis from a longitudinal perspective. *Academy of Management Review, 24,* 346–357.

Dansereau, F., Yammarino, F. J., & Markham, S. E. (1995). Leadership: The multiple-level approaches. *Leadership Quarterly, 6,* 97–109.

Dansereau, F., Yammarino, F. J., Markham, S. E., Alutto, J. A., Newman, J. M., Dumas, M., Nachman, S. A., Naughton, T. J., Kim, K., Al-Kelabi, S.A.H., Lee, S., & Keller, T. (1995). Individualized leadership: A new multiple-level approach. *Leadership Quarterly, 6,* 413–450.

Firebaugh, G. (1980). Groups as contexts and frog ponds. In K. H. Roberts & L. Burstein (Eds.), *Issues in aggregation.* New Directions for Methodology of Social and Behavioral Science, no. 6. San Francisco: Jossey-Bass.

Friedman, H. (1968). Magnitude of experimental effect and a table for its rapid estimation. *Psychological Bulletin, 70,* 245–251.

Friedman, H. (1982). Simplified determinations of statistical power, magnitude of effect and research sample sizes. *Educational and Psychological Measurement, 42,* 521–526.

George, J. M. (1990). Personality, affect, and behavior in groups. *Journal of Applied Psychology, 75,* 107–116.

George, J. M., & James, L. R. (1993). Personality, affect, and behavior in groups revisited: Comment on organization, levels of analysis, and a recent application of within and between analysis. *Journal of Applied Psychology, 78,* 798–804.

Hays, W. L. (1981). *Statistics.* Austin, TX: Holt, Rinehart and Winston.

Hays, W. L. (1985). Review of theory testing in organizational behavior: The varient approach. *Contemporary Psychology, 30,* 160–161.

House, R. J. (1987). Review of theory testing in organizational behavior: The varient approach. *Administrative Science Quarterly, 32,* 459–464.

Huselid, M. A. (1995). The impact of human resource management practices on turnover, productivity, and corporate financial performance. *Academy of Management Journal, 38,* 635–672.

James, L. (1998). Implications of a multiple levels of analysis Ohio State leadership study for estimating interrater agreement. In F. Dansereau & F. Yammarino (Eds.) *Leadership: The multiple-level approaches. Part A: Classical and new wave* (pp. 61–64). Greenwich, CT: JAI Press.

Klein, K. J., Dansereau, F., & Hall, R. J. (1994). Levels issues in theory development, data collection, and analysis. *Academy of Management Review, 19,* 195–229.

Klein, K. J., & House, R. J. (1995). On fire: Charismatic leadership and levels of analysis. *Leadership Quarterly, 6,* 183–198.

Markham, S. E. (1988). Pay-for-performance dilemma revisited: An empirical example of the importance of group effects. *Journal of Applied Psychology, 73,* 172–180.

Markham, S. E., & McKee, G. H. (1991). Declining organizational size and increasing unemployment rates: Predicting employee absenteeism from a within-plant and between-plant perspective. *Academy of Management Journal, 34,* 952–965.

Markham, S. E., & McKee, G. H. (1995). Group absence behavior and standards: A multi-level analysis. *Academy of Management Journal, 38(4),* 1174–1190.

Miller, J. G. (1978). *Living systems.* New York: McGraw-Hill.

Pfeffer, J. (1977). The ambiguity of leadership. *Academy of Management Review, 2,* 104–112.

Raudenbush, S. (1995). Hierarchical linear models to study the effects of social contexts on development. In J. Gottman (Ed.), *The analysis of change* (pp. 165–201). Mahwah, NJ: Erlbam.

Rousseau, D. M. (1985). Issues of level in organizational research: Multi-level and cross-level perspectives. In L. L. Cummings & B. Staw (Eds.), *Research in organizational behavior* (Vol. 7, pp. 1–37). Greenwich, CT: JAI Press.

Schriesheim, C. A. (1995). Multivariate and moderated within-and between-entity analysis (WABA) using hierarchical linear multiple regression. *Leadership Quarterly, 6,* 1–18.

Schriesheim, C., Cogliser, C., & Neider, L. (1995). Is it "trustworthy"? A multiple-levels-of-analysis reexamination of an Ohio State leadership study, with implications for future research. *Leadership Quarterly, 6,* 111–145.

Schriesheim, C. A., Cogliser, C. C., & Neider, L. L. (1998). "Trustworthy" is a judgment call. In F. Dansereau & F. J. Yammarino (Eds.), *Leadership: The multiple-level approaches. Part A: Classical and new wave* (pp. 65–72). Greenwich, CT: JAI Press.

Schriesheim, C., Neider, L., & Scandura, T. (1998). Delegation and leader-member exchange: Main effects, moderators, and measurement issues. *Academy of Management Journal, 41,* 298–318.

Stogdill, R. N., & Coons, A. E. (1957). *Leader behavior: Its descriptions and measurement.* Columbus: Bureau of Business Research, Ohio State University.

Weick, K. (1976). Educational organizations as loosely coupled systems. *Administrative Science Quarterly, 21,* 1–19.

Yammarino, F. J. (1990). Individual-and group-directed leader behavior descriptions. *Educational and Psychological Measurement, 50,* 739–759.

Yammarino, F. J. (1998). Multivariate aspects of the varient/WABA approach for multi-level theory testing: A discussion and leadership illustration. *Leadership Quarterly, 9,* 203–227.

Yammarino, F. J. (in press). A conceptual-empirical approach for testing meso and multi-level theories. In H. L. Tosi (Ed.), *Extensions of the environment/organization/person model.* Greenwich, CT: JAI Press.

Yammarino, F., & Dubinsky, A. J. (1992). Superior-subordinate relationships: A multiple-level-of-analysis approach. *Human Relations, 45,* 575–600.

Yammarino, F. J., & Dubinsky, A. J. (1994). Transformational leadership theory: Using levels of analysis to determine boundary conditions. *Personnel Psychology, 47,* 787–811.

Yammarino, F. J., Dubinsky, A. J., Comer, L. B., & Jolson, M. A. (1997). Women and transformational and contingent reward leadership: A multiple-levels-of-analysis perspective. *Academy of Management Journal, 40,* 205–222.

Yammarino, F. J., & Markham, S. E. (1992). On the application of within and between analysis: Are absence and affect really group-based phenomena? *Journal of Applied Psychology, 77,* 168–176.

CHAPTER 11

The Application of Hierarchical Linear Modeling to Organizational Research

David A. Hofmann
Mark A. Griffin
Mark B. Gavin

Hierarchically ordered systems are an integral and defining aspect of organizations. How one chooses to investigate these hierarchically ordered systems has been discussed in a number of disciplines (sociology, economics, education, marketing, management, and psychology) for quite some time. The principal issue of concern is how to analyze and interpret data that reside at different levels of analysis. Hierarchical linear models provide a conceptual and statistical mechanism for investigating and drawing conclusions regarding relationships that cross levels of analysis. This chapter discusses the hierarchical nature of organizations and organizational research, provides an overview of the hierarchical linear modeling (HLM) methodology, and, using example research questions and simulated data, provides a step-by-step analytical introduction to these models. In addition, a number of other more specific issues are discussed, including statistical power and sample-size requirements, the implications of the statistical assumptions underlying these models, how the scaling of variables can change the interpretation and meaning of the estimated model, and how hierarchical linear models relate to other multilevel analytic approaches.

The inherent hierarchical order and structure of organizations is apparent throughout the various theoretical and methodological contributions to this volume. Hall (1987) noted implicitly this hierarchical structure when he defined organizations as individuals organized into a collective residing in an environment—a definition that encompasses three hierarchical levels consisting of individuals, a collective or system, and an environment. For organizational researchers, this hierarchical structure manifests itself in the observation of hierarchical relationships. Hierarchical relationships occur when events at one level of analysis influence or are influenced by events at another level of analysis. Given the structure of organizations, a wide variety of hierarchical relationships can be observed and, in fact, have frequently been discussed and investigated in the organizational sciences. For example, researchers have investigated the relationships between organizational environmental factors and organizational structures (Aldrich & Pfeffer, 1976; Pfeffer & Salancik, 1978), organizational/subunit technologies and individual attitudes (Hulin & Roznowski, 1985), group norms/stimuli and individual behavior (Hackman, 1992), departmental characteristics/structure and individual attitudes (Brass, 1981; James & Jones, 1976; Oldham & Hackman, 1981; Rousseau, 1978), and climate/culture and individual behavior (Hofmann & Stetzer, 1996; James, James, & Ashe, 1990; Kozlowski & Hults, 1987; Martocchio, 1994). In each of these examples, at least two different levels of analysis were involved.

Although it might not be initially obvious, hierarchical structures also occur in longitudinal studies when, for example, a time series of measurements is taken on a variable of interest for a number of different units (Nesselroade, 1991). Several researchers have suggested that such longitudinal data can be investigated by first analyzing patterns of change within units over time and then relating these patterns to between-unit variables (Bryk & Raudenbush, 1987; Deadrick, Bennett, & Russell, 1997; Eyring, Johnson, & Francis, 1993; Hofmann, Jacobs, & Gerras, 1992; Hofmann, Jacobs, & Baratta, 1993). Organizational studies of change that could be considered from this perspective range from micro investigations of individual work performance to macro investigations of organizational growth and decline (Austin & Villanova, 1992; Child, 1974,

1975; Deadrick et al., 1997; Hofmann et al., 1992, 1993). For example, at the organizational level, Child (1974, 1975) has investigated managerial influences on organizational performance, using a sample of eighty-two British firms spanning six industries. Although Child examined predictors of the average growth in income, assets, and sales over a five-year period by averaging these performance indices, an alternative approach would have been first to investigate the change pattern for each firm over time and then investigate predictors of these change patterns. This type of approach would have taken into account the nested and hierarchical nature of the data (that is, nested time series within firms).

As can be seen from the diversity of the examples just cited, hierarchical data structures occur in a large number of content areas within organizational science. As will be seen, the principal benefit of using multilevel methods is that they allow researchers to examine the relationship between variables that span different levels of analysis. Often in the past these hierarchical data structures have been either implicitly or explicitly ignored. In this chapter, we provide an introduction to and overview of hierarchical linear models—an approach to multilevel data that greatly facilitates the explicit recognition and investigation of these types of data structures.

Overview of Hierarchical Linear Modeling Methodology

Consistent with the hierarchical linear modeling approach, we will discuss an example in which a researcher is interested in investigating a dependent variable at the lowest level of analysis and independent variables at the same level of analysis as well as at higher levels. These types of research questions have been referred to as either *cross-level* (Rousseau, 1985) or *mixed-determinant* models (Klein, Dansereau, & Hall, 1994). It should be noted that the choice to focus on these models is more than coincidental. In fact, it is for these types of questions that hierarchical linear models are best suited. Although there has been some initial work using these models to investigate upward relationships (Griffin, 1997a), the traditional application will be to research questions taking the form of those described in this chapter.

Dealing with Hierarchical Data

As an example of this type of model, say that a researcher is interested in the relationships among individual employees' helping behavior toward their co-workers, their current affective state (that is, mood), and the level of work-group cohesion. We will assume, for this example, that work-group cohesion is a group-level variable that has been measured by having each group member complete a survey, and that sufficient within-group agreement and between-group variance exist to warrant the aggregation of these individual perceptions to the group level (Bliese, Chapter Eight, this volume). Therefore, the focus will be on the group mean as an indicator of the work group's level of cohesion. In this case, individual-level helping behavior is the dependent variable, and mood and cohesion are the independent variables. Notice that, given our assumptions about the level of analysis of our variables, these independent variables span two levels of analysis; that is, mood is an individual-level variable, and cohesion is a group-level variable. When one is confronted with a research design and variables of this kind, there are primarily three options from which one can choose.

First, one can disaggregate the data so that the lower-level units are assigned a score representing their value on the higher-level variable. In our example, this would take the form of assigning to each individual a score representing the level of the work group's cohesion. In other words, everyone in the group would receive the same cohesion score. After this is done for each group included in the study, one can proceed with traditional ordinary least squares (OLS) regression analysis, investigating mood and cohesion as predictors of individual-level helping behavior. As we will discuss in our comparison between OLS regression and hierarchical linear models, this approach has several shortcomings, including the likely violation of statistical assumptions.

The second major option is to aggregate the lower-level variables to the same level as the higher-level variables. In our example, this would entail aggregating individual-level helping behavior as well as mood to the group level of analysis (that is, the level of analysis at which the cohesion measure resides) and then using the group means of these variables in subsequent analyses. The disadvantage of this approach, however, is that potentially meaningful individual-level variance is ignored both in the outcome measure and in one of the predictors. This ignored variance may indeed be meaningful and informative. In addition, if there is meaningful individual-level variance (in mood, for example), then the aggregation of this variable to represent a group-level property (for example, group affective tone) might result in a group-level variable with questionable construct validity (Klein et al., 1994).

Hierarchical linear models represent the third major option for dealing with hierarchically nested data structures. These models are specifically designed to overcome the weaknesses of the disaggregated and aggregated approaches discussed above. For one thing, they explicitly recognize that individuals within a group may be more similar to one another than they are to individuals in another group and may not, therefore, provide independent observations. In other words, these approaches explicitly model both the lower-level and the higher-level random-error components, therefore recognizing the partial interdependence of individuals within the same groups. This aspect of hierarchical linear models is in contrast to OLS approaches, where individual- and group-level random errors are not separately estimated. In addition, these models allow one to investigate both lower-level and higher-level variance in the outcome variable while maintaining the appropriate level of analysis for the independent variables.

A Brief Overview of Hierarchical Linear Models

The hierarchical linear modeling approach is a two-stage strategy that investigates variables occurring at two levels of analysis. (Software is available to analyze more than two levels of analysis. For the sake of clarity of presentation, however, we will focus on two-level models.) In the first stage, or level 1 analysis, relationships among level 1 variables are estimated separately for each higher-level unit. With respect to our example, this entails regressing individual-level helping behavior onto mood for each group. The outcome of this first stage is intercept and slope terms estimated separately for each group. Thus, for each group there will be a level 1 intercept term as well as a slope term summarizing the relationship between mood and helping behavior. These intercept and slope estimates from the level 1 analysis are then used as outcome variables in the level 2 analysis. In our example, we will investigate the degree to which cohesion predicts the variance across groups in the level 1 intercepts and slopes.

Viewing hierarchical linear models in equation form, the level 1 component of our example regresses individual level helping behavior onto individual levels of mood separately for each group:

$$\text{Helping behavior}_{ij} = \beta_{0j} + \beta_{1j}(\text{Mood}_{ij}) + r_{ij} \tag{1}$$

where Helping behavior$_{ij}$ is the degree of helping of individual i in group j, Mood$_{ij}$ is the mood score for the same individual, and r_{ij} represents random individual error. β_{0j} is the intercept value for group j, and β_{1j} is the regression slope for group j.

Equation 1 differs from the usual regression equation in that the parameters are estimated for each of the j groups separately. For this reason, the parameters can vary across groups. The subscript j associated with the parameters indicates that the parameter estimates can have a different value for each group.

In the second stage of the this approach, the level 1 parameters are used as dependent variables for analysis at the group level. In equation format, and using our ongoing example, one can envision the following model:

$$\beta_{0j} = \gamma_{00} + \gamma_{01} (\text{Cohesion}_j) + U_{0j} \tag{2}$$

$$\beta_{1j} = \gamma_{10} + \gamma_{11} (\text{Cohesion}_j) + U_{1j} \tag{3}$$

where β_{0j} and β_{1j} are defined as before (that is, as the level 1 intercept and slope respectively), Cohesion$_j$ is a group-level measure of the psychological attraction among group members, γ_{00} and γ_{10} are level 2 intercept terms, γ_{01} and γ_{11} are level 2 slope terms, and U_{0j} and U_{1j} are level 2 residuals. Equation 2 represents the main-effect model, which investigates whether cohesion is related to the between-group variance in helping behavior after controlling for mood. Equation 3 represents a cross-level interaction in such a way as to assess the degree to which cohesion moderates the within-group relationship between mood and helping behavior. Therefore, one could summarize this approach as a regression of regressions because the level 1 regression parameters (that is, intercepts and slopes) are themselves regressed onto higher-level variables in the level 2 analysis (Arnold, 1992).

Hierarchical Linear Models: History, Background, and Applications

Now that a brief overview of hierarchical linear models has been provided, it might be useful to discuss the literatures within which this approach has been applied. Even though the problems associated with hierarchically ordered data have been discussed in a number of different literatures—for example, in sociology (Blalock, 1984; Mason, Wong, & Entwistle, 1983), economics (Hanushek, 1974; Saxonhouse, 1976), biology (Laird & Ware, 1982), marketing (Wittink, 1977), and statistics (Longford, 1993)—the approach described here primarily emerged from educational research, where students are nested in classrooms and classrooms are nested in schools. In this case, researchers are primarily interested in assessing student as well as classroom and school effects on student learning and performance. Clearly, these data are multilevel in nature. In addition, the outcome variable is usually at the lowest level of analysis (that is, the student level), with both lower-level and higher-level predictors (that is, student, classroom, and school characteristics).

The relatively modern precursor of the present class of hierarchical linear models emerged from a conference convened in 1976 on data-aggregation problems in educational research (Burstein & Hannan, 1976; Burstein, Kim, & Delandshere, 1989). One of the outcomes of this conference was a proposal by Burstein (1980) to use a slopes-as-outcomes model; hence the initiation of the general form of the multilevel model presented earlier. Although statistical estimation problems initially stalled the full development of these models, Raudenbush (1988) noted a series of statistical developments that made these models more technically feasible by the middle of the 1980s (see also Bryk & Raudenbush, 1992). Under several different labels—*hierarchical linear models* (Bryk & Raudenbush, 1992), *multilevel linear models* (Goldstein, 1987), *variance-components models* (Longford, 1986), and *random-coefficient models* (Longford, 1993)—these models have become increasingly complex. As a result, specialized software packages have been developed and are commonly available (Kreft, DeLeeuw, & van der Leeden, 1994). In the discussion that follows, we use *hierarchical linear models* as a broad term encompassing this general approach to multilevel data. When we use the HLM nomenclature, we will be specifically referring to the HLM software (Bryk, Raudenbush, & Congdon, 1996).

Since the widespread development of these models, they have been applied in a number of different research domains outside the organizational sciences. For example, recent applications and discussions of hierarchical linear models have spanned the following domains and topics:

- Meta-analysis (Kalaian & Raudenbush, 1996)
- Psychological change and distress in married couples (Barnett, Raudenbush, Brennan, Pleck, & Marshall, 1995; Raudenbush, Brennan, & Barnett, 1995)
- Psychotherapy (Joyce & Piper, 1996)
- Cognitive growth (Plewis, 1996)
- Information processing after a head injury (Zwaagstra, Schmidt, & Vanier, 1996)
- Educational research (Battistich, Solomon, Kim, Watson, & Schaps, 1995; Raudenbush, Rowan, & Cheong, 1993)
- Sociology (Jones, 1995)
- Program evaluation (Osgood & Smith, 1995)

In the organizational sciences, these models have been used to investigate questions arising in a number of different substantive domains. For example, they have been used to investigate the following topics:

- Goal congruence (Vancouver, Millsap, & Peters, 1994)
- The interaction of environment, person, and behavior (Vancouver, 1997)
- The interaction between individuals and situations (Griffin, 1997a)
- The dynamic nature of performance criteria (Deadrick et al., 1997; Hofmann et al., 1993)
- The relationship between group factors and unsafe behaviors/accident-cause interpretation (Hofmann & Stetzer, 1996, 1998)
- The moderating influence of leadership climate (Gavin & Hofmann, in press)

- Contextual effects on organizational citizenship behavior (Kidwell, Mossholder, & Bennett, 1997)
- Procedural-justice context (Mossholder, Bennett, & Martin, 1998)
- The effects of work group cohesiveness on performance and organizational commitment (Wech, Mossholder, Stéel, & Bennett, 1998)
- Perceptions of client satisfaction with health services (Jimmieson & Griffin, 1998)
- Individual skill acquisition (Eyring et al., 1993; Gully, 1997)
- Individual and organizational predictors of pay satisfaction (Griffin, 1997b).

Although this list of topics does convey the growing popularity of these models, it might be useful to review one or two of these studies in more depth, to give an idea of the types of questions and interpretations that they allow. Kidwell and colleagues (1997), for example, report a study investigating the relationship between group cohesion and organizational citizenship behavior. Specifically, they proposed that citizenship behaviors within work groups would be influenced by individual differences in job satisfaction and by group-level differences in cohesion. They also proposed that group cohesion would be a cross-level moderator so that the relationship between job satisfaction and citizenship behavior would be stronger in groups that were more cohesive.

Using a sample of 260 employees in forty-nine work groups, they found that citizenship behavior varied systematically across groups, and that the level of group cohesion predicted differences in citizenship behavior even after individual differences in job satisfaction were controlled for. They also found that the relationship between satisfaction and citizenship behavior varied across groups, and that this relationship was stronger when groups were more cohesive. In other words, the relationship between job satisfaction and citizenship behavior was accentuated in more cohesive work groups. Thus work-group cohesion acted as a cross-level moderator of the relationship between job satisfaction and citizenship behavior.

Another example, from a longitudinal perspective, is a recent paper by Deadrick and colleagues (1997). These authors have investigated the dynamic nature of individual performance over time. When longitudinal data are investigated with hierarchical linear models, the level 1 model becomes a within-person analysis summarizing an individual's performance trajectory over time (see also Hofmann et al., 1993). The level 2 model then investigates individual-level predictors of these performance trajectories. In their study, Deadrick and colleagues (1997) investigated the performance of sewing-machine operators over the first twenty-four weeks of employment. They found significant differences across individuals, both in initial performance (that is, the performance-trajectory intercept) and in linear trend, or change in performance over time (that is, the linear slope of the performance trajectory). With respect to predicting individual differences on these trajectories, the authors found that cognitive ability and previous job-related experience predicted both initial performance and linear change in performance over time. Specifically, the results indicated that those sewing-machine operators with higher cognitive abilities and more previous job-related experience had higher initial job performance but improved less over time, which suggests that there may have been a ceiling effect with respect to performance over time.

As can be seen by the breadth of applications already noted, hierarchical linear models constitute a generalized tool for investigating multilevel relationships. Although this approach to multilevel data emerged primarily out of the education literature, it has more recently expanded and been integrated into a number of different literatures. Although its use in the organizational sciences has been increasing only recently, the widespread applicability and generalized nature of this approach, coupled with the nested nature of much organizational data, should make hierarchical linear models more popular in the future.

Using Hierarchical Linear Models to Investigate Substantive Research Questions

Now that a brief overview of hierarchical linear models has been presented, along with several substantive examples, it might be useful to consider in greater depth the process a researcher would likely follow in using this approach to investigate substantive questions. In this section, we return to our ongoing substantive example and specify a set of possible research questions and hypotheses. We then walk through the hierarchical linear modeling approach to testing these hypotheses. (This section is based, in part, on the overview provided by Hofmann, 1997.)

To illustrate the procedure for testing the hypotheses using the HLM program, we generated simulated data consisting of fifty groups with twenty individuals in each one. (The data used to illustrate the HLM procedure are available from any of the three coauthors.) Recall that our substantive example is focused on the relationship among helping behavior, mood, and work-group cohesion. Furthermore, helping behavior and mood are assumed to be individual-level variables, whereas work-group cohesion is assumed to be a group-level variable. The content of these hypotheses is as follows:

H1. *Individual-level mood will be positively related to helping behavior.*

H2. *Cohesion will be positively related to helping behavior after controlling for individual-level mood.*

H3. *Cohesion will moderate the relationship between mood and helping behavior so that mood and helping behavior will be more strongly related when the group is more cohesive.*

In the following section, we will describe how to test these hypotheses with the HLM program.

Hierarchical Linear Models: Equations, Effects, and Statistical Tests

Before detailing the sequence of models estimated to investigate these hypotheses, it is necessary to define some of the basic components of the hierarchical linear model. In our brief overview of hierarchical linear models, we presented three equations (see equations 1, 2, and 3).

Although the level 1 and level 2 models were discussed earlier as separate equations, it should be noted that they are estimated simultaneously. Three key terms that arise in estimating these models are *fixed effects, random coefficients,* and *variance components.* Fixed effects are parameter estimates that do not vary across groups. For example, equations 2 and 3 are estimated at the group level (that is, across groups) and so there is only one parameter that summarizes the relationship across all groups. As a result, the parameters estimated in these equations do not vary across groups. The parameters in equations 2 and 3 are therefore fixed effects (γ_{00}, γ_{01}, γ_{10}, and γ_{11}).

Hierarchical linear models, and the HLM software specifically (Bryk et al., 1996), estimate these fixed effects by using a generalized least squares (GLS) regression approach. Although these level 2 regression parameters could be estimated with an OLS approach, this is not appropriate, given that the precision of the level 1 parameters (that is, the level 2 dependent variable) will likely vary across groups. In other words, because the standard errors of the level 1 parameters can vary across groups, the reliability of the level 2 outcome variable can be different for each group. Some level 1 parameters will be better estimates of the underlying relationship, and it is this variation in precision that is taken into account in the level 2 analysis. This GLS estimation provides a weighted level 2 regression so that groups with more reliable (that is, more precise) level 1 estimates receive more weight and therefore have more influence in the level 2 regression; t-test statistical tests are provided for these fixed effects.

The variance of the level 1 residuals (that is, the variance in r_{ij}) and the variance-covariance of the level 2 residuals (that is, the variance-covariance matrix of U_{0j} and U_{1j}) comprise the variance components. The variances and covariances of the level 2 residuals are contained in the τ matrix. The HLM procedure uses the EM algorithm (Dempster, Laird, & Rubin, 1977; Raudenbush, 1988) to produce maximum-likelihood estimates of the variance components. With regard to statistical tests, HLM provides a chi-square test for the level 2 residual variances—in our example, U_{0j} and U_{1j}—assessing whether the particular variance component departs significantly from zero.

Random coefficients are those coefficients that are allowed to vary across groups. In the current example, the level 1 intercepts and slopes (that is, β_{0j} and β_{1j}) are random coefficients. The HLM procedure does not provide any statistical tests for these parameters. However, as will be shown, one can assess whether the mean and variance of these parameters depart significantly from zero.[1]

One-Way Analysis of Variance: Partitioning Outcome Variance into "Within" and "Between" Components

In looking at the three example hypotheses listed earlier, one thing to notice is that helping behavior is hypothesized to be predicted by both individual- and group-level independent variables. For these hypotheses to be supported, there must be variation in helping behavior at both the individual and the group level. In other words, if group-level variables are going to be significantly related to helping behavior, then helping behavior, by definition, must contain meaningful between-group variance. This first model investigates the amount of between-group variance in helping behavior by partitioning the total variance in helping behavior into its within-group and between-group components. This model is conceptually equivalent to a one-way analysis of variance (ANOVA), with helping behavior as the dependent variable and with group membership serving as the independent variable. To do this, the following equations can be estimated:

Level 1: $\text{Helping}_{ij} + \beta_{0j} + r_{ij}$

Level 2: $\beta_{0j} = \gamma_{00} + U_{0j}$

where

β_{0j} = mean for helping for group j

γ_{00} = grand mean helping

Variance $(r_{ij}) = \sigma^2$ = within-group variance in helping

Variance $(U_{0j}) = \tau_{00}$ = between-group variance in helping

In this set of equations, the level 1 equation includes no predictors; therefore, the regression equation includes only an intercept term. To compute intercept terms in regression, the analysis includes a unit vector as a predictor in the equation. The parameter associated with this unit vector represents the intercept term in the final regression equation. In regression software packages, the researcher typically does not explicitly model this unit vector. Similarly for hierarchical linear models, when a researcher specifies no predictors in a level 1 or level 2 equation, the variance in the outcome measure is implicitly regressed onto a unit vector, producing a regression-based intercept estimate. In the level 1 equation, the β_{0j} parameter will be equal to that group's mean level of helping behavior (that is, if a variable is regressed only onto a constant unit vector, the resulting parameter is equal to the mean).

The level 2 model regresses each group's mean helping behavior onto a constant; that is, β_{0j} is regressed onto a unit vector, resulting in a γ_{00} parameter equal to the grand mean helping behavior (the mean of the group means, β_{0j}). Given that each of the respective dependent variables is regressed onto a constant, it follows that any within-group variance in helping behavior is forced into the level 1 residual (r_{ij}) and any between-group variance in helping behavior is forced into the level 2 residual (U_{0j}).

Although HLM does not provide a significance test for the within-group variance component (σ^2), it does provide a significance test for the between-group variance (τ_{00}). In addition, the ratio of the between-group variance to the total variance can be described as an intraclass correlation (Bryk & Raudenbush, 1992). In the preceding model, the total variance in helping behavior has been decomposed into its within- and between-group components:

$$\text{Variance (Helping}_{ij}) = \text{Variance } (U_{0j} + r_{ij}) = \tau_{00} + \sigma^2$$

Therefore, an intraclass correlation can be computed by investigating the following ratio:

$$\text{ICC} = \frac{\tau_{00}}{\tau_{00} + \sigma^2}$$

This intraclass correlation represents a ratio of the between-group variance in helping behavior to the total variance in helping behavior. In summary, the one-way ANOVA provides the following pieces of information regarding the helping behavior measure:

1. The amount of variance residing within groups
2. The amount and significance of variance residing between groups
3. The intraclass correlation specifying the percentage of the total variance residing between groups (see Bliese, Chapter Eight, this volume, for a more detailed discussion of intraclass correlations)

Table 11.1 presents the results of this analysis, using the example data. The grand mean of helping behavior—that is, the average helping behavior pooled across individuals and groups—is 31.39:

$$t\,(49) = 22.05, p < .01$$

The within-group variance on the helping-behavior measure is 31.76 (σ^2), whereas the between-group variance in helping is 99.82.

The chi-square test indicates that this between-group variance is significant:

$$\chi2(49) = 3,129.25, \, p < .01$$

The intraclass correlation for the helping-behavior measure is .76—that is, 99.82 / (99.82 + 31.76)—indicating that 76 percent of the variance resides between groups.[2]

Random-Coefficient Regression Model

The presence of significant between-group variance in helping behavior is the first requirement for testing hypotheses 2 and 3. In addition, these hypotheses propose that group-level cohesion will be significantly associated with the variance in the level 1 intercepts (hypothesis 2) and variance in the slopes (hypothesis 3). For these hypotheses to be supported, there must be significant variance in intercepts and slopes across groups. In other words, significant variance in the intercepts and slopes can be considered a precondition for the testing of hypotheses 2 and 3. The following model is designed to test these preconditions. In addition, this model will also directly test hypothesis 1. This model is called the *random-coefficient regression model* because it is similar to ordinary regression analysis, but in this model the coefficients are allowed to vary across groups. It takes on the following form:

Level 1: $\text{Helping}_{ij} = \beta_{0j} + \beta_{1j}(\text{Mood}_{ij}) + r_{ij}$

Level 2: $\beta_{0j} = \gamma_{00} + U_{0j}$

$\beta_{1j} = \gamma_{10} + U_{1j}$

where

γ_{00} = mean of the intercepts across groups

γ_{10} = mean of the slopes across groups (hypothesis 1)

variance $(r_{ij}) = \sigma^2$ = level 1 residual variance

Variance $(U_{0j}) = \tau_{00}$ = variance in intercepts

Variance $(U_{1j}) = \tau_{11}$ = variance in slopes

Table 11.1. Results of the Estimated Models, Based on Example Data Set.

Model	Parameter Estimates[a]						
	γ_{00}	γ_{01}	γ_{10}	γ_{11}	σ^2	τ_{00}	τ_{11}
One-way ANOVA							
L1: $Helping_{ij} = \beta_{0j} + r_{ij}$	31.39	—	—	—	31.76	99.82	—
L2: $\beta_{0j} = \gamma_{00} + U_{0j}$							
Random-coefficient regression							
L1: $Helping_{ij} = \beta_{0j} + \beta_{1j}(Mood_{ij}) + r_{ij}$	31.42	—	3.01	—	5.61	45.63	.13
L2: $\beta_{0j} = \gamma_{00} + U_{0j}$							
L2: $\beta_{1j} = \gamma_{10} + U_{1j}$							
Intercepts-as-outcomes							
L1: $Helping_{ij} = \beta_{0j} + \beta_{1j}(Mood_{ij}) + r_{ij}$	24.92	1.24	3.01	—	5.61	41.68	.13
L2: $\beta_{0j} = \gamma_{00} + \gamma_{01}(Cohesion_j) + U_{0j}$							
L2: $\beta_{1j} = \gamma_{10} + U_{1j}$							
Slopes-as-outcomes							
L1: $Helping_{ij} = \beta_{0j} + \beta_{1j}(Mood_{ij}) + r_{ij}$	25.14	1.19	2.06	.18	5.61	42.95	.02
L2: $\beta_{0j} = \gamma_{00} + \gamma_{01}(Cohesion_j) + U_{0j}$							
L2: $\beta_{1j} = \gamma_{10} + \gamma_{11}(Cohesion_j) + U_{1j}$							

[a] Parameters defined as follows:

γ_{00} = Intercept of level-2 regression predicting β_{0j}

γ_{01} = Slope of level-2 regression predicting β_{0j}

γ_{10} = Intercept of level-2 regression predicting β_{1j}

γ_{11} = Slope of level-2 regression predicting β_{1j}

σ^2 = variance in level-1 residual (i.e., variance in r_{ij})

τ_{00} = variance in level-2 residual for models predicting β_{0j} (i.e., variance in U_{0j})

τ_{11} = variance in level-2 residual for models predicting β_{1j} (i.e., variance in U_{1j})

Because there are no level 2 predictors of either β_{0j} or β_{1j}, the level 2 regression equation is simply equal to an intercept term and a residual. In this form, the γ_{00} and γ_{10} parameters represent the level 1 coefficients averaged across groups (they represent the pooled β_{0j} and β_{1j} parameters). Similarly, given that β_{0j} and β_{1j} are regressed onto constants, the variance of the level 2 residual terms (U_{0j} and U_{1j}) represent the between-group variance in the level 1 parameters. HLM provides a *t*-test related to the γ_{00} and γ_{10} parameters, where a significant *t*-value indicates that the parameter departs significantly from zero. In the case of the γ_{10} parameter, this *t*-test provides a direct test of hypothesis 1. In other words, this tests whether mood is significantly related to helping behavior. Note that this test is actually assessing whether the pooled level 1 slope between mood and helping behavior differs significantly from zero (whether, on average, the relationship between mood and helping is significant).

HLM also provides a chi-square test for the two residual variances (τ_{00} and τ_{11}). These chi-square tests indicate whether the variance components differ significantly from zero and, in this case, determine whether the variance in the intercepts (τ_{00}) and slopes (τ_{11}) across groups is significantly different from zero. Thus the random-coefficient regression model provides two primary pieces of information: it tests the significance of the pooled level 1 slopes used to test level 1 hypotheses, and it tests whether there is significant variance surrounding the pooled level 1 intercepts and slopes. In other words, the random regression model provides a significance test for the mean of the level 1 regression coefficients as well as for the variance in the level 1 regression coefficients.

Table 11.1 provides the results for the random-coefficient regression model for the example data. Both γ_{00} and γ_{10} indicate that the average, or pooled, intercept and slope is significantly different from zero:

$$\gamma_{00} = 31.42, \ t(49) = 32.74, \ p < .01$$

$$\gamma_{10} = 3.01, \ t(49) = 43.68, \ p < .01$$

The direction of the pooled slope of the regression of helping behavior onto mood (γ_{10}) indicates that, on average, individuals in a more positive mood are more likely to help their co-workers, thereby supporting hypothesis 1. The results in Table 11.1 also illustrate that, across groups, there is significant variance in the intercepts:

$$\tau_{00} = 45.63, \chi^2(49) = 4{,}605.68, p < .01$$

There is also significant variance, across groups, in the slopes:

$$\tau_{11} = .13, \chi^2(49) = 110.17, p < .01$$

Thus the preconditions for hypotheses 2 and 3 are also supported.

The random-coefficient regression model allows us to do one more thing. Although we know that, on average, mood is significantly related to helping behavior, we do not know the magnitude of this relationship. However, we do have from the ANOVA model an estimate of the within-group variance in helping behavior ($\sigma^2 = 31.76$), and from the current model we have an estimate of the residual within-group variance after controlling for mood ($\sigma^2 = 5.61$). Comparing these two variance estimates allows us to compute an R^2 for the relationship between helping behavior and mood. Specifically, one can obtain the R^2 for helping behavior by computing the following ratio:

R^2 for level 1 model = $(\sigma^2\text{oneway ANOVA} - \sigma^2\text{random regression})$ $/\sigma^2\text{oneway ANOVA}$

This ratio compares the amount of variance accounted for by mood to the total within-group variance in helping in the denominator. Therefore, this ratio represents the percentage of the level 1 variance in helping that is accounted for by mood. In our example data, this R^2 is equal to .82:

$$(31.76 - 5.61) \, / \, 31.76$$

It should be emphasized that this R^2 value is computed with the use of the within-group variance as the denominator, not with the use of the total variance in the outcome variable (see Snijders & Bosker, 1994, for several alternative computations of R^2 values). Thus it is important to keep in mind that this R^2 value, as well as those to be discussed, are computed relative to the variance that can be predicted by a given independent variable; they are not computed relative to the total variance in the outcome variable. For example, level 1 variables are evaluated versus the within-group variance in the outcome variable, whereas level 2 variables (as will be shown) are evaluated relative to the between-group variance in the intercepts and slopes, respectively.

Intercepts-as-Outcomes Model

Given that our example data demonstrated significant between-group variance in the intercept term across groups, the next step is to see if this variance is significantly related to work-group cohesion (hypothesis 2). The HLM model takes the following form:

Level 1: $\text{Helping}_{ij} = \beta_{0j} + \beta_{1j}(\text{Mood}_{ij}) + r_{ij}$

Level 2: $\beta_{0j} = \gamma_{00} + \gamma_{01}(\text{Cohesion}_j) + U_{0j}$

$\beta_{1j} = \gamma_{10} + U_{1j}$

where

γ_{00} = level 2 intercept

γ_{01} = level 2 slope (hypothesis 2)

γ_{10} = mean (pooled) slopes

Variance $(r_{ij}) = \sigma^2$ = level 1 residual variance

Variance $(U_{0j}) = \tau_{00}$ = residual intercept variance

Variance $(U_{1j}) = \tau_{11}$ = variance in slopes

This model is similar to the random-coefficient regression model discussed earlier, with the addition of cohesion as level 2 predictor of β_{0j}. The t-tests associated with the γ_{01} parameter provide a direct test of hypothesis 2. Given that the level 2 equation for β_{0j} now includes a predictor (cohesion), the variance in the U_{0j} parameter (τ_{00}) represents the residual variance in β_{0j} across groups. If the chi-square test for this parameter is significant, it indicates that there remains systematic level 2 variance that could be modeled by additional level 2 predictors. All other parameters take on the same meaning as they did under the estimation of the random-coefficient regression model.

Inspection of Table 11.1 indicates that, in our example data, cohesion is a significant predictor of the between-group variance in the intercept term:

$$\gamma_{01} = 1.24; \ t(48) = 2.47, \ p = .02$$

The chi-square test associated with the residual variance in the intercept across groups indicates that there is still significant variance remaining in this parameter across groups:

$$\tau_{00} = 41.68; \ \chi^2(48) = 4{,}127.70, \ p < .01$$

The γ_{10} parameter takes on the same meaning (and same value) as in the previous model and indicates that, on average, mood is significantly and positively related to helping behavior. The chi-square test for the variance in the τ_{11} indicates that there is significant variance in the slope term:

$$\tau_{11} = .13, \ \chi^2(49) = 110.18, \ p < .01$$

The modeling of this variance and the testing of hypothesis 3 is taken up in the next model.

After the estimation of the intercepts-as-outcomes model, we know that cohesion was significantly related to the variance in the intercept term across groups. In order to assess the magnitude of this relationship, we can compare the variance in the τ_{00} from the random-coefficient regression model (the total between-group variance in the intercept term across groups) with the variance in the τ_{00} for the current model (the residual variance in the intercept after accounting for cohesion). Specifically, by comparing these two τ's one can obtain the R^2 for cohesion by computing the following ratio:

$$R^2 \text{ for level 2 intercept model} =$$
$$(\tau_{00} \text{ random regression} - \tau_{00} \text{ intercepts-as-outcomes})/$$
$$\tau_{00} \text{ random regression}$$

For our example data, this R^2 is equal to .09—that is, $(45.63 - 41.68)/45.63$. Once again, note that this R^2 value is computed relative to the between-group variance in the intercepts; it is not computed relative to the total variance in the outcome variable (Snijders & Bosker, 1994).

Slopes-as-Outcomes Model

Given that the preceding model indicates significant variance in the level 1 slopes across groups (τ_{11}), we can see if this variance is significantly related to cohesion (hypothesis 3). The HLM model takes the following form:

Level 1: $\text{Helping}_{ij} = \beta_{0j} + \beta_{1j} (\text{Mood}_{ij}) + r_{ij}$

Level 2: $\beta_{0j} = \gamma_{00} + \gamma_{01} (\text{Cohesion}_j) + U_{0j}$

$\beta_{1j} = \gamma_{10} + \gamma_{11} (\text{Cohesion}_j) + U_{1j}$

where

γ_{00} = level 2 intercept

γ_{01} = level 2 slope (hypothesis 2)

γ_{10} = level 2 intercept

γ_{11} = level 2 slope (hypothesis 3)

Variance = $(r_{ij}) = \sigma^2$ = level 1 residual variance

Variance = $(U_{oj}) = \tau_{00}$ = residual intercept variance

Variance $(U_{1j}) = \tau_{11}$ = residual slope variance

The differences between this slopes-as-outcomes model and the intercepts-as-outcomes model are that cohesion is now included as a predictor of the β_{1j} parameter and, as a result, the U_{1j} variance is now the residual variance in the β_{1j} parameter across groups instead of the total variance across groups. Once again, if the chi-square test associated with this parameter variance is significant, it indicates that there remains systematic variance in the β_{1j} parameter that could be modeled by additional level 2 predictors. In addition, the t-test associated with the γ_{11} parameter provides a direct test of hypothesis 3. This hypothesis represents a cross-level moderator or cross-level interaction because a group-level variable is hypothesized to moderate the relationship between two individual-level variables.

Inspection of Table 11.1 indicates that, for our example data, γ_{11} is significant, thereby supporting hypothesis 3:

$$\gamma_{11} = .18, \, t(48) = 6.32, \, p<.01$$

The positive parameter estimate indicates that as cohesion increases, the slope relating mood to helping behavior becomes more positive (that is, stronger). Table 11.1 also reveals that the remaining variance in the β_{1j} parameter is not significantly different from zero:

$$\gamma_{11} = .02, \, \chi^2(48) = 59.22, \, ns$$

Once again, we use the value of the τ_{11} parameter from the previous model with the value of the τ_{11} parameter from the current model to compute an R^2 for cohesion as a level 2 moderator of the relationship between individual-level mood and helping behavior. Specifically, one can obtain the R^2 as follows:

$$R^2 \text{ level 2 slope model} =$$
$$(\tau_{11} \text{ intercept-as-outcomes} - \tau_{11} \text{ slopes as outcomes}) \, /$$
$$\tau_{11} \text{ intercept as outcomes}$$

For the example data, this R^2 value is .85—that is, $(.13 - .02) \, / \, .13$—which indicates that cohesion accounts for 85 percent of the variance in the relationship between mood and helping behavior.

Looking across the preceding models, the data have supported each of our three hypotheses, listed earlier. Specifically, the random-coefficient regression model provides support for hypothesis 1, the intercepts-as-outcomes model provides support for hypothesis 2, and the slopes-as-outcomes model provides support for hypothesis 3. Although the preceding sequence of models provides a test of a series of relatively simple hypotheses, the extension of these models to include more level 1 and level 2 predictors is relatively straightforward. Additional details regarding the testing of more complex models can be found in Bryk and Raudenbush (1992), Goldstein (1995), and Longford (1993).

Key Assumptions of Hierarchical Linear Models

Hierarchical linear models carry with them certain assumptions concerning the organizational systems under investigation, the data structures that can be analyzed, and the distributional properties of variables. In the passages that follow, we review some of the methodological and statistical assumptions on which these models are based.

Methodological Assumptions

The first assumption is that lower-level units (for example, individuals) are nested within identifiable higher-level units (for example, groups/teams or departments). In collecting data from such organizational systems, it is necessary that each lower-level unit be linked to an identifiable higher-level unit. A second assumption for both the organizational system and the data, the lower-level units are exposed to and influenced by characteristics and/or processes of the higher-level units. For example, in studying individuals nested within teams, it is assumed that team membership matters, and that individuals are influenced by characteristics and processes of the team. This is a general assumption underlying the hierarchical linear modeling approach. Whether a given characteristic and/or process of the higher-level unit has an impact on the lower-level outcome is, of course, an empirical question, which is tested via the estimation of the specific model(s).

A third assumption regarding the data is that the outcome variable is measured at the lowest level of interest to the researcher. In our example, for instance, the lowest level of interest is the individual level, and the outcome variable is individual-level helping behavior. Although the outcome variable will reside at the lowest level of interest to the researcher, the predictor variables can include both this level and higher levels of analysis. This is also illustrated in our example by the inclusion of both individual-level mood and group-level cohesion.

Finally, hierarchical linear models assume that the outcome variable varies both within the lower-level units and between the higher-level units. This is because these models investigate the influence of higher-level variables on lower-level outcomes, and this necessitates variance in the outcome both within and between units.

Statistical Assumptions

Hierarchical linear models, like any other statistical technique, require certain assumptions about the nature of the data. For two-level models, the following assumptions apply (Bryk & Raudenbush, 1992, p. 200):

1. Level 1 residuals are independent and normally distributed with a mean of zero and variance σ^2 for every level 1 unit within each level 2 unit.
2. Level 1 predictors are independent of level 1 residuals.
3. Random errors at level 2 are multivariate normal, each with a mean of zero, a variance of τ_{qq}, and a covariance of τ_{qq}', and are independent among level 2 units.
4. The set of level 2 predictors is independent of every level 2 residual. (This assumption is similar to assumption 2, but for level 2.)
5. Residuals at level 1 and level 2 are also independent.

To continue with our example, these assumptions entail the following meanings:

1. After taking into account the effect of mood, the within-group errors are normal and independent, with a mean of zero in each group and equal variances across groups (assumption 1).
2. If any additional level 1 predictors of helping are excluded from the model (and if their variance is thereby forced into the level 1 residual), they are independent of individual mood (assumption 2).
3. The group effects (that is, the level 2 residuals) are assumed multivariate normal, with variances τ_{00} and τ_{11} and covariance τ_{01} (assumption 3).

4. The effects of any group-level predictors excluded from the model for the intercept and mood slope are independent of cohesion (assumption 4).
5. The level 1 residual r_{ij} is independent of the residual group effects U_{0j} and U_{1j}.

Although Bryk and Raudenbush (1992) discuss these assumptions and the influence of possible violations, James (1995) noted several issues not discussed by Bryk and Raudenbush. First, hierarchical linear models assume multivariate normality and, on the basis of this assumption, proceed with maximum-likelihood estimation. The assumption of multivariate normality can be problematic, however, especially in the presence of interactions. This is clearly the case when level 1 slopes are predicted with level 2 variables. Second, hierarchical linear models treat independent variables as random variables; that is, processes beyond the control of the researcher determine the level of an individual's value on the independent variable. (This is by contrast with fixed variables, where individuals are randomly assigned to particular levels of the independent variable.) Given this assumption, it is possible that the independent variables will be correlated with the associated residuals. This could occur if an omitted variable is both correlated with the predictor variable included in the model and with the dependent variable (James, 1980). Finally, with regard to longitudinal data (Bryk & Raudenbush, 1987), hierarchical linear models assume that the level 1 residuals are independent, which may not be the case when one is modeling time-series data. Given the relative newness of hierarchical linear models, it remains to be seen how robust these techniques are to violations of these assumptions and, therefore, how robust this approach is to multilevel analysis.

Additional Issues in the Use of Hierarchical Linear Models

There are several additional issues that should be considered by researchers investigating multilevel relationships. In particular, the following section discusses the implications of alternative scalings of the level 1 predictors, as well as sample-size requirements.

Alternative Scales for Level 1 Predictors

Because hierarchical linear models use the level 1 parameters (that is, intercepts and slopes) as dependent variables in the level 2 equations, it is imperative that researchers understand the interpretation of these parameters. Regression textbooks (e.g., Cohen & Cohen, 1983) note that the slope parameter represents the expected increase in the outcome variable, given a unit increase in the independent variable, whereas the intercept represents the expected value of the outcome measure when all the independent variables take on a value of zero. In the organizational sciences, it is often the case that variables do not have meaningful, or true, zero points. For example, it means little for a person to have zero mood, job satisfaction, or organizational commitment, or for an organization to have zero structure, technology, centralization, or formalization. Therefore, it is useful to ask whether there are alternative scalings that would render the intercept more interpretable.

In hierarchical linear models, three alternative scalings of the level 1 independent variables have traditionally been discussed:

1. Raw-metric approaches, where the level 1 predictors are used in their original form
2. Grand-mean centering, where the grand mean of the level 1 variable is subtracted from each individual's score (for example, $\text{mood}_{ij} - \text{mood}_{\text{grand mean}}$)
3. Group-mean centering, where the group mean is subtracted from each individual's score on the predictor (for example, $\text{mood}_{ij} - \text{mood}_{\text{group mean}}$)

Although grand-mean and raw-metric approaches yield equivalent models, group-mean centering generally is not equivalent to these other two scaling options (Kreft, DeLeeuw, & Aiken, 1995). Recently, a number of researchers have discussed how group-mean centering versus raw-metric/grand-mean centering options can change the estimation and interpretation of hierarchical linear models (Bryk & Raudenbush, 1992; Hofmann & Gavin, 1998; Kreft et al., 1995; Longford, 1989; Plewis, 1989; Raudenbush, 1989a, 1989b). In particular, these scaling options can influence the interpretation of level 2 intercept and slope models. Each of these will be discussed in turn.

Scaling Options and Level 2 Intercept Models

In level 2 intercept models, group-mean centering versus raw-metric/grand-mean centering influences the interpretation of the variance of the level 2 intercept term. Specifically, when either grand-mean or raw-metric approaches are adopted, the variance in the intercept term represents the adjusted between-group variance in the outcome measure, after controlling for the level 1 predictors. In our example, and with these centering options, the variance in the intercept term across groups represents the between-group variance in helping behavior after controlling for mood. Given the wording of our three hypotheses, grand-mean or raw-metric centering of the level 1 predictors would be appropriate.

In using group-mean centering, alternatively, the level 1 intercept variance simply reflects the between-group variance in the outcome variable; that is, it reflects the unadjusted between-group variance in the outcome variable. In our example, and with group-mean centering, the intercept would reflect the between-group variance in helping behavior (the effects of individual mood have not been controlled for). Therefore, it would have been inappropriate for us to have tested hypothesis 2 by using group-mean centering, because all the effects of mood (within and between groups) would not have been taken into account. Put more simply, the level 2 model regressing the intercept term onto cohesion would be providing a test of the group-level relationship between helping and cohesion (equivalent to the group-level regression of the mean of helping behavior onto cohesion). Clearly, given the wording of hypothesis 2, this would have been an inappropriate analysis because the variance in mood—in particular, the between-group variance—has not been controlled for in the regression equation.

It is critical for researchers to understand that when group-mean centering is chosen as the scaling option for level 1 predictors, the between-group variance in these variables is excluded from the model. Therefore, the only way to completely control for the effects of level 1 variables (both within-group and between-group variance) under group-mean centering is to add this eliminated variance back in to the model. With respect to our example, the only way to control for the effects of mood before investigating the relationship between helping and cohesion would be to estimate a level 2 model with two predictors of helping behavior—namely, group-level mood and cohesion. This model would include the between-group variance in mood that was eliminated via the group-mean centering and would therefore provide results similar to those of a grand-mean or raw-metric model. The important point to emphasize here is that when group-mean centering is used, the effects of the level 1 variables are not controlled for in estimating the level 2 models.

Scaling Options and Level 2 Slope Models

The distinction between group-mean centering and raw-metric/ grand-mean centering can also be important in level 2 slope models. This is true because, with raw-metric or grand-mean centering, the level 1 slope summarizing the relationship between the level 1 predictor and the outcome variable is actually a function of two different relationships: the within-group relationship between the predictor and the outcome, and the between-group relationship between the predictor and the outcome. To illustrate, let us assume that a researcher has an independent and a dependent variable, and that both contain meaningful variance within and between groups. Given this meaningful within-and between-group variance, the researcher could actually create three independent variables: one consisting of the within-group variance (group-mean–centered), one consisting of the between-group variance (group means), and one consisting of the raw metric, which would contain both within- and between-group variance. Three regression equations could then be estimated with the use of the within-group variance, the between-group variance, and the raw-metric variance. The first equation would provide an estimate of the within-group relationship, the second an estimate of the between-group relationship, and the third an estimate of the total, or composite, relationship.

This logic applies to hierarchical linear modeling as well. In particular, raw-metric–centered models or grand-mean–centered models produce level 1 slopes that are actually composites of the within-group and between-group relationships among the independent and dependent variable. In fact, it is only when one group mean centers the level 1 predictors (that is, eliminates the between-group variance in the level 1 predictor from the level 1 model) that the level 1 slopes provide a pure estimate of the within-group relationship (Raudenbush, 1989b). As Raudenbush (1989b) has pointed out, this inclusion of both the within-group relationship and the between-group relationship in the level 1 slope estimates, under either raw-metric or grand-mean centering, can result in spurious cross-level interactions (see Hofmann & Gavin, 1998, for an example using simulated data).

We think that researchers should at least investigate this possibility when evaluating cross-level interactions. For instance, in the case of our substantive example, we hypothesized that work-group cohesion would act as both a cross-level main effect and as a moderator—that is, it would predict both the level 2 intercepts and the slopes. We also hypothesized that the main effect of cohesion would incrementally predict helping behavior (that is, over and above the effect of mood). Thus raw-metric or grand-mean centering would be the appropriate choice for our main-effect model. But we also hypothesized that cohesion would act as a cross-level moderator as well, by significantly predicting the level 1 slopes. As already noted, raw-metric or grand-mean centering can, on occasion, produce spurious cross-level interactions (Hofmann & Gavin, 1998; Raudenbush, 1989b). With respect to practical recommendations, we would recommend that the researcher first estimate all the models (both level 2 intercept and slope models) by using either raw-metric or grand-mean centering and then estimate one additional model before concluding the analyses. This last model would specify group-mean centering for the level 1 predictor, add in the group mean of the level 1 predictor in the level 2 intercept model (to reintroduce the between-group variance in the level 1 predictor, variance that was eliminated via group-mean centering), and re-estimate the cross-level interaction. In the case of our substantive example, this final model would take on the following form:

Level 1: $\text{Helping}_{ij} = \beta_{0j} + \beta_{1j} (\text{Mood}_{\text{group centered}}) + r_{ij}$

Level 2: $\beta_{0j} = \gamma_{00} + \gamma_{01} (\text{Mean Mood}_j) + \gamma_{02} (\text{Cohesion}_j) + U_{0j}$

$\beta_{1j} = \gamma_{10} + \gamma_{11} (\text{Cohesion}_j) + U_{1j}$

$\beta_{2j} = \gamma_{20} + U_{2j}$

If the γ_{11} parameters across these two final models are virtually identical, then, in order to be consistent with the investigation of all other hypotheses, we would report the grand-mean–centered results and footnote that we checked the cross-level interaction, using group-mean centering to ensure that the result was not spurious. This way, the results are easier for the reader to follow because the choice of centering is not changing halfway through the results section, but the researcher is confident that the results are not spurious.

It is important to emphasize that neither of these scaling options is statistically more correct than the other; instead, these decisions must be based on the theoretical model under consideration and on the nature of the hypotheses under investigation (for more details, see Hofmann & Gavin, 1998; Kreft et al., 1995). With respect to the organizational sciences, Hofmann and Gavin (1998) treat, at greater depth, these different centering options for different cross-level paradigms that traditionally have been investigated by organizational researchers.

Sample-Size Requirements

In the literature on hierarchical linear models, Kreft (1996) is, to our knowledge, the most comprehensive and complete summary of the work conducted on power and sample-size requirements. Summarizing simulation studies by Kim (1990) and Bassiri (1988), Kreft (1996) concludes that, in general, relatively large sample sizes are required. With regard to specific recommendations, two studies have indicated that in order to have sufficient power (.90) to detect cross-level interactions (that is, a level 2 slope relationship), it is necessary to have a sample of thirty groups containing thirty individuals each (Bassiri, 1988; van der Leeden & Busing, 1994).[3] There does appear to be a trade-off, however, between the number of groups and the number of individuals per group. For example, if there is a large number of groups (say, one hundred fifty), then the requirements regarding the number of individuals per group are reduced, to maintain the same level of power. Similarly, if there is a large number of individuals in each group, then the requirements regarding the number of groups will be reduced. All in all, however, there is still much work to be done regarding the power of these models and the sample size required in order for there to be adequate power (Bryk & Raudenbush, 1992).

Conclusion

In the preceding sections, we have provided a general introduction to and overview of hierarchical linear models. In an effort to provide a few summary conclusions regarding hierarchical linear models, we turn now to a discussion of the questions that we believe these models are both most and least effective at answering. In addition, we briefly compare hierarchical linear models to two commonly used methods of investigating multilevel models: OLS regression and within-and-between analysis. We close with some thoughts about what we believe the future holds for this approach to multilevel modeling.

Questions That Hierarchical Linear Models Answer Most Effectively

The following questions are particularly well suited to investigation by hierarchical linear models. The first four are related to one another and, in combination, build a picture of relationships across levels of analysis:

1. *Does the group in which individuals work make a difference?* This question concerns the degree to which individual measures vary across work groups. Hierarchical linear models address this question by estimating the proportion of total variance in individual responses that can be attributed to differences between groups and the proportion of total variance that can be attributed to differences among individuals. For example, the first step in the analysis of our substantive example was to investigate the extent to which the variance in helping behavior resided within groups versus between groups.

Similar questions can be answered by a variety of ANOVA procedures that partition variance in individual responses (Shrout & Fleiss, 1979). However, hierarchical linear models also provide a framework for incorporating predictors of this variance at both the individual level and the work-group level. In this way, information provided about the degree of variation between work groups is a precursor to questions about the predictors of this variance. The influence of predictors at the individual level is the basis for the following question.

2. *What is the impact of individual differences across work groups?* This question concerns the nature of relationships in the level 1 units. The question about the impact of individual differences can be broken into two smaller questions. Returning to our substantive example, we see that the first question asks whether, on average, individual-level mood is related to helping behavior. As we

have seen, hierarchical linear models provide a pooled estimate of the overall impact of individual factors. The second question addresses the variability in this relationship across groups. This question is investigated by estimating the systematic variance in the slope of helping behavior when regressed onto mood. If there is variation across groups, we know that individual mood has different effects, depending on the work groups to which individuals belong.

3. *Are individuals influenced by characteristics of the work group?* This question asks whether particular characteristics of the work group are related to the variance in individual outcomes that resides between work groups. It is essentially a main-effect question, addressing whether group characteristics predict individual-level outcomes after controlling for individual differences (that is, level 1 predictors). Hierarchical linear models enable an assessment of the relative contribution of multiple work-group characteristics so that the unique proportion of variance in the individual outcome associated with a given work-group characteristic can be obtained.

4. *Do properties of the work group modify individual-level relationships?* Provided that the answer to the second question reveals significant variance in the level 1 relationship across groups, this question addresses the extent to which group-level predictors can account for this variance. The answer to this question is perhaps what constitutes the most distinct advantage that hierarchical linear models offer to organizational researchers. Organizations are often concerned with the impact of aggregate-level interventions on relationships at the individual level. For example, an incentive program may aim to influence the degree to which perceived fairness is related to contextual performance. A job-design intervention may aim to increase the relationship between individual skills and task performance. In both examples, the relationship between two measures at the individual level is moderated by a characteristic of the work group. Hierarchical linear models are helpful here because its two-stage strategy enables assessment of the degree to which the relationship varies across work groups before an estimate is made of whether group characteristics moderate the relationship.

5. *Do individual differences influence individual change over time?* This question is somewhat different from the previous questions. It assumes that repeated measures have been obtained, and it asks whether the change in individuals over time is related to individ-

ual differences. Multiple measurements enable the assessment of specific growth patterns. For example, a linear and quadratic trend in work performance can be estimated for each individual. Subsequently, the researcher can investigate whether these trajectories are related to such individual differences as cognitive ability or previous work experience (Deadrick et al., 1997).

Questions That Hierarchical Linear Models Answer Least Effectively

The preceding five questions form the basis for a range of related questions that can be used to investigate multilevel relationships. Some questions that span levels of analysis are not readily answered by hierarchical linear models because they do not correspond to the assumptions made about the structure of the data and the types of relationships that are proposed. Three questions not addressed specifically by hierarchical linear models are described here:

1. *How do individuals influence work-group characteristics?* The difficulty of answering this question via hierarchical linear models is due to the assumption that the outcome measure is measured at the lowest level of analysis. Specifically, the question asks about the extent to which individual-level characteristics influence or predict aggregate phenomena. The examples discussed earlier were all constructed so that the dependent variable was measured at the lower level of analysis. When the outcome of interest is not at the lowest level, then this approach will not usually be the most appropriate analytical tool.

2. *At what level of analysis should a variable be measured?* Hierarchical linear models do not identify the most appropriate level at which a variable should be analyzed, although information obtained from the preceding question can shed light on the nature of the variation between work groups, which in turn can be used to support decisions about aggregation. For example, if a large proportion of variance in a measure occurs between work groups, then this result can be used to support aggregation of the measure to the work-group level. However, hierarchical linear models assume that the level of analysis for each measure has been determined before analysis, and that other techniques (for example, r_{wg}) are more appropriate for making decisions about level of measurement and data aggregation.

3. *To which group should an individual be assigned?* Hierarchical linear models require clear definition of the hierarchical structure in which measurements are embedded. The analysis does not provide information about the most appropriate group for an individual, as determined on the basis of ambiguous information about group membership. In this case, cluster-analytic procedures provide a more appropriate analytical tool.

Hierarchical Linear Models and OLS Regression

As already mentioned, OLS approaches present some problems with respect to multilevel modeling, but it is worthwhile to address several issues in greater depth. It will be recalled that OLS regression analog to this model is carried out by assigning the score on higher-level variables down to each of the respective lower-level units (for example, each member of a given group gets the same score on cohesion) and then conducting the analysis at the individual level. Given that OLS can approximate the hierarchical linear models, there are similarities in the sense that the same variables (both lower-level and higher-level) can be analyzed and the same types of relationships can be investigated (in-unit effects and both cross-level main effects and cross-level interaction effects).

This solution, however, is not without problems. OLS regression assumes, for example, that the random errors are independent, are normally distributed, and have constant variance. As Bryk and Raudenbush (1992) note, this assumption will likely be violated because the random errors will include a group-level component in addition to an individual-level component. This group-level error brings into question the independence of observations within groups because a portion of the random error is group random error (that is, measurement error of the group score), which is constant across individuals in a given group. In other words, the random errors of individuals in the same group are likely to be more similar than those of individuals in different groups, thus violating the assumption of independence. In addition, this group-level random error is also likely to vary across groups, thereby violating the assumption of constant variance (Bryk & Raudenbush, 1992). Finally, the assignment of group-level variables down to the individual level results in the use of statistical tests that are based on the number of individuals instead of on the number of groups. Therefore, standard errors associated with the tests of the group-level variable may be underestimated (Bryk & Raudenbush, 1992; Tate & Wongbundhit, 1983).

Hierarchical linear modeling, however, provides a more complex analysis and, in the process, more information than its OLS counterpart. Additionally, hierarchical linear modeling provides a more statistically appropriate analysis than OLS regression, for several reasons. First, hierarchical linear models explicitly partition the variance in the outcome variable and provide information about the magnitude (and significance) of these variance components. Second, separate regression analyses are performed for each group, relating the lower-level predictor(s) to the lower-level outcome. Because this is done, the level 1 intercepts and slopes are allowed to vary between level 2 units. OLS regression, by contrast, conducts a single regression analysis, pooling the lower-level units across groups, and subsequently does not allow the intercepts and slopes to vary. Fourth, as a result of the partitioning of the variance in the outcome into its within-group and between-group components, hierarchical linear modeling yields a more complex error term than its OLS counterpart. Specifically, the lower-level and higher-level errors are separately estimated, whereas the OLS regression approach combines them into a single term. Among other things, this has implications for assessing the explanatory power of variables at each of the different levels via the calculation of the R^2's (which is dependent on the error terms).

Hierarchical Linear Models and Within-and-Between Analysis

Another option for analyzing multilevel data is to use within-and-between analysis (Dansereau, Alutto, & Yammarino, 1984). In its basic form, WABA strives to answer two fundamental questions. The first question examines the variance within and between groups on a particular variable, in an effort to determine whether the variable is best represented at the individual or the group level. The second question examines the relationship between two variables, in an effort to determine whether the relationship resides primarily at the individual or the group level. It assumes that the two variables are measured at the same level of analysis—specifically, the lower level. Although the basic WABA analysis is bivariate, it should be noted that Schriesheim (1995) has made the extension to a multivariate WABA.

In our view, the primary distinction between hierarchical linear models and WABA is the basic type of question that each technique was designed to answer. Hierarchical linear models are geared toward answering questions about how higher-level variables influence lower-level outcomes and lower-level relationships (that is, level 1 slopes). WABA is more geared toward answering questions about the level at which the relationship between two variables (both measured at the same level) resides. Thus, whereas WABA is concerned with identifying the level at which the relationship between two variables exists, hierarchical linear modeling prespecifies the level at which variables are expected to relate, and it specifies that their relationships will cross levels.

Another distinction, touched on earlier but made explicit here, is that WABA analyses involve only variables measured at the same level. For example, WABA can be used to investigate the relationship between two individual-level variables among individuals nested within groups. The analysis provides insight into whether the relationship between these two variables resides predominantly within groups, between groups, or both. Alternatively, hierarchical linear models allow for the investigation of the relationship between an outcome and variables measured and/or residing at two or more levels. For example, these models can be used to investigate, simultaneously, the influence of individual as well as team characteristics on individuals.

A final distinction between hierarchical linear models and WABA emerges when one is interested in investigating cross-level interactions. Hierarchical linear models were specifically designed to investigate how level 2 variables can moderate the relationship between two level 1 variables (that is, the slopes-as-outcomes model). WABA provides no such analysis and implicitly assumes that these slopes are homogeneous across groups (George & James, 1993). Thus, although the WABA model has recently been expanded to include interactions at each level, cross-level interactions are not possible, to our knowledge. Although WABA does not enable a researcher to investigate one of the central questions for which hierarchical linear models were developed (that is, cross-level interactions), it does provide evidence surrounding questions that must be answered in advance of the application of hierarchical linear models (for example, the level at which a variable, or a relationship, resides).

The Future of Hierarchical Linear Models

At the beginning of this chapter, we noted the diverse fields in which hierarchical linear modeling has been applied. We believe that the popularity of these methods will continue to increase over the next five to ten years. In fact, we believe that the breadth of the fields in which these models have been adopted testifies to both the flexibility and the conceptual forthrightness of the method. Although levels-of-analysis issues have been discussed for a number of years in the organizational sciences (Rousseau, 1985), there seems to be a recent and growing emphasis on integrating levels of analysis into theory building (Cappelli & Sherer, 1991; House, Rousseau, & Thomas-Hunt, 1995; Klein et al., 1994; Morgeson & Hofmann, 1998). This volume speaks to this growing emphasis on integrating levels of analysis into organizational theory building. This increasing emphasis on multilevel theory building will result in a growing demand for multilevel data-analytic tools. We believe that hierarchical linear models will provide a mechanism for testing at least some of these theories (for example, those that specify predictors at multiple levels of analysis and an outcome variable at the lowest level).

Concurrent with this emphasis on multilevel theory, a number of applications of hierarchical linear modeling have started to appear in the organizational science literature. For example, in a special issue devoted to hierarchical linear models, the *Journal of Management* provided an overview of the technique (Hofmann, 1997), followed by four applications of these models to substantive questions (Deadrick et al., 1997; Griffin, 1997a; Kidwell et al., 1997; Vancouver, 1997). In addition, articles using hierarchical linear models have recently appeared in a number of other organizationally focused journals (Griffin, 1997b; Hofmann et al., 1993; Hofmann & Stetzer, 1996, 1998; Jimmieson & Griffin, 1998; Mossholder et al., 1998; Vancouver et al., 1994; Wech et al., 1998). The co-occurrence of this increasing demand for multilevel theory building and the emerging use of hierarchical linear models, as well as the use of other multilevel techniques described in this volume, will, we believe, create a synergy in the organizational sciences so that both development and testing of multilevel models of organizational phenomena will greatly increase over the next five to ten years. We hope that this chapter, as well as the other chapters in this volume, will help to increase not only the strength of multilevel theories but also the degree to which these theories can be tested.

Notes

1. In some contexts, researchers are interested in obtaining the most accurate estimate for a level 1 parameter for a particular group. For example, often in educational research the level 1 parameters convey information about a particular school's effectiveness (Raudenbush, 1988). The inspection of equations 1, 2, and 3, however, reveals that there are actually two estimates of these level 1 parameters. Specifically, one can obtain an OLS estimate of a particular group's level 1 coefficients via equation 1, or use equations 2 and 3 to compute predicted values of a particular group's intercept and slope. Thus, the OLS equation 1 provides one estimate of the intercept and slope, whereas the computation of predicted values in equations 2 and 3 provides a second estimate. If the researcher is interested in obtaining the most accurate estimate of the level 1 coefficients for a particular group, the question remains: Which of the two is best?

   The HLM approach does not force the researcher to make a choice between these two different estimates of a unit's intercept and slope. Specifically, the HLM procedure can produce empirical Bayes estimates, which are optimally weighted composites of the two different estimates discussed earlier—that is, the estimates emerging from equation 1 and those coming from equations 2 and 3 (Bryk & Raudenbush, 1992; Morris, 1983; Raudenbush, 1988). Both Bryk and Raudenbush (1992) and Raudenbush (1988) provide more extended discussions of these empirical Bayes estimates and their computation. Suffice it to say here that these empirical Bayes estimates can be computed and will provide more accurate estimates of a particular group's level 1 coefficients, which in some contexts will be quite useful. Although it is important to point out that the ability to obtain these empirical Bayes estimates is an important strength of the HLM approach, they likely will not be relevant to most organizational researchers. Specifically, most organizational researchers are interested in obtaining level 2 predictors of the level 1 parameters instead of merely obtaining the best estimates of the level 1 parameters.

2. It should be noted here that 76 percent of the variance residing between groups is quite large when compared to published studies investigating cross-level models (e.g., Campion, Medsker, & Higgs, 1993;

Hofmann & Stetzer, 1996; James, 1982). The reader is reminded that these are simulated data.

3. The sample-size requirements to detect a cross-level main effect (that is, the level 2 intercept model) are likely to be less, given that intercept estimates are typically more precisely estimated than are slope estimates (that is, they have small standard errors). In fact, Hofmann and Stetzer (1996) have found significant cross-level main effects by using data on twenty-one teams containing approximately ten individuals each.

References

Aldrich, H. E., & Pfeffer, J. (1976). Environments of organizations. *Annual Review of Sociology, 2,* 79–105.

Arnold, C. L. (1992). An introduction to hierarchical linear models. *Measurement and Evaluation in Counseling and Development, 25,* 58–90.

Austin, J. T., & Villanova, P. (1992). The criterion problem: 1917–1992. *Journal of Applied Psychology, 77,* 836–874.

Barnett, R. C., Raudenbush, S. W., Brennan, R. T., Pleck, J. H., & Marshall, N. L. (1995). Change in job and marital experiences and change in psychological distress: A longitudinal study of dual-earner couples. *Journal of Personality and Social Psychology, 69,* 839–850.

Bassiri, D. (1988). *Large and small sample properties of maximum likelihood estimates for the hierarchical linear model.* Unpublished doctoral dissertation, Michigan State University.

Battistich, V., Solomon, D., Kim, D., Watson, M., & Schaps, E. (1995). Schools as communities, poverty levels of student populations, and students' attitudes, motives, and performance: A multilevel analysis. *American Educational Research Journal, 32,* 627–658.

Blalock, H. M. (1984). Contextual-effects models: Theoretical and methodological issues. In R. H. Turner & J. F. Short, Jr. (Eds.), *Annual review of sociology* (Vol. 10, pp. 353–372). Palo Alto, CA: Annual Reviews.

Bliese, P. D. (2000). Within-group agreement, non-independence, and reliability: Implications for data aggregation and analysis. In K. J. Klein & S.W.J. Kozlowski (Eds.), *Multilevel theory, research, and methods in organizations* (pp. 349–381). San Francisco: Jossey-Bass.

Brass, D. J. (1981). Structural relationships, job characteristics, and worker satisfaction and performance. *Administrative Science Quarterly, 26,* 331–348.

Bryk, A. S., & Raudenbush, S. W. (1987). Application of hierarchical linear models to assessing change. *Psychological Bulletin, 101,* 147–158.

Bryk, A. S., & Raudenbush, S. W. (1992). *Hierarchical linear models: Applications and data analysis methods.* Thousand Oaks, CA: Sage.

Bryk, A. S., Raudenbush, S. W., & Congdon, R. T., Jr. (1996). *HLM: Hierarchical linear and nonlinear modeling with the HLM/2L and HLM/3L programs.* Chicago: Scientific Software International.

Burstein, L. (1980). The role of levels of analysis in the specification of educational effects. In R. Dreeben & J. A. Thomas (Eds.), *Analysis of educational productivity: Issues in microanalysis.* Cambridge, MA: Ballinger.

Burstein, L., & Hannan, M. T. (1976). *Data aggregation in educational research.* Unpublished paper.

Burstein, L., Kim, K. S., & Delandshere, G. (1989). Multilevel investigations of systematically varying slopes: Issues, alternatives, and consequences. In R. D. Bock (Ed.), *Multilevel analysis of educational data* (pp. 233–276). Orlando, FL: Academic Press.

Campion, M. A., Medsker, G. J., & Higgs, A. C. (1993). Relations between work group characteristics and effectiveness: Implications for designing effective work groups. *Personnel Psychology, 46,* 823–850.

Cappelli, P., & Sherer, P. D. (1991). The missing role of context in OB: The need for a meso-level approach. In L. L. Cummings & B. M. Staw, (Eds.), *Research in organizational behavior* (Vol. 13, pp. 55–110). Greenwich, CT: JAI Press.

Child, J. (1974). Managerial and organizational factors associated with company performance. Part 1. *Journal of Management Studies, 11,* 175–189.

Child, J. (1975). Managerial and organizational factors associated with company performance. Part 2. *Journal of Management Studies, 12,* 12–27.

Cohen, J., & Cohen, P. (1983). *Applied multiple regression/correlation analysis for the behavioral sciences.* Mahwah, NJ: Erlbaum.

Dansereau, F., Alutto, J. A., & Yammarino, F. J. (1984). *Theory testing in organizational behavior: The varient approach.* Englewood Cliffs, NJ: Prentice Hall.

Deadrick, D., Bennett, N., & Russell, C. (1997). Using hierarchical linear modeling to examine dynamic performance criteria over time. *Journal of Management, 23,* 745–757.

Dempster, A. P., Laird, N. M., & Rubin, D. B. (1977). Maximum likelihood from incomplete data via the EM algorithm. *Journal of the Royal Statistical Society,* series B, *39,* 1–38.

Eyring, J. D., Johnson, D. S., & Francis, D. J. (1993). A cross-level units of analysis approach to individual differences in skill acquisition. *Journal of Applied Psychology, 78,* 805–814.

Gavin, M. B., & Hofmann, D. A. (in press). Using hierarchical linear modeling to investigate the moderating influence of leadership climate. *Leadership Quarterly.*

George, J. M., & James, L. R. (1993). Personality, affect, and behavior within-groups revisited: Comment on aggregation, levels of analysis, and a recent application of within-and-between analysis. *Journal of Applied Psychology, 78,* 798–804.

Goldstein, H. (1987). *Multilevel models in educational and social research.* New York: Oxford University Press.

Goldstein, H. (1995). *Multilevel statistical models.* London: Edward Arnold.

Griffin, M. A. (1997a). Interactions between individuals and situations: Using HLM procedures to estimate reciprocal relationships. *Journal of Management, 23,* 759–773.

Griffin, M. A. (1997b). Multilevel influences on work attitudes: Organizational and individual predictors of pay satisfaction. *Australian Psychologist, 32,* 190–195.

Gully, S. M. (1997). *The influences of self-regulatory processes on learning and performance in a team training context.* Unpublished doctoral dissertation, Michigan State University.

Hackman, J. R. (1992). Group influences on individuals in organizations. In M. D. Dunnette & L. M. Hough (Eds.), *Handbook of industrial and organizational psychology* (2nd ed., pp. 199–268). Palo Alto, CA: Consulting Psychologists Press.

Hall, R. H. (1987). *Organizations: Structures, processes, and outcomes* (4th ed.). Englewood Cliffs, NJ: Prentice Hall.

Hanushek, E. A. (1974). Efficient estimators for regressing regression coefficients. *The American Statistician, 28,* 66–67.

Hofmann, D. A. (1997). An overview of the logic and rationale of hierarchical linear models. *Journal of Management, 23,* 723–744.

Hofmann, D. A., & Gavin, M. B. (1998). Centering decisions in Hierarchical Linear Models: Theoretical and methodological implications for organizational science. *Journal of Management, 23,* 623–641.

Hofmann, D. A., Jacobs, R., & Baratta, J. (1993). Dynamic criteria and the measurement of change. *Journal of Applied Psychology, 78,* 194–204.

Hofmann, D. A., Jacobs, R., & Gerras, S. (1992). Mapping individual performance over time. *Journal of Applied Psychology, 77,* 185–195.

Hofmann, D. A., & Stetzer, A. (1996). A cross level investigation of factors influencing unsafe behavior and accidents. *Personnel Psychology, 49,* 307–339.

Hofmann, D. A., & Stetzer, A. (1998). The role of safety climate and communication in accident interpretation: Implications for learning from negative events. *Academy of Management Journal, 41,* 644–657.

House, R., Rousseau, D. M., & Thomas-Hunt, M. (1995). The meso paradigm: A framework for the integration of micro and macro organizational behavior. In L. L. Cummings & B. M. Staw (Eds.), *Research in organizational behavior* (Vol. 17, pp. 71–114). Greenwich, CT: JAI Press.

Hulin, C. L., & Roznowski, M. (1985). Organizational technologies: Effects on organizational characteristics and individuals responses. In S. Bachrach & N. DiTomaso (Eds.), *Research in the sociology of organizations* (Vol. 7, pp. 39–53). Greenwich, CT: JAI Press.

James, L. R. (1980). The unmeasured variables problem in path analysis. *Journal of Applied Psychology, 65,* 415–421.

James, L. R. (1982). Aggregation bias in estimates of perceptual agreement. *Journal of Applied Psychology, 67,* 219–229.

James, L. R. (1995). Comments offered as part of a presentation (Introduction, explanation, and illustrations of hierarchical linear modeling as a management research tool) at the annual conference of the Academy of Management, Vancouver, British Columbia.

James, L. R., James, L. A., & Ashe, D. K. (1990). The meaning of organizations: The role of cognition and values. In B. Schneider (Ed.), *Organizational climate and culture* (pp. 40–84). San Francisco: Jossey-Bass.

James, L. R., & Jones, A. P. (1976). Organizational structure: A review of structural dimensions and their conceptual relationships with individual attitudes and behavior. *Organizational Behavior and Human Performance, 16,* 74–113.

Jimmieson, N., & Griffin, M. A. (1998). Linking staff and client perceptions of the organization: A field study of client satisfaction with health services. *Journal of Occupational and Organizational Psychology, 71,* 81–96.

Jones, F. L. (1995). Micro-macro linkages in sociological analysis: Theory, method, and substance. *Australian and New Zealand Journal of Sociology, 31,* 74–92.

Joyce, A. S., & Piper, W. E. (1996). Interpretive work in short-term individual psychotherapy: An analysis using hierarchical linear modeling. *Journal of Consulting and Counseling Psychology, 64,* 505–512.

Kalaian, H. A., & Raudenbush, S. W. (1996). A multivariate mixed linear model for meta-analysis. *Psychological Methods, 1,* 227–235.

Kidwell, R. E., Jr., Mossholder, K. M., & Bennett, N. (1997). Cohesiveness and organizational citizenship behavior: A multilevel analysis using work groups and individuals. *Journal of Management, 23,* 775–793.

Kim, K. S. (1990). *Multilevel data analysis: A comparison of analytical alternatives.* Unpublished doctoral dissertation, University of California, Los Angeles.

Klein, K. J., Dansereau, F., & Hall, R. J. (1994). Levels issues in theory development, data collection, and analysis. *Academy of Management Review, 19,* 195–229.

Kozlowski, S.W.J., & Hults, B. M. (1987). An exploration of climates for technical updating and performance. *Personnel Psychology, 40,* 539–563.

Kreft, I.G.G. (1996). *Are multilevel techniques necessary? An overview, including simulation studies.* Unpublished paper, California State University, Los Angeles.

Kreft, I.G.G., DeLeeuw, J., & Aiken, L. S. (1995). The effect of different forms of centering in Hierarchical Linear Models. *Multivariate Behavioral Research, 30,* 1–21.

Kreft, G. G., DeLeeuw, J., & van der Leeden, R. (1994). Review of five multilevel analysis programs: BMDP-5V, GENMOD, HLM, ML3, VARCL. *American Statistician, 48,* 324–335.

Laird, N. M., & Ware, H. (1982). Random-effects models for longitudinal data. *Biometrics, 38,* 963–974.

Longford, N. T. (1986). VARCL—Interactive software for variance component analysis: Applications for survey data. *Professional Statistician, 5,* 28–33.

Longford, N. (1989). To center or not to center. *Multilevel Modeling Newsletter, 1*(2), 7, 8, 11.

Longford, N. T. (1993). *Random coefficient models.* New York: Oxford University Press.

Martocchio, J. J. (1994). The effects of absence culture on individual absence. *Human Relations, 47,* 243–262.

Mason, W. M., Wong, G. M., & Entwistle, B. (1983). Contextual analysis through the multilevel linear model. In S. Leinhardt (Ed.), *Sociological methodology* (pp. 72–103). San Francisco: Jossey-Bass.

Morgeson, F. P., & Hofmann, D. A. (1998). *Collective constructs in the organizational sciences: An essay on their structure and function.* Unpublished manuscript.

Morris, C. N. (1983). Parametric empirical Bayes inference: Theory and applications. *Journal of the American Statistical Association, 78,* 47–65.

Mossholder, K. W., Bennett, N., & Martin, C. L. (1998). A multilevel analysis of procedural justice context. *Journal of Organizational Behavior, 19,* 131–141.

Nesselroade, J. R. (1991). Interindividual differences in intraindividual change. In L. M. Collins, & J. L. Horn (Eds.), *Best methods for the analysis of change: Recent advances, unanswered questions, future directions* (pp. 92–105). Washington, DC: American Psychological Association.

Oldham, G. R., & Hackman, J. R. (1981). Relationships between organizational structure and employee reactions: Comparing alternative frameworks. *Administrative Science Quarterly, 26,* 66–83.

Osgood, D. W., & Smith, G. L. (1995). Applying hierarchical linear modeling to extended longitudinal evaluations: The Boys Town follow-up study. *Evaluation Review, 19,* 3–38.

Pfeffer, J., & Salancik, G. (1978). *The external control of organizations: A resource dependence perspective.* New York: HarperCollins.

Plewis, I. (1989). Comment on "centering" predictors. *Multilevel Modeling Newsletter, 1*(3), 6, 11.

Plewis, I. (1996). Statistical methods for understanding cognitive growth: A review, a synthesis and an application. *British Journal of Mathematical and Statistical Psychology, 49,* 25–42.

Raudenbush, S. W. (1988). Educational applications of hierarchical linear models: A review. *Journal of Educational Statistics, 13,* 85–116.

Raudenbush, S. W. (1989a). "Centering" predictors in multilevel analysis: Choices and consequences. *Multilevel Modeling Newsletter, 1*(2), 10–12.

Raudenbush, S. W. (1989b). A response to Longford and Plewis. *Multilevel Modeling Newsletter, 1*(3), 8–10.

Raudenbush, S. W., Brennan, R. T., & Barnett, R. C. (1995). A multivariate hierarchical model for studying psychological change in married couples. *Journal of Family Psychology, 9,* 161–174.

Raudenbush, S. W., Rowan, B., & Cheong, Y. F. (1993). Higher order instructional goals in secondary schools: Class, teacher, and school influences. *American Educational Research Journal, 30,* 523–553.

Rousseau, D. M. (1978). Characteristics of departments, positions, and individuals: Contexts for attitudes and behavior. *Administrative Science Quarterly, 23,* 521–540.

Rousseau, D. M. (1985). Issues of level in organizational research: Multi-level and cross-level perspectives. *Research in Organizational Behavior, 7,* 1–37.

Saxonhouse, G. R. (1976). Estimated parameters as dependent variables. *American Economic Review, 66,* 178–183.

Schriesheim, C. A. (1995). Multivariate and moderated in-and-between-entity analysis (WABA) using hierarchical linear regression. *Leadership Quarterly, 6,* 1–18.

Shrout, P. E., Fleiss, J. L. (1979). Intraclass correlations: Uses in assessing rater reliability. *Psychological Bulletin, 86,* 245–282.

Snijders, T.A.B., & Bosker, R. J. (1994). Modeled variance in two-level models. *Sociological Methods and Research, 22,* 342–363.

Tate, R. L., & Wongbundhit, Y. (1983). Random versus nonrandom coefficient models for multilevel analysis. *Journal of Educational Statistics, 8,* 103–120.

Vancouver, J. B. (1997). The application of HLM to the analysis of the dynamic interaction of environment, person, and behavior. *Journal of Management, 23,* 795–818.

Vancouver, J. B., Millsap, R. E., & Peters, P. A. (1994). Multilevel analysis of organizational goal congruence. *Journal of Applied Psychology, 79,* 666–679.

van der Leeden, R., & Busing, F.M.T.A. (1994). First iteration versus igls/rigls estimates in two-level models: A monte carlo study with ML3. *Psychometrics and Research Methodology,* preprint PRM 94–03.

Wech, B. A., Mossholder, K. W., Steel, R. P., & Bennett, N. (1998). Does work group cohesiveness affect individuals' performance and organizational commitment? A cross-level examination. *Small Group Research, 29,* 472–494.

Wittink, D. R. (1977). Exploring territorial differences in the relationship between marketing variables. *Journal of Marketing Research, 14,* 145–155.

Zwaagstra, R., Schmidt, I., & Vanier, M. (1996). Recovery of speed of information processing in closed-head-injury patients. *Journal of Clinical and Experimental Neuropsychology, 18,* 383–393.

CHAPTER 12

Multilevel Analytical Techniques
Commonalities, Differences, and Continuing Questions

Katherine J. Klein   Mark A. Griffin
Paul D. Bliese   David A. Hofmann
Steve W. J. Kozlowski   Lawrence R. James
Fred Dansereau   Francis J. Yammarino
Mark B. Gavin   Michelle C. Bligh

A variety of statistical procedures are available to establish agreement within groups and/or to analyze multilevel data. These procedures include r_{wg}, eta-squared, ICC(1), ICC(2), within-and-between analysis (WABA), hierarchical linear modeling (HLM), and cross-level operator (CLOP) analyses in regression and analysis of variance. These procedures in are described in detail in Chapters Eight through Eleven. Because each of these chapters addresses a different procedure or set of procedures, readers may gain an appreciation of each procedure in isolation but may nevertheless wonder how the

Note: Preparation of this chapter was a collaborative effort. Katherine J. Klein conceived of the idea for the chapter and was the primary contact person, talking and e-mailing with the chapter authors as the chapter developed. Klein, Paul D. Bliese, and Steve W. J. Kozlowski wrote the chapter. Bliese developed the simulated data set, conducted the cross-level-operator data analyses (on the basis of Chapter Nine in this volume, by Lawrence R. James and Larry J. Williams), and conducted several of the other data analyses reported in the chapter. Michele C.

procedures compare, and whether the procedures answer the same or different questions. Indeed many debates in the literature revolve around these issues. In this chapter, we offer some answers to these questions.

We do not present an overview of each procedure. Instead, we describe commonalities and differences among the various data-analytic procedures. Accordingly, we urge readers to study Chapters One, Eight, Nine, Ten, and Eleven before reading this chapter. Our goal is to help readers make informed choices about which procedures to use when, and why; our goal is not to evaluate or advocate, nor is it to resolve differences among the procedures.

The chapter is organized into four sections. In the first section, we describe a number of dimensions that differentiate the indices often used to justify aggregation of lower-level (for example, individual) data to a higher level of analysis (for example, groups). These indices are r_{wg}, WABA, ICC(1), ICC(2), and eta-squared. In the second section, we describe dimensions that differentiate three procedures commonly used in multilevel data analysis. These procedures are WABA, HLM (one of a class of random-coefficient modeling techniques), and CLOP. In the third section, we use these indices and procedures to analyze a simulated data set, thereby illustrating similarities and differences among the approaches. In the fourth section, we offer a brief summary and concluding comments.

Aggregation of Lower-Level Data to Higher Units of Analysis

Multilevel researchers often gather data from lower-level units (for example, individuals) to assess higher-level (for example, group) constructs. In doing so, multilevel researchers typically propose, implicitly or explicitly, a composition model linking the individual-level data to the group-level construct they seek to measure (see Chan,

---

Bligh conducted the WABA analyses under the guidance of Fred Dansereau and Francis J. Yammarino. Mark B. Gavin conducted the HLM data analyses in consultation with David A. Hofmann and Mark A. Griffin. This chapter is based in part on Chapters Eight, Nine, Ten, and Eleven, whose authors had the opportunity to provide comments on and sign off on this chapter. Although supportive of this chapter, Williams was unavailable to provide detailed comments and therefore opted not to be included as a chapter author.

1998; Rousseau, 1985; see also Kozlowski & Klein, Chapter One, this volume). Composition models of this type propose that the lower-level data are sufficiently homogeneous within units that the data may be meaningfully aggregated to the unit level. The lower-level data are thus "candidates" for aggregation to the higher level. A number of procedures are available to determine whether these candidates are "contenders"—that is, whether the lower-level data are indeed sufficiently homogeneous to justify aggregation. These procedures include r_{wg}, WABA, ICC(1), ICC(2), and eta-squared. We distinguish between WABA and eta-squared because, although WABA utilizes eta-squared values in drawing inferences, not all multilevel researchers interpret eta-squared values in the same way that WABA researchers do. Here, we highlight five dimensions that differentiate the various procedures most commonly used to justify aggregation.

1. *Does the procedure assess variability within one unit at a time, or does the procedure assess within- and between-unit variability across the entire sample of units?*

Of the five procedures commonly used to justify aggregation of lower-level data to the higher-level of analysis, only r_{wg} (James, Demaree, & Wolf, 1984) provides an assessment of agreement within a specific group. The r_{wg} procedure compares the observed within-group variability to the within-unit variability expected from a hypothetical random distribution—that is, an expected variance, or EV. Thus a researcher uses r_{wg} to obtain a separate assessment of within-unit agreement on the measure of interest for each unit in his or her sample. Kozlowski and Klein (Chapter One, this volume) call this a *construct-by-unit approach*. This approach allows one to test whether within-group agreement is uniform across all the units in the sample.

In contrast, the remaining procedures—ICC(1), ICC(2), eta-squared, and WABA I—assess within-unit homogeneity by comparing between-group variance to the total variance across a researcher's entire sample of units. These procedures provide an omnibus index of homogeneity and do not allow one to assess whether a specific unit shows greater than chance homogeneity. Kozlowski and Klein (Chapter One, this volume) call this a *construct-by-sample approach.* Using this approach, a researcher may conclude that a variable is homogeneous within units across the entire sample even if some specific units show little within-unit homogeneity.

Different procedures used to justify aggregation may yield different conclusions. If agreement within each unit is high but the means for the units vary little from unit to unit, then a researcher using r_{wg} alone will conclude that aggregation to the unit level is appropriate. (If so, the researcher may discover, in testing group-level hypotheses, that the sample lacks sufficient between-unit variability to provide an adequate test of the hypotheses.) In contrast, a researcher using ICC(1), ICC(2), eta-squared, or WABA may conclude that aggregation is not appropriate, given the lack of between-group variability. Conversely, if the means for the units vary considerably across a sample but variability within each unit is also relatively high, then researchers using ICC(1), ICC(2), eta-squared, or WABA may conclude that aggregation is warranted, whereas a researcher using r_{wg} may conclude that aggregation is not warranted. This potential for disagreement stems, in large part, from how random variance is defined: either in terms of an expected random distribution within a group or in terms of total (within-and between-group) variance. For more detail, see Bliese (Chapter Eight, this volume) and Dansereau and Yammarino (Chapter Ten, this volume).

2. *Is the procedure commonly used to decide between two patterns of variability (either homogeneous groups or independent individuals), or is the procedure commonly used to decide among three patterns of variability (homogeneous groups, independent individuals, or heterogeneous interdependent individuals within groups)?*

In using r_{wg}, ICC(1), ICC(2), and/or eta-squared to determine whether it is appropriate to aggregate an individual-level variable to the unit level, most researchers consider just two possibilities:

1. Yes, the variable shows sufficient within-group agreement and/or sufficient between-group variability to justify aggregating the variable to the unit level; the variable is indeed a measure of a unit property.
2. No, the variable does not show sufficient within-group agreement and/or sufficient between-group variability to justify aggregation; the variable is a measure of individual differences.

There is, however, a third possibility: specifically, a variable may show high variability within groups and low variability between groups (that is, greater within-group variability than expected by chance), which is potentially indicative of a heterogeneous or frog-pond property. This possibility, potentially overlooked by researchers using r_{wg}, ICC(1), ICC(2), and eta-squared, plays an integral role in WABA (Dansereau & Yammarino, Chapter Ten, this volume). Researchers using other procedures might dismiss substantial within-unit variability as between-individual variability or as error rather than seeing it as evidence for meaningful interdependence of individuals within groups (parts).

Note, however, that this focus on the parts condition is based more on convention than on mathematical limitations of the other approaches. For example, evidence of the parts or frog-pond condition is provided by a negative ICC(1) value, when ICC(1) is calculated from a one-way random-effects ANOVA (see Bartko, 1976; Bliese, Chapter Eight, this volume). Similarly, r_{wg} will also yield negative values potentially indicative of a frog-pond condition when within-group variance exceeds the expected variance (Brown, Kozlowski, & Hattrup, 1996).

3. Does the procedure consider each variable separately, or does it consider the entire set of hypothesized independent and dependent variables?

Researchers using WABA typically examine within- and between-group variability in all their measures before deciding whether to analyze the relationships among all their measures at a single level of analysis—that is, at the unit-level (wholes), within units (parts), or within and between units (equivocal or individual-level analyses). In contrast, researchers using r_{wg}, eta-squared, ICC(1), and/or ICC(2) focus on what these indices reveal about a *specific* variable in isolation, without necessarily considering implications for other variables in the data set. As we explain in more detail in the following section, this difference between WABA and the other aggregation indices reflects the fact that WABA is primarily designed to identify the key level or levels at which a set of relationships should be analyzed. WABA researchers seek to learn at what level or levels an effect—a relationship—occurs. Finding evidence that a relationship occurs at two different levels of analysis, WABA researchers would typically analyze the relationship at the two different levels of analysis but would do so sequentially—in two separate equations.

Other analytical tools—most notably hierarchical linear modeling and cross-level operator analyses—allow researchers to test models that simultaneously incorporate variables at multiple levels of analysis. Before testing these cross-level models (see Kozlowski & Klein, Chapter One, this volume), researchers may use r_{wg}, eta-squared, ICC(1), and/or ICC(2) to justify aggregating only the specific measures that presumably reflect higher-level constructs.

4. *How and where does the procedure draw the line in determining whether the data should or should not be aggregated to the unit level?*

Researchers have long debated—and seem likely to continue to debate—the precise standards to use in deciding whether aggregation to the unit level is or is not justifiable. A common rule of thumb is that aggregation is justifiable if the r_{wg} for a unit is .70 or higher. If one is using r_{wg} to test the appropriateness of aggregation, should one remove variables and/or units with r_{wg} values that fall below .70? The answer is open to debate. Many researchers who use r_{wg} simply report the average r_{wg} for their groups (for each measure they wish to aggregate to the group level), using average r_{wg} values near or above .70 to justify aggregation. Reporting the range of r_{wg} values and the percentage of units with values greater than .70 seems reasonable. Often overlooked, however, is the importance of testing the statistical significance of r_{wg}, given various assumptions about its distribution (see Bliese, Chapter Eight, this volume).

Researchers who use eta-squared or ICC(1) to justify aggregation typically assert that aggregation is warranted if the F-test is statistically significant. A statistically significant F-test indicates that the between-group variance of a measure is significantly greater than the within-group variance of the measure. Note that the same F-test is used to evaluate the statistical significance of both eta-squared and ICC(1).

WABA researchers argue that aggregation of a measure to the unit level is justified if the F-test for the measure is statistically significant *and* if between-group variability in the measure is also "practically significant." WABA researchers calculate the E-test to evaluate practical significance (see Dansereau and Yammarino, Chapter Ten, this volume). Their goal in assessing practical significance is to identify effects that are expected to hold regardless of sample size.

Yet another perspective is that aggregation is appropriate if the group means of the aggregate variable can be reliably differentiated (see Bliese, Chapter Eight, this volume). ICC(2) provides such a measure. One can interpret the ICC(2) as one would any other reliability measure. Common practice suggests that values equal to or above .70 are acceptable, values between .50 and .70 are marginal, and values lower than .50 are poor. Note that small between-unit differences, as evidenced by relatively small ICC(1) values, may lead to reliable mean differences if the units are relatively large.

In summary, the existing literature provides few hard-and-fast (and several varying) standards to use to determine whether a variable has an acceptable amount of homogeneity to justify aggregation. In many cases, the differing procedures and criteria used to justify aggregation may yield similar conclusions. Thus r_{wg}, ICC(1), ICC(2), eta-squared, and WABA may all suggest that the same variable(s) should be aggregated, but this is not always the case, as we show in our analyses of the simulated data set in the third section of this chapter.

5. *To what extent are the values obtained in using the procedure influenced by the size of the groups in the sample?*

Clearly, this is an important question for evaluating the quality of any statistical procedure used to justify data aggregation. Indeed, this question was one of the important issues underlying the debate between Schmidt and Hunter (1989) and Kozlowski and Hattrup (1992) regarding r_{wg}. Kozlowski and Hattrup (1992) demonstrated that the method for indexing within-group homogeneity recommended by Schmidt and Hunter (1989)—the standard error of the mean and its associated confidence interval—was biased by sample size. The larger the size of the groups, the more likely Schmidt and Hunter's approach was to indicate within-group homogeneity, even when actual within-group agreement was low. In contrast, r_{wg} was relatively unaffected by group size. However, r_{wg} was somewhat attenuated when group size was ten or smaller and when actual agreement was moderate to low.

The influence of group size also lies at the heart of a quite recent and by no means resolved controversy in the levels-related literature, but this one involves bias due to small group size. WABA relies on the calculation of the E-ratio (based on eta-squared) to determine the practical significance of within- and between-unit variability in an individual-level measure. WABA advocates argue that the E-ratio is valuable because the practical significance of the E-ratio does not vary as a function of sample size (see Dansereau & Yammarino, Chapter Ten this volume). In contrast, the statistical significance of the F-ratio—considered, in WABA, in conjunction with the E-ratio—does vary as a function of sample size.

Bliese and Halverson (1998) have argued, however, that eta-squared (on which the E-ratio rests) varies as a function of sample—specifically, unit size. Bliese (Chapter Eight, this volume) suggests that small units typically yield larger eta-squared values than do large units, and that therefore a sample of two hundred individuals grouped in small units (for example, two-person dyads) is more likely to yield a practically significant E-ratio than is a sample of the same number of individuals grouped into larger units (say, twenty-person teams). Bliese proposes that ICC(1) provides a measure of between-unit variability that is not influenced (biased) by the size of the units in one's sample. Dansereau and Yammarino (Chapter Ten, this volume) counter that such results will occur in random data but not necessarily in field data, and that ICC(1) values do not vary as a function of group size precisely because the formula for ICC(1) includes and thus controls for degrees of freedom.

We have no resolution to offer. Suffice it to say that additional research is needed regarding the influence of sample size (that is, the number and size of the units in a sample) on the indices—particularly ICC(1), eta-squared, and the E-test—used in justifying aggregation to the unit level.

To summarize, we know that, within the limits already noted, r_{wg} values are generally not influenced by the size of the units in a sample (see Kozlowski & Hattrup, 1992, for details). Further, we know that ICC(2) and the significance of the F-test for ICC(1) and eta-squared are influenced by the number and size of the units in a sample. But experts, for now at least, disagree about the influence that the number and size of the units in a sample have on eta-squared and the E-test used in WABA.

Summary Comments

Table 12.1 summarizes our comparison of r_{wg}, eta-squared, ICC(1), ICC(2) and WABA. We urge researchers to use a number of these indices before aggregating their measures. A researcher's theoretical framework may suggest that one or more of the indices is most appropriate. The different indices that we have compared are most likely to lead to the same conclusion in relatively unambiguous cases—that is, when a measure's variability lies quite predominantly between units, or when a measure's variability lies quite predominantly within units, or when a measure shows random variability within and between units. When the indices lead to differing conclusions regarding the merits of aggregation, researchers may rely on theory, prior research, and/or belief in the superior merits of one of the indices in deciding whether to aggregate their measure(s). Our analyses of the simulated data set allow us to compare the conclusions that a researcher would reach in using differing indices to justify aggregation. But we have analyzed just one data set, a simulated one at that. Additional research is needed to clarify the merits of the differing indices available to justify aggregation and to clarify the frequency with which the indices yield differing conclusions.

Analysis of Multilevel Data

In analyzing multilevel data, researchers typically use one of three procedures: multilevel random-coefficient modeling (for example, HLM), WABA, or cross-level operator analyses. In this section, we highlight five key differences among the procedures.

1. *Does the procedure include guidelines for determining whether the set of variables is best treated at the unit, individual, or interdependent level?*

WABA researchers use WABA criteria to determine whether their variables are best conceptualized and analyzed as the properties of homogeneous groups, independent individuals, or interdependent individuals within groups. WABA researchers then analyze their data accordingly. This approach is unique to WABA. The two parts of WABA are inextricably linked:

Table 12.1. Summary of Procedures Used to Justify Aggregation of Lower-Level Data to Higher Units of Analysis.

Question	r_{wg}	ICC(1)	ICC(2)	WABA
1. Does the procedure assess variability within one unit at a time or across the entire sample?	Within	Across	Across	Across
2. Is the procedure commonly used to decide between two patterns of variability (homogeneity or independence) or among three patterns (homogeneity, independence, or heterogeneity)?	Two	Two	Two	Three
3. Does the procedure consider each variable separately or the entire set of variables?	Each separately	Each separately	Each separately	Entire set
4. Where does the procedure draw the line in determining whether data should be aggregated?	.70 rule of thumb	Significant F-test	.70 rule of thumb	Significant F-test and E-test
5. Are the values obtained in using the procedure influenced by group size?	No	No	Yes	Uncertain

1. The determination that a data set should be analyzed between groups (wholes), within groups (parts), or between and within groups (equivocal)
2. The subsequent analysis of the data at the appropriate level of analysis (based on WABA criteria)

Thus, for WABA, the answer to the preceding question is yes: WABA does provide guidelines for determining at what level a set of variables should be treated.

HLM and CLOP analyses are quite different. HLM and CLOP do not provide guidelines for determining the level of a researcher's variables. HLM and CLOP, unlike WABA, are not designed to test the merits of aggregation; rather, they are designed to test cross-level models, in which one or more higher-level variables is posited to have a direct or moderating effect on lower-level variables (see Kozlowski & Klein, Chapter One, this volume). Before conducting HLM and/or CLOP, a researcher must determine whether a given variable should be aggregated to and analyzed at the unit level of analysis. Thus a researcher using HLM and/or CLOP typically relies on theory, r_{wg}, ICC(1), ICC(2), and/or eta-squared to justify the aggregation of some predictors to a higher unit level before analyzing the effects of these measures on a lower-level dependent variable.

2. Does the procedure allow a researcher to test multilevel models, assessing whether the relationship between two or more variables holds at two or more levels of analysis?

Multilevel models posit that a relationship between two variables holds at two or more levels of analysis (House, Rousseau, & Thomas-Hunt, 1995; Klein, Dansereau, & Hall, 1994; Rousseau, 1985; see also Kozlowski & Klein, Chapter One, this volume). Thus, for example, climate for service and performance exhibit a multilevel relationship if group climate for service is positively related to group performance and if organizational climate for service is positively related to organizational performance. It is possible to use HLM and CLOP in conjunction with r_{wg}, ICC(1), ICC(2), or eta-squared to test multilevel models, but WABA was specifically designed to test such models and thus does so explicitly and effectively.

To test multilevel relationships, WABA researchers conduct sequential analyses, first testing the relationship between two or more variables at one level of analysis in one equation and subsequently testing the relationship between the variables at a different level of analysis in a second equation. Consider again the relationship of climate to service and performance. To test whether the variables have the multilevel relationship that has been suggested, a WABA researcher would examine whether measures of climate for service and performance are homogeneous within groups and covary between groups (indicative of a group wholes relationship), and whether they are homogeneous within organizations and covary between organizations (indicative of an organizational wholes relationship). WABA allows a researcher to test more complex multilevel models as well. For example, WABA might be used to show that the relationship between two variables reflects not only between-group differences and within-group homogeneity (indicative of a group wholes relationship) but also group heterogeneity within organizations (indicative of a relationship reflecting group parts within organizations).

Multilevel models are complex conceptually, methodologically, and analytically. Yet another complexity is lexical. Most current organizational writers (e.g., House et al., 1995; Klein et al., 1994; Rousseau, 1985; see also Kozlowski & Klein, Chapter One, this volume) define a multilevel relationship as we have here: as a relationship between two or more variables that holds at more than one level of analysis. However, following Miller (1978), WABA researchers (e.g., Dansereau, Alutto, & Yammarino, 1984) refer to these relationships not as multilevel relationships but as *cross-level relationships*. As the next section indicates, however, most current organizational writers (e.g., House et al., 1995; Klein et al., 1994; see also Kozlowski & Klein, Chapter One, this volume) mean something quite different by that term. For clarity in the remainder of this chapter, we use the term *multilevel model* as we have defined it here, and we use the term *cross-level model* as we define it in the following sections.

3. *Does the procedure allow a researcher to test cross-level direct-effect models, simultaneously assessing the effects of independent variables at different levels of analysis on a lower-level dependent variable?*

A cross-level direct-effect model suggests that one or more higher-level variables has a main effect on a lower-level variable (House et al., 1995; Klein et al., 1994; Rousseau, 1985; see also Kozlowski & Klein, Chapter One, this volume). For example, the characteristics of an organization's reward system may influence individual employees' pay satisfaction. Both hierarchical linear modeling and cross-level operator analyses allow a researcher to test cross-level direct-effect models, simultaneously assessing the effects of independent variables at two or more levels of analysis (for example, organization and individual) on a lower-level (for example, individual) dependent variable. WABA, unlike cross-level operator and HLM analyses, does not allow a researcher to assess simultaneously the effects of independent variables at different levels of analysis. (Question 5, later in this section, highlights differences between HLM and CLOP analyses of cross-level direct-effect models.)

4. *Does the procedure allow a researcher to test cross-level moderator-effect models, assessing the extent and correlates of between-unit variability in the slope of the relationship between two lower-level variables?*

A cross-level moderator-effect model posits that the strength of the relationship between two lower-level (for example, individual-level) variables varies from unit to unit, typically as a function of particular unit characteristics. Thus, to take a simple example, the relationship between individual pay and individual performance (two individual-level variables) may be stronger in units that award pay raises for performance and weaker in units that award pay raises for seniority. A unit's pay policy is a unit-level variable that moderates the relationship between individual pay and individual performance.

HLM is explicitly designed to test cross-level moderator-effect models; that is, HLM is designed to identify whether lower-level slopes vary across higher-level units, and whether lower-level slope variability is related to higher-level variables. HLM is well suited to these types of analyses because it allows researchers to treat slope variation as a random factor. This is accomplished by including a specific error term for slope variation (see Hofmann, Griffin, & Gavin, Chapter Eleven, this volume). This "random effect" for slope variation is unique to HLM and is not estimated in either cross-level operator analyses or WABA. In HLM, cross-level interaction effects are assessed by determining the degree to which higher-level factors explain slope variation.

To some extent, CLOP and WABA can be used to estimate the consistency of slopes across groups. Using CLOP, one can test for slope differences by examining the block of interactions between group membership (coded as $J - 1$ dummy codes) and the independent variable. If the interaction is significant, it suggests that the slope between the independent and dependent variable varies across groups. Note that this test can be "expensive" in terms of degrees of freedom, particularly if J (the number of groups) is large because it requires an additional $J - 1$ degrees of freedom. In contrast, HLM performs this test using only two degrees of freedom— one for the estimate of slope variance, and one for the estimate of slope-intercept covariance. One may also use CLOP to test whether the slope of the relationship between a lower-level independent variable and the dependent variable varies as a function of a specific group characteristic (for example, group structure) by forming a moderator variable. This is not so "expensive" in terms of degrees of freedom, because the interaction term in this case has just one degree of freedom. In WABA, one can also test for slope variation among groups by either creating subsets or using a multiple regression WABA approach (see Dansereau & Yammarino, Chapter Ten, this volume). Nevertheless, it is worth reiterating that neither CLOP nor WABA explicitly allows for a random slope term; consequently, neither approach integrates tests of slope differences as explicitly or as efficiently as HLM does.

5. *In testing cross-level direct-effect models, does the procedure evaluate the effects of group-level predictors at the group level of analysis, or does the procedure evaluate the effects of group-level predictors at the individual level of analysis?*

This question captures key differences between the ways in which CLOP and HLM test both cross-level direct-effect models and cross-level moderating-effect models. (Because WABA does not allow researchers to test cross-level direct-effect models and was not designed to test cross-level moderating-effect models, this section focuses exclusively on CLOP and HLM.)

In testing cross-level models, HLM first estimates the relationships between the dependent variable and the lower-level (for example, individual-level) independent variables within each unit. HLM then examines the relationship between the outcomes of this analysis (the unit intercepts and slopes) and the higher-level (that is, unit-level) independent variables. Thus HLM uses unit-level independent variables to explain between-unit variance in the dependent variable intercepts and slopes.[1] In contrast, CLOP uses both individual-level independent variables and unit-level independent variables to explain total (within- and between-unit) variance in the dependent variable. CLOP analyses do not partition variance into within- and between-unit components. This difference between CLOP and HLM has potentially important implications for estimated main-effect sizes, estimates of standard error, degrees of freedom, and interpretation of the results. We briefly consider each of these implications.

In HLM, higher-level independent variables—that is, independent variables varying solely between units—are used, as we have noted, to explain between-unit variability. Thus, in using HLM to test a cross-level direct-effect model, one may find that an organizational characteristic (for example, organizational climate) explains 60 percent of the between-organization variance in employee turnover intentions. This means that 60 percent of the variance among the organizational intercepts for employee turnover intentions is explained by the variable organizational climate. Organizational climate does not explain 60 percent of the total (within- and between-organization) variance in employee turnover intentions. If, for example, just 10 percent of the variance in employee turnover intentions lies between organizations, then organizational climate will explain approximately 6 percent of the total variance (60 percent of 10 percent of the total variance = 6 percent of the total variance).

In cross-level operator analyses, by contrast, higher-level independent variables are used to explain total variance (that is, between- and within-unit variance) in the dependent variable. Thus a researcher using cross-level operator analyses to assess the same cross-level direct-effect relationship between organizational climate and employee turnover intentions (within the same data set already described) will obtain results that look quite different from the results obtained by the researcher using HLM. Because CLOP analyses reveal the percentage of total variance explained (not the percentage of between-unit variance explained), CLOP reports effect sizes much smaller than in HLM. Thus, in the example just described, organizational climate will explain approximately 6 percent of the total variance. Accordingly, great care must be taken in interpreting and comparing the results of CLOP and HLM. The finding that a variable explains 60 percent of the between-unit variance in a dependent variable may appear, at first glance, far more consequential than the finding that the variable explains 6 percent of the total variance in the dependent variable (Bryk & Raudenbush, 1992). In fact, both findings capture the same relationship between (in this example) climate and turnover intentions—the same relationship, assessed with different metrics.

The results obtained with HLM and with cross-level operator analysis differ not only in effect size but also in the standard error used in testing the significance of the cross-level effect. In cross-level operator analyses, standard error estimates (provided in the statistical output) are based on total variance because the analysis does not partition variance into the "between" and "within" components for computation of the standard errors. In HLM, by contrast, standard errors are based on partitioned variance: standard errors for lower-level variables (called level 1 variables in HLM) are based on lower-level (for example, within-group) variance, and standard errors for higher-level variables (called level 2 variables in HLM) are based on higher-level (for example, between-group) variance. One well-documented consequence is that results from cross-level operator analyses will, in general, provide standard error estimates for the higher-level variables that are too small (Bryk & Raudenbush, 1992; Kreft & de Leeuw, 1998). This means that cross-level operator analyses may show that a group-level variable was significantly related to the outcome variable, whereas HLM analyses of the same data and the same relationship may show that the group-level variable was not significantly related to the outcome. Standard error estimates for lower-level (level 1) variables are also affected, although the exact form of the bias is less well documented. In short, HLM and cross-level operator analyses calculate standard errors differently, and this can lead to quite different estimates of statistical significance.

CLOP and HLM also treat the degrees of freedom for higher-level variables differently. In HLM, the degrees of freedom for a higher-level variable are $J - 1$ (where J is the number of higher-level units). In cross-level operator analyses, the degrees of freedom for the higher-level variable are $N - 1$ (where N is the number of total observations) when the higher-level variable is a single, metric variable (for example, a measure of a specific characteristic of higher-level units, such as group structure). When, however, the higher-level variable is a nominal measure of unit membership (dummy coded), then HLM and CLOP test the effects of the higher-level measure-of-unit measure, using comparable degrees of freedom (that is, $J - 1$).

In sum, a researcher who used both HLM and cross-level operator analyses to analyze the same cross-level relationship in the same data would be likely to find that the two analytical procedures yield very similar parameter estimates (regression coefficients) but different—perhaps quite different—effect sizes, standard errors, and significance levels. As we shall show in the third section of this chapter (and as discussed in Chapter Nine), it is not difficult to use the results from cross-level operator analyses to approximate the results that would have been obtained with HLM. Although this renders effect sizes from CLOP quite similar to those obtained with HLM, this does not obviate issues regarding statistical significance and standard error.

Summary Comments

Our comparison of WABA, CLOP, and HLM highlights important differences among the techniques (see Table 12.2). WABA was designed to identify the appropriate level or levels to describe the relationships among the variables in a data set. In contrast, CLOP and HLM were designed to test cross-level models. Unlike WABA, neither CLOP nor HLM incorporates any decision rules to determine the appropriate level or levels at which the relationships should be described. Researchers using CLOP and HLM must use other procedures, such as r_{wg}, ICC(1), ICC(2), and eta-squared, to justify the aggregation of their measures to the unit level. CLOP and HLM differ insofar as HLM allows one to model the non-independence or clustering present in the data; CLOP does not. Thus, in testing the effects of higher-level (for example, group) independent variables on a lower-level (for example, individual) dependent variable, HLM and cross-level operator analyses will yield very similar parameter estimates but different estimates of effect sizes, standard errors, and statistical significance. Finally, because HLM allows one to specify a random slope term, HLM is particularly effective in testing cross-level moderating-effect models. Understanding these key differences among the approaches can help one select an approach that is matched to one's theoretical question.

Table 12.2. Summary of Procedures Used to Analyze Multilevel Data.

Question	WABA	HLM	CLOP
1. Does the procedure include guidelines for determining whether variables are best treated at the unit, individual, or interdependent level?	Yes	No	No
2. Does the procedure allow a researcher to test multilevel models?	Yes, designed to do so	Yes, but not designed to do so	Yes, but not designed to do so
3. Does the procedure allow a researcher to test cross-level direct-effects models?	No	Yes	Yes
4. Does the procedure allow a researcher to test cross-level moderator-effect models?	Yes, but not designed to do so	Yes	Yes
5. In evaluating cross-level models, does the procedure evaluate the effects of group-level predictors at the group or individual level of analysis?	Not applicable	Group level of analysis	Individual level of analysis

Analyses of a Simulated Data Set

In this section, we report the results of our analyses of a simulated data set created by our coauthor Paul Bliese. The goal was to create a data set that would both be of interest to organizational researchers and illustrate similarities and differences among the statistical procedures commonly used to analyze multilevel data. Clearly, the complexity of the various multilevel approaches prohibits us from providing detailed descriptions of the results from each of the data-analytic techniques. Further, only a series of Monte Carlo studies could provide a definitive analysis of the similarities and differences among the multilevel procedures described in the preceding section of the chapter. Nevertheless, we believe that the analyses of the mock data set are helpful in clarifying similarities and differences among the multilevel data-analytic procedures. We begin by providing a detailed description of the data set. Next, we describe the results of several analyses of the merits of aggregating specific variables to the unit level. Finally, we present the results of WABA, HLM, and cross-level operator analyses of the simulated data set.[2]

Using a random-number generator, Bliese created a data set that contained 750 individual-level observations. The 750 observations were nested within fifty groups, and each group contained fifteen members. Thus the data were created to simulate a condition in which a researcher gathered measures of eight constructs (one dependent variable and seven predictors) from 750 employees nested within fifty groups of fifteen members each. Using variations of procedures discussed in Bliese and Halverson (1998) and Bliese (1998), Bliese created the data set, specifying target ICC(1) values and intercorrelations among the variables. Because Bliese used a random-number generator to create the data set, the actual ICC(1) values and intercorrelations among the variables in the data set do not conform precisely to his specifications. As with any simulated data set, one would expect the average ICC(1) values and intercorrelations to match the original specifications if the data set were repeatedly created. In the present case, however, the original specifications provided guidelines for how the data were created, and so the conformity of the data to the exact specifications is less important.

Variables

The simulated data set contains eight variables. The first variable was created to simulate an individual-level measure of Job Satisfaction, the dependent variable for the data set. This variable was created to vary both within and between groups, with an expected ICC(1) of .15 (actual ICC(1) = .11). The remaining variables were created as possible predictors of Job Satisfaction.

The first independent variable was created to simulate a measure of Cohesion. This variable was created to have an ICC(1) of .20 (actual ICC(1) = .22). The variable was created to have a group-level correlation of .50 with Job Satisfaction (that is, a correlation of .50 between the Cohesion group means and the Job Satisfaction group means) and a within-group correlation of zero with Job Satisfaction.

The second independent variable was created to simulate a measure of Positive Affect. This variable was created to be unrelated to group membership, with an expected ICC(1) value of zero (actual ICC(1) = .02) and a raw correlation of .25 with Job Satisfaction.

The third independent variable was created to simulate a measure of Pay. This variable was created to have more within-group variability than between-group variability, with an expected negative ICC(1) value (the actual ICC(1) value was −.01, suggesting a weak frog-pond variable). The variable was created to have a within-group (or frog-pond) correlation of .40 with Job Satisfaction.

The fourth independent variable was created to simulate a measure of Negative Leader Behaviors. The variable was created to have an ICC(1) value of .10 (actual ICC(1) = .04). Further, the variable was created to have a group-level correlation with Job Satisfaction of −.70 and a within-group (frog-pond) correlation with Job Satisfaction of −.30.

The fifth and sixth independent variables were created to simulate measures of Workload and Task Significance, respectively. Further, these variables were generated to interact with each other in their relationships with Job Satisfaction. Workload items were generated to have an ICC(1) of 0 (actual ICC(1) = 0), and Task Significance items were created to have an ICC(1) of .10 (actual ICC(1) = .11). Workload was created to have a correlation of −.40 with Job Satisfaction when Task Significance was low. When Task Significance was high, however, Workload was created to be unrelated to Job Satisfaction.

The seventh variable was created to simulate a measure of perceptions of the Physical Work Environment. Presumably there would be low variability among group members on a rating of this nature; consequently, this variable was generated to have an ICC(1) of .70 (actual ICC(1) = .67). The Physical Environment variable was created to have a group-level correlation of .40 with Job Satisfaction and a within-group correlation of 0 with Job Satisfaction.

The development of the mock data set was guided by several implicit hypotheses:

1. Job Satisfaction is positively related to Cohesion, Positive Affect, Pay, and Physical Work Environment
2. Job Satisfaction is negatively related to Negative Leader Behaviors and Workload
3. The relationship between Job Satisfaction and Workload is moderated by Task Significance.

Preliminary Analyses: Making the Decision to Aggregate

Table 12.3 lists each variable's mean, standard deviation, ICC (1), ICC(2), eta-squared, within-eta correlation, between-eta correlation, F-test, E-ratio, and inverse-F. Note that the eta-squared is simply the square of the between-eta correlation. Further, the F-test provides a test of the significance of eta-squared, the between-eta correlation, and ICC(1). The inverse-F is used by WABA researchers when a variable's within-eta correlation is larger than its between-eta correlation (see Dansereau et al., 1984; see also Dansereau & Yammarino, Chapter Ten, this volume, for further details).

Unfortunately, we cannot provide r_{wg} values for the variables in this data set. r_{wg}, or more appropriately, $r_{wg.j}$, assesses variability among group members' responses to the survey items within a scale, but the data set simulates scale means, with no information whatsoever regarding mock scale items. That is, r_{wg} cannot be calculated in the absence of information regarding the number of items within a scale and the variability of item scores within each group.

Table 12.4 presents the raw-score, group-level (between-group), and within-group correlations between the independent variables and the dependent variable, Job Satisfaction. The raw-score correlation is the individual-level correlation between the 750 dependent and independent variables. The group-level (between-group)

Table 12.3. Means, Standard Deviations, and Summary Statistics for the Simulated Data Set.

Variable	M	SD	ICC(1)	ICC(2)	Eta-squared	Eta-between	Eta-within	F	E-ratio	Inverse F
Job satisfaction	0.08	2.48	.11	.65	.17	.41	.91	2.87**	.45	.35
Cohesion	0.23	2.51	.22	.81	.27	.52	.85	5.26**	.61	.19
Positive affect	0.06	0.98	.02	.28	.09	.30	.95	1.38**	.32	.72
Pay	0.04	1.01	−.01	−.27	.05	.23	.97	.79	.24	1.27
Negative leadership	0.00	1.09	.04	.38	.10	.32	.95	1.60**	.34	.62
Workload	0.00	1.04	−.00	−.07	.06	.25	.97	.93	.26	1.08
Task significance	−0.01	1.01	.11	.65	.17	.41	.91	2.89**	.45	.35
Physical environment	0.07	1.43	.67	.97	.71	.84	.55	33.79***	1.52	

*p < .05; **p < .01; ***p < .001

correlation is the correlation among the fifty group means, and the within-group correlation is the correlation of X and Y deviation scores. (See Dansereau & Yammarino, Chapter Ten, this volume, for the calculation of these correlations.) Intercorrelations among the independent variables are not presented because, given the way the data were generated, the correlations among the independent variables were near zero (the average intercorrelation among the independent variables was .002).

The preliminary analyses presented in Tables 12.3 and 12.4 provide the information necessary to compare different standards commonly used to justify aggregation to the unit level of analysis. As already noted, we cannot calculate r_{wg} values for the simulated data. However, we can compare the conclusions a researcher would make in basing the decision to aggregate on ICC(1), eta-squared, ICC(2), and WABA. The identical F-test is used to test the statistical significance of ICC(1) and of eta-squared. Thus, if a researcher relied solely on the presence of a statistically significant F (that is, on significantly greater between-group than within-group variance in the data) to determine whether to aggregate a measure to the

Table 12.4. Correlations Between Independent Variables and Satisfaction.[a]

Variable	Raw Correlation	Between-Group Correlation	Within-Group Correlation
1. Cohesion	0.05	0.38**	−0.04
2. Positive affect	0.18**	0.21	0.17**
3. Pay	0.37**	−0.08	0.42**
4. Negative leadership	−0.29**	−0.61**	−0.25**
5. Workload	−0.25**	−0.32*	−0.24**
6. Task significance	0.02	−0.00	0.03
7. Physical environment	0.10*	0.33**	−0.03

[a] n = 750 for the individual-level correlations; 700 (750 − 50) for the within-group correlations; and 50 for the between-group correlations

*p < .05, two-tailed

**p < .01, two-tailed

group level of analysis, the researcher would aggregate six of the eight simulated variables to the group level: Job Satisfaction, Cohesion, Positive Affect, Negative Leader Behavior, Task Significance, and Physical Work Environment. The F-test for eta-squared, and for ICC(1), is statistically significant for each of these variables. If, instead, a researcher chose to aggregate only those measures showing reliable group differences, as evidenced by ICC(2) values over the conventional reliability standard of .70, then the researcher would aggregate just two of the eight variables: Cohesion and Physical Environment.

WABA combines the information presented in Table 12.3 (specifically, the between- and within-eta correlations) with the information presented in Table 12.4 (the between-group, within-group, and total correlations), to yield the information presented in Table 12.5. (See Dansereau & Yammarino, Chapter Ten, this volume, for more information regarding the calculations on which Table 12.5 is based.) The WABA researchers examined the information in these tables to determine at what level the data should be analyzed: at the level of wholes (that is, between groups), at the level of the equivocal condition (that is, between and within groups), or at the level of parts (that is, within groups).

Table 12.5. WABA-Components Analysis.

Variables and Relationships	Between Components	Within Components	Total Correlation	Inference from WABA
Satisfaction and				
Cohesion	.08	−.03	.05	Individual
Positive affect	.03	.15	.18	Individual
Pay	.01	.37	.37	Parts
Negative leadership	−.08	−.21	−.29	Individual
Workload	−.03	−.22	−.25	Individual
Task significance	−.00	.03	.02	Individual
Physical environment	.11	−.01	.09	Wholes

More specifically, the WABA researchers began by examining the F-ratio and E-test values (see Table 12.3) to compare the between-eta and within-eta correlations. The WABA researchers concluded that, with the exception of Physical Environment, the variables as a whole showed no clear indication of predominant between-group variation or of predominant within-group variation. Examining the relationships among the variables (shown in Table 12.4), as well as Z-tests and A-tests of these relationships (not shown in Table 12.4 but described in Chapter Ten), the WABA researchers made the following observations:

1. The relationship between Job Satisfaction and Pay is primarily a function of within-group differences.
2. The relationships between Job Satisfaction and Cohesion, Negative Leadership, and Physical Environment are primarily a function of between-group differences.

Given that Job Satisfaction is related to some variables primarily as a function of between-group differences and related to other variables primarily as a function of within-group differences, the WABA researchers concluded that the relationships among the variables are most appropriately conceptualized and analyzed at the individual level of analysis. WABA researchers define the pure individual level—the equivocal condition—as one that varies freely within and between groups.

Finally, the WABA researchers examined the "between" and "within" components underlying the raw correlations among the variables (see Table 12.5). The "between" components are formed by multiplying the between-eta correlations for x and y by the between-group correlation. The "within" components are formed by multiplying the within-eta correlations for x and y by the within-group correlation. The two components sum to the total individual-level, raw-score correlation. The findings in Table 12.5 reveal that only the within-group component for the correlation of Pay Satisfaction and Job Satisfaction supports a parts inference. Only the between-group component for the correlation of Physical Environment and Job Satisfaction supports a wholes inference. The relationships of the remaining variables and Job Satisfaction support an equivocal, or individual-level, inference. For WABA researchers, these results lend further support to the assertion that the variables in the data set vary both within and between groups and should thus be conceptualized and analyzed at the individual level of analysis. Accordingly, the WABA analysts concluded that none of the variables in the mock data set should be aggregated to the unit level.[3]

Summary Comments

Researchers using different criteria to justify aggregation may indeed reach very different conclusions regarding the merits of aggregation. This could lead to differences in the specification of the theoretical model to be tested. Researchers relying on a statistically significant F-test for ICC(1) or eta-squared would report that six of the eight variables in the simulated data set could justifiably be aggregated. Researchers relying on ICC(2) values exceeding .70 would report that two of the eight variables could justifiably be aggregated. Researchers using WABA, however, determined that none of the variables should be aggregated.

Using WABA to Analyze the Relationship Between Predictors and Job Satisfaction

Building on the results just discussed, the WABA researchers analyzed the relationship between the independent variables and Job Satisfaction at the individual level of analysis. The WABA researchers did not aggregate any of the independent variables. This is an important detail because several of the measures—Cohesion, Negative Leader Behavior, Physical Environment, and Task Significance—were aggregated to the group level in the HLM and CLOP analyses. Thus the WABA analysts simply regressed Job Satisfaction on the raw, individual-level measures of all the independent variables. The results appear in the first column of Table 12.6.

The results indicate that three of the predictors—Positive Affect, Pay, and Physical Environment—are significantly positively related to Job Satisfaction. Two of the predictors—Negative Leader Behavior and Workload—are significantly negatively related to Job Satisfaction. Neither Cohesion nor Task Significance is significantly related to Job Satisfaction. Finally, the interaction of Task Significance and Workload is significant: the greater the Task Significance, the weaker the relationship between Workload and Job Satisfaction. Together, the eight predictors explain 29 percent of the total, individual-level variance in Job Satisfaction (that is, 29 percent of the total between- and within-group variance) in Job Satisfaction.

Table 12.6. Comparison of Unstandardized Parameter Estimates for the Equations Predicting Job Satisfaction.

Variable	WABA	HLM	CLOP
Positive affect (raw)	0.34**	0.31**	0.33**
Pay (raw)	0.82**	0.83**	0.83**
Workload (raw)	−0.42**	−0.34**	−0.35
Group cohesion (mean)	—	0.15*	0.20*
Cohesion (raw)	0.04	—	—
Group negative leadership (mean)	—	−1.17**	−1.06**
Negative leadership (raw)	−0.58**	−0.43**	−0.43**
Group physical environment (mean)	—	0.17*	0.15*
Physical environment (raw)	0.18**	—	—
Group task significance (mean)	—	−0.24	−0.34
Task significance (raw)	0.01	—	—
Group task significance by workload interaction (cross-level)	—	1.24**	1.28**
Task significance by workload interaction (raw)	0.22**	—	—

$*p < .05$

$**p < .01$

$***p < .001$

Using HLM to Analyze the Relationship Between Predictors and Job Satisfaction

The HLM analyses of the relationship between the predictors and Job Satisfaction were guided by nine hypotheses. The HLM hypotheses are identical in direction to the hypotheses outlined previously. However, the HLM hypotheses differ from the previous ones insofar as the HLM hypotheses specify the level (individual or group) of each predicted relationship. Together, the hypotheses describe a cross-level model that specifies lower-level effects (hypotheses 1 through 4), cross-level main effects (hypotheses 5 through 8), and a cross-level moderating effect (hypothesis 9).

Hypotheses 1 to 4 focus on individual-level (or level 1) relationships:

H1. *Individual Positive Affect will be positively related to individual Job Satisfaction.*

H2. *Individual Negative Leader Behavior will be negatively related to individual Job Satisfaction.*

H3. *Individual Pay will be positively related to individual Job Satisfaction within groups so that the higher an individual's Pay, relative to the pay of other group members, the higher the individual's Job Satisfaction.*

H4. *Individual Workload will be negatively related to individual Job Satisfaction.*

Hypotheses 5 to 8 focus on cross-level main effects. Analyses testing these hypotheses examine intercepts as outcomes (see Hofmann et al., Chapter Eleven, this volume).

H5. *After controlling for the individual-level predictors, Group Cohesion (that is, the group mean for Cohesion) will be positively related to the average Job Satisfaction of group members.*

H6. *After controlling for the individual-level predictors (including Negative Leader Behaviors), Group Negative Leader Behaviors (that is, the group mean for Negative Leader Behaviors) will be negatively related to average level of Job Satisfaction of group members above and beyond the individual effects of Negative Leader Behaviors on individual Job Satisfaction.*

H7. *After controlling for the individual-level predictors, Group Physical Work Environment (that is, the group mean of perceptions of the Physical Work Environment) will be positively related to average level of Job Satisfaction of group members.*

H8. *After controlling for the individual-level predictors, Group Task Significance (that is, the group mean of Task Significance) will be positively related to average level of Job Satisfaction of group members.*

Finally, hypothesis 9 tests whether a group-level predictor moderates the relationship between two individual-level variables. The analysis tests a cross-level moderating effect, examining slopes as outcomes (again, see Hofmann et al., Chapter Eleven, this volume):

H9. *Group Task Significance (that is, the group mean of Task Significance) will moderate the relationship between individual Workload and individual Job Satisfaction. Specifically, whereas individual Workload is expected to be negatively related to individual Job Satisfaction, this relationship will be weak in groups in which Task Significance is high.*

In the WABA analyses, as we have noted, none of the measures was averaged and aggregated to the unit level. Guided first by the implicit theoretical model that determined the creation of the mock data set, and then by supporting ICC(1) and ICC(2) values for the measures, the HLM researchers aggregated (averaged) four measures to the unit level within the HLM analyses: Cohesion, Negative Leader Behaviors, Physical Work Environment, and Task Significance. In the remainder of the chapter, we refer to the aggregated measures as *Group Cohesion, Group Negative Leader Behaviors, Group Physical Work Environment,* and *Group Task Significance,* respectively. Further, within the HLM analyses, the effects of Negative Leadership Behavior were tested both at the individual level of analysis (Negative Leadership Behaviors) and at the group level of analysis (Group Negative Leader Behaviors).

A total of four models was specified to test the nine hypotheses just identified. The HLM analysts opted for this sequence because it provided a minimum number of models for testing the hypotheses and ultimately resulted in a final model that simultaneously accounted for all the hypothesized effects. The first model run by the HLM analysts was a null model with no predictors. This model partitioned the variance in Job Satisfaction into between- and within-group components. The second model was an individual-level model specifying the four individual-level predictors of Job Satisfaction but containing no predictors at the group level. The third model was a group-level model that included the four individual-level predictors from the previous model as well as the four group-level predictors of Job Satisfaction. The fourth and final model included the specified cross-level interaction in addition to the four previously identified individual-level predictors and the four previously identified group-level predictors.

Null model. The null model specified no individual-level or group-level predictors, only Job Satisfaction as an outcome. This model revealed that 11 percent of the variance in Job Satisfaction resided between groups; note that this is equivalent to the ICC(1) reported earlier. Although this certainly indicates that the majority of the variance in Job Satisfaction lies at the individual level, the group-level variance component is significant (χ^2 = 140.78, 49 df, p < .001) and suggests that exploration of its antecedents is a worthwhile pursuit.

Individual-level model. Next, the HLM analysts modeled the four individual-level predictors of Job Satisfaction. These predictors were Positive Affect, Negative Leader Behaviors, Pay, and Workload. In specifying this model, all predictors with the exception of Pay were centered around their grand means. Pay was centered around its group mean because it was hypothesized to operate as a within-group, or frog-pond, effect in which the effect of an individual's Pay on his or her Job Satisfaction was dependent on his or her level of Pay relative to the pay of other group members. These centering decisions are consistent with earlier discussions (see Hofmann et al., Chapter Eleven, this volume) and with the recommendations of Hofmann and Gavin (1998).

In this model, each of the coefficients is significant in the anticipated direction: Positive Affect (β_{1j} = .30, t-ratio = 4.01, p < .001), Negative Leader Behaviors (β_{2j} = –.49, t-ratio = –6.19, p < .001), Pay (β_{3j} = .85, t-ratio = 10.31, p < .001), and Workload (β_{4j} = –.39, t-ratio = –3.39, p < .01). Collectively, the four predictors account for 38 percent of the within-group variance in Job Satisfaction. For two reasons, this estimate of variance explained differs from the estimate of variance explained in the regression performed by the WABA researchers:

1. The WABA researchers included all the predictor variables in their regression, whereas the HLM researchers included only the four variables (already noted) in this model.
2. The WABA researchers assessed the percentage of total (within- and between-group) variance explained, whereas the HLM analysis assessed the percentage of within-group variance explained.

One other finding of interest from the HLM model is that the slope of the relationship between Workload and Job Satisfaction varies significantly across groups (χ^2 = 100.94, 49 df, p < .001). This between-group variability in the slope of the Workload–Job Satisfaction relationship is the focus of hypothesis 9. None of the other predictors had slope effects that varied across groups.

Group-level model. Next, the four group-level predictors of Job Satisfaction (Group Cohesion, Group Negative Leader Behaviors, Group Physical Work Environment, and Group Task Significance) were added to the previous model. The level 1 (here, the individual level) portion of the model remained the same in terms of the predictors included and the centering options specified. Each of the group-level predictors in this cross-level main-effect model was significant: Group Cohesion ($\gamma01 = .16$, t-ratio = 2.23, $p < .05$), Group Negative Leader Behaviors ($\gamma02 = -1.17$, t-ratio = -4.23, $p < .001$), Group Physical Work Environment ($\gamma03 = .18$, t-ratio = 2.42, $p < .05$), and Group Task Significance ($\gamma04 = -.51$, t-ratio = -2.31, $p < .05$). As a set, the four group-level predictors account for 45 percent of the between-group variance in Job Satisfaction. There is still a significant amount of remaining variance between groups in Job Satisfaction ($\chi^2 = 78.41$, 45 df, $p < .01$). However, there are no other group-level predictors in the data set to model this remaining variance.

Full model. The final model builds on the previous model by adding into the model a test of the cross-level moderating effect of Group Task Significance on the Workload–Job Satisfaction relationship. The results of this model are shown in the second column of Table 12.6. (The table also includes the final coefficient estimates for all the variables in the model.) Of specific interest is the significant cross-level moderating effect; see "Group Task Significance by Workload Interaction (Cross-Level)" in Table 12.6. This finding indicates that when Group Task Significance is high, the negative within-group relationship between Workload and Task Significance is attenuated. The pattern of significance for the other coefficients is the same as in the preceding models except that in this model the main effect of Group Task Significance is no longer significant. Although a significant 68 percent of the variance in the Workload–Job Satisfaction relationship was successfully modeled with group Task Significance, significant variance remains across groups in that relationship ($\chi^2 = 65.21$, 48 df, $p < .05$), variance that could be modeled with other group-level predictors, theory and data permitting.

Using CLOP to Analyze the Relationship
Between Predictors and Job Satisfaction
As we have noted, HLM and cross-level operator analyses are quite similar. Both are designed to test cross-level models. They differ, however, in their partitioning of the variance in the lower-level dependent variable (and thus in their modeling of non-independence or clustering in the data). HLM evaluates the effects of lower-level independent variables on lower-level outcomes and the effects of higher-level independent variables on higher-level variance in intercepts and slopes. Traditional cross-level operator analyses, in contrast, predict total variance in the dependent variable. Thus, as we have noted, cross-level operator analyses assess the extent to which both individual- and group-level predictors explain total (within- and between-group) variability in the dependent variable. The analyses in the first part of this section illustrate traditional cross-level operator analyses.

As explained in Chapter Nine (James & Williams, this volume), analysts may take the results of traditional cross-level operator analyses and estimate the effects of higher-level independent variables on higher-level variance in intercepts and slopes, thereby approximating the results of hierarchical linear modeling. The analyses in the second part of this section illustrate this strategy. To facilitate the comparison of cross-level operator analyses and HLM, the CLOP researchers patterned their analyses on the HLM analyses just reported.

Traditional CLOP analyses. As the first step in the traditional cross-level operator analyses, the researchers regressed Job Satisfaction on the four individual-level predictors: Positive Affect, Negative Leader Behaviors, Pay, and Workload. (Following the HLM researchers, the CLOP researchers centered all predictors around their grand means with the exception of Pay, which was group-mean–centered.) Each of the coefficients is significant in the anticipated direction: Positive Affect ($\beta = .35$, t-ratio = 4.38, $p < .001$), Negative Leader Behaviors ($\beta = -.59$, t-ratio = -8.27, $p < .001$), Pay ($\beta = .87$, t-ratio = 10.88, $p < .001$), and workload ($\beta = -.43$, t-ratio = -5.72, $p < .001$). The beta coefficients are similar (though not identical) to those from the HLM analysis. Collectively, the four predictors account for 27.6 percent of the total (within- and between-group) variance in Job Satisfaction.

As the next step, the researchers assigned the group-mean scores for Cohesion, Negative Leadership, Task Significance, and Physical Environment back to the individual and used these scores as predictors. The four cross-level predictors are significantly related to Job Satisfaction: Group Cohesion ($\beta = .23$, t-ratio = 3.90, $p < .001$), Group Negative Leadership ($\beta = -1.07$, t-ratio = -4.58, $p < .001$), Group Work Environment ($\beta = .17$, t-ratio = 2.73, $p < .01$), and Group Task Significance ($\beta = -.39$, t-ratio = -2.13, $p < .05$). Together, the four cross-level predictors explain an additional 5.2 percent of the variance in Job Satisfaction, over and above the variance explained by the individual-level predictors. Thus the group- or cross-level predictors and the individual-level predictors explain a total of 32.8 percent of the variance in Job Satisfaction.

As the final step of the traditional cross-level operator analyses, the researchers examined the hypothesized cross-level moderating effect of Group Task Significance on the Workload–Job Satisfaction relationship. The interaction term is statistically significant ($\beta = 1.27$, t-ratio = 7.45, $p < .001$), explaining an additional 4.7 percent of the total variance in Job Satisfaction. Thus, all together, the individual-level predictors, the group-level predictors, and the interaction of Group Task Significance and Workload explain 37.5 percent of the total variance in Job Satisfaction. The parameter estimates for the full regression model are shown in Table 12.6. Note that the total variance explained by the CLOP regression (37.5 percent) exceeds the total variance explained by the WABA regression (29 percent). This reflects the fact the CLOP researchers aggregated four of the variables to the group level, whereas the WABA researchers did not. These four variables (Cohesion, Negative Leadership, Task Significance, and Physical Environment) were created in the mock data set to covary with Job Satisfaction more strongly between than within groups. Therefore, the aggregated variables had more predictive power (in the CLOP analysis) than the raw, disaggregated measures had (in the WABA analysis).

"Translating" the results of traditional CLOP analyses to estimate between-group (level 2) variance. The CLOP researchers performed a series of additional analyses to estimate the extent to which the group-level variables explained between-group variability (not total vari-

ability) in Job Satisfaction. Their first step was simply to obtain an estimate of the extent of between-group (versus within-group) variability in Job Satisfaction. To do this, the CLOP researchers regressed Job Satisfaction on $J - 1$ dummy codes representing Group Membership (J equals the number of groups). This model is identical to a one-way ANOVA (Cohen & Cohen, 1983). It partitions Job Satisfaction variance into its between-group and within-group components. The R-Squared value for this model is .17, suggesting that about 17 percent of the variation in Job Satisfaction resides between groups. It is important to recognize that this estimate is a slightly biased overestimate (as is its ANOVA analogue, eta-squared). It is an overestimate because the regression model includes forty-nine independent variables (the dummy codes for the fifty groups) but does not correct for this large number of predictors. A better estimate of the variance "explained by" Group Membership is provided by the shrunken R-square (Cohen & Cohen, 1983). This measure adjusts for the number of predictors. The shrunken R-square estimate is .11, or approximately 11 percent of the variance. Not coincidentally, the shrunken R-square estimate of .11 matches the ICC(1) estimate of .11 and the ICC estimate from the HLM analysis.

The next step for the CLOP analysts was to estimate the percentage of the between-group variance accounted for by the group-level predictors (Group Cohesion, Group Negative Leadership, Group Task Significance, and Group Physical Environment). Recall that the group-level predictors explained an additional 5.2 percent of the variance in Job Satisfaction, over and above the variance explained by the individual-level predictors. This 5.2 percent of the total variance represents 47 percent of the between-group variance ($5.2/11 = 47$). Note that this "translation" of the results of traditional CLOP analyses does not change the parameter estimates for the predictor variables, but only the estimate of the percentage of variance explained. In comparison, the HLM analysis showed that the group-level predictors explain 45 percent of the between-group variance in Job Satisfaction.

Finally, to estimate the extent to which Task Significance explained between-group variability in the slope of the Workload–Job Satisfaction relationship, the researchers first needed an estimate of between-group variability in this relationship. To estimate between-group variability in the Workload–Job Satisfaction relationship, the researchers conducted a three-step hierarchical regression. In the first step, they regressed Job Satisfaction on Workload. In the second step, they added the forty-nine ($J-1$) dummy codes for Group Membership to the model. In the third step, they added the forty-nine Workload by Group Membership interaction terms to the model. At each step, the significance of the block was assessed. The important step in the detection of cross-level interaction effects is the third block. This block accounts for significant variance [$F(49,650) = 2.84$, $p < .001$], indicating that the relationship between Workload and Job Satisfaction varies significantly between groups. The R-square for the model with only Workload is .06. The R-square for the model with Workload and Group Membership is .22, with a shrunken R-square of .16. Finally, the R-square for the third model, including the interaction term and both main effects, is .36, with a shrunken R-square of .26. Thus the researchers concluded (using the shrunken R-square) that the interaction of Group Membership and Workload accounts for 10 percent (.26 minus .16) of the total individual-level variance in Job Satisfaction; that is, between-group variability among the slopes explains 10 percent of the total variance in Job Satisfaction.

The traditional CLOP analyses, reported in the preceding subsection, showed that the interaction of Group Task Significance and Workload explained 4.7 percent of the total variance in Job Satisfaction. Accordingly, the CLOP researchers concluded that Group Task Significance accounts for 47 percent (4.7/10) of the between-group variation in the Workload–Job Satisfaction relationship. (As in the previous "translation," this translation of the results does not change the parameter estimates for the predictor variables.) In contrast, the results of the HLM analyses suggest that Group Task Significance explained 68 percent of the variation in this relationship.

Summary of Analyses

The results of each of the three sets of analyses, summarized in Table 12.6, provide strong support for the hypotheses. Of course, the data were developed to illustrate the hypotheses, so this is hardly a surprising result! More intriguing is a comparison of the results of the three analytical techniques. A critical consideration, of course, is that the WABA results are based on the raw, individual-level data; the WABA researchers aggregated no variable to the group level. In contrast, both the HLM researchers and the CLOP researchers aggregated four variables to the group level: Cohesion, Negative Leadership Behaviors, Physical Environment, and Task Significance. Before discussing in more detail the differing results in Table 12.6, we must caution again that the results are illustrative, not definitive. They are based on one mock data set. Our three analyses of this data set are a useful beginning, not a final statement.

We begin our discussion with a comparison of the HLM and CLOP results. As the results in Table 12.6 indicate, the parameter estimates for the two models are very similar. This is to be expected because estimates of these "fixed" effects tend to vary little across estimation technique (Bryk & Raudenbush, 1992). The parameter estimates do differ somewhat in statistical significance, particularly for the group-level variables. For example, in the CLOP analysis, Group Cohesion is significant with a p value less than .01 (the exact p-value is .0005), but the p value in the HLM analyses is significant, with a p value of .036. This difference reflects the fact that HLM adjusts the standard errors for group-based non-independence (see Bliese, Chapter Eight, this volume, for a discussion of this form of non-independence), whereas CLOP makes no such adjustment. As we and many others have noted, this difference between HLM and CLOP may cause standard errors for the group-level variables in CLOP analyses to be too small, thus leading to Type I errors.

The HLM analyses and the traditional CLOP analyses do yield very different estimates of the variance explained by the predictors. This reflects the fact that HLM uses higher-level (for example, group) predictors to explain higher-level (for example, between-group) variance in intercepts and slopes, whereas traditional cross-level operator analyses use higher-level predictors to explain total variance in the dependent variable. While one may "translate" the results of traditional cross-level operator analyses to obtain estimates of the between-group variance explained, the results are similar but not identical to those obtained in using HLM. Further, it is not entirely clear how to evaluate the statistical significance of the "translated" (and thus transformed) CLOP results.

Researchers must use great care in interpreting the differing estimates of explained variance that HLM and CLOP provide. For example, the HLM analyses indicate that the four group-level predictors explain 45 percent of the between-group variance in the Job Satisfaction. The traditional cross-level operator analyses, in contrast, indicate that the same four group-level predictors explain just 5.2 percent of the total variance in Job Satisfaction. The difference lies neither in the data nor in the relationships among the variables but in the reference point. The HLM analyses are conducted "with reference to" (that is, for the dependent variable of) the Job Satisfaction group intercepts; the CLOP analyses are conducted "with reference to" (that is, for the dependent variable of) the raw individual Job Satisfaction scores. The correct reference point depends in part on the researcher's theory. HLM analyses are commonly viewed as statistically superior to CLOP analyses; HLM analyses assess cross-level effects, using statistically appropriate degrees of freedom and estimates of standard error. HLM analyses may be difficult to interpret, however, if the between-unit intercepts of the dependent variable are not conceptually meaningful. (For further discussion of the meaning of aggregated variables, such as the group intercepts in HLM, see Kozlowski & Klein, Chapters One, this volume; Bliese, Chapter Eight, this volume; and Dansereau & Yammarino, Chapter Ten, this volume.)

The WABA analyses stand in rather sharp contrast to the HLM and CLOP analyses. A key difference, of course, is that the WABA researchers chose not to aggregate any of the independent variables; rather, the WABA researchers concluded that the relationships among the set of variables were best conceptualized and analyzed at the individual level of analysis. The WABA parameter estimates for the individual-level predictors are quite similar to the HLM and CLOP parameter estimates for these measures. The parameter and effect-size estimates for the variables left disaggregated by the WABA researchers, but aggregated by the HLM and CLOP researchers, are of course quite different. WABA, as we have noted, was designed to identify the single level or levels at which a set of relationships is best conceptualized and analyzed. WABA may analyze a set of relationships at "single levels" insofar as WABA allows one to conduct such analyses sequentially, but not simultaneously. In this sense, WABA is perhaps more constraining than HLM or CLOP, but WABA does allow a researcher to avoid at least some of the conceptual and statistical complexities that can arise in interpreting the results of HLM and CLOP analyses. In the present case, for example, it is relatively simple, both conceptually and statistically, to interpret the end results of the WABA analyses as indicative of the influence of a set of individual-level perceptual variables on individual-level Job Satisfaction. In contrast, the HLM and CLOP analyses suggest that Job Satisfaction is the product of both group and individual characteristics and, further, that the relationship between Job Satisfaction and one of its individual-level predictors (Workload) varies from group to group, in part as a function of the group's Task Significance.

Concluding Comments

In this chapter, we have compared and demonstrated a set of procedures commonly used to justify aggregation (r_{wg}, WABA, ICC(1), ICC(2), eta-squared) and a set of procedures commonly used to analyze multilevel data (WABA, HLM, and CLOP). We hope that we have, in the process, clarified commonalities and differences among these procedures.

The procedures used to justify aggregation are most likely to lead to the same conclusion in relatively unambiguous cases—that is, when a measure's variability lies quite predominantly between units, or when a measure's variability lies quite predominantly within units, or when a measure shows random variability within and between units. In more ambiguous cases, the procedures used to justify aggregation may yield differing conclusions.

Ultimately, aggregation is a judgment call informed by theory and data. Theory provides—or, at least, should provide—a detailed and convincing explanation of how and why lower-level measures may be combined to yield meaningful measures of unit characteristics. Each of the procedures used to justify aggregation provides a slightly different piece of evidence that the theory is correct—that aggregation is warranted. For example, r_{wg} provides evidence of the extent to which each of the units in a sample is characterized by within-unit agreement on the measure in question. Eta-squared and ICC(1) provide evidence of the extent to which the sample as a whole varies within and between units on the measure in question. ICC(2) provides evidence of the stability or reliability of the unit means on the measure in question. WABA provides evidence of the extent to which not one measure but all the measures in a sample vary and covary primarily within units, between units, or within and between units. The pieces of evidence are related but by no means identical.

Within-and-between analysis, hierarchical linear modeling, and cross-level operator analyses allow researchers to examine the relationships among higher-level and lower-level measures. When higher-level variables are derived from lower-level measures, aggregation decisions have profound implications for the conceptualization and analysis of multilevel and cross-level models. We drew a rather sharp distinction between the first and second parts of this chapter. The third part of this chapter—the analysis of the mock data set—shows how integrally related aggregation decisions may be to the design and testing of multilevel and cross-level models. The differing aggregation decisions made by the WABA researchers, by contrast with the decisions made by the CLOP and HLM researchers, led to sharp differences in the researchers' respective analyses and interpretations of the data.

Even in the absence of differing aggregation decisions, however, WABA, HLM, and CLOP are quite distinct. WABA, we have emphasized, was designed to identify the level or levels describing a set of relationships within a data set. WABA is thus particularly well suited to the testing of multilevel theoretical models, as we have used that term in this chapter. HLM and CLOP, in contrast, were designed to test cross-level models, as we have used that term in this chapter, and are particularly well suited to this task. HLM offers statistical advantages that may be important in testing cross-level moderating-effect models.

We hope that our examination of the commonalities and differences among multilevel analytical techniques will assist organizational researchers in using these techniques. There is no one best technique for analyzing multilevel data. The procedures, we have shown, provide differing pieces of evidence, which may be used to answer differing kinds of theoretical questions. This chapter has described the current state of the art in multilevel data analysis, not the end state. As organizational scholars devote increasing attention to multilevel issues, our theoretical models will grow in sophistication, complexity, and variety (see Kozlowski & Klein, Chapter One, this volume). And with these changes will come the need for, and surely the development of, new ways to test multilevel theory. As authors, we do not look forward to when this chapter is out-of-date; as researchers, however, we do.

Notes

1. Note that individual-level independent variables may explain not just within-unit variance but also between-unit variance in the dependent variable if the individual-level independent variable itself varies both within and between units. If an individual-level independent variable is group-mean centered, it varies only within units and thus can only explain within-unit variance in the dependent variable. See Hofmann and colleagues, Chapter Eleven, this volume, for further discussion of these issues.

2. The simulated data set is available on the Web site of the Society for Industrial and Organizational Psychology: http://www.siop.org. Individuals may download the data set and analyze it with WABA, CLOP, and HLM to gain hands-on experience in multilevel data analysis.

3. The WABA researchers also examined the homogeneity of the data set by splitting the sample into two groups: those with more within-group agreement on the dependent variable, and those with less within-group agreement on the dependent variable. They then conducted additional WABA analyses on the two subsamples. In the first subsample (characterized by relatively high within-group variability), none of the between-group correlations differed from the within-group correlations. In the second subsample (characterized by relatively low within-group variability), three of the between-group correlations were significant and differed from the analogous correlations in the high-variability subsample. On the basis of these results, the WABA researchers concluded that the sample was not homogeneous and thus that aggregated analyses would not represent the data. The WABA researchers believed that in these circumstances the best that could be done was to use the individual scores, recognizing that this was a violation of the homogeneity requirements of most statistical analyses.

References

Bartko, J. J. (1976). On various intraclass correlation reliability coefficients. *Psychological Bulletin, 83,* 762–765.

Bliese, P. D. (1998). Group size, ICC values, and group-level correlations: A simulation. *Organizational Research Methods, 1,* 355–373.

Bliese, P. D. (2000). Within-group agreement, non-independence, and reliability: Implications for data aggregation and analysis. In K. J. Klein & S.W.J. Kozlowski (Eds.), *Multilevel theory, research, and methods in organizations* (pp. 349–381). San Francisco: Jossey-Bass.

Bliese, P. D., & Halverson, R. R. (1998). Group size and measures of group-level properties: An examination of eta-squared and ICC values. *Journal of Management, 24,* 157–172.

Brown, K. G., Kozlowski, S.W.J., & Hattrup, K. (1996, August). *Theory, issues, and recommendations in conceptualizing agreement as a construct in organizational research: The search for consensus regarding consensus.* Paper presented at annual meeting of the Academy of Management, Cincinnati, OH.

Bryk, A. S., & Raudenbush, S. W. (1992). *Hierarchical linear models: Applications and data analysis methods.* Thousand Oaks, CA: Sage.

Chan, D. (1998). Functional relations among constructs in the same content domain at different levels of analysis: A typology of composition models. *Journal of Applied Psychology, 83,* 234–246.

Cohen, J., & Cohen, P. (1983). *Applied multiple regression/correlation analysis for the behavioral sciences* (2nd ed.). Mahwah, NJ: Erlbaum.

Dansereau, F., Alutto, J. A., & Yammarino, F. J. (1984). *Theory testing in organizational behavior: The varient approach.* Englewood Cliff, NJ: Prentice-Hall.

Dansereau, F., & Yammarino, F. J. (2000). Within and Between Analysis: The varient paradigm as an underlying approach to theory building and testing. In K. J. Klein & S.W.J. Kozlowski (Eds.), *Multilevel theory, research, and methods in organizations* (pp. 425–466). San Francisco: Jossey-Bass.

Hofmann, D. A., & Gavin, M. B. (1998). Centering decisions in hierarchical linear models: Theoretical and methodological implications for organizational science. *Journal of Management, 23,* 623–641.

Hofmann, D. A., Griffin, M., & Gavin, M. (2000). The application of hierarchical linear modeling to organizational research. In K. J. Klein & S.W.J. Kozlowski (Eds.), *Multilevel theory, research, and methods in organizations* (pp. 467–511). San Francisco: Jossey-Bass.

House, R., Rousseau, D. M., & Thomas-Hunt, M. (1995). The meso paradigm: A framework for the integration of micro and macro organizational behavior. In L. L. Cummings & B. M. Staw (Eds.), *Research in organizational behavior* (Vol. 17, pp. 71–114). Greenwich, CT: JAI Press.

James, L. R., Demaree, R. J., & Wolf, G. (1984). Estimating within group interrater reliability with and without response bias. *Journal of Applied Psychology, 69,* 85–98.

James, L. R., & Williams, L .J. (2000). The cross-level operator in regression, ANCOVA, and contextual analysis. In K. J. Klein & S.W.J. Kozlowski (Eds.), *Multilevel theory, research, and methods in organizations* (pp. 382–424). San Francisco: Jossey-Bass.

Klein, K. J., Dansereau, F., & Hall, R. J. (1994). Levels issues in theory development, data collection, and analysis. *Academy of Management Review, 19,* 195–229.

Kozlowski, S.W.J., & Hattrup, K. (1992). A disagreement about within-group agreement: Disentangling issues of consistency versus consensus. *Journal of Applied Psychology, 77,* 161–167.

Kozlowski, S.W.J., & Klein, K. J. (2000). A multilevel approach to theory and research in organizations: Contextual, temporal, and emergent processes. In K. J. Klein & S.W.J. Kozlowski (Eds.), *Multilevel theory, research, and methods in organizations* (pp. 3–90). San Francisco: Jossey-Bass.

Kreft, I., & de Leeuw, J. (1998). *Introducing multilevel modeling.* Thousand Oaks, CA: Sage.

Miller, J. G. (1978). *Living systems.* New York: McGraw-Hill.

Rousseau, D. (1985). Issues of level in organizational research: Multilevel and cross-level perspectives. In L. L. Cummings & B. M. Staw (Eds.), *Research in organizational behavior* (Vol. 7, pp. 1–37). Greenwich, CT: JAI Press.

Schmidt, F. L., & Hunter, J. E. (1989). Interrater reliability coefficients cannot be computed when only one stimulus is rated. *Journal of Applied Psychology, 74,* 368–370.

PART 3

Commentary

CHAPTER 13

Networks and Frog Ponds
Trends in Multilevel Research
Daniel J. Brass

"A continuing and frequently stated challenge that we ought to keep trying to meet is to forge a stronger link between the macro and micro parts of the field. This argues for giving more attention to what have been labeled meso phenomena and also to research attempts to show how individual and group actions can affect organizational actions, as well as vice versa. A focus on only the macro side or only the micro side of the organizational studies coin, as it were, will keep giving us an incomplete and ultimately unsatisfying picture."

Although this quote might have appeared in any of the chapters in this volume, it comes from Lyman Porter (1996), commenting in the fortieth-anniversary issue of *Administrative Science Quarterly* (*ASQ*). To celebrate this anniversary, *ASQ* asked nine leading organizational scholars, all of whom had been active researchers in 1956, to reflect on the field. Porter was advocating the research philosophy of James D. Thompson, first editor of *Administrative Science Quarterly*. He did not need to convince the other eight scholars. It is notable that all nine essays in the anniversary issue include multilevel issues. Even Philip Selznick's reflections on institutional theory—a decidedly macro approach to organizations—emphasize the multilevel orientation of these early scholars; he quotes from his own book, *Leadership in Administration*: "No social process can be understood save as it is located in the behavior of individuals, and especially in their perceptions of themselves and each other. The problem is to link the larger view to the more limited one, to see how institutional change is produced by, and in turn shapes, the interaction of individuals in day-to-day situations" (Selznick, 1996, p. 274).

Each of the essays in the anniversary issue provides some of the author's reflections on what the multidisciplinary field of "organizational behavior" (OB) looked like in the 1950s. That decade was a time when the study of organizations was dominated by organizational sociologists and industrial psychologists. The label *organizational behavior* was meant to reflect both the macro emphasis on organizations and the micro emphasis on individual behavior. Today, the term *organizational behavior* is typically used to label the micro orientation, but it was this historic view of organizational behavior that led House, Rousseau, and Thomas-Hunt (1995) to argue that if it's not meso, it's not OB.

Have we lost the integrative flavor of the multilevel approach to organization studies that was evident in the 1950s? Perhaps it was never there, or perhaps it was evident only in the classics that have survived since the 1950s. As Edgar Schein remembers, "For their part, the organizational sociologists paid equally little attention to what the psychologists had learned about individual differences, testing and selection methods, training and development, incentives, motivation, and rewards" (Schein, 1996, p. 230).

Although some things remain the same, it is evident that the field has changed. As in industrial/organizational (IO) psychology, the number of scholars and the number of journals have grown tremendously over the past forty years. With this growth has come the emergence of many subfields. Although he is concerned about the fragmentation, Zald (1996, p. 252) notes, "The fragmentation and change of organizational studies is in some ways a measure of its success." But March (1996, p. 280) writes, "As the field has grown and elaborated new perspectives, it has continually been threatened with becoming not so much a new integrated semidiscipline as a set of independent, self congratulatory cultures of comprehension." And as Porter (1996, p. 264) notes, "Probably the most significant failure of micro-OB, in my view, is that we have tended to ignore the 'O' in our studies of micro phenomena. We have clearly emphasized the 'B,' especially in recent years, but we have by and large been remiss in considering organizations as critical contexts affecting the behavior occurring within them." Similarly, in this volume, Schneider, Smith, and Sipe (Chapter Two) and DeNisi (Chapter Three) suggest that the "I" in I/O psychology might more accurately have stood for "individual" than "industrial."

For those of us in business schools, it is encouraging to note that the number of multilevel articles published in such mainstream journals as *Administrative Science Quarterly, Academy of Management Journal (AMJ)*, and *Academy of Management Review (AMR)* has increased dramatically over the past ten years (House et al., 1995; Brass & House, in press). Likewise, it is equally heartening to see the number of citations in this volume to multilevel publications in the *Journal of Applied Psychology*, often thought of as a micro journal. Our niche as I/O departments within psychology or organizational behavior departments in business schools depends on our distinguishing ourselves from the more general psychologists and sociologists. According to House and colleagues (1995, p. 73), "The distinguishing feature of organizational phenomena is that processes at several levels of analysis are in some way linked."

It is noteworthy that the multilevel frameworks suggested by Rousseau (1985); by Klein, Dansereau, and Hall (1994); and by Kozlowski and Klein in Chapter One of this volume have provided a useful multilevel lens for assessing research in various topic areas. Anyone looking for research ideas need go no further than the chapters in this volume. One quickly becomes aware of the gaps in the empirical research when one attempts to find studies that correspond to the multilevel arrows linking independent and dependent variables at the individual, group, and organizational levels of analysis. In addition to research in specific topic areas, these frameworks also provide a handy reference for assessing multilevel trends in research.

Recent Trends in Multilevel Research

In suggesting trends in multilevel research, I rely heavily on the classifications and counts from *ASQ, AMJ,* and *AMR* provided by House and colleagues (1995) and by Brass and House (in press), as well as on my own reading of the other journals and the citations and chapters in this volume. As noted, the number of multilevel articles continues to increase in the 1990s. The importance of crossing levels of analysis arises from the likelihood that variables at one level of analysis will be correlated with variables at another level of analysis. Research that does not cross levels of analysis will likely be incorrectly specified, and estimates of variance explained will be biased. As research continues to identify cross-level relationships, more and more research crosses levels of analysis.

Just as the number of multilevel articles has increased, so has the number of different levels of analysis considered in these articles. In addition to the typically noted individual, group, and organizational levels, there are the dyadic level, the triadic level, the business unit level, the occupational level, the organizational-chains level, the industry or organizational population level, the national level, the cultural level, and the societal level. Is there a finite set of appropriate units of analysis that can be considered in studying organizational behavior? As Glick (1992) asks, "Do we get a better understanding of the world by examining the wall, the bricks in the wall, or the sand and mortar between the bricks?" Klein and her colleagues (1994), Kozlowski and Klein (Chapter One, this volume), and several of the other chapters in this volume have provided a detailed analysis of methods for testing levels of analysis. As the authors note, however, these methods are designed to confirm the researcher's theory and corresponding measurement; they are not, absent any theory, meant to determine the appropriate levels of analysis.

Determining the appropriateness of a particular unit of analysis for organizational studies is largely a theoretical question. Depending on one's theory and interest, any of a variety of levels of analysis may lead to insights into the functioning of organizations. The problems and debates seem to arise when we do not measure our constructs at the same level of analysis as our theory. We are faced with questions about the appropriateness of aggregating measures to higher levels of analysis, or about disaggregating to lower levels of analysis (although recent reviews of published articles show few examples of disaggregation). Most of the recent journal articles seem to suggest that homogeneity of variance on the lower-level measures is justification for aggregating to the higher level. However, Kozlowski and Klein, in Chapter One, note that many higher-level constructs are not theoretically dependent on homogeneity of variance in the lower-level measures. As they remark, the performance of a baseball team does not assume homogeneity of the performances of the individual members of the team.

In addition, we have seen an increase in articles dealing with statistical techniques for assessing the appropriateness of aggregation to higher levels (Bliese, Chapter Eight, this volume; Dansereau & Yammarino, Chapter Ten, this volume; Hofmann, Griffin, & Gavin, Chapter Eleven, this volume). These statistical tests are extremely helpful in confirming theoretical arguments, but, as the authors note, they are not substitutes for theory.

The theoretical questions surrounding aggregation deal with the issue of entitivity, a question that group researchers have struggled with for years. What constitutes the entity we call a group? Shaw (1976, pp. 6–14) summarizes many definitions of groups and concludes that we classify entities on the basis of our perceptions of them. He argues that the only basis we have for attributing reality to any object is our perception of it. When we establish boundaries to differentiate entities, our perceptions are commonly affected by such factors as a common fate (two or more elements are in the same place at the same time, move together, and share the same outcome), similarity (on one or more attributes), proximity (they are close to each other in physical or psychological space), and pregnance (the extent to which the elements forming a pattern tend to be perceived as the best possible figure in relation to the ground). Whether an aggregate constitutes a distinct entity is a question of perception: the perception of the (possible) members (Do these people perceive themselves to be a group?) and of the others around them (Do others perceive these people to be a group?). If they are perceived to be a group, is it then appropriate to aggregate individual-level measures to the group level? Not yet. We now need to ask, "Is the aggregated measure the same as the group-level construct?" Again, this is a theoretical question. For example, we would not suggest that the age of a group (the amount of time the group has been in existence) is appropriately measured by the average age of the members of the group (even if the members of the group are all of the same age and if their average age differs from the average ages of the members of other groups). Labeling it a group construct depends on providing a theoretical argument for why the aggregated measure is the same thing as the group construct. The inclination to provide such an argument may depend on whether the researcher theorizes that groups are aggregations of individuals or whether the researcher theorizes that groups are intact entities with properties that cannot be disaggregated to the individual level of analysis.

Almost all the chapters in this volume address aggregation, and many insightful discussions and solutions are provided. I do not wish to repeat them in these short comments. The chapters exemplify the many interesting subtleties of aggregation. My brief comments are meant only to emphasize one of the points that crosses all these articles: ultimately, we must rely on theory. As Kozlowski and Klein note in Chapter One, "Theory takes precedence—that is the one overarching principle."

An increase in multilevel theoretical models is also evident in the journals; indeed, it is difficult to find a nonempirical review article in *AMR* that does not cross adjacent levels of analysis. Typically, these articles have taken a top-down approach, looking at the effects of contextual variables on individuals or groups (e.g., Dutton, Dukerich, & Harquail, 1994). In addition to the individual/group/organization classification of levels of analysis, recent increases are noted in the effects of industrial or societal/cultural variables on lower level variables (e.g., Earley, 1994; see also Chao, Chapter Seven, this volume). The recent interest in top management teams and CEOs has provided most of the examples of bottom-up effects of individuals or teams on organizational strategy and performance (e.g., Hayward & Hambrick, 1997).

Research conducted at more than two different levels of analysis is still infrequent (e.g., Allmendinger & Hackman, 1996; Thomas, Shankster, & Mathieu, 1994). Full-fledged multilevel models that attempt to consider independent/dependent-variable relationships at three levels of analysis remain rare. Staw, Sandelands, and Dutton's article on threat-rigidity effects (1981) is still the most often cited example. Lindsley, Brass, and Thomas's theory of efficacy-performance spirals (1995) is one of the few full-fledged models to include compositional effects, but a recent article by Chan (1998), as well as the chapters in this volume, suggest that interest in composition effects is increasing.

Also noticeable by their absence are studies in which a variable at one level of analysis moderates a relationship at another level of analysis (e.g., Erez & Somech, 1996). I have also seen few examples of the mediating effects of in-between levels of analysis, such as group-level variables mediating relationships between individual-level and organization-level variables. We still know very little about if and how one level of analysis may mediate relationships between higher and lower levels of analysis.

Frogs and Ponds

Ever since Firebaugh (1980) emphasized the importance of "frog-pond effects," there has been a dramatic increase in the number of empirical articles that consider an individual relative to a group (Kozlowski & Klein, Chapter One, this volume; Dansereau & Yammarino, Chapter Ten, this volume). Two topic areas account for many of these articles: the interest in diversity and relative demographics (e.g., Wagner, Pfeffer, & O'Reilly, 1984; Tsui, Egan, & O'Reilly, 1992), and articles investigating the fit between individuals and organizations (e.g., Chatman, 1991; Chatman & Brasade, 1995).

Frog-pond effects present some interesting twists to compositional models that attempt to explain the relationship between functionally similar constructs at different levels of analysis. For example, a researcher might want to investigate the effects of individual power on group power, and vice versa. Because power is a relational concept, my interpersonal power in a group depends on my relative standing with regard to other members of the group. Likewise, the group's power is relative to other groups. The group may gain (or lose) power, with no effect on the internal relative hierarchy of the members. However, if a powerful individual joins the group (likely increasing the overall external perception of the power of the group), my relative interpersonal power will likely decrease within the group (another individual who is more powerful than I am has been added). I become a smaller frog in a bigger pond. At the same time, it may increase my power in relation to those outside the group (some of the powerful individual's power accrues to the group and hence to me because I am a member of the group). If I leave the group for a less powerful group, it may decrease my external power reputation but may increase my internal standing (I'm more powerful than most of the others in my new group). I've become a bigger frog in a smaller pond. Therefore, there are some interesting complexities in considering frog-pond effects in compositional models.

Networks

In addition to "frog-pond effects" and "fit" articles, another dramatic increase has occurred in the number of network-related articles published. House and colleagues (1995) add networks as an additional classification when they note that more than 10 percent of the multilevel articles involve social networks. The analysis of social networks does not easily fit our traditional notions of levels of analysis because the unit of analysis is the *relationships* among the actors rather than the actors themselves. A network is typically defined as a set of nodes and the set of ties representing some relationship, or lack of relationship, between the nodes. In the case of social networks, the nodes represent actors (individuals, groups, organizations, and so on). The links often involve some form of interaction, such as communication, or represent a more abstract relationship, such as trust or friendship. In the case of organizations as actors (Klein, Palmer, & Conn, Chapter Six, this volume), the relationship might be understood in terms of joint ventures, trade associations, or corporate interlocks.

Social network analysis assumes that actors are embedded, with other actors, in a complex web of relationships. The basic building block of social network analysis is the relationship; the focus is on the link, or lack of a link, rather than on the actors. Therefore, our normal method of classifying levels of analysis (individual, group, organization) does not seem to apply to networks. At least two actors are needed to form a link; therefore, the individual level of analysis does not exist. The idea of a network implies more than one link. Whereas the dyad is the building block of the network, one link connecting two actors likely would not be considered a network. Therefore, it may not be appropriate to refer to networks as representing the dyadic or interpersonal (intergroup or interorganizational) level of analysis. A minimum of two links connecting three actors is required in order to have a network and establish such notions as indirect links and paths. Although measures of network position can be assigned to actors, these measures are not the properties of isolated actors or dyads; rather, they represent the actor's relation to the other actors in the network. A change in any position affects all the other positions.

When the individual is the actor (representing the nodes in the network), the network typically is measured by asking each person to indicate with whom he or she interacts (communicates, is friends with, goes to for advice, and so on). These individual responses are then aggregated to form the network. Aggregation in this case is a form of compilation: the network is a complex combination of relationships (Kozlowski & Klein, Chapter One, this volume). The network is "drawn" through the addition of each person's links to the "picture." The "picture" is a matrix, with each actor listed across the top as well as down the left side. A number is placed in the intersecting cell of the matrix that corresponds to two actors, indicating whether they interact with each other (1) or not (0); some larger number may indicate the frequency or intensity of the interaction (for example, a number on a Likert-type scale, from 1 to 7). This method of aggregating individual responses to a higher level of analysis (the network) does not present the typical aggregation problems discussed as levels-of-analysis issues (e.g., Robinson, 1950).

The compilation of the network on the basis of individual interactions is also consistent with theory that suggests that networks are the result of interpersonal interactions. As Barley notes (1990, pp. 64–65), "While people's actions are undoubtedly constrained by forces beyond their control and outside their immediate present, it is difficult to see how any social structure can be produced or reproduced except through ongoing action and interaction." Therefore, social networks typically focus on relatively stable patterns of interaction. These patterns emerge and become institutionalized as recurrent interaction takes on, over time, the status of predictable, socially shared regularities—that is, "taken-for-granted facts" (Barley, 1990, p. 67). People then behave within these institutionalized patterns as if these structures (networks) were external to and constraints upon their interactions. The constrained behavior in turn underwrites and reinforces the observed, socially shared patterns. These shared patterns also facilitate interaction, just as language facilitates as well as constrains communication.

However, a few peculiar problems arise when the focus is on relationships rather than on actors. The question of entitivity is particularly troublesome because networks can be extended almost infinitely as researchers continue to add indirect ties (friends of friends). Where do we draw the boundary around the network? Organizational researchers have typically relied on the convenience of formally designated units, such as work groups, departments, divisions, or organizations. However, theory must again be the overarching guide. For example, limiting the network to organizational members would not be useful in studying boundary spanners.

Additional problems arise when we study relationships rather than actors. What do we do when actor A says she talks with actor B, but actor B says he does not talk with actor A? In network terms, this represents a nonreciprocated link, and we can assess the degree of reciprocation for the entire network as some indication of the reliability of the data. In many cases, these nonreciprocated ties can be resolved through checking with the actors involved, if that is possible. A similar question arises in using a scale to indicate the frequency or intensity of interaction. What do we do if actor A represents the link as a 2 and actor B represents the link as a 6? Do we represent the link as the minimum, the maximum, or the average score? No easy answer currently exists, but it is to be hoped that our theory may provide some guidance.

Relationships also exist in which reciprocation is not necessarily expected. For example, we may be interested in advice relationships (A goes to B for advice, but B does not go to A for advice) or influence relationships (A has power over B, but B does not have power over A). Such relationships are inherently asymmetric. When reciprocation is not expected, we can compose a directed network of asymmetric links in which the links have arrows showing the direction of relationships. Most network measures can be calculated on matrices of symmetric relationships (cells above the diagonal are the same as cells below the diagonal) or asymmetric relationships (cells above the diagonal are different from cells below the diagonal).

Additional questions arise when researchers wish to study relationships between groups or organizations (see Klein et al., Chapter Six, this volume) rather than individuals. As Labianca, Brass, and Gray note (1998, p. 55), "Every individual may be perceived as a representative of a group, and every interpersonal interaction may be perceived in part as an intergroup interaction." If so, does every relationship between two people represent a relationship between two groups (or organizations, or nations, or races) to which those two individuals belong? As a practical question of measurement, do we count any interaction between two members of different groups as constituting interaction between those different groups? Social network researchers have often answered yes to this question. This answer is supported in part by findings that interpersonal relationships (as friends, acquaintances, or enemies) between members of different groups affect perceptions of intergroup conflict (Labianca et al., 1998). However, it is not clear how individual interactions between members of different groups might be aggregated to form some measure of intergroup interaction. Do four interpersonal relationships between members of different groups represent more intergroup interaction than two interpersonal relationships between members of different groups? In addition, it is likely that people distinguish between interpersonal interactions (such as friendships) and intergroup interactions in which they speak as representatives of their groups to representatives of other groups. When a person is officially speaking for a group or an organization, the interaction may be quite different from when the person is speaking as a friend. However, each type of interaction (official or personal) may be affected by the other. Personal connections provide potential avenues for preliminary testing of official communication (for example, "How would your group react to the idea of forming an alliance with my group?"), or problems may occur when personal interactions are misinterpreted as official interactions: "I told you that information as a friend; I didn't expect that you would tell everyone in your group."

Network researchers have also suggested that common membership in groups (as when CEOs sit on the same corporate boards of directors) constitute evidence of interaction. For example, as Breiger (1988, p. 83) argues, there is a duality of persons and groups: "Individuals come together (or, metaphorically, 'intersect' one another) within groups, which are collectives based on the shared interest, personal affinities, or ascribed status of members who participate regularly in collective activities. At the same time, the particular patterning of an individual's affiliations (or the 'intersection' of groups within the person) defines his or her points of reference and (at least partially) determines his or her individuality." Nevertheless, Breiger suggests that we distinguish between membership ties (based on common membership in groups) and social relationship ties (based on interpersonal interaction). Membership ties may represent only potential interaction, whereas interpersonal social relationships represent actual interaction.

These questions and problems arise as we begin to consider relationships rather than actors as the unit of analysis. The trends indicate that research on relationships, such as research focusing on networks and interorganizational relationships (see Klein et al., Chapter Six, this volume), is increasing. In addition, several key constructs in organizational studies (power, conflict, leadership, and so on) represent relationships. Therefore, researchers will continue to confront these issues in the future.

Conclusion

It is encouraging to see the many interesting research questions generated by the multilevel perspective adopted by the authors of the chapters in this volume. I have tried to complement these articles by reviewing some of the recent trends in multilevel research and focusing on the dramatic increases in networks and frog ponds. It appears that multilevel research is alive and well and being challenged by many interesting issues. The chapters in this volume provide excellent answers to some of the most perplexing questions in multilevel research. Just as the chapters in this volume were organized around topic areas, it appears that future research will also be organized around topic areas rather than around distinctions between micro and macro. It also appears that, as in this volume, topic areas will be multilevel and discussions will center on multilevel issues. Undoubtedly, we will see more articles like these.

References

Allmendinger, J., & Hackman, J. R. (1996). Organizations in changing environments: The case of the East German symphony orchestras. *Administrative Science Quarterly, 41,* 337–369.

Barley, S. R. (1990). The alignment of technology and structure through roles and networks. *Administrative Science Quarterly, 35,* 61–103.

Bliese, P. D. (2000). Within-group agreement, non-independence, and reliability: Implications for data aggregation and analysis. In K. J. Klein & S.W.J. Kozlowski (Eds.), *Multilevel theory, research, and methods in organizations* (pp. 349–381). San Francisco: Jossey-Bass.

Brass, D. J., & House, R. J. (in press). The meso perspective: Reflections and trends. In W. Joyce (Ed.), *Perspectives on organization science.*

Breiger, R. L. (1988). The duality of persons and groups. In B. Wellman & S. D. Berkowitz (Eds.), *Social structures: A network approach* (pp. 83–93). Cambridge, England: Cambridge University Press.

Chan, D. (1998). Functional relations among constructs in the same content domain at different levels of analysis: A typology of composition models. *Journal of Applied Psychology, 83,* 234–246.

Chao, G. T. (2000). Multilevel issues and culture: An integrative view. In K. J. Klein & S.W.J. Kozlowski (Eds.), *Multilevel theory, research, and methods in organizations* (pp. 308–346). San Francisco: Jossey-Bass.

Chatman, J. A. (1991). Matching people and organizations: Selection and socialization in public accounting firms. *Administrative Science Quarterly, 36,* 459–484.

Chatman, J. A., & Brasade, S. B. (1995). Personality, organizational culture, and cooperation: Evidence from a business simulation. *Administrative Science Quarterly, 40,* 423–443.

Dansereau, F., & Yammarino, F. J. (2000). Within and Between Analysis: The varient paradigm as an underlying approach to theory building and testing. In K. J. Klein & S.W.J. Kozlowski (Eds.), *Multilevel theory, research, and methods in organizations* (pp. 425–466). San Francisco: Jossey-Bass.

DeNisi, A. S. (2000). Performance appraisal and performance management: A multilevel analysis. In K. J. Klein & S.W.J. Kozlowski (Eds.), *Multilevel theory, research, and methods in organizations* (pp. 121–156). San Francisco: Jossey-Bass.

Dutton, J. E., Dukerich, J. M., & Harquail, C. V. (1994). Organizational images and member identification. *Administrative Science Quarterly, 39,* 239–265.

Earley, C. P. (1994). Self or group? Cultural effects of training on self-efficacy and performance. *Administrative Science Quarterly, 39,* 89–117.

Erez, M., & Somech, A. (1996). Is group productivity loss the rule or the exception? Effects of culture and group-based motivation. *Academy of Management Journal, 39,* 1512–1537.

Firebaugh, G. (1980). Groups as contexts and frog ponds. In K. H. Roberts & L. Burstein (Eds.), *Issues in aggregation*. New Directions for Methodology of Social and Behavioral Science, no. 6. San Francisco: Jossey-Bass.

Glick, W. H. (1992, May). *Sand, bricks, or walls: A matter of realism*. Paper presented at seventh annual conference of the Society for Industrial and Organizational Psychology, Montreal.

Hayward, M.L.A., and Hambrick, D. C. (1997). Explaining the premiums paid for larger acquisitions: Evidence of CEO hubris. *Administrative Science Quarterly, 42,* 103–127.

Hofmann, D. A., Griffin, M., & Gavin, M. (2000). The application of hierarchical linear modeling to organizational research. In K. J. Klein & S.W.J. Kozlowski (Eds.), *Multilevel theory, research, and methods in organizations* (pp. 467–511). San Francisco: Jossey-Bass.

House, R., Rousseau, D. M., & Thomas-Hunt, M. (1995). The meso paradigm: A framework for the integration of micro and macro organizational behavior. In L. L. Cummings & B. M. Staw (Eds.), *Research in organizational behavior* (Vol. 17, pp. 71–114). Greenwich, CT: JAI Press.

Klein, K. J., Dansereau, F., & Hall, R. J. (1994). Levels issues in theory development, data collection, and analysis. *Academy of Management Review, 19,* 195–229.

Klein, K. J., Palmer, S. L., & Conn, A. B. (2000). Interorganizational relationships: A multilevel perspective. In K. J. Klein & S.W.J. Kozlowski (Eds.), *Multilevel theory, research, and methods in organizations* (pp. 267–307). San Francisco: Jossey-Bass.

Kozlowski, S.W.J., & Klein, K. J. (2000). A multilevel approach to theory and research in organizations: Contextual, temporal, and emergent processes. In K. J. Klein & S.W.J. Kozlowski (Eds.), *Multilevel theory, research, and methods in organizations* (pp. 3–90). San Francisco: Jossey-Bass.

Labianca, G., Brass, D. J., & Gray, B. (1998). Social networks and perceptions of intergroup conflict: The role of negative relationships and third parties. *Academy of Management Journal, 41,* 55–67.

Lindsley, D. H., Brass, D. J., & Thomas, J. B. (1995). Efficacy-performance spirals: A multilevel perspective. *Academy of Management Review, 20,* 645–678.

March, J. G. (1996). Continuity and change in theories of organizational action. *Administrative Science Quarterly, 41,* 278–287.

Porter, L. W. (1996). Forty years of organization studies: Reflections from a micro perspective. *Administrative Science Quarterly, 41,* 262–269.

Robinson, W. S. (1950). Ecological correlations and the behavior of individuals. *American Sociological Review, 15,* 351–357.

Rousseau, D. M. (1985). Issues of level in organizational research: Multi-level and cross-level perspectives. In L. L. Cummings & B. M. Staw (Eds.), *Research in organizational behavior* (Vol. 7, pp. 1–37). Greenwich, CT: JAI Press.

Schein, E. H. (1996). Culture: The missing concept in organizational studies. *Administrative Science Quarterly, 41,* 229–240.

Schneider, B., Smith, D. B., & Sipe, W. P. Personnel selection psychology: Multilevel considerations. In K. J. Klein & S.W.J. Kozlowski (Eds.), *Multilevel theory, research, and methods in organizations* (pp. 91–120). San Francisco: Jossey-Bass.

Selznick, P. (1996). Institutionalism "old" and "new." *Administrative Science Quarterly, 41,* 270–277.

Shaw, M. E. (1976). *Group dynamics.* New York: McGraw-Hill.

Staw, B. M., Sandelands, L. E., & Dutton, J. E. (1981). Threat-rigidity effects in organizational behavior: A multilevel analysis. *Administrative Science Quarterly, 26,* 501–524.

Thomas, J. B., Shankster, L. J., & Mathieu, J. E. (1994). Antecedents of organizational issue interpretation: The roles of single-level, cross-level, and content cues. *Academy of Management Journal, 37,* 1252–1284.

Tsui, A. S., Egan, T. D., & O'Reilly, C. A. (1992). Being different: Relational demography and organizational attachment. *Administrative Science Quarterly, 37,* 549–579.

Wagner, G. W., Pfeffer, J., & O'Reilly, C. A. (1984). Organizational demography and turnover in top-management groups. *Administrative Science Quarterly, 29,* 74–92.

Zald, M. N. (1996). More fragmentation? Unfinished business in linking the social sciences and the humanities. *Administrative Science Quarterly, 41,* 251–261.

CHAPTER 14

Multilevel Competencies and Missing Linkages

Denise M. Rousseau

The multilevel quality of behavior in organizations is one defining feature of the organizational behavior field and its related discipline of industrial/organizational psychology, and one of the field's core competencies is its ability to understand multilevel issues. This volume is a splendid example of the field's intellectual contribution as well as of its continued promise, based on its multilevel competence and essential character. This commentary builds on this volume's contributions and offers some thoughts on where we are and where we might go from here.

In this commentary, I make three basic points. First, although multilevel research is inherent in the field, rigorous multilevel thinking may not be. Second, the field faces a critical challenge to develop rich and rigorously specified theory regarding the nature of linkages across levels. Third, if we pay greater attention to the role of time in cross-level processes and to the study of events where individual, group, and organizational processes converge, we will be closer to understanding the cross-level linkages that are inherent in organizations. To address these points, I first consider how critical multilevel issues are to the study of behavior in organizations and examine why these issues have received insufficient attention, despite their importance.

The Long-Standing Multilevel Character of Organizational Research

It is virtually impossible to take a core concept in organizational research, from motivation and performance to decision making and leadership, and not find that theory and research about it spans several levels. Take, for example, Lawler's research on motivation and performance. His early research focused primarily on individuals (Lawler, 1968), work that was followed by studies of subunit performance (Lawler & Hackman, 1969) and that culminated in an extensive body of recent research on high-performing work systems (Lawler, Mohrman, & Ledford, 1998).

Moreover, practices such as training and incentives, commonly studied for their effects on individuals, have also been addressed at higher levels of complexity as "bundles" of human resource practices that characterize firms with different strategies (Pil & MacDuffie, 1996; Ostroff & Bowen, Chapter Five, this volume). Throughout organizational behavior research, the most common shift in focus appears to be from an individual level to a higher one. However, even higher-level concepts, such as the effects of leadership on groups of followers, have shifted from a focus on groups and organizations (Fielder, 1972) to a focus on dyads (Graen & Scandura, 1987) and even to so individual an aspect as self-management (Batt, 1999). Organizational concepts frequently take an elevator ride, to lower as well as higher levels. As a doctoral student in the 1970s, it was exciting for me to learn how organizations affect individuals. More recent research also suggests that individual and group enactments can be organization-creating (Weick, 1995), a shift in the directionality of influence (and of research interest) that is proving to be at least as productive as the traditional view. But there are consequences of the dynamism surrounding levels of theory in organizational research, and these consequences may be cause for concern.

Although research interests span many levels within and around firms, and although organizational behavior constructs frequently are applied at several levels, I wonder whether we really do "think" in a multilevel way. Do we really have our eyes on the whole as well as on the parts? I have been puzzled about why recent reviewers of the field's progress have reported few "new" developments (O'Reilly,

1990; Mowday & Sutton, 1993), despite what seems to be a powerful cumulation of research on the complexity of behavior in organizations (Goodman & Whetton, 1998; Rousseau, 1997). My hunch is that the dynamism of level shifting can mean that the innovations and complexity characteristic of a multilevel field can be missed if one assumes a single vantage point.

Nevertheless, it is reasonable to consider whether organizational research might become too broad, thus making it difficult for us to build on other research and learn from one another. In a provocative address and subsequent article, Pfeffer (1993) argued that the field of organizational behavior is undermining its academic standing by providing a broad tent for scholars who pursue such fundamentally different perspectives as sensemaking, neoinstitutionalism, behaviorism, and rational choice. I suspect that he was being purposely provocative rather than advocating any one paradigm. I would argue that the strength and the comparative advantage of organizational behavior lies in the diversity of the paradigms incorporated under its big tent, by contrast with a field that is constricted in its narrow purity. Our challenge is to transform these differences into greater insight regarding the complexity of organizational behavior. For us to meet this challenge, there is a need for integration that capitalizes on the learning provided by different paradigms. The multilevel perspective can provide this integration. The real danger of having a big tent is in becoming so engrossed by discovering a variety of organizational processes (or by making a case for one's particular piece of organizational complexity) that the patterns and synergies among paradigms are overlooked.

Cross-level researchers—those scholars in the field who have focused simultaneously on processes at several levels—have long advocated integration rather than the supremacy of any one concept. This is consistent with the large body of work that Schneider and his colleagues have contributed to the field, and for which Schneider, Smith, and Sipe make a case in Chapter Two of this volume. An openness of mind and spirit is very much in keeping with social science traditions. One purpose of social science is to get away from what Selznick (1999) has called the "ego problem" and focus on what we can learn from each other. In this regard, organizational behavior may be the quintessential social science.

It is the nature of organizations and the behavioral processes of their constituents to contain hierarchically nested systems, which means that it is difficult to find relations on a single level that are not influenced by those of other levels. In Chapter One, Kozlowski and Klein make a cogent case for how the multilevel perspective brings rigor to the process of building and testing theories of organizational behavior. As they indicate, the traditional micro perspective assumes that aggregation masks important individual differences, whereas the macro perspective generally ignores how individuals shape higher-level phenomena. Lateral relations also have been increasingly recognized for their effects on how work is organized, as in the case of Chinese family firms (Granrose and Chua, 1996; Chao, Chapter Seven, this volume). Issues of linkages, both horizontally across levels and laterally among components, are a core problem in our field.

The field of organizational behavior is distinct for its deep appreciation of complexity, to the point of tolerating a certain degree of messiness. But we need to bring more careful thinking and scientific rigor to studying how cross-level processes work. The compilation processes described in this volume begin to portray the complex interactions among individuals and the integration of their unique skills to bring about higher-level outcomes (see Kozlowski, Brown, Weissbein, Cannon-Bowers, & Salas, Chapter Four, this volume). Thus, in the case of training in organizations, cross-level effects occur as a function of individuals' skill fit within the organization's context and the congruence of one individual's skills with those of others. Compilation of individual skills into higher outcomes is an emergent developmental process: lower-level changes occur more quickly, but they take time to rise to a higher level. Within a specific organization, the effects of training can come from the embedded ties among individual workers, their interactions with their work groups, and the organizational responses to the results of their skill deployment. The appreciation that this volume's authors demonstrate for the bundling of training with other human resource practices, such as performance appraisal and coaching, points the way. The next step is to identify the processes that emerge when different practices combine and give rise to individual and organizational responses. But unless we become more discerning about the mechanisms through which such cross-level effects occur, the larger potential for intellectual growth and cumulation in multilevel organizational research will remain unrealized.

The Challenge of Developing Theory Regarding Linkages

Linkages among individuals, groups, and organizations must be brought to the forefront of organizational research. First and foremost, we must address the problem of specification: What social, psychological, and systemic processes account for observed effects? Specification requires us to identify linkages among causes, effects, and moderating conditions across a spectrum of potentially pertinent levels.

To further enhance our science, researchers need to develop more coherent multilevel theories addressing linkages. Several chapters in this book argue that there is a need to make the forms, time lags, and causal specifications of linkages more explicit. Linkages are indeed often implicit: high-performing firms presumably bring economic benefits to their workers, skilled workers arguably perform more reliably than their less able counterparts, and so on. But where are the data? Consider again the example of training effects in organizations. Research on training has been undertaken by everyone from economists and sociologists to macro-organizational behavior researchers and dyed-in-the-wool industrial psychologists. These researchers assume that training (at the level of the society, region, firm, or person) affects organizational outcomes, and yet the specific nature of this linkage is rarely well articulated. Ostroff and Bowen, in Chapter Five, effectively make a similar case regarding the role that human resource practices play in promoting organizational effectiveness. How, then, can we understand the ways in which individuals, groups, and the bundles of practices that firms deploy contribute to organizational effectiveness? What are the developmental processes whereby multilevel practices such as training (and related processes of creativity and learning) unfold?

Let us begin with some familiar cross-level processes. Two linkage mechanisms implicit in a good deal of the multilevel organizational research, which includes this volume, are cross-level feedback and congruence. Feedback mechanisms, positive and negative, have been widely used to study organizational settings; their effects on individuals, groups, and firms are evident. Negative feedback in hierarchical settings, which typically represents forms of control, is spurred by deviance from rules, standards, norms, or tolerances (for example, individuals' absences in relation to personnel policies regarding attendance, or subunits' adherence to standardized accounting practices). We know that negative feedback from a higher level limits the variability in behavior of lower-level units. Negative feedback mechanisms can play a role in training by reinforcing desired behaviors acquired through training and extinguishing undesirable ones. However, it is often only when negative feedback mechanisms fail (or have never been put in place) that the role of linkages becomes apparent. The amount of time required before a substandard act is noted or generates a higher-level response is indicative of the role that higher-level processes play in shaping lower-level behavior. It also serves as an indicator of organizational effectiveness, differentiating efficiency from inefficiency and financial losses from profitability.

Positive feedback mechanisms are operating when responses at one level accelerate rates of behavior at another. Whereas negative feedback tends to engender stability over time, positive feedback generates disequilibrium and nonlinearity (DeGreene, 1973). Early interventions into positive feedback cycles tend to yield low-level responses, which in turn accelerate over time. On the adaptive side, individual learning can promote group or organizational learning, which in turn can increase the ability to adapt to environmental changes. Rewards for innovation and communication channels that promote idea sharing can be the devices through which positive feedback mechanisms lead to more rapid change and adaptiveness over time and across levels. Positive feedback is associated with accelerated rates of change, and in certain circumstances it can also promote errors, particularly when higher-level units exhibit insufficient control over the performance of lower-level components. At Barings, for example, one individual broker's risky trades, combined with his accelerated risk taking to cover losses and coupled with the halo that successful brokers possessed in the eyes of his superiors (positive feedback), ultimately led to the financial collapse of a centuries-old bank (Goodman, 2000).

Congruence is another linkage mechanism that has been widely studied by organizational researchers (e.g., Edwards, 1996). In this context, the term *congruence* means that the capacities of various components match in a way that promotes effective higher-level processing and sustained lower-level performance. The different mental models that team members have of their collective task can create congruence, producing a whole whose capabilities are greater than those of its parts. The workings of congruence are implicit in the compilation processes described by Kozlowski and colleagues (Chapter Four, this volume) and by Ostroff and Bowen (Chapter Five, this volume). Congruence mechanisms account for many situations in organizational research where the mere study of individuals, separately or in the aggregate, would miss the point: variability among individuals may be the critical quality that creates the larger whole. A simple way to explain such phenomena is through the notion of *fit* with the larger environment. But what exactly does that mean? A complex technology operated by people with multiple skills entails fit, but the actual mechanism accounting for the joint effect of the two might actually be coordination: multiple skills coupled with complex technology make coordination simpler to achieve. In any case, congruence can take a variety of forms and demands attention in its own right.

The explicit specification and empirical study of such mechanisms is the critical next step in building the field's multilevel character. Thirty years ago a new focus on climate made salient the emergent phenomena manifest at higher levels, and ten years ago a new interest in sensemaking and enactment brought managerial cognition into firm-level studies of behavior; simultaneous top-down and bottom-up perspectives, with a touch of lateral movement, permeate this volume as well as other recent works (Chan, 1998; Goodman, 2000). Sustained attention to multilevel linkages is key to promoting greater cumulation in organizational research. To accomplish this objective, we might be well served by a slightly different approach to the empirical study of organizational processes, one that emphasizes the influence of time on these processes.

Time and Events

One way to actively use the multilevel intellectual tools we have at present, and thereby expand their coherence and richness, would be to place more emphasis on the role of time in organizational processes. It is no coincidence that several chapters of this volume address the role of time in the specification of causal models (see, for example, Chapters One, Four, and Five). Ample empirical evidence suggests that the effects of organizations on persons are better seen in conditions of stability, whereas the opposite is true in conditions of uncertainty. Simon (1973) points out the existence of time-scale variations across levels, with lower-level processes generally being faster than higher-level ones. The recognition of such patterns informs both measurement design and sampling strategies in research as we seek to better understand and better specify why relationships are bottom-up or top-down and how processes differ between new units (for example, groups or firms) and established ones.

Longitudinal studies are valuable for the insights they offer into issues regarding time. However, from the perspective of organizational research, both issues of time and related cross-level processes can often be more readily understood from the study of events. Events are interactions among combinations of activities that lead to an outcome—for example, a plane landing on an aircraft carrier (Roberts, 1990) or the collision of two aircraft (Weick, 1990). By studying organizational events, we can better inform ourselves about multilevel processes because the activities of individuals, groups, and larger organizations, which include communications, coordinations, and conflicts that arise among them, combine in ways that affect performance. The processes surrounding the intersection of individual, group, and organizational dynamics in shaping such singularities as the collapse of Barings, the explosion of the space shuttle *Challenger*, and the Tenerife disaster are inherently multilevel, as indicated in work by Ramanujam (1999), Vaughn (1996), and Weick (1990). Collections of events within a single organization, as in the case of research on such high-reliability organizations as naval aircraft carriers, are particularly able to illustrate the multilevel character of organizational processes. In these cases, both repeated patterns and unpredicted variations can be discerned, allowing cross-level mechanisms to reveal themselves.

Conclusion

We have an opportunity to accelerate developments in organizational behavior by paying sustained attention to multilevel issues. Building theory that respects variability and the array of cross-level processes operating within organizations moves us closer to well-specified models of organizational effectiveness, to better appreciation of how humans organize themselves in accomplishing tasks, and to deeper understanding of how organizations shape the human experience. This volume offers a variety of concepts that are useful in specifying the linkages between lower-level behaviors and higher-level effectiveness. These concepts can help us understand the cycles through which higher-level organizational processes arise and subsequently shape the behavior and experiences of workers. Ultimately, this volume offers ways for us to (in Kozlowski and Klein's wonderful phrase) "understand the whole and keep an eye on the parts."

References

Batt, R. (1999). Work organization, technology, and performance in customer service and sales. *Industrial and Labor Relations Review, 52,* 539–564.

Chan, D. (1998). Functional relations among constructs in the same content domain at different levels: A typology of composition models. *Journal of Applied Psychology, 83,* 234–246.

Chao, G. T. (2000). Multilevel issues and culture: An integrative view. In K. J. Klein & S.W.J. Kozlowski (Eds.), *Multilevel theory, research, and methods in organizations* (pp. 308–346). San Francisco: Jossey-Bass.

DeGreene, K. B. (1973). *Sociotechnical systems: Factors in analysis, design, and management.* Englewood Cliffs, NJ: Prentice-Hall.

Edwards, J. R. (1996). An examination of competing versions of the person-environment fit approach to stress. *Academy of Management Journal, 39,* 292–340.

Fielder, F. E. (1972). Predicting the effects of leadership training and experience from the contingency model. *Journal of Applied Psychology, 56,* 114–119.

Goodman, P. S. (2000). *Missing organizational linkages: Tools for cross-level organizational research.* Thousand Oaks, CA: Sage.

Goodman, P. S., & Whetton, D. A. (1998). Fifty years of organizational behavior from multiple perspectives. In M. Neufeld & J. McKelvey (Eds.), *A half-century of challenge and change in employment relations.* Ithaca, NY: ILR Press.

Graen, G. B., & Scandura, T. A. (1987). Toward a psychology of dynamic organizing. In L. L. Cummings & B. M. Staw (Eds.), *Research in organizational behavior* (Vol. 9, pp. 175–208). Greenwich CT: JAI Press.

Granrose, C. S., & Chua, B. L. (1996). Global boundaryless careers: Lessons from Chinese family businesses. In M. B. Arthur & D. M. Rousseau (Eds.), *The boundaryless career: A new employment principle for a new organizational era* (pp. 201–217). New York: Oxford University Press.

Kozlowski, S.W.J., Brown, K. G., Weissbein, D. A., Cannon-Bowers, J. A., & Salas, E. (2000). A multilevel approach to training effectiveness: Enhancing horizontal and vertical transfer. In K. J. Klein & S.W.J. Kozlowski (Eds.), *Multilevel theory, research, and methods in organizations* (pp. 157–210). San Francisco: Jossey-Bass.

Kozlowski, S.W.J., & Klein, K. J. (2000). A multilevel approach to theory and research in organizations: Contextual, temporal, and emergent processes. In K. J. Klein & S.W.J. Kozlowski (Eds.), *Multilevel theory, research, and methods in organizations* (pp. 3–90). San Francisco: Jossey-Bass.

Lawler, E. E. (1968). A correlational causal analysis of the relationship between expectancy attitudes and job performance. *Journal of Applied Psychology, 52,* 462–468.

Lawler, E. E., & Hackman, J. R. (1969). Impact of employee participation in the development of pay incentive plans. *Journal of Applied Psychology, 53,* 467–471.

Lawler, E. E., Mohrman, S. A., & Ledford, G. E. (1998). *Strategies for high-performance organizations.* San Francisco: Jossey-Bass.

Mowday, R., & Sutton, R. I. (1993). Organizational behavior: Linking individuals and groups to organization contexts. *Annual Review of Psychology, 44,* 195–229.

O'Reilly, C. A. (1990). Organizational behavior: Where we've been, where we're going. *Annual Review of Psychology, 42,* 427–458.

Ostroff, C., & Bowen, D. E. (2000). Moving HR to a higher level: HR practices and organizational effectiveness. In K. J. Klein & S.W.J. Kozlowski (Eds.), *Multilevel theory, research, and methods in organizations* (pp. 211–266). San Francisco: Jossey-Bass.

Pfeffer, J. (1993). Barriers to the advancement of organizational science: Paradigm development as a dependent variable. *Academy of Management Review, 18,* 599–621.

Pil, F. K., & MacDuffie, J. P. (1996). The adoption of high-involvement work practices. *Industrial Relations, 35,* 423–455.

Ramanujam, R. (1999). *Organizational errors and the case of Barings.* Unpublished manuscript, Carnegie Mellon University.

Roberts, K. H. (1990). Some characteristics of high-reliability organizations. *Organization Science, 2,* 1–17.

Rousseau, D. M. (1997). Organizational behavior in the new organizational era. *Annual Review of Psychology, 48,* 515–546.

Schneider, B., Smith, D. B., & Sipe, W. P. Personnel selection psychology: Multilevel considerations. In K. J. Klein & S.W.J. Kozlowski (Eds.), *Multilevel theory, research, and methods in organizations* (pp. 91–120). San Francisco: Jossey-Bass.

Selznick, P. (1999, March 27). Keynote address, Western Academy of Management, Redondo Beach, CA.

Simon, H. A. (1973). The organization of complex systems. In H. H. Pattee (Ed.), *Hierarchy theory* (pp. 1–27). New York: Braziller.

Vaughn, D. (1996). *The Challenger launch decision: Risky technology, culture and deviance at NASA.* Chicago: University of Chicago Press.

Weick, K. E. (1990). The vulnerable system: An analysis of the Tenerife air disaster. *Journal of Management, 16,* 571–593.

Weick, K. E. (1995). *Sensemaking in organizations.* Thousand Oaks, CA: Sage.

Name Index

583

Subject Index

Printed in the United States
105066LV00004B/19/A